Moulines/Niebergall (Hrsg.) · Argument und Analyse

Perspektiven der Analytischen Philosophie
Neue Folge

Herausgegeben von Georg Meggle und Julian Nida-Rümelin

Carlos Ulises Moulines /
Karl-Georg Niebergall (Hrsg.)

Argument und Analyse

mentis
PADERBORN

Die Deutsche Bibliothek – CIP-Einheitsaufnahme

Ein Titeldatensatz für diese Publikation ist bei
Der Deutschen Bibliothek erhältlich.

Gedruckt auf umweltfreundlichem, chlorfrei gebleichtem
und alterungsbeständigem Papier ∞ ISO 9706

© 2002 mentis Verlag GmbH
Schulze-Delitzsch-Straße 19, D-33100 Paderborn
www.mentis.de

Alle Rechte vorbehalten. Dieses Werk sowie einzelne Teile desselben sind urheberrechtlich
geschützt. Jede Verwertung in anderen als den gesetzlich zulässigen Fällen ist ohne vorherige
Zustimmung des Verlages nicht zulässig.

Printed in Germany
Einbandgestaltung: Anna Braungart, Regensburg
Satz und Herstellung: Rhema – Tim Doherty, Münster, www.rhema-verlag.com
Druck: WB Druck, Rieden/Allgäu
ISBN 3-89785-253-5

Inhaltsverzeichnis

Carlos Ulises Moulines / Karl-Georg Niebergall: Vorwort 7

Teil I
Erkenntnistheorie, Wissenschaftstheorie, Logik

Jay Rosenberg: Was epistemische Externalisten vergessen 13
Wolfgang Lenzen: Realität und „Wirklichkeit". Kritische Bemerkungen zu Gerhard Roths „neurobiologischem Konstruktivismus" 33
Manfred Stöckler: 42 Jahre danach – Ein neuer Blick auf Oppenheim, Putnam und die Einheit der Wissenschaften 55
Ulrich Gähde: Ist der Ramsey-Satz eine empirische Behauptung? 67
José A. Diez: Possession Conditions for Scientific Concepts 83
Karl-Georg Niebergall: On the Limits of Gödel's Second Incompleteness Theorem 109

Teil II
Sprachphilosophie, Philosophie des Geistes, Metaphysik

Stephen Schiffer: The Things We Believe 139
Joëlle Proust: Are Empirical Arguments Acceptable in Philosophical Analyses of the Mind? 163
Pierre Jacob: Is Meaning Intrinsically Normative? 187
Manuel García-Carpintero: A Vindication of Sense-data 203
E. J. Lowe: A Defense of the Four-Category Ontology 225
Uwe Meixner: How to Reconcile Non-Physical Causation with the Physical Conservation Laws 241

Teil III
Ethik und politische Philosophie

Günther Patzig: Gibt es Grenzen der Redefreiheit? 259
Peter Railton: Kant Meets Aristotle Where Reason Meets Appetite 275

Georg Meggle: NATO-Moral & Kosovo-Krieg: Ein ethischer Kommentar ex post 295

Dietmar von der Pfordten: Politisches Handeln 313

Teil IV
Ästhetik

Catherine Z. Elgin: Originals, Copies and Fakes 339

Reinold Schmücker: Sind Fälschungen Originale? 357

Christel Fricke: Kunstwerke und ihre nicht-künstlerischen Gegenstücke – Ein Kantisch inspirierter Beitrag zur Debatte über das Ende der Kunst 371

Teil V
Religionsphilosophie

Richard Swinburne: The New Programme of Natural Theology 391

Christoph Jäger: Religious Experience and Epistemic Justification: Alston on the Reliability of „Mystical Perception" 403

Namenregister 424

Autoren 429

Vorwort

Auch wenn aus heutiger Sicht wegen der Schriften Gottlob Freges die 80er Jahre des 19. Jahrhunderts üblicherweise als die „Geburtsstunde" der analytischen Philosophie angesehen werden, so wurde diese neue Form des Philosophierens erst durch die Arbeiten von Bertrand Russell und G.E. Moore dem allgemeinen philosophischen Publikum um 1900 bekannt, so daß wir gegenwärtig auf ziemlich genau hundert Jahre des Bestehens analytischer Philosophie zurückblicken können. In diesem Sinn konnte der 4. Kongreß der deutschsprachigen *Gesellschaft für Analytische Philosophie*, der im September 2000 in Bielefeld stattfand und aus dem der vorliegende Proceedings-Band hervorgegangen ist, als eine Art „Jahrhundertfeier" verstanden werden. Daher auch die Wahl des allgemeinen Titels sowohl des Kongresses wie auch dieses Bands: „Argument und Analyse". In der Tat stellt das ständige Bemühen um schlüssige *Argumentation* auf allen philosophischen Gebieten und bei sämtlichen philosophischen Fragestellungen und die klare und präzise *Analyse* der dabei verwendeten Begriffe und Voraussetzungen ein Markenzeichen analytischen Philosophierens überhaupt dar. Im Laufe eines Jahrhunderts haben die analytisch vorgehenden Philosophen der verschiedensten Richtungen ihre Interessen, Thesen und Schlußfolgerungen auf allen möglichen Gebieten ständig verändert und revidiert, manchmal sogar ganz radikal aufgegeben bzw. umgebaut – eine beständige, gemeinsame Einstellung, eine unleugbare „Familienähnlichkeit" sind trotzdem geblieben. Wie bei jeder anderen Art von Familienähnlichkeit ist es sehr schwer, wenn nicht sogar unmöglich, die analytische genau zu definieren, aber nichtsdestoweniger ist sie ganz real. So läßt es sich ziemlich schnell feststellen, ob eine vorgegebene Gedankenausführung analytisch vorgeht oder nicht, und auch in welchem Maß sie dies tut. Begriffsanalytische Sorgfalt und möglichst gut fundierte Argumentation sind zwar nicht die ausschließlichen, wohl aber die bedeutendsten „Symptome" dafür, daß wir es mit einem echten analytischen Text zu tun haben – was immer die konkret eingesetzten Begrifflichkeiten und die durchgeführten Argumente sein mögen.

Von diesem Geist zeugen die im vorliegenden Band enthaltenen Aufsätze. Wir meinen, daß ihnen eine sorgfältige, kritischen Analyse der involvierten

Begrifflichkeiten und Positionen, sowie der genauesten Durchführung der relevanten Argumente gemeinsam ist. Gleichzeitig stellen die hier gesammelten Aufsätze eine repräsentative Auswahl des Spektrums des gegenwärtigen analytischen Philosophierens dar.

Abgesehen von ihrem intrinsischen Wert für die Weiterführung der Diskussion auf dem jeweiligen philosophischen Gebiet möge die Gesamtheit der vorliegenden Aufsätze dazu beitragen, ein Vorurteil zu zerstreuen, das, wenn auch weniger intensiv als in früheren Zeiten, beim philosophisch interessierten Publikum nach wie vor ein ziemlich hartnäckiges Leben führt: daß nämlich außerhalb ihrer „Stammgebiete" der Logik, Wissenschaftstheorie und Sprachphilosophie die analytische Philosophie wenig Anregendes zu den traditionelleren Problemkreisen der Philosophie zu sagen hat. Dagegen zeigen zahlreiche Beiträge in diesem Band, daß die Reflexion über zentrale Fragen der „klassischeren" Gebiete der Erkenntnistheorie, der Philosophie des Geistes, der Metaphysik, der Ethik, und sogar der Ästhetik und der Religionsphilosophie in der analytischen Philosophie seit geraumer Zeit weit über eine marginale Präsenz hinausgegangen ist.

Der vorliegende Band stellt eine strenge, kleine Auswahl der Beiträge, die auf dem Bielefelder Kongreß präsentiert wurden, dar. Denn natürlich war es unmöglich, die Gesamtheit der etwa 200 Kongreß-Beiträge zu publizieren, auch wenn die meisten von ihnen von sehr hoher Qualität waren. Etwa die Hälfte der hier veröffentlichten Aufsätze wurden von deutschen Philosophen verfaßt, die andere Hälfte stammt von renommierten US-amerikanischen, britischen, französischen und spanischen Autoren, womit u. a. auch die Anbindung der deutschsprachigen analytischen Philosophie an die internationale Diskussion klar dokumentiert wird.

Auch wenn die Grenzen zwischen den philosophischen Problemgebieten naturgemäß fließend sind, so haben die Herausgeber versucht, zur Orientierung des Lesers die Beiträge nach dem Gesichtspunkt der inhaltlichen und/ oder methodologischen Affinität zu gruppieren. Dadurch sind fünf verschiedene Sektionen entstanden: Sektion I: *Erkenntnistheorie, Wissenschaftstheorie, Logik*, mit den Beiträgen von Jay Rosenberg, Wolfgang Lenzen, Manfred Stöckler, Ulrich Gähde, José A. Diez und Karl-Georg Niebergall; Sektion II: *Sprachphilosophie, Philosophie des Geistes, Metaphysik*, mit den Beiträgen von Stephen Schiffer, Joëlle Proust, Pierre Jacob, Manuel Garcia-Carpintero, E. J. Lowe und Uwe Meixner; Sektion III: *Ethik und politische Philosophie*, mit den Beiträgen von Günther Patzig, Peter Railton, Georg Meggle und Dietmar von der Pfordten; Sektion IV: *Ästhetik*, mit den Beiträgen von Catherine Elgin, Reinold Schmücker und Christel Fricke; Sektion V: *Religionsphilosophie*, mit den Beiträgen von Richard Swinburne und Christoph Jäger. Die hier veröffentlichten Aufsätze dieser Autorinnen und Autoren stellen ein reichhaltiges Panorama der aktuellen Reflexionen und Ergebnisse im Geist der analytischen Philosophie auf all diesen Gebieten dar.

Die Herausgeber   München, Januar 2002

Teil I

Erkenntnistheorie, Wissenschaftstheorie, Logik

Jay F. Rosenberg

Was epistemische Externalisten vergessen

Wilfrid Sellars war bekanntlich ein epistemischer Internalist. In „Der Empirismus und die Philosophie des Geistes"[1] schrieb er:

> Möglicherweise wird man nun denken, daß es offenbar keinen Sinn hat, wenn man annimmt, daß ein Vorkommnis [„Dies ist grün"], welches z. B. von Jones geäußert wird, erst dann Beobachtungswissen zum Ausdruck bringen würde, wenn Jones bereits wüßte, daß öffentliche verbale Episoden dieser Art verläßliche Anzeichen für die Existenz grüner Gegenstände sind, die sich in einer geeigneten Beziehung zum Sprecher befinden. Ich bin da anderer Meinung. Ich halte tatsächlich etwas Vergleichbares für richtig. (Sellars 1999, § 36, S. 65)

Das drückt in wenigen Worten zusammengefaßt eine Art von epistemischem Internalismus aus, also die allgemeine These, daß jemand nur dann etwas weiß, wenn er (wenigstens im Prinzip) in der Lage ist, seine Meinung durch geeignete Rechtfertigungen zu begründen.

Robert Brandom ist bekanntlich ein Verehrer von Sellars, aber er ist trotzdem ein epistemischer Externalist. In seinem *opus magnum Making It Explicit*[2] findet man z. B. folgende Überlegungen:

> Nehmen wir an, daß man Monique beigebracht hat, Weißbuchen anhand ihrer Blätter zu erkennen. In Folge dessen [...] tendiert sie dazu, auf den Anblick von Blättern der richtigen Art häufig so zu reagieren, daß sie nicht-inferentiell die Anwesenheit einer Weißbuche berichtet. Sie versteht, was es bedeutet zu behaupten, daß etwas eine Weißbuche ist und [...] ist tatsächlich überzeugt, daß eine Weißbuche zugegen ist. Trotzdem kann es sein, daß sie sich ihrer Diskriminationsfähigkeit nicht sicher ist, auch lange nachdem sie eigentlich schon zuverlässig ist. In dieser Situation könnte sie die wahre Überzeugung haben, daß eine Weißbuche vor ihr steht, aber total außerstande sein, jene Behauptung zu rechtfertigen [...], ja es könnte sogar sein, daß sie dementiert, eine zuverlässige nicht-inferentielle Zeugin über Weißbuchen zu sein.
> Trotzdem kann es [...] für jemand, der sie für eine zuverlässige Zeugin hält, völlig in Ordnung sein, nicht nur auf der Basis ihres Berichts zu der Überzeugung zu

---

[1] Von Thomas Blume übersetzt und herausgegeben (mentis Verlag; Paderborn: 1999).
[2] Harvard University Press; Cambridge, MA: 1992. Die Übersetzungen sind meine.

kommen, daß eine Weißbuche anwesend ist, sondern auch ihren Bericht [...] zu zitieren, als das, was seine Überzeugung rechtfertigt. Dabei wird ihre Behauptung genau in der Weise autoritativ behandelt, die für Wissen erforderlich ist. (Brandom 1992, S. 219)

Beide Zitate befassen sich mit der Glaubwürdigkeit von Äußerungen, die Beobachtungen ausdrücken. Wie Sellars betont, hängt die Glaubwürdigkeit solcher Äußerungen nicht nur von den geäußerten Satz-Typen, sondern wesentlich von den Umständen ihres Vorkommens ab, d. h. die epistemische Autorität einer solchen Äußerung wird irgendwie von der Tatsache abgeleitet, „daß [sie] auf eine bestimmte Weise und unter einer bestimmten Menge von Umständen entstanden ist" (Sellars 1999, § 32, S. 61). Die Vermutung liegt nahe, daß es sich um eine Variante des Externalismus anzunehmen, der zufolge das bloße *Bestehen* einer passenden Tatsache bezüglich des Ursprungs der Äußerung sowohl notwendig als auch hinreichend ist, um ihr die Art von Autorität zu verleihen, die wahre Überzeugungen in Wissen verwandelt.

Alvin Goldmans „kausale Theorie des Wissens" wird häufig als Musterbeispiel eines solchen strengen Externalismus betrachtet. Der Grundgedanke des Externalismus ist, daß eine Überzeugung sich kraft ihres Ursprungs als Wissen qualifiziert. S weiß, daß p, genau dann, wenn S' Überzeugung, daß p, auf passende Weise aus der *Tatsache*, daß p entsteht (und also unter anderem wahr ist). Goldman hat vorgeschlagen, dieses Entstehen „auf passende Weise" *kausal* zu verstehen: S' Überzeugung, daß p, gilt nur dann als Wissen, wenn sie von der Tatsache, daß p, richtig *verursacht* worden ist.

Der Vorbehalt ‚richtig' ist in dieser Analyse unentbehrlich, weil es ein Problem mit *abweichenden* Kausalketten gibt. Hier ist, leicht modifiziert, eines von Goldmans phantasiereichen Szenarios: Ein Vulkan bricht aus; Lava ergießt sich über die Landschaft. Kurz danach entfernt jemand aber wieder die ganze Lava und bringt sie in ein verstecktes Lager. Jahrhunderte später endeckt jemand dieses versteckte Lager und verteilt die Lava (erneut) in der Gegend, um einen örtlichen Vulkanausbruch vorzutäuschen. S sieht die Lava und erschließt daraus, zufälligerweise richtig, daß der Vulkan vor mehreren Jahrhunderten ausgebrochen ist. Obwohl der ursprüngliche Ausbruch mit der späteren wahren Überzeugung von S kausal verbunden ist, würden wir nur ungern sagen, daß S weiß, daß der Vulkan ausgebrochen ist. S' wahre Überzeugung wurde (allgemein gesprochen) von dem Vulkanausbruch verursacht, aber die kausale Verbindung war nicht „von der richtigen Sorte"

Goldmans erste Strategie, mit diesem Problem fertig zu werden, ist merkwürdigerweise unverkennbar *internalistisch*. Sie verlangt von dem Subjekt S, daß es die relevante kausale Kette „richtig rekonstruieren" können müsse, d. h., daß S weitere Überzeugungen haben müsse, die die kausale

Verbindung zwischen der Tatsache, daß p, und S' entsprechender wahrer Meinung genau wiedergeben. Weil S in dem geschilderten Szenario normalerweise nicht nur annehmen würde, daß die zum Indiz dienende Lava von dem daraus erschlossenen Ausbruch verursacht worden war, sondern auch, daß die Lava danach mehr oder weniger ungestört an ihrer jetzigen Stelle gelegen habe, wird die Bedingung einer „richtigen Rekonstruktion" der Kausalkette – die den bizarren Umweg der Lava über Einsammeln, Lagerung und Wiederverteilung einschließen müsste – nicht erfüllt.

Obwohl diese internalistische Strategie mit Gegenbeispielen dieses Typs fertig werden konnte, wurde es schnell klar, daß sie gegen verschiedene andere Gegenbeispiele machtlos war. Wenn z. B. kurz vor fünfzehn Uhr ein Fleck am Horizont als das sich nähernde Postschiff identifiziert wird, zufälligerweise richtig, weil man das Postschiff ohnehin um fünfzehn Uhr erwartet, würden wir diese wahre Überzeugung wieder nur ungern als Wissen bezeichnen, obwohl die kausalen Verhältnisse hier völlig normal sind und, wie wir annehmen dürfen, auch „richtig rekonstruiert" worden sind. Man *sieht* das Postschiff, und man glaubt, *daß* man das Postschiff sieht. Die Schwierigkeit ist aber, daß man nicht in der Lage ist zu bestimmen, daß das, was man sieht, wirklich das Postschiff ist. Um das zu wissen, schließt Goldman, muß man zwischen dem Postschiff und anderen relevanten Möglichkeiten, z. B. Fähren, Segeljachten, Frachtern usw., *unterscheiden* können, was man in dem Beispiel aber nicht kann.

Dem Anschein nach wird dieser Test der relevanten Diskriminationsfähigkeit auch mit verschiedenen anderen schwierigen Geschichten erfolgreich fertig, z. B. der bekannten „potemkinschen Scheune" von Carl Ginet. Hier befindet sich Person S, die normalerweise auf Spazierfahrten Scheunen anhand ihres Aussehens gut identifizieren kann, unwissentlich in einer Gegend, die mit geschickten Nachbildungen von Scheunenvorderseiten bestückt ist – im Scheunenfassadenbezirk. Aus ihrem Wagenfenster hinausschauend, kommt S zu der Überzeugung, daß da rechts auf dem Acker eine Scheune steht – und das stimmt. Licht, das von einer echten Scheune gespiegelt worden ist, hat S' Wahrnehmungserfahrung verursacht. Trotzdem wollen wir wieder nicht sagen, daß S in dieser Situation weiß, daß da rechts auf dem Acker eine Scheune steht, und Goldmans Prinzip unterstützt diese Einstellung: So wie sie situiert ist, ist S nicht in der Lage, zwischen echten Scheunen und nachgebildeten Fassaden zu unterscheiden.

Diese Geschichte kann man aber auch anders beschreiben, nämlich so, daß S kein Wissen hat, weil sie Scheunen im Scheunenfassadenbezirk nicht *zuverlässig* erkennen kann. Obwohl das Verfahren, einfach hinzuschauen und dabei zu sehen, ob eine Scheune auf einem Acker steht, *normalerweise* verläßlich ist, ist es *in diesem Bezirk* unzuverlässig. Sich hier auf solche einzelnen Wahrnehmungen zu verlassen, bürgt deshalb nicht für die Wahrheit der daraus resultierenden Überzeugungen. *Zuverlässigkeit* ist ein Hauptthema der meisten externalistischen Erkenntnistheorien. Der leitende Gedanke ist, daß sich Überzeugungen nur dann als Wissen qualifizieren, wenn die epistemischen Verfahren, die sie verursachen, verläßliche Wahrheitsindikatoren sind.

Eine starke externalistische Haltung dieser Art legt eine radikale externalistische Deutung des *Begriffs* des Wissens nahe, der zufolge die Erklärung dieses Begriffs überhaupt keinen Hinweis auf Rechtfertigungsargumente enthält. Wesentlich für das Wissen ist nur wahre Überzeugung. Ein solcher „Begriffsexternalismus" wird gelegentlich vertreten. Vielleicht ist Crispin Sartwell heute sein bekanntester Verteidiger[3], aber die These wurde schon von Franz von Kutschera in seinem Buch *Grundfragen der Erkenntnistheorie*[4] entwickelt, und die folgenden Überlegungen sind dort entstanden.

Die Argumente, die den Begriffsexternalismus unterstützen, sind trügerisch einfach: Wissen hat objektive und subjektive Aspekte, und es ist der optimale epistemische Zustand. Also verfügt man nur dann über Wissen von einer empirischen Tatsache wenn man hinsichtlich dieser Tatsache sowohl objektiv als auch subjektiv in der bestmöglichen epistemischen Lage ist. Erstens gibt es aber keine mögliche objektive Eigenschaft einer empirischen Überzeugung, die stärker ist als ihre Wahrheit. Die objektive epistemische Lage von jemandem, dessen (relevante) Überzeugung wahr ist, läßt sich nicht verbessern. Folglich läßt sie sich nicht dadurch verbessern, dass er über irgendeine Rechtfertigung verfügt oder sie anwendet. Wenn eine solche Rechtfertigung also eine Rolle für das Wissen spielen soll, muß es im Zusammenhang mit seinem subjektiven Aspekt sein. Dem Anschein nach kann ein Mensch aber zweitens in keiner stärkeren Beziehung zu einer empirischen Wahrheit stehen, als sie rückhaltlos zu glauben. Die subjektive epistemische Lage von jemandem, der von einer (bestimmten) empirischen Wahrheit völlig überzeugt ist, kann also ebenfalls nicht verbessert werden. Solche Überzeugungen können aus Rechtfertigungsüberlegungen entstehen, aber sie können vermutlich auch von irgenwelchen rein kausalen Mechanismen verursacht werden. Die subjektive Lage des Überzeugten bleibt die gleiche. Also spielen Rechtfertigungen für das Wissen keine essentielle Rolle. Wesentlich ist nur, dass es sich um wahre Überzeugungen handelt. Von Kutschera faßt diese Überlegungen so zusammen:

---

[3] „Knowledge is Merely True Belief", *American Philosophical Quarterly*, 28, 1991, S. 157–65; „Why Knowledge is Merely True Belief", *The Journal of Philosophy*, 89, 1992, S. 167–80.
[4] Walter de Gruyter; Berlin: 1982.

Überzeugung ist [...] ein hinreichendes subjektives Kriterium für Wissen. Eine Suche nach stärkeren subjektiven Kriterien für Wissen ist also illusorisch: Sicherer als ganz sicher kann man nicht sein. Stärkere objektive Kriterien für Wissen als die Wahrheit des Sachverhalts sind aber ebenfalls nicht denkbar: Richtiger als wahr kann ein Satz ebenfalls nicht sein. Wissen wird hier also in zwei Komponenten aufgespalten: in die subjektive Komponente der Überzeugung und in die objektive Komponente der Wahrheit, und beide sind einer Steigerung nicht fähig. (Kutschera 1982, S. 16)

Ein traditioneller Externalist wird hier protestieren, daß es doch eine objektive Eigenschaft von Überzeugungen gibt, die stärker als die Wahrheit ist. Jemand, dessen Überzeugung nicht nur wahr, sondern auch von einem zuverlässigen meinungsbildenden Verfahren erzeugt worden ist, ist epistemisch besser dran als jemand, dessen Überzeugung nur wahr ist. Und dabei deuten manche Externalisten den Begriff der Rechtfertigung so, daß eine Überzeugung *nur dann* gerechtfertigt ist, *wenn* sie von verläßlichen meinungsschaffenden Mechanismen erzeugt wird. Aber stimmt es, daß eine derartige Herkunft den objektiven epistemischen Wert einer Überzeugung steigern kann?

Mir scheint das zweifelhaft. Erstens sind zuverlässige Verfahren, die Überzeugungen herstellen, normalerweise nicht unfehlbar. Aber die objektive epistemische Lage von jemandem, der mittels solcher Verfahren ausnahmsweise eine *falsche* Überzeugung bekommen hat, ist sicherlich *nicht* besser, als die von jemandem, der die gleiche falsche Überzeugung nur zufällig hat, z.B., als reine Vermutung. Und wenn eine bestimmte Entstehungsgeschichte den objektiven epistemischen Wert einer falschen Überzeugung nicht generell steigert, ist es schwierig zu verstehen, wieso die gleiche Entstehungsgeschichte den objektiven epistemischen Wert einer Überzeugung steigern soll, wenn diese wahr ist.

Zweitens ist normalerweise jeder Externalist der Meinung, daß die Wahrheit die *grundlegende* positive objektive epistemische Eigenschaft ist. D.h., die Zuverlässigkeit eines meinungsbildenden V*erfahrens* wird durch die überwiegende Wahrheit seiner Erzeugnisse *definiert*. Wenn eine Überzeugung überhaupt irgendeinen objektiven epistemischen Wert kraft ihrer Entstehung durch ein derartiges Verfahren besitzt, wird dieser Wert selbst den objektiven epistemischen Wert der wahren Überzeugungen als solcher voraussetzen und aus diesem herstammen. Also kann eine Entstehung mittels derartiger Verfahren diesen Wert nicht steigern. Von Kutschera stimmt zu:

Man kann daher zwar den Begriff des Wissens [...] einschränken auf wahre Überzeugungen, die auf gewisse Weise gewonnen sind – und das entspricht manchen umgangssprachlichen Verwendungen des Wortes ‚Wissen‘ besser [...] –, aber man gelangt dadurch nicht zu einer qualitativ höheren Art des Wissens. (Kutschera 1982, S. 24)

Ich ziehe also das Schluß, daß ein konsequenter Externalist auf die These festgelegt ist, daß keine objektive epistemische Eigenschaft einer Überzeugung stärker als ihre Wahrheit sein kann. Der Begriffsexternalismus spiegelt einfach diese Festlegung wider.

Aber wenn Wissen nur wahre Überzeugung sein soll, was wird dann aus der traditionellen und sicher korrekten Beobachtung, daß eine glückliche Schätzung oder richtige Ahnung kein Wissen ist? Eine Schätzung gilt genau dann als glücklich oder eine Ahnung als richtig, wenn sie *wahr* ist. Wenn sie trotzdem nicht als Wissen gilt, muß es aus begriffsexternalistschen Sicht daran liegen, daß sie keine *Überzeugung* im relevanten Sinn ist. So schreibt z. B. Sartwell, daß

> Argumente, die versuchen zu zeigen, daß das Wissen irgendeine dritte Bedingung erfordert, oft von einem inhaltlich zu wenig bestimmten Begriff der Überzeugung abhängig sind. Solche Argumente bestehen häufig nur in einem Hinweis auf die Tatsache, daß eine glückliche Schätzung nicht als Wissen gilt. Aber natürlich ist normalerweise eine glückliche Schätzung noch nicht eine Überzeugung. (Sartwell 1991, S. 159)[5]

Was eine begriffsexternalistische Darstellung des Wissens braucht, ist also ein ziemlich enger Begriff der Überzeugung, der eine epistemische Haltung der Sicherheit oder uneingeschränkten subjektiven Zuversicht umfaßt. Von Kutchera legt z. B. fest, daß eine Person S nur dann im relevanten Sinn der Überzeugung ist, daß p, wenn die (subjektive) Wahrscheinlichkeit von p für S genau 1 ist (Kutschera 1982, S. 2). Wir sollten also fragen, unter welchen Bedingungen ein Mensch in diesem eingeschränkten, für die begriffsexternalistische Darstellung des Wissens erforderlichen Sinn eine wahre Überzeugung hat.

Bei Keith Lehrer finden wir z. B. die Geschichte von Herrn Truetemp. Ohne sein Wissen oder seine Zustimmung ist ihm ein zuverlässiges Temperaturmeßgerät eingepflanzt worden. Die Angaben dieses Geräts sind so mit seinem Zentralnervensystem verschaltet, daß er regelmäßig wiederkehrende spontane Gedanken über die präzise Temperatur in seiner unmittelbaren Nähe hat, die tatsächlich überwiegend wahr sind. Herr Truetemp hat also das nötige Rüstzeug für höchst zuverlässige Berichte über die Temperatur in seiner Umgebung. Aber welche Art von Temperaturberichten können wir vernünftigerweise von ihm erwarten?

---

[5] „[Arguments] to the effect that some third condition is required for knowledge often play on an insufficiently rich notion of belief. Such arguments ... often take the form simply of pointing out that a lucky guess does not count as knowledge. But of course, in the usual case, a lucky guess is not even a belief."

So wie Lehrer den Fall ursprünglich beschrieb, weiß Herr Truetemp nicht, daß er zuverlässig ist. Er hat spontane Überzeugungen über die Temperatur in seiner Nähe, aber er hat überhaupt keinen Grund anzunehmen, daß diese Überzeugungen richtig sind. Vom epistemischem Gesichtspunkt, argumentiert Lehrer, ist Herr Truetemp in der gleichen Lage wie die vertrauensselige Sue (wie ich sie nennen will), deren Urteile über die Temperatur auf der Anzeige eines alten Thermometers an der Wand der Laube in ihrem Schrebergarten basieren. Weil Thermometer, die sich an solchen Stellen befinden, häufig *un*genau anzeigen, ist Sue, selbst wenn dieses Thermometer zufälligerweise genau anzeigt und seine Anzeige deswegen vertrauenswürdig ist, solange nicht berechtigt, sich auf die Anzeige dieses Thermometers zu verlassen, wie sie keinen positiven Beleg für seine Zuverlässigkeit hat.

Das epistemische Verhältnis zwischen Herrn Truetemp und seinen spontanen Gedanken über die Temperatur ist das gleiche wie das zwischen der vertrauensseligen Sue und den Anzeigen ihres alten Schrebergartenthermometers. Weil spontane Meinungen über die präzise Temperatur häufig (und sogar typischerweise) *un*genau sind, ist Herr Truetemp auch dann, wenn seine Gedanken zufällig genau und also vertrauenswürdig *sind* – was wir vorausgesetzt haben –, solange nicht berechtigt, sich auf seine nicht-inferentiellen Temperatururteile zu verlassen, wie er keinen positiven Beleg ihrer Zuverlässigkeit hat. Der springende Punkt ist nun aber, daß Herr Truetemp, wenn er ein vernünftiges und epistemisch verantwortungsbewußtes Subjekt ist, selbst *den Schluß ziehen kann, soll und wird*, daß er dazu nicht berechtigt ist – was wiederum die Stärke seines subjektiven Vertrauens zu seinen spontanen Temperatururteilen beeinflussen wird.

Dieses Wechselspiel zwischen objektiver Rechtfertigung und subjektivem Vertrauen spiegelt die tief verwurzelte Rolle der Vernunft in reifer menschlicher Wahrnehmung wider. Ernest Sosa hat diesen Punkt besonders klar formuliert:

> Kein mit Vernunft gesegneter Mensch hat bloßes animalische Wissen von der Sorte, das Tiere besitzen. Denn selbst wenn eine Wahrnehmungsüberzeugung so direkt wie möglich von sinnlichen Reizen hergeleitet wird, bleibt es relevant, daß man *keine* Anzeichen von entgegengesetzten Umständen wahrgenommen hat. Ein mit Vernunft ausgestattetes Wesen überwacht automatisch seine Hintergrundinformationen und sensorischen Inputs mit Blick auf mögliche entgegengesetzte Anzeichen und wählt, selbst wenn es am direktsten auf sinnliche Reize reagiert, automatisch die kohärenteste Hypothese. Denn auch wenn seine Reaktion auf Reize am direktsten ist, würde seine Reaktion sich ändern, *wenn* es auch Zeichen von glaubwürdigen entgegengesetzten Aussagen hören oder sehen würde. Die Überzeugungen eines *vernunftbegabten* Wesens rühren also anscheinend nie von *bloßer* Selbstbeobachtung, Erinnerung oder Wahrnehmung her. Die Vernunft ist immer

wenigstens ein stiller Teilhaber, der Ausschau nach weiteren relevanten Daten hält, und dessen *Schweigen* deshalb immer eine Mitursache der Überzeugungen ist. (Sosa 1991, S. 240)[6]

Die Hintergrundinformationen, die Herrn Truetemp und der vertrauensseligen Sue zugänglich sind, schließen die Tatsache ein, daß Meinungen über die örtliche Temperatur, die auf ihre besondere Weise erreicht worden sind – d. h. über spontane unüberlegte Urteile bzw. aufgrund der Anzeige eines alten Schrebergartenthermometers – im allgemeinen *nicht* genau und zuverlässig sind. Und gerade deswegen sollte sich der „stille Teilhaber" Vernunft in diesen Fällen klar und deutlich *zu Wort melden*, insbesondere um die beiden zu warnen, daß es hier epistemisch unangebracht ist, die Art von bedingungslosem Vertrauen in die Korrektheit ihrer Überzeugungen zu haben, die für vorbehaltlose *Berichte* über die örtlichen Temperaturen geeignet wäre.

Zu diesem Zeitpunkt sollten wir uns an Brandoms Beschreibung von Monique und ihrem Verhältnis zu ihren spontanen Überzeugungen über Weißbuchen erinnern:

> Es kann sein, daß sie sich ihrer Diskriminationsfähigkeit nicht sicher ist, auch lange nachdem sie eigentlich schon zuverlässig ist. In dieser Situation könnte sie eine wahre Überzeugung haben, daß eine Weißbuche vor ihr steht, aber total außerstande sein, jene Behauptung zu rechtfertigen [...], ja es könnte sogar sein, daß sie dementiert, eine zuverlässige nicht-inferentielle Zeugin über Weißbuchen zu sein. (Brandom 1992, S. 219)

In Anbetracht unserer Diskussion des Falles Truetemp können wir jetzt eine Spannung innerhalb des Komplexes aus epistemischen Haltungen und Verhalten erkennen, den Brandom Monique zuschreibt. Einerseits setzt er voraus, daß sie „dazu [tendiert], auf den Anblick von Blättern der richtigen Art häufig so zu reagieren, daß sie nicht-inferentiell die Anwesenheit einer Weißbuche berichtet". Aber andererseits demonstriert sie mit der vorbehaltlosen Behauptung „Das ist eine Weißbuche" einen Grad von Sicherheit und epistemischem Vertrauen, auf den sie, weil sie ihrer Diskriminierungsfähigkeit ja nicht sicher ist, und es sogar sein könnte, „daß sie dementiert, eine zuverlässige nicht-inferentielle Zeugin über Weißbuchen zu sein ", keinen Anspruch hat – und das soll, kann und wird sie normalerweise selbst erkennen. Insofern Monique eine gewissenhafte und vernünftige epistemisch Handelnde ist, sollten wir also erwarten, daß sie nur *vorbehaltliche* Behauptungen darüber machen wird, welche Bäume Weißbuchen sind – „Das scheint eine Weißbuche zu sein", „Ich denke, daß das vielleicht eine Weißbuche ist",

---

[6] Ernest Sosa, *Knowledge in Perspective: Selected Essays in Epistemology* (Cambridge University Press; Cambridge: 1991).

„Wahrscheinlich ist das eine Weißbuche", „Ich neige dazu zu sagen, daß es eine Weißbuche ist", usw.

Ebenso gilt, daß auch die vertrauensselige Sue und Herr Truetemp, wenn sie erst ihr epistemisches Vertrauen in das richtige Verhältnis dazu gebracht haben, was sie über die Vertrauenswürdigkeit des ihnen zugänglichen Beweismittels zu glauben berechtigt sind, geneigt sein werden, nur vorbehaltliche Behauptungen über die örtliche Temperatur zu machen. Anders gesagt, weder Herr Truetemp, noch Sue oder Monique werden die Art von vorbehaltlosen Überzeugungen haben, die vom Standpunkt des Begriffsexternalismus nötig sind, damit ihre wahren Überzeugungen als Wissen gelten können.

Ex hypothesi sind wir wissenden Außenseiter berechtigt, Moniques Identifikation von Weißbuchen, wie immer gemäßigt und mit Vorbehalt sie sie ausdrückt, als vertrauenswürdig zu betrachten. Gleichfalls werden wir, in Anbetracht der Tatsache, daß wir über Herrn Truetemps Implantate informiert sind, mit Recht seine vielleicht zögernden oder ausweichenden Temperaturberichte als vollkommen zuverlässig behandeln. Brandom nimmt also ganz richtig an, daß wir dazu neigen werden, solche Behauptungen „als autoritativ in genau der Weise, die für Wissen erforderlich ist" zu *betrachten*. Wenn wir unsere Überzeugungen auf Moniques oder Truetemps Aussagen stützen, brauchen *unsere* Urteile über Weißbuchen oder die Temperatur in Truetemps Nähe *nicht* vorsichtig und mit Vorbehalt zu sein. Unsere epistemische Lage berechtigt uns, Monique und Truetemp sozusagen als verläßliche intentionale Indikatoren zu behandeln.

Aber das ist sicherlich nur deshalb so, weil wir unsere auf Moniques oder Truetemps Aussagen gegründeten Urteile dadurch stützen können, daß wir uns ausdrücklich auf deren Verläßlichkeit berufen. Wir verfügen eben über die passenden rechtfertigenden Argumente:

Wenn gefragt, berichtet Monique zögernd, daß dieses eine Weißbuche ist.
Moniques zögerliche Identifikationen von Weißbuchen sind tatsächlich sehr zuverlässig.
Also dürfen wir berechtigt schließen, daß es doch eine Weißbuche ist.
Herr Truetemp berichtet mit leichtem Vorbehalt, daß die örtliche Temperatur 38° beträgt.
Solche spontane Überzeugungen über die Temperatur sind bei Truetemp sehr zuverlässig.
Also dürfen wir berechtigt schließen, daß die Temperatur in seiner Nähe wirklich 38° beträgt.

Natürlich gibt es im Prinzip keinen Hinderungsgrund, daß auch Monique und Truetemp selbst die Richtigkeit ihrer eigenen spontanen Urteile untersuchen. Sie könnten dadurch berechtigt an einen Punkt gelangen, an dem sie die gleichen allgemeinen Zuverlässigkeitsprämissen für wahr halten, die uns wissenden Außenseitern zugänglich sind. Sie könnten also in die epistemische Lage kommen, Rechtfertigungsargumente in der Ichform auf ihre eigenen spontanen Urteile und Überzeugungen anzuwenden, die genau von der gleichen Art sind wie die, die wir eben in der dritten Person erläutert haben. Dann und nur dann würden Monique und Truetemp selbst geneigt und berechtigt sein, diejenigen vorbehaltlosen Behauptung zu machen, die das notwendige epistemische Vertrauen widerspiegeln – Behauptungen die derart uneingeschränkte Überzeugungen manifestieren, daß sie dem Begriffsexternalismus, wenn wahr, als Wissen gelten.

Nach diesen Überlegungen erweist sich der Begriffsexternalismus also als dialektisch instabil. Er schlägt vor, die traditionelle Rolle der Rechtfertigungen zu eliminieren, indem er Wissen bloß als zugleich subjektive und objektive *epistemische Optimalität* charakterisiert, die sich auch als das Überzeugtsein und das Wahrsein der Überzeugung interpretieren läßt. Aber wie wir eben gesehen haben, spielen Rechtfertigungen, obwohl sie den objektiven epistemischen Status einer wahren Überzeugung nicht verbessern können, eine wesentlichen Rolle für deren subjektiven Aspekt. Wahrscheinlich war Platon der erste, der das betont hat.

> [Mit] den wahren Meinungen hat es keine Not, solange sie ausharren, und ihre Wirkungen sind durchweg gut. Aber lange Zeit auszuharren, ist nicht ihre Sache, sondern sie entweichen aus der Seele des Menschen; sie haben also keinen rechten Wert, den bekommen sie erst dann, wenn man sie festbindet durch denkende Erkenntnis des Grundes. [...] Wenn sie aber befestigt sind, so werden aus ihnen erstens sichere Erkenntnisse, und zweitens erhalten sie dadurch die Kraft des Beharrens. Und darum ist denn das Wissen von höherem Wert als die richtige Meinung, und das befestigende Band ist es, was das Wissen von der richtigen Meinung unterscheidet. (Platon, Menon 98a)[7]

Selbst wenn es als epistemische Optimalität konstruiert wird, ist und bleibt Wissen eine *normative* Angelegenheit. Das ist die tiefste Wurzel von Sellars' Internalismus:

> Der springende Punkt liegt darin, daß wir keine empirische Beschreibung dieser Episode oder dieses Zustandes liefern, wenn wir eine Episode oder einen Zustand als ein *Wissen* bezeichnen. Wir stellen sie vielmehr in den logischen Raum der Gründe, der Rechtfertigung und der Fähigkeit zur Rechtfertigung des Gesagten. (Sellars 1999, § 36)

---

[7] Herausgegeben von Klaus Reich (Felix Meiner Verlag; Hamburg: 1972).

Ein epistemisch gewissenhaft reflektierender Handelnder wird also seine subjektiven Überzeugungen immer im richtigen Verhältnis zu seinen objektiven epistemischen Ansprüchen halten. Diese Ansprüche ergeben sich wiederum aus den ihm verfügbaren Rechtfertigungen. Das ist der erste wesentliche Punkt, den epistemische Externalisten vergessen, und er hat auch Konzequenzen für traditionelle epistemologische Auseinandersetzungen zwischen „Fundamentalisten" and „Kohärentisten". Denn er impliziert, daß einzelne spontane Gedanken und Urteile, die „unmittelbar" oder „fundamental" sind, in dem Sinne, daß die *unabgeleitet* oder *nicht-inferentiell* sind, trotzdem ihren Status als Ausdrücke von (Beobachtungs-)*Wissen* der Tatsache verdanken, daß sie in Rechtfertigungsargumenten nicht nur als Prämisse vorkommen können, aus denen sich empirische Allgemeinheiten „induktiv" schließen lassen, sondern auch selbst als Konklusionen rechtfertigender Argumente, die sich auf allgemeine Prämissen über den Beweisführungswert von genau solchen Episoden gründen. Aus eben diesem Grund schließt Sellars daß

> [...] die Metapher einer ‚Grundlage' irreführend ist, und zwar insofern, als sie uns nicht sehen läßt, daß dann, wenn es eine logische Dimension gibt, innerhalb deren sich andere empirische Propositionen auf Beobachtungsberichte stützen, eine weitere logische Dimension existiert, innerhalb derer sich letztere auf erste stützen. (Sellars 1999, § 38)

Aber wir sind noch nicht mit dem Begriffsexternalismus fertig. Eine weitere Perspektive findet man bei Ansgar Beckermann, dessen Aufsatz „Wissen und wahre Meinung"[8] mit einer Untersuchung und teilweisen Verteidigung von Kutscheras „minimalem Wissensbegriff" anfängt. Was wir verstehen sollen, argumentiert Beckermann, ist, daß

> von Kutschera in seinen Überlegungen zum Wissensbegriff ein ganz anderes Ziel verfolgt als die meisten anderen Autoren. Ihm geht es nicht um eine Definition, die die Intension (oder zumindest die Extension) des alltagssprachlichen Wissensbegriffs möglichst genau einfängt, sondern um die Entwicklung eines Wissensbegriffs, der den systematischen Bedürfnissen der Erkenntnistheorie am besten entspricht. Für ihn lautet die entscheidende Frage daher: Gibt es *systematische* Gründe dafür, alternative, engere Wissensbegriffe dem minimalen Begriff (MinW) vorzuziehen? (Beckermann 1997, S. 31)

Auf diese Frage antwortet von Kutschera anscheinend mit „Nein", und Beckermann gibt ihm dabei in wenigstens einem Sinne Recht.

---

[8] In Wolfgang Lenzen (Hrsg.), *Das weite Spektrum der analytischen Philosophie: Festschrift für Franz von Kutschera* (Walter de Gruyter; Berlin: 1997), S. 24–43.

Beckermanns eigene Hauptthese ist, daß

> [der] traditionelle dreigliedrige Wissensbegriff [...] systematisch gesehen ein Unding [ist]. Er bringt Dinge zusammen, die nicht zusammengehören und die zusammenzubringen nur Verwirrung stiften kann. *Dieser* Begriff hat in einer *systematisch* betriebenen Erkenntnistheorie keinen Platz. Es hat deshalb – von einem systematischen Standpunkt aus gesehen – auch gar keinen Zweck, zu versuchen, die Intension (oder zumindest die Extension) *dieses* Begriffs durch einen präziseren einzufangen. (Beckermann 1997, S. 42)

Was die traditionelle Analyse des Wissens als gerechtfertigte wahre Überzeugung (GWÜ) irrtümerweise zusammenbringt, argumentiert Beckermann, sind Antworten auf verschiedene epistemologische Fragen. Eine systematische epistemologische Theorie, schlägt er vor, schließt Antworten auf drei Grundfragen ein:

1) Was ist das Ziel unserer Erkenntnisbemühungen?
2) Wie – mit welchen Mitteln und Verfahren – können wir dieses Ziel erreichen? (Und in welchen Bereichen können wir es erreichen?)
3) Wie – mit Hilfe welcher Kriterien – können wir überprüfen ob bzw. inwieweit wir dieses Ziel erreicht haben? (Beckermann 1997, S. 39)

Begriffsexternalismus gibt die Antwort auf die *erste* dieser Fragen: „Was wir anstreben, sind wahre Überzeugungen – nicht mehr und nicht weniger." (Beckermann 1997, S. 39) Im Gegensatz dazu beziehen sich Hinweise auf *zuverlässige meinungsbildende Verfahren* typischerweise auf die *zweite* Frage. Solche Verfahren sind nicht an sich epistemologisch wichtig, sondern nur als wesentliches und unverzichtbares *Mittel*, um unser einziges epistemisches Ziel zu erreichen.

> Gerade wer die Auffassung vertritt, das Ziel unserer Erkenntnisbemühungen seien wahre Überzeugungen und sonst nichts, wird sich daher in besonderer Weise um verläßliche Methoden der Erkenntnisgewinnung bemühen. Denn ohne solche Methoden kann er sein Ziel nicht erreichen. Allerdings wird das Ziel selbst durch diese Methoden nicht definiert. D.h., Antworten auf die Frage nach verläßlichen Methoden der Erkenntnisgewinnung sind Antworten auf die zweite, nicht auf die erste der drei Grundfragen der Erkenntnistheorie. (Beckermann 1997, S. 39)

Letztlich beziehen sich Hinweise auf *Rechtfertigungen* auf die *dritte* Grundfrage. Wenn wir eine Rechtfertigung suchen, argumentiert Beckermann, wollen wir wissen,

> ob wir uns auf das, wovon andere (oder auch wir selbst) überzeugt sind, *verlassen* können, ob wir in unserem Denken und Handeln von ihren Überzeugungen ausgehen können, mit anderen Worten: ob diese Überzeugungen (wahrscheinlich) wahr sind. (Beckermann 1997, S. 40)

Aus dieser Perspektive ist eine Überzeugung genau dann gerechtfertigt wenn sie ein Merkmal der wahrscheinlichen Wahrheit besitzt. Ihre Entstehung aus einem zuverlässigen meinungsbildenden Verfahren und die Fähigkeit des Glaubenden, sie durch das Zitieren guter Gründe zu unterstützen, sind solche Merkmale (Beckermann 1997, S. 41).[9]

Beckermann schließt also, daß

> *Wahrheit* und *Rechtfertigung* [...] Antworten auf zwei ganz verschiedene Fragen der Erkenntnistheorie [sind]. Wahrheit ist das Ziel und Rechtfertigung nur ein Mittel bzw. ein Kriterium. Was wir anstreben, sind *wahre Überzeugungen*. Ob eine Überzeugung *gerechtfertigt* ist, interessiert uns nur deshalb, weil ihre Wahrheit in der Regel nicht auf der Hand liegt. (Beckermann 1997, S. 41)

Demnach ist die klassische GWÜ-Analyse des Wissens das Produkt einer unglücklichen Begriffsvermengung. Statt immer wieder über die Frage zu streiten, welche Analyse *den* Wissensbegriff am besten vertritt, wäre es am vernünftigsten, so Beckermann, auf den Begriff des Wissens einfach zu verzichten, und nur über wahre Überzeugungen und gerechtfertigte Überzeugungen zu sprechen. Aber wenn wir trotzdem unsere systematische epistemologische Theorie so entwickeln wollen, daß sie nach wie vor *einem* Wissensbegriff eine Schlüsselrolle zuteilt, dann, schließt Beckermann,

> scheint es am vernünftigsten, den Ausdruck ‚Wissen' als Ausdruck für das Ziel unserer Erkenntnisbemühungen zu verwenden. Wenn man dies tut, gibt es jedoch keine Alternative zum minimalen Wissensbegriff, d.h., zur Identifikation von Wissen mit wahrer Überzeugung. Denn das Ziel aller Erkenntnisbemühungen sind wahre Überzeugungen und nichts anderes. (Beckermann 1997, S. 42-3)

Wie sollen wir die These verstehen, daß wahre Überzeugungen das *Ziel* unserer Erkenntnisbemühungen, paradigmatisch unserer Forschungen, sind? Normalerweise ist das Festlegen eines Ziels der erste Schritt einer Überlegung, die dazu dienen soll, die Mittel dem Zwecke anzupassen. Traditionell stellt man solch eine Überlegung mit Hilfe eines praktischen Syllogismus dar:

P1 Ich will (wir wollen) das Ziel Z erreichen.
P2 Die besten (die einzigen) Mittel, um Z zu erreichen, sind M.
P3 Also verwende ich (verwenden wir) M.

---

[9] Hier trifft sich Beckermann mit Crispin Sartwell: „[Justification] (a) gives procedures by which true beliefs are obtained, and (b) gives standards for evaluating the products of such procedures with regard to that goal. From the point of view of (a), justification prescribes techniques by which knowledge is gained. From the point of view of (b), it gives a criterion for knowledge. But in neither case does it describe a logically necessary condition for knowledge." (Sartwell 1992, S. 174)

Ich habe diese Überlegung so formuliert, um ihr Verhältnis zu wirklichem Verhalten zu betonen. D.h., P3 stellt einen *Entschluß* dar, der als dauerhafte oder unmittelbare *Absicht* zu verstehen ist. Wenn das Beabsichtigte sozusagen „ausführbar" ist, geht so eine Absicht unter den passenden Umständen *ceteris paribus* direkt in Handeln über. In der Tat, die Gedanken- und Sprachepisoden, die unsere Absichten und Willensakte ausdrücken, würden den dazu nötigen intentionalen Inhalt überhaupt nicht haben, wenn sie, als Ereignisse betrachtet, nicht solche kausalen Rollen spielten.

Kurzum, Ziele und Zwecke sind – typischerweise durch Vorhaben und Strategien spezifiziert – *kausal* mit dem Entstehen von (Dispositionen zu) individuellen Handlungen verbunden. Wir befassen uns hier nun speziell mit epistemischen Zielen, daher auch mit epistemischen Handlungen. Also brauchen wir, um die Idee, daß wahre Überzeugungen das Ziel der Forschung sind, verständlich zu machen, ein Beispiel dieser allgemeinen praktischen Syllogismusform, das eine Verbindung zwischen einer Festlegung auf dieses Ziel und dem tatsächlichen *Ausführen* der Forschung herstellt, das also zeigt, *wie* sich unsere Verpflichtung auf das Ziel der Wahrheit in unseren konkreten kognitiv-epistemischen Aktivitäten niederschlagen kann.

Wenn wir uns nach Beckermann richten, stoßen wir zuerst auf ungefähr folgendes:

P1a Wir wollen, daß unsere Überzeugungen wahr sind.
P2a Das beste (das einzige) Mittel, um das zu bewirken, ist nur das zu glauben, was gerechtfertigt ist,
P3a Also glauben wir nur das, was gerechtfertigt ist.

Diese Formulierung setzt jedoch einen offensichtlich unannehmbaren Voluntarismus hinsichtlich von Überzeugungen voraus. Obwohl etwas zu glauben sehr allgemein gesprochen ein Tun ist, ist Glauben keine ausführbare Handlung. Wovon man überzeugt ist, entscheidet man nicht und wählt es nicht aus. Man stellt bloß fest, daß man von diesem oder jenem überzeugt ist (oder nicht), und eine Erklärung dieser Tatsache kann, muß aber nicht, irgendeine Begründung, ein Beweismittel oder eine Rechtfertigung erwähnen. Dieses Beispiel zeigt also noch nicht die gesuchte Verbindung zwischen dem Ziel der Wahrheit und wirklichen konkreten epistemischen Aktivitäten.

Wir können trotzdem Beckermanns Behauptung zustimmen, daß das beste (oder das einzige) Mittel, um zu wahren Überzeugungen zu gelangen, darin besteht, das zu glauben, was gerechtfertigt ist, aber nur weil Beckermann das Gerechtfertigtsein einer Überzeugung damit *identifiziert*, daß sie eine wahrheitshinweisende Eigenschaft besitzt. „Eine Überzeugung, daß *p*, ist genau dann gerechtfertigt, wenn sie ein Merkmal besitzt, aus dem hervorgeht, daß *p* (wahrscheinlich) wahr ist" (Beckermann 1997, S. 41). Weil es kein wirksames Verfahren gibt (noch geben kann), wahre Überzeugungen als solche zu erkennen, d. h. keine epistemisch zugänglichen *wahrheits-bestimmenden* Eigenschaften von Überzeugungen, fällt es uns schwer, uns irgendeine Alternative zur Suche nach Rechtfertigungen vorzustellen, von *besseren* Alternativen ganz zu schweigen.

Aber eben weil es unmöglich ist, epistemisch zugängliche wahrheits*bestimmende* Eigenschaften von Überzeugungen zu finden, wird es sehr problematisch, die notwendigen wahrheits*hinweisenden* Eigenschaften der Überzeugungen zu identifiziern. Im Einklang mit der Tradition schlägt Beckermann zwei solcher Eigenschaften vor:

> Überzeugungen, die durch verläßliche Methoden gewonnen wurden, sind ... gerechtfertigt; aber auch Überzeugungen, für die die jeweilige Person S gute Gründe anführen kann. Denn auch dieses Merkmal spricht dafür, daß das, was S glaubt, wahr ist. (Beckermann 1997, S. 41)

Natürlich können wir zustimmen, daß Überzeugungen, die durch verläßliche Methoden gewonnen wurden, wahrscheinlich wahr sind, aber nur weil unter der normalen Voraussetzung eine überzeugungsschaffende Methode nur dann *verläßlich* ist, wenn sie *tatsächlich* überwiegend wahre Überzeugungen liefert. Wenn die Zuverlässigkeit einer Methode so *definiert* wird, folgt es trivialerweise, daß die Überzeugungen, die aus ihrer Anwendung entstehen, wahrscheinlich wahr sind.

Ähnliches gilt für Beckermanns zweiten Vorschlag, daß die Tatsache, daß eine Person gute Gründe für eine Überzeugung anführen kann, ein Hinweis auf die wahrscheinliche Wahrheit dieser Überzeugung ist. Denn aufgrund wessen wird ein angeführter Grund, z. B. daß r, für eine bestimmte Überzeugung, z. B. daß p, ein *guter* Grund sein? Traditionell lautet die Antwort: die Tatsache, daß r, erhöht beträchtlich die Wahrscheinlichkeit, daß p wahr ist. Und wenn der Wert einer Begründung so *definiert* wird, folgt wieder trivialerweise, daß Überzeugungen, die sich gut begründen lassen, wahrscheinlich wahr sind.

Die Schwierigkeit entsteht, wenn wir versuchen, solche trivialen Notwendigkeiten in konkrete epistemische Verfahrensweisen umzuwandeln. Denn um zu *bestimmen*, daß eine überzeugungsschaffende Methode verläßlich ist, brauchen wir offensichtlich ein *unabhängiges* Mittel um festzustellen, ob die Überzeugungen, die aus Anwendungen dieser Methode entstehen, überwiegend wahr *sind*. Und dementsprechend gilt, daß wir, um zu bestimmen, daß ein *gegebener* Grund r für eine Überzeugung p ein *guter* Grund für p ist, bestimmen können müssen, daß die Tatsache, daß r, die Wahrscheinlichkeit, daß p wahr ist, tatsächlich steigert – und es ist abermals schwierig zu sehen, wie das möglich wäre, ohne ein zugängliches *unabhängiges* Mittel, um festzustellen, daß *p* immer oder oft wahr *ist*, wenn *r* besteht.

Hier würde ein epistemischer Externalist höchstwahrscheinlich einwenden, daß wir die Zuverlässigkeit unserer überzeugungsschaffenden Methoden (bzw. den wahrheitshinweisenden Charakter unserer Begründungen) nicht *bestimmen* müssen, um in unseren Überzeugungen gerechtfertigt zu sein. Es reicht aus, daß diese Überzeugungen aus der Anwendung von Methoden, die *tatsächlich* zuverlässig sind, entstehen (bzw. auf Gründen basieren, die *tatsächlich* gut sind).

Aber das Problem ist nicht, daß wir keine Garantie haben können, daß unsere Versuche, objektive Wahrheiten zu erreichen, gelingen werden. Die Schwierigkeit liegt vielmehr grob gesprochen darin, daß wir keinen Grund haben zu glauben, daß unsere wirklichen epistemischen Aktivitäten *überhaupt* eine, wie auch immer geartete Beziehung zu solchen objektiven Wahrheiten haben. Wir können gar keinen *Zusammenhang* feststellen, zwischen unseren konkreten epistemischen Vorgehensweisen und dem angeblichen Ziel, (nur) objektive wahre Überzeugungen zu haben. Wenn wir eine Erklärung der bloßen Möglichkeit suchen, daß wahre Überzeugungen das Ziel unserer epistemischen Aktivitäten sind, ist der traditionelle Externalismus nur eine Sackgasse. Denn wenn wir nicht *feststellen* können, welche überzeugungsschaffenden Methoden verläßlich sind (bzw. welche gegebenen Gründe gute Gründe sind), dann können wir unsere angeblich vorrangige Verpflichtung auf das Ziel der Wahrheit keineswegs in konkrete epistemische Verhaltensweisen und Strategien ummünzen.

Das Ergebnis dieser Überlegungen scheint also zu sein, daß objektive Wahrheit trotz fast universeller Einmütigkeit einfach nicht als Ziel unserer epistemischen Aktivitäten dienen *kann*. Richard Rorty hat den springenden Punkt prägnant so formuliert, „Es ist einfach nicht das, was der gesunde Menschenverstand als ein Ziel bezeichnen würde. Denn es ist weder etwas, das wir als erreicht erkennen könnten, noch etwas, an das wir uns heranarbeiten könnten" (Rortry 1998, S. 39).[10] Damit ist nicht gesagt, daß es kein erklärbares Verhältnis zwischen wahren Überzeugungen und unseren konkreten epistemischen Vorgehensweisen geben könnte, aber es läßt sich daraus schließen, daß die traditionelle Vorstellung von diesem Verhältnis, als einem Verhältnis zwischen epistemischem Zweck und epistemischem Mit-

---

[10] „It is not what common sense would call a goal. For it is neither something we might realize we had rached, nor something to which we might get closer." Richard Rorty, „Is Truth a Goal of Inquiry?", in *Truth and Progress*, Philosophical Papers, Vol. 3 (Cambridge University Press; Cambridge and New York: 1998), S. 19–42.

tel, wesentlich falsch ist. Der Philosoph, der das wahrscheinlich am klarsten gesehen hat, ist C. S. Peirce:

> Wir mögen uns zwar einbilden, [daß] wir [...] nicht bloß eine Meinung, sondern eine wahre Meinung [suchen]. Aber stelle diese Einbildung auf die Probe, und sie erweist sich als grundlos, denn sobald eine feste Überzeugung erreicht ist, sind wir völlig zufriedengestellt, gleichgültig ob die Überzeugung wahr oder falsch ist. Und es ist klar, daß nichts außerhalb des Bereiches unserer Erkenntnis das Ziel unseres Forschens sein kann, denn was unseren Verstand nicht beeinflußt, kann auch nicht Motiv einer Anstrengung des Verstandes sein. Das Äußerste, was wir behaupten können, ist, daß wir nach einer Überzeugung suchen, die wir *für wahr halten*. Aber wir halten jede unserer Überzeugungen für wahr, und daher ist die zuletzt vorgeschlagene Ausdrucksweise eine bloße Tautologie. (Peirce 1967, 5.375)[11]

Peirces Bemerkung, daß das, was den Verstand nicht beeinflußt, auch nicht als Beweggrund geistiger Bemühung dienen kann, spiegelt das Leitmotiv unserer letzten Überlegungen wider, daß etwas, was das Wesen und die Struktur unserer wirklichen konkreten epistemischen Vorgehensweisen nicht bestimmen kann, auch nicht als Ziel dieser Aktivitäten dienen könne. Denn ein vermeintliches Ziel kann den Verstand nur dann beeinflussen, wenn wir gelegentlich bestimmen können, ob das angebliche Ziel schon erreicht ist, oder ob wir uns ihm wenigstens angenähert haben.

Andererseits spiegelt Peirces Bemerkung, daß wir jede unserer Überzeugungen für wahr halten, die Platitüde wider, daß das Überzeugtsein ein Fürwahrhalten *ist*. *Alles*, wovon wir derzeit überzeugt sind, halten wir für wahr. Rortys „ironistische" Perspektive wandelt diese Platitüde in die Behauptung um, daß unsere Wahrheitsbewertungen immer „whiggisch", d.h. rückwärtsgewandt, sind, und Robert Brandom behandelt sie im Wesentlichen als eine Äquivalenz: Etwas für wahr zu halten bedeutet so viel wie: die Rechtfertigungsverpflichtungen, die das Überzeugtsein ausmachen, selbst zu übernehmen, d.h., kurz gesagt, selbst davon überzeugt zu sein. Folglich kann eine solche „immanente" Wahrheit auch nur dem Namen nach ein Ziel

---

[11] „We may fancy [...] that we seek, not merely an opinion, but a true opinion. But put this fancy to the test and it proves groundless; for as soon as a firm belief is reached we are entirely satisfied, whether the belief be true or false. And it is clear that nothing out of the sphere of our knowledge can be our object, for nothing which does not affect the mind can be a motive for mental effort. The most that can be maintained is, that we seek for a belief that we shall *think* to be true. But we think each one of our beliefs to be true, and, indeed, it is mere tautology to say so." (Peirce 1967, 5.375) C.S. Peirce, „The Fixation of Belief", in *Collected Papers of Charles Sanders Peirce*, 6 vols., ed. C. Hartshorne and P. Weiss; (Cambridge, MA: 1931–35), vol. 5, S. 358–87. Zitiert aus „Die Festlegung einer Überzeugung", in Charles Sanders Peirce, *Schriften I: Zur Entstehung des Pragmatismus*, herausgegeben von Karl-Otto Apel, (Suhrkamp Verlag; Frankfurt a.M.: 1967).

sein. Wie das angebliche Ziel der „epistemisch-transzendenten" objektiven Wahrheit lenkt sie keineswegs die wirkliche konkrete Ausführung unserer Forschung. Und wie wir in jenem Fall keinen Grund haben können zu glauben, daß wir unser angebliches Ziel erreicht haben, können wir in diesem Fall keinen Grund haben zu glauben, daß wir unser angebliches Ziel *noch nicht erreicht* haben. Aber ein echtes Ziel wird nur dann festgelegt, wenn es einen wirklichen, greifbaren Unterschied impliziert, zwischen den Verhaltensweisen, die zu seiner Verwirklichung führen oder tendieren, und denen, die das nicht tun. Das ist der zweite wesentliche Punkt, den epistemische Externalisten vergessen.

Wir sind somit zum Schluß gekommen, daß kein Wahrheitsbegriff eine bestimmende Rolle für unsere epistemischen Aktivitäten spielen kann, weder der transzendente Begriff objektiver Wahrheit, noch der minimalistische Begriff immanenter Wahrheit. Der Verdacht liegt also nahe, daß ein Wahrheitsbegriff überhaupt keine wesentlichen Rolle in einer angemessenen epistemologischen Theorie zu spielen hat. Tatsächlich, wenn das Wort ‚wahr', wie u. a. Simon Blackburn bemerkt hat [12], „ausschweifend" ist – d. h. nicht nur auf Aussagen angewandt wird, sondern auch auf Sätze, die z. B. Normen oder Absichten ausdrücken – und wenn es zudem, wie u. a. Donald Davidson argumentiert hat [13], undefinierbar ist, dann ist es vielleicht am vernünftigsten, den Wahrheitsbegriff einfach beiseite zu lassen und das Ziel unserer kognitiv-epistemischen Aktivitäten direkt in *gerechtfertigten* Überzeugungen zu suchen. Das Ziel aller Erkenntnisbemühungen sind gerechtfertigte Überzeugungen und nichts anderes.

Diese „begriffsinternalistische" Darstellung des Wissens ist natürlich genau das Gegenteil von Beckermanns „begriffsexternalistischem" Schluß. Aber es sollte jetzt klar sein, daß sich Beckermanns Verteidigung des „minimalen Wissensbegriffs" von Kutscheras auf eine tief problematische und letztlich unhaltbare Form einer systematischen epistemologischen Theorie stützt. Denn wenn der Kern einer solchen Theorie darin besteht, die drei Fragen:

1) Was ist das Ziel unserer Erkenntnisbemühungen?
2) Wie [...] können wir dieses Ziel erreichen? [und]
3) Wie [...] können wir überprüfen ob bzw. inwieweit wir dieses Ziel erreicht haben? (Beckermann 1997, S. 39)

befriedigend zu beantworten, dann schneidet, wie wir gesehen haben, die traditionelle Theorie, nach der wahre Überzeugungen das vorrangige

---

[12] Cf. „Wittgenstein, Wright, Rorty and Minimalism", *Mind*, 107, 1998, S. 157–81.
[13] Cf. „The Folly of Trying to Define Truth", *Journal of Philosophy*, 93, 1996, S. 263–78.

Ziel und Rechtfertigungen die dazu geeigneten Mittel sind, sehr schlecht ab.[14]

Literatur

Beckermann, A.: Wissen und wahre Meinung. In: *Das weite Spektrum der analytischen Philosophie: Festschrift für Franz von Kutschera*, hrsg. von W. Lenzen, de Gruyter, Berlin 1997, 24–43.

Blackburn, S.: Wittgenstein, Wright, Rorty and Minimalism, *Mind* 107 (1998), 157–81.

Brandom, R.: *Making it explicit*, Harvard University Press, Cambridge, MA 1992.

Davidson, D.: The Folly of Trying to Define Truth, *Journal of Philosophy* 93 (1996), 263–78.

Kutschera, F. von: *Grundfragen der Erkenntnistheorie*, de Gruyter, Berlin 1982.

Peirce, C.S.: Die Festlegung einer Überzeugung. In: *C. S. Peirce, Schriften I: Zur Entstehung des Pragmatismus*, hrsg. von K.-O. Apel, Suhrkamp Verlag, Frankfurt am Main 1967. Original: The Fixation of Belief. In: *Collected Papers of Charles Sanders Peirce, 6 vols.*, ed. by C. Hartshorne and P. Weiss, Cambridge, MA 1931–35, vol. 5, 358–87.

Platon: *Menon*. Hrsg. von K. Reich, Felix Meiner Verlag, Hamburg 1972.

Rorty, R.: Is Truth a Goal of Inquiry?. In R. Rorty: *Truth and Progress, Philosophical Papers, Vol. 3*, Cambridge University Press, Cambridge and New York 1998, 19–42.

Sartwell, C.: Knowledge is Merely True Belief, *American Philosophical Quarterly* 28 (1991), 157–65.

Sartwell, C.: Why Knowledge is Merely True Belief, *The Journal of Philosophy* 89 (1992), 167–80.

Sellars, W.: *Der Empirismus in der Philosophie des Geistes*, mentis, Paderborn 1999.

Sosa, E.: *Knowledge in Perspective: Selected Essays in Epistemology*, Cambridge University Press, Cambridge 1991.

---

[14] Für eine letzte sprachliche Korrektur meines Textes bin ich Ralf Stoecker unaussprechlich dankbar.

Wolfgang Lenzen

Realität und „Wirklichkeit"

Kritische Bemerkungen zu Gerhard Roths „neurobiologischem Konstruktivismus"

Abstract

In *Das Gehirn und seine Wirklichkeit* Gerhard Roth develops a so-called „neurobiological constructivism" the main theses of which can be summarized as follows:

- The task of brain science is to find out which neural processes underlie mental processes like consciousness and thinking. These processes together form our world of experience („Wirklichkeit") which is a construction of the brain.
- The subjective „Wirklichkeit" must be distinguished from an „objective" trans-phenomenal world which exists independent of our conscious experience, which cannot be experienced, and which is referred to by Roth as „reality" („Realität").
- Sensory experiences of a subject S must not be interpreted as relations between S and the objective „reality" but rather as relations between S and her subjective „Wirklichkeit".

This paper aims to show that the neurobiological constructivism rests on confusions concerning the ontological relation between the two realms of „Wirklichkeit" vs. „Realität" and concerning the epistemological status of the relation of sensual experience.

1. Der „neurobiologische Konstruktivismus"

In seinem 1994 erschienenen Buch *Das Gehirn und seine Wirklichkeit* hat der Bremer Hirnforscher Gerhard Roth die Position eines neurobiologischen Konstruktivismus entwickelt, deren Kernthesen sich folgendermaßen zusammenfassen lassen:

(*K1*) Aufgabe der Hirnforschung ist es herauszufinden, „welche neuronalen Prozesse den geistigen oder mentalen Prozessen wie Bewusstsein und Denken in unserem Gehirn zugrunde liegen und wie sich dies alles zu einer Einheit zusammenfügt. Diese Prozesse zusammen bilden [...] unsere Erlebniswelt, die *Wirklichkeit*" (19; 21).[1]

(*K2*) „Die Wirklichkeit, in der ich lebe, ist [...] ein Konstrukt des Gehirns" (19; 21). Diese auch als „phänomenale Welt" bezeichnete „Wirklichkeit" bzw. die „Welt unserer Empfindungen besteht aus drei Bereichen: der Außenwelt, der Welt unseres Körpers und der Welt unserer geistigen und emotionalen Zustände" (278; 314).

(*K3*) „Dieser Wirklichkeit wird gedanklich eine *transphänomenale* Welt gegenüber gestellt, die unerfahrbar ist und dementsprechend in der phänomenalen Welt nicht vorkommt" (280; 316). „Diese Welt wird als „objektive", bewusstseinsunabhängige oder transphänomenale Welt bezeichnet [... und] der Einfachheit halber *Realität* genannt" (288; 324).

(*K4*) Die Wahrnehmungen eines Subjekts *S* ebenso wie seine kausalen Interaktionen mit der Außenwelt sind jedoch nicht als Relationen zwischen *S* und der *Realität* zu deuten, sondern so, „daß alle erlebten Vorgänge zwischen mir [...] und der Außenwelt *innerhalb der Wirklichkeit* ablaufen. Wenn ich einen Gegenstand anfasse oder mit einer Person spreche, so fasse ich einen *wirklichen* Gegenstand an und spreche mit einer *wirklichen* Person" (280; 316).

(*K5*) „Wir sind damit zu einer *Aufteilung der Welt* in Realität und Wirklichkeit [...] gelangt. *Die Wirklichkeit wird in der Realität durch das reale Gehirn hervorgebracht*. Sie ist damit Teil der Realität, und zwar derjenige Teil, in dem wir vorkommen. Dies ist eine höchst *plausible* Annahme, die wir allerdings innerhalb der Wirklichkeit treffen und die nicht als eine Aussage über die tatsächliche Beschaffenheit der Realität mißverstanden werden darf" (289; 325).

Wie im folgenden gezeigt werden soll, beruhen entscheidende Teile dieser Aussagen auf fundamentalen Verwirrungen bezüglich des logischen Zusammenhangs zwischen Realität und „Wirklichkeit" und der erkenntnistheoretischen Beziehung des Wahrnehmens, wie sie im Kern bereits 1918 in Gottlob Freges Aufsatz „Der Gedanke" aufgedeckt wurden.

---

[1] Seitenangaben ohne nähere Literaturverweise beziehen sich auf die erste Auflage Roth 1994; zur Kontrolle werden hinter dem Semikolon die Seitenangaben der wohl häufiger benutzten, leicht revidierten Ausgabe im Rahmen der Reihe *stw* angegeben.

2. Realität und „Wirklichkeit"

Im Lichte des üblichen alltäglichen und philosophischen Sprachgebrauchs erscheint eine Unterscheidung zwischen „Wirklichkeit" und Realität zunächst einigermaßen *unnatürlich*. Doch dies ist nur ein linguistischer Punkt, kein Sachproblem. Folgen wir also Roth und verstehen unter der „Wirklichkeit" (des Subjekts S) gemäß *K1* die phänomenale Erlebniswelt von S, d.h. die Menge aller Empfindungen oder Erlebnisse von S bzw. die Menge der *Vorstellungen* von S. Solche Vorstellungen sind nun keineswegs, wie Philosophen früher vielleicht glaubten, einfache *Abbilder* einer zugrundeliegenden Realität, sondern durchweg *Konstruktionen* des jeweiligen Subjekts. Wegen des Löwenanteils von Arbeit, die das Gehirn bei solcher Konstruktion zu leisten hat, erscheint es durchaus vernünftig, gemäß *K2* die „Wirklichkeit", d.h. die Gesamtheit der Vorstellungen von S, als „Konstrukt des Gehirns" zu bezeichnen.

Dieser Ansatz führt jedoch logisch zwingend zu der Annahme, dass es außer(halb) der „Wirklichkeit" von S zumindest *eine* weitere Entität gibt, die nicht selber ein Konstrukt des Gehirns von S sein kann, nämlich das *Subjekt S* bzw. dessen Gehirn – $G(S)$ – selber. Auf dieses elementare, aber erkenntnistheoretisch äußerst bedeutsame Faktum hatte Frege schon 1918 aufmerksam gemacht, als er gegen die idealistische Annahme, *alles* in der Welt sei eine bloße Vorstellung, den schlagenden Einwand vorbrachte:

> Wenn alles Vorstellung ist, so gibt es keinen Träger der Vorstellungen. Und so erlebe ich nun wieder einen Umschlag ins Entgegengesetzte. Wenn es keinen Träger der Vorstellungen gibt, so gibt es auch keine Vorstellungen; denn Vorstellungen bedürfen eines Trägers, ohne den sie nicht bestehen können. [...] Kann es ein Erleben geben, ohne jemanden, der es erlebt? Was wäre dieses ganze Schauspiel ohne einen Zuschauer? Kann es einen Schmerz geben, ohne jemanden, der ihn hat? Das Empfundenwerden gehört notwendig zum Schmerze, und zum Empfundenwerden gehört wieder jemand, der empfindet. Dann aber gibt es etwas, was nicht meine Vorstellung ist und doch Gegenstand meiner Betrachtung, meines Denkens sein kann, und ich bin von der Art. (Frege 1918, 47)

In ähnlicher Weise sah auch Roth ein: „Wenn ich aber annehme, dass die Wirklichkeit ein Konstrukt des Gehirns ist, so bin ich gleichzeitig gezwungen, eine Welt anzunehmen, in der dieses Gehirn, der *Konstrukteur*, existiert" (288; 324). Denn wenn man „die Existenz einer bewusstseinsunabhängigen Welt, der Realität, leugnen [würde], dann [...] wären [...] alle Befunde über das Zustandekommen der „Welt im Kopf" völlig rätselhaft" (289; 325). Oder noch etwas detaillierter:

Wenn ich [...] davon ausgehe, daß die Wirklichkeit durch das reale Gehirn erzeugt [wird], so folgt daraus logisch, daß es eine Entität geben muß, welche nicht Teil der Wirklichkeit ist. Die gesamten Ausführungen darüber, welche Funktion Wahrnehmung hat, wofür Sinnesorgane nötig sind, was sie tun, wie das Gehirn funktioniert, all dies ist natürlich unsinnig, wenn ich nicht gleichzeitig annehme, daß es eine Realität gibt, in de[r] ein Gehirn existiert, auf das ich diese Aussagen beziehen kann. (321; 358/9)

Das folgende Diagramm illustriert in schematischer Weise die konstruktivistische Aufteilung der Welt in „Realität" und „Wirklichkeit", wie sie sich aus der Perspektive eines einzelnen Subjekts S darstellt. Dabei symbolisiert der Pfeil ⇒ die Relation des Erzeugens bzw. Konstruierens:

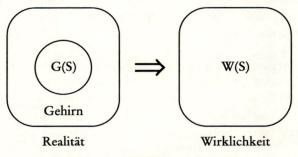

Diagramm 1: Die Welt (eines Subjekts S)

Roths Erörterungen erfolgen über weite Strecken des Werks aus der „solipsistischen" Perspektive des einen (eigenen) Ichs und seiner „Wirklichkeit". Erst gegen Ende des Buchs bemerkt der Autor beiläufig, dass „es eben-

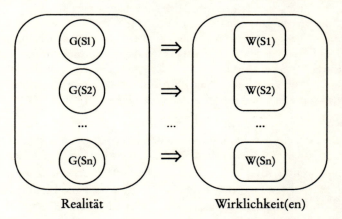

Diagramm 2: Die Welt aus intersubjektiver Perspektive

soviele individuelle Wirklichkeiten [gibt], wie es reale Gehirne gibt" (297; 333). Deshalb muss der neurobiologische Konstruktivist allgemeiner für *jedes* erkenntnisfähige Subjekt S_i die Existenz eines realen Gehirns, $G(S_i)$, anerkennen, welches die je subjektive Wirklichkeit von S_i, $W(S_i)$, konstruiert. Aus transsubjektiver Perspektive wäre die Aufteilung der Welt in Realität und „Wirklichkeit(en)" deshalb schematisch wie oben (S. 36, unten) darzustellen.

Des weiteren soll man gemäß *K2* die Erlebniswelt oder „Wirklichkeit" eines Subjekts *S* in drei Teilbereiche aufspalten, nämlich (i) in die sog. Außenwelt (relativ zu *S*), (ii) in den Körper von *S* und (iii) in die geistigen und emotionalen Zustände – bzw. kurz: die Psyche – von *S*. Im einfachsten, „solipsistischen" Fall ließe sich dies durch das folgende Diagramm verdeutlichen:

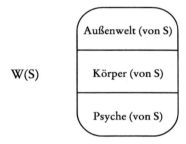

Diagramm 3: Dreiteilung der „Wirklichkeit"

Aus intersubjektiver Perspektive wäre das frühere Diagramm 2 entsprechend wie folgt zu modifizieren:

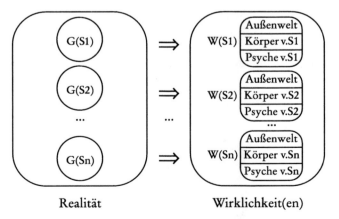

Diagramm 4: Realität und „Wirklichkeit"

Aus dieser Darstellung geht hervor, dass Roth sich etwas ungenau und fehlerhaft ausdrückt, wenn er in These *K5* die „Wirklichkeit" als jenen „Teil der Realität" bezeichnete, „in dem wir [Menschen] vorkommen", und wenn er anschließend behauptet, dass die Unterscheidung zwischen Realität und Wirklichkeit „innerhalb der Wirklichkeit" selber getroffen würde und „nicht als eine Aussage über die tatsächliche Beschaffenheit der Realität mißverstanden werden" dürfe. Zwar bleibt die in Diagramm 3 dargestellte Unterteilung in sog. Außenwelt, Körper und Psyche trivialerweise innerhalb der „Wirklichkeit" des jeweiligen Subjekts *S*. Aber die in Diagramm 4 veranschaulichte globalere und fundamentalere Unterteilung der *Welt* in bewusstseinsunabhängige Realität einerseits und phänomenale „Wirklichkeit(en)" andererseits geht bereits aus sprachlogischen Gründen über die Grenzen der je subjektiven „Wirklichkeit(en)" hinaus. Wie übrigens auch der erste Satz von *K5* eindeutig zum Ausdruck bringt, muss diese Unterscheidung notwendigerweise als Aussage über die *tatsächliche Beschaffenheit der umfassenden Welt* verstanden werden, die für jedes erkenntnisfähige Subjekt S_i neben dem realen Gehirn $G(S_i)$ auch die von ihm konstruierte Erfahrungswelt $W(S_i)$ (samt deren Teilbereichen Psyche, Körper und Außenwelt) enthält. Ingesamt muss der neurobiologische Konstruktivist also zumindest die folgenden Behauptungen über die objektive Realität unterschreiben:

(*R1*) Es gibt eine von den je subjektiven „Wirklichkeiten" unabhängige Realität.

(*R2*) Für jedes erkenntnisfähige Subjekt S_i ist das reale Gehirn $G(S_i)$, welches die je subjektive Erlebniswelt $W(S_i)$ erzeugt, ein Bestandteil dieser objektiven Realität.

Wenn man sich über das so präzisierte Verhältnis von Realität und „Wirklichkeit" erst einmal klar geworden ist, braucht man bei diesen Thesen allerdings keineswegs stehen zu bleiben. Aufgrund elementarer biologischer Annahmen können Gehirne wohl kaum ohne einen entsprechenden *Körper* existieren, d.h. die folgende „Hypothese" ist zumindest überaus „plausibel":

(*R3*) In der Realität wird das *reale* Gehirn von einem *real* existierenden Organismus mit *realem* Blut versorgt.

So gestand übrigens auch Roth beiläufig die (hypothetische) Existenz von *realen* Organismen zu, die u.a. *reale* Gehirne und Sinnesorgane enthalten.[2]

---

[2] Vgl. S. 288; 324: „In dieser Welt [der Realität] – so nehmen wir an – gibt es viele Dinge, unter anderem auch Organismen. Viele Organismen haben Sinnesorgane, auf die physikalische und chemische Ereignisse als Reize einwirken, und sie haben Gehirne, in denen aufgrund dieser Einwirkungen und interner Prozesse eine phänomenale Welt entsteht, eben die Wirklichkeit."

Weil aber weiterhin das „*reale* Gehirn [...] in seiner Realität kaum auf Dauer durch imaginäre Speisen sich und seinen Organismus am Leben erhalten" (294; 330) kann, müsste Roth im nächsten Schritt konsequenterweise auch die Existenz von *realer Nahrung* anerkennen, z. B. vom realem Brot, das aus realem Weizen gebacken wurde, welcher auf einem realen Weizenfeld heranwuchs, dessen Wachstum die Existenz von realen Nährstoffen, realer Feuchtigkeit und realer Sonneneinstrahlung voraussetzt, usw. In Fortsetzung dieses Gedankengangs erscheint es „höchst plausibel", aufgrund weiterer naturgesetzlicher Hypothesen die reale Existenz (fast) aller noch so kleinen Details der Welt anzuerkennen, die wir ansonsten – im Alltag wie im Wissenschaftsbetrieb – als ‚Realität' zu bezeichnen gewohnt sind.[3]

Gegen eine solche Ausdehnung von Aussagen über die „tatsächliche Beschaffenheit der Realität" würde Roth vermutlich den Einwand erheben, dass zwischen den „Axiomen" *R1*, *R2* und den hieraus mit Hilfe von naturwissenschaftlichen Hypothesen abgeleiteten „Theoremen" à la *R3* ein gravierender Unterschied hinsichtlich ihres *epistemischen Status* bestehe. Die Basisprinzipien *R1* und *R2* ergeben sich aus den Grundvoraussetzungen des neurobiologischen Konstruktivismus mit *logischer* bzw. *analytischer* Notwendigkeit; sie sind deshalb *subjektiv völlig gewiss*. Hingegen führe bereits der „hypothetische" Schluss von der Existenz eines realen menschlichen Gehirns auf die Existenz eines realen menschlichen Körpers zu einer logisch keineswegs mehr zwingenden, sondern prinzipiell *fehlbaren* und deshalb auch subjektiv nicht völlig sicheren Annahme, für die man keine *objektive Wahrheit* beanspruchen dürfe.

Auf das Problem der „objektiven Wahrheit" und Roths diesbezüglicher Skepsis wird in Abschnitt 5 weiter unten näher eingegangen. Im Moment sei bloß festgehalten, dass die *Fehlbarkeit* einer Aussage A *alleine* noch keinen hinreichenden Grund für die skeptische Schlussfolgerung darstellt, es gäbe kein objektive Wahrheit bzw. objektives Wissen sei unmöglich.[4] Von wenigen Ausnahmen (wie z. B. dem Cartesischen ‚Cogito ergo sum') abgesehen, sind *alle* Aussagen sowohl über die Existenz als auch über die Beschaffenheit irgendwelcher realer Objekte der Außenwelt *fehlbar*. Wie Frege in der bereits zitierten Kritik des Idealismus feststellte, ist der Verzicht auf Unfehlbarkeit der unvermeidbare Preis, den man zahlen muss, wenn man sich anheischt, Behauptungen über die objektive Realität aufzustellen:

---

[3] Es war z. B. mit Sicherheit eine *reale* Kugel, die am 15. Juli 1997 das reale Gehirn von Gianni Versace durchdrang und damit nicht nur dem realen Leben, sondern zugleich auch der subjektiven Wirklichkeit des homosexuellen Modezaren ein jähes Ende bereitete.

[4] Für eine ausführliche Begründung dieser Position vgl. Kutschera 1982, Kap. 1, spez. Abschnitt 1.7.

> Mit dem Schritte, mit dem ich mir eine Umwelt erobere, setze ich mich der Gefahr des Irrtums aus. Und hier stoße ich auf einen weiteren Unterschied meiner Innenwelt von der Außenwelt. [...] So finden wir im Gegensatz zu weit verbreiteten Meinungen in der Innenwelt Sicherheit, während uns bei unsern Ausflügen in die Außenwelt der Zweifel nie ganz verlässt. Dennoch [... können] wir es wagen [...], über die Dinge der Außenwelt zu urteilen. Und wir müssen das sogar wagen auf die Gefahr des Irrtums hin, wenn wir nicht weit größeren Gefahren erliegen wollen. (Frege 1918, 49)

Dies trifft selbstverständlich auch auf die überwältigende Mehrheit von Roths Aussagen in *Das Gehirn und seine Wirklichkeit* zu.[5] Die Ausführungen in den nicht-philosophischen Kapiteln des Werks, in denen der Aufbau und die Funktionsweise des Gehirns bzw. des Nervensystems beschrieben wird, sind klarerweise als (fehlbare) Behauptungen über die objektive Realität interpretieren, und nicht als (unfehlbare) Erfahrungsberichte über die phänomenale Erlebniswelt des Subjekts Gerhard Roth. Naturwissenschaftler beschäftigen sich generell mit den *objektiven* Gesetzmäßigkeiten der Natur, und dem Neurobiologen kommt dabei die spezielle Aufgabe zu, wissenschaftlich zu erklären, wie Lebewesen mit hinreichend komplexen Nervensystemen es schaffen, sich eine innere Repräsentation eben dieser Außenwelt – also eine, wie Roth es nennt, subjektive „Wirklichkeit" – zu erzeugen. Dass der *Philosoph* G. R. dem *Naturwissenschaftler* G. R. nicht die Aufgabe zugestehen will, die „objektive" Realität zu erforschen[6], hat seinen Grund offenbar darin, dass er aufgrund seines früheren Studiums der Kantschen Erkenntnistheorie meinte, die folgende Frage im Sinne der ersten Alternative beantworten zu müssen:

3. Was nehmen wir wahr: die „Wirklichkeit" oder die Realität?

Für jeden Naturwissenschaftler sollte eigentlich feststehen, dass es sich bei den verschiedenen Formen sinnlicher Wahrnehmung – Sehen, Hören, Riechen, Schmecken, Tasten – um Prozesse handelt, bei denen ein wahrnehmungsfähiges Subjekt sich Informationen über Dinge bzw. Ereignisse seiner *realen Umwelt* verschafft. Dabei muss allerdings eingeschränkt werden, dass Wahrnehmung erstens *selektiv* ist, d.h. die Umwelt wird „nur in dem Maße

---

[5] In der Tat handelt es sich auch bei der fundamentalen Aussage *R2* bzw. *K2*, der zufolge das (reale) Gehirn für die Konstruktion der subjektiven „Wirklichkeit" verantwortlich ist, um eine solche fehlbare – wenngleich „völlig plausible" – biologische *Hypothese*!
[6] Vgl. das allzu bescheidene Schlusscredo (326; 363), wo Roth meint, den Anspruch, „als Wissenschaftler [...] objektive Wahrheiten zu verkünden", aufgeben zu müssen.

...fasst, in dem Merkmale und Prozesse der Welt für einen Organismus überlebensrelevant sind" (72; 85). Zweitens besteht Wahrnehmung nicht einfach in einer direkten *Abbildung* „der Welt durch das Gehirn [...]. Vielmehr werden die physikalisch-chemischen Umweltereignisse in den Sinnesorganen in die „Sprache des Gehirns" übersetzt, d.h. in neuroelektrische Erregungszustände und ihre neurochemischen Äquivalente" (100/101; 114). Kurz und gut: „Wahrnehmung hängt zwar mit Umweltereignissen zusammen, welche die verschiedenen Sinnesorgane erregen; sie ist jedoch nicht abbildend, sondern *konstruktiv*" (112; 125).

Aufgrund dieser Einsicht glaubt der Philosoph nun schließen zu dürfen, dass die *wahrgenommenen Gegenstände bzw. Prozesse selber* ebenfalls nur Konstruktionen des (realen) Gehirns und damit Elemente der je subjektiven „Wirklichkeit" sind. So bezeichnet Roth generell „diejenigen Dinge und Vorgänge, die ich anschaulich wahrnehme, als Konstrukte des Gehirns" (292; 328) und behauptet z.B. ganz konkret: „Wenn ich einen Gegenstand anfasse oder mit einer Person spreche, so fasse ich einen *wirklichen* Gegenstand an und spreche mit einer *wirklichen* Person" (280; 316). An anderer Stelle lautet es entsprechend: „Ich sehe wirkliche, nicht reale Gegenstände. Dies gilt auch für mein Handeln. Wenn ich nach etwas greife, so bewege ich meine wirkliche, nicht meine reale Hand, die nach einem wirklichen, nicht nach einem realen Gegenstand greift" (289; 325).

Diese Ansicht ist jedoch völlig unhaltbar! Sowohl die sinnliche Wahrnehmung von Dingen (bzw. Ereignissen) der Umwelt als auch die im Handeln vollzogene kausale Interaktion mit solchen Dingen lässt sich konsistenterweise nur als eine Relation zwischen dem *realen* Subjekt und der es umgebenden *Realität* auffassen. Dass zunächst auf der *einen* Seite der Relation ein reales Subjekt erforderlich ist, ergibt sich aus der zentralen Rolle, die nach Roths Ausführungen dem Gehirn (inklusive den Sinnesorganen) bei jeglicher Wahrnehmung zukommt. Wie im letzten Abschnitt betont wurde, ist es ja jeweils das *reale* Gehirn eines (deshalb ebenfalls *realen*) Subjekts S, welches die phänomenale Erlebniswelt von S erzeugt. Nun erfolgt die Konstruktion der „Wirklichkeit" gemäß Roth aber gerade so, dass „die physikalisch-chemischen Umweltereignisse in den Sinnesorganen in die „Sprache des Gehirns" übersetzt, d.h. in neuroelektrische Erregungszustände und ihre neurochemischen Äquivalente" verwandelt werden. Aufgrund dieses kausalen Mechanismus müssen dann auch die neuroelektrischen Erregungszustände der Sinneszellen bzw. die dadurch hervorgerufenen neurochemischen Vorgänge im Gehirn bzw. im Nervensystem als Elemente der *Realität* aufgefasst werden. So wie gemäß *R3* das *reale* Gehirn nur durch einen *realen* Organismus ernährt werden kann, gilt also analog:

(*R4*) Beim Prozess sinnlicher Wahrnehmung empfängt das *reale* Gehirn die elektrochemischen Impulse durch Vermittlung *realer* Sinnesorgane.

Nun wird aber ein reales Sinnesorgan normalerweise ebenfalls durch reale physikalisch-chemische Umweltereignisse erregt, so dass insgesamt bewiesen ist: Die sinnliche Wahrnehmung von Dingen bzw. Ereignissen der Umwelt ist in aller Regel eine Relation zwischen einem *realen* Subjekt S und der es umgebenden *Realität*.[7]

Was für den Fall der Wahrnehmung gilt, gilt aber analog auch für das Handeln. Betrachten wir Roths eigenes Beispiel des Greifens bzw. Tastens. Wenn ich als reales Subjekt bzw. als realer Akteur mit meiner Hand etwas ergreife, so ist bzw. impliziert das Tasten eine spezielle Form von Wahrnehmen. Wie gerade gezeigt wurde, setzt diese Wahrnehmung jedoch eine reale Hand voraus, und ebenso wird diese in aller Regel durch einen realen Gegenstand innerviert, welcher einen physikalischen Reiz auf die realen Sinneszellen der Hand ausübt. Wenn man Roths Verdoppelung der Welt in Realität und „Wirklichkeit" überhaupt mit vollziehen will, muss man also im konträren Gegensatz zum neurobiologischen Konstruktivismus feststellen: Ich sehe reale, nicht „wirkliche" Gegenstände. Und wenn ich nach etwas greife, so bewege ich meine reale, nicht meine „wirkliche" Hand, die wiederum nach einem realen, nicht nach einem „wirklichen" Gegenstand greift.

Andererseits sind diese Vorgänge in der objektiven Realität normalerweise mit entsprechenden Erlebnissen oder *Vorstellungen* korreliert, die sich das jeweilige Subjekt von diesen Vorgängen macht. Deshalb könnte man *zusätzlich* zur obigen Beschreibung des realen Vorgangs auch noch davon sprechen, dass in der „Wirklichkeit", d.h. in der phänomenalen Erlebniswelt des Subjekts S, die „wirkliche" Hand nach einem „wirklichen" Gegenstand greift. Doch beide Beschreibungsebenen sind völlig miteinander verträglich, und es ist überaus wichtig, beide immer strikt auseinander zu halten und sich außerdem darüber im klaren zu sein, dass die erlebten Vorgänge in der „Wirklichkeit" in aller Regel auf entsprechenden Ereignissen in der Realität beruhen.

Wie die Klausel ‚in aller Regel' signalisiert – und wie durch Sinnestäuschungen, Halluzinationen, Träume und ähnliche Phänomene illustriert wird –, sind allerdings Ausnahmen von eben dieser Regel möglich. In solchen Fällen erzeugt das Gehirn Vorstellungen bzw. Elemente der „Wirklichkeit", die man vielleicht ebenfalls als Sinnesempfindungen oder als Wahrnehmungsbilder bezeichnen könnte, die jedoch nicht durch kausale Einwirkung von

---

[7] Vgl. auch Roths (in Anm. 2 zitiertes) Eingeständnis, dass die jeweilige phänomenale Welt oder „Wirklichkeit" durch Einwirkungen von physikalischen und chemischen Ereignisse als Reize auf das *reale* Gehirn entsteht.

realen Gegenständen oder Prozessen hervorgerufen werden. Aber auch in solchen Ausnahmefällen sollte man nicht davon sprechen, dass das Subjekt *S* statt eines realen Gegenstandes nun bloß einen „wirklichen" Gegenstand, d.h. eine Vorstellung wahrnimmt. Bei einer Sinnestäuschung, Halluzination oder Fata Morgana *hat S* eine (visuelle) *Vorstellung*, im üblichen Sinne des Wortes ‚sehen' *sieht S* diese Vorstellung aber nicht. Wenn man – wie im Alltag üblich – ‚sehen' als ein Erfolgsverb auffasst, muss man in solchen Ausnahmesituationen genauer sagen: *S sieht* gar nichts, *S glaubt* nur, etwas zu sehen.[8]

Roths eigene naturwissenschaftliche Erklärung „normaler" sinnlicher Wahrnehmung gestattet jedenfalls nur die folgende erkenntnistheoretische Analyse. Wenn ein Subjekt *S* z.B. eine Rose sieht (oder riecht oder fühlt), dann werden „physikalisch-chemische Umweltereignisse in den Sinnesorganen in die „Sprache des Gehirns" übersetzt, d.h. in neuroelektrische Erregungszustände und ihre neurochemischen Äquivalente". Diese neuronalen Prozesse im Gehirn sind mit geistigen Prozessen im Bewusstsein korreliert und erzeugen so den Sinneseindruck, die subjektive Vorstellung, bzw. das Wahrnehmungsbild einer Rose. Auch wenn man beachtet, dass solche Wahrnehmungsbilder nicht in naiv abbildender, sondern in konstruktiver Weise hergestellt werden, bleiben die logischen Beziehungen völlig klar: Das, was das Subjekt *S sieht* bzw. riecht bzw. fühlt, ist die reale Rose als ein Teil der *Außenwelt*; das, was *S* dabei phänomenal *erlebt* bzw. in seinem Bewusstsein *hat*, ist hingegen die Vorstellung oder das Wahrnehmungsbild der Rose als ein Teil der *Innenwelt*, d.h. der Erlebniswelt bzw. der „Wirklichkeit" von *S*. *Indem S* die reale Rose sieht, riecht oder fühlt, entsteht in ihrem Bewusstsein die „wirkliche" Rose als subjektive Vorstellung oder Empfindung. Eine solche *Vorstellung* kann jedoch weder von *S* selber noch von irgendeinem anderen Subjekt gesehen, gerochen oder ertastet werden! Als *mentale Konstrukte* des (realen) Gehirns haben Vorstellungen keine physischen Oberflächen, von denen elektromagnetische Wellen reflektiert werden könnten, um die Sinneszellen irgendeines Auges zu erregen. Ebenso sind Vorstellungen nicht in der Lage, chemische Moleküle auszusenden, um die Sinneszellen irgendeiner Nase zu erregen; und Vorstellungen haben auch keine soliden Oberflächen, die durch mechanischen Druck die Tastzellen irgendei-

---

[8] In einem abgeleiteten Sinn kann man zwar davon sprechen, dass das, was *S* zu sehen glaubte, in Wirklichkeit nur eine Einbildung oder eine „Vorstellung" von *S* war. Das bedeutet freilich nicht, dass *S* ihre eigene Vorstellung wortwörtlich gesehen hätte, sondern lediglich, dass das vermeintlich Gesehene eben nur in ihrer Einbildung bzw. in ihrer Vorstellung existierte. Vgl. in diesem Zusammenhang auch die Unterscheidung zwischen Sehen in „phänomenaler" und Sehen in „relationer" Bedeutung in Hoffman 2000, 21.

ner Hand innervieren könnten. In diesem Sinn ist die gesamte „Wirklichkeit", d.h. die phänomenale Welt der Erlebnisse, Vorstellungen und Empfindungen irgendeines Subjekts S, grundsätzlich unsichtbar, unhörbar, unriechbar, unschmeckbar und untastbar. Wer anders denkt, wiederholt nur den Hauptfehler des erkenntnistheoretischen Idealismus à la Berkeley [9] und verwechselt die phänomenal erlebten Wahrnehmungsbilder mit den wahrgenommenen Gegenständen selber.[10] Man darf also nicht wie Roth (292; 328) „diejenigen Dinge und Vorgänge, die ich anschaulich wahrnehme, als Konstrukte des Gehirns" bezeichnen. Nur die *Wahrnehmungsbilder* sind Konstrukte des Gehirns, nicht hingegen die wahrgenommenen Dinge bzw. Vorgänge selber, die den fraglichen Konstruktionsvorgang durch physikalisch-chemische Einwirkung auf die Sinnesorgane erst in Gang setzen![11]

---

[9] Vgl. z.B. Hylas' Eingeständnis gegen Ende des ersten Dialogs von Berkeley 1713, 61, dass die äußeren, materiellen Dinge „an sich nicht empfindbar" sind: „Im eigentlichen Sinne oder unmittelbar können nur Vorstellungen wahrgenommen werden." Für eine ausführliche Analyse dieses Fehlers vgl. Kutschera 1982, Kap. 3 und 4.

[10] So ist z.B. der Eiffelturm gut 300 m hoch und viele Tausend Tonnen schwer und kann deshalb schwerlich Teil meines Gehirns bzw. der hiervon erzeugten phänomenalen Erlebniswelt sein. Aber in meinem Gehirn bzw. in meiner Erlebniswelt ist selbstverständlich Platz für die *Vorstellung* oder den Sinneseindruck eines 300 m hohen und viele Tausend Tonnen schweren Turms!

[11] Die Genese dieses Fehlers lässt sich übrigens recht gut an einer Passage aus einer früheren Arbeit beobachten, wo Roth (1991, 128) im Einklang mit der Gehirnforschung davon ausgeht, „[...] daß die phänomenale Welt ein Konstrukt unseres kognitiven Systems und damit des Gehirns ist. Diese phänomenale Welt umfaßt alles, was wir überhaupt erleben können, nämlich sinnliche Wahrnehmungen, Gedanken, Empfindungen, Vorstellungen und natürlich auch Konstrukte unseres Denkens. Ebenso ist die grundsätzliche Untergliederung der phänomenalen Welt in drei Bereiche, nämlich die uns umgebende Welt, unseren Körper und unsere mentale Welt, eine Konstruktion unseres Gehirns." Roth übersieht aber, dass diese von ihm als „ontologisch" bezeichnete Untergliederung der „*Wirklichkeit*" Hand in Hand geht mit einer fundamentaleren, im eigentlichen Sinn *ontologischen* Untergliederung der *Realität*, die er als Wissenschaftler immer schon voraussetzt, wenn er z.B. fortfährt: „Das Gehirn nimmt diese Unterscheidung vor, da sie von entscheidender Bedeutung für das Überleben des Organismus ist: es muß für den Organismus stets klar sein, was Ereignisse der Umwelt sind, was den eigenen Körper betrifft und was „bloß" gedacht, gefühlt, erinnert, gewollt ist." Da hier vom *realen* Gehirn (als dem Konstrukteur der je subjektiven „Wirklichkeit") die Rede ist, macht der Satz nur dann Sinn, wenn es sich um das Überleben des *realen* Organismus handelt: Für *diesen* ist es überlebensnotwendig herauszufinden, „was Ereignisse der [*realen*] Umwelt sind, was den eigenen [*realen*] Körper betrifft, und was „bloß" gedacht, gefühlt, erinnert, gewollt", d.h. was bloße *Vorstellung* des realen Gehirns ist.

4. Das Ich und seine zwei Gehirne

Nach diesen Klarstellungen können wir nun das Problem analysieren, mit dem Roth sich herumschlägt, wenn er die Frage zu beantworten versucht „Wo existiert mein Gehirn?":

> Ich habe diejenigen Dinge und Vorgänge, die ich anschaulich wahrnehme, als Konstrukte des Gehirns bezeichnet. Was aber ist mit *meinem* Gehirn, das ich ja ebenfalls anschauen kann, zum Beispiel mithilfe eines Computertomographen? Ich könnte mir auch in einem heroischen Selbstversuch den Schädel öffnen und dann mein Gehirn im Spiegel oder mithilfe einer Videokamera ansehen.
> Ich stelle dann folgende Vermutung an: Wie alles, was ich wahrnehme, ist auch dieser Sinneseindruck ein Konstrukt des Gehirns. Das Gehirn erzeugt also ein Konstrukt von sich selbst. Dies tut es ganz offensichtlich deshalb, weil die Netzhaut von bestimmten optischen Reizen in bestimmter Weise erregt wird und das visuelle System in der geschilderten Weise mithilfe des Gedächtnisses hieraus eben dieses Bild meines Gehirns zusammensetzt.
> Das bedeutet aber, daß dieses Gehirn, das ich betrachte und als meines identifiziere, *nicht* dasjenige Gehirn sein kann, welches mein Wahrnehmungsbild von diesem Gehirn hervorbringt. Würde ich beide Gehirne miteinander identifizieren, so käme ich zu der Schlußfolgerung, daß mein Gehirn sich als echte Teilmenge enthält. Ich wäre nämlich dann zugleich in mir und außer mir, und der Operationssaal, in dem ich mich dann befinde, wäre zugleich in meinem Gehirn, und das Gehirn (zusammen mit dem Kopf und Körper) in dem Operationssaal.
> Um derartige absurde Schlußfolgerungen zu vermeiden, müssen wir zwischen einem *realen* Gehirn, welches die Wirklichkeit hervorbringt, und dem *wirklichen* Gehirn, unterscheiden. Daraus folgt: Dasjenige Gehirn, das mich hervorbringt, ist mir selbst unzugänglich, genauso wie der reale Körper, in dem es steckt, und die reale Welt, in welcher der Körper lebt. (292/3; 328/9)

Zur genaueren Analyse dieser Überlegung wollen wir zunächst ein paar Konventionen einführen. Ist S irgendeine Person, so bezeichne ‚$G(S)$' das Gehirn von S, wobei im Einzelfall konkreter die Abkürzung ‚$G_r(S)$' bzw. ‚$G_w(S)$' verwendet wird, wenn feststeht, dass es sich um das *reale* bzw. das *wirkliche* Gehirn von S handelt. Ferner stehe ‚R' für die Person des Autors G. R.; dann lässt sich die Ausgangsprämisse des obigen Gedankenexperiments zunächst durch die schematische Aussage darstellen: R betrachtet $G(R)$. Die entscheidende Frage lautet nun: Handelt es sich bei dem *betrachteten* Gehirn um $G_r(R)$ oder um $G_w(R)$?[12] Nach Roths Auffassung führt die Hypothese

---

[12] Auf den ersten Blick erscheint die Alternative sogar noch komplizierter, denn außer dem realen und dem wirklichen Gehirn wäre eigentlich noch ein „drittes Gehirn" in Betracht zu ziehen, nämlich der „*Sinneseindruck*", den das reale Gehirn, $G_r(R)$, in konstruktiver Weise beim Betrachten von $G(R)$ erzeugt, indem „die Netzhaut von bestimmten optischen Reizen in

(B₁) R betrachtet $G_r(R)$.

zu einem Widerspruch, weil das „Gehirn, das ich betrachte und als meines identifiziere, *nicht* dasjenige Gehirn sein kann, welches mein Wahrnehmungsbild von diesem Gehirn hervorbringt. Würde ich beide Gehirne miteinander identifizieren, so käme ich zu der Schlußfolgerung, daß mein Gehirn sich als echte Teilmenge enthält."

In der Tat käme man zwangsläufig zu einem Widerspruch, wenn man im Kontext der konstruktivistischen Aufspaltung der Welt in Realität einerseits und Wirklichkeit andererseits *irgendeinen* realen Gegenstand mit seinem „wirklichen" Pendant identifiziert. Dies geht unmittelbar aus den obigen Diagrammen hervor. Laut Diagramm 1 ist ja die gesamte „Wirklichkeit" des Subjekts R, $W(R)$, ein *Produkt* des realen Gehirns $G_r(R)$. Das „wirkliche" Gehirn $G_w(R)$ hingegen ist gemäß Diagramm 3 ein kleiner Teil des „wirklichen" Körpers von R, der selber einen Teil von $W(R)$ darstellt. Dieses banale Faktum erweist jedoch These B₁ keineswegs als falsch. Denn Roths gegenteilige These

(B₂) R betrachtet $G_w(R)$

beruht in entscheidender Weise auf der *zusätzlichen* Annahme, dass für das betrachtete Gehirn $G(R)$ gilt: „Wie alles, was ich wahrnehme, ist auch dieser Sinneseindruck[!] ein Konstrukt des Gehirns." Zwar muss trivialerweise zugestanden werden: *Wenn* $G(R)$ ein vom realen Gehirn, $G_r(R)$, erzeugter bzw. konstruierter *Sinneseindruck* wäre, dann könnte unmöglich $G(R) = G_r(R)$ sein, denn das Konstrukt eines Konstrukteurs ist niemals mit dem Konstrukteur identisch! Doch genau in der hervorgehobenen Prämisse verbirgt sich die Crux des gesamten Gedankengangs, nämlich die erkenntnistheoretische Verwechselung zwischen den wahrgenommenen *Objekten* und den Wahrnehmungs*bildern* eben dieser Objekte.

Es ist und bleibt philosophisch unhaltbar, das, „was ich wahrnehme", als einen bloßen „Sinneseindruck" zu interpretieren, den das Gehirn (bzw. allgemeiner: das visuelle bzw. sonstige Wahrnehmungssystem) produziert. *Indem* ich etwas beobachte, sehe, höre, rieche, schmecke oder fühle, *habe* ich entsprechende *Sinneseindrücke*. Doch das, *was* ich wahrnehme, sind nicht diese Sinneseindrücke, sondern in aller Regel[13] reale Objekte meiner Außenwelt. Nur die Sinneseindrücke bzw. Wahrnehmungsbilder sind Konstrukte

---

bestimmter Weise erregt wird und das visuelle System [...] hieraus eben dieses Bild" von $G(R)$ zusammensetzt. In Sinne des neurobiologischen Konstruktivismus darf man jedoch diesen Sinneseindruck – der von Roth ausdrücklich als *Konstrukt* des realen Gehirns bezeichnet wird – mit dem „wirklichen" Gehirn, $G_w(R)$, identifizieren.

[13] Vgl. dazu die einschränkende Bemerkung im vorherigen Abschnitt.

des Gehirns, nicht aber die *Dinge, von denen* sie Eindrücke bzw. „Bilder" darstellen.

Das Problem von Roth's „zwei Gehirnen" reduziert sich somit auf folgende simple Feststellung: Das *wahrgenommene* Gehirn, G(R), unterscheidet sich selbstverständlich von dem *Wahrnehmungsbild*, welches sich das Subjekt R vermittels seines reales Gehirns, $G_r(R)$, von eben jenem Objekt macht. Wenn Roth sich in einem anderen, ebenso heroischen Selbstversuch statt des Schädels die Brust geöffnet und sein reales Herz bei der Arbeit beobachtet hätte, müsste man entsprechend konstatieren: Das beobachtete Herz unterscheidet sich von dem *Wahrnehmungsbild*, das R sich von diesem Herzen macht. Und was für das eigene Herz oder Hirn gilt, gilt analog auch für Hirne oder Herzen anderer Leute. Stets ist das beobachtete (reale) *Objekt X* ungleich dem Wahrnehmungsbild, das irgendein Subjekt S sich von X macht. Doch hieraus folgt mitnichten die skeptische Konklusion: „Dasjenige Gehirn, das mich hervorbringt, ist mir selbst unzugänglich, genauso wie der reale Körper, in dem es steckt, und die reale Welt, in welcher der Körper lebt." Erstens handelt es um eine grobe sprachliche Ungereimtheit, wenn Roth davon redet, dass das reale Gehirn, $G_r(R)$, „*mich* hervorbringt". Was Roths reales Hirn „hervorzubringen" vermag, ist – in der Terminologie des Konstruktivismus – allenfalls die gesamte „Wirklichkeit" der Person R, d.h. deren subjektive Erlebnis- oder Erfahrungswelt, nicht jedoch die *Person R* selber. Zweitens mag diese „*Wirklichkeit*" – primär – immer nur dem betroffenen Subjekt R unmittelbar „zugänglich" sein. Doch das reale Gehirn von R, das diese „Wirklichkeit" hervorbringt, ist als Teil der objektiven Realität nicht nur R, sondern im Prinzip auch jedem anderen Beobachter zugänglich.

5. Objektive Wahrheit

Roths Konzeption von „Wirklichkeit" und Realität und seine Weigerung, die objektive Erkennbarkeit der Realität anzuerkennen, ist durch eine *Erkenntnisskepsis* motiviert, die sich insbesondere in den folgenden Bemerkungen äußert:

(W1) „Wahrnehmung ist eine Grundleistung von Lebewesen [..., die jedoch] primär nichts mit dem Erkennen „wahrer" oder „objektiver" Sachverhalte zu tun" hat (65[14]).

---

[14] In der *stw*-Ausgabe fehlt hier (am Anfang von Abschnitt 4, 78) der Satz „Obwohl das Wort „Wahrnehmung" es nahelegt, hat diese Leistung primär nicht mit dem Erkennen „wahrer" oder „objektiver" Sachverhalte zu tun."

(*W2*) „Wahrnehmung ist stets selektiv, erfaßt nie die „ganze Wahrheit" im philosophischen Sinn, weil so etwas für das Überleben völlig irrelevant ist. Die Welt wird nur in dem Maße erfaßt, in dem Merkmale und Prozesse der Welt für einen Organismus überlebensrelevant sind" (72; 85).

(*W3*) „Wahrnehmungen sind immer nur *Hypothesen* über die Umwelt" (73; 86).

(*W4*) „Wahrnehmung kann [...] aus vielen Gründen nicht in einer direkten Abbildung der Welt durch das Gehirn bestehen. Vielmehr werden die physikalisch-chemischen Umweltereignisse in den Sinnesorganen in die „Sprache des Gehirns" übersetzt" (100/101; 113/4).

(*W5*) „[Unsere Sinnesorgane können] mit ihren Rezeptoren die Umweltereignisse (z. B. ein Gesicht, ein gesprochener Satz, ein Blumenduft) überhaupt nicht in ihrer natürlichen [...] Komplexität erfassen. [...] Die Sinnesrezeptoren können nur auf bestimmte physikalische und chemische Ereignisse [nämlich Lichtstärke und Wellenlänge] reagieren" (101; 114/5).

(*W6*) „Wahrnehmung hängt zwar mit Umweltereignissen zusammen, welche die verschiedenen Sinnesorgane erregen; sie ist jedoch nicht abbildend, sondern *konstruktiv*" (112; 125).

Die hier angerissenen und vor allem im Kapitel über „Wirklichkeit und Wahrheit" weiter diskutierten „klassischen philosophischen" Fragen lauten: „1. Welchen Erkenntniswert haben unsere Wahrnehmungen? Liefern sie uns Informationen über die Dinge der Außenwelt oder sind sie reine Konstrukte? 2. In welchem Maße ist objektive Erkenntnis, Wahrheit, möglich? 3. Welchen ontologischen Status hat die Realität? Existiert sie überhaupt? Wenn ja, kann man über sie etwas Sinnvolles aussagen?" (303; 339). Roths Antworten lauten:

1) „Alles, was wir überhaupt bewusst wahrnehmen können, ist ein Konstrukt unseres Gehirns und keine unmittelbare Widerspiegelung der Realität" (306; 342).

2) „Die Entwicklung der modernen Naturwissenschaft hat [...] gezeigt, daß objektive Erkenntnis unmöglich ist" (316; 353).

3) „Obwohl erkenntnistheoretisch die Realität vollkommen unzugänglich ist, muß ich erstens ihre Existenz annehmen, um nicht in elementare Widersprüche zu geraten, und zweitens kann mir niemand verbieten, mir Gedanken über die Beschaffenheit der Realität zu machen, und zwar zu dem Zwecke, die Phänomene *in meiner Wirklichkeit* besser erklären zu können. Ich darf nur keine objektive Gültigkeit hierfür beanspruchen" (321/2; 359).

Diese erkenntnisskeptischen Thesen werden jedoch durch Roths neurobiologische Theorie der Wahrnehmung nicht schlüssig begründet.

Erstens ist anzumerken, dass die von Roth unterstellte *Unverträglichkeit* zwischen dem hypothetisch-konstruktivem Charakter der Wahrnehmung einerseits und ihrer Funktion andererseits, dem Individuum „wahre" bzw. „objektive" Informationen über die Dinge der Außenwelt zu liefern, so überhaupt nicht gerechtfertigt ist. Auch wenn Wahrnehmung keine „direkte Abbildung der Welt" darstellt, sondern auf konstruktiven Leistungen des Gehirns beruht, kann sie dem Individuum dennoch richtige bzw. – wie Roth selber betont – geradezu *überlebensrelevante* Informationen über die Umwelt verschaffen. Nehmen wir z.B. an, auf einer Wiese am Waldrand sitzt ein Hase friedlich im Sonnenschein; plötzlich riecht, hört oder sieht er, wie ein Fuchs sich nähert. Diese Wahrnehmung, wie konstruktiv-hypothetisch sie auch immer sein mag, liefert dem Tier eine wichtige Information über die „objektive" Realität. Dabei ist zunächst noch einmal zu betonen, dass es sich tatsächlich um die *Realität* und nicht bloß um die „Wirklichkeit", d.h. um die Erlebniswelt des Hasen handelt, denn das *reale* Leben des *realen* Nagers steht (mutmaßlich) auf dem Spiel. Laut Roths These *W1* hat eine solche, wiewohl überlebensrelevante Wahrnehmungsleistung des Hasen „nichts mit dem Erkennen „wahrer" oder „objektiver" Sachverhalte zu tun". Dies ist aber, im üblichen Verständnis der Worte ‚wahr' und ‚objektiv', schlicht und einfach *falsch*.

Das Wort ‚objektiv' wird – im Alltag ebenso wie in philosophischen Diskursen – als Gegenbegriff zu ‚subjektiv' gebraucht, und ‚wahr' entsprechend als Gegenbegriff zu ‚falsch'. Speziell ist es in manchen Situationen extrem wichtig, das subjektive Für-wahr-halten vom objektiven Wahrsein zu unterscheiden. In diesem Sinne dürfte man z.B. die Vermutung des Hasen, ein Fuchs am Waldrand wolle sich ihm nähern und ihn fressen, als *subjektiv* bezeichnen. Ob sie auch *objektiv* wahr ist, hängt davon ab, was der Fuchs wirklich will. Vielleicht ist der vermeintliche Fuchs gar kein wirklicher Fuchs sondern ein Dackel, oder es handelt sich zwar um einen Fuchs, aber der hat es gar nicht auf den Hasen abgesehen, sondern auf ein Rebhuhn, das sich gleichfalls auf der Wiese sonnt. Die Wahrnehmung des Hasen impliziert jedenfalls nicht *automatisch* die Wahrheit des fraglichen Sachverhalts, und in diesem Sinn ist Roths Behauptung *W3* völlig korrekt, der zufolge „Wahrnehmungen immer nur *Hypothesen* über die Umwelt" darstellen. Das schließt aber keineswegs aus, dass Wahrnehmungen *manchmal* (oder sogar ziemlich *häufig*) einen tatsächlich bestehenden Sachverhalt betreffen. *Wenn* der Fuchs den Hasen wirklich fressen will, dann braucht man sich jedenfalls nicht mit der zurückhaltenden Beschreibung à la *W2* zufrieden geben, dass das Tier seine Umwelt „nur" in dem Maße erfasst hat, „in dem Merkmale und Prozesse der Welt für [s]einen Organismus überlebensrelevant sind". Man darf mit Fug und Recht behaupten, dass der Hase durch Riechen, Hören oder Sehen einen *objektiv wahren* Sachverhalt erkannt hat.

Roths gegenteilige Auffassung beruht offenbar auf einem fehlgeleiteten, allzu strikten Verständnis von „objektiver Wahrheit". In einem diesbezüglichen Abschnitt (317 ff.; 354 ff.) referiert er zunächst die sog. Korrespondenztheorie der Wahrheit, die in einer modernen Variante besagt, dass „ein Satz genau dann wahr [ist], wenn der Sachverhalt besteht, den er behauptet". Hieraus zieht Roth den Schluss:

> Wahrheit bemißt sich also danach, ob es möglich ist, festzustellen, ob der behauptete Sachverhalt tatsächlich vorliegt oder nicht. Dies ist an *Beobachtungen* gebunden, und alles, was wir soeben über den Aussagewert von Beobachtungen gesagt haben, gilt natürlich auch in diesem Zusammenhang. Danach kann es keine objektiven Wahrheiten geben. (317; 354)

Nun ist aber erstens Wahrheit nicht dasselbe wie Verifizierbarkeit. Eine Aussage der Art, dass auf der Erde vor 3 Milliarden Jahre noch kein Leben existierte, konnte damals natürlich nicht durch Beobachtung eines Erdenbewohners überprüft werden. Und auch mit heutigen und zukünftigen wissenschaftlichen Methoden lässt sie sich vermutlich weder verifizieren noch falsifizieren. Dennoch erscheint es sinnvoll, von der Wahrheit bzw. Falschheit dieser Aussage zu reden, und aus rein logischen Gründen wissen wir, dass entweder diese Aussage oder aber ihre Negation *wahr* ist. Doch auch wenn man dem Argument zuliebe zugesteht, dass die Wahrheit (zumindest *empirischer*) Aussagen an die Möglichkeit gekoppelt ist, durch Beobachtung zu überprüfen, „ob der behauptete Sachverhalt tatsächlich vorliegt oder nicht", bleibt uneinsichtig, wieso „es keine objektiven Wahrheiten geben" können soll.

Leider hat Roth keine expliziten und präzisen Kriterien benannt, die für das Vorliegen *objektiver* Wahrheit(en) erfüllt sein müssen.[15] Welche Bedingungen ihm vorschwebten, geht allenfalls indirekt aus einzelnen Passagen hervor, so etwa, wenn er Vollmers Auffassung kritisiert „Objektive Wahrheit existiert *an sich*, unabhängig von menschlichem Denken" (319; 357), oder wenn er Poppers „Idee des objektiven und absoluten Wahrheitsbegriffs" (320; 357) zurückweist, weil man ihr keinerlei „Eigenschaften zuschreiben [kann]

---

[15] Zwar referiert er zu Anfang von Kap. 14 traditionelle philosophische Positionen zur Frage des objektiven *Wissens* bzw. der objektiven *Erkenntnis*, und lässt dabei durchblicken, dass ein „objektives Wissen" bedeuten würde, „daß die Sachverhalte der bewußtseinsunabhängigen Welt zumindest teilweise so zu erkennen sind, wie sie *tatsächlich* sind" (304; 340). Was dies für die gesuchte Unterscheidung von „objektiver" vs. „nicht-objektiver" (= „subjektiver"?) Wahrheit impliziert, bleibt jedoch unklar.

außer der, [...] *unerkennbar*" zu sein. Nun ist hier nicht der Ort, die Wahrheitskonzeption der Evolutionären Erkenntnistheorie oder Poppers Konzeption „absoluter" Wahrheit näher zu diskutieren oder sogar zu verteidigen. Ich persönlich würde „absolute" Wahrheiten eher im Bereich *nicht-empirischer* Sachverhalte wie $2+2=4$ oder $(p \wedge q \rightarrow p \vee q)$ suchen. Und wenn es darum geht, *empirische* Aussagen anzugeben, deren Wahrheit „unabhängig von menschlichem Denken" bzw. unabhängig von der Beobachtung irgendeines Lebewesens besteht bzw. bestanden hat, würde ich primär an das zuvor genannte Beispiel denken „Vor mehr als drei Milliarden Jahren existierte noch kein Leben auf der Erde".[16]

Roths Ablehnung „objektiver" Wahrheit betrifft jedoch vermutlich ganz gewöhnliche Sachverhalte wie das Beispiel vom Hasen und Fuchs, und er führt für seine Skepsis zwei Gründe ins Feld. Erstens ist die Wahrheit eines empirischen Sachverhalts „an *Beobachtungen* gebunden" und diese Beobachtungen bzw. „Wahrnehmungen von „tatsächlich Vorhandenem" sind – wie wir alle aus Erfahrung wissen – nicht immer verläßlich von Sinnestäuschungen, Halluzinationen, Tagträumen oder bloßen Vorstellungen zu unterscheiden" (285; 321). Zweitens ist Wahrnehmung – wie es in These *W2* bzw. *W5* hieß – „selektiv [und] erfaßt nie die „ganze Wahrheit" im philosophischen Sinn", „denn die [menschlichen] Sinnesorgane können mit ihren Rezeptoren die Umweltereignisse [...] überhaupt nicht in ihrer natürlichen [...] Komplexität erfassen. Die Sinnesrezeptoren können nur auf bestimmte physikalische und chemische Ereignisse [nämlich Lichtstärke und Wellenlänge] reagieren" (101; 114).

Roths erstes Argument (der Sinnestäuschung) wurde vor mehr als drei Jahrhunderten im fünften Paragraphen von Descartes' *Erster Meditation* wie folgt vorweggenommen:

> Alles nämlich, was ich bisher am ehesten für wahr angenommen, habe ich von den Sinnen oder durch Vermittlung der Sinne empfangen. Nun aber bin ich dahinter gekommen, dass diese uns bisweilen täuschen, und es ist ein Gebot der Klugheit, niemals denen ganz zu vertrauen, die auch nur einmal uns getäuscht haben. (Descartes 1641, 12)

Gegen die bloße *Maxime*, sich im alltäglichen Handeln bzw. beim wissenschaftlichen Argumentieren niemals 100%ig auf den Augenschein zu verlassen, wäre an und für sich nichts einzuwenden. Doch der Versuch, die angebliche Unmöglichkeit sicheren Wissens bzw. objektiver Erkenntnis durch Rekurs auf Sinnestäuschungen zu begründen, scheint mir zum Scheitern ver-

---

[16] *Sofern* diese Aussage wahr ist; wenn sie hingegen falsch ist, nehme man als Beispiel stattdessen die Negation „Auf der Erde gab es bereits vor mehr als drei Milliarden Jahren Leben".

urteilt. Descartes versichert uns aufrichtig, er sei früher einmal durch seine Sinne getäuscht worden. Er sei *„dahinter gekommen,* dass diese uns bisweilen täuschen", d. h. er habe ihre Unzuverlässigkeit *erkannt.* Aber wie konnte er:

> [...] überhaupt *erkennen,* daß seine Sinne ihn einmal im Stich gelassen haben. Doch nur vermittels dieser – als generell unzuverlässig deklarierten – Sinne selber! Er hat – durch *Sinneswahrnehmung* – erkannt, daß, obwohl er aufgrund vorhergehender Sinneswahrnehmungen meinte, p sei er Fall, in Wirklichkeit non-p der Fall ist. Descartes' Erkenntnis eines früheren Irrtums, die seiner Argumentation nach die generelle Fallibilität empirischer Urteile begründen soll, setzt also die Erkenntnis der Falschheit (und damit zugleich die Erkenntnis der Wahrheit) zumindest *eines* empirischen Urteils voraus. Sein Argument der Sinnestäuschung wird damit zirkulär bzw. logisch inkonsistent. (Lenzen 1982, 125)

Trotzdem bleibt es natürlich richtig, dass Wahrnehmung keine Wahrheitsgarantie in sich trägt. *Jede* empirisch-kontingente Aussage, wie gut sie auch immer durch Beobachtung bestätigt sein mag, könnte sich als falsch herausstellen. Doch die von Roth behauptete Unmöglichkeit „objektiver Wahrheit" folgt hieraus nur dann, wenn man ein unangemessen strenges Kriterium von „Objektivität" zugrundelegt und nur solche Aussagen bzw. Sachverhalte als „objektiv wahr" deklariert, bezüglich derer ein Irrtum logisch ausgeschlossen ist. Ein solcher Begriff „perfekten Wissens" ist jedoch, wie Kutschera (1982, 28 ff.) betont hat, erkenntnistheoretisch unbrauchbar und beruht wahrscheinlich auf einem modallogischen Fehlschluss. Zwar setzt im üblichen philosophischen Verständnis Wissen Wahrheit voraus. Deshalb folgt aus der stets vorhandenen Möglichkeit, dass ein Subjekt S sich bzgl. eines empirischen Sachverhalts p irrt, die *Möglichkeit,* dass S nur zu wissen glaubt, aber nicht wirklich *weiß,* dass p. Aber daraus folgt keineswegs, dass es *nicht möglich* wäre, dass S weiß, dass p.

Betrachten wir abschließend Roths zweites Argument gegen „objektive" Wahrheit, das auf der „Selektivität" der menschlichen Wahrnehmung beruht. Dieser Punkt wurde z. B. auch in Johnson 1991, 166/7 wie folgt formuliert:

> Wo wir die Trennungslinie zwischen dem Subjektiven und dem Objektiven auch immer ziehen, klar ist, daß wir nicht die Macht haben, die Welt wirklich objektiv zu betrachten. Wir beeinflussen das Beobachtete nicht nur dadurch, daß wir es beobachten, wir filtern die Welt auch mit unseren Sinnen, verarbeiten die dadurch gewonnenen Daten, und unser Gehirn ordnet sie zu Strukturen. Wir können Licht nur in einem kleinen Bereich seines vollen elektromagnetischen Spektrums sehen. Wir nehmen lediglich das wahr, was unser Nervensystem uns wahrzunehmen erlaubt. Für ein Lebewesen mit einem nach einer anderen Blaupause aufgebauten Gehirn wäre das Universum ein völlig anderer Ort, und es stünden ihm Türen offen, von denen wir nun träumen können.

Diese Ausführungen verdeutlichen noch einmal das Dilemma, das sich bei vielen prominenten Naturwissenschaftlern beobachten lässt, wenn sie parallel die „normale" Perspektive ihrer Fachdisziplin einnehmen und sich von philosophischer Warte her mit den erkenntnistheoretischen Konsequenzen ihrer Forschungsergebnisse auseinandersetzen. Ein *Naturwissenschaftler* darf durchaus behaupten, dass die menschlichen Sinnesorgane die Umweltereignisse nicht in ihrer vollen Komplexität erfassen und dass wir insbesondere „Licht nur in einem kleinen Bereich seines vollen elektromagnetischen Spektrums sehen" können. Speziell mag ein vergleichender Neurobiologe triftige Gründe für die Vermutung besitzen, dass Lebewesen mit „einem nach einer anderen Blaupause aufgebauten Gehirn" die gleiche Umwelt gänzlich anders wahrnehmen als wir Menschen. *Er* darf zu Recht darauf hinweisen, dass die menschlichen Sinnesorgane „mit ihren Rezeptoren die Umweltereignisse […] überhaupt nicht in ihrer natürlichen [d.h. *objektiven*!] Komplexität erfassen" können; dass unsere Sinnesrezeptoren „nur auf bestimmte physikalische und chemische Ereignisse" reagieren und dass diese physikalischen Reize „sehr verschieden von unseren komplexen visuellen und auditorischen Wahrnehmungsinhalten" sind. Aber wer als *Philosoph* die skeptische These vertritt, die objektive Realität sei „vollkommen unzugänglich", der kann nicht konsistenterweise behaupten, dass wir Menschen diese Realität nur „selektiv" bzw. „nicht in ihrer natürlichen Komplexität" wahrzunehmen vermögen. Denn das hieße ja, *erkannt* zu haben, dass die „unzugängliche" und damit *unerkennbare* Realität Eigenschaften besitzt, zu denen wir Menschen mit unserer Sinnesorganisation überhaupt keinen perzeptionellen Zugang besitzen sollen.

6. Fazit

Es ist sicher ein wichtiges Verdienst von Roths Buch, deutlich gemacht zu haben, dass Wahrnehmung keine schlichte *Abbildung* oder Widerspiegelung der objektiven Realität, sondern ein komplexer neurobiologischer Vorgang ist, der zur Konstruktion von je subjektiven „Wirklichkeiten" oder Erlebniswelten führt, die von Spezies zu Spezies (und vielleicht sogar von Individuum zu Individuum) stark divergieren können. Wir haben – um die berühmte Metapher von Thomas Nagel aufzugreifen – nicht die geringste Vorstellung davon, wie es ist, eine Fledermaus zu sein, und erst recht wird uns die Erlebniswelt eines Frosches, einer Fliege oder eines Flamingos für immer fremd und verschlossen bleiben. Dennoch ist unsere subjektive „Wirklichkeit", d.h. das Bild, das wir Menschen mit unserer spezifischen Sinnesorganisation uns von der Welt machen, trivialerweise ein Bild der *objektiven Realität*, und dieses Bild kann mit den Bildern, die sich andere Lebewesen mit völlig anderer Sinnesorganisation von eben der gleichen objektiven Realität machen, völlig kompatibel sein.

Daraus folgt natürlich nicht, dass *jede* subjektive Annahme über einen Sachverhalt der objektiven Realität automatisch *wahr* sein müsste. Das Zugeständnis, dass die gleiche Realität durch verschiedene Individuen verschiedener Spezies möglicherweise in sehr verschiedenen Weisen wahrgenommen wird, hebt den wichtigen Unterschied zwischen dem bloß subjektiven Fürwahr-halten und dem objektiven Wahrsein keineswegs auf. Irren ist nicht allein menschlich – auch Fledermäuse können einem Irrtum erliegen! Doch wo immer, in Bezug auf einen objektiv vorliegenden Sachverhalt, ein Irrtum möglich ist, ist eben auch Wahrheit, Wissen bzw. Erkenntnis möglich sein. Dass ein (menschliches oder nichtmenschliches) Individuum die objektive Realität erkennt, bedeutet nicht, dass sein subjektives Bild das *einzig* richtige oder das *einzig* wahre wäre. Es bedeutet lediglich, dass sein subjektives Bild mit einem objektiv bestehenden Sachverhalt übereinstimmt. In diesem Verständnis ist Roths Dogma der Unerkennbarkeit oder Unzugänglichkeit der objektiven Realität jedenfalls unhaltbar.

Literatur

Berkeley, G.: *Drei Dialoge zwischen Hylas und Philonous*, 1713; zitiert nach der Ausgabe Hamburg (Meiner), 1980.

Descartes, R.: *Meditationen über die Grundlagen der Philosophie*, 1641; zitiert nach der Ausgabe Hamburg (Meiner), 1972.

Frege, G.: Der Gedanke – Eine logische Untersuchung, *Beiträge zur Philosophie des deutschen Idealismus* 1 (1918), 58–77; zitiert nach dem Abdruck in G. Frege, *Logische Untersuchungen*, hrsg. von G. Patzig, Vandenhoeck & Ruprecht, Göttingen 1966, 30–53.

Hoffman, D. D.: *Visuelle Intelligenz – Wie die Welt im Kopf entsteht*, Klett-Cotta, Stuttgart 2000.

Johnson, G.: *In den Palästen der Erinnerung – Wie die Welt im Kopf entsteht*, Droemer Knaur, München 1991.

Kutschera, F. von: *Grundfragen der Erkenntnistheorie*, de Gruyter, Berlin 1982.

Lenzen, W.: Die Verwirrungen des Skeptizismus – Descartes und seine Folgen, *Grazer Philosophische Studien* 18 (1982), 123–135.

Roth, G.: Kognition: Die Entstehung von Bedeutung im Gehirn. In: *Die Entstehung von Ordnung, Organisation und Bedeutung*, hrsg. von W. Krohn, G. Küpper, Suhrkamp, Frankfurt 1991, 104–133.

Roth, G.: *Das Gehirn und seine Wirklichkeit*, Suhrkamp, Frankfurt 1994; Taschenbuchausgabe in der Reihe *stw* 1997.

Manfred Stöckler

42 Jahre danach

*Ein neuer Blick auf Oppenheim, Putnam und
die Einheit der Wissenschaften*

Abstract

1958 erschien der legendäre Aufsatz „Unity of Science as a Working Hypothesis" von Paul Oppenheim und Hilary Putnam. Die beiden Autoren verteidigen die These, daß die Einheit der Wissenschaft eines Tages durch aufeinander folgende Schritte von Mikroreduktionen erreichbar ist. In meiner Untersuchung konfrontiere ich ihre Ergebnisse mit heutigen Auffassungen und analysiere ihre Argumente. Welche Prämissen sind auch nach heutiger Sicht noch überzeugend, welche nicht? Was haben die Autoren übersehen? Welche Form der Einheit der Wissenschaften kann auch heute noch verteidigt werden?

1. Einleitung

Im Jahre 1958 war in den *Minnesota Studies* eine starke These zu lesen: Die Einheit der Wissenschaft ist durch aufeinanderfolgende Schritte von Mikroreduktionen erreichbar (etwa in der Art, wie intuitiv die Chemie auf Physik reduzierbar zu sein scheint). Vor 42 Jahren lag es sicherlich viel näher als heute, die Einheit der Wissenschaft zu verteidigen. Gegenwärtig beschäftigen sich die Wissenschaftstheoretiker nicht mehr so intensiv mit den grundlegenden Fragen der fundamentalen Physik. Die Untersuchung von komplexen Phänomenen, wie etwa der Supraleitung oder, noch viel wichtiger, die Vorgänge in lebendigen Organismen, sind zunehmend ins Zentrum des Interesses gerückt. Fast durchweg wird dabei die Autonomie schichtspezifischer, „spezieller" Wissenschaften betont. Kann und soll die Einheit der Wissenschaft unter diesen Umständen überhaupt noch verteidigt werden?

Die Frage, wieviel Einheit die Wissenschaft braucht, ist nicht nur von philosophisch-akademischem Interesse. Kann man in den empirischen Naturwissenschaften mit einer bunten Sammlung von Modellen und Minitheorien zufrieden sein (darauf scheinen Programme wie das von Nancy Cartwright (1994 und 1995) hinauszulaufen), oder muß man doch danach suchen, wie alles zusammenhängt, ob die Vielfalt der Phänomene auf wenige einheitliche Gesetze zurückführbar ist? Die Antwort auf diese Frage wird unser Weltbild beeinflussen, von ihr werden aber auch einzelne Fragen der Wissenschaftsorganisation abhängen.

Gerade in einer Zeit, in der die Einheit der Wissenschaft unter den Wissenschaftsphilosophen keinen guten Ruf hat, kann es sich lohnen, auf die frühen Kämpfer für die Einheit der Wissenschaft zurückzuschauen. Paul Oppenheim und Hilary Putnam entwickeln in ihrem legendären Aufsatz von 1958 „Unity of Science as a Working Hypothesis" nach verschiedenen Begriffsklärungen eine ganze Reihe von Argumenten für die Glaubwürdigkeit ihrer These. Es sind empirische, methodologische und pragmatische Gründe, die für die Möglichkeit der Vereinheitlichung der Wissenschaften sprechen. Zu den vielfältigen Indizien gehören z. B. Erfolge des Reduktionsprogramms in der Vergangenheit und Hinweise aus neuen Theorien über die Evolution des Kosmos und über die Entstehung und Entwicklung des Lebens. Während Oppenheim und Putnam 1958 noch von einer breiten Zustimmung ausgehen konnten („Die Wünschbarkeit dieses Ziels wird weithin anerkannt [...]", S. 3), sind wir heute skeptischer. An der Einheitswissenschaft wurde viel Kritik geübt. Einheit gilt als Gefahr, Pluralismus ist das neue Ideal. Tatsächlich werden die meisten von uns die Konklusion der damaligen Argumente von Oppenheim und Putnam für falsch halten. Die Entwicklung der Einzelwissenschaften und der Wissenschaftstheorie läßt die Hoffnung der beiden Autoren als zu optimistisch erscheinen. Differenzierte Analysen des Reduktionsbegriffs und die genaue Untersuchung von Fallbeispielen zeigen die Schwierigkeit von Reduktionen schon innerhalb der Physik. Die Philosophie des Geistes kämpft mit zusätzlichen Erklärungslücken (besonders im Umkreis der Intentionalität und der Qualia).

Im folgenden werde ich die Ergebnisse von Oppenheim und Putnam mit heutigen Auffassungen konfrontieren und ihre Argumente einer genauen Analyse unterziehen. Welche Prämissen sind auch nach heutiger Sicht noch überzeugend, welche nicht? Wenn die Argumente heute nicht mehr überzeugen: worin lag der Fehler? Was haben die Autoren übersehen? Worin haben sie sich geirrt? So begeben wir uns zugleich in eine Fallstudie zur Frage, was man in der Philosophie auch bei ausreichender Intelligenz, klarem Kopf und gutem Willen alles falsch machen kann. Bei Oppenheim und Putnam gibt es Fehlleistungen an überraschenden Stellen, z. B. auf der Ebene der Elementarteilchen. Andererseits werde ich aber auch zeigen, daß das Programm der Einheit durchaus gute Gründe hat, und daß man vielen Einwänden begegnen kann, wenn zwischen ontologischen und pragmatischen bzw. methodischen

Fragen hinreichend unterschieden wird. Im *Teil 2* werde ich zunächst die Arbeit von Oppenheim und Putnam mit ihren Begriffsklärungen und Argumenten vorstellen. Der *Teil 3* enthält Analysen und Fehlerdiagnosen und im *Teil 4* untersuche ich die Frage, welche Form der Einheit der Wissenschaft auch heute noch verteidigt werden kann.

2. Oppenheim/Putnam (1958)

In ihrem Aufsatz unterscheiden die beiden Autoren zunächst zwischen *verschiedenen Formen* von Einheit: Eine einheitliche Sprache der Wissenschaft muß z. B. noch nicht bedeuten, daß auch die jeweiligen Gesetze vereinheitlicht werden können. Weiter werden von Oppenheim und Putnam verschiedene Varianten von Reduktionsbegriffen untersucht. Sie selbst schließen sich der Konzeption von Kemeny und Oppenheim an. Danach ist eine *Theorie T_2 auf eine Theorie T_1 reduziert* genau dann, wenn

1. T_2 Terme enthält, die nicht in der Sprache von T_1 enthalten sind,
2. jegliche Beobachtungsdaten, die durch T_2 erklärt werden können, auch durch T_1 erklärbar sind,
3. T_1 mindestens so gut systematisiert ist wie T_2.

In dieser Definition von Reduktion spiegeln sich zeitgenössische Vorstellungen über eine wissenschaftliche Theorie. Die Grundidee ist jedoch, daß die Theorie T_2 auf T_1 reduziert wird, wenn T_1 im Hinblick auf die Beobachtungsdaten die gleichen Erklärungserfolge hat wie T_2. Insbesondere wird nicht (wie etwa bei E. Nagel) gefordert, daß die Terme von T_2 mit Hilfe von T_1 *definiert* werden, oder die Gesetze von T_2 aus den Gesetzen von T_1 *abgeleitet* werden müssen.

Die Reduktion einer Teilwissenschaft B_2 (z.B. der Chemie) auf eine Teilwissenschaft B_1 (z.B. die Physik) wird über die Reduktion der jeweiligen Theorien definiert. Wichtig ist der Begriff der *Mikroreduktion*, in dem die Reduktionsrichtung mit einer Teil-Ganze-Relation verknüpft wird. Die Teilwissenschaft B_2 redet über Ganze, die eine Zerlegung in echte Teile zulassen, die zum Grundbereich der Teilwissenschaft B_1 gehören. Daraus ergibt sich:

Die Reduktion von B_2 auf B_1 ist eine *Mikroreduktion*, wenn

- B_2 auf B_1 reduziert ist,
- die Objekte des Grundbereichs von B_2 Ganze sind, die eine Zerlegung in echte Teile haben, welche alle dem Grundbereich von B_1 angehören.

Da die reduzierende Theorie T_1 mindestens die gleiche Erklärungskraft hat wie die reduzierte Theorie T_2, kann sie in dieser zentralen Funktion T_2

ersetzen. Einheit wird in dieser Konzeption erreicht, indem die reduzierte Theorie durch die reduzierende Theorie *ersetzt* wird.

Eher umstandslos werden von Oppenheim und Putnam sechs *Reduktionsstufen* eingeführt:

6 soziale Gruppen
5 (mehrzellige) lebende Dinge
4 Zellen
3 Moleküle
2 Atome
1 Elementarteilchen

Dabei wird die Annahme gemacht, daß es eine niedrigste Stufe, nämlich die der Elementarteilchen gibt. Die Einteilung in die Reduktionsstufen orientiert sich offenbar an Wissenschaftsbereichen bzw. Wissenschaftsgruppen. Aufgrund der Teil-Ganze-Relation ist die Zuordnung zu einer Stufe auch von einer bestimmten Sichtweise bestimmt: „Also spricht ein Physiker, wenn er über ‚alle physikalischen Objekte' redet, auch über lebende Dinge aber nicht über diese als lebende Dinge" (Oppenheim/Putnam 1958, S. 10).

Nach der Klärung dieser Voraussetzungen bringen Oppenheim und Putnam nun verschiedene Argumente für die Glaubwürdigkeit der Annahme, daß die Einheit der Wissenschaft eines Tages erreicht werden kann. Die erste Gruppe von Argumenten stützt sich auf *methodologische* Überlegungen. Das Streben nach der Einheit der Wissenschaft ist fruchtbarer und verspricht im Einzelfall mehr Erfolg, als wenn man sich von vornherein mit einer bunten Vielfalt nicht zusammenhängender Theorien begnügt. Diese Argumente sind allerdings eher Argumente dafür, daß es sinnvoll ist, nach der Einheit der Wissenschaft zu suchen, und weniger Argumente dafür, daß man diese Einheit auch finden kann.

Das ist anders mit dem *Evolutionsargument*. Oppenheim und Putnam berufen sich auf Ergebnisse der empirischen Wissenschaften, um zu zeigen, daß die höheren Reduktionsstufen nach und aus den tieferen Stufen entstanden sind. Dies, so ist die Überlegung, kann nur verständlich gemacht werden, wenn die höheren Stufen auf die tieferen reduzierbar sind.

Die dritte Gruppe von Argumenten sind die induktiven Argumente. Die Autoren zeigen, daß es in der Vergangenheit *Reduktionserfolge* auf jeder Stufe gegeben hat. Besonders eindrucksvoll sind dabei sicherlich die Erfolge der Molekularbiologie bei der Entschlüsselung des genetischen Codes durch Watson, Crick und andere zu Beginn der 50er Jahre.

Ich glaube, daß man diese Argumentation so interpretieren kann, daß aus den Erfolgen eines atomistischen Erklärungsprogramms metaphysische Konsequenzen gezogen werden können. Da der Rückgang auf tiefere Reduktionsstufen, d.h. auf Theorien, die für die Komponenten zuständig sind, auch für das Ganze zu fruchtbaren Erklärungen führt, liegt die Annahme nahe, daß die fundamentalen Gesetze der Physik für die Naturerklärung ausreichen, insbesondere, daß vitalistische Positionen falsch sind. Die Vielfalt der Phänomene in den verschiedenen Schichten käme danach durch spezielle Randbedingungen zustande.

Eine solche metaphysische Konzeption wird in dem Aufsatz von 1958 nicht explizit angesprochen. Die Diskussion darüber ist jedoch für unser Naturbild wichtig. Im folgenden Abschnitt sollen daher die Argumente von Oppenheim und Putnam genauer analysiert und ihre Korrektheit untersucht werden.

3. Analyse und Fehlerdiagnose

Ich möchte zunächst das *Evolutionsargument* analysieren. Unter seinen Prämissen enthält es die Auskünfte der Kosmologie und anderer historischer Naturwissenschaften, nach denen die *höheren Schichten* (Reduktionsstufen) jeweils *nach* und *aus* den tieferen Schichten *entstanden* sind. Die Konklusion des Arguments ist, daß die höheren Stufen auch mit Hilfe der tieferen Stufen *erklärt* werden können.

Dieses Argument hat zwei Prämissen.

Erste Prämisse:

> *Die tieferen Stufen existierten zeitlich vor den höheren Stufen.*

Das ist eine Aussage über die Evolution des Kosmos. Hinzu kommt die

Zweite Prämisse:

> „[...] Wir wollen annehmen, daß den Dingen, die zeitlich später auftreten, mit Hilfe von zeitlich früheren Dingen und Prozessen Rechnung getragen werden kann." (S. 15)

Daraus ergibt sich folgende Konklusion:

> *Die höheren Stufen können mit Hilfe der tieferen Stufen erklärt werden.*

Dieses Argument ist nicht ganz einfach zu beurteilen. Seine Überzeugungskraft hängt offenbar an der zweiten Prämisse und dem in ihr verwendeten Kausalbegriff. Diese zweite Prämisse setzt eine spezielle Konzeption von Kausalität voraus. Die beiden Autoren erläutern ihre Auffassung des Kausalprinzips auf folgende Weise:

> Wir wollen, wie es in der Wissenschaft üblich ist, kausale Determiniertheit als leitendes Prinzip annehmen, d.h. wir wollen annehmen, daß den Dingen, die zeitlich später auftreten, mit Hilfe von zeitlich früheren Dingen und Prozessen Rechnung getragen werden kann. Wenn wir dann herausfinden, daß es eine Zeit gab, zu der ein bestimmtes Ganzes nicht existierte und Dinge auf einer niedrigeren Stufe zusammenkamen, um dieses Ganze zu bilden, so ist es sehr natürlich anzunehmen, die Charakteristika dieses Ganzen könnten unter Bezug auf diese früheren Ereignisse und Teile ursächlich erklärt werden. Zugleich ist es nur natürlich anzunehmen, daß die Theorie dieser Charakteristika durch eine Theorie mikroreduziert werden kann, die sich nur mit den Charakteristika dieser Teile befaßt. (Oppenheim/Putnam 1958, S. 15)

Hier scheinen Oppenheim und Putnam jedoch einen wichtigen Punkt zu übersehen. Es ist durchaus denkbar, daß auf den höheren Stufen spezifische Gesetze zur Geltung kommen, die in den tieferen Stufen noch nicht sichtbar sind (etwa Gesetze, die die Wechselwirkung der Komponenten in zusammengesetzten Systemen betreffen). Dennoch würde man darin keine Verletzung des Kausalprinzips (als eines methodologischen Prinzips) sehen. Was die Autoren hier offenbar zusätzlich benötigen, ist die stillschweigende Annahme der kausalen Abgeschlossenheit und Vollständigkeit der Physik als Theorie der tiefsten Stufe. Diese Zusatzannahme ist aber in einer gewissen Hinsicht schon fast mit der Konklusion identisch.

Dennoch scheint mir das Evolutionsargument nicht ohne Wert zu sein (vgl. dazu auch Vollmer 1986, S. 225f.). Für Anhänger einer reduktionistischen These, wie sie die beiden Autoren vertreten, ist die Evolution der Schichten, beginnend mit der niedrigsten, genau das, was man zu erwarten hat. Für Gegner der Einheitswissenschaft oder für Pluralisten ist dieser Verlauf der Evolution zunächst nicht vor anderen denkbaren Verläufen ausgezeichnet. Anhänger der Einheitswissenschaft haben für die zeitliche Abfolge der Entstehung der Schichten offenbar die bessere Erklärung, die weniger willkürliche Annahmen erfordert. Die Bewertung des Evolutionsarguments hängt davon ab, welches Gewicht man solchen Schlüssen auf die beste Erklärung zugestehen will.

Ich möchte jetzt zum induktiven Argument übergehen. Hier geht es um die Frage, wie bisherige Erfolge von Mikroreduktionen einzuschätzen sind. Am problematischsten ist sicherlich die Stufe 6. Die Autoren haben hier aber vorgebaut. Sie räumen ein, daß die Mikroreduktion der Stufe 6 noch nicht allzu viele Erfolge vorweisen kann und sie begründen diese Lage damit, daß „wohlbegründete theoretische Kenntnis der Stufe 6 ... noch ziemlich rudimentär [ist], so daß es nicht viel gibt, was mikroreduziert werden kann" (S. 16). Hier wird man sicherlich Bedenken haben, ob die Beschreibung des entsprechenden Forschungsfeldes adäquat ist. Liegen die Reduktionshindernisse im Einzelfall wirklich darin, daß das Wissen rudimentär ist? Oder liegt es daran, daß die verschiedenen Stufen unterschiedliche Begriffe und Perspektiven verwenden? Ist es wirklich so, daß es zum methodischen Individualismus keine Alternative gibt? Unklar ist auch, in welchem Sinne man sagen kann, daß der Grundbereich der Stufe 6 aus Elementen der Stufe 5 *besteht*. Gibt es auf der Stufe 5 z.B. *handelnde* Individuen, die gesellschaftliche Institutionen der Stufe 6 bilden könnten? Wie würde man Begriffe wie *Handlung* oder *Rationalität* mikroreduzieren? Die Probleme liegen hier offenbar weniger in der mangelnden Qualität der schichtspezifischen Theorien auf der Stufe 6 als in der Schwierigkeit, diese Theorien mit den Theorien tieferer Schichten in Beziehung zu setzen.

Ganz andere Probleme gibt es auf der Stufe 1. Überlegungen aus der Quantenfeldtheorie, die unter dem Namen „Effektive Feldtheorien" bekannt geworden sind, zeigen, daß es hier möglicherweise keine einfache Basis gibt, keinen Satz letzter Bausteine, aus denen alles andere zusammengesetzt ist. Es gibt zwar eine Basisdisziplin „Elementarteilchenphysik" (was für eine epistemisch abgeschwächte Variante des Einheitsprogramms ausreichen mag), aber ihre Theorien zeichnen keine Basiselemente von der aus der atomistischen Tradition gewohnten Art aus. Vielmehr wird das Bild nahegelegt, daß jedem Energiebereich eine eigene Teilchenontologie zugeordnet werden muß (vgl. Hartmann 1995, Kap. 3). Die verschiedenen Energiebereiche sind also durch für sie jeweils typische Teilchensorten gekennzeichnet, wobei die Teilchen (oder Felder) eines Bereichs nicht aus den Teilchen (oder Feldern) eines anderen Bereichs zusammengesetzt sind. Die Teilchen unterschiedlicher Bereiche sind nicht durch eine Teil-Ganze-Relation miteinander verbunden. Die Diskussion um die Effektiven Feldtheorien zeigt, wie man zu einer Schichteneinteilung kommen kann, ohne auf eine Teil-Ganze-Beziehung zurückgreifen zu müssen. Vor 42 Jahren war es allerdings unproblematisch, die Stufe 1 als Startpunkt für die Mikroreduktionen anzunehmen.

Es fällt auf, daß bei Oppenheim und Putnam kein Hinweis auf *antireduktionistische Argumente* (vgl. Hoyningen-Huene 1992) zu finden ist, d.h. sie diskutieren nicht die Möglichkeit von Argumenten, die prinzipiell die Reduktion zweier Wissensbereiche aufeinander ausschließen und damit auch Reduktionserfolge in Teilbereichen entwerten. Solche Argumente wurden in letzter Zeit insbesondere im Bereich der Philosophie des Geistes vorgebracht. Die Probleme, z.B. Intentionalität (vgl. Carrier 1991) oder Qualia zu reduzieren, passen auch nicht recht in die von den Autoren vorgeschlagene Stufeneinteilung. Das Verhältnis des Mentalen zum Physischen ist nicht in einfacher Weise als Teil-Ganze-Beziehung aufzufassen.

Es ist eine interessante methodologische Frage, welches Gewicht man Beispielen und Gegenbeispielen von Reduktionen beimessen will. Sicherlich gibt es klassische *Erfolge*. So kann man heute die Eigenschaften von Kochsalz auf physikalischer Grundlage verstehen, auch wenn Kochsalz z. B. bei Mill als Musterbeispiel eines Stoffes mit nicht reduzierbaren Eigenschaften galt. Die Gefahr dabei ist allerdings, daß man die Erfolge bei den „leichten" Fällen fälschlicherweise verallgemeinert, daß man sich durch eine *einseitige Diät* ernährt. Andererseits zeigen auch die Gegenbeispiele, d. h. die Beispiele für Mißerfolge von Reduktionsversuchen nicht unbedingt das Scheitern des Reduktionsprogramms. So hat z. B. Fodor (1974) betont, daß es genauso viele Spezialisierungen wie Vereinheitlichungen gibt (ähnlich argumentieren auch Carrier und Mittelstrass (1990, S. 24)). Dabei ist aber zu bedenken, daß Spezialisierungen in der Frühphase der Entwicklung eines Gebietes (wie z. B. der Elektrodynamik) später durch Vereinheitlichungen wieder aufgehoben werden können, während Vereinheitlichungen in der Regel nicht mehr verloren gehen. Hier scheint es eine Asymmetrie zu geben, die eher in die Richtung der Vereinheitlichung weist. Man kann nicht das Scheitern der klassischen Mechanik bei der Erklärung der elektromagnetischen Strahlung gegen die Erfolge der Quantenmechanik bei der Erklärung der chemischen Bindung aufrechnen.

Es fällt weiter auf, daß Oppenheim und Putnam sehr wenig über die Motive zur Einheit schreiben. Das Streben nach Einheit wird als selbstverständlich vorausgesetzt. Die Frage, *warum Einheit*, wird nicht diskutiert (vgl. dazu Stöckler 2000). Ein wichtiger Teil dieser Frage ist, ob die Vereinheitlichungen für den praktischen Umgang und die Anwendung der Wissenschaft nützlich sind. Dabei besteht wenig Zweifel, daß ein Lehrbuch der Agrikulturchemie durch die Übersetzung in die Sprache der Quantenfeldtheorie wenig gewinnt. Der Reduktionsbegriff, den Oppenheim und Putnam verwenden, legt eine Elimination der Begriffe der höheren Stufe nahe, aber gegen diese Elimination sprechen praktische Gründe. Die Einheit der Wissenschaft ist zunächst vor allem ein Thema der Metaphysik, speziell ein Thema eines naturalistischen Erklärungsprogramms. Über den Rahmen der Naturphilosophie hinaus kann das Streben nach Einheit zu einem fruchtbaren heuristischen Motor werden. In der heuristischen Perspektive wird man allerdings auch viele Beispiele finden, in denen pluralistische Ansätze in der jeweiligen Forschungssituation dem Vereinheitlichungsstreben überlegen waren.

Vereinheitlichungen entfalten ihre Kraft in der Erklärungsperspektive. Es stellt sich die Frage, inwieweit umgekehrt jede Vereinheitlichung schon eine Erklärung ist. Wäre Erklären ein Spezialfall von Vereinheitlichen, hätte man prinzipielle methodologische Gründe für die Einheit: Vereinheitlichung folgt aus dem Streben nach Erklärung. Dabei ist aber eine bestimmte Theorie der Erklärung vorausgesetzt, die nicht unumstritten ist. Weiterhin folgt aus solchen prinzipiellen Überlegungen nicht unbedingt, daß die Vereinheitlichung durch *Mikroreduktionen* vorangehen muß. Der *Erfolg* der Mikroreduktionen ist nicht schon *methodologisch* festgelegt, er ist eines der *empirischen* Elemente in der Theorie von Oppenheim und Putnam.

Ein weiterer Mangel der Arbeit von Oppenheim und Putnam ist, daß sie nicht diskutieren, was eigentlich eine Reduktionsstufe oder eine Schicht definiert. Fixsterne sind aus viel mehr Teilchen zusammengesetzt als Maikäfer. Trotzdem gehören Maikäfer zu einer neuen Schicht, aber nicht die Fixsterne. Offenbar geht es bei der Bildung einer neuen Stufe nicht nur um die reine Zusammensetzung. Es scheinen pragmatische Gründe im Spiel zu sein, die es erforderlich machen, neue Eigenschaften einzuführen und eine Fülle von Informationen in ökonomischer Weise erfassen zu müssen.

Eine weitere Schwäche des Aufsatzes ist der verwendete Reduktionsbegriff. Offenbar braucht man schon in der Physik verschiedene Arten von Reduktionen (vgl. Scheibe 1997/1999), und insgesamt wäre aus der Sicht der heutigen Reduktionsdebatten zu diesem Problem einiges mehr sagen. Generell kann man konstatieren, daß die mit Hilfe heutigen Wissens auszumachenden Fehler im Aufsatz von Oppenheim und Putnam meist darin bestehen, daß die Komplexität eines Problems unterschätzt und alternative Denkansätze übersehen oder voreilig ausgeschlossen werden.

Wenn auch die Analyse zeigt, daß das Programm von Oppenheim und Putnam an vielen Stellen präzisierungsbedürftig ist und daß die Autoren mögliche Alternativen übersehen haben, so erscheint doch das Ziel der Einheit der Wissenschaft auch heutzutage noch immer attraktiv. Welche Form der Einheit der Wissenschaft verteidigt werden kann, soll im nächsten Abschnitt untersucht werden.

4. Welche Form der Einheit der Wissenschaft kann verteidigt werden?

Ich möchte mich hier auf die empirischen Wissenschaften beschränken. Zur Verteidigung einer naturalistischen Metaphysik (ein Unternehmen, das eng mit der Einheit der Wissenschaft zusammenhängt), müßte man allerdings auch untersuchen, wie weit Mathematik und andere Strukturwissenschaften, aber auch Konzepte wie Rationalität auf die tieferen Reduktionsstufen reduzierbar sein sollten. Ich möchte noch einmal betonen, daß ich nicht dafür argumentiere, daß die reduzierende Theorie im Wissenschaftsalltag der reduzierten überlegen ist. Die Einheit der Wissenschaft bringt in der Regel keine praktischen Vorteile. Häufig wird natürlich die Tieferlegung punktuelle Erklärungserfolge mit sich bringen. So kann die Zellbiologie punkt-weise durch molekularbiologische Überlegungen ergänzt werden. Durch solche partiellen oder punktweisen Reduktionen entstehen Hybridtheorien. Das entscheidende Argument für die praktischen Grenzen der Reduktionen stammt von einem der beiden Autoren der hier untersuchten Studie. In einer späteren Arbeit hat Hilary Putnam (1975) folgendes deutlich gemacht und sich dabei selbst korrigiert: Gute Erklärungen beginnen nicht immer auf der tiefsten Stufe.

Pragmatische Gründe sprechen eher für die Existenz von Schichten. Dafür sind Grenzen der Handhabbarkeit mathematischer Gleichungen und die übergroße Informationsfülle schuld, an denen auch leistungsfähige Computer nichts ändern können. Neue Begriffe müssen eingeführt werden, die helfen, die Komplexität zu reduzieren. Dies schließt nicht aus, daß man anstrebt, die schichtenspezifischen Theorien mit den Theorien der tieferen Schichten jedenfalls im Prinzip zu verknüpfen. Der Reduktionsbegriff von Kemeny und Oppenheim scheint für ein solches Unternehmen nicht unbedingt geeignet zu sein, da die erklärende Kraft dieser Theorien in verschiedenen Bereichen liegt und aufgrund unterschiedlicher schichtenspezifischer Frageperspektiven beurteilt werden muß.

Die Reduktion sieht eher so aus, daß der Erfolg der Theorie der höheren Schicht mit Hilfe der Theorie der tieferen Schicht *und* der jeweiligen schichtenspezifischen Beschreibungsperspektive verständlich gemacht werden kann. Deswegen sind auch schichtenspezifische Begriffe nicht allein durch die Begriffe der tieferen Theorie definierbar. So sind durchaus auch spezielle Methoden denkbar, z.B. Modellierungen und Simulationen, die z.B. zeigen, wie im Prinzip die Bewegung eines Fischschwarms auf Verhaltenstendenzen der einzelnen Fische zurückgeführt werden kann.

In der Methodologie der Wissenschaften, die sich mit komplexen Systemen beschäftigen, scheint sich ein Weg zu öffnen zwischen einem streng exakten Reduktionismus und einem totalen schichtenrelativen Pluralismus von Theorien. Man könnte eines Tages gute Gründe für die Annahmen haben, daß

– es fundamentale Gesetze nur in der Physik gibt (das Ohmsche Gesetz $U = R \times I$ ist in diesem Sinne nicht fundamental),
– Prozesse auf höherer Stufe immer durch Mechanismen bzw. durch die Relation von Funktion und Realisierung (Ausfüllen der entsprechenden Rolle) mit Prozessen auf der tieferen Stufe verbunden sind.

Die Voraussetzung für diesen Optimismus ist,

– daß es keine überzeugenden antireduktionistischen Argumente gibt, daß also an keiner Stelle prinzipielle Gründe eine Reduktion ausschliessen,

- daß die fehlende de facto-Reduzierbarkeit plausible Gründe hat (etwa weil man eine Gleichung mit 10^{23} Variablen hinschreiben und lösen müßte),
- daß bessere Methoden (neue Theorieansätze oder raffiniertere Berechnungsmethoden) im Laufe der Zeit zu einer Verbesserung der „Reduzierbarkeit" führen.

Wenn die Grenzen der Reduzierbarkeit pragmatische Ursachen haben, dann müssen neue, wirksamere Methoden dazu führen, daß diese Grenzen verschoben werden können. Der Grad der Vereinheitlichung muß sich durch neue Ansätze verbessern. Ein Beispiel für einen Erfolg in dieser Richtung ist die Reduktion der Laser-Gleichung auf ein quantenfeldtheoretisches Modell in der Synergetik von Hermann Haken (vgl. Stöckler 1991). In dieser Perspektive gibt es durchaus Fortschritte in Richtung einer Einheit der Wissenschaft, die, so verstanden, auch heute noch als Arbeitshypothese akzeptiert werden kann.

Literatur

Carrier, M.: On the Disunity of Science or Why Psychology is not a Branch of Physics. In: *Einheit der Wissenschaften*, hrsg. von der Akademie der Wissenschaften zu Berlin, 1991, 39–59.

Carrier, M., Mittelstrass, J.: The Unity of Science, *International Studies in the Philosophy of Science* 4 (1990), 17–31.

Cartwright, N.: Fundamentalism vs. the Patchwork of Laws, *Proceedings of the Aristotelian Society* 93/2 (1994), 279–292.

Cartwright, N.: The Metaphysics of the Disunified World. In: *PSA 1994*, ed. by M. Forbes, 1994, East Lansing (Mich.), 357–364.

Fodor, J. A.: Special Sciences, *Synthese* 28 (1974), 97–115.

Hartmann, S.: *Metaphysik und Methode*, Konstanz 1995.

Hoyningen-Huene, P.: On the Way to a Theory of Antireductionist Arguments. In: *Emergence or Reduction?*, hrsg. von A. Beckermann, H. Flohr und J. Kim, Berlin 1992, 289–301.

Oppenheim, P., Putnam, H.: Unity of Science as a Working Hypothesis. In: *Concepts, Theories, and the Mind-Body Problem, Minnesota Studies in the Philosophy of Science, Volume II*, hrsg. von H. Feigl und M. Scriven, G. Maxwell, Minneapolis 1958, 3–36 (deutsche Übersetzung: Einheit der Wissenschaft als Arbeitshypothese. In: *Erkenntnisprobleme der Naturwissenschaften*, hrsg. von L. Krüger, Köln 1970, 339–371).

Putnam, H.: Philosophy and Our Mental Life. In: H. Putnam, *Mind, Language and Reality, Philosophical Papers, Volume 2*, Cambridge 1975, 291–303.

Scheibe, E.: *Die Reduktion physikalischer Theorien. Ein Beitrag zur Einheit der Physik*, 2 Bände, Heidelberg 1997/1999.

Stöckler, M.: Reductionism and the New Theories of Self-Organization. In: *Advances of Scientific Philosophy*, hrsg. von G. Schurz und G. Dorn, Amsterdam 1991, 233–254.

Stöckler, M.: Why unify? Bemerkungen zur Einheit der Physik. In: *Die Einheit der Wirklichkeit*, hrsg. von B.-O. Küppers, München 2000, 165–183.

Vollmer, G.: Reduktion und Evolution – Argumente und Beispiele. In: G. Vollmer, *Was können wir wissen? Band 2: Die Erkenntnis der Natur*, Stuttgart 1986, 211–233.

Ulrich Gähde

Ist der Ramsey-Satz eine empirische Behauptung?

Abstract

In scharfem Gegensatz zur etablierten Sichtweise wird gezeigt, dass es sich bei dem Ramsey-Satz von Theorie-Elementen und Theorien-Netzen in sämtlichen üblichen Formulierungen nicht um eine empirische, sondern vielmehr um eine mathematisch determinierte Behauptung handelt. Weiterhin wird dafür argumentiert, dass die Kluft zwischen dem *statement view* und dem *non statement view* empirischer Theorien keineswegs so tief und unüberbrückbar ist, wie allgemein angenommen. Schließlich werden Gründe dafür angegeben, warum die Wahl zwischen beiden Ansätzen sich weniger an philosophischen Grundsatzüberlegungen, als vielmehr an pragmatischen Kriterien orientieren sollte. Kandidaten für derartige pragmatische Kriterien werden diskutiert.

Von Stegmüller und anderen ist das strukturalistische Theorienkonzept als *non statement view* charakterisiert und klar von einer Aussagenkonzeption empirischer Theorien abgegrenzt worden.[1] In dieser Sichtweise werden Theorien als nicht-propositionale Gebilde gedeutet; sie stellen danach Werkzeuge dar, mit denen umfassende empirische Hypothesen in Gestalt von Ramsey-Sätzen formuliert werden. Die Aufgabe der folgenden Überlegungen besteht darin, diese Sichtweise einer genaueren Prüfung zu unterziehen. Sie werden insbesondere gravierende Zweifel daran begründen, dass der Ramsey-Satz tatsächlich eine adäquate Wiedergabe der mit einer Theorie verbundenen *empirischen Behauptung* darstellt.

Den Ausgangspunkt bildet die Erörterung der Leitidee, die hinter der Formulierung des Ramsey-Satzes steht (Abschnitt 1). Danach kann die theoretische Beschreibung eines physikalischen, biologischen, ökonomischen etc. Systems als eine spezielle Form der *Ergänzungsbildung* interpretiert werden. Was damit genau gemeint ist, wird an einem Beispiel erläutert. In Abschnitt 2 wird der methodische Status der entsprechenden Ergänzbarkeitsbehauptung, d.h. des Ramsey-Satzes, näher untersucht. In scharfem Gegensatz zum

---

[1] Vgl. etwa Stegmüller 1973, Einleitung.

strukturalistischen *Credo* wird gezeigt, dass es sich beim Ramsey-Satz in allen üblichen Formulierungen keineswegs um eine empirische Behauptung handelt. Der Ramsey-Satz stellt vielmehr eine Hypothese dar, deren Wahrheitswert mit ausschließlich mathematischen Hilfsmitteln bestimmt werden kann. Die Aufgabe der folgenden Abschnitte besteht darin zu zeigen, dass der Bezeichnung *empirische Behauptung einer Theorie* dennoch eine sinnvolle Bedeutung verliehen werden kann. Dabei wird die Unterscheidung zwischen partiellen Modellen und Datenstrukturen eine wichtige Rolle spielen; sie wird in Abschnitt 3 erläutert. Die Bedeutung dieser Unterscheidung für die Frage, was mit der *empirischen Behauptung* einer Theorie gemeint sein kann, wird in Abschnitt 4 diskutiert. Der abschließende Abschnitt 5 enthält eine kritische Anmerkung zum Thema *non statement view*: Es werden Gründe dafür angeben, warum die Wahl zwischen *statement view* und *non statement view* nicht zur philosophischen Grundsatzfrage stilisiert, sondern vielmehr nach *pragmatischen* Kriterien entschieden werden sollte. Einige Kriterien, die eine solche Wahl leiten können, werden diskutiert.

1. Theoretische Beschreibung als Ergänzungsbildung

Nach strukturalistischer Auffassung kann die theoretische Beschreibung eines Systems als *Ergänzungsbildung* aufgefasst werden. Dabei ist eine Datenbasis vorgegeben, die zu einem Modell der in Frage stehenden Theorie komplettiert werden soll. Was damit gemeint ist, kann leicht an einem einfachen Beispiel illustriert werden: Angenommen, die Bahnkurven zweier Doppelsterne um den gemeinsamen Schwerpunkt sollen mit Hilfe der Newtonschen Axiome sowie des allgemeinen Gravitationsgesetzes erklärt werden. Dabei sollen insbesondere die Massen der beiden Objekte sowie die zwischen ihnen wirkenden Kräfte bestimmt werden.

Strukturalistisch betrachtet bedeutet das Folgendes: Angenommen, das System ist weit genug von allen anderen stellaren Objekten entfernt, um Wechselwirkungen ausschließen zu können. Dann besteht die Objektmenge P dieser intendierten Anwendung nur aus den beiden Komponenten des Doppelsternsystems. Die Bahnkurven der beiden Objekte werden über ein Zeitintervall T gemessen und in einer Ortsfunktion s zusammengefasst. Das Tripel $z = \langle P, T, s \rangle$ wird in der strukturalistischen Terminologie als *partielles Modell* der klassischen Mechanik bezeichnet. Es repräsentiert die betreffende intendierte Anwendung. Die Aufgabe der theoretischen Beschreibung besteht nun darin, dieses partielle Modell durch Anfügung geeigneter Massen- und Kraftfunktionen zu einem Modell der Theorie zu ergänzen.

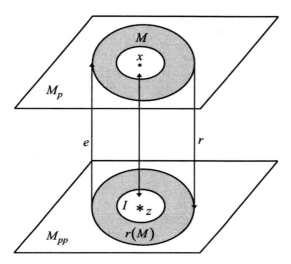

Formal kann dieser Ergänzungsvorgang wie folgt dargestellt werden: Sei M die Modellmenge der Theorie. $r(M)$ sei die Menge aller derjenigen partiellen Modelle, die erfolgreich zu einem Modell der Theorie komplettiert werden können.[2] Dann wird behauptet, dass z zu dieser Menge gehört

$$z \in r(M).$$

Wenn man auf das Modell x der Theorie Bezug nehmen möchte, zu dem das partielle Modell ergänzt werden kann, dann kann man diesen Sachverhalt auch wie folgt ausdrücken:

$$\exists x\, [x \in M \wedge r(x) = z].$$

Im allgemeinen wird man es nicht mit einem einzelnen System zu tun haben, das theoretisch beschrieben werden soll, sondern mit einer mehrelementigen Klasse derartiger Systeme. Falls man sog. Brückenstrukturen (*Constraints* und *Links*) ignoriert, die die theoretische Beschreibungen verschiedener intendierter Anwendungen untereinander korrelieren, so erhält man die folgende Formulierung des Ramsey-Satzes:[3]

(1) $\quad \forall z\, [z \in I \rightarrow z \in r(M)] \quad$ bzw.

(2) $\quad \exists X\, [X \subseteq M \wedge r(X) = I] \quad$ bzw. $\quad I \subseteq r(M)$

---

[2] r ist die sog. *Restriktionsfunktion*, die jedem Modell ein zugehöriges partielles Modell zuordnet, indem sie – anschaulich gesprochen – jeweils die theoretischen Funktionen ‚abschneidet'.

[3] Brückenstrukturen sind für die folgenden Überlegungen, die sich ausschließlich mit dem methodischen Status des Ramsey-Satzes beschäftigen, irrelevant.

Damit liegt eine besonders einfache (und in vielen Hinsichten unzulängliche) Version des Ramsey-Satzes vor.

Normalerweise wird der Ramsey-Satz so interpretiert, dass er die Theoretisch-nichttheoretisch-Unterscheidung voraussetzt: Ergänzt werden sollen gerade die *theoretischen* Funktionen – nach strukturalistischem *Credo* im Fall der klassischen Mechanik also die Massen- und Kraftfunktion. Man verdeutlicht sich jedoch leicht, dass der mit dem Schlagwort *theoretische Beschreibung als Ergänzungsbildung* bezeichnete Grundgedanke von der Theoretisch-nichttheoretisch-Unterscheidung mit ihren zahlreichen Problemen weitgehend unabhängig ist. Entscheidend für diesen Grundgedanken ist vielmehr die Tatsache, dass, anschaulich formuliert, *Bruchstücke* eines Modells vorliegen und behauptet wird, dass diese Bruchstücke zu einem vollständigen Modell der Theorie komplettiert werden können. So lassen sich etwa leicht Situationen denken, in denen man nicht nur die Ortsfunktionen der beteiligten Objekte kennt, sondern auch die Masse eines oder mehrerer Objekte bereits in früheren Untersuchungen ermittelt wurden und es nun nur noch darum geht, die Masse der restlichen zum System gehörenden Körper sowie die zwischen ihnen wirkenden Kräfte zu bestimmen. Die Problematik ist in diesem Fall völlig analog, obwohl sie quer zur üblichen Theoretisch-nichttheoretisch-Unterscheidung verläuft.

Die eben angegebene Formulierung des Ramsey-Satzes ist in vielen Hinsichten stark vereinfacht. So bleiben in ihr etwa die folgenden drei Aspekte unberücksichtigt:

1. Ein entscheidender Vorteil des strukturalistischen Theorienkonzepts gegenüber herkömmlichen metatheoretischen Ansätzen besteht darin, dass man zum Ausdruck bringen kann, dass empirische Theorien nicht alle intendierten Anwendungen „über einen Leisten spannen", sondern vielmehr verschiedene Anwendungen unter Verwendung verschiedener spezieller Varianten des formalen Apparats beschreiben können. Konkret bedeutet das: Einerseits werden sehr allgemeine Fundamentalprinzipien formuliert, die in *sämtlichen* Anwendungen einer Theorie gelten müssen. Andererseits wird aber zugleich wesentlich von Spezialgesetzen Gebrauch gemacht, die nur in bestimmten Anwendungen Gültigkeit beanspruchen. Gerade durch die Kooperation von Grund- und Spezialgesetzen gewinnen empirische Theorien ihre spezifische Leistungsfähigkeit, ihren ‚Biss'. Sie ermöglicht es empirischen Theorien, konkrete Anwendungen in sehr differenzierter Weise zu beschreiben, ohne dass die dabei verwendeten spezielleren Annahmen auch in alle anderen Anwendungen hineingetragen werden müssten. Eine komplexere Version des Ramsey-Satzes muss diesen Sachverhalt widerspiegeln.

2. Empirische Theorien beschreiben die Wirklichkeit immer nur im Rahmen einer bestimmten Messgenauigkeit: Sie sind nur approximativ richtig. Um diesen Sachverhalt adäquat erfassen zu können, wird eine *approximative* Version des Ramsey-Satzes benötigt.

3. Theorien beanspruchen in aller Regel, eine in sich schlüssige, *konsistente* theoretische Beschreibung ihrer Anwendungsmenge zu liefern. Die Aufgabe, eine entsprechende Konsistenzforderung in adäquater Weise zu formulieren und in den Ramsey-Satz zu integrieren, ist keineswegs trivial.[4] Das gilt vor allem dann, wenn eine solche Konsistenzforderung für die *approximative* Version des Ramsey-Satzes formuliert werden soll.

Auf technische Details von raffinierteren Formulierungen des Ramsey-Satzes, die die zuvor genannten drei Aspekte berücksichtigen, muss im Rahmen dieser Arbeit nicht näher eingegangen werden. Sie sind irrelevant für die Problematik, die im Zentrum dieses Artikel steht: „Welchen methodischen Status besitzt der Ramsey-Satzes? Handelt es sich um eine empirisch oder um eine mathematisch bestimmte Behauptung?" Auf diese Fragen wird nun näher eingegangen.

2. Überlegungen zum Status des Ramsey-Satzes

Der mit einer Theorie (genauer: mit einem Theorie-Element oder einem Theorien-Netz) assoziierte Ramsey-Satz wird in der einschlägigen Literatur häufig als *empirische Behauptung* (*empirical claim*) bezeichnet.[5] In diesem Abschnitt soll gezeigt werden, dass es sich beim Ramsey-Satz in allen üblicherweise verwendeten Formulierungen nicht um eine *empirische* Hypothese handelt, sondern vielmehr um eine Behauptung, deren Wahrheitswert mit ausschließlich *mathematischen* Hilfsmitteln bestimmt werden kann.

Betrachtet werde zunächst die im vorigen Abschnitt angegebene Formulierung (1) des Ramsey-Satzes für eine Anwendungsmenge I:

$$(1) \quad \forall z [z \in I \rightarrow z \in r(M)]$$

Für die verbreitete Auffassung, nach der es sich dabei um eine *empirische* Behauptung handelt, wird häufig die folgende Begründung angeführt: „Bei den partiellen Modellen aus I handelt es sich um *empirisch interpretierte* Strukturen. Aus diesem Grund ist die Behauptung ihrer Ergänzbarkeit zu einer entsprechenden Modellmenge eine *empirische* Hypothese." Dass diese

---

[4] Vgl. Gähde 1996.
[5] Vgl. etwa Balzer/Moulines/Sneed 1987, S. 89ff., 177ff.

Begründung nicht zutrifft, zeigen die folgenden Überlegungen am Beispiel des Doppelsternsystems: Angenommen, dieses System wird durch ein bestimmtes partielles Modell z erfasst. Dann behauptet der Ramsey-Satz, dass z zu einem Modell $x \in M$ ergänzt werden kann. x enthält als Komponenten zunächst diejenigen Basismengen, die bereits Komponenten des partiellen Modells z waren. In unserem Fall handelt es sich dabei um die Objektmenge P und das Zeitintervall T. Darüber hinaus enthält x nur mathematische Hilfsbasismengen (hier: $\mathbb{N}$ und $\mathbb{R}$) sowie Funktionen, die auf den genannten Basis- und Hilfsbasismengen definiert sind (f und m). x enthält dagegen keine weiteren Mengen empirischer Entitäten, die nicht bereits in z auftraten. Aus diesem Grund kann die Frage, ob z zu einem Modell aus M ergänzbar ist, mit ausschließlich mathematischen Mitteln beantwortet werden: Obwohl die partiellen Modelle und die Modelle empirisch interpretierte Strukturen darstellen, stellt der Ramsey-Satz in der oben angegebenen Konditionalform (1) dennoch keine empirische, sondern vielmehr eine mathematische Ergänzbarkeitsbehauptung dar.

Etwas schwieriger ist die Frage nach dem Status des Ramsey-Satzes zu beantworten, wenn auf die im letzten Abschnitt angegebene Version (2) zurückgegriffen wird, die nicht in Konditionalform formuliert ist. Hier scheint eine Existenzbehauptung über eine Modellmenge X und damit zugleich über die empirischen Entitäten ausgesprochen zu werden, die in diesen Modellen vorkommen. Ob man dieser Interpretation zustimmt oder nicht, hängt jedoch wesentlich davon ab, ob man I bereits als vorgegeben annimmt oder nicht. Angesichts der Tatsache, dass man die Ergänzbarkeitsfrage im allgemeinen erst dann stellen wird, wenn das der Fall ist, dürfte der Ramsey-Satz auch in diesem Fall so zu interpretieren sein, dass er nur eine *mathematische Ergänzbarkeitsbehauptung* zum Ausdruck bringt. Alles, was an Empirie benötigt wird, ist dann bereits in die Formulierung der entsprechenden partiellen Modelle eingeflossen.

Dennoch kann der Bezeichnung *empirische Behauptung einer Theorie* eine sinnvolle Bedeutung gegeben werden. Das wird im Folgenden erläutert. Den Ausgangspunkt bildet dabei die Unterscheidung zwischen *partiellen Modellen* und *Datenstrukturen*, die im folgenden Abschnitt erläutert wird.[6] Ihre Relevanz für die Interpretation des Ramsey-Satzes wird anschließend in Abschnitt 4 analysiert.

---

[6] Eine entsprechende Unterscheidung ist bereits vor mehreren Jahren vorgeschlagen worden, ohne das ihre grundlegende Bedeutung für das strukturalistische Theorienkonzept in vollem Umfang erkannt worden wäre; vgl. Balzer/Lauth/Zoubek 1993.

3. Datenstrukturen

Bei der Verwendung von partiellen Modellen wird von der Annahme ausgegangen, dass *sämtliche* Funktionswerte aller nichttheoretischen Funktionen bekannt sind. Im Beispiel des Doppelsternsystems würde das etwa bedeuten, dass die Bahnkurven beider Objekte *vollständig* bekannt sind. Diese Annahme ist jedoch aus mindestens zwei Gründen unzutreffend. Erstens enthalten die Definitionsbereiche nichttheoretischer Funktionen i. a. unendlich viele Argumentwerte, denen stets nur endlich viele *de facto* durchgeführte Messungen gegenüberstehen. Zweitens gibt es im allgemeinen zusätzliche situationsspezifische Gründe, die die Menge der Funktionswerte, die durch Messung bestimmt werden können, weiter einschränken. So kann man etwa die Bahn einer Komponente des Doppelsternsystems nicht bestimmen, wenn diese Komponente durch die andere Komponente oder ein weiteres Objekt verdeckt wird. Die Annahme von partiellen Modellen mit vollständig bekannten nichttheoretischen Funktionen ist demnach eine Fiktion. Statt dessen verfügt man stets nur über eine endliche, begrenzte Datenbasis. Aus dieser endlichen Datenbasis werden dann in einem weiteren und keineswegs unproblematischen Schritt die Bahnkurven dieser Objekte gewonnen.

Eine ähnliches Problem liegt bei den meisten Experimenten bzw. Beobachtungssituationen vor: Anstelle von partiellen Modellen, bei denen *per definitionem* sämtliche Funktionswerte der nichttheoretischen Funktionen gegeben sein müssen, liegen stets nur endliche, begrenzte Datenbasen vor. Derartige Bruchstücke von partiellen Modellen werden im Folgenden als *(nichttheoretische) Datenstrukturen* bezeichnet.

Um den Begriff der Datenstruktur formal zu definieren, kann auf den Hilfsbegriff der *Substruktur* zurückgegriffen werden:

Def.: Seien z und z' zwei Tupel. z ist eine Substruktur von z' ($z \sqsubset z'$) gdw. gilt:
  a) z und z' besitzen dieselbe Stellenzahl.
  b) Jede Komponente von z ist eine (eventuell leere) echte oder unechte Teilmenge der entsprechenden Komponente von z'.

Ebenso kann die Relation $\sqsubset$ auch für Mengen von Tupeln eingeführt werden:

Def.: Seien Z und Z' zwei Klassen von Tupeln. Dann gelte $Z \sqsubset Z'$ gdw. die folgenden beiden Bedingungen erfüllt sind:
  a) Für jedes $z \in Z$ gibt es genau ein $z' \in Z$ mit $z \sqsubset z'$.
  b) Z' enthält keine weiteren Elemente.

Unter Verwendung dieser Relationen können wir nichttheoretische Datenstrukturen als Substrukturen partieller Modelle definieren:

Def.: z ist eine *nichttheoretische Datenstruktur* gdw. es ein $z' \in M_{pp}$ gibt, so dass gilt: $z \sqsubset z'$. Mit anderen Worten: Eine nichttheoretische Datenstruktur ist eine Substruktur eines partiellen Modells.

Die Formulierung des Ramsey-Satzes kann leicht so verallgemeinert werden, dass sie auch auf den Fall von Datenstrukturen anwendbar ist. $\tilde{I}$ bezeichne eine Klasse intendierter Anwendungen, die in Form von Datenstrukturen vorgegeben sind. Dann kann der Ramsey-Satz für Datenstrukturen wie folgt reformuliert werden:

$$\forall z \left[z \in \tilde{I} \rightarrow \exists x \left[x \in M \wedge z \sqsubset r(x) \right] \right], \quad \text{oder kurz} \quad \tilde{I} \sqsubset r(M).$$

Die Ersetzung von partiellen Modellen durch Datenstrukturen mag auf den ersten Blick als bloß technische Modifikation von untergeordneter Bedeutung erscheinen. Das wäre jedoch eine Fehleinschätzung. In Wirklichkeit wirft diese Modifikation grundlegende wissenschaftstheoretische Fragestellungen auf. Das wird besonders dann deutlich, wenn man von der *strikten* zur *approximativen* Version des Ramsey-Satzes übergeht. In diesem Fall tritt ein Problem auf, dass für zahlreiche Einzelwissenschaften von grundlegender Bedeutung ist – das Problem, wie man durch eine vorgegebene Menge von Messwerten einen Funktionsgraphen legt, der diese Messdaten möglichst gut approximiert. Bekanntlich gibt es hier eine Fülle von Kriterien, an denen man sich orientieren kann. Diese Kriterien weisen teilweise deutlich differierende Leistungsmerkmale auf. So gewichtet etwa der *least mean square fit* (also dasjenige Kriterium, bei dem die Summe der Quadrate der Abstände der Funktionswerte von dem Funktionsgraphen minimiert wird) ‚Ausreisser' besonders stark. Die Diskussion über diese Kriterien ist vor allem deswegen wichtig, weil die Wahl eines bestimmten Approximationskriteriums wesentliche Bedeutung für die theoretische Beschreibung des betreffenden Systems gewinnen kann. Die gesamte einschlägige Diskussion, die in den Einzelwissenschaften intensiv geführt wird, konnte bisher im strukturalistischen Ansatz nicht nachgezeichnet werden. Wenn man dagegen von partiellen Modellen zu Datenstrukturen und zudem zu einer approximativen Version des Ramsey-Satzes übergeht, kann sie in diesem Rahmen nachvollzogen und analysiert werden.

Der Übergang von partiellen Modellen zu Datenstrukturen hat zudem für die Fragestellung, die im Zentrum dieses Artikels steht, eine grundlegende Bedeutung: für die Frage, was unter der *empirischen Behauptung* einer Theorie zu verstehen ist und wie diese Behauptung mit dem Ramsey-Satz korreliert ist. Das wird nun näher ausgeführt.

4. Datenstrukturen, Ramsey-Satz und empirische Behauptung

Kehren wir noch einmal zum Beispiel des Doppelsternsystems zurück. Die Messwerte, die in Datenstrukturen zusammengefasst werden, dienen zwei verschiedenen Aufgaben. Zunächst liefern sie selbstverständlich empirische Informationen über das in Frage stehende System. Im Fall des Doppelsternsystems wird eine entsprechende Datenstruktur insbesondere Informationen über die Bahnkurven enthalten, auf denen sich die beiden Komponenten um den gemeinsamen Schwerpunkt bewegen. Zugleich dient die Datenstruktur aber noch einem weiteren Zweck: Sie legt fest, *um welches System es sich überhaupt handelt*. Konkret wird man etwa im Fall des Doppelsternsystems für einige Zeitpunkte angeben, wo die beiden Komponenten von der Erde aus zu beobachten sind. Datenstrukturen dienen damit keineswegs nur dazu, Informationen über ein bestimmtes, bereits vorher eindeutig identifiziertes System zu liefern. Sie erfüllen vielmehr zugleich die Aufgabe festzulegen, um welches System es sich überhaupt handelt.

Für die folgenden Überlegungen ist es wichtig, dass Datenstrukturen nicht statisch sind. Vielmehr sind sie ständiger Veränderung unterworfen: Erstens wird durch neue Messungen die Datenbasis ständig erweitert. Zweitens müssen alte Daten eventuell korrigiert oder ersetzt werden. Mit anderen Worten: Ein und dasselbe System wird im Laufe der Zeit durch eine Sequenz verschiedener Datenstrukturen beschrieben.

Diesen Überlegungen kommt eine Schlüsselrolle zu, wenn es darum geht, den Behauptungskomplex zu entwirren, der mit Hilfe einer empirischen Theorie über ein System bzw. eine Klasse von Systemen formuliert wird. Dieser Behauptungskomplex enthält drei Teilbehauptungen, die der Einfachheit halber an einem einzelnen System erläutert werden:

1. Es wird behauptet, dass die vorliegende Datenstruktur das betreffende System im Rahmen der Messgenauigkeit adäquat erfasst, d.h. dass die Messwerte korrekt sind. Dabei handelt es sich offenbar um eine empirische Behauptung.

2. Es wird behauptet, dass die vorliegende Datenstruktur unter Wahrung von *Constraints* und *Links* zu einem Modell der betreffenden Theorie (bzw. eines speziellen Theorie-Elements) ergänzt werden kann. Diese Behauptung kommt im Ramsey-Satz in der Formulierung für Datenstrukturen zum Ausdruck. Wie in Abschnitt 3 dargestellt, handelt es sich dabei in allen üblichen

Formulierungen gerade nicht um eine empirische Hypothese, sondern vielmehr um eine Behauptung, deren Wahrheitswert mit ausschließlich mathematischen Methoden bestimmt werden kann.

3. Schließlich wird man häufig die wesentlich weitergehende Hypothese aufstellen, dass das durch die Datenstruktur gekennzeichnete System *generell* einen erfolgreichen Anwendungsfall des betreffenden Theorie-Elements darstellt. Damit ist gemeint, dass sich nicht nur die *gegenwärtig verfügbare* Datenstruktur zumindest näherungsweise zu einem Modell des betreffenden Theorie-Elements ergänzen lässt, sondern dass eine entsprechende Aussage auch für alle diejenigen Datenstrukturen gilt, die sich auf dasselbe System beziehen und die durch Hinzunahme oder Korrektur von Messwerten aus der gegenwärtig verfügbaren Datenstruktur hervorgehen. So wird man etwa vermuten, dass das genannte Doppelsternsystem *generell* – und nicht nur in Bezug auf eine zu einem bestimmten Zeitpunkt verfügbare Datenbasis – eine erfolgreiche Anwendung der klassischen Mechanik darstellt. Das ist offenbar eine sehr starke empirische Behauptung, die zwar – in Übereinstimmung mit Poppers Überlegungen – niemals endgültig verifiziert, wohl aber im Grenzfall durch einen einzigen Datensatz falsifiziert werden kann.

Die sorgfältige Unterscheidung zwischen diesen drei Teilbehauptungen erscheint aus mehreren Gründen als wünschenswert. Erstens: Wie zuvor erläutert kann sie dazu beitragen, den Behauptungskomplex zu entwirren, der mit Hilfe einer empirischen Theorie über eine intendierte Anwendung bzw. eine Klasse intendierter Anwendungen formuliert wird. Dabei handelt es sich bei der ersten und der dritten Teilbehauptung jeweils um eine empirische Hypothese. Dagegen stellt die zweite Teilbehauptung – die Ergänzbarkeitsbehauptung in Gestalt des Ramsey-Satzes – eine mathematische Behauptung dar.

Zweitens: Die im Strukturalismus übliche Identifizierung von intendierten Anwendungen mit konkreten partiellen Modellen oder Datenstrukturen hat eine stark anti-intuitive Konsequenz: Jedesmal, wenn sich die Messwerte ändern, müsste man streng genommen von einer *neuen* intendierten Anwendung sprechen. Man kann also z.B. das Doppelsternsystems nicht als *eine* intendierte Anwendung der klassischen Mechanik betrachten. Statt dessen liegt jedesmal eine neue intendierte Anwendung vor, wenn sich die verfügbare Datenbasis ändert. Das entspricht aber selbstverständlich keineswegs dem Sprachgebrauch. Man möchte von „dem Planetensystem", „dem Gezeitenproblem" oder eben „dem konkreten Doppelsternsystem" als einer Anwendung der klassischen Mechanik sprechen können.[7] Die Entkopplung von

---

[7] Schon diese wenigen Beispiele zeigen, dass der Anwendungsbegriff mehrdeutig ist: Auf der einen Seite werden wie in den oben angegebenen Beispielen damit *konkrete* Systeme bezeich-

intendierten Anwendungen und partiellen Modellen bzw. Datenstrukturen ermöglicht die sinnvolle Formulierung der folgenden Frage: „Wann beziehen sich zwei Datenstrukturen auf dieselbe Anwendung?." Am Beispiel des Doppelsternsystems lässt sich gut erläutern, warum diese Frage nichttrivial ist. So können (und werden) sich hier nicht nur die verfügbaren Bahndaten für die beiden bekannten Komponenten des Systems ständig ändern, sondern auch die Objektmenge selbst. Das wird immer dann der Fall sein, wenn neue Objekte oder Materieverteilungen entdeckt werden, die über Gravitationskräfte mit den beiden bekannten Komponenten des Doppelsternsystems wechselwirken. Ab wann wird man hier von einer *neuen* Anwendung sprechen? Wie identifiziert man intendierte Anwendungen? Vermutlich wird die nähere Untersuchung dieser Frage eine irreduzible Vagheit im Anwendungsbegriff zu Tage führen, die bisher im strukturalistischen Konzept in seiner jetzigen Form nicht zum Ausdruck kommt. Interessant ist dabei insbesondere die Frage, ob nicht doch theoretische Überlegungen – und zwar Überlegungen, die sich auf diejenige Theorie beziehen, mit deren Hilfe die Beschreibung erfolgen soll – in die Identifikation von intendierten Anwendungen einfließen.

5. Eine Schlussbemerkung zum Schlagwort ‚*non statement view*'

Wie eingangs erwähnt, wird im strukturalistischen Ansatz scharf zwischen Theorien und den mit ihnen formulierten Behauptungen unterschieden. Theorien stellen danach keine Entitäten dar, die selbst einen propositionalen Gehalt besitzen. Statt dessen werden sie als *Werkzeuge* interpretiert, mit deren Hilfe komplexe Hypothesen formuliert werden können. Auf Grund dieser Trennung hat man vom strukturalistischen Ansatz als vom *non statement view* gesprochen und diese Sichtweise vom üblichen *statement view*, d.h. einer Aussagenkonzeption empirischer Theorien, abgegrenzt. Insbesondere Stegmüller hat diese Unterscheidung hervorgehoben und die Auseinandersetzung zwischen beiden Sichtweisen zu einer philosophischen Grundsatzfrage erklärt.[8]

---

net, auf die eine empirische Theorie angewendet werden soll. Auf der anderen Seite wird der Begriff *Anwendung* häufig auch im Sinne von *Anwendungstypen* (‚der harmonische Oszillator', ‚der freie Fall', ‚das Zwei-Körper-Problem') verwendet. Derartige Anwendungstypen werden im Rahmen des strukturalistischen Theorienkonzepts üblicherweise durch Klassen von partiellen Modellen erfasst. In diesem Artikel wird jedoch nur auf intendierte Anwendungen eingegangen, die sich auf konkrete Systeme beziehen.

[8] Vgl. etwa Stegmüller 1973.

Diese scharfe Trennung zwischen beiden Theoriekonzeptionen ist aus mehreren Gründen problematisch. Zum einen ist die Kluft zwischen *statement view* und *non statement view* keineswegs so tief, wie Stegmüllers Ausführungen das suggerieren. Wie die folgenden Überlegungen zeigen werden, sollten bei der Wahl zwischen beiden Ansätzen weniger philosophische Grundsatzüberlegungen, als vielmehr pragmatische Kriterien ausschlaggebend sein. Zum anderen hat die einseitige Betonung der Auseinandersetzung zwischen *statement view* und *non statement* dazu geführt, dass andere, wesentlich wichtigere Unterschiede zwischen dem strukturalistischen Ansatz und konkurrierenden wissenschaftstheoretischen Konzeptionen in den Hintergrund getreten sind. Die Diskussion ist dadurch auf die falsche Fährte gesetzt worden. Auf beide Punkte wird nun nacheinander eingegangen.

Dass die Kluft zwischen dem *non statement view* und der Aussagenkonzeption empirischer Theorien keineswegs so unüberbrückbar ist wie häufig behauptet, zeigen schon die folgenden Überlegungen: In die Definition von Theorie-Elementen und Theorien-Netzen – also den strukturalistischen Substituten für empirische Theorien – fließen an zahlreichen Stellen *Aussagen* ein. Ein Beispiel: Die Modellmengen von Theorie-Elementen werden mit Hilfe von mengentheoretischen Prädikaten ausgezeichnet, die unter Verwendung von *Aussagen* – nämlich Gesetzen, Charakterisierungen, Typisierungen etc. – definiert werden. Dasselbe gilt für Brückenstrukturen, also für *Constraints* und *Links*: Auch hier wird wesentlich auf Aussagen über bestehende Korrelationen zwischen verschiedenen Modellen eines oder mehrerer Theorie-Elemente zurückgegriffen. Ein drittes Beispiel: Die Konstruktion eines Theorien-Netzes enthält bereits die Zuordnung von bestimmten Anwendungsmengen zu speziellen Varianten der in Frage stehenden Theorie. Damit nimmt sie den entscheidenden Punkt des zugehörigen Ramsey-Satzes – und damit der entscheidenden Aussage, die mit Hilfe dieser Theorie über ihren Anwendungsbereich formuliert werden soll – bereits implizit vorweg.

Schon diese wenigen Beispiele zeigen, dass die Kluft zwischen *statement view* und *non statement view* keineswegs so tief ist wie häufig behauptet. Aus diesem Grund sollte die Wahl zwischen beiden Ansätzen nicht zu einer philosophischen Grundsatzfrage stilisiert, sondern vielmehr von pragmatischen Kriterien geleitet werden. Wenn man dieser Auffassung folgt, dann lassen sich allerdings gewichtige Argumente finden, die für den Einsatz modelltheoretischer Hilfsmittel, wie sie im strukturalistischen Ansatz bereitgestellt werden, sprechen. Drei Argumente, die zum Teil schon in der Literatur behandelt worden sind, seien an dieser Stelle hervorgehoben.[9]

---

[9] Vgl. Bartelborth 1996, S. 270 ff.

Erstens: Durch die Betonung der Bedeutung des Modellbegriffs wird eine weitgehende Unabhängigkeit von der konkreten sprachlichen Formulierung einer Theorie gewonnen. Verschiedene äquivalente Formulierungen ein und derselben empirischen Theorie können als solche dadurch identifiziert werden, dass sie die gleiche Modellmenge auszeichnen. Bas C. van Fraassen (1991, S. 5) hat deswegen zu Recht den Übergang von syntaktischen zu semantischen Ansätzen in der Wissenschaftstheorie mit dem Übergang von Koordinatendarstellungen zu koordinatenfreien Darstellungen in der theoretischen Physik verglichen.

Zweitens: Approximation und Idealisierung spielen eine entscheidende Rolle, wenn empirische Theorien auf konkrete Systeme angewendet werden sollen. Theorien passen immer nur näherungsweise auf reale Systeme. Ein wesentlicher Vorteil semantischer Ansätze besteht darin, dass gerade in ihrem Rahmen Approximation und Unschärfe besonders gut erfasst werden können. So lässt sich in einem modelltheoretischen Rahmen vergleichsweise leicht präzisieren, was damit gemeint ist, dass sich ein Modell in einer näher zu spezifizierenden Nachbarschaft zu einem anderen Modell befindet.

Drittens: Der modelltheoretische Ansatz bietet einen leistungsfähigen formalen Rahmen, um approximative Reduktionsbeziehungen zwischen verschiedenen empirischen Theorien zu explizieren.

Das sind nur drei Beispiele für Argumente, die für semantische, mit modelltheoretischen Hilfsmitteln arbeitende Ansätze in der Wissenschaftstheorie sprechen. Dabei handelt es sich um pragmatische Argumente, die zeigen, dass bestimmte Leistungen in einem modelltheoretischen Rahmen in besonders einfacher und nahe liegender Weise erbracht werden können. Damit ist natürlich nicht gesagt, dass diese Leistungen nicht auch im Rahmen einer entsprechend verfeinerten und erweiterten Aussagenkonzeption empirischer Theorien erbracht werden können. Schon aus diesem Grund erscheint es als wenig sinnvoll, die Auseinandersetzung zwischen der Aussagenkonzeption empirischer Theorien und dem *non statement view* zu einer philosophischen Grundsatzfrage zu stilisieren und in den Mittelpunkt der philosophischen Diskussion über diesen Ansatz zu rücken. Ein solches Vorgehen lenkt zudem von den eigentlich bedeutenden Unterschieden zwischen dem strukturalistischen Ansatz und konkurrierenden wissenschaftstheoretischen Konzeptionen ab. Drei dieser Unterschiede seien abschließend genannt:

1. Der strukturalistische Ansatz unterscheidet sich von anderen wissenschaftstheoretischen Konzeptionen dadurch, dass er nicht nur eine Präzisierung der Fundamentalgesetze einer Theorie liefert, sondern auch eine beliebige Anzahl spezieller Varianten dieser Theorie erfassen kann. Dieser Um-

stand ist insbesondere für die Analyse theoriendynamischer Phänomene wichtig: Bei den meisten zur *normal science* (in Kuhns Terminologie) gehörenden Entwicklungsphasen einer empirischen Theorie bleiben deren Grundgesetze weitgehend unangetastet. Modifikationen werden dagegen an spezielleren Theorieteilen vorgenommen: an Spezialgesetzen, Hilfshypothesen, Randbedingungen usw. Gerade diese spezielleren Komponenten einer Theorie bleiben jedoch in den meisten herkömmlichen wissenschaftstheoretischen Darstellungen unexpliziert. Die im Rahmen dieser Ansätze bereitgestellten Informationen beziehen sich damit auf diejenigen Komponenten einer empirischen Theorie, die sich bei der Mehrzahl der wissenschaftshistorischen Prozesse gerade *nicht* ändern. Und selbst dann, wenn man sich speziell für wissenschaftliche Revolutionen interessiert, wird man sich zugleich intensiv mit den weniger radikalen, letztlich erfolglosen Modifikationsversuchen beschäftigen, die den revolutionären Veränderungen vorausgegangen sind. Ein wesentlicher Vorteil des strukturalistischen Ansatzes besteht darin, dass man in seinem Rahmen auch derartige feinere wissenschaftshistorische Vorgänge, die die Grundgesetze einer Theorie (zunächst) nicht in Mitleidenschaft ziehen, analysieren kann. Trotz seiner offenkundigen Bedeutung ist dieser grundlegende Vorteil des strukturalistischen Ansatzes in der Diskussion bisher nur am Rande thematisiert worden.

2. Grundgesetze einer empirischen Theorie gelten *per definitionem* in allen Anwendungen dieser Theorie. Spezialgesetze beanspruchen dagegen nur in bestimmten Anwendungen Gültigkeit. Sofern man in einer wissenschaftstheoretischen Analyse auch speziellere Varianten einer empirischen Theorie berücksichtigen will, muss der verwendete metatheoretische Rahmen deswegen zwei Anforderungen erfüllen: Erstens muss er ein explizites Konzept *intendierter Anwendungen* zur Verfügung stellen. Zweitens müssen in ihm formale Hilfsmittel bereitgestellt werden, mit denen erfasst werden kann, wie spezielle Varianten einer Theorie speziellen intendierten Anwendungen zugeordnet werden. Der Strukturalismus hat auf diese doppelte Herausforderung zunächst in der Weise reagiert, dass in ihm intendierte Anwendungen mit *partiellen Modellen* identifiziert wurden.[10] Nun ist, wie zuvor dargestellt, das Konzept der *partiellen Modelle* in mehreren Hinsichten stark idealisierend bzw. fiktiv: Zum einen wird von der Existenz einer vollständigen Datenbasis ausgegangen, d.h. sämtliche Funktionswerte der nichttheoretischen Funktionen werden als gegeben angenommen. Zum anderen bleiben Fragen im Zusammenhang mit der stets begrenzten Messgenauigkeit darin

---

[10] Genauer formuliert, ist die Klasse intendierter Anwendungen einer empirischen Theorie im allgemeinen eine *echte* Teilklasse der zugehörigen Klasse partieller Modelle.

unberücksichtigt. Angesichts der zentralen Rolle, die der kontinuierliche Anstieg der Messgenauigkeit bei vielen wissenschaftshistorischen Prozessen gespielt hat, ist offensichtlich, dass alle derartigen Vorgänge im ursprünglichen strukturalistischen Konzept nicht adäquat widergespiegelt werden können. Mit dem Übergang von partiellen Modellen zu Datenstrukturen wird zumindest ein Teil dieser Idealisierungen beseitigt. Der strukturalistische Ansatz wird dadurch deutlich realistischer. Zugleich tritt jedoch die in Abschnitt 4 angesprochene Frage in den Vordergrund, wie sich Datenstrukturen auf reale Systeme beziehen: Der Strukturalismus benötigt eine *Referenztheorie für Datenstrukturen*, von der sich bisher bestenfalls die Umrisse abzeichnen.

3. Wie zuvor erläutert steht hinter dem Ramsey-Satz die Leitidee, dass die theoretische Beschreibung einer Anwendungsmenge als *Ergänzungsbildung* aufgefasst werden kann. Die Diskussion darüber, wie diese Ergänzungsbildung möglichst differenziert erfasst werden kann, erstreckt sich inzwischen über mehrere Jahrzehnte. Sie hat zu sukzessive komplexeren Formulierungen des Ramsey-Satzes geführt. Den Ausgangspunkt bildete die Formulierung des Ramsey-Satzes für einzelne, isoliert betrachtete Theorie-Elemente. Ein wesentlicher Entwicklungsschritt ermöglichte dann die Formulierung des Ramsey-Satzes für Theorien-Netze, in dem unterschiedliche intendierte Anwendungen unter Verwendung verschiedener spezieller Varianten einer Theorie beschrieben werden. Weitere wichtige Entwicklungsschritte ermöglichen es, die vielfältigen Korrelationen zwischen verschiedenen Modellen einer Theorie nachzuzeichnen. Schließlich zielten neuere Bemühungen darauf ab, eine Konsistenzforderung in den Ramsey-Satz zu integrieren. Durch diese Forderung kommt der mit einer Theorie verbundene Anspruch zum Ausdruck, eine in sich widerspruchsfreie, eben konsistente Beschreibung der zugehörigen Menge intendierter Anwendungen zu liefern.[11]

Die Diskussion über eine adäquate Formulierung des Ramsey-Satzes ist damit keineswegs abgeschlossen. Sie steht vielmehr gegenwärtig vor einem besonders wichtigen Schritt: Es geht darum, eine adäquate *approximative Version des Ramsey-Satzes für Datenstrukturen* zu formulieren. Dieser Schritt ist deswegen von besonderer Bedeutung, weil er die für viele Einzelwissenschaften essentielle Problematik enthält, wie man eine vorgegebene Menge von Messdaten durch eine Funktion am besten approximiert bzw. ‚fittet'. Bekanntlich existieren zahlreiche konkurrierende Approximationskriterien, deren Anwendungsbereiche sowie Vor- und Nachteile in den Einzelwissenschaften intensiv diskutiert werden. Im Zusammenhang mit der Formulie-

---

[11] Vgl. Gähde 1996.

rung einer approximativen Version des Ramsey-Satzes für Datenstrukturen könnte diese Diskussion im Detail nachgezeichnet und analysiert werden. Dadurch würde der strukturalistische Ansatz erneut erheblich an Realitätsnähe und praktischer Relevanz auch für die Einzelwissenschaften gewinnen.

Die drei zuvor skizzierten Aspekte der strukturalistischen Konzeption sind trotz ihrer offenkundigen Relevanz bisher in der Diskussion über diesen Ansatz nur am Rande thematisiert worden. Dennoch dürfte ihre eingehende Analyse wesentlich fruchtbarer sein als die bisher vorherrschende Debatte über die vermeintliche Grundsatzfrage *statement view* versus *non statement view* empirischer Theorien.

Literatur

Balzer, W., Moulines, C.U., Sneed, J.D.: *An Architectonic for Science. The structuralist Program*, Reidel, Dordrecht 1987.

Balzer, W., Lauth, B., Zoubek, G.: A Model for Science Kinematics, *Studia Logica* 52 (1993), 519–548.

Bartelborth, T.: *Begründungsstrukturen. Ein Weg durch die analytische Erkenntnistheorie*, Akademie-Verlag, Berlin 1996.

Gähde, U.: On Innertheoretical Conditions for Theoretical Terms, *Erkenntnis* 32 (1990), 215–233.

Gähde, U.: Holism and the Empirical Claim of Theory-Nets. In: *Structuralist Theory of Science. Focal Issues, New Results*, ed. by W. Balzer and C.U. Moulines, de Gruyter, Berlin – New York 1996, 167–190.

Stegmüller, W.: *Probleme und Resultate der Wissenschaftstheorie und Analytischen Philosophie*, Band II, *Theorie und Erfahrung*, 2. Halbband: *Theorienstrukturen und Theoriendynamik*, Springer, Berlin – Heidelberg – New York 1973.

van Fraassen, B.: *Quantum Mechanics*, Clarendon, Oxford 1991.

José A. Díez

Possession Conditions for Scientific Concepts[1]

The aim of this contribution is to present the main traits of a general framework for the individuation of scientific concepts. The goal is to provide conditions for concepts, not only to capture the same property, but to be the very same concept. In doing so, the framework combines three originally independent departure points: (a) the metascientific tools provided by net-like model-theoretic analysis of scientific theories; (b) the possession-condition version of the conceptual-role theory for the individuation of concepts; and (c) the three main proposals on the content of scientific concepts, namely, Received View's „laws plus correspondence rules", Kuhn's „laws applied to exemplars" and moderate, non reductive operationalism. Here we can offer only the basic guide lines of the project.[2] To carry it out, further conceptual and metaempirical work must be done, mainly: (i) a full defense of some controversial thesis dogmatically assumed here (remarkably, the concept-constitutive character of some empirical facts, and the relevance of a neutral observational basis), and (ii) to incorporate metaempirical data about scientists beliefs/behavior provided by historians and psychologist of science. A project of this kind, if successfully developed, can provide a better basis for approaching conceptual change in science, and other important related issues such as incommensurability and scientific progress.

First, I briefly deal with two epistemological topics in order to introduce some desiderata and assumptions. Then, I introduce five different components of the content of scientific concepts and present the general traits of the theory of possession conditions we will make use for the integration of such components. Finally, I propose the kind of possession condition that corresponds to each of these five components, I present some problems and point out some possible ways of dealing with them.

---

[1] Research for this work has been supported by the projects PB98-0495-C08-07 and PFF2000-1073-C04-04, funded by DGES, Spanish Government. I thank Susan Carey, José Luis Falguera, Manuel García Carpintero, Ulises Moulines and Ernest Sosa for their helpful comments on previous versions of this work.

[2] For a more complete, but still programmatic, presentation of the project see Díez 2002.

Introduction

One of the most prominent antirealist arguments of the last decades is the following version of traditional instrumentalism (cf. e.g. van Fraassen 1980):

EMP The justification of our beliefs about the physical world relies on our experience.
INFR For every theory T, there are infinitely many other theories incompatible with T but empirically equivalent to T.

INST When T is well confirmed, we are justified in believing only T(obs).

The first premise, EMP, is an empiricist principle that seems plausible according to some minimal empiricism everybody (in our surroundings) is prima facie ready to endorse: the justification of our empirical beliefs relies on our „experiential" interaction with the world. The second premise, INFR, is the infradetermination thesis, which also seems plausible according to a common mathematical fact everybody is ready to accept: every finite set of points may be embedded in infinitely many incompatible functions. The conclusion that seems to follow is instrumentalism: confirmation of T amounts to justified beliefs only about T(obs), that is, about the observable consequences of T. The latest prominent version of the argument, van Fraassen's, has been sometimes objected to arguing against his notion of observability, for it is anthropocentric and time-dependent. This reply, however, is unsound, for the intended conclusion of the argument is not about „what exists" but about „what we are justified in believing exists", and what *we* are justified to believe may depend, of course, on the nature of *our* cognitive system.

Nevertheless, the argument may be resisted in a different vein, due to the ambiguity of ‚experience' and ‚rely'. There are different readings of the argument depending on the way we disambiguate these terms. On a first reading, ‚experience' is understood as „observational experience" and ‚rely' as „immediately rely". Then the realist may object to EMP as question begging: this reading of EMP is, according to him, stronger than what a reasonable (i.e. non-instrumentalist) empiricism commits us to. His point is that „indirect" or „inferential" justification from observation is allowed as well (though he must specify what this inferential justification exactly consists of). On a second reading, ‚experience' is understood in the same way but ‚rely' is understood as „rely in the long run". Now the realist accepts EMP, but rejects INFR: he doesn't accept that these theories are (always) empirically equivalent (i.e. equally justified) „in the long run" (though, again, the challenge for him is to specify the precise sense in which they are not „empirically" equivalent in the long run). On a last reading³, ‚experience' is understood simply as „testing basis". But now the argument is not formally valid, unless we add the following hidden premise (Local Observability of Testing Basis):

LOTB: For every theory T, its testing basis involves only observable entities.

There are good reasons for not endorsing this hidden premise, if we understand, as we should, that the testing basis of a theory T is described within the vocabulary of T, i.e. using only T-terms/concepts. On a model-theoretic account, theories are sets of models which are made up of the denotation of T-(primitive-)terms/concepts, and the testing basis (the „T-testable facts") is identified with the *empirical substructures* of such models. On the specific structuralist model-theoretic approach, these substructures obtain applying the *T-theoretical/T-non theoretical* distinction to T-vocabulary (and to their denotation in the models). According to this distinction, a T-concept is T-non theoretical iff it (it's denotation) can be determined/measured without presupposing any law of T (e.g., position and time are Classical Mechanics-non theoretical), and it is T-theoretical iff it is not T-non theoretical, i.e. all its determination methods presuppose some law of T (e.g. mass and force are CM-theoretical). Thus, the testing basis for T, *T-intended applications*, is made of T's empirical substructures, i.e. of the „T-non theoretical part" of T-models (structuralist's *partial models*) whose determination does not presuppose the laws of T. This is why T-facts, even if they are „theory-laden", are not T-laden. In Classical Mechanics, then, models are structures of the kind $\langle P, s, t, m, f \rangle$, and partial models are purely cinematic structures of the kind $\langle P, s, t \rangle$.

The key point for us here is that the „T-non theoretical/T-theoretical" and „observational/non observational" distinctions do not coincide, neither intensionally *nor* extensionally.⁴ The former is local, relative to theories (a T-concept may be T-non theoretical but T'-theoretical), the latter is global (a concept – perhaps at a given time – is observational or it is not, period). T-theoreticity has to do with T-dependence of determination

---

³ One might think that there is a further reading according to which the conclusion just says „When T is well confirmed, we are justified to believe only that T is empirically adequate". But ‚empirically adequate' means either „T(obs)-true" (this is the normal use, e.g. in van Fraassen) or „well confirmed". The former coincides with our version, the latter makes the conclusion trivial.

⁴ Contrary to what van Fraassen seems to presuppose: „Empirical substructures of models are the candidates for the representation of observable phenomena" (1989, p. 227). Kuhn 1993 explicitly endorses a similar T-theoretical/T-non theoretical distinction, traces it back to the structuralist foundational work Sneed 1971 (cf. fn. 17) and mentions as one of its advantages that „it ends the apparent equivalence of ‚observational' and ‚non-theoretical' " (p. 333).

methods, irrespective of whether these methods are, or are not, „observational". And they do not coincide extensionally either: there are observational T-theoretical entities (e.g. genes are Genetics-theoretical, enzymes are Biochemistry-theoretical) and non observational T-non theoretical (e.g. utility is T-non theoretical for some economic theories, weight is Stoichiometry-non theoretical – if somebody protests that weight is observational, then he should say the same about the CM-theoretical mass).

So, I take LOTB to be false: there may very well be theories whose T-non theoretical conceptual machinery, the one T uses for describing the relevant facts in predicting and testing, is non observational. I also, however, take it that *this does not imply that observation plays no role in testing*. It implies only that, if observation does play a role, it does not (always) play it „directly through" the T-non theoretical machinery of theories. Then we have to look for this role elsewhere, *outside T's* vocabulary, hence *outside T's* models. Although Quantum Mechanics does not include within its vocabulary expressions like ‚path-cloud', nor Electromagnetism expressions like ‚pin movement', paths in clouds and pin movements „matter" for testing Quantum Mechanics and Electromagnetism. So, even if the role of observation may sometimes rely directly on T-non theoretical concepts, other times it may rely on something else. Actually, this role relies on something else more often than it may seem at first sight, for the *relevant* role of observation may rely on something else even for theories whose T-non theoretical concepts are observational in a broad sense. Even if there is a (broad) sense in which Classical space and time, and Relativistic space-time, are observable, this is not the relevant sense. Why? Because in the very same sense that we say that white paths in black clouds confirm Quantum Mechanics, we also say that light-dots moving in the sky (Mercury's trajectory), confirm Relativistic better than Classical Mechanics. The relevant sense in which trajectories are observable must be common to both CM and RM. However, CM and RM T-non theoretical machinery, i.e. Classical and Relativistic Kinematics, do not coincide. Therefore, there must be *outside* CM and RM a *neutral* way of identifying trajectories to which both theories are related (this „relation" does not have to imply any kind of „translation").

There is quite a lot of literature against this old-fashioned point of view, but though I cannot argue for it here, I take it to be the only way to avoid a radical *empirical* relativism.[5] In a famous passage, Hanson (1971) tells us

---

[5] By ‚radical empirical relativism' I mean the thesis that no part of our cognitive interaction with the world is at the same time (a) essential for the understanding of science/knowledge, and (b) human „neutral", not subject to rational disagreement (irrespective to differences in – other parts of – belief systems). Enemies of a neutral basis may not be committed to radical

that there is a sense in which, when they look at the sky, the Copernican and the Aristotelian do see the same and there is a sense in which they don't, and the relevant sense for the understanding of science is the one in which they don't. We have devoted great effort during the last decades to understanding the grain of truth Hanson's dictum contains. Now it is time to devote some effort to the understanding of its grain of falsehood. So, I take the following as a desideratum: A theory for the individuation of scientific concepts must show a conceptual link between the testing of scientific propositions and a basis of neutral observational prescientific concepts.

Another traditional antirealist argument, the incommensurability argument, states, in its most common version, that propositional *contents* expressed by homophonic sentences belonging to different theories/disciplinary matrix/research traditions are not „comparable" (in this version, incommensurability amounts to content-incomparability but not, as many of its advocates emphasize, to incomparability *tout court*). This thesis presupposes some relation between different modalities of scientific propositions, mainly between nomic and conceptual modalities (also between nomic and metaphysical ones, but we won't deal with this relation here). I'll use conceptual and nomic modalities in the following standard senses (much of this is intrinsically controversial, but to our present concerns it does not matter). A proposition P is conceptually necessary, or C-necessary, iff P is a consequence of (the propositions that fix the content of) the concepts involved in P (e.g. „every green surface is colored", „every grandfather is a male", „nothing is heavier than itself"). P is nomically necessary, or N-necessary, iff P is a consequence of the laws of nature (and the concepts involved, e.g. „metals expand when heated", „every spheroid made of Uranium is less than 1 km diameter").[6]

The relation between N-necessity and C-necessity for scientific propositions directly involves the identity of scientific concepts, for a scientific „law", which is N-necessary, will be C-necessary depending on whether it is constitutive of the content of some of the concepts involved. Though we can not argue for this here, there is nothing wrong in some N-necessities being C-necessities. Empirical facts, laws of nature, may be constitutive facts of conceptual/meaning content, therefore there may be empirically „revisable"

---

relativism *tout court*, for they may say, and many do, that evaluative distinctions can be made according to non-empirical criteria. I find radical *empirical* relativism unacceptable, though I find its „moderate" weakening acceptable (moderate: *some* parts, but *not every*, of our ... are (a) but not (b)).

[6] There is the well known problem that not every logical consequence of a law seems to be a law. But this does not concern us here for even if lawlikeness is not closed under logical implication, N-necessity is.

conceptual truths.[7] The question is which laws are constitutive, and to what extent. This is part of what a theory of scientific concept identity should elucidate. We'll try to say something about it later. Now, we just make clear in advance that, in doing so, we will allow some nomic truths to be also conceptual truths (e.g. „masses attract each other"). Nevertheless, even if N-necessity and C-necessity overlap, they cannot collapse. It is C-necessary that not every N-necessity is a C-necessity. Otherwise, the smallest change in a superspecific law would amount to a change in the concepts, and it would be almost impossible for two scientist to share any content. But I take it (I guess everybody takes it) scientists do normally share content, at least within one single theory. Therefore, besides C-necessary N-necessities there are also non C-necessary N-necessities. A theory of concepts must show how both things are possible.

The multifactorial nature of scientific contents

During the last four decades, different proposals for the content of scientific concepts have been made. We believe that such proposals are not in opposition but complement each other. All of them are different versions, or emphasize different aspects, of a quite natural idea, namely, that the content of scientific concepts is determined by both the formal laws in which they occur and the way scientists apply the formal apparatus to empirical situations (cf. e.g. Carnap 1966 and Lewis 1970). The view of theoretical content we propose here is a fusion and an expansion of the different versions of this traditional *laws plus empirical applications* view. Though this general idea is quite natural and hard to resist, the problem is how to make it precise enough. Almost everybody agrees on how the formal part has to be understood: formal connections for a concept C are connections between C and other theoretical concepts (belonging to the same or to a different theory) by means of „laws". There is less agreement, however, on how to understand the second, empirical component. According to the orthodox Received View, the empirical content enters through a set of *correspondence rules*, sentences/propositions that relate the term/concept C with some observational terms/concepts. According to the operational variant, the connection is made up of *operational definitions* or, in the non-reductivist version, *operational rules* that state the way C is

---

[7] The question is partly terminological. If by ‚empirical proposition' we understand „proposition that belongs to an empirical theory", then there are empirical conceptual propositions; if we understand „non conceptually constitutive" then of course there are no conceptual empirical propositions. The non terminological substantive issue is how to understand the first reading.

related to a set of operational procedures of measurement or (for non metrical concepts) determination. According to Kuhn (and others), empirical content enters when scientists apply laws to specific systems (Kuhn's exemplars, which do not need to be described within an observational vocabulary). As we have suggested, and contrary to what a quick glance may show, these different elucidations of the empirical component are not incompatible but partially complementary. There is no single source where empirical content comes from, and I take these elucidations as a basis for a multi-directional analysis of that component. Though I cannot justify this here, a proper reading of the different elucidations of the empirical part of the content shows four different, complementary, factors that contribute to the empirical content. Together with the formal component, we propose then, as a first approximation to be developed, the following penta-factorial analysis of the content of scientific concepts.

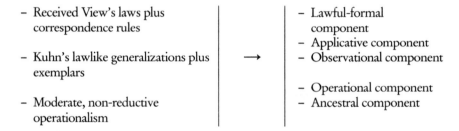

Lawful-formal component: It intends to capture the *formal* part of the content. It is determined by relations between C and
(i) other theoretical concepts of T, through the T-laws, and
(ii) other theoretical concepts of other theories T', T'', ..., through bridge-laws.
Because of the difference between N-necessity and C-necessity, not every T-law/bridge-law may be relevant for the content; the main problem is to specify which and how.

Applicative component: It is the heritage of Kuhn's understanding of the empirical component. It is determined by relations between C and concrete empirical applications/systems of T (e.g. the moon turning around the earth, a kid swinging in a swing, etc.). These systems are described with T-concepts, but T-non theoretical ones (which need not be observational). Not every empirical application is essential to the content.

Observational component: It is partially related with the traditional understanding of correspondence rules. It is determined by relations between C

and some family of observational neutral prescientific concepts/scenarios/ whatsoever. This relation is not necessarily direct, and generally it is not. It does not relate C directly with observational concepts, but indirectly through empirical applications.

Operational component (if any): It is the heritage of moderate operationalism. It is determined by relations between C and some (fundamental) operational procedures of measurement/determination. This component directly applies only to T-theoretical concepts for which there exist such operational procedures. Not every theoretical concept has it (e.g. *entropy* does not). A concept that does not have it directly, may indirectly acquire it via constitutive dependence relations with others that do have it directly.

Folk-ancestral component (if any): It is determined by relations between C and some prescientific folk explanatory practices. Its recognition comes from a view of scientific knowledge in continuity with prescientific, folk *explanatory* knowledge. Some parts of prescientific knowledge, though not fully structured, are explanatory, and some explanatory concepts of scientific theories are refinements of their folk ancestors. As we shall argue, when this is the case, such a relation matters for the identity of the scientific concept. Not every scientific concept has, or is strongly related to, folk ancestors (e.g. *quark* doesn't, *entropy* probably doesn't either), but some do (e.g. *mass*[8]). As before, when a theory has some concept with this component, then its other concepts indirectly acquire it via their relation with the former; and again, even if no concept of a theory T directly contains this component, T-concepts *may* partially acquire it via *constitutive* intertheoretical relations (if any) between T and other theories with concepts with ancestral content. I think this component is implicitly present in some Received View's correspondence rules[9], but I won't argue for this here (I will give an independent, non-historical motivation later).

What we need now is a way of integrating these components into a unified theory of content and, within this framework, to make their logical form and some relevant aspects more precise. Our proposal here is to integrate them within a theory of concept-identity, rather than of meaning or of properties. A theory of meaning seems too broad for our aims. We want to identify the

---

[8] Typical folk explanations involving an ancestor of *mass* are „the truck went off the road because it was too heavy and it took the turn too fast", or „the ship will sink because the cargo is too heavy".

[9] E.g. Carnap's „if temp(x) is greater than temp(y) then x is hotter than y", for the folk concept of „hotter than" is clearly explicative („the pressure cooker exploded because we heated it too much").

entities in virtue of which we can say that, when both Newton and Laplace believed that mass is conservative, both believed literally the same content. There are many senses of ‚meaning‘, some of which are not relevant for this aim (at least not at first sight). Meanings can be references, which can be, in turn, extensional sets, or intensional properties. We do need something intensional, so sets do not help us. But we also want contents about „nonexisting properties" (phlogiston, caloric, etc.), and properties will doubtfully help for that. What we need is some intensional entity like „ways of thinking", senses, whose existence is guaranteed when we think. I call these entities ‚concepts‘, and I propose to individuate them using a specific version of conceptual-role theories, namely, the possession condition version according to which to individuate a concept is to give its possession conditions.

Possession conditions

I have said that our targets are „meanings-as-senses" or „ways of thinking", what we shall call ‚concepts‘. Yet, there may also be different kinds of these entities. It may be argued that there is some sense of ‚meaning-as-a-sense‘ according to which the meaning of ‚mass‘ changed from Newton to Laplace. I do not want to argue against this sense (a kind of meaning-as-a-sense whose change would not affect communication). I just want to state that there is another sense in which the content remains the same. There is a sense according to which when both Newton and Laplace believed that mass is conservative they both believed literally the same content; and when Stahl believed and Lavoissier denied that combustible substances have phlogiston, what one believed was literally what the other denied. Our target here is the kind of entity involved in their entertaining literally the same content. The concepts we want to individuate are the components of these propositional contents. As I have said, I do not want to argue here against the view that there is a sense of ‚concept‘ according to which the concept *mass* changes from Newton to Laplace. To our present concerns, it suffices if, as I take it, there is an intensional sense of ‚content‘ such that Newton and Laplace literally believed the same content. The components of such contents are the entities in whose individuation we are interested here. I call these entities ‚concepts‘ (irrespective of whether there is a different, more fine-grained, sense of the word).

The general principle that applies to our concepts, as epistemic entities, is a principle of substitution *salva* content-attitude, that is, concepts are different iff they make some cognitive difference:

For all concepts C, D: $C = D$ iff for every content $K(C)$ that has C as a constituent, and for every (ideal) thinker x and epistemic attitude A, (in ideal circumstances) x has the attitude A towards $K(C)$ iff x has the attitude A towards $K(D)$.

Nowadays, it is broadly accepted that to individuate a concept is to give its possession conditions.[10] It must be emphasized that these are conditions for the individuation of concepts themselves, not for the attribution of beliefs that involve the concepts. It is possible to entertain a content $K(C)$ without possessing the concept C (Putnam's elm-beliefs), therefore we have to distinguish between *using* a concept, in the sense of being capable of entertaining contents with the concept as a constituent, and *possessing* a concept, in the sense of satisfying its individuation-conditions.[11] Usually, possession conditions are set in terms of a conceptual role, i.e. of the function the concept has in the thinker's psychology. In some versions, this role is determined by the so-called *central beliefs*: X is the unique concept C to possess which a thinker must believe $K_1, ..., K_n$. We can make it somewhat wider if we determine the role, not by central beliefs but by *central belief relations*: ... must believe ... if he believes .... Or even *central attitude relations*: ... must have the attitude ... towards ... if he has attitudes ... towards .... All these versions, however, allow for narrow contents only, whereas a general scheme of concept possession should be neutral to the narrow/wide issue, i.e. it should preclude neither wide nor narrow contents. For this reason, I favor Peacocke's version of conceptual-role possession conditions for the individuation of concepts. The general form of Peacocke's possession condition is approximately the following.[12] (This applies only to concepts for which there is no explicit definition, which are the most common and interesting cases; concepts with explicit, eliminative definitions in terms

---

[10] Cf. e.g. Peacocke 1992, Bealer 1998; for a criticism, Fodor 1998.

[11] The origin of this distinction goes back to Putnam 1975 and Burge 1979; cf. also Peacocke's possession condition vs. attribution conditions distinction (1992), Bealer's full possession vs. possession (1998), and Higginbotham's mastery vs. possesion (1988). Using conditions are weaker than possession ones, and essentially deferential.

[12] Cf. Peacocke 1992, ch. 1. Here I follow Peacocke only in this general schema and some general features I'll comment later on, but not in many of his epistemological and metaphysical theses about concepts (e.g. his strong Platonism, or his defense of non-conceptual scenarios-contents); they are independent of the kind of issues we deal with here, so I prefer to leave them open. For a self-criticism of his former approach, see Peacocke 1998. As far as I understand his criticisms, they don't essentially affect the use of PC we make for scientific concepts here (cf. also: „offering, for a given concept F, an implicit conception [...] is consistent with the existence of an $A(C)$-conforming conceptual role which individuates F", p. 74).

of other concepts, such as *bachelor*, are individuated by the definition, *given the individuation of the concepts involved in the definiens.*)

(PC) X is the unique concept C to possess which a thinker must:
in conditions D_1 have the attitude A_1 towards content K_1 (…),
…,
in conditions D_n have the attitude A_n towards content K_n (…).[13]

- The variable ‚C' must appear at least in one of the expressions ‚K_i(…)', but some K_i may not have C as a constituent; they can have concepts other than C as constituents, or no concept at all (in cases of non-conceptual contents – e.g. Peacocke's scenarios and protopropositions – if such things exist).
- In order to possess X, it is not necessary for the thinker to possess the concepts in terms of which the theorist describes conditions, attitudes and contents.
- Other concepts G_1, …, G_k may be constituents of contents K_i. When this is the case, in order to possess X, the thinker must possess these G_i. In this case, we say that (the possession of) X presupposes (the possession of) G_i. When a family of concepts X_1, …, X_k is such that every one presupposes the others, we say that this family of concepts is *holistic*. When such a holism occurs, one cannot, properly speaking, give the possession conditions just for one member of the family, but to „all together" at the same time.
- The constant that a specific PC puts in X's position (e.g. ‚red') cannot appear in ‚K_i' content clauses, (instead, for these clauses the use of the variable ‚C' must suffice). But this constant can be used elsewhere, e.g. in the description of conditions D_i.

These are the general traits of PC individuation conditions that we have to take into account in what follows. The idea, now, is to single out the kinds of possession conditions for scientific concepts. The above five components are, or are not, plausible independently of the way we integrate them. They do need, however, some integration, for, as they stand now, it is not clear how they „work together". The possession condition scheme provides a way of „putting together" these components: each component will provide its specific serie(s) of conditions, attitudes and contents. The hard part is to make precise enough the specific serie(s), mainly the attitude-contents, for

---

[13] To simplify the exposition, I use „contents" as the objets of epistemic attitudes, but for some formal concepts, e.g. logical connectives, the possession condition may involve another kind of objets and attitudes, like „finding primitively compelling such and such inferences" (cf. Peacocke 1992, ch. 1).

each component. In the discussion of some problems, I'll use as an example the classical or Newtonian concept of mass, C-MASS.[14] As I said above, in order to determine the concrete possession conditions *for a specific concept*, e.g. C-MASS, we need further metaempirical information about its user's (conceptual) intuitions coming mainly from historians and psychologists of science (this does not make this program suspicious of socio-psychologism, but I cannot argue for this here).

What follows is quite programmatic and needs further justification and more elaboration in many of its details. For our present programmatic aims, I confine myself singling out the logical form of the possession condition that corresponds to each component, and to point out the main problems in fixing the parameters involved.[15]

Possession conditions for scientific concepts

What we must offer here is, basically, the logical form of the possession condition with which each component contributes to the content of the concept. Before beginning the task, three preliminary remarks are in order. First, in identifying the relevant contents, full precision cannot be expected. This is so not only because of the limited and programmatic character of the task, but also and mainly because, as we'll see, some intrinsic vagueness *may* be involved. Second, we are going to express these contents in model-theoretic terms, but because what we have just said above, this does not presuppose the scientist to possess the model-theoretic conceptual machinery we use to describe this content. Finally, we must keep in mind that we are looking for concept-*possession* conditions, not for concept-*using* conditions. This is important because some elements (laws, applications, ...) may appear in the completion of CP, the knowledge of which does not coincide with the origin of the theory, i.e. they were not known (either explicitly *or* implicitly) at the very beginning of the theory.

---

[14] What I say here about the C-MASS example is highly speculative and for illustrative purposes only.

[15] For a more developed presentation of this program, cf. Díez 2002, were I propose, even in schematic way, some answers to the problems pointed out here.

Formal content

This component is determined by relations between the concept and other theoretical concepts, concepts of T through the T-laws and perhaps concepts of other theories T', ..., through bridge-laws that link T with T', ... For the sake of simplicity, let's focus on the relations with other T-concepts through T-laws.[16] This component intends to capture the *formal* part of the content of C. The attitude involved here seems to be some kind of belief, but it is difficult to see what the content is. It cannot be „these specific laws/models are *true of (apply to)* these specific empirical systems". This is an important concept-identity belief-content, but it does not belong to this formal component, it belongs to the next, applicational component.

Maybe, one could say, the applicational component suffices, for it also carries out the formal component, i.e. the formal content always comes „together with" or „within" the applicative one. This, however, is implausible. If this were the case, we then would lose something essential to the traditional formal component. We can realize it as soon as we pay attention to the tree-like structure of many scientific theories. As Kuhn and Lakatos emphasized, and structuralism develops in its central notion of *theory-net*, not all laws are on the same level. Some are more important or central than others, e.g., Newton's Second Law is very central, the general law for elastic movements is less central, and the specific law for the simple pendulum is still less. At a given time, a theory has the structure of an inverted tree-like net, with its central parts/laws on the top, from where different specialization-branches open, making room for specific laws for specific applications; e.g. in CM, one theory-element opens the distance-dependent forces branch, another opens the velocity-dependent branch, etc.; within the first branch, we have further specializations, for instance, direct versus inverse distance-dependent forces; and so on. As an enduring entity, during its history, a theory is identified with a sequence of different (but connected) theory-nets.

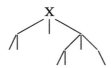

---

[16] Something similar would apply to intertheoretical links. When some such link is constitutive, we have a case of intertheoretical concept presupposition; if it is constitutive for concepts of both theories, then we have a case of local holism (cf. preceding section).

The only formal component that comes with an application, comes within one specific branch of the net. Of course, the formal components of other branches would come with other applications, but we still lose the part of the formal component that comes from cross-branch connections, i.e. from the fact that the concept that appears in the laws of one branch is the same that appears in the laws of other branches not connected with the first by bottom-to-top paths (remember that no application belongs to every branch). In order to capture all the (relevant) connections, cross-branch ones included, the belief must involve the whole (relevant part of) the theory-net.

The relevant belief for the possession condition must be something like the following: „every possible intended application is embeddable in one branch or another of the (relevant part of the) net". Note that the reference to *possible* applications does not make this belief part of the applicative component, for such component requires reference to actual *specific* applications. So, this condition involves every empirical system scientists did, do or will try to subsume under T. In colloquial terms, the relevant concept-constitutive belief is like a guide for empirical research: „every thing the theory wants to deal with must be treated within the following [...] frame of laws". I take this to be the intuitive sense of the traditional formal component.

Now, the question is which laws are the *relevant* ones, that is, which parts of the theory-net (better, of the sequence of theory-nets) matter for the content of the concept. Not every law in every branch may be relevant, for then N-necessity and C-necessity would collapse; any change, no matter how small, would affect the individuation of the concept, which is quite implausible. So, which laws matter and to what extent?[17]

- It seems plausible that at least „the general law(s)", e.g. Newton's second law, must be included. They are especially central in those cases where they function like *guide principles*. And these laws bring with them the ontological-typological part of the content, i.e. the kind and general features of the possible referents of concepts; e.g. that mass is conservative (i.e. it is a function only of particles, not of time, or position, or velocity, etc.).
- This, however, may not suffice. It is plausible that, or at least open whether, in some cases „some part" of the more specific laws must be included as

---

[17] Peacocke (1999) seems to deny that this law's role, what he calls ‚theoretical role', is concept constitutive: if the theoretical role is highly specific, it is implausible for such specific roles are revisable without abandoning the concept; and if the role is unspecific, it can be hardly individuative (pp. 14–15). What follows tries to escape this dilemma, even though at the price of some vagueness (but there are some laws that are constitutive, against Peacocke; as we shall see, this answer depends essentially on the tree-like structure of the theory were the concepts occur).

well. First of all, some *structural* facts concerning the main branches of the theory-net. For instance, in Classical Mechanics, it may be constitutive of C-MASS that masses suffer forces that depend on distance, or that depend on velocity, etc.
- This, though, may not suffice either. Some more specific laws might be constitutive as well, at least in some of their *general traits*. For instance, it could be constitutive of C-MASS, not only that masses cause forces on each other, but also that this force is one of attraction, instead of repulsion. And it also could be constitutive that their attraction decreases, instead of increases, with distance. Similar considerations apply to recuperation-elastic forces and their increasing with distance from equilibrium, and probably to some other cases.
- If these general traits were constitutive, would they suffice? The answer depends on whether some other more specific traits of the laws might be constitutive as well. Would C-MASS be different if the distance-exponential of the gravitational law were 2.1 instead of 2?, and 3?, and 10^3? Something like this *may* also matter: If masses' attraction decreased with distance, but *so fast(er than now)*, would the concept be the same? If the answer is „no" (and it may be, at least for some range of changes), then relatively specific or detailed traits of certain laws would be constitutive. Something similar also applies to details of non-quantitative laws. Of course, the question about the limit arises, and as in many other borderline issues, there is no sharp line. This amounts to a specific vagueness of concept-identity, which actually was already implicit in the previous considerations. If such a vagueness arises, to formally deal with it we would need some fuzzy tool or another. Whatever the tool we use, it has as a consequence the blurriness of the relevant sets of models (laws).

The formal component of the concept-content is then linked to the belief that a certain net „works", i.e. that any possible intended application is embeddable in one branch or another of such a net. This net is not a theory-net. The knots of a theory-net N are theory-elements, and theory-elements $T = \langle K, I \rangle$ are made both of a formal part, the formal core K, *and* of a set of intended applications I. What we need is a net of laws, i.e. a net N_k of formal cores. And we need a specific N_k^*, made up of the more general guide-principles, with the relevant, and only the relevant, specialization branches; and within every branch, going down till the relevant more specific laws in their relevant (probably vague) traits. Let $\underline{N_k}^*$ be the fuzzy entity that captures the relevant extent of the relevant traits of such laws (probably, the deeper we go in the net, the wider the fuzzy threshold will be). I take $\underline{N_k}^*$ to be the *extended guide-principle* of the theory, the part that allows for revision only under conceptual revision. This net is what matters for the formal component of concept-content, and it takes into account, not only (part) of the content of (some) laws but also how they are related, i.e. their „position" in the net. It is what possessors of the concept believe that applies, *through some of its branch-extensions*, to every possible application. We have then, as a possession condition, something like:

(FOR-PC) Every *possible* intended application is embeddable in $\underline{N_k}^*$.

Applicative content

Here, the general possession condition is that, confronted with certain *specific* empirical systems, the scientist believes that certain laws apply, i.e. that the systems are embeddable in some specific parts of the theory-net.[18] These content-attitudes are, then, typical empirical claims: this specific application x is embeddable in this specific set of actual models M (or better, in this specific formal core K). Remember that this content involves only T-concepts, T-theoretical as well as T-non-theoretical, for intended applications are fully identified-described, as T-testing/empirical basis, only by means of T-non-theoretical conceptual machinery. In order to clarify this component, two remarks are in order. As we'll see, for this component to be plausible the net-like structure of the theory will be essential.

First, not every intended application is involved. Of course, a scientist that belongs to T's scientific community must believe that (almost) every intended application is embeddable in the net, but the relevant belief for the possession condition is not this strong belief, but a weaker one. He has to believe, for example, that tides are embeddable in such and such mechanical laws, but that tides are mechanical systems is doubtfully constitutive of the concept C-MASS. The relevant belief for concept-identity involves, then, only a subset Ip of the set I of intended applications. We will call these members of Ip, the *paradigmatic* intended applications, for paradigms constitute concept-identity. I take this as the right way of defining what counts as a paradigmatic application. Which specific Ip corresponds to a given theory is not a question we can answer by just philosophizing. To determine which applications are concept-constitutive requires (meta)empirical investigation. In the case of

---

[18] Peacocke (1999, p. 14), seems to argue against the constitutive character of some applications. But he is discussing there a kind of concepts that are *epistemically individuated*, concepts whose possession conditions require not mere belief but knowledge. What he says is plausible only against the (wrong) idea that theoretical concepts are epistemically individuated, not against the constitutive character of some *beliefs* involving intended applications.

Classical Mechanics, the system earth-moon is probably a paradigm, and probably a cannon shot and pendulae as well, but tides are probably not (and light surely not, pace Newton). Some vagueness will also be inescapable here. So, we'll use the blurred version $\underline{I_p}$. Note, again, that it is not necessary that paradigmatic applications belong to the theory „from its very beginning", though they do usually appear rather early.

Second, and crucial, the belief cannot be that such and such specific systems are embeddable in such and such laws, *in all the laws' details*. This would be an inadmissible reading of the applicative component of concept-identity that would provoke a natural reaction: „How can the earth-moon system satisfying the law of gravitation (and some other laws) *in all its (their) details* be constitutive of the concept C-MASS? This seems, prima facie, hardly *conceptually* necessary. If this is the way we must understand the constitutive character of the applicative component, it is clearly implausible". The target of this sound criticism, however, is not what we propose here. The relevant *constitutive* belief is not that the earth-moon system satisfies the law of gravitation (and others) *in its (their) full details*, but a weaker one: *the earth-moon system is a case of distance-decreasing mass attraction mechanical system* (including some – vague – quantitative threshold; and an analogous weakening applies to other laws involved here). That the full details apply to the paradigmatic system, though believed, cannot be concept-constitutive. Therefore, the right hand side of „*x* is embeddable in …" constitutive beliefs must be weakened in a similar manner as we did for the formal component. In terms of core-nets, the relevant net for the constitutive applicational component does not include everything, it includes very central general laws and „part" of the content of more specific laws in the specialization-branches that apply to paradigmatic applications. It is an open question whether this formal net coincides with the relevant one for the formal component N_k^*. Leaving this issue open, we must denote differently the relevant formal net whose branches apply to the different (kinds of) paradigmatic applications: N_k+. As before, and for the same reason, what is relevant is not this entity but its blurred version $\underline{N_k+}$.

The belief-content with which the applicative component contributes to the concept-identity is then the following „empirical" claim:

(APP-PC) $\underline{I_p}$ is embeddable in $\underline{N_k+}$

Observational content

In the first section, I tried to make plausible that: (a) observation does not necessarily play a direct role in testing a theory *through its intended applications*, for this T-testing basis is described with T-non-theoretical concepts and there are (many) theories whose T-non-theoretical concepts are not observational in the relevant sense; nevertheless, (b) observation must play *some* role in testing; therefore, (c) the relevant „observational" concepts for such a role must be found (for many theories) „outside" T. The idea is that even when (as it often happens) intended applications are not observable in character, they must amount to *observable differences*. This is what provides a *common basis* for (partial) comparison of competing theories when they don't share their T-non-theoretical vocabulary. The firm intuition that friends of strong incommensurability have not been able to rule out is that, even though Classical and Relativistic Mechanics do not share their T-non-theoretical vocabulary (classical and relativistic cinematic concepts do not coincide), the latter succeeds with Mercury's „trajectory" whereas the former does not, so there must be some way of identifying „that path" which is independent of both theories *and* relevant for their epistemic evaluation.

I take the relation to these observational concepts as constitutive of T's concept-identity, for I think that a user that shares everything else but lacks any belief connecting the concepts with observational scenarios, even if she can *use* them, she does not have a perfect understanding of the concepts. This was part of the right aim of the Received View's correspondence rules, the part that tried to capture the grain of truth of a moderate non-reductive verificationism. Nevertheless, things are more complex than they assumed. Even if constitutive of T-theoretical concept identity, the relation between T-theoretical concepts and observational concepts is not *direct* (as far as this component is involved). The constitutive relation is in this case indirect, through (i) a direct relation between observational concepts and the T-non-theoretical concepts in terms of which intended applications are conceptualized, and (ii) a direct-explicative relation between T-theoretical concepts and intended applications. But such *indirectness* does not make the relation less constitutive. Before saying something about the possession conditions related to this component, I just state here without justification how I understand this observational basis.

- These observational concepts must be *neutral* in the sense that „what they amount to" (e.g. the shapes, *and just the shapes*, in the telescope lens, for Aristotelians and Copernicans) is not object of possible disagreement among normal human beings, irrespective of differences in other parts of the cognitive/believe systems.

- I do not presuppose, and I do not need, that what this observational basis amounts to are *beliefs*. Since I wanted to leave this issue open, I'll use now ‚(observational) scenes' with an intended neutral reading.
- These observational scenes are not necessarily *universal*, in the sense that they are actually shared by normal human beings. I tend to think so, but it is controversial whether there might be „normal" human beings lacking one part or another of these resources. It suffices that they are neutral in the above-mentioned sense.
- These observational concepts are neutral with respect to the realism debate. According to the use we make of them here, they are not subjective-psychological entities, but they allow a realist as well as a projectivist reading (in their nomic aspects).
- The postulation of these basic observational scenes amounts to a certain kind of foundationalism, but not necessarily to one of a *justificational* kind. These observational scenes, even if basic, do not necessarily carry the whole *justificatory burden*; they are *compatible* with a notion of justification that makes room for (partial) non-fundamental justification. Arguments for or against it must be found elsewhere.
- If they are beliefs, their neutrality does not necessarily imply their certainty, infallibility, undefeasibility, or the like.
- Whatever they are, they are not influenced by theoretical-relative beliefs, but it is also open whether they can be influenced by some other kind of beliefs, provided these beliefs are also universal (in the above-mentioned sense).
- Often this bottom level is only implicit in scientific testing, for agreement on „data" is found earlier at some higher level (not necessarily neutral, i.e. probably theory-laden).
- These observational scenes do not determine everything. When competing theories make predictions, i.e. have intended applications that amount to different observational scenes, then they are decisive; but if competing theories do not make such a difference, there is no empirical way of arguing for one over the other.

I won't even try to give an explication of this universal observational basis. What I have in mind are things like white dots on a blue sky, paths in a black cloud chamber, moving pins, colored rings on a computer screen, and the like. I have no idea how to characterize them. The history of philosophy is full of a variety of attempts, and of a no fewer variety of refutations. Sense data do not work, nor does phenomenal language, nor things-language, … But I think that the long history of failed attempts is not a good reason to object to them. Failures of singular elucidations of neutral observation do not amount to an argument against it. On the other hand, general arguments against it (remember that our „it" is not necessarily the only source of justification) are not much less controversial than their target. They succeed in pointing out the non-neutrality, the theory-ladeness, of T-testing basis (T's intended applications) but I insist that this is not what we consider neutral observation here.

This last point is crucial. I have been talking about paths in black cloud chambers, pin movements, etc. Everybody knows, though, that these things do not mean anything „as such". It is not a pin movement what matters, nor just a cloud-path in a jar, but pin movements and cloud-paths *in specific instrumental devices* (galvanometer, ...). And everybody knows also that the way from, say, pin movements to galvanometer readings is a long experimental theory-laden non-neutral way. Feyerabend (1975) reminds us very well how this is true even in the simple case of the telescope. Aristotelians objected to the significance of the „shapes" on the telescope's lens as data about Venus' phases for, according to them, „that" did not correspond with any relevant thing happening in the supra-lunar world (since the different nature of this world makes common infra-lunar optic laws inapplicable). Feyerabend's, Hanson's and many other's insistence made it definitely clear that intended applications are theory-laden (though they did not fully clarify that T-intended application are *not* T-laden). Yet nothing in what they say amounts to the fact that what „obtained in the lens" was theory-relative. Aristotelians and Copernicans *agreed* on „what was going on in the lens", on the shapes and colors that obtained; they *agreed* then on the shape-color-scene. The disagreement was about its *significance*. They disagreed, then, in the way intended applications are construed from observable, neutral scenes. The construction of T-intended applications, T-testing basis, from something else is an extremely important and hard issue. My point is simply that, whatever the path from neutral observation to non-neutral intended applications is, this path has at one of its ends such a neutral observation, and we cannot make the path clear, nor its function, without paying attention to this end. These scenes clearly matter for confirmation and empirical import: if Aristotelians agreed on the use of the telescope, then (*other things being equal*) they had to agree on the refutation *because they could not rationally disagree on the shape-color-scene*. Once this is recognized, of course, effort must be focused on the elucidation of this basis and on the reconstruction of the path. For our present aims, though, it suffices to recognize its existence.

We then have the following possession condition (a more sophisticated version should include some reference to instrumental situations):

(OBS-PC) In the presence of a certain intended application, the scientist must *expect* a certain observational scene, or that a certain observational scene obtains.

Operational content

The previous three components are of general application, they apply to every *T*-theoretical concept. The present component (and perhaps the next one) are not that general, at least not in a direct way. It applies directly only to *T*-theoretical concepts with fundamental determination procedures[19] and through them, indirectly, to other *T*-theoretical concepts and to other *T'*-theoretical concepts linked to them via intertheoretical constitutive relations (if any).

Fundamental determination procedures are procedures that determine (part of) the extension of the concept – for metrical concepts, (part of) the values of the functions – without using previous determinations/values. We'll focus here only on fundamental procedures for metrical concepts. Typical examples are the fundamental measurement of mass by means of a pan balance, of lengths by means of rigid rods, or of temperature by means of a thermometer. We can determine the mass-values of a range A of objects without any previous measurement using a qualitative comparison relation R and a combination operation $*$. The intended interpretation of R is „x is more massive than, or as massive as, y", and the operationalist definition (definition of *this* relation, not of the concept) corresponding to the pan balance procedure is „xRy iff y's pan does not go below x's pan" (if the comparison procedure were a spring balance, we had „xRy iff y's elongation is no longer than x's"). The intended interpretation of $*$ is physical concatenation. If certain conditions obtain, by an arbitrary choice of a standard and of its value, all the bodies in the range can be valued.

The intuition that supports the idea that fundamental determination procedures like these are constitutive of concept-identity is the following. We have seen that C-MASS is CM-theoretical, which means that it cannot be measured without presupposing CM-laws, i.e. the existence of successful intended applications. The existence of fundamental measurement, however, seems to amount to a different conclusion, for in measuring masses with pan balances we have not made explicit use of any law. But this is an illusion.

---

[19] Derived determination procedures, to the extent that they are concept-constitutive, are included in the applicative component, for such procedures are basically specific intended applications.

The illusion is not that we have measured *something* without using CM-laws. This is true. The illusion is that we have measured c-mass, i.e. the property that CM talks about, the property that C-MASS allegedly denotes. If we do not suppose that the pan balance satisfies momentum CM-laws, i.e. if we do not suppose that it is an intended application of (one branch) of CM, we cannot say that we are measuring the very same mass that CM talks about, that we are determining the concept C-MASS. So, as far as it is clear (as it is) that with such procedures we are measuring the very same mass that CM talks about, it is then constitutive of C-MASS that there are certain relations between CM-intended applications and operational fundamental measurement procedures which can be described using a qualitative language. If a scientist does not think that the qualitative system $\langle A, R,^* \rangle$ „is" a CM-system, a successful intended application, she does not possess the concept C-MASS. The difficulty here is how to make this belief precise: the „is" is not a plain identity, for fundamental measurement systems are described/conceptualized with qualitative machinery, different to the quantitative machinery with which we describe CM-systems.

In order to make the relevant relation precise, we should make reference to the qualitative theory that studies fundamental measurement systems, (Fundamental) Measurement Theory (MT).[20] Because we cannot extend on MT here, we'll just give an informal characterization of the corresponding possession condition. The intuitive idea is simply that, when confronted with a specific fundamental measurement model, the scientist must believe that:

(a) quantitative functions (denoted by the concept, say mass-functions) belonging to actual models of the quantitative theory are coherent with the functions MT specifies in the representation theorem linked to the measurement model; and
(b) the T-non-theoretical description of the measurement model is an intended application of T.

Ancestral content

The last component aims to capture the essential role of folk explanations for the identity of concepts with ancestors involved in such explanations. The idea is that, for example in mechanics, when such an ancestor does exist, a

---

[20] Cf. the summa *Foundations of Measurement*, by Suppes, Krantz, Luce and Tversky. For the history of MT cf. Díez 1997; for a metatheoretical reconstruction of MT, cf. Díez 1992 and Moulines-Díez 1994.

scientist that does not relate the sophisticated mechanical explanation with the folk one hardly *possesses* the concept C-MASS. That is, a scientific concept being a refinement of a previous folk one may be partially constitutive of the concept. The possession condition that corresponds to this relation must capture these refinements. In order to do that, what we propose here is to consider these cases as partially similar to cases of scientific reduction: the Newtonian concept C-MASS „refines" its folk ancestor in a similar way as relativistic R-MASS „refines" C-MASS. The notion of reduction we have in mind here is the model-theoretic relation of *reductive approximation* (cf. Balzer, Moulines, Sneed 1987, ch. VII). Though there are a great variety of reductive relations, the core model-theoretic idea is that T reduces T' when the applicability of T implies the applicability of T'. More precisely: when there is a correlation between T'-models and (some) T-models so that, every successful T'-intended application corresponds to some successful T-intended application. That is, when the correlation is so that, for every successful T'-intended application, the fact that it is effectively embedded in T'-actual models (better, in some specific part of T's formal net) is implied by the fact that some specific T-intended application is effectively embedded in T-actual models (better, in some specific part of T's formal net). The approximative character comes from the fact that the implication works only under certain approximative assumptions (e.g. in mechanics, that the body's velocity is negligible in comparison to light's velocity).

There are two possible ways to apply this scheme to determine the possession condition of this component (for the sake of simplicity I omit approximative complications):

(ANC-PC) (a) In presence of a specific phenomenon and a folk explanation of it, the scientist believes, of a correlated T-non-theoretical description of the phenomenon, that it is embeddable in a T-model correlated to the folk explanation.

(b) In presence of a phenomenon and a folk explanation of it, the scientist believes that, the fact that a correlated T-non-theoretical description of the phenomenon is embeddable in a T-model correlated to the folk-explanation, implies that the phenomenon is embeddable in the folk explanation.

The second condition is stronger in two ways: it implies that the scientist possesses folk concepts, for they are involved in the content of the belief; and the content is a full reductive content, namely, that certain scientific explanations imply certain folk explanations. The constitutive character of this component may be more plausible under the first reading than under the second.

One difficulty to apply this framework to scientific-folk pairs is that it is not clear how folk explanations are structured. The two main alternatives discussed in the literature are that these explanations are structured like either „naive" scientific theories-laws or just as a series of „prototypes".[21] To avoid connotations in either way, I'll use the neutral ‚naive conceptions'.

What may be controversial is that relations to these folk explanations are constitutive of scientific concepts content. I cannot give a general argument that applies to any scientific concept, for there is no such argument. Many scientific concepts do not have ancestors, so the constitutive character of the relation with folk ancestors is not a consequence of general features common to all scientific concepts. That possession of scientific concepts without ancestors does not (directly) presuppose any belief involving their folk ancestors is trivially true. The question is whether the opposite is non-trivially true of concepts with folk ancestors. Might not a Martian become a Classical Mechanics physicist, without our folk explanations? The question, again, is not about *using*, there is no doubt about that. The question is about *possession*, and if the Martian fully possesses C-MASS, it is hard for me to see how this is possible without any connection with our folk explanations. Remember that the issue is *not* whether she can refer to the same *property*, or to make the same right predictions, i. e. to be equally successful with intended applications. This is perfectly conceivable without „folk connections" if she shares the other four components. The issue is whether with the previous four components, but lacking the connection to our folk explanations, she does all that *possessing our concept*, i. e. with literally the same conceptual tools than we use doing so. I think she doesn't. Of course, this is only to repeat that, according to our view, the fact that a scientific concept is a refinement of a previous folk one is partially constitutive of the concept. This seems to me especially plausible at least on the weak reading of the possession condition, which does not presuppose the possession of folk concepts.

References

Balzer, W., Moulines, C. U., Sneed, J. D.: *An Architectonic for Science. The Structuralist Program*, Reidel, Dordrecht 1987.

Bealer, G.: A Theory of Concepts and Concept Possession. In: *Concepts. Philosophical Issues 9,* ed. by E. Villanueva, Ridgeview, Atascadero 1998, 261–301.

Burge, T.: Individualism and the Mental, *Midwest Studies in Philosophy* 4 (1979), 73–121.

Carnap, R.: *Philosophical Foundations of Physics*, Basic Books, New York 1966.

---

[21] For a general characterization and discussion of these approaches, cf. Yates *et al.* (1988).

Díez, J. A.: *Metrización y Teoricidad*, Doctoral Dissertation, Univ. Barcelona 1992.
Díez, J. A.: A Hundred Years of Numbers. An Historical Introduction to Measurement Theory, *Studies in History and Philosophy of Science* 21 (1997), Part I: 167–181, Part II: 237–265.
Díez, J. A.: A Program for the Individuation of Scientific Concepts, *Synthese* 130 (2002), 13–48.
Feyerabend, P.: *Against Method*, New Left Books, London 1975.
Fodor, J.: *Concepts*, Clarendon, Oxford 1998.
Haack, S.: *Evidence and Inquiry*, Blackwell, Oxford 1993.
Hanson, N. R.: *Observation and Explanation*, Harper and Row, London 1971.
Higginbotham, J.: Conceptual Competence. In: *Concepts. Philosophical Issues 9*, ed. by E. Villanueva, Ridgeview, Atascadero 1998, 149–161.
Kuhn, T. S.: Possible Worlds in History of Science. In: *Possible Worlds in Humanities, Arts and Sciences'*, ed. by S. Allén, de Gruyter, New York 1989, 9–32.
Kuhn, T. S.: Dubbing and Redubbing: The Vulnerability of Rigid Designation. In: *Scientific Theories. Minnesota Studies in the Philosophy of Science 14*, ed. by C. W. Savage, University of Minnesota Press, Minneapolis 1990, 298–318.
Kuhn, T. S.: Afterwords. In: *World Changes*, ed. by P. Horwich, MIT Press, Cambridge 1993, 311–341.
Lewis, D.: How to Define Theoretical Terms (1970). In: D. Lewis, *Philosophical Papers I*, Oxford University Press, Oxford 1983, 78–95.
Moulines, C. U. and Díez, J. A.: Theories as Nets: Combinatorial Measurement Theory. In: *Patrick Suppes, Mathematical Philosopher*, ed. by P. Humphreys, Kluwer Academic Press, Dordrecht 1994, 275–297.
Peacocke, C.: *A Study of Concepts*, MIT Press, Cambridge 1992.
Peacocke, C.: Implicit Conceptions and The Phenomenon of Abandoned Principles. In: *Concepts. Philosophical Issues 9*, ed. by E. Villanueva, Ridgeview, Atascadero 1998, 43–88.
Peacocke, C.: *Being Known*, Clarendon, Oxford 1999.
Putnam, H.: The Meaning of ‚Meaning'. In: H. Putnam, *Mind, Language and Reality, Philosophical Papers, Volume 2*, Cambridge University Press, New York 1975, 215–271.
Sneed, J. D.: *The Logical Structure of Mathematical Physics*, Reidel, Dordrecht 1971.
van Fraassen, B.: *The Scientific Image*, Clarendon, Oxford 1980.
van Fraassen, B.: *Laws and Symetry*, Clarendon, Oxford 1989.
Yates, J. et al.: Are conceptions of motion based on a naive theory or on prototypes?, *Cognition* 29 (1988), 251–275.

Karl-Georg Niebergall

On the Limits of Gödel's Second Incompleteness Theorem*

Abstract

As they are commonly stated, Gödel's incompleteness theorems hold for recursively enumerable theories which are formulated in sufficiently rich languages and have "enough" proof-theoretic strength – e.g., for recursively enumerable extensions of PA. Now, while it is rather clear that Gödel's first theorem does not transfer to, e.g., each consistent extension of PA, the situation with respect to Gödel's second theorem is more complicated.

In this paper, it will be shown that outside the domain of recursively enumerable theories there are theories T proving their own consistency – employing, moreover, only "natural" formalizations of T. Natural though these formalizations may be, they do not satisfy all conditions from some set $\mathscr{C}$ of canonicity-conditions. I close with the result that for a wide range of theories T, T indeed cannot prove "Con$_\tau$" if all these conditions hold.

1. Introduction

Gödel's incompleteness theorems (see Gödel 1931) belong to the most important results in modern logic; in the words of Kleene 1986, p. 126: "Gödel's 1931 was undoubtedly the most exciting and the most cited article in mathematical logic and foundations to appear in the first eighty years of this century". Moreover, they are often thought to be of particular philosophical relevance. E.g., Stegmüller writes "Der heutige Erkenntnistheoretiker kann an den Resultaten der logischen und mathematischen Grundlagenforschung

---

* This paper was presented at the Fourth International Congress of the *Gesellschaft für Analytische Philosophie*, "Argument und Analyse", Bielefeld 2000. Thanks to Ulises Moulines and Nicole Ehlers for their support, to Volker Halbach, Hannes Leitgeb and Göran Sundholm for their remarks at the GAP-conference, and Godehard Link and Stefan Iwan for the many discussions on the topic. Part of this work was supported by a DFG-grant entitled "Ontologische Reduktion im Lichte metamathematischer Methoden" (given to G. Link).

nicht mehr vorbeigehen. Insbesondere sind viele der innerhalb der Metamathematik gewonnenen Ergebnisse von einer so außerordentlichen Bedeutung und Tragweite, daß deren genaues Studium für jeden, der erkenntnistheoretische Untersuchungen betreiben will, welche auf der Höhe der Zeit stehen, ganz unerläßlich ist." (Stegmüller 1959, p. 1)

Let me first remind you of some of the most important examples of the application of the incompleteness theorems and related results in philosophy: They have been used to discredit one of the most influential approaches to the foundation of mathematics – Hilbert's program (see Hilbert 1964). They have been taken to show that a formalist conception of language, even when it is restricted to mathematics, is inadequate: this claim had an impact both on the philosophy of mathematics and the philosophy of language. There have even been applications in the philosophy of mind, where it has been claimed that they show that the mind is no machine (see Lucas 1961).[1]

Yet, it has to be noted that, at the same time, an elaboration of what the philosophical relevance or implications of Gödel's incompleteness theorems *precisely* are is only seldom attempted, let alone carried out in detail (this holds even for Stegmüller 1959). Moreover, one thing should be clear: those philosophical claims are not *implied* by the incompleteness theorems (when they are understood as purely (meta-)mathematical results) alone. In fact, there is no way to derive philosophical claims (other then logical truths) – if they are stated in a language which does not contain any mathematical vocabulary – from statements formulated in a purely mathematical language.

Let's call this observation the *"nonderivability-objection"*. I have two replies to it: (a) Philosophical claims *need* not be formulated in languages which contain no mathematical vocabulary at all. In general, which statements are taken to be "philosophical" and which are not (but are considered to belong to, e.g., the special sciences) is determined by the philosophers, or, say, by the scientific community or "the culture" they belong to. The circumstance that so many influential analytic philosophers mention and use the incompleteness theorems in their philosophical writings simply bestowes philosophical relevance upon them. From this point of view, Gödel's incompletenss theorems should be regarded to be on a par with claims like "There are synthetic judgements a priori" or "Reference is inscrutable", i.e., as philosophical claims in their own right.

Admittedly, reply (a) is not quite satisfactory. First, the procedure suggested by it of explaining merely by examples what philosophy is opens the door to *ad hoc* decisions and should be particularly unconvincing for

---

[1] Other applications in philosophy have been less intelligible; see Sokal/Bricmont 1998 for both an entertaining and illuminating presentation.

the philosopher, with all his interest in general principles.[2] Second, whereas statements of the type "There are synthetic judgements a priori" or "Reference is inscrutable" are integrated into full-fledged systems of philosophy and are multiply connected with further philosophical work, it is doubtful if this is so for, say, "Each consistent recursively enumerable extension of PA is incomplete" (i.e. Gödel's first incompleteness theorem).[3] Thus, even if it is granted that the incompleteness theorems belong to philosophy, it could still be held that they are *undeveloped* philosophy. Finally, if the nonderivability-objection addresses the point that Gödel's theorems have no implications for *preexisting* philosophical theses, i.e. for theses which have an existence and are recognized as having some importance as philosophical claims independently of Gödel's theorems, then answer (a) is irrelevant.

The third objection leads me to reply (b). Surely, the philosophical positions and areas of inquiry addressed in the above examples – Hilbert's program, verificational semantics (and scepticism about metaphysics) and the mind-body problem – existed and were taken to have philosophical importance prior to Gödel's discovery of the incompleteness results. And even though the latter may not imply philosophical statements or statements belonging to preexisting philosophy by themselves, they may certainly do so when they are conjoined with further premises – premises, that contain both (meta-)mathematical vocabulary and vocabulary which is used in formulating the statements from the preexisting philosophical area (let's call them bridge principles).[4]

But several questions remain: Do Gödel's incompleteness theorems in conjunction with plausible bridge principles really imply what they are supposed to imply? What *exactly* are these "plausible bridge principles"? Are they true? And what *exactly* are the philosophical statements which are claimed to rest on Gödel's theorems (like "the mind is no machine")?

Personally, I do not think that Gödel's theorems support, e.g., the claims that the mind is no machine or that Hilbert's program (in its classical form of the 1920's) failed (I will not argue for this here; see Niebergall/Schirn 1998 and Niebergall/Schirn (forthcoming)). But, e.g. in case of the latter, this is so mainly because it has – *qua* philosophical program – not been presented precisely enough. In fact, metamathematical results do have implications for

---

[2] But it should be added that, at some point, one has to start labelling sentences as "philosophical". This holds from a theoretical perspective, too. For if the only way to grant the predicate "philosophical" to a statement were to show that it is of relevance to another statement which already has been accepted as philosophical, we would enter a regress.

[3] At least, the connection to other claims whose philosophical character is not in doubt has not been made as explicit as in the foregoing examples.

[4] For more on this see Benacerraf (1998), who prefers the name "Princess Margeret premisses".

reconstructions or successor programs of Hilbert's program (see, e.g., Tait 1981, Feferman 1988, Simpson 1988); for these are already formulated under the influence of, e.g., the incompleteness theorems. Put more generally, it is certainly the case that the way we are formulating the above mentioned areas of inquiry were influenced, if not *shaped* by Gödel's theorems and related research.[5] I think with this remark, we are almost back to reply (a): only that here it is the mutual influence of distinct areas of reseach which is stressed, whereas in (a) it has been that boundaries between these areas may vanish.

If I pursued this line of thought further, I should discuss the bridge-principles in somewhat more detail: for they are, at least for the philosopher of logic, certainly the most interesting and the most problematic component of the above reasoning. One may even have the idea that it all comes down to them when one is attempting to obtain philosophical theses from Gödel's incompleteness theorems. But I think this is an exaggeration. The reason is that the metamathematical results themselves do not speak such an unequivocal language.

I think that the fact that Gödel's incompleteness theorems are considered to be so important – both in (mathematical) logic and in philosophy – has, eventually, two (or three) reasons:

(i) the most "natural" and most important mathematical theories, in particular when it comes to theories as the *means* of investigation, and not only as its *objects*, are Peano Arithmetic (PA) and Zermelo-Fraenkel Set Theory (ZF) (plus several variants of them).[6] For these theories, Gödel's incompleteness theorems hold.
(ii) Gödel's incompleteness theorems apply to a wide range of theories. And generality is, both in philosophy and in mathematics, an end in itself.

In addition, (i) and (ii) support each other: if PA and ZF were the only theories for which Gödel-type incompleteness hold, one could regard them as "exotic" and would probably prefer other theories. If the incompleteness theorem held for many theories, but not for PA and ZF, one could consider this to be just a further argument for the distinguished character of PA and ZF and simply care less for incomplete theories.

---

[5] This is particularly interesting in the philosophy of mind, where (besides Lucas' and related work) the *Turing Test* plays quite a central role in several texts.
[6] I think that it is almost unexceptionally accepted that PA and ZF *do have* these properties. That this is so has several causes; personally, I think that some of them can be transferred to reasons for accepting PA and ZF. But here, I will not give arguments for their naturality.

Thus, we have a wide range of theories for which Gödel's incompleteness theorems hold, some of them being very natural and important not only for mathematics, but for the whole scientific enterprise. But neither does this mean that *all* theories (even when only those are taken into account which are formulated, say, in the language L[PA] of first-order arithmetic) nor does it yield that all theories which could be regarded as *natural* satisfy the incompleteness theorems. What is certainly not implied by Gödel's incompleteness theorems is that all and the only theories one has to care about are those for which the incompleteness theorems hold.[7] Thus, if the refutation of Hilbert's program were really implied by Gödel's second theorem and some plausible bridge-principle, not only the latter could be challenged, but the specific formulation of Gödel's second theorem could also be put into question – as irrelevant to the philosophical position dealt with.

Having this as a background, I will deal with the questions, which from a systematic point of view are prior to at least the first 3 of the questions asked above, namely: "What exactly are – rather general versions of – Gödel's incompleteness theorems?", and "Are they true?". In fact, my main interest will be the second incompleteness theorem.

2. Gödel's incompleteness theorems: precise renderings

2.1 *The first incompleteness theorem and generalizations*

As a starting-point for my investigation, I suggest the following statement as a fairly general formulation of Gödel's First Incompleteness Theorem

Gödel's First Theorem; G1: Each consistent recursively enumerable theory T such that $PA \subseteq T$ is incomplete.[8]

---

[7] What about non axiomatizable theories? As an example, take PA extended by one application of the ω-rule (in short, PA^1_ω). I would take it that this is a natural theory, for I think that the acceptance of the induction principle rests on the acceptance of the ω-rule. PA^1_ω is certainly not axiomatizable: it proves all true Π^0_2-sentences. Of course, some would "reject" such a theory out of hand, i.e. claim that it is of no importance. But why? Because PA^1_ω is an infinite set? But so is the theory PA. Because PA^1_ω is not axiomatizable? But why should this be a reason. Because we cannot comprehend (understand, control, …) it? But can we do this in the case of PA, i.e. PA as a whole, and not only a finite piece of it? More generally, once we have jumped from the assumption of only finitely many objects (here: sentences) to infinitely many, why should we be able to comprehend the recursively enumerable ones, but not those that are not recursively enumerable?

[8] I assume some basic knowledge of recursion theory; see Rogers 1967. In particular, I will usually write "r.e." instead of "recursively enumerable".

Let me first make a comment on the terminology used in G1. When dealing with Gödel's incompleteness theorems, especially with the second, one has to be attentive to the distinction between arbitrary sets of formulas, theories and the sets of formulas "giving" a theory. (a) A theory T is, as usual, understood as a set of formulas which is closed under some sort of consequence relation. For the latter, classical first-order consequence will be chosen here; for the languages investigated in this paper will mainly be first-order languages. When dealing with, e.g., theories formulated in second order languages, the standard second-order consequence could be interesting, too; but it will often lead to trivializations of G1.[9] (b) The theories T which will be of primary interest for generalizations of G1 later on are not r.e., i.e., not *axiomatizable*. That is, given a common understanding of the word "axiom", a set S having such a T as its deductive closure is certainly no set of axioms. On may say that T is *given* by S or that S is *a set of principles* for T in this case. Here, I prefer to use the phrase "S is an *axiom-set* for T" for "T is the deductive closure of S" even when S is not r.e.

Of course, G1 is not exactly what Gödel showed. First, he obtained his metatheorem merely for one special theory (called "P" by him), which is a variant of PA (see Gödel 1931). But because of the method of proof employed by Gödel to obtain his result it was clear that it would be possible to get similar theorems for a wide range of theories. In fact, Gödel himself mentioned such extensions at various places (e.g. already in Gödel 1930 and in a discussion at the conference on the foundations of mathematics held in Königsberg 1930 (see Erkenntnis 2, 1931)); other important "classical" contributions to this field of research are Mostowski 1952 and Tarski et.al. 1953. – Second, Gödel's original proof of incompleteness rested on PA_G being ω-consistent; it was discovered by Rosser that the assumption of consistency suffices (see Rosser 1936).

Let me also note that the incompleteness of T which is addressed in G1 (as it is formulated) need not be established by a *self-referential* construction – more technically speaking, by an application of the diagonalization lemma. Since even the latter phrase is somewhat imprecise and since it may well be that one can prove the incompleteness of T both by a self-referential

---

[9] There are finite sets A of sentences of second-order number theory such that the set T of all their consequences in standard second order semantics is a complete theory extending PA. But first, this does does not mean that these T provide counterexamples to G1: for such a T is not r.e. And second, the set T_0 of consequencs of A in generalized second order semantics is r.e., but it also is incomplete. In other words, none of T and T_0 provides a counterexample to G1; but this holds for T for a trivial reason.

construction and without one, I leave it with the statement of Gödel's first theorem that I have actually chosen.

Coming to generalizations of G1, several possibilities suggest themselves now:

(1) Theories formulated in languages which differ from L[PA] may be considered.

Of course, it is the case that some of those theories are incomplete and that this can be shown using self-referential constructions; but since they are formulated in a language L different, maybe even disjoint, from L[PA], their incompleteness is not really covered by G1.[10] Moreover, there are examples like DLO, the theory of dense linear orderings without endpoints, formulated in a language L with vocabulary $\{<,=\}$, which are complete (in L), though being r.e.; speaking of "extension of PA" may be nonsensical in such a case. – Changes of languages are not of primary interest in this paper. It is usually rather obvious how to deal with them in principle, but to carry out the details is often awkward (see Feferman 1960 and Lindström 1997 for more details).

(2) Theories which do not extend PA may be considered.

In the case of Gödel's first incompleteness theorem, it would indeed be adequate to consider extensions of Robinson Arithmetic (Q) (see Tarski et.al. 1953 and Monk 1976) instead of extensions of PA.[11] In addition, Q constitutes sort of a "minimal" (natural) theory S such that "Each consistent r.e. extension T of S is incomplete." For, although all proper subtheories of Q are surely incomplete (even if they do not represent all primitive recursive functions or prove the diagonalization lemma), some of them have complete r.e. completions U (see Tarski et.al. 1953).[12] – But Q is no good choice for a "base theory" when it comes to Gödel's second theorem for T. The reason is that in order to obtain that metatheorem, one has to formalize metamathematical statements about syntactical features in the theory T. And Q is simply too weak to be able to prove the relevant formalizations. Since

---

[10] ZF is an well known example; surely, though, the incompleteness of ZF follows from the fact that PA is relatively interpretable in ZF; see Lindström 1997 for the relevant definitions.

[11] The incompleteness of Q can be shown by using the usual selfreferential construction; moreover, the second incompleteness theorem holds for Q, too (see Hájek/Pudlák 1993).

[12] That is, such a U is *complete with respect to L[PA]*. One should not forget that completeness of a theory has to be understood relative to a language: Presburger-Arithmetic, for example, is well known for being a complete theory. Yet, as a subtheory of PA, it must be incomplete. Of course, there is no paradox here: Presburger-Arithmetic does not decide all sentences of L[PA], but it does decide all sentences of a sublanguage L[P] of L[PA] whose vocabulary does not include the multiplication sign.

generalizations of the second incompleteness theorem constitute this paper's main goal, I am content with G1.

(3) What remains is to loosen the restriction to the class of r.e. theories found in G1. A first suggestion could thus be

G1.a   Each consistent extension T of PA is incomplete
(or *G1.b*   Each consistent extension T of PA in L[PA] is incomplete).

Yet, G1.a and G1.b are (completely) false: Th($\mathcal{N}$) is a simple counterexample. – But Th($\mathcal{N}$) is not an arithmetically definable theory. Let's be more cautious then and try

G1.c   Each consistent arithmetically definable extension T of PA in L[PA] is incomplete.

Yet, G1.c is false, too – as shown by (at least) Hasenjaeger and Kleene already around 1950 (see Kleene 1952, Hasenjaeger 1953 and Tarski et.al. 1953).[13] In particular, there are complete consistent extensions of PA which are Δ_2^0.[14] In distinction from PA, which is Σ_1^0 and proves all true Σ_1^0-sentences, the completions of PA which are Δ_2^0 are far from being able to prove all true Δ_2^0-sentences. Moreover, they necessarily prove false Σ_1^0-sentences (i.e., they are not Σ_1^0-sound). This suggests

G1.d   Each sound arithmetically definable extension T of PA in L[PA] is incomplete,

which is true, but rather unexciting. For a more interesting generalization of G1, one should have a look at the interplay between the complexity of T and the extent of its soundness or completeness, to put it vaguely. The (in terms of the arithmetical hierarchy) optimal extension of G1 that can be achieved here is:

Theorem A:[15] Let T be in Σ_{k+1}^0, PA $\subseteq T$, and let T be k-consistent; then T is incomplete.
Moreover, there are T in Σ_{k+1}^0, PA $\subseteq T$, such that T is complete and sound for Σ_{k-1}^0-sentences.

---

[13] See, e.g., Feferman 1960, Visser 1991 and Hájek/Pudlak 1993 for strengthenings of this result.
[14] Vaguely put, a Σ_k^0 (Π_k^0) formula is a formula from L[PA] with a quantifier prefix which begins with an existential (universal) quantifier and has k changes between existential und universal quantifiers; a Δ_k^0 formula is defined as being equivalent to a Σ_k^0- and a Π_k^0-formula (for a precise definition, see Kaye 1991).
[15] For a proof, see Niebergall 1996.

2.2 The second incompleteness theorem: correct versions

After these preparatory remarks on general forms of Gödel's first theorem, I now come to the main subject of this paper's investigation: attempts to formulate and (dis-)prove general versions of Gödel's second theorem. Let me first give a precise rendering of it which is correct for consistent r.e. extensions T of PA; in a second step, this formulation will be generalized to a wider domain of theories. Taking G1 as an inspiration, the following statement is suggested as a precise form of Gödel's second incompleteness theorem

G2.? No consistent r.e. extension T of PA proves the consistency of T.[16]

When compared with Gödel's first incompleteness theorem[17], what is of crucial importance here is that "S proves the consistency of T" has to be analyzed appropriately. This is in strong contrast to G1, where it is only claimed that *some* sentence in $L[T]$ is independent from T: what this sentence "expresses" is simply not mentioned; and it is debatable whether it enters into its proof or to which extent it does so.[18]

As a sort of minimal assumption, I presuppose that "S proves the consistency of T" has to be explained as

$$S \vdash \mathrm{CON},$$

where "CON" is supposed to be a (single) sentence[19] in $L[S]$ *expressing* "T is consistent". What remains to be done is to give an explication of

---

[16] I will not consider the "dual" of G2.?, "No consistent r.e. extension T of PA proves the inconsistency of T" (or extensions of it) in this paper. First, it is false (take $PA + \{\neg Con_{pa}\}$ for T); second, its "repaired" variant "No sound r.e. extension T of PA proves the inconsistency of T" is correct, but trivial.

[17] It may be noted that in the premise of G2.?, mention of consistency is absolutely sufficient. In addition, what may be added to the historical comments made above is that in his 1931 paper, Gödel merely announced a proof of his second theorem (for PA_G); but he never published one. It remained for Hilbert and Bernays 1939 to do this.

[18] Let me remark that, in comparison with the first incompleteness theorem, almost nothing has been published on possible generalizations of the second incompleteness theorem. The most important exception is Feferman 1960, a paper to which this text owes a lot; cf. also Jeroslov 1971 and 1975 and Niebergall 1996.

[19] Although the domain of *explicantia* of "S proves the consistency of T" admitted by this scheme is already (much) too wide, it seems that consistency proofs as understood by Hilbert in his classical papers on proof theory (see Hilbert 1964) could provide examples outside of this domain; cf. Niebergall and Schirn 1998 for what they call "approximative consistency proofs".

"'CON' expresses 'T is consistent'".[20] For this, one could, as a first attempt, contemplate an *extensionally* adequate definition:

(i) "CON" expresses "T is consistent" : $\iff$ (T is consistent $\iff$ $\mathcal{N} \vDash$ CON).

But if T is consistent[21], the choice of "$0 = 0$" for "CON" would make the *definiens* true, whence "$0 = 0$" would turn out to express "T is consistent" – which is certainly an inacceptable consequence.

It is rather obvious that the definition just suggested does not make much sense: for T is not even mentioned in its *definiens*. Accordingly, for "CON" to express "T is consistent", the least one should demand is that a *representation* of T or of a set of axioms of T has to occur in "CON". Here, "representation" is defined as follows: let $A \subseteq \omega^k$, α a k-place formula (from L[PA]); then

α is a representation of A : $\iff \forall \vec{n} \in \omega^k (\vec{n} \in A \iff \mathcal{N} \vDash \alpha(\vec{n}))$.

The condition that a representation τ of T should occur in "CON" if "CON" is to express "T is consistent" is certainly a necessary one. But the definition

(ii) "CON" expresses "T is consistent" : $\iff$ (T is consistent $\iff$ $\mathcal{N} \vDash$ CON) and a representation τ of T occurs in "CON"

is as unacceptable as (i). One simply has to notice that, τ being a representation of (an axiomset of) T,

T is consistent $\iff \mathcal{N} \vDash \forall x(\tau(x) \vee \neg \tau(x))$

holds, if T is consistent. But $\forall x(\tau(x) \vee \neg \tau(x))$ does not express "T is consistent".

Nonetheless, the mere assumption of this necessary condition already suffices to falsify the following possible generalization of G2.?:

G2.?? No consistent extension T of PA proves the consistency of T.

Whereas Th($\mathcal{N}$) provided a counterexample to G1.a and G1.b, this is not so in the case of G2.?. For if Th($\mathcal{N}$) were to prove the consistency of Th($\mathcal{N}$), Th($\mathcal{N}$) $\vdash$ CON would hold. Hence "CON" would belong to the language of Th($\mathcal{N}$), i.e. the language of first order arithmetic, and so would a representation τ of Th($\mathcal{N}$). Yet, this contradicts that Th($\mathcal{N}$) is not arithmetically definable.

---

[20] I will often also use the phrase "'CON' is a natural formalization of 'T is consistent'" instead.

[21] Since for inconsistent theories it is impossible to be incomplete, it is only for consistent theories that a discussion of what "expresses" could mean is of any relevance for the second incompleteness theorem.

Of course, I did not seriously suggest the "*definientia*" for "'CON' expresses 'T is consistent'" discussed above. For a proper understanding of how to arithmetize "T is consistent" correctly, one should first get a clearer picture about the usual metatheoretical definitions of "T is consistent".[22] On the one hand, we can surely assume that, in informal metalogic, "T is consistent" is defined as "$\bot$ is not provable in T", or as a sentence trivially (e.g. logically) equivalent to it. Moreover, "φ is provable in T" is often – but not always – explicitly defined as "there is a b such that b is a proof for φ in T". For there is the well-known and popular method of defining the set of theorems *inductively* instead. Yet, since the natural way of transforming inductive definitions into explicit ones uses set theoretic notions – whence it is not available in L[PA] – and since the standard method of formalizing inductive definitions in L[PA] leads to "built-up sequences", i.e., in the case of "φ is provable in T" back to proofs anyway, I will only consider the explicit definitions of "theorem" mentioned above.

On the other hand, a lot of different *definientia* for "b is a proof for a in T" are in use: often, b is supposed to be a finite sequence of formulas; but sometimes it is also taken to be a tree, and sometimes its entries are ordered pairs, sequences, sets or multisets. Furthermore, there are a lot of different calculi, like Tableau, sequent, natural deduction or Hilbert-style calculi. And even when only, say, Hilbert-type calculi are dealt with, they may differ from each other in their primitive rules: in particular, they may or may not have the cut-rule as a basic rule. Of course, the theorems (or closed theorems) obtained by these different calculi are (or should be) "the same". But this does not mean that the formalizations of these calculi need to be *provably* equivalent (in, say, PA).

So, let me simply *decide* at this point to deal only with Hilbert-type proofs in a logic with cut, or *modus ponens*, as a base rule. Here, "b is a proof for a in T" is defined as "b is a finite sequence of formulas; the last formula of b is a; all the formulas belonging to b are logical axioms or belong to T or are obtained from formulas occuring 'earlier' in b by *modus ponens* (or from an "earlier" one by some version of the rule of generalization)."

If this much is accepted, and given that τ is a representation of an *axiom-set* of T (T arithmetically definable), the following arithmetical formulas suggest themselves as formalizations of the concepts discussed here:

---

[22] When speaking about "metatheoretical definitions", I mean definitions where *definiens* and *definiendum* are already stated in an *informal*, yet precise, e.g. mathematical, language. In particular, I am not concerned here with the step from phrases like "T is consistent" in ordinary language to their *explications* in an informal language of informal metalogic.

Definition 1: $\text{Proof}_\tau(x,y) : \iff \text{Seq}(x) \wedge y = x_{\text{lh}(x)-1} \wedge$
$\forall v < \text{lh}(x)\, [\text{LogAx}(x_v) \vee \tau(x_v) \vee \exists u w < v (x_w = \text{imp}(x_u, x_v))]$ [23]
("x is a proof for y in τ (or T)"),

$\text{Pr}_\tau(y) : \iff \exists x \text{Proof}_\tau(x,y)$ ("y is τ-provable (or T-provable)"),

$\text{Con}_\tau : \iff \neg \text{Pr}_\tau(\ulcorner \bot \urcorner)$ ("τ (or T) is consistent").

Certainly, these are the common arithmetizations of "x is a proof for y in T", "y is T-provable" and "T is consistent". Now, it may be agreed that they are natural formalizations; but it may still be insisted that they are merely very special cases of possible formalizations of the metatheoretical predicates mentioned. An alternative which is well known is provided by, e.g., the so called *Rosser proof and provability-predicate* and the *Rosser consistency assertion*:

$\text{Proof}_\tau^R(x,y) : \iff \text{Proof}_\tau(x,y) \wedge \forall z \leq x \neg \text{Proof}_\tau(z, \text{neg}(y))$,

$\text{Pr}_\tau^R(y) : \iff \exists x \text{Proof}_\tau^R(x,y)$,

$\text{Con}_\tau^R : \iff \neg \text{Pr}_\tau^R(\ulcorner \bot \urcorner)$.

What follows from these definitions is that $\text{PA} \vdash \text{Con}_{\text{pa}}^R$.[24] Does this mean that, after all, PA *does* prove its own consistency? Maybe so. But recall the examples discussed above: clearly, they did not show that PA can prove its own consistency but rather that the definitions (i) and (ii) of "'CON' expresses 'PA is consistent'" were inadequate. This is a possible response to Rosser's definition, too – though the latter is surely not as easily rejected as those earlier definitions.

Given the goal of this section, I need not answer that quite vague (hence difficult) question, however. For what I aim at is to find and investigate formulations of the second incompleteness theorem which are as *strong* as possible. By a "strong formulation (of the second incompleteness theorem)" I understand not only one that is precise and general; it also should not be refutable *easily*. For example, such a formulation of the incompleteness theorem should not turn out to be false already for PA. In particular, I will happily add further conditions to the *definiens* of "'CON' expresses 'PA is consistent'" in order to circumvent *weak renderings* of the incompleteness theorems – if only these conditions have *some* plausibility and if they can be stated in precise terms.[25] The "refutation" provided by the Rosser provability predicate is thus too cheap for my aims. To be candid, at the

---

[23] "imp" and "neg" are function signs in L[PA] representing the conditional and negation.

[24] See Rosser 1936. Further nice examples for consistency assertions for theories T which are provable in T are provided by those consistency assertions that stem from (the formalizations of) cut-free calculi; see Kreisel/Takeuti 1974 and Hájek/Pudlák 1993 for details.

[25] Being "natural" is, for example, no precise condition.

On the Limits of Gödel's Second Incompleteness Theorem

background of this approach there is the belief that generalizations of the second incompleteness theorem *are* refutable for many theories. Now, the *stronger* such a generalization, the harder its refutation – whence the more interesting it is to obtain one.

When comparing "Proof(x,y)" and "Proof$^R(x,y)$", an important difference is obvious: whereas the former has the same quantificational structure as the (definiens of the) metatheoretical "*b* is a proof for *a*", the latter is rather a structure preserving formalization of "*b* is a proof for *a* (understood in the previous sense) and there is no shorter proof for the negation of *a*". Now, the least one should demand from a formalization of the proof-predicate is that it should have the same *structure* – in particular, quantificational structure – as the informal proof-predicate "*b* is a proof for *a*" itself. This leads to the formula "Proof(x,y)" and excludes "Proof$^R(x,y)$" as a formalization. Accordingly, the formalization of "*b* is a proof for *a* in *T*" should be *uniform* in the "*b* is a proof for *a*"-part: only different choices of τ, i.e. different ways of representing *axiom-sets* of *T*, should make a difference.

This leads back to Definition 1 and, moreover, motivates the following definition as an answer to the problem I started with:

(iii) "CON" expresses "*T* is consistent" : $\iff$ there is a representation τ of an *axiom-set* of *T* such that "CON" is the formula "Con$_\tau$" (where "Con$_\tau$" is defined as above).

Yet, this *definiens* it too narrow: for example, its prevents "$\forall x \neg \text{Proof}_\tau(x, \ulcorner \bot \urcorner)$" from expressing "*T* is consistent". Three amendments to the *definiens* of (iii) seem plausible: replace " 'CON' is the formula 'Con$_\tau$' " by " 'CON' is a formula which is equivalent to 'Con$_\tau$' in first-order logic / in *T* / in PA". Now, what we had is

G2.?+ For no consistent r.e. extension *T* of PA *T* ⊢ CON,

where "CON" expresses "*T* is consistent". Fortunately, it does not depend on whether this phrase is defined by (iii) or by any of its variants that two versions of G2.?+ suggest themselves

G2.???   For each consistent r.e. extension *T* of PA and for each representation τ of an *axiom-set* of *T*, *T* ⊬ Con$_\tau$,
G2.???? For each consistent r.e. extension *T* of PA, there exists a representation τ of an *axiom-set* of *T* such that *T* ⊬ Con$_\tau$.

When comparing G2.??? and G2.????, the latter seems to be too weak a claim. Be that as it may – following the general approach outlined above, I will take the G2.??? variant as a basis for further investigations. Indeed, G2.??? is much *stronger* than G2.????: for whereas G2.???? is true, G2.??? is false.

This rather surprising result has been obtained already in the late 1950's by Feferman (see Feferman 1960). There, Feferman constructed a representation pa* of an *axiom-set* of PA such that, notwithstanding PA's consistency, PA ⊢ Con$_{\text{pa}^*}$ nevertheless holds.[26] pa* is defined as follows (here, "pa(x)" is the usually chosen representation for the usually chosen axiom system of PA):

$$\text{pa}^*(x) :\iff \text{pa}(x) \land \forall z \leq x \text{Con}_{\text{pa} \restriction z}.$$

Note that the proof- and provability-predicate and the consistency assertion for pa* are defined in the uniform way fixed above. It is only the representation pa* of an *axiom-set* of PA which is unusual. Feferman's construction is indeed sophisticated; but this does not mean that we have to swallow that we should be content with G2.???, after all. For it is possible to find a precise condition of a general nature which distinguishes formula "pa(x)" from "pa*(x)": whereas PA is Σ_1^0 and both the set of its axioms usually chosen and the formula "pa(x)" representing it may be taken to be Σ_0^0, formula "pa*(x)" is Π_1^0.[27] I. e., the complexity of pa* in terms of the arithmetical hierarchy is higher then that of the theory which is the deductive closure of the *axioms-set* represented by pa* itself.[28]

---

[26] Feferman's construction is very general; in particular, it applies to all arithmetically definable extensions of PA in L[PA] (as an analysis of Feferman's proof reveals).

[27] Hence, the provability-predicate Pr$_{\text{pa}^*}$ is Σ_2^0, whereas Pr$_{\text{pa}}$ is Σ_1^0.

[28] I agree that a convincing explication of "'CON' is a natural formalization of '*T* is consistent'" does not exist and has, in particular, also not been presented in this paper. But this does not mean that we have no understanding at all of what a natural representation could be. It is rather like in the time before Church (and others, of course) had presented a general explication of "computable function": examples of what was taken to be a computable function were known and could be used as test cases for suggested definitions (one may think of, e.g., the Ackermann function). Similarly, there is nothing inacceptable about calling the usually used representation "pa(x)" of an axiomatization of PA "natural"; the question is rather whether there are other natural ones.

This leads to my second remark: It seems that, e.g., the Rosser-proof predicate (for PA) is a rather natural formalization of what a proof in PA is relative to the following metatheoretical definition of the latter, which has already been presented above:

"*b* is a proof for *a* (understood in the original sense) and there is no shorter proof for the negation of *a*". Likewise, the Feferman-proof predicate (for PA) is doubtlessly natural relative to the *axiom-set* of PA represented by pa* (cf. Visser 1989 for a similar remark). That suggests that it could be appropriate to replace the consideration of statements of, e.g., the form "'CON' is a natural formalization of '*T* is consistent'" *simpliciter* by the consideration of statements of the type "'CON' is a natural formalization of '*T* is consistent' with respect to the *axioms-set* S of *T*". The goal of finding an explication of what it is to be a natural representation would then be transferred to the question what a *natural axiomatization* of a theory *T* or a *natural way of "givenness"* of *T* could be. I cannot answer this question, but I think that it should be investigated more thoroughly.

Here, then, we finally have a correct version of Gödel's second incompleteness theorem (see Feferman 1960):

Gödel's Second Theorem; G2: For each consistent r.e. extension T of PA and for each representation τ of an *axiom-set* of T, which is itself Σ^0_1, $T \nvdash \mathrm{Con}_\tau$, i.e.

Gödel's Second Theorem; G2: For each consistent extension T of PA which is Σ^0_1 and for each representation τ of an *axiom-set* of T, which is itself Σ^0_1, $T \nvdash \mathrm{Con}_\tau$.[29]

Given this way of stating G2, the generalization to arbitrary arithmetically definable extensions of PA is now obvious:

Gödel's Second Theorem – generalized; G2.gen: For each consistent arithmetically definable extension T of PA and for each representation τ of an *axiom-set* of T, if the complexity of τ is not higher then the complexity of T, then $T \nvdash \mathrm{Con}_\tau$.[30]

3. Refuting the generalized second incompleteness theorem

3.1 *A first attempt – complete theories*

Having formulated a correct version (G2) of Gödel's second incompleteness theorem and a generalization (G2.gen), the question that forces itself upon us is clearly: is the "generalized second incompleteness theorem" really a (meta-)theorem?

---

[29] It may be that very weak theories formulated in L[PA] or languages with similar expressive richness prove their own consistency (see Willard 1993 and Willard 2001 for work going in this direction). In fact, whether this might be so for Q had been an open question for several years before it was solved in the negative in Bezboruah/Shepherdson 1976. See this text for some remarks about how to interpret such a result correctly, and Hájek/Pudlak 1993 for generalizations of it. Let me note that the examples T presented here are not touched by any doubts which might stem from the proof theoretical weakness of T: for they will be extensions of PA.

[30] When one wants to formalize syntactical metamathematical statements about r.e. theories, theories like IΣ_1 or even IΔ_0 and IΔ_0 + Supexp usually suffice (cf. Hájek/Pudlak 1993). But this is not so when one is dealing with arithmetically definable theories of unbounded complexity, i.e. with those theories that are addressed in G2.gen. For in this context formalizations of, e.g., metatheoretical inductive proofs on the length of derivations have to be carried out time and again. If one wants to do all this in a single theory, PA is unavoidable. Moreover, PA and its extensions in L[PA] are reflexive, i.e. prove the consistency of their finitely axiomatizable subtheories; this is sometimes advantageous, too.

To start with, under G2 it is evident that no r.e. theory can present a counterexample to G2.gen.[31] Furthermore, instantiating T to $\text{Th}(\mathcal{N})$ in G2.gen results in a conditional with an unsatisfiable premise – for there is no representation of $\text{Th}(\mathcal{N})$ in $\text{L}[\text{Th}(\mathcal{N})]$ – whence that conditional is true. As before, it is for trivial reasons that $\text{Th}(\mathcal{N})$ lacks relevance: one has to look for theories which are definable in the languages in which they are formulated. Turning to *arithmetically definable completions* of PA in L[PA] seems to be a promising move here. For it should be quite unlikely that each of these theories proves its own inconsistency. But if just one of them should not prove its own inconsistency, by its completeness, it would have to prove its consistency.

Indeed, the idea just sketched works (at least) to some extent.

Lemma 1: There exists a completion Λ of PA (in L[PA]) with complexity Δ_2^0 and a representation $\sharp\lambda$ of the *theory* Λ such that $\sharp\lambda$ is a Δ_2^0-formula and $\Lambda \vdash \neg\sharp\lambda(\ulcorner\bot\urcorner)$.

Proof: For each consistent axiomatizable theory S with representation σ in Σ_0^0, it is possible to construct a complete theory Λ (extending S) in Δ_2^0 with representation λ, such that Λ is (PA + Con_σ)-provably complete. More explicitly,

$$\text{PA} + \text{Con}_\sigma \vdash \text{Con}_\lambda \wedge \forall x(\text{Pr}_\sigma(x) \to \lambda(x)) \wedge \text{QCmp}_\lambda$$

holds.[32] By construction, $\lambda(x)$ is in Σ_2^0 und (PA + Con_σ)-provably equivalent to a Π_2^0-formula λ'.[33]

Now, let $\sharp\lambda(x) := \lambda(x) \wedge \text{Con}_\sigma$ and $\sharp\lambda'(x) := \lambda'(x) \wedge \text{Con}_\sigma$.

Then $\sharp\lambda$ is a representation of the *theory* Λ: for λ is closed under a formalization of the rules of inference (even (PA + Con_σ)-provably so), and therefore represents not only an *axiom-set* of Λ, but Λ itself. And since "Con_σ" is true, the same holds for $\sharp\lambda$. Moreover, $\sharp\lambda \in \Sigma_2^0$ and $\sharp\lambda' \in \Pi_2^0$, and it is the case that $\text{PA} \vdash \forall x(\sharp\lambda(x) \leftrightarrow \sharp\lambda'(x))$.

---

[31] In fact, the r.e. theories which prove their own consistency defined by Rogers 1967 (p. 186 ff.), Jeroslov 1975, Girard 1987 (p. 79) and Visser 1989 do not violate G2 or G2.gen: the formalized consistency assertions employed there rest on nonstandard formalizations of the proof predicates or on representations of *axiom-sets* which are not Σ_1^0.

[32] See Feferman 1960 and, for more details, Visser 1991. Here, "QCmp$_\lambda$" is a formalization of "Λ is quantificationally complete".

[33] Of course, for a consistency proof for Λ in Λ, $\Lambda \vdash \text{Con}_\sigma$ would suffice. But this is not guaranteed – whence a change of representation is in order. The change of representation presented here is inspired by Hájek 1977. In fact, it may be regarded as a simplification of the nonstandard representation considered in Feferman 1960.

Finally, it is clear that $PA \vdash \neg\sharp\lambda(\bot)$, for

$$\begin{aligned}
PA \vdash \sharp\lambda(\bot) &\rightarrow \lambda(\bot) \wedge Con_\sigma \\
&\rightarrow Pr_\lambda(\bot) \wedge Con_\lambda \\
&\rightarrow \bot.
\end{aligned}$$

By choosing PA for S and "$pa(x)$" for "$\sigma(x)$", the claim of the lemma follows.

Of course, the theory presented in Lemma 1 is not really an example for the theories I would like to find. For the consistency assertion employed it in is far from being of the type "$\neg Pr_\alpha(\ulcorner\bot\urcorner)$". Moreover, the representation $\sharp\lambda$ used for Λ is not chosen as a "natural" representation of (an *axiom-set* of) Λ.[34] Finally, none of the arithmetically definable completions of PA is sound (you may recall that those completions that are Δ_2^0 prove false Σ_1^0-sentences).

The problems addressed here provide the background for a method of obtaining theory-internal consistency proofs which is thoroughly different from the one presented above. As a preparatory step, some general considerations on (finite) intersections of theories are useful.

3.2 *Intersections*

Let S and T be arithmetically definable theories and $\sigma(x)$ and $\tau(x)$ be representations of *axiom-sets* of S and T. Then "$Pr_\sigma(x)$" and "$Pr_\tau(x)$" are representations of S and T, and "$Pr_\sigma(x) \wedge Pr_\tau(x)$" is a representation of $S \cap T$. Moreover, it is usually taken for granted (though not explicitly mentioned) that, if $\sigma(x)$ and $\tau(x)$ are *natural* representations of *axiom-sets* of S and T, then "$Pr_\sigma(x)$", "$Pr_\tau(x)$" and "$Pr_\sigma(x) \wedge Pr_\tau(x)$" are natural representation of S, T and $S \cap T$, too. Given the definition

$$(\sigma \wedge \tau)(x) :\iff Pr_\sigma(x) \wedge Pr_\tau(x)$$

---

[34] If a natural representation and a formalization of a natural Hilbert-style provability predicate can be used here instead, I do not know. – A sort of a counterpart to Lemma 1, which strikingly illustrates how much metatheorems of this type may depend on the representation employed, is the following metatheorem:

Theorem B: Let S be a r.e. extension PA, σ be a Σ_1^0-representation of a set of axioms of S, and let T be a completion of $S + Pr_\sigma(\bot)$ with representation τ. Then there exist a representation τ' of T such that τ and τ' are of the same complexity and $T \vdash \neg Con_{\tau'}$.
(**Idea of the proof:** Define $\tau'(x) :\iff \sigma(x) \vee \tau(x)$ and apply the formalized completeness theorem; see Niebergall 1996.)

That is, there are consistent theories which, in some sense, prove both their consistency and their inconsistency (with different representations, of course).

this suggests the following "principle for natural representations": if σ and τ are natural representations of *axiom-sets* of S and T, then $\sigma \wedge \tau$ is a natural representation of $S \cap T$.

Now, consider $\overline{S \cap T}$, i.e. the deductive closure of $S \cap T$; since $(\sigma \wedge \tau)(x)$ is a natural representation of $S \cap T$, by the type of reasoning just employed, "$\Pr_{\sigma \wedge \tau}(x)$" is a natural representation of $\overline{S \cap T}$. But since, by assumption, $S = \overline{S}$ and $T = \overline{T}$ hold, $\overline{S \cap T} = S \cap T$ holds, too. Thus, we have two representations – "$\sigma \wedge \tau$" and "$\Pr_{\sigma \wedge \tau}$" – for one theory – $S \cap T$. Does this create a problem? No, for *first*, it is not clear whether, if $A = B$ and α is a natural representation of A, it has to be a natural representation of B. *Second*, even if "is a natural representation of x" is assumed to be extensional (in x), one theory may still have many natural representations. For example, if $\alpha(x) \vee \beta(x)$ is a natural representation of X, the distinct formula $\beta(x) \vee \alpha(x)$ should count as a natural representation, too. Of course, we could "identify" representations which are provably equivalent in, say, PA. But, finally, note that "$(\sigma \wedge \tau)(x)$" and "$\Pr_{\sigma \wedge \tau}(x)$" *are* PA-provably equivalent:

Lemma 2:
 (a) $\text{PA} \vdash \forall x((\sigma \wedge \tau)(x) \leftrightarrow \Pr_{\sigma \wedge \tau}(x))$.
 (b) $\text{PA} \vdash \text{Con}_\sigma \vee \text{Con}_\tau \leftrightarrow \text{Con}_{\sigma \wedge \tau}$.

Proof: What has to be shown is $\text{PA} \vdash \forall x((\Pr_{\sigma \wedge \tau}(x) \rightarrow (\sigma \wedge \tau)(x))$ (the rest follows easily). This is done by formalized induction on the length of proof in $\sigma \wedge \tau$ (cf. Feferman 1960).

3.3 *Mutual and system-internal consistency proofs*

I now present a general method for obtainig theories which prove their own consistency. Besides forming intesections of theories in the way just discussed, it's main ingredient is a somwhat surprising result from Niebergall 1996 – the existence of *mutual consistency proofs*: there exists theories S and T such that S proves the consistency of T and vice versa, while Gödel's incompleteness theorems hold for both. – In fact, there are many theories which mutually prove their consistency.[35] As a (trivial) example for mutual consistency proofs consider the theories

$S := \text{PA} + \text{Tr}_{\Pi_1^0}$ and $T_0 := \text{PA} + \text{Con}_{\text{pa}+\text{Tr}_{\Pi_1^0}}$, with natural representations

$\sigma(x) (:= \text{pa}(x) \vee \text{Tr}_{\Pi_1^0}(x))$ and $\tau_0(x)(:= \text{pa}(x) \vee x = \overline{\ulcorner \text{Con}_{\text{pa}+\text{Tr}_{\Pi_1^0}} \urcorner})$ of

---

[35] See Niebergall 1996 for more details and and Niebergall/Schirn (forthcoming) for an application to Hilbert's program.

On the Limits of Gödel's Second Incompleteness Theorem

their "natural" *axiom-sets*.[36] By definition of T_0, $T_0 \vdash \text{Con}_\sigma$. And since T_0 is r.e. and consistent, its consistency assertion Con_{τ_0} is a true Π_1^0-sentence, whence provable in S.

An even better example for this phenomenon is the following:

$S := \text{PA} + \text{Tr}_{\Pi_1^0}$ and $T_1 := \text{PA} + \text{RFN}[\text{pa}]$[37], both provided with natural representations σ and τ_1 of their "natural" *axiom-sets*.[38]

Having theories proving mutually their consistency at hand, it is easy to establish that there are theories proving their own consistency.

Example 1: Let S, T_1 and σ, τ_1 be chosen as above and let the representation of $S \cap T_1$ be $\sigma \wedge \tau_1$.
Since $S \vdash \text{Con}_{\tau_1}$, it follows that $S \vdash \text{Con}_{\sigma \wedge \tau_1}$. Since $T_1 \vdash \text{Con}_\sigma$, it follows that $T_1 \vdash \text{Con}_{\sigma \wedge \tau_1}$.
Therefore, $S \cap T_1 \vdash \text{Con}_{\sigma \wedge \tau_1}$.

Evidently, this example is obtained as a special case of a general procedure for building theories which prove their own consistency. That method can, of course, by varied in a lot of ways. For example, it provides us with theories proving their own *correctness* (to an arbitrary extent):

Example 2: Let $k \geq 1$, $A := \text{PA} + \text{Tr}_{\Pi_{k+1}^0}$ with natural representation α of its "natural" *axiom-set*, and let $B := \text{PA} + \text{RFN}[\text{pa}]$ with natural representation β of its "natural" *axiom-set*.

In Niebergall 1996, it is shown that $B \vdash \text{RFN}[\alpha]$. Since "$\text{RFN}_{\Sigma_k^0}[\beta]$", i.e. the restriction of the uniform reflection principle for β to Σ_k^0-formulas, is a set of true Π_{k+1}^0-sentences, $A \vdash \text{RFN}_{\Sigma_k^0}[\beta]$. By Lemma 2,

$$A \cap B \vdash \text{RFN}_{\Sigma_k^0}[\alpha \wedge \beta].$$

Moreover, it should be emphasized that the representations of the theories considered in these examples are clearly "natural" formalizations of consistency assertions. In particular, this means that the problems put forward above for complete theories are almost solved. *Almost* (but not quite), because one still has to take care for the complexity conditions on $S \cap T_1$ and $\sigma \wedge \tau_1$.

---

[36] $\text{Tr}_{\Pi_k^0}$ and $\text{Tr}_{\Sigma_k^0}$ are the set of true Π_k^0-sentences and the set of true Σ_k^0-sentences ($k \geq 1$). I use the same expressions also for the arithmetical formulas representing these sets.

[37] RFN[pa] is the so called "uniform reflection principle" for PA, i.e. the set of all formulas "$\forall x (\text{Pr}_{\text{pa}}(\ulcorner \psi(x) \urcorner) \rightarrow \psi(x))$" for arbitrary formulas ψ in L[PA].

[38] For a proof of $T_1 \vdash \text{Con}_\sigma$, see Niebergall 1996 and Niebergall/Schirn (forthcoming).

In order to deal with this problem, let me consider a slightly more complicated variant of Example 1.

Example 3: Let $S := \text{PA} + \text{Tr}_{\Pi_1^0}$ with representation σ and let

$$T := \text{PA} + \text{RFN[pa]} + \text{Pr}_{\text{pa+RFN[pa]}}(\ulcorner \bot \urcorner)$$

with natural representation τ of its "natural" *axiom-set*.

Then $S \vdash \text{Con}_\tau$, for T is consistent (by Gödel's second incompleteness theorem), whence "Con_τ" is a true Π_1^0-sentence. Also, $T \vdash \text{Con}_\sigma$, for $T \supseteq T_1$.

Arguing along the lines presented in Example 1, this implies

$$S \cap T \vdash \text{Con}_{\sigma \wedge \tau}.$$

Moreover, $S \cap T$ is sound, and $\sigma \wedge \tau$ in Σ_2^0.

It remains to show that $S \cap T$ is not Π_2^0: First note that S is inconsistent with T [39]; hence, there exists a sentence ψ such that $T \vdash \neg \psi$ and $S \vdash \psi$. This implies $(S \cap T) + \psi = S$. If $S \cap T$ were in Π_2^0, then $(S \cap T) + \psi$, i.e. S, would be, too. But this is impossible since S is Σ_2^0-complete.

4. The limit of the refutations: numerations

4.1 *A further generalization of the second incompleteness theorem*

The picture suggested by the foregoing discussion is that there are quite a lot of consistent theories which prove their own consistency. Moreover, these theories are extensions of PA, are (in part) sound and not too unnatural; and for some of them, "prove their own consistency" is formalized in a natural way. In other words, G2.gen is *quite false*. Is this the end of the story of generalizations of Gödel's second incompleteness theorem? I don't think so. Let me first propose a new generalization of G2, and make some motivating comments afterwards.

Gödel's Second Theorem – strictly generalized; G2.GEN: For each consistent arithmetically definable extension T of PA and for each representation τ of an *axiom-set* of T, if τ is a numeration of this *axiom-set* in T and if the complexity of τ is not higher then the complexity of T, then $T \nvdash \text{Con}_\tau$.

A *numeration* (see Feferman 1960)[40] is sort of a representation relativized to a theory (in fact, a representation is a numeration in $\text{Th}(\mathcal{N})$). The precise

---

[39] This did not hold for S and T_1 in Example 1.
[40] A further strengthening of numerations, binumerations, will not be considered any further in this paper. Let me merely note that Feferman's representation of an *axiom-set* of PA, though not being Σ_1^0, is certainly a binumeration of this *axiom-set* in PA; cf. Feferman 1960.

definition is as follows: let $A \subseteq \omega^k$, α be a k-place formula (from L[PA]), T be a theory (in L[PA]); then

$$\alpha \text{ is a numeration of } A \text{ in } T : \iff \forall \vec{n} \in \omega^k (\vec{n} \in A \iff T \vdash \alpha(\vec{n})).$$

There are several reasons for taking G2.GEN into account. First, one method of proving Gödel's *first* incompleteness theorem for T employs numerations of an *axiom-set* of T in T; this works to some extent even for non r.e. theories (the other method uses, e.g. when restricted to r.e. theories T, that the provability predicate for T can be chosen to be Σ^0_1). Second, the condition that τ should numerate an *axiom-set* of T in T seems to be quite reasonable. It is motivated by the idea of *control* (instead of *structure preservation*): Speaking in anthropomorphical terms: if a theory T does not recognize that it is T whose consistency is expressed in "Con$_\tau$", one need not wonder that T proves "Con$_\tau$". In particular, T might treat τ as if it were a representation of a finitely axiomatizable subtheory of T, whence T – given that is, being an extension of PA in L[PA], reflexive – could well be able to prove "Con$_\tau$". Third, considering G2.GEN is motivated by my goal to investigate strong formulations of the second incompleteness theorem.

Does G2.GEN hold? In order to answer this question, a plausible *first step* is to have a look at the theories dealt with in Lemma 1 and Examples 1 and 3. In Lemma 1, we had a change of representation; hence, it will probably come as no surprise that the representation $\sharp\lambda$ of Λ employed there is no numeration of Λ. What may be surprising, though, is that there is *no* representation of an *axiom-set* of Λ *at all* which is a numeration of this *axiom-set* in Λ. In fact, such a result holds for each complete extension of PA.

Theorem 1: If T is an arithmetically definable completion of PA, then there exists no formula τ which is a representation of an *axiom-set* of T and a numeration of this *axiom-set* in T.

Proof: Assume there is an *axiom-set* of T which is numerated by τ in T. Then, "Proof$_\tau$" is a numeration of the T-proof relation in T (cf. Feferman 1960, Theorem 4.4(i)), i.e.: for all $n, m \in \omega$

$$T \vdash \text{Proof}_\tau(\overline{n}, \overline{m}) \iff \mathcal{N} \vDash \text{Proof}_\tau(\overline{n}, \overline{m}) \qquad (*)$$

Hence, for all $n, m \in \omega$

$$T \vdash \text{Proof}_\tau(\overline{n}, \overline{m}) \wedge \forall z \leq \overline{n} \neg \text{Proof}_\tau(z, \text{neg}(\overline{m})) \iff$$
$$\mathcal{N} \vDash \text{Proof}_\tau(\overline{n}, \overline{m}) \wedge \forall z \leq \overline{n} \neg \text{Proof}_\tau(z, \text{neg}(\overline{m})),$$

which implies, in particular, that if $\mathscr{N} \models \mathrm{Pr}_\tau^R(\ulcorner R\urcorner)$, then $T \vdash \mathrm{Pr}_\tau^R(\ulcorner R\urcorner)$. By an application of the diagonalization lemma (cf. Kaye 1991 and Hájek/Pudlak 1993), let R be the *Rosser fixed point*, i.e.

$$Q \vdash R \longleftrightarrow \neg \mathrm{Pr}_\tau^R(\ulcorner R\urcorner).$$

- If $T \vdash R$ then $\mathscr{N} \models \mathrm{Pr}_\tau^R(\ulcorner R\urcorner)$, whence $T \vdash \mathrm{Pr}_\tau^R(\ulcorner R\urcorner)$. Therefore, $T \vdash \neg R$; contradiction.
- If $T \nvdash R$, then $T \vdash \neg R$ because T is complete. Hence $\exists n \mathscr{N} \models \mathrm{Proof}_\tau(\bar{n}, \ulcorner \neg R\urcorner)$ and, by $(*)$,

$(**) \ \exists n T \vdash \mathrm{Proof}_\tau(\bar{n}, \ulcorner \neg R\urcorner).$

Moreover, $T \vdash \exists x (\mathrm{Proof}_\tau(x, \ulcorner R\urcorner) \wedge \forall z \leq x \neg \mathrm{Proof}_\tau(z, \ulcorner \neg R\urcorner))$, which, taken in conjunction with $(**)$, implies $\exists n T \vdash \exists x < \bar{n} \mathrm{Proof}_\tau(\bar{n}, \ulcorner R\urcorner)$, i.e. $\exists n T \vdash \mathrm{Proof}_\tau(\bar{0}, \ulcorner R\urcorner) \vee \ldots \vee \mathrm{Proof}_\tau(\bar{n}, \ulcorner R\urcorner)$. Because of the completeness of T, $\exists n (T \vdash \mathrm{Proof}_\tau(\bar{0}, \ulcorner R\urcorner) \vee \ldots \vee T \vdash \mathrm{Proof}_\tau(\bar{n}, \ulcorner R\urcorner))$ follows from this, which yields (by $(*)$)

$$\exists n (\mathscr{N} \models \mathrm{Proof}_\tau(\bar{0}, \ulcorner R\urcorner) \vee \ldots \vee \mathscr{N} \models \mathrm{Proof}_\tau(\bar{n}, \ulcorner R\urcorner)).$$

Therefore, $T \vdash R$; contradiction.

Eventually, this shows that the assumption that there is an *axiom-set* of T which has a numeration τ in T is false.[41]

Coming to Examples 1 and 3 the situation is not as bad, but bad enough. In fact, the representations $\sigma \wedge \tau_1$ and $\sigma \wedge \tau$ of $S \cap T_1$ and $S \cap T$ – natural though they may be – are *no numerations* of *axiom-sets* of these theories in $S \cap T_1$ and $S \cap T$, resp. Thus, the examples presented here do not constitute refutations of G2.GEN.[42]

So, let's go a *second step* and look for other theories which might provide counterexamples to G2.GEN. Presently, the only procedures I know of for obtainig theories of this kind are the ones illustrated by the examples above. These fall under two types:

(Theories of type (A)) Finite intersections $T_1 \cap \ldots \cap T_n$ such that some of the T_i are arithmetically definable completions of PA.

(Theories of type (B)) Finite intersections $T_1 \cap \ldots \cap T_n$ such that the T_i prove that they are complete for their complexity class.

---

[41] By a simpler type of argument, employing the Gödel fixed point of τ instead of the Rosser fixed point, it can also be shown:
Lemma C: If T is a completion of PA, then: T is closed under τ-necessitation $\Longleftrightarrow$ $T \vdash \mathrm{Pr}_\tau(\ulcorner \bot \urcorner)$.

[42] I will show a more general result in the next subsection.

Though Examples 1 and 3 provide no counterexampels to G2.GEN, one might still conjecture that there are theories of type (A) or (B) which will do. But, depending on some properties of the theories T_i involved, this is also not the case. To be more explicit, the following holds for theories of type (A):

Theorem C: If S is an arithmetically definable completion of PA, T an arbitrary arithmetically definable theory (extending PA) which is not a proper subtheory of S, and if α is a representation of an *axiom-set* of $S \cap T$ such that $\forall n(S \cap T \vdash \mathrm{Rfn}[\alpha \lceil n \rceil])$, then α is not a numeration of this axiom-set in $S \cap T$.[43]

For theories of type (B), a similar metatheorem is true (see the next subsection for a precise statement and a detailed proof of it).

These results suggest that G2.GEN could be a remarkebly stable generalization of Gödel's second incompleteness theorem. Whether there are any theories violating even G2.GEN, I do not know.

4.2 *Theories of type (B)*

For the theories S, T_1 and T considered in Examples 1 and 3, Gödel's second incompleteness theorem can be proved in the uniform way which is well known from r.e. theories: first the so called "Löb derivability conditions" are established, and then, by a general "modal" method, the incompleteness theorems are derived from those conditions. The derivability condition which is of decisive importance when it comes to the proof of the second theorem, I call "LÖB3+": for r.e. theories T with representation τ, ist says that for each Σ_1^0-sentence φ, $T \vdash \varphi \rightarrow \mathrm{Pr}_\tau(\lceil \varphi \rceil))$. The vague formulation "T_i proves that it is complete for its complexity class" employed in the above statement about theories of type (B) is rendered more precise through the condition that LÖB3+ has to hold for T_i.

Hence, let me use $\Delta(T_1, \ldots, T_k; \tau_1, \ldots, \tau_k; \gamma)$ as an abbreviation for

(I) $T_1, \ldots, T_k$ are arithmetically definable extensions of PA, having representations $\tau_1, \ldots, \tau_k$ of complexity $\Sigma_{i_1}^0, \ldots, \Sigma_{i_k}^0$, such that $\mathrm{PA} \vdash \forall x(\mathrm{Pr}_q(x) \rightarrow \mathrm{Pr}_{\tau_i}(x))$ $(1 \leq i \leq k)$;

(II) For convenience, let's assume that $i_1 \leq i_2 \leq \ldots \leq i_k$. Then $T_1, \ldots, T_k; \tau_1, \ldots, \tau_k$ satisfy LÖB3+ in the following strong sense (for $1 \leq j \leq k$)

---

[43] This can be proved along the lines of Theorem 2, but using an Orey-type fixed point instead of the Rosser fixed point and employing some additional reasoning about relative interpretations. For reasons of space, I cannot give a proof of Theorem C here.

$$\forall \varphi (\varphi \text{ is a } \Sigma^0_{i_j}\text{-sentence} \Longrightarrow \text{PA} \vdash \varphi \to \text{Pr}_{\tau_j}(\ulcorner \varphi \urcorner)).$$

(III) γ is a sentence from L[PA] which is consistent with $(T_1 \cap T_2 \cap \ldots \cap T_k)$.

Lemma 3: If $\Delta(T_1, \ldots, T_k; \tau_1, \ldots, \tau_k; \gamma)$, then for $1 \leq j \leq k$

(1) $\forall \varphi \ \text{PA} \vdash \text{Pr}_{\tau_j + \gamma}(\ulcorner \varphi \urcorner) \to \text{Pr}_{\tau_j}(\overline{\ulcorner \text{Pr}_{\tau_j + \gamma}(\ulcorner \varphi \urcorner) \urcorner})$

(2) $\forall \varphi \ \text{PA} \vdash \text{Pr}_{\tau_j}(\ulcorner \varphi \urcorner) \to \text{Pr}_{\tau_j \wedge \ldots \wedge \tau_k + \gamma}(\overline{\ulcorner \text{Pr}_{\tau_j}(\ulcorner \varphi \urcorner) \urcorner})$

(3) $\forall \varphi \ \text{PA} \vdash \text{Pr}_{\tau_j + \gamma}(\overline{\ulcorner \neg \text{Pr}_{\tau_j + \gamma}(\ulcorner \varphi \urcorner) \urcorner}) \to \text{Pr}_{\tau_j + \gamma}(\ulcorner \bot \urcorner)$.

Proof:
(1) follows immediately from the assumption of LÖB3+, for "$\text{Pr}_{\tau_j + \gamma}$" is $\Sigma^0_{i_j}$.

(2) Since the theories are supposed to be ordered in weakly ascending complexity, the assumption of LÖB3+ for i with $j \leq i \leq k$ yields

$$\forall \varphi \text{PA} \vdash \text{Pr}_{\tau_j}(\ulcorner \varphi \urcorner) \to \text{Pr}_{\tau_i}(\overline{\ulcorner \text{Pr}_{\tau_j}(\ulcorner \varphi \urcorner) \urcorner}).$$

The claim follows by Lemma 2.

(3) follows from *Löb's theorem* in its formalized version. Employing (1), both the proof of the latter and the derivation of (3) from it are the same as the ones known from the domain of r.e. theories.[44]

Before I state and prove the main result, let me note that, if α is a numeration of A in T, then the following holds: $\forall \psi (A \vdash \psi \Longrightarrow T \vdash \text{Pr}_\alpha(\ulcorner \psi \urcorner))$; in short: "$T$ is closed under Pr_α-necessitation".

Therefore it is clear that, in order to establish that theories T of type (B) cannot prove their own consistency while employing proof-predicates formulated with *numerations* τ of *axiom-sets* of T, is suffices to show that theories of type (B) closed under Pr_τ-necessitation cannot prove their own consistency. More precisely:

Theorem 2: If $\Delta(T_1, \ldots, T_k; \tau_1, \ldots, \tau_k; \gamma)$ and if $(T_1 \cap T_2 \cap \ldots \cap T_k)$ is closed under $\text{Pr}_{\tau_1 \wedge \ldots \wedge \tau_k}$-necessitation, then:

(i) $(T_1 \cap T_2 \cap \ldots \cap T_k) + \gamma \vdash \text{Con}_{\tau_1 \wedge \ldots \wedge \tau_k + \gamma} \Longrightarrow$
$\forall j (1 \leq j < k \Longrightarrow (T_1 \cap T_2 \cap \ldots \cap T_k) + \gamma \vdash \text{Con}_{\tau_1 \wedge \ldots \wedge \tau_{k-j} + \gamma}))$

(ii) $(T_1 \cap T_2 \cap \ldots \cap T_k) + \gamma \vdash \text{Con}_{\tau_1 \wedge \ldots \wedge \tau_k + \gamma} \Longrightarrow (T_1 \cap T_2 \cap \ldots \cap T_k) + \gamma \vdash \text{Con}_{\tau_1 + \gamma}$.

(iii) $(T_1 \cap T_2 \cap \ldots \cap T_k) + \gamma \nvdash \text{Con}_{\tau_1 \wedge \ldots \wedge \tau_k + \gamma}$.

---

[44] See Boolos 1993. Let me remark that this is the place where the assumption in (I) that the T_i PA-provably extend Q is used.

Proof: (i) Induction on j.

$j = 1$: Assume $(T_1 \cap T_2 \cap \ldots \cap T_k) + \gamma \vdash \text{Con}_{\tau_1 \wedge \ldots \wedge \tau_k + \gamma}$, i.e.

$$(T_1 \cap T_2 \cap \ldots \cap T_k) + \gamma \vdash \neg \text{Pr}_{\tau_1 \wedge \ldots \wedge \tau_k}(\overline{\ulcorner \neg \gamma \urcorner}).$$

Then, by Lemma 2, $(T_1 \cap T_2 \cap \ldots \cap T_k) + \gamma \vdash \neg \text{Pr}_{\tau_1}(\overline{\ulcorner \neg \gamma \urcorner}) \vee \ldots \vee \neg \text{Pr}_{\tau_k}(\overline{\ulcorner \neg \gamma \urcorner})$, whence

$$(T_1 \cap T_2 \cap \ldots \cap T_k) \vdash \gamma \to (\text{Pr}_{\tau_1}(\overline{\ulcorner \neg \gamma \urcorner}) \to (\text{Pr}_{\tau_2}(\overline{\ulcorner \neg \gamma \urcorner}) \to$$

$$\ldots (\text{Pr}_{\tau_{k-1}}(\overline{\ulcorner \neg \gamma \urcorner}) \to \neg \text{Pr}_{\tau_k}(\overline{\ulcorner \neg \gamma \urcorner}) \ldots).$$

Now, by assumption, $(T_1 \cap T_2 \cap \ldots \cap T_k)$ is closed under $\text{Pr}_{\tau_1 \wedge \ldots \wedge \tau_k}$-necessitation. Therefore

$$(T_1 \cap T_2 \cap \ldots \cap T_k) \vdash \text{Pr}_{\tau_1 \wedge \ldots \wedge \tau_k + \gamma}(\overline{\ulcorner \text{Pr}_{\tau_1}(\overline{\ulcorner \neg \gamma \urcorner}) \to (\text{Pr}_{\tau_2}(\overline{\ulcorner \neg \gamma \urcorner}) \to}$$

$$\overline{\ldots (\text{Pr}_{\tau_{k-1}}(\overline{\ulcorner \neg \gamma \urcorner}) \to \neg \text{Pr}_{\tau_k}(\overline{\ulcorner \neg \gamma \urcorner}) \ldots) \urcorner}),$$

which by distribution and Lemma 2 in turn implies

$$(T_1 \cap T_2 \cap \ldots \cap T_k) \vdash \text{Pr}_{\tau_1 \wedge \ldots \wedge \tau_k + \gamma}(\overline{\ulcorner \text{Pr}_{\tau_1}(\overline{\ulcorner \neg \gamma \urcorner}) \urcorner}) \to$$

$$\text{Pr}_{\tau_2 \wedge \ldots \wedge \tau_k + \gamma}(\overline{\ulcorner \text{Pr}_{\tau_2}(\overline{\ulcorner \neg \gamma \urcorner}) \to (\ldots \neg \text{Pr}_{\tau_k}(\overline{\ulcorner \neg \gamma \urcorner}) \ldots) \urcorner}).$$

With Lemma 3(2), this yields that

$$\text{Pr}_{\tau_1}(\overline{\ulcorner \neg \gamma \urcorner}) \to \text{Pr}_{\tau_2 \wedge \ldots \wedge \tau_k + \gamma}(\overline{\ulcorner \text{Pr}_{\tau_2}(\overline{\ulcorner \neg \gamma \urcorner}) \to (\ldots \neg \text{Pr}_{\tau_k}(\overline{\ulcorner \neg \gamma \urcorner}) \ldots) \urcorner}) \quad (*)$$

is $(T_1 \cap T_2 \cap \ldots \cap T_k)$-provable.

Moreover, by distribution and Lemma 2 it is the case that

$$\text{PA} \vdash \text{Pr}_{\tau_2 \wedge \ldots \wedge \tau_k + \gamma}(\overline{\ulcorner \text{Pr}_{\tau_2}(\overline{\ulcorner \neg \gamma \urcorner}) \to (\ldots \neg \text{Pr}_{\tau_k}(\overline{\ulcorner \neg \gamma \urcorner}) \ldots) \urcorner}) \to$$

$$(\text{Pr}_{\tau_2 \wedge \ldots \wedge \tau_k + \gamma}(\overline{\ulcorner \text{Pr}_{\tau_2}(\overline{\ulcorner \neg \gamma \urcorner}) \urcorner}) \to$$

$$\text{Pr}_{\tau_3 \wedge \ldots \wedge \tau_k + \gamma}(\overline{\ulcorner \text{Pr}_{\tau_3}(\overline{\ulcorner \neg \gamma \urcorner}) \to (\ldots \neg \text{Pr}_{\tau_k}(\overline{\ulcorner \neg \gamma \urcorner})) \ldots) \urcorner})).$$

This, Lemma 3(2) and $(*)$ imply

$$(T_1 \cap T_2 \cap \ldots \cap T_k) \vdash \text{Pr}_{\tau_1}(\overline{\ulcorner \neg \gamma \urcorner}) \to (\text{Pr}_{\tau_2}(\overline{\ulcorner \neg \gamma \urcorner}) \to$$

$$\text{Pr}_{\tau_3 \wedge \ldots \wedge \tau_k + \gamma}(\overline{\ulcorner \text{Pr}_{\tau_3}(\overline{\ulcorner \neg \gamma \urcorner}) \to (\ldots \neg \text{Pr}_{\tau_k}(\overline{\ulcorner \neg \gamma \urcorner})) \ldots) \urcorner})).$$

An iteration of this type of reasoning will eventually lead to the $(T_1 \cap T_2 \cap \ldots \cap T_k)$-probability of

$$\mathrm{Pr}_{\tau_1}(\overline{\ulcorner \neg \gamma \urcorner}) \wedge \ldots \wedge \mathrm{Pr}_{\tau_{k-1}}(\overline{\ulcorner \neg \gamma \urcorner}) \to \mathrm{Pr}_{\tau_k + \gamma}(\overline{\ulcorner \neg \mathrm{Pr}_{\tau_k}(\overline{\ulcorner \neg \gamma \urcorner})\urcorner}).$$

Therefore, by Lemma 3(3)

$$(T_1 \cap T_2 \cap \ldots \cap T_k) \vdash \mathrm{Pr}_{\tau_1}(\overline{\ulcorner \neg \gamma \urcorner}) \wedge \ldots \wedge \mathrm{Pr}_{\tau_{k-1}}(\overline{\ulcorner \neg \gamma \urcorner}) \to \mathrm{Pr}_{\tau_k + \gamma}(\overline{\ulcorner \bot \urcorner}) \quad (**)$$

Moreover, by assumption and Lemma 2,

$$(T_1 \cap T_2 \cap \ldots \cap T_k) + \gamma \vdash \mathrm{Pr}_{\tau_1}(\overline{\ulcorner \neg \gamma \urcorner}) \wedge \ldots \wedge \mathrm{Pr}_{\tau_{k-1}}(\overline{\ulcorner \neg \gamma \urcorner}) \to \neg \mathrm{Pr}_{\tau_k + \gamma}(\overline{\ulcorner \bot \urcorner}) \quad (***)$$

(**) and (***) establish $(T_1 \cap T_2 \cap \ldots \cap T_k) + \gamma \vdash \neg(\mathrm{Pr}_{\tau_1}(\overline{\ulcorner \neg \gamma \urcorner}) \wedge \ldots \wedge \mathrm{Pr}_{\tau_{k-1}}(\overline{\ulcorner \neg \gamma \urcorner}))$, i.e.

$$(T_1 \cap T_2 \cap \ldots \cap T_k) + \gamma \vdash \mathrm{Con}_{\tau_1 \wedge \ldots \wedge \tau_{k-1} + \gamma}.$$

Induction step j to $j+1$: Assume $(T_1 \cap T_2 \cap \ldots \cap T_k) + \gamma \vdash \mathrm{Con}_{\tau_1 \wedge \ldots \wedge \tau_k + \gamma}$, and let it be the case (by I.H.) that

$$(T_1 \cap T_2 \cap \ldots \cap T_k) + \gamma \vdash \mathrm{Con}_{\tau_1 \wedge \ldots \wedge \tau_{k-j} + \gamma} \quad (+)$$

In the same way as it was done above – with $k - j$ instead of k – one shows that

$$(T_1 \cap T_2 \cap \ldots \cap T_k) \vdash \mathrm{Pr}_{\tau_1}(\overline{\ulcorner \neg \gamma \urcorner}) \wedge \ldots \wedge \mathrm{Pr}_{\tau_{k-j-1}}(\overline{\ulcorner \neg \gamma \urcorner}) \to \mathrm{Pr}_{\tau_{k-j} + \gamma}(\overline{\ulcorner \bot \urcorner}).$$

Since $(T_1 \cap T_2 \cap \ldots \cap T_k) \vdash \neg(\mathrm{Pr}_{\tau_1}(\overline{\ulcorner \neg \gamma \urcorner}) \wedge \ldots \wedge \mathrm{Pr}_{\tau_{k-j-1}}(\overline{\ulcorner \neg \gamma \urcorner}))$[45] is implied by (+),

$$(T_1 \cap T_2 \cap \ldots \cap T_k) + \gamma \vdash \mathrm{Con}_{\tau_1 \wedge \ldots \tau_{k-j+1} + \gamma}$$

follows.

---

[45] (+) is equivalent to $(T_1 \cap T_2 \ldots \cap T_k) \vdash \gamma \to (\mathrm{Pr}_{\tau_1}(\overline{\ulcorner \neg \gamma \urcorner}) \to (\mathrm{Pr}_{\tau_2}(\overline{\ulcorner \neg \gamma \urcorner}) \to \ldots (\mathrm{Pr}_{\tau_{k-j-1}}(\overline{\ulcorner \neg \gamma \urcorner}) \to \neg \mathrm{Pr}_{\tau_{k-j}}(\overline{\ulcorner \neg \gamma \urcorner}))\ldots)$. Since $(T_1 \cap T_2 \ldots \cap T_k)$ is assumed to be closed under $\mathrm{Pr}_{\tau_1 \wedge \ldots \wedge \tau_k}$-necessitation, the $(T_1 \cap T_2 \ldots \cap T_k)$-probability of
$\mathrm{Pr}_{\tau_1 \wedge \ldots \wedge \tau_k + \gamma}[\mathrm{Pr}_{\tau_1}(\overline{\ulcorner \neg \gamma \urcorner}) \to (\mathrm{Pr}_{\tau_2}(\overline{\ulcorner \neg \gamma \urcorner}) \to \ldots (\mathrm{Pr}_{\tau_{k-j-1}}(\overline{\ulcorner \neg \gamma \urcorner}) \to \neg \mathrm{Pr}_{\tau_{k-j}}(\overline{\ulcorner \neg \gamma \urcorner}))\ldots)]$
follows, whence $(T_1 \cap T_2 \ldots \cap T_k) \vdash$
$\mathrm{Pr}_{\tau_1 \wedge \ldots \wedge \tau_{k-j} + \gamma}[\mathrm{Pr}_{\tau_1}(\overline{\ulcorner \neg \gamma \urcorner}) \to (\mathrm{Pr}_{\tau_2}(\overline{\ulcorner \neg \gamma \urcorner}) \to \ldots (\mathrm{Pr}_{\tau_{k-j-1}}(\overline{\ulcorner \neg \gamma \urcorner}) \to \neg \mathrm{Pr}_{\tau_{k-j}}(\overline{\ulcorner \neg \gamma \urcorner}))\ldots)]$
holds, too. The rest is now as before.

(ii) results from (i) by taking $j = k - 1$.
(iii) If (iii) does not hold, (ii) yields

$$(T_1 \cap T_2 \cap \ldots \cap T_k) + \gamma \vdash \text{Con}_{\tau_1 + \gamma}.$$

Now this plus the closure of $(T_1 \cap T_2 \cap \ldots \cap T_k)$ under $\text{Pr}_{\tau_1 \wedge \ldots \wedge \tau_k}$-necessitation and Lemma 2 imply

$$(T_1 \cap T_2 \cap \ldots \cap T_k) \vdash \text{Pr}_{\tau_1 + \gamma}(\overline{\ulcorner \text{Con}_{\tau_1 + \gamma} \urcorner}).$$

By Lemma 3(3),

$$(T_1 \cap T_2 \cap \ldots \cap T_k) \vdash \text{Pr}_{\tau_1 + \gamma}(\overline{\ulcorner \bot \urcorner})$$

follows. But this contradicts the assumption that $(T_1 \cap T_2 \cap \ldots \cap T_k) + \gamma$ is consistent.

Corollary 1: $\sigma \wedge \tau_1$ and $\sigma \wedge \tau$ are no numerations of *axiom-sets* of $S \cap T_1$ and $S \cap T_2$.

References

Bezboruah, A., Shepherdson, J.: Gödel's second incompleteness theorem for Q, *The Journal of Symbolic Logic* 41 (1976), 503–512.

Boolos, G.: *The Logic of Provability*, Cambridge University Press, Cambridge 1993.

Feferman, S.: Arithmetization of metamathematics in a general setting, *Fundamenta Mathematicae* 49 (1960), 35–92.

Feferman, S.: Hilbert's program relativized: proof-theoretical and foundational reductions, *The Journal of Symbolic Logic* 53 (1988), 364–384.

Girard, J.Y.: *Proof Theory and logical Complexity, vol. I*, Bibliopolis, Naples 1987.

Gödel, K.: Einige metamathematische Resultate über Entscheidungsdefinitheit und Widerspruchsfreiheit, *Anzeiger der Akademie der Wissenschaften in Wien* 67 (1930), 214–215.

Gödel, K.: Über formal unentscheidbare Sätze der *Principia Mathematica* und verwandter Systeme I, *Monatshefte für Mathematik und Physik* 38 (1931), 173–198.

Hájek, P.: Experimental logics and Π_3^0-theories, *The Journal of Symbolic Logic* 42 (1977), 515–522.

Hájek, P., Pudlak, P.: *Metamathematics of First-Order Arithmetic*, Springer, Berlin, Heidelberg, New York 1993.

Hasenjaeger, G.: Eine Bemerkung zu Henkin's Beweis für die Vollständigkeit des Prädikatenkalküls der ersten Stufe, *The Journal of Symbolic Logic* 18 (1953), 42–48.

Hilbert, D.: *Hilbertiana*, Wissenschaftliche Buchgesellschaft, Darmstadt 1964.

Hilbert, D., Bernays, P.: *Grundlagen der Mathematik II*, Springer-Verlag, Berlin, Heidelberg 1939.

Jeroslov, R.: Experimental logics and Δ_2^0-theories, *Journal of Philosophical Logic* 4 (1975), 253–267.
Kaye, R.: *Models of Peano Arithmetic*, Oxford University Press, Oxford 1991.
Kleene, S.C.: *Introduction to Metamathematics*, North-Holland, Amsterdam 1952.
Kleene, S.C.: Introductory note to 1930b, 1931 and 1932b. In: *Kurt Gödel, Collected Works, Volume I*, ed. by S. Feferman et al., Oxford University Press, New York 1986, 126–141.
Kreisel, G., Takeuti, G.: *Formally self-referential propositions in cut-free classical analysis and related systems*, Disssertationes Mathematicae 118, Warschau 1974.
Lindström, P.: *Aspects of Incompleteness*, Springer, Berlin 1997.
Lucas, J.R.: Minds, machines and Gödel, *Philosophy* 36 (1961), 112–127.
Monk, D.: *Mathematical Logic*, Springer, Berlin 1976.
Mostowski, A.: *Sentences undecidable in Formalized Arithmetic*, North-Holland, Amsterdam 1952.
Niebergall, K.G.: *Zur Metamathematik nichtaxiomatisierbarer Theorien*, München 1996.
Niebergall, K.G., Schirn, M.: Hilbert's finitism and the notion of infinity. In: *The Philosophy of Mathematics Today*, ed. by M. Schirn, Oxford University Press, Oxford 1998, 271–305.
Niebergall, K.G., Schirn, M.: Hilbert's programme and Gödel's theorems, forthcoming.
Rogers, H.: *Theory of recursive Functions and effectice Computability*, McGraw-Hill, New York 1967.
Rosser, J.B.: Extensions of some theorems of Gödel and Church, *The Journal of Symbolic Logic* 1 (1936), 87–91.
Simpson, S.G.: Partial realizations of Hilbert's program, *The Journal of Symbolic Logic* 53 (1988), 349–363.
Sokal, A., Bricmont, J.: *Fashionable Nonsense. Postmodern Intellectuals' Abuse of Science*, Picador, New York 1998.
Stegmüller, W.: *Unvollständigkeit und Unentscheidbarkeit*, Springer, Wien 1959.
Tait, W.W.: Finitism, *The Journal of Philosophy* 78 (1981), 524–546.
Tarski, A., Mostowski, A., Robinson, R.M.: *Undecidable Theories*, North-Holland, Amsterdam 1953.
Visser, A.: Peano's smart children: a provability logical study of systems with built-in consistency, *Notre Dame Journal of Formal Logic* 30 (1989), 161–196.
Visser, A.: The formalization of interpretability, *Studia Logica* 59 (1991), 81–105.
Willard, D.: Self-verifying axiom systems. In: *Computational Logic and Proof Theory*, ed. by G. Gottlob, A. Leitsch, D. Mundici, Lecture Notes in Computer Science 713, Springer, Berlin 1993, 325–336.
Willard, D.: Self-verifying axiom systems, the incompleteness theorem and related reflection principles, *The Journal of Symbolic Logic* 66 (2001), 536–596.

Teil II

Sprachphilosophie, Philosophie des Geistes, Metaphysik

Stephen Schiffer

The Things We Believe

1. The Face-Value Theory and a Further Question

A theory about belief reports which at face value looks right holds that utterances of the form

(1) *A* believes that *S*

are true just in case the referent of the '*A*' term stands in the belief relation to the proposition to which the 'that *S*' term refers. The face-value plausibility of this theory is made plain in the following way.

The part which implies that (1) consists of a two-place transitive verb flanked by slots for two argument singular terms gets its default status by way of being the most straightforward way of accounting for the validity of inferences like these:

> Harold believes that there is life on Venus, and so does Fiona.
> So, there is something that they both believe – to wit, that there is life on Venus.

> Harold believes everything that Fiona says.
> Fiona says that there is life on Venus.
> So, Harold believes that there is life on Venus.

> Harold believes that there is life on Venus.
> That there is life on Venus = Fiona's theory.
> So, Harold believes Fiona's theory.

The remaining part of the face-value theory, which says propositions are the referents of that-clauses in utterances of form (1), gets its *prima facie* status in the following way. Consider

> Ramona believes that eating carrots improves eyesight

If, as the face-value theory has it, 'that eating carrots improves eyesight' has a referent, then, obviously, its referent is *that eating carrots improves eyesight*, and we can straightway say the following things about it:

- *That eating carrots improves eyesight* is *abstract*: it has no spatial location, nor anything else that can make it a physical object.
- It's *mind- and language-independent* in two senses. First, its existence is independent of the existence of thinkers or speakers. *That eating carrots improves eyesight* wasn't brought into existence by anything anyone said or thought. Second, *that eating carrots improves eyesight* can be expressed by a sentence of just about any natural language but itself belongs to no language.
- It has a *truth condition*: *that eating carrots improves eyesight* is true iff eating carrots improves eyesight.
- It has its truth condition *essentially*: it's a *necessary truth* that *that eating carrots improves eyesight* is true iff eating carrots improves eyesight. The contrast here is with sentences. The *sentence* 'Eating carrots improves eyesight' is also true iff eating carrots improves eyesight, but that is a *contingent* truth that would have been otherwise had English speakers used 'carrots' the way they now use 'bicycles'.
- It has its truth condition *absolutely*, i.e., without relativization to anything. The contrast is again with sentences. The sentence 'Eating carrots improves eyesight' has its truth condition only *in English* or *among us*. There might be another language or population of speakers in which it means that camels snore; but *that eating carrots improves eyesight* has its truth condition everywhere and everywhen.

From all this we may conclude, by an obvious generalization, that things believed are *propositions*: abstract, mind- and language-independent entities that have truth conditions, and have their truth conditions both essentially and absolutely.

The foregoing considerations establish not the truth of the face-value theory but only its *prima facie* status. I'll assume as a working hypothesis that the theory is true; the rest of this paper is about the further nature of the propositions we believe given that working hypothesis.

2. Compositionality, Unstructured Vs. Structured Propositions, and Russellian Vs. Fregean Propositions

There's plenty of room for face-value theorists to disagree about the nature of the propositions we believe, but nearly all of them accept a hypothesis that keeps their disagreements within certain bounds. I'll call this hypothesis the *compositionality hypothesis* (CH). To a first approximation CH holds that the referent of a that-clause token is determined by its structure and the referents its component expressions have in that token.[1] This is a first approximation because it needs to be qualified in order to deal with implicit references sometimes made in the utterance of a that-clause, such as the reference to a place made in the that-clause in 'Henrietta believes that it's raining'. CH, then, is better put by saying that the referent of a that-clause token is determined by its structure and the referents of its (explicit and implicit) component expressions.

One issue that immediately arises relative to CH is whether the propositions to which that-clauses refer, and thus the propositions we believe, are *structured* or *un*structured, in a technical sense of 'structured' that can be glossed in the following way. First, let's say that an expression has a *primary* reference in a that-clause if it has reference in the that-clause, and its referent doesn't function to help determine the referent of some other expression in the that-clause. Thus, in the that-clause in 'Ralph believes that that guy standing next to Betty is a pickpocket', 'that guy standing next to Betty' has a primary reference, but 'Betty' doesn't. Second, let's assume, untendentiously, that, given CH, the primary references made in the utterance of a that-clause determine an ordered pair of the form

$$\langle\langle x_1, \ldots, x_n\rangle, X^n\rangle$$

where X^n is the referent of the main verb of the that-clause and the members of the n-tuple are the referents of the other (explicit or implicit) expressions having primary references in the that-clause. Then, given CH, there is a function f such that

p is the referent of the that-clause which determines $\langle\langle x_1, \ldots, x_n\rangle, X^n\rangle$ iff $f(\langle\langle x_1, \ldots, x_n\rangle, X^n\rangle) = p$

If f effects a one-one mapping, mapping no two ordered pairs onto the same proposition, then the propositions to which that-clauses refer are structured, and they are unstructured if f effects a many-one mapping, mapping some distinct ordered pairs onto the same proposition. If that-

---

[1] I would've said 'syntax' instead of 'structure' if syntax always mirrored logical form.

clauses refer to structured propositions, then two that-clauses can refer to the same proposition only if their component expressions make the same primary references; but if that-clauses refer to unstructured propositions, then two that-clauses can refer to the same proposition even if their component expressions make different primary references.

I'll assume, with just about every other philosopher, that, given CH, we can pretty much dismiss unstructured propositions out of hand. This is because it would seem that the only way of individuating such propositions, given CH, is by their possible-worlds truth conditions, which has the counter-intuitive consequence that George W. Bush believes every mathematical truth just by virtue of believing that every dog is a dog. Robert Stalnaker has gone to some lengths to explain away the counter-intuitiveness of such consequences[2], but there is some question whether he has succeeded.

Virtually every proponent of the face-value theory takes believing to be a relation to structured propositions, and here the big contest, for all intents and purposes, is between the Russellian conception of structured propositions and the Fregean conception of them.

Russellian propositions are structured entities whose basic components, or propositional building blocks, are the objects and properties our beliefs are about. For example, a typical Russellian would hold that the references made in the that-clause in 'Alice believes that Bob loves Carol' determine the ordered pair

⟨⟨Bob, Carol⟩, the love relation⟩

which in turn determines, by the aforementioned one-one mapping, the Russellian proposition to which the that-clause refers. The basic components of the Russellian proposition are the same as the ones in the ordered pair that determines the proposition. In fact, Russellians typically *identify* their propositions with ordered pairs like the one displayed[3], although a more cautious theorist may want to say that while structured propositions stand in one-to-one correspondence with ordered pairs, the propositions themselves are *sui generis* abstract entities not identifiable with any set-theoretic constructions. Still, there can be no harm in *representing* Russellian propositions by the ordered pairs that determine them. For the Russellian, every proposition may be taken to be an ordered pair of the form $\langle\langle x_1, ..., x_n\rangle, R^n\rangle$, where $\langle x_1, ..., x_n\rangle$ is an n-ary sequence of things of any ontological category and R^n is an n-ary relation (properties are one-place relations). For example, the proposition that roses are red and violets are blue becomes

---

[2] See, e.g., Stalnaker 1984.
[3] See, e.g., Kaplan 1978, Salmon 1986, and Soames 1988.

⟨⟨the proposition that roses are red, the proposition that violets are blue⟩, the conjunction relation⟩

and the proposition that there are tigers becomes

⟨⟨the property of being a tiger⟩, the property of being instantiated⟩

(*vide* Soames 1988). For any possible world w, $\langle\langle x_1, ..., x_n\rangle, R^n\rangle$ is true in w iff $\langle x_1, ..., x_n\rangle$ instantiates R^n in w, false in w otherwise.[4]

The Fregean position is best thought of as a reaction to certain problems encountered by the Russellian position on its most straightforward construal.[5] Think of the Fregean as a theorist who began as a Russellian, encountered problems with her position, and then developed Fregeanism as the antidote to those problems. There were three problems that motivated the switch.

One was the problem of "empty names." According to the Russellian, the referent of 'George Eliot' in

(2) Ralph believes that George Eliot was a man

is George Eliot, and the proposition to which (2)'s that-clause refers is the "singular proposition" ⟨George Eliot, the property of being a man⟩. Suppose, however, that it transpires that there never was such a person as George Eliot, that *Middlemarch* and the other novels brandishing that name as the name of its author were in fact written by a committee. Then it would seem that the Russellian would have to say that (2)'s that-clause fails to refer to anything, since it contains a term that fails to refer to anything, and that therefore (2) would have no truth-evaluable content. At the same time, however, it seems intuitively that

(3) Ralph believes that George Eliot was a man, but in fact there was no such person; a committee wrote all the novels

might well be true if there were no such person as George Eliot. Yet it can't be that (3) but not (2) would be true should George Eliot not exist.

---

[4] Perhaps this is slightly tendentious. A possible Russellian position may refuse to assign the "singular proposition" that Pavarotti sings a truth-value in possible worlds in which Pavarotti does not exist. Nothing in the context of the present discussion turns on this.

[5] According to the Russellian, every that-clause refers to a Russellian proposition, even one whose contained sentence is an existential generalization. Hence, one doesn't give up being a Russellian by claiming, as Russell did, that the proposition to which a that-clause containing a name refers is a general proposition, or any other kind of Russellian proposition. But such a move is made only in response to the problems being raised; the initial Russellian position, which I'll usually simply refer to as the Russellian position, treats names and certain other singular terms as "directly referential."

A second problem manifested itself in examples like (4) and (5):

(4) Ralph rationally believes that George Eliot adored groundhogs and Mary Ann Evans didn't adore woodchucks
(5) Ralph rationally believes that George Eliot adored groundhogs and George Eliot didn't adore groundhogs

Intuitively, (5) can't be true, but (4) can easily be true. All it would take would be for Ralph not to be aware either that George Eliot was Mary Ann Evans or that the property of being a groundhog is the property of being a woodchuck. Yet, and this was the problem, the Russellian who also accepts the face-value theory must evidently hold that (4) and (5) can't differ in truth-value, since they differ only in their that-clauses and both that-clauses refer to the same Russellian proposition.

A third problem was similar to, but significantly different from, the second problem, and came to light with an example like

(6) Ralph believes that George Eliot adored groundhogs but doesn't believe that Mary Ann Evans adored woodchucks

It seems obvious that (6) might be true, notwithstanding that George Eliot = Mary Ann Evans and the property of being a groundhog = the property of being a woodchuck. But the Russellian must hold that both that-clauses in (6) refer to the same Russellian proposition, and that therefore, assuming the face-value theory, (6) is not only false, but necessarily false.

They were the problems for which the Fregean sought a circumventing theory; she thought she found it in Fregeanism. The Fregean holds that the referents expressions have in that-clauses are not the objects and properties our beliefs are about but are rather things she calls *concepts*, or *modes of presentation* (or *guises*, or *ways of thinking*), of the objects and properties our beliefs purport to be about. (Henceforth, I'll for the most part drop 'mode of presentation', which was Frege's own metaphor, and use just 'concept', even though this use of 'concept' differs from Frege's own technical use.) Fregean propositions, then, are structured entities whose basic building blocks are concepts of the objects and properties our beliefs purport to be about. As regards 'Alice believes that Bob loves Carol', this theorist holds that there are concepts c_b, c_c, and C_L of Bob, Carol, and the love relation, respectively, such that 'Bob' refers to c_b, 'Carol' to c_c, and 'loves' to C_L, and that, therefore, the Fregean proposition to which the that-clause refers may be represented by

$\langle\langle c_b, c_c \rangle, C_L \rangle$

Just as the Russellian may take $\langle\langle x_1, ..., x_n \rangle, R^n \rangle$ to represent the form of every proposition, so the Fregean may take it to be represented by $\langle\langle c_1, ...,$

$c_n \rangle$, $C^n \rangle$. For any possible world w, $\langle \langle c_1, \ldots, c_n \rangle, C^n \rangle$ is *true in w* iff $\exists x_1, \ldots, x_n, R^n(x_1, \ldots, x_n, R^n$ fall under $c_1, \ldots, c_n, C^n$ respectively in w & $\langle x_1, \ldots, x_n \rangle$ instantiates R^n in w), and *false in w* if $\exists x_1, \ldots, x_n, R^n(x_1, \ldots, x_n, R^n$ fall under $c_1, \ldots, c_n, C^n$ respectively in w & $\langle x_1, \ldots, x_n \rangle$ doesn't instantiate R^n in w). Fregeans are free to dispute whether $\langle \langle c_1, \ldots, c_n \rangle, C^n \rangle$ is false in w or neither true nor false in w if $\sim \exists x_1, \ldots, x_n, R^n(x_1, \ldots, x_n, R^n$ fall under $c_1, \ldots, c_n, C^n$ respectively in w).

For the Fregean, then, propositional building blocks are not the objects and properties our beliefs are about, but rather "concepts" of them. But what are they? Although the word 'concept' and its ilk – 'mode of presentation', 'way of thinking', 'guise', etc. – are chosen for the suggestiveness of their pretheoretic meanings, no one of those pretheoretic meanings does all the technical work the Fregean requires. There isn't much to be gleaned about concepts from the generic Fregean theory, and Fregeans can, and do, disagree among themselves about what exactly concepts are. What we do get from generic Fregeanism is that concepts are whatever propositional building blocks must be in order to avoid the problems that arise for Russellianism. As regards the problem of empty names, the Fregean can hold that in the counterfactual situation in which George Eliot never existed, we can account for the truth of 'Ralph believes that George Eliot was a man, but in fact there was no such person; a committee wrote all the novels' by claiming that 'George Eliot' there refers not to George Eliot but to a concept of her. As regards the problems of rational belief and disbelief, the Fregean can account for how 'Ralph rationally believes that George Eliot adored groundhogs and Mary Ann Evans did not adore woodchucks' and 'Ralph rationally believes that George Eliot adored groundhogs and George Eliot did not adore groundhogs' can take different truth-values by claiming either that the occurrences of 'George Eliot' and 'Mary Ann Evans' refer to distinct concepts (albeit of the same person) or that 'groundhog' and 'woodchuck' refer to distinct concepts (albeit of the same property), which means that in either case Ralph is not believing both a proposition and its negation, but rather a proposition and the negation of some other proposition. The Fregean handles the third problem for the Russellian in similar fashion. Nothing prevents 'Ralph believes that George Eliot adored groundhogs but doesn't believe that Mary Ann Evans adored woodchucks' from being true, since its two that-clauses refer to distinct propositions.

Although I can't go into the matter here, I believe there is no promising way of combining a Russellian conception of propositions with the face-value theory.[6] At the same time, Fregeanism is also not without problems. A couple

---

[6] Nathan Salmon (2001) seeks to resolve the problem of empty names for the Russellian by

of alleged problems are problems only if one underestimates the Fregean's resources, in particular the Fregean's ability to invoke object-dependent concepts, concepts that are individuated in terms of the things of which they are concepts and which wouldn't exist unless those things existed. For example, the Fregean can easily allow that the proposition to which a that-clause containing a name refers has possible-worlds truth conditions suitable to the name's functioning in the that-clause as a rigid designator if the Fregean holds that the referent of the name is an object-dependent concept.

Other problems for the claim that every that-clause refers to a Fregean proposition seem not to be based on misunderstanding or underestimation.

First, one should suspect there's something fishy about the Fregean's claim that occurrences of terms in that-clauses refer to concepts. The problem is most salient in cases where the Fregean is constrained to say that a term makes a contextually-determined reference to a concept. Consider first a typical case of contextually-determined reference. Walking down the street with a friend, you point to an unusually coifed man and say, 'That's how my father combed his hair', where your utterance of 'that' refers to a certain hair style. A large part, if not the whole part, of what makes it the case that your utterance of 'that' referred to that hair style is that your intention in uttering the demonstrative was to refer to that hair style. Now, intending is a propositional attitude like believing, and if the Fregean is right, then what she says about believing applies, *mutatis mutandis*, to intending. One thing this means is that the proposition that provides the content of an intention is a Fregean proposition, so that your referential intention in uttering 'that' must, if the Fregean is right, involve a proposition containing a concept, a mode of presentation, of the hair style to which you referred. This is not unintuitive for the case at hand. But now suppose you say to your friend,

(7) I met a high school English teacher who actually believes that George Eliot was a man!

According to the Fregean, in uttering 'George Eliot' you are referring to some concept, or mode of presentation, of Eliot, and in uttering 'man', you are referring to some concept, or mode of presentation, of the property of being a man. On any version of Fregeanism worth considering, these will be contextually-determined references, since it's implausible that 'George Eliot' and 'man' have associated with them particular concepts involved in every

---

arguing that even when a speaker intends her use of a name in a that-clause to refer to a bearer of the name, the occurrence of the name refers to a certain sort of *mythical entity* should it turn out that the intended bearer of the name doesn't exist. This makes it very hard to be an atheist.

literal use of those expressions. Very well, then you, *qua* utterer of (7), should be able to answer these questions:

– According to the Fregean, whenever you refer to anything, you do so under some particular concept of that thing. What then is the concept under which you're referring to a concept of George Eliot in uttering the token of 'George Eliot' in your utterance of (7), and what then is the concept under which you're referring to a concept of the property of being a man in uttering the token of 'man' in your utterance of (7)? Might the Fregean say that concepts, or modes of presentation, are the one sort of thing we can think about directly, in a way unmediated by a concept, or mode of presentation, of it? What would explain that strange anomaly?
– And what is the concept of George Eliot to which you are referring in uttering 'George Eliot' in (7), and what is the concept of the property of being a man you are there referring to in uttering 'man'? Since the referents in (7) of the tokens of 'George Eliot' and 'man' are determined by your referential intentions, one would think you should be able to say. After all, in every clear case of contextually-determined reference one has no trouble in saying to what one is referring. And if one cannot say, what, again, would explain this strange anomaly?

I dare say it's clear that no one can say what concepts are the referents of 'George Eliot' and 'man' in (7) or what the concepts are under which one is referring to those concepts, and no one can say why it is that one can't say.

Second, it's apt to seem that, whatever concepts turn out to be, there are cases where it's implausible to think anything that could be called reference to a concept is going on. An example of such a case is the belief report

Just about everyone who visits New York City believes that it's noisy,

which is both true and easily understood, even though, one would think, there is nothing to which the occurrence of 'it' might there refer that could, in any sense, constitute the way in which nearly every visitor to New York thinks of the city. Similarly, you may believe what I tell you when I say

Hilda believes that that guy is on his way there from Paris

but would you thereby know the concepts under which Hilda, who is not party to the utterance, is thinking about Jacques Derrida, the *x-is-on-the-way-to-y-from-z* relation, Bielefeld, and Paris?

Third, there is an argument against the Fregean theory – due to Adam Pautz, an NYU graduate student – which complements the first problem. The argument may be put thus:

(1) If the Fregean theory is true, then (a) the referent of 'Fido' in 'Ralph believes that Fido is a dog' is a concept of Fido.
(2) If (a), then the following inference is valid:
Ralph believes that Fido is a dog
∴ $\exists x(x$ is a concept & Ralph believes that x is a dog)
(3) But the inference is not valid; given the truth of the premise, the conclusion is also true only in the unlikely event that Ralph mistakes a concept for a dog.
(4) ∴ The Fregean theory is not true.

If this argument is unsound, it's most likely because premise (2) is false. The problem is that (2) is based on an evidently well-established logico-semantical principal: if o is the referent of t in the true sentence $S(t)$ [and – thinking of 'Giorgione was so-called because of his size' – t makes no other contribution to the truth-value of $S(t)$], then o makes true the existential generalization $\exists x S(x)$. But if (2) is false, one should be able to say why it constitutes an exception to the principle; one should be able, in other words, to make a good case for its being false. What is that case? It's no objection to the premise that the Fregean theory precludes substitution *salva veritate* of 'the concept of Fido' for 'Fido' in the that-clause, since when ensconced in the that-clause, 'the concept of Fido' would refer not to the concept of Fido but to the concept of the concept of Fido. The argument proceeds in full awareness of that aspect of Frege's theory and does not challenge it; the force of the argument turns only on the fact that, if the Fregean theory is right, a concept is *the referent* of 'Fido' in the that-clause. In this connection, it may be helpful to keep in mind that for the Fregean, the position of the that-clause is entirely referential and transparent, so that if the that-clause refers to the Fregean proposition $\langle c_f, C_d \rangle$, then from 'Ralph believes that Fido is a dog' we get, *salva veritate*, 'Ralph believes $\langle c_f, C_d \rangle$' (which does unproblematically entail '$\exists x(x$ is a concept & Ralph believes $\langle x, C_d \rangle)$').

Neither Russellianism (the claim that only Russellian propositions are the referents of that-clauses) nor Fregeanism (the claim that only Fregean propositions are the referents of that-clauses) is plausible. The distinction between Russellianism and Fregeanism is not an exhaustive classification of theories of structured propositions, but, for all that matters, it does yield an exhaustive and exclusive distinction concerning the referent of a given expression in a given that-clause: given what the generic Fregean means by 'concept', this referent will either be an object or property or else a concept of one. This in turn yields the following partitioning of theories of structured propositions, which is exhaustive as regards structured propositions:

– The referent of a that-clause is always/sometimes a Russellian proposition.

- The referent of a that-clause is always/sometimes a Fregean proposition.
- The referent of a that-clause is sometimes a Fressellian proposition (if I may), such as the proposition represented by

$$\langle\langle \text{Bob}, c_c\rangle, C_L\rangle,$$

which could result from the referent of 'Bob' in 'Alice believes that Bob loves Carol' being Bob, while the other terms have Fregean referents.[7]

I'll take it to be obvious on reflection that none of these positions is plausible if neither Russellianism nor Fregeanism is plausible for the reasons given.

We seem to be in the following position: we can't combine the face-value theory of belief reports with the compositionality hypothesis because no account of the nature of propositions consistent with that combination is plausible. What should we do next – start over, hoping to find a misstep in the steps that brought us to this point, question the face-value theory, or question CH? It would be unsatisfying to try to cook up an account of propositions to satisfy what we might now recognize to be requirements imposed by the face-value theory, but I think there may be an independently plausible account of propositions that sustains the face-value theory's plausibility.

3. Pleonastic Propositions

Pleonastic entities are entities that enter our conceptual schemes via what I call *something-from-nothing transformations*. Such a transformation is a valid inference from a statement involving no reference to a thing of a certain kind to a statement that does involve reference to a thing of that kind. It's because the statement that does involve the reference is often a pleonastic equivalent of the statement from which it's inferred that I call the entities in question "pleonastic" entities. Properties and propositions are pleonastic entities; from

   Fido is a dog,

whose only singular term is 'Fido', we may infer two pleonastic equivalents:

   Fido has the property of being a dog,

which contains the new singular term 'the property of being a dog', whose referent is the property of being a dog, and

   That Fido is a dog is true

---

[7] Cf. Horwich 1998, p. 122.

(more colloquially, 'It's true that Fido is a dog'), which contains the new singular term 'that Fido is a dog', whose referent is the proposition that Fido is a dog. What makes these something-from-nothing transformations valid is that their corresponding conditionals are *conceptual truths*. The concept of a property is such that grasp of it enables one to know *a priori* the necessary truth that if Fido is a dog, then Fido has the property of being a dog, and grasp of the concept of a proposition – i.e., grasp of the concept that goes with the use of that-clauses – enables one to know *a priori* the necessary truth that if Fido is a dog, then that Fido is a dog is true.

Some philosophers doubt there can ever be an F such that the mere concept of an F can secure that a truth whose intrinsic specification involves no mention of an F can entail the existence of an F. Thus Hartry Field:

> An investigation of conceptual linkages can reveal conditions that things must satisfy if they are to fall under our concepts; but it can't yield that there are things that satisfy those concepts (as Kant pointed out in his critique of the ontological argument for the existence of God). (Field 1989, p. 5)

For consider the concept of a *wishdate*, which I hereby stipulatively introduce thus:

> x is a *wishdate* $=_{df}$ x is a person whose existence supervenes on someone's wishing for a date, every such wish bringing into existence a person to date

Field's point implies that while this is a perfectly kosher definition, it doesn't result in its being true that there are any wishdates, no matter who wishes for a date. All that follows from the stipulative definition of a wishdate is that *if* (*per impossibile*) wishdates exist, *then* their existence supervenes on the mere wish for a date.

But there is a crucial difference between the concept of a wishdate and the concept of a proposition (or of any other kind of pleonastic entity, although from now on my focus will be just on propositions). To a first approximation, the difference is that:

> There are numerous theories T such that when we add the concept of a wishdate to T, the resulting theory is *not* a *conservative extension* of T. But if we add the concept of a proposition to *any* theory T, the resulting theory *is* a conservative extension of T.

A theory T' is a *conservative extension* of a theory T provided that T' includes T and nothing statable in the vocabulary of T is entailed by T' but not by T. The notion of "adding a concept" is vague; it should be taken to mean that the canonical expression for the new concept has its full meaning when introduced, and that as much of that meaning as can be made explicit via defining conditions is made explicit, especially whatever existence-entailing something-from-nothing conditionals are partly definitive of the concept.

Suppose T is a fairly rich true physical theory that doesn't employ the concept of a wishdate or the concept of a proposition, but does entail that someone wished for a date. Adding the concept of a wishdate to T will entail that there exists a person – the person brought into existence by the wish for a date – whose existence wasn't recognized in T but was statable in the vocabulary of T. The resulting theory is therefore clearly not a conservative extension of T. Indeed, should the new person exist, he or she would be a substantial physical object that would enormously disturb the preexisting causal order. But when we add the concept of a proposition to T, what can we get that we couldn't get from T alone? If T entails that Lester wished for a date, then the new theory entails that the proposition that Lester wished for a date is true, but we can assert nothing new that can be said in the language of T. Adding propositions to one's ontology does nothing to disturb the preexisting causal order. That is why adding the concept of a proposition to T yields a conservative extension of T.

The first shot needs refinement; as it stands it's too strong to account for what makes the truths expressed by instances of 'If S, then it's true that S' conceptual truths. This is because there are ways of adding the concept of a proposition to a theory and getting a theory that isn't a conservative extension of the original theory. For example:

- The new theory, but not the original theory, may entail that more than such-and-such many things exist, which was statable in the original theory.
- The original theory may assert that if there are abstract entities, then it will snow in Miami in August. When we add the concept of a proposition to that theory, the resulting theory will entail that it will snow in Miami in August, which, we may assume, was assertible but unasserted in the original theory.
- The original theory may assert that there are no abstract entities. When we add the concept of a proposition to that theory, we get an inconsistent theory from which everything follows.

The qualification these examples motivate is that the new theory must be a conservative extension not of the original theory, T, but of the theory obtained from T by restricting the latter's quantifiers to things in the recognized ontology of T. A thing is in the "recognized ontology" of T provided it falls under a sortal category that imposes criteria of individuation – *dog, electron, restaurant*, but not, say, *thing* or *created thing* – and that

T claims to be instantiated. This is vague, but I trust it's the notion whose precisification I need, and that it will serve present purposes well enough.[8]

It enables me to put together a definition that will capture what I want from the notion of a pleonastic entity. The definition should be regarded as stipulative, substantive claims coming in the form of claims about what kinds of things are pleonastic entities. For now, the definition needs only to get right the distinction between wishdates and propositions. I start with some preliminary definitions.

> Where '$\Rightarrow$' expresses metaphysical entailment, '$S \Rightarrow \exists x Fx$' is a *something-from-nothing F-entailment claim* iff (i) its antecedent is metaphysically possible but doesn't *logically* entail either its consequent or any statement of the form '$\exists x(x = a)$', where 'a' refers to an F, and (ii) the concept of an F is such that if there are Fs, then $S \Rightarrow \exists x Fx$. (I'll say that the concept of an F "implies" a something-from-nothing F-entailment claim if it satisfies (ii).)
>
> A *pleonastic entity* is an entity that falls under a *pleonastic concept*; and a pleonastic concept is the concept of an F which implies *true* something-from-nothing F-entailment claims.
>
> For any theory T, T^τ is the theory obtained from T by restricting T's quantifiers to things in the recognized ontology of T.

I now offer the following conservative-extension criterion for being a pleonastic concept.

> (CE) The concept of an F implies true something-from-nothing F-entailment claims – and is therefore a *pleonastic concept* – iff (i) it implies something-from-nothing F-entailment claims, and (ii) for any theory T, the theory obtained by adding the concept of an F to T^τ is a conservative extension of T^τ.[9]

We can see how CE handles the problems for the first shot in the following way.

---

[8] The idea of accommodating certain difficulties for the conservative extension test in this way derives from Hartry Field 1980, p. 11. The idea is also used by Bob Hale and Crispin Wright (2000) in their discussion of conservativeness in connection with Hume's Principle. Their way of putting the qualification is that the extending theory "must not introduce fresh commitments which (i) are expressible in the language as it was prior to the introduction of its [additional material] and which (ii) concern the previously recognized ontology of concepts, objects, and functions, etc., whatever in detail they may be" (302). I'm also indebted to Field for getting me to see that the qualification I proposed in a previous draft had more in it than I needed.

[9] CE supercedes the criterion proposed in Schiffer 2001.

Let T be a theory that doesn't use the concept of a proposition. For simplicity, we may suppose that "physical objects" comprise T's recognized ontology (and never mind that *physical object* isn't a sortal concept in the intended sense), and let 'Px' abbreviate 'x is a physical object'. Thus, if T contains

$$\forall x Gx$$

then T^τ contains

$$\forall x(Px \rightarrow Gx)$$

And if T contains

$$\exists x Gx$$

then T^τ contains

$$\exists x(Px \ \& \ Gx)$$

Now, the first problem was that the theory obtained by adding the concept of a proposition to T may entail that more than such-and-such many things exist, when this isn't entailed by T. But since the new theory doesn't entail that more than such-and-such many *physical* things exist, it's a conservative extension of T^τ, whose claims about how many things exist are limited to claims about how many *physical* things exist.

The second problem for the first shot was that T may assert that if there are abstract entities, then it will snow in Miami in August. But T^τ merely says that if any physical objects are abstract objects, then it will snow in Miami in August, and thus nothing statable but unstated in T^τ is forthcoming when we add the concept of a proposition to T^τ.

The third problem was that T may assert that there are no abstract entities. But since T^τ merely asserts that nothing exists that is both a physical object and an abstract entity, there is again no problem for CE.

The concept of a proposition, I submit, satisfies CE and is thereby a pleonastic concept, that of a wishdate isn't. We over-generalize Kant's insight when we lump concepts that satisfy CE with the concept of a wishdate and the concept of God. Propositions are mere shadows of the sentences yielding them in something-from-nothing transformations; they come softly into existence, without disturbing the preexisting causal order in any way. That is why claims that they exist may be conservatively added to the truths we had before those claims were added.[10]

---

[10] The metaphor of propositions as shadows of sentences is adapted from David Armstrong's (1989) metaphor of properties as shadows of predicates.

Propositions are pleonastic entities that enter our conceptual scheme via something-from-nothing transformations, but the language game we play with that-clauses is not limited to something-from-nothing transformations, or even to what is indirectly implied by them. Crucially, there is also the use of that-clauses in ascriptions of speech acts and psychological states like belief. These practices presuppose the validity (subject to certain qualifications[11]) of the something-from-nothing transformation that yields the familiar truth schema for propositions – viz.,

The proposition that S is true iff S

– but the role of that-clauses in propositional-attitude discourse isn't deducible from the something-from-nothing practice and is essential to completing the account of pleonastic propositions. What we're about to see is of signal importance for the theory of propositional attitudes – namely, that, in certain crucial respects, the relation between that-clauses and the propositions to which they refer is importantly different from the usual relation between singular terms and their referents.

Assume that the face-value theory is correct and that, therefore, utterances of the form 'A believes that S' share the form $R(a, b)$ with other sentences containing a two-place relational predicate flanked by two argument singular terms, such as 'She loves him' and 'Austria is next to Germany'. Trivially, if in an utterance of

(9) t_1 R s t_2

the uttered token of t_1, $ô_1$, refers to a and the uttered token of t_2, $ô_2$, refers to b (and assuming that 'R' expresses the R relation), then the utterance will be true just in case a R s b. Thus, the referent of $ô_2$ will in this logical sense help "determine" the truth condition for the utterance. This much holds for every utterance of form (9), including belief reports. It's after this commonality that important differences take over. I'll list a few things that normally hold of utterances of form (9) when the term in the t_2 slot is other than a that-clause which, as we'll presently see, don't hold when the term is a that-clause in a belief report.

a. Typically, in order to evaluate an utterance of form (9), we must first identify the referent of $ô_1$ and the referent of $ô_2$, and then determine whether the former stands in the R relation to the latter. Consequently, the referent of $ô_2$, once itself determined, partially determines the criteria for evaluating

---

[11] I allude to the semantic paradoxes. In Schiffer (forthcoming) I argue that the paradoxes actually support the pleonastic construal of propositions.

the statement made by the utterance of (9): we fix the referent of $ô_2$, and thereby partially fix the criteria for truth-evaluating the utterance of (9). What we absolutely do *not* do is *first* fix the criteria for evaluating the utterance of (9) and *then* use that to fix the referent of $ô_2$. This is an obvious and familiar point, but it's important to me that it be made vivid. To this end, consider the pair of statements

(10a) Henri admires Picasso

(10b) Henri admires Braque

In order to evaluate the utterance of (10a), we must first identify the referents of 'Henri' and 'Picasso'; likewise, *mutatis mutandis*, for (10b). It would be laughable to suppose we *first* fix the criteria of evaluation and *then* use those criteria to determine the referents. We evaluate the statements made in (10a,b) by glomming onto the referents of 'Henri', 'Picasso', and 'Braque' and then determining whether the first stands in the admire relation to the other two. This is brought home by the absurdity of supposing that we know that Picasso ≠ Braque because we know that the statements made in (10a) and (10b) may differ in truth-value. Just the opposite, of course: we know that the two statements may differ in truth-value *because we know that Picasso ≠ Braque*.

b. If $ô_2$ in the utterance of (9) refers to b, there will be a condition Cxy such that (i) $ô_2$ refers to b by virtue of $\langle ô_2, b \rangle$ satisfying Cxy and (ii) the condition Cxy is independent of both (9) and the fact that its utterance has the truth condition it has: satisfaction of Cxy entails nothing *per se* about those things, and its specification involves no mention of them. For example, the occurrence of 'Picasso' in (10a) refers to Picasso by virtue of a certain conventional practice of referring to Picasso by the name 'Picasso', and if in uttering 'She fed that pigeon' my utterance of 'that pigeon' refers to a certain pigeon, then that is by virtue of the fact that the pigeon was the contextually salient pigeon to which I intended to refer in uttering 'that pigeon'.

c. If $ô_2$ is a semantically complex singular term, then the referent of $ô_2$ is determined by its structure and the referents – broadly construed so as to include the extensions of predicates, functors, and so on – of its component expressions.

d. A consequence – indeed, a precondition – of (a) is that in the normal case the identity and individuation of the referent of $ô_2$ owes nothing to the criteria of evaluation it helps to determine. It's because Picasso and Braque each has an identity and individuation that is entirely independent of the criteria for evaluating the statements about them that we immediately see the absurdity of supposing that we know that Picasso ≠ Braque because we know that the statements made in (10a) and (10b) may differ in truth-value.

That-clause reference, as I suggested, differs with respect to each of (a)–(d).

a′. As we just observed in (a), when t_2 in an utterance of (9) is not a that-clause, we first fix the referent of the token of t_2, $ô_2$, and then use that to help fix the criteria for evaluating the utterance of (9), as illustrated in the examples (10a) and (10b). Matters are just the opposite when we turn to that-clauses and their referents. In a belief report, we *first* have contextually-determined criteria of evaluation, and *then* those criteria determine the proposition to which the that-clause refers. These criteria of evaluation are in part determined by contextual factors pertaining to the communicative interests of speakers and their audiences, even after disambiguation and obvious reference-fixing has taken place.[12] It should be fairly uncontentious that the referent of a that-clause is nearly always contextually determined. Two literal utterances of

(11) Ralph believes that George Eliot was a woman

may have different truth-values, owing to the fact that in one conversational context but not the other the truth of the utterance requires thinking of George Eliot as a famous author. If, as I am defeasibly assuming, the face-value theory is correct, then the two utterances of 'that George Eliot was a woman' refer to different propositions – albeit, no doubt, to propositions with the same possible-worlds truth condition: each is true in a possible world w just in case George Eliot is a woman in w. But I'm saying considerably more than that the referent of a that-clause is contextually determined; I'm also saying something about the way that referent is determined. If we were evaluating an utterance of 'Ralph admires her' we would first determine the referent of 'her' and that would in turn complete the determination of the criteria for evaluating the statement. In evaluating the statement made in the utterance of (11), however, we first implicitly fix the criteria for evaluating the statement, and that is what fixes the referent of the that-clause. This isn't to deny that the semantic properties of expressions in a that-clause are not crucial to the determination of the that-clause's reference; in order to fix the criteria of evaluation for the utterances of (11) we must first know to whom the utterances of 'George Eliot' refer. My point is that these semantic properties on their own don't determine the referents of that-clauses; rather, those semantic properties help to determine the criteria of evaluation for belief reports, which criteria in turn fix the referents of that-clauses.

---

[12] The point of the "obvious" qualification will soon be apparent.

In glossing (a), I illustrated the left-to-right direction of

fixing the referent of $ô_2$ $\rightarrow$ determining the criteria of evaluation

for the normal case when $ô_2$ is not a that-clause by the absurdity, as regards (10a,b), of supposing that we know that Picasso ≠ Braque because we know that (10a) and (10b) can differ in truth-value. When we compare (10a,b) with the following two pairs of utterances, we see how the following two pairs nicely illustrate the right-to-left direction of

fixing the referent of $ô_2$ $\leftarrow$ determining the criteria of evaluation

when $ô_2$ is a that-clause in a belief report:

(13a) Nobody doubts that whoever believes that all ophthalmologists are ophthalmologists believes that all ophthalmologists are ophthalmologists
(13b) Nobody doubts that whoever believes that all ophthalmologists are ophthalmologists believes that all ophthalmologists are eye doctors[13]
(14a) Lois believes that Superman flies
(14b) Lois believes that Clark Kent flies

We know that the two members of all three pairs – (10a,b), (13a,b) and (14a,b) – may well differ in truth-value, but there is a very important difference between (10a,b), on the one hand, and, on the other hand, (13a,b) and (14a,b). As already noted, it's absurd to suppose we know that Picasso ≠ Braque because we know that (10a) and (10b) may differ in truth-value; rather, we know that (10a) and (10b) may differ in truth-value *because* we know that Picasso ≠ Braque. But just the opposite obtains as regards the other two pairs. We don't know that (13a) and (13b) may differ in truth-value because we know that the proposition that whoever believes that all ophthalmologists are ophthalmologists believes that all ophthalmologists are ophthalmologists ≠ the proposition that whoever believes that all ophthalmologists are ophthalmologists believes that all ophthalmologists are eye doctors; rather, we know that the proposition that whoever believes that all ophthalmologists are ophthalmologists believes that all ophthalmologists are ophthalmologists ≠ the proposition that whoever believes that all ophthalmologists are ophthalmologists believes that all ophthalmologists are eye doctors *because we know (13a) and (13b) may differ in truth-value*. Likewise for (14a) and (14b): we first know that they may differ in truth-value, and on this basis we know that the proposition that Superman flies ≠ the proposition that Clark Kent flies.

---

[13] The examples, but not the use to which they're put, are borrowed from Mates 1952.

b′. When t_2 is not a that-clause, there is associated with it a condition Cxy that is independent of the truth condition and criteria of evaluation for the utterance of (9) and which determines the referent of the utterance of t_2. There is no such condition when t_2 is a that-clause. This is because the truth conditions for the utterance fix the referent, not the other way around, as is usually the case. There is the utterance, and the contextually-determined criteria for evaluating the utterance, which fixes the truth conditions of the utterance, and therewith the proposition to which the that-clause refers.

c′. When $ô_2$ is a semantically complex term other than a that-clause, its referent is determined by its structure and the referents of its component expressions. Consequently, in the normal case one fixes the referent of $ô_2$ by first fixing the referents of its component expressions. It follows from (a′) that we don't fix the referent of a that-clause by first fixing the referents of its component expressions; what fixes the referent of the that-clause are the criteria for truth-evaluating the belief report. The fact that we don't fix the referent of a that-clause by way of fixing the referents of its component expressions doesn't preclude the referent of a that-clause from being a function of the referents of its component expressions. It may be that the criteria of evaluation that determine the proposition to which the that-clause refers also determine, *pari passu*, entities suitable to play the role of Fregean concepts *qua* components of those propositions, and thereby suitable to be the referents of expressions in that-clauses, so that, once those referents are in place, we can say that the referent of the that-clause is a function of the referents of its component expressions. It's important, however, to see that the criteria of evaluation don't *have* to determine referents for a that-clause's component expressions in order to determine a referent for the that-clause, for the criteria of evaluation already provide the way of determining the referent of $ô_2$ that would normally be provided by the referents of $ô_2$'s component expressions.

Still, a stronger point can be made: the contextually-determined criteria of evaluation don't determine anything adequate to be propositional building blocks, the referents of expressions in that-clauses. Certainly they don't determine anything with an identity and individuation that's independent of the propositions they're supposed to build. If pleonastic propositions have components – that is to say, if they're Fregean propositions – then the pleonastic concepts composing pleonastic propositions would have to be abstractions from the propositions containing them, with no identity of their own apart from those propositions. They would perforce be individuated in terms of the propositions containing them and would be tantamount to equivalence classes of propositions: the concept to which an expression in a that-clause refers would, for all intents and purposes, be *the class of propositions equivalent in such-and-such respect to the proposition to which the that-clause refers*. For example, the that-clause in a particular utterance of 'Ralph believes that George Eliot was a man' may refer to a proposition that, intuitively speaking, requires thinking of George Eliot as a famous author, along with various other George Eliot related things not so easily articulated, and we may trivially think of the token of 'George Eliot' as associated with a certain equivalence class of propositions: the class of propositions equivalent to the one in question with respect to how they require thinking of George Eliot. To suppose that such equivalence classes, determined in the way they are determined, might be construed as the referents of expressions in that-clauses would be to render vacuous the idea that the referent of a complex expression is determined by the referents of its parts. If someone proposes that the referent of a that-clause isn't determined by the referents of its constituent expressions, we hardly refute her claim by pointing out that we can trivially get the same referent by associating with each part of the that-clause a certain equivalence class of propositions. I conclude, then, that when $ô_2$ is a that-clause, then we can't construe its referent as determined by its structure and the referents of its component expressions.

d'. When $ô_2$ is other than a that-clause, its referent enjoys criteria of individuation that are independent of the criteria of evaluation which that referent helps to determine. Think of Picasso and Braque. When, however, $ô_2$ is a that-clause in a belief report, the criteria of individuation for the proposition to which the that-clause refers depend on the criteria of evaluation. More specifically, the propositions we believe enjoy no more intrinsic conditions of individuation than those provided by their truth conditions and the requirements for believing those propositions that are determined by the criteria for truth-evaluating belief reports in which reference is made to those propositions. This doesn't mean that there must be believers in order for there to be propositions; it means the conditions that individuate propositions in the range of the belief relation can be individuated only with respect to what it would take to believe them. This is a consequence of the points made in (c'), since it's the only option for the identity and individuation of propositions if they're not structured entities whose basic components themselves have an identity and individuation that is independent of the propositions they build.

4. Pleonastic Propositions and the Face-Value Theory

The face-value theory of sentences of the form 'A believes that S' holds that these sentences say, as it were, that A believes the proposition that S. If the face-value theory is to be plausible, it must allow us to recognize the truth of a sentence such as 'Ralph believes that George Eliot adored groundhogs but not that Mary Ann Evans adored woodchucks'. This rules out both Stalnakerian, unstructured propositions, which are individuated by their possible-worlds truth conditions, and Russellian propositions, which are individuated by the objects and properties they're about. Fregean propositions are, literally, tailor-made for the face-value theory, but, alas, they may not be well enough made to help anyone. Both Russellian and Fregean propositions are structured entities whose ultimate components are propositional building blocks, the Russellian and the Fregean disagreeing about the nature of those blocks. The need for such structured entities was thought to be motivated, in part, by the compositionality hypothesis, CH, which holds that the referent of a that-clause token is determined by its structure and the references made in its utterance. If CH is rejected, then the face-value theory can look to unstructured but fine-grained propositions, which is what pleonastic propositions are. Whatever evidence there is for pleonastic propositions is evidence against CH. It behooves us, therefore, to ask what was supposed to motivate CH in the first place. The most immediate answer is that it was thought to be needed to account for how a semantically complex singular can have its reference; but we've seen that it's not needed for that if that-clauses refer to pleonastic propositions, for then the referent of a that-clause token is determined by the criteria for evaluating the belief report in which the token occurs. Questions, some with a hint of potential problems, remain, but I find (not for the first time) that I've exhausted my allotted number of pages before I've exhausted my subject. A more complete treatment is given in Schiffer (forthcoming).

References

Armstrong, D.: *Universals: An Opinionated Introduction*, Westview Press, 1989.
Field, H.: *Science without Numbers*, Princeton University Press, 1980.
Hale, B., Wright, C.: Implicit Definition and the A Priori. In: *New Essays on the A Priori*, ed. by P. Boghossian and C. Peacocke, Oxford University Press, 2000.
Horwich, P.: *Meaning*, Oxford University Press, 1998.
Kaplan, D.: Dthat. In: *Syntax and Semantics 9: Pragmatics*, ed. by P. Cole, Academic Press, 1978.

Mates, B.: Synonymity. In: *Semantic and the Philosophy of Language*, ed. by L. Linsky, University of Illinois Press, 1952.
Salmon, N.: *Frege's Puzzle*, MIT Press, 1986.
Salmon, N.: Mythical Objects. In: *Essays on Meaning & Truth*, ed. by J. Campbell, M. O'Rourke, and D. Shier, Seven Bridges Press, 2001.
Schiffer, S.: *The Things We Mean*, Oxford University Press, forthcoming.
Schiffer, S.: Meanings. In: *Essays on Meaning & Truth*, ed. by J. Campbell, M. O'Rourke, and D. Shier, Seven Bridges Press, 2001.
Soames, S.: Semantics and Semantic Competence. In: *Cognition and Representation*, ed. by S. Schiffer and S. Steele, Westview Press, 1988.
Stalnaker, R.: *Inquiry*, MIT Press, 1984.

Joëlle Proust

Are Empirical Arguments Acceptable in Philosophical Analyses of the Mind?

Is it appropriate for philosophy to borrow from science theoretical concepts or to invoke experimental evidence in order to do its explanatory work? One central argument for a positive answer is that rational explanation in general has a holistic character. Such holism applies both to the inferential procedures taken to be valid and to the beliefs taken to be true. Discussions of the notion of reflective equilibrium have developed during the last decades these two central themes. 1) The principle of *reflective equilibrium* as described by Nelson Goodman (Goodman 1965) shows that the process through which our forms of inference are justified is virtuously circular: particular deductive inferences are justified by valid general rules that are themselves justified by the fact that they allow valid inferences. 2) What holds for inference can be generalized to the whole explanatory process. John Rawls (1971) offered a wider picture of reflective equilibrium, including not only the inferential part of the justificatory process, but the substantial part as well: our inferences constrain and are constrained by all the semantic, epistemological, metaphysical and psychological knowledge available. What holds for justification in general seems to hold *a fortiori* for philosophical arguments in epistemology, independently of their authors' specific claims and doctrines.

Other arguments however have been offered in favour of the autonomy of philosophical explanations relative to science. The main one is that philosophical analyses in general should be *a priori*, i.e. established independently of empirical investigation. The notion of a prioricity here at work is aimed at reflecting the particular stance that philosophy should adopt towards experience: not as something simply given, which might be offered an empirical description, but as a something to be known and justified in a rational discourse, involving a "logical space of reasons" rather than "a logical space of nature".[1]

---

[1] The latter expression is meant by McDowell (1994) to offer a symmetrical phrase to Sellars' "logical space of reasons".

There is clearly a tension between these two approaches of rationality, a tension that may be eased with a more thorough discussion of the kind of empiricism to be endorsed, as can be found in the recent literature. Let us assume for now that the question whether empirical considerations may be used in general philosophy is settled one way or another; the question of their use in the *philosophy of mind* would still remain unsolved. For even if one accepts that experts are in better position to know what the concepts we borrow from them mean, one may resist deferring to experts when it comes to one's own mental experience. In the theory of collective rationality sketched above, experts are a central ingredient in the justification of most of our judgements. For a state of reflexive equilibrium can only be reached if everyone recognizes that *mathesis universalis* is a socially distributed matter. To be able to reach knowledge, one needs to justify one's beliefs against the backdrop of a coherent set of beliefs as available in any potentially relevant domain of thought and inquiry. Obviously a social division of labour is needed here: an individual thinker has to defer to the experts of specialized domains both for offering theoretically justified definitions as well as for providing lawful regularities and testable explanations. Indeed, as Putnam (1975) suggested, speakers do defer to experts to provide the precise definitions of terms they use. Scientific research itself works in part on the assumption that the terms now used may be later redefined as part of the explanation which the researchers are presently striving to provide.[2]

Now although the basic structure of explanation should be the same in all the parts of philosophy, the philosophy of mind offers an additional source of difficulty. A single "unsophisticated" individual, with no particular scientific training in theoretical psychology and sociology, seems indeed entitled to justify thoughts about herself. She is thus in a position to explain her own conduct, to plan and make rational decisions even though she is lacking any theoretical knowledge about psychological and sociological facts. More important, still, she can do so even though she does not know that such a theoretical knowledge is available at all. It seems that the principle of rejecting such an unsophisticated individual from the realm of rational agents would introduce a dangerous segregation among thinkers, and would also put intolerable constraints on successful communication between speakers of different cultures.

It would also invite scepticism about self-knowledge. For once the instability of the knowledge presently available in the neurosciences is recognized, a thinker, however "sophisticated" she may be, would also have to accept a principled deference in time. A rational thinker would thus have

---

[2] See also Rey (1997).

to accept that she may not be able to justify presently her own mental concept use, or the way she derives her decisions from her past experiences. There is a new tension here, that does not concern the possible gap between experience as *given* (in the scientific scheme) and experience as *justified* (in the philosophical scheme), but rather between *everyday understanding of oneself* and *theoretical explanations about the self*. This tension will be the focus of the present article.

Two contrasting positions, expressed by Jennifer Hornsby and Georges Rey, will help us sketch the two opposing positions.

Jennifer Hornsby:
"We ought not to assume at the outset that the basis of our everyday understanding of one another is susceptible of correction and refinement by experts in some specialist field where empirical considerations of some non-commonsensical kind can be brought to bear". (1997, 3-4)

Georges Rey:
"Surely it is obvious 'at the outset' with regard to any explanatorily interesting project that people who have studied the phenomena more systematically than is ordinarily possible will be in a position to correct and refine the basis of our ordinary thought." (2001)

Both authors are concerned here with the question how autonomous philosophical reasoning about the mind should be from a scientific view of the world – including theoretical psychology and the neurosciences. Or, in other words, they are discussing how close and exclusive is the connection of a philosophical approach of intention, action and self-understanding with a commonsense, folk-psychological approach of the mental. This question has been addressed mostly by authors who fight or defend naturalism. My first section however will attempt to show that the question is not to be simply identified with a general stance on the naturalistic program. It is not to be assimilated with the question of how philosophy generally relates to science, although clearly this general problem has consequences on the present discussion. It has to do with the acceptability of empirical arguments in the philosophy of mind, which is clearly an epistemological topic, dealing with justification of claims of a certain kind. I will then turn to the philosophical claims that are generally brought to the fore to justify the autonomy thesis relative to the philosophy of mind. I will discuss how independent these claims can be, with their respective bearing on the autonomy thesis, and will discuss their validity.

1. Empirical considerations and the naturalistic program

To be clearer about the relation of our present question with a general position on the naturalistic program, we need to determine at the outset what is understood under this term. Dewey defined "naturalism" (in Baldwin's *Dictionary of philosophy and psychology*) as a methodological project for philosophy: it is "the theory that the whole of the universe or of experience may be accounted for *by a method like that of the physical sciences,* and with recourse only to the current conceptions of physical and natural science; more specifically, that mental and moral processes may be reduced to the terms or categories of the natural sciences".

Now all the work in this definition is done by the notion of "a method like that of the physical sciences". How can a philosophical argument *resemble* one in the physical sciences? By being couched in causal terms, whose relata do not differ from the entities usually recognized in the natural sciences – in particular in a non-normative way? But if such was the case, a philosophical argument would become indistinguishable from a scientific argument, and therefore philosophy would dissolve into specific scientific inquiries.

The notion of likeness may however be understood in a methodologically less constraining way, meaning that a naturalistic approach rejects "spiritual or transcendental arguments" in the terms of Dewey. In this sense, naturalism is a metaphysical claim, according to which only material entities matter causally; naturalism boils down to materialism, i.e. the monist claim that the substance supporting causal relations in nature is one and the same in all the diverse phenomena, whether mental or physical.

It is generally believed that most modern naturalistic philosophers belong to the methodological rather than to the metaphysical kind of materialism.[3] In other words, most of them do not have as a goal to show that the mind can be reduced to a material or a physical system, in the strong sense that mental regularities should be explained entirely in non-mental terms. They are content with a view in which although mental states are identical with physical states, mental laws cannot be directly expressed at a physical-causal level.

But we will not examine any longer the various positions that are currently debated on the question of which kind of physicalism can be found acceptable to account for the mental causal power. For the question we are dealing with *cuts across* specific views one may have towards the metaphysics of the mind. The difficulty noted above has to do with how justified someone is to refer to one's mental states in one's own terms, irrespective of the teachings of

---

[3] See for ex. Gary Hatfield's *The Natural and the Normative*, (17).

science on the metaphysics of the mental. The specific way in which a theory of the mental is dealing with physicalism is irrelevant to it. A second reason why naturalistic considerations are of no help is that while naturalism offers a *general* approach in which philosophy is not insulated from the sciences, but on a par with them, – depending on a common lore of knowledge and rational constraints –, it does not offer any *specific* recommendation on how philosophy is able to play its own score within the general symphony of the sciences. The methodological recommendation of being attuned to a scientific view of the world does not bring with it a specific set of rules for using science, or mimicking scientific method. Surely it won't do to simply clothe one's own reflections in a scientific garb, as Hume presenting his study of the mind under Newton's authority. Naturalism does not recommend that philosophy becomes a kind of loose registration of facts: surely naturalism does not invite philosophers to making scientific results accessible to the many. A third reason is that the very idea of following a naturalistic method may not be the relevant kind of question that should be addressed in *every* philosophical inquiry. Using or not empirical arguments might be decided differently according to the specific subject matter one deals with. For example, someone studying the philosophy of biology might want to apply, say, the concept of function, in a way compatible with the facts stated in contemporary evolution theory and genetics; whereas someone studying moral value or formal demonstration might be justified, at least to a certain extent, in ignoring psychological and sociological facts about morality or reasoning. The deep reason is that natural science does not cover all there is to think about, even in a world exhaustively composed of matter.

A way of generalizing the three arguments above is to claim that the question of the validity of empirical considerations is also raised within non-naturalistic frameworks. Even if one defends the view that thought is inherently normative and irreducible to scientific description, one will need to appeal to "normative intuitions", concerning what seems right or wrong to individual subjects, and even to "normative facts", as Kant does when reflecting on the conditions of possibility of true knowledge as ascertained in the various existing sciences. Here again, one needs to establish how a subject would be in a position to reach rational evaluations about her own beliefs and plans if she does not master the kind of normative facts and intuitions that are best exemplified in the mature sciences.

For all these reasons, I will detach the question of the acceptability of empirical arguments in the philosophy of mind, from the stance one should take on naturalism as a view on the architecture of knowledge.

2. The autonomy of philosophy in the philosophy of mind.

The autonomy of philosophy, in this context, is the claim that an appropriate answer to the central questions of the philosophy of mind should be delivered by philosophical investigation and argument alone, without relying on data or arguments from the empirical sciences. More specifically, the view is that, unlike natural kind concepts, such as chemical elements or pathological syndromes, whose definitions have to be established by scientific investigations, mental concepts are essentially defined through their ordinary usage, i.e. through common-sense psychology. Of course, presented in this way, the view is expressed in a question-begging way. For why should common-sense psychology be more akin to philosophical investigation and argument than theoretical psychology? Why, in other words, would philosophy be more "at home" in common-sense psychology than in theoretical psychology or in neuroscience? And why should common-sense arguments and reasoning belong to the realm of *a priori* reasoning?

A response to this question has been offered by various philosophers of this century and the last, including Wittgenstein, Anscombe, McDowell, and many others. The central role of common sense psychology in the philosophy of mind can be established through a distinction between *two kinds of intelligibility*. McDowell presents the latter in the following way. A first kind of explanations is one "in which things are made intelligible by being revealed to be, or to approximate to being, as they rationally ought to be". A second kind is that "in which one makes things intelligible by representing their coming into being as a particular instance of how things generally tend to happen".[4] The idea then is that, whereas philosophy brings intelligibility to mental facts by showing how these facts explain rationally an agent's action through *her own* access to psychological and external facts, science explains mental facts by showing *how they are generated* and *"tend to happen"*. Obviously, the distinction between two kinds of intelligibility is tightly related to the contrast between a normative and a descriptive perspective on things. For in the first case the analysis essentially comes up with reasons to act, whereas in the second kind of case, things are represented as they happen in certain causal contexts. In the case of the philosophy of mind, it also is conceptually connected with the contrast between a first person and a third-person perspective on mental facts. Granted that common-sense psychology allows deploying the kind of normative intelligibility pinpointed by McDowell, whereas scientific psychology explains behavior in a purely

---

[4] McDowell 1985.

causal-descriptive way, commonsense psychology is all there is to know to construct arguments in the philosophy of mind.

The distinction between two kinds of intelligibility is obviously not to be taken itself as a simple descriptive fact about knowledge. It depends on a more fundamental, overarching claim called the constitutive ideal of rationality, and it entertains conceptual relations with other claims about causality and self-knowledge, which we will need to explore.

A – *The constitutive ideal of rationality*

The notion of intelligibility in general which plays a fundamental role in McDowell's considerations in his 1985 paper, "Functionalism and anomalous monism", is borrowed from Davidson's central claim in "Mental Events"[5], about the holistic and rationally constrained character of a theory of mental attribution:

> [...] When we use the concepts of belief, desire, and the rest, we must stand prepared, as the evidence accumulates, to adjust our theory in the light of considerations of overall cogency: the *constitutive ideal of rationality* partly controls each phase in the evolution of what must be an evolving theory. (223)[6]

Many philosophers, among whom McDowell, base their appreciation of what functionalism can and cannot achieve, on the role played by what Davidson called the "constitutive ideal of rationality". We shall see that this claim also drives philosophers' stances on how scientific evidence can, or cannot, be incorporated to a philosophical analysis of the mental.

The idea of a constitutive ideal of rationality is that the understanding of other beings and of oneself is governed by principles that are articulated not by the laws of science but by rationality itself; these principles are not only used to understand others, they also make any interpretation possible. This last feature is what makes the ideal a "constitutive" one.

Recognizing that the constitutive concept of rationality is a norm rather than a fact allows to appreciate, as McDowell does in his 1985 article, that beliefs and desires are involved in explanations "of a special sort", i.e. explanations putting "things" – thoughts, propositional attitude and actions – in perspective with what they ought to be. This indeed provides quite a different kind of explanation from one that predicts that, given P, Q tends to

---

[5] Davidson 1980, 207–227.
[6] see also *ibid*. 222: "It is a feature of the mental that the attribution of mental phenomena must be responsible to the background of reasons, beliefs, and intentions of the individual".

happen. If being thirsty, I take a beer in the fridge, this is not to be explained as a disposition to move in a particular way in a given context, but rather as a piece of behavior to be evaluated as rational, given the totality of my beliefs and desires at the time.

Even a theory that would model specific sets of deductive relations between beliefs that an agent may use to think and act, according to McDowell, would fail to credit rationality with a constitutive role, and therefore would not reach the level of normativity that is needed for the mental. Two features are of special importance:

- The kind of normativity involved is such that rationality is presented in an *entirely general way*. A norm is said to be "categorical"; in contrast, a set of domain-specific rules and inferences as specified in a functional approach would only offer *hypothetical* imperatives, i.e. *conditions* under which something qualifies as a system of beliefs.
- Mental normativity must be one in which rationality is presented in a way that captures the *applicability of forms to contents*. Common sense displays this kind of understanding, when it allows a subject to grasp that violating the norm of rationality automatically brings unintelligibility with it.[7]

B – *The essential subjectivity of the mental*

The notion of a constitutive ideal of rationality thus drives in turn an appeal to a subjective grasp, contrasted with an objective conformity, that will allow for spelling out how a norm can be espoused rather than simply followed. Thomas Nagel initially introduced his contrast between objective and subjective approaches of reality to emphasize the dynamics of objective knowledge and the limits of objectivity when it comes to understanding the self and other mental phenomena:

> A succession of objective advances may take us to a new conception of reality that leaves the personal or merely human perspective further and further behind. But if what we want is to understand the whole world, we can't forget about those subjective starting points indefinitely; we and our personal perspectives belong to the world. One limit encountered by the pursuit of objectivity appears when it turns back on the self and tries to encompass subjectivity in its conception of the real. The recalcitrance of this material to objective understanding requires both a modification of the form of objectivity and recognition that it cannot by itself provide a complete picture of the world, or a complete stance toward it. (Nagel 1986, 6)

---

[7] See McDowell 1985, in McDowell 1998, 330–1.

Nagel's problem however did not consist in emphasizing the *a priori* incompatibility between the approaches but rather in exploring the possibility of *integrating* them and clarifying the limits of such integration. In his perspective, "objectivity is a method of understanding". The method in question consists in stepping back from our own particular position in space and time, thus taking our own location as one unspecific position in the world, that we mean to characterize independently from ourselves, or "as it is in itself" (Nagel 1986, 5). Nagel's suggestion consists in modifying the form of objectivity to accommodate subjective facts. The subjective form, which is for him the essence of raw feels and intentional states can be only grasped by having them oneself, or else, by imagining that one has them. One can therefore think of oneself "from outside" while preserving the subjective way in which mental states are given to a subject, relying on "how far our subjective imagination can travel" (1986, 18).

In the philosophy of mind, the objective pull can however lead us astray: it is the case with what Nagel calls "objective blindness", a condition linked to ignoring the resources of imagination necessarily involved in any adequate understanding of minds and selves. This misleading attempt results in an "external theory" of the mental, i.e. a theory mimicking the natural sciences. Physics is clearly a science in which reality can be understood independently of a human perspective on the world. Philosophers draw on the case of physics to develop an approach of the mind that would similarly be detached from any particular perspective. Physicalism and functionalism are philosophical theories of the mental illustrating that strategy. Nagel feels that an unbearable separation within the self results from this vain effort of denying one's own subjectivity while studying mental properties.

This separation creates in turn the problem of "reintegrating" the external properties into living subjects:

> One has to *be* the creature whom one has subjected to detached examination, and one has in one' entirety to *live* in the world that has been revealed to an extremely distilled fraction of oneself. (Nagel 1986, 9)

Nagel does not explicitly indicate how his own method for grasping objectively subjective mental facts allows such a fusion between the creature and her mind. Part of the difficulty of Nagel's view is that it is expressed at a level of generality that does not bring much light to the way of conducting specific appropriate research on the mind.

In close agreement with Nagel, McDowell dismisses the view that "reality [about the mental] is objective, in the sense of being fully describable from no particular point of view" (McDowell, 336). There is "a natural intuition to the effect that the mental is both real and essentially subjective", he writes, now dissociating himself from Davidson's own position on this matter.[8] A fundamental mistake, according to McDowell, consists in "forcing the mental into an objective mould" (McDowell, 336).

McDowell understands "subjectivity" as covering not only phenomenal experience and its qualitative content, but also propositional attitudes. Two reasons are offered for treating propositional attitudes as subjective facts. First, entertaining them presupposes "comprehending the content of someone's outlook on the world". Second, distinguishing what does and what does not make sense involves "representing the idea that we might learn from others and thereby find them intelligible". What McDowell wants to show is that the subjective character of the notion of a limit to intelligibility has to do with the constitutive role of rationality. He explains the relationship between the two claims in the following way:

> Achieving the kind of understanding for which rationality plays its constitutive role requires a sensitivity to the specific detail of the subjective stance of others, and an openness to learning from it, that is bound to be falsified if one supposes that explanations involving the constitutive ideal *work by locating their explananda in a structure specifiable from outside content*. (McDowell 1985, 337) (my italics)

This last claim provides the *closure* of the subjective experience and knowledge posited as the essence of the mental. It is in fact this central claim which *excludes an objective approach* as non-relevant in philosophy, and in particular forbids any illumination through scientific evidence. For without it, one might both concede that there is a subjective twist to propositional attitudes and to the openness of an individual to others, *and* defend the view that subjective properties can adequately be rephrased in equivalent objective terms (for example in sentences held true in response to given stimuli, or in dispositions to believe and desire).

Let us summarize claim 2. Objectivism consists in taking a third person point of view on the mind, i.e. adopting an external stance in which the mind is an object in the world among others, endowed with specific representational capacities. Using scientific results necessarily commits one to objectivism. Therefore another method, rejecting such commitments, should be used. This alternative method consists in approaching the mind in the subject's own terms, i.e. in common-sense idiom.

---

[8] For although McDowell says that Davidson "respects" this intuition, the latter does not dwell on it and even writes explicitly that "On the proposed test of the mental, the distinguishing feature of the mental is not that it is private, subjective, or immaterial, but that it exhibits what Brentano called intentionality", (*ibid*. 211).

C – Mental causation and the common-sense view of the mental

Among the methodological consequences of the contrast between a subjective and an objective approach to the mind is the question of causality: should it be restricted to the objective realm, and shown irrelevant in the subjective domain of reasons? Or should a new causal picture, coherent with the contrast, be spelled out in more detail? In Nagel's perspective, there is only one kind of causation in the world, and the subjective realm does not provide ontology for a separate kind of causation. Even though the external perspective on the mind seems to dissolve the impression of freedom that subjects enjoy, no jumping out of individual minds outside time, space and physical causality is allowed: objectivity comes with an exclusivist view on causation. There is only one level of causation holding between events in the world.

> The objective view *seems* to wipe out such autonomy [of the subjective intentional realm] because it admits only one kind of explanation of why something happened – causal explanation – and equates its absence with the absence of any explanation at all. (Nagel 1986, 115)

According to Nagel, this seeming however resists careful analysis. The search for an autonomous intentional explanation is seen as leading at best to a very limited kind of intelligibility[9]; it cannot explain "why I did what I did rather than the alternative that was causally open to me" (Nagel 1986, 116). Furthermore, physico-bio-sociological causation is also part of our subjective experience: the objective pull maintains its grip on our sense of receiving passively from the world our capacities, our opportunities and even our own self:

> We remain, as pursuers of knowledge, creatures inside the world who have not created ourselves, and some of whose processes of thought have simply been given to us (Nagel 1986, 118) [...] The objectivity that seems to offer greater control also reveals the ultimate givenness of the self. (Nagel 1986, 119)

Those philosophers who, like Nagel, recognize only one level of causation in the world, thus tend to recognize that empirical considerations may enrich the subjective stance through a process of self-distanciation and reappropriation. But another lesson on causation can be drawn from the existence of a subjective domain.

In contrast with Nagel, Jennifer Hornsby maintains that there is a distinctive level of causation in that domain that allows to completely account for actions "in the terms that we use as agents":

---

[9] At worst, it leads to incoherence.

> There is the thought, which Thomas Nagel has made especially vivid, that it is essential to our conceiving of ourselves as agents that we take our actions to be completely accounted for in the terms that we use as agents; the possibility of treating actions from the impersonal point of view would then subvert our ordinary conception of ourselves. (Hornsby 1993, in Heil & Mele, 161).

The crucial notion in that argument is that of "conceiving ourselves as agents". For as we saw, this conception is in Nagel's perspective largely unsupported, and constitutes an irresistible article of faith for which no intelligible account can be provided.

Hornsby's particular way of arguing for this autonomous level of causal efficacy of the mental consists in maintaining that there is no overlap between internal, subjective causation, on the one hand, and external, objective causation, on the other hand. A defender of the subjective view should maintain, according to her, that a direct causal foundation for intentional states and for agency can be found in what we might call a commonsense "world-and-psychology-view", characterisable independently from the world as described by physics, theoretical psychology and neuroscience. A typical question of an 'action explanation' is "Why did the agent do action A?" whereas a purely causal question is "Why was there an event of kind E?" The first question concerns a person, able to articulate her reasons in various propositional attitudes; the second has to do with an impersonal event in the objective causal order. For Hornsby, there is no common ground on which to deal with both questions. What we need only consider in explaining A's action is "a network of intelligible dependencies between the facts about what an agent thinks, what she wants, and what she does".[10]

She maintains that the causal-explanation view in the first sense (relevant for agency) is compatible with rejecting a view in which an action results causally from "discrete things interacting" (for ex. token states of belief and desire). (Hornsby 1993, 167) Wanting and believing, in this view, are not events. Let us take for example the case of Peter wanting to boil some water. Peter's intentional states result in changing the world causally. The question how his intentional states are converted in physical forces is entirely external to philosophical concerns. There indeed is a gap between the subjective and the objective order, which Hornsby gladly acknowledges. The agent may see the gap, but need not be concerned by it. He will notice that the gap is bridged when his action is successfully accomplished: "There is no need to invent an item to bridge the gap between Peter's states of mind and the event of his want's being satisfied: when his want was satisfied, the gap was bridged – he switched on the kettle".

---

[10] Hornsby 1993, 168.

Actions are initiatings of series of events (178) in this sense: there is something an agent intentionally does, there is some change in the world brought about by a person. In other words, an action is the event of a person's causing something, a movement of her own body, a letter written, a kettle of water being boiled, etc.[11] But what a person does, she insists, "is not an event, and it is therefore not a 'component of the flux of events in the world'". Or, as she also presents the view, "there are events that are not in the world "of nature"." (184). This makes a whole range of reductive questions irrelevant: At what stage in the neural chain shall we find an agent's action? "Our concepts of action may not contain the precision needed to determine an answer for it".[12]

The gap between the causal-explanatory approach in philosophy, on the one hand, and the causal-explanatory approach in psychology and the neurosciences is taken to be foreign to philosophical purpose by J. Hornsby. She writes:

> If the causal reality of belief and desire is just their causal-explanatory reality, then it need make no use of a further idea – of items inside people that we latch on to when we give action explanations. (1993, 168)

The upshot is that commonsense psychology is the proper medium for doing philosophy of mind; the ontological level on which causation normally supervenes being here bracketed, the only relevant level for philosophy of mind is the way people understand one another, i.e. commonsense psychology. (Hornsby prefers the term of *commonsense psychology* to the more usual expression of "*folk psychology*", because the latter implies that we are speaking of a kind of knowledge that specialists will reorganize around more efficient and testable concepts).[13]

---

[11] Davidson defends a similar view in his 1963 "Actions, reasons and causes". An intention to do A "does not refer to an entity, state, disposition or event" (in 1980, 8). Justifying and explaining an action "go hand in hand", but justifying depends on the explanatory role played by some intentional content (what Dadvidson calls "the primary reason"), and not conversely: the belief alone explains the action.
Davidson also claims that "there is something very odd in the idea that causal relations are empirical rather than logical" (14). His reason for this claim is that "a reason rationalizes an action only when the descriptions are appropriately fixed, and the appropriate descriptions are not logically independent" (14). The difference between Davidson's and Hornsby's treatments of action is that, for Davidson, causation can be accessed "impersonally", i.e. through mental states, whereas for Hornsby, only a person can have a causal power in acting. (see her 1993, 169).

[12] Hornsby 1997, 67.

[13] Hornsby 1997, 3–4.

3. Discussing the three claims

Let us summarize the discussion at this point. We suggested that a stance on the value of empirical considerations in the philosophy of mind stems from three general claims concerning the study of the mental:

1) The claim of the constitutive role of rationality
2) The claim of the subjective essence of the mental
3) The claim of the causal specificity of common-sense view on action and subjectivity.

The three claims that I summarized define a certain way of approaching mental concepts; my analysis emphasized their inter-relations. Let us observe again that the autonomy of the philosophy of mind can be defended in various ways. The stronger view presented above results from accepting the three claims, as Jennifer Hornsby. The concept of a person, in Hornsby, is understood on the basis of a joint acceptance of the three claims. The person, rather than her mental states, causally determines her actions. She has a personal level access to her motives, and thus is able both to rationalize her actions and those of others.

It is possible however to defend only one or two of these claims while rejecting the remainder; significantly different stances on the mental would result, as well as different ways of dealing with the autonomy of philosophy (i.e. different ways of blocking, allowing or requiring empirical-scientific considerations into philosophy). McDowell, who espouses the first two claims, occupies an only slightly weaker position than Hornsby's does. Many non-reductionist philosophers of mind would agree with claim 1 (sometimes in a revised form) and with claim 2, while rejecting 3 (for example, Dennett 1969). Davidson would only accept 1. Some hard-core naturalist philosophers would deny 1, 2 and 3.

Thus each particular combination of stances taken on the three claims implies a specific stance on empirical arguments in the philosophy of mind. The three claims listed above are obviously not jointly *necessary* to exclude recourse to scientific evidence from philosophical analysis of the mind (for there are certainly many other ways of concluding that empirical-scientific considerations are out of place in philosophy). As I just suggested, but did not have time to prove, they are separately *sufficient* to constrain the recourse to scientific neurology and psychology. I will concentrate on each of them.

Claim 1 and the autonomy of philosophy

It certainly is impossible in a few lines to discuss in detail the importance which McDowell attributes to the "constitutive ideal" of rationality, and how scientific reasoning, as a result, is taken to belong to a derived kind of rationality. We will concentrate on what explains that there should be such a constitutive link between truth and rationality, on the one hand, and intentional description and mental attribution on the other. Steven Stich (1990) has offered an explanation along these lines: "for a person's cognitive states to be intentionally characterizable, the states, the interactions among them, and their interactions with the environment must all be similar to our own".[14] Given the role which inferences play in the interactions between states, at least minimal rationality principles must be shared, as well as reference, meaning and truth. Davidson's work furthermore suggested that interpretation necessarily presupposes some trade-off between meaning and truth; in particular it presupposes that familiar semantic hypotheses will be made about the meanings of the terms used in the to-be interpreted language.

Now there are various ways in which this antecedence of the thinker's thought in the process of interpretation can be understood. There seems to be a natural way to understand this procedure in terms of how *language use constrains* meaning and reference, rather than as a feature of a *subjective* grasp of language. Being subjective is obviously a property of a thought *as entertained by someone*. But there are objective features explaining why the thought is entertained, and that reach deeper in the causal explanation of intentional states than the brute fact that it is being thought *by me*. In particular, thought has definite informational/representational properties, that allow it to be generated, semantically evaluated, communicated, etc., given the epistemic and motivational properties of the thinker(s) involved. Finding that something makes sense or not thus does not seem to *result essentially* from a subjective impression; it may be characterized through sentence and speech analysis in syntactic, in semantic or in pragmatic terms. Such an understanding is inferential if anything is, and the inferences may be considered independently from a subjective stance. In this view, subjective appraisal of what makes sense is not a primary fact from which philosophical examination should start. It is a fact derived from properties of representational systems. Note that our reading consists in using a denial of claim 2 to weaken claim 1, just as claim 1 draws its full strength from a full adhesion to claim 2.

If the claim for the constitutive character of rationality is weakened in this way, and made independent from claim 2, then it allows to appreciate as a

---

[14] Stich 1990, 38.

substantial possibility that a particular subject might fail to recognize rules of inference or misapply them in the process of interpreting other speakers. Two crucial preliminary steps in epistemology will thus consist in learning from science the mechanisms through which information is generated, collected and communicated, and from psychopathology and neurology in which particular way misrepresenting and miscommunicating can occur.

Alvin Goldman[15] exemplifies such a view, in which rational justification cannot be conducted in full independence from scientific investigation: he maintains that the aim of philosophy is evaluative (epistemology, ethics, philosophy of law illustrate most clearly a normative interest in philosophy). According to him, this aim invites rather than it precludes a rational interest in scientific (descriptive) evidence on reasoning capacities. Granted that justification is grounded in beliefs of a certain kind, and that evaluations of beliefs derive from evaluations of belief-forming processes, an epistemologist has to assess the reliability of the processes involved in belief formation and in reasoning. As Goldman notes, "Which processes are suitable cannot be certified by logic alone, but depend on properties of our basic cognitive equipment". In this task, empirical facts about social organisation may also be relevant.[16]

Let us now consider our second basic claim.

Claim 2 and the subjective essence of the mental

In *Simple Mindedness*, Hornsby complains that philosophers of mind talk about action in an impersonal language that makes it easy to forget that the agents are people:

> So we find "two beliefs produce a third" standing for a person's arriving at a conclusion. We find "an experience causes a belief" in place of the idea that a person believes something because things look to her to be a certain way. We find "pains result in avoidance reactions", substitution for a conception of a person's behavior as intelligible in the light of the fact that she suffers pain. (Hornsby 1997, 157)

One may agree here with Hornsby: confusions between informational and subjective levels should be avoided.[17] There may be a good reason however to use a subpersonal language instead of the personal one when it comes

---

[15] See in particular Goldman 1986.
[16] What Goldman calls "social epistemology" is concerned with the truth-getting impact of different patterns and arrangements of social intercourse. See Goldmann (1999).
[17] A similar complaint is voiced by thinkers of a different inclination, like Dennett (1969).

to expressing representational properties. While the philosophers under Hornsby's critical review might perhaps express more clearly their arguments, they may still have a point using subpersonal rather than personal properties. What is needed in Hornsby's argument is a proof that *all* the facts relevant to epistemic states and agency lie within a person's subjective access and conscious control. The point again is that of the intentional closure of the subjective view. Let us develop briefly this point.

According to the subjective view, one cannot be in pain, have an emotion, form an intention, without simultaneously forming the belief that one has it.[18] One might object that pains, emotions, physical postures, intentions, often fail to be acknowledged by their bearer; the underlying states may be currently active in an individual (i.e. be contextually triggered and control her behavior in a way essentially similar to conscious pains, emotions, physical postures and intentions), while being, at least for some time, undetected by the subject. The agent herself may well acknowledge that later on, and recognize a corresponding disposition in herself in a retrospective way.[19]

If an emotion, or rather a quasi-emotional state can control behavior without the agent noticing it, we have a dilemma. Should we take such a state as mental, because it controls behavior, can be acknowledged retrospectively and belongs to the kinds of states that are normally felt in a subjective way? Or should we refrain from including it in mental states, because it is currently unnoticed? These two competing features – access to consciousness or ability to control – seem to make it worthwhile to try articulating in more detail a theory of the kind of access that an organism has to her own proprioceptive and intentional states, thus grounding conscious or currently unconscious knowledge of one's current deeds, intentions and well-being in specific informational facts.

One might also object to Hornsby's attempt at recapturing the agent's overarching role with respect to his/her mental life that the sense of being the thinker of one's thought falls short of occupying a temporally continuous stream of consciousness; many of the subject's states are of an elusive kind, not states that a subject really controls or experiences as her own, but states

---

[18] see Shoemaker 1996.
[19] Naomi Eilan (1997): "It is unfair to claim that "our personal level concept of remembering is wholly independent of any reference to the mechanisms that make remembering possible. It fails to do justice to the passivity involved in asking oneself questions, for the passivity here is partly a function of the fact that in doing what one is doing (asking and answering the question) there is something going on that makes this possible that one does not have access to. (...) The fact that there is this non-conscious cognitive ingredient just is what introduces the passivity."

that occur within her with varying results (either positively helping her solve a problem, as in directed memory and in reasoning, or as intruding her personal sphere, as in obsessive thoughts). Even in the course of controlled thinking, there is a wide spectrum of mental states that are passively entertained by a thinker, instead of being the result of controlled attention. In remembering, for example, there is clearly a contrast between the decision to try and remember, and the actual experience of retrieving from memory. Remembering is a good example of the necessity of articulating personal experience with subpersonal mechanisms in order to account for the passivity experienced by a rememberer, who depends on them without knowing which they are and how they work. Should all these psychological events in which an agent is passive towards her mental life be counted among the "external" or the internal sphere?

Some might certainly argue that as far as these mechanisms are studied scientifically, in an "objective" perspective, they fail to coincide with what a subject experiences from the inside. In this light, therefore, there is apparently a decisive "aspectual" gap between what the subject feels as a passive experience where she allows her brain to work towards a solution, and the active operations of the brain described in theoretical psychology and in neuroscience. But such a gap consists in the unavailability of a description of the same phenomenon common to the scientist and the subject, not in a complete absence of a common *reference* between the two descriptions. What guarantees this reference is the capacity of a subject to come up with an indexical reference to all kinds of passive mental operations for which he may indeed have no description and only an indirect marker. In the case of an experience of passivity, for example, the subject may still refer to her "tip-of-the-tongue" impression, or to her "letting the name of that person surface". The subject who tries to remember a name knows that she does not know the mechanism for memory retrieval, but knows however that somehow she will manage to retrieve it; she spontaneously describes her experience as one of passivity, as one of "letting things follow their course". Another example of mental passivity is experienced when letting "sink in" an information of a radically new and potentially threatening nature: in such a case, the subject experiences that time is needed for her system to draw the needed inferences before she can face the new facts and handle the emotions involved. This sense of "extraneity" is thus quite common outside psychiatry. Any subject, "sophisticated" or not, is clearly able to refer to these episodes of her mental life through indexicals, referring possibly first to episode tokens, and later on to types of them.

If this line of reasoning is correct, expert knowledge does not need to conflict with a subject's ability to justify rationally her own plans, beliefs and actions. Even though the subject does not possess the explicit knowledge that the expert has, she is in a position to justify her own mental concept use, or the way she derives her decisions from her past experiences on the basis of her procedural knowledge of how her thought develops, through more or less controlled mental processes.

We do not want to deny that there are two faces for each mental process; on the one hand it develops as a more or less controllable procedure, identifiable indexically by a thinker; on the other hand it can be studied as a sequence of informational processing or neuronal activation. We do not deny either that the contrast procedure/process parallels the contrast subjective/objective. What we deny is that the contrast has a deep metaphysical significance and, in particular that it grounds the subjective as such. Just as one can interpret Jackson's puzzle (in Jackson 1986) about what Mary knows as illustrating a distinction between what Mary knows propositionally and the procedural way in which Mary displays her knowledge, one can interpret the subjective-objective opposition as two sides of the same procedural coin (put to use or studied as a sequence of informational processes).

Claim 3 and the causal specificity of a common-sense view on action and subjectivity.

According to claim 3, there is a complete dissociation between the causal mechanisms that are activated when we think and act and the causal relations between our intentional states and our actions. When a person explains her actions or justifies her decisions, she need not invoke any kind of mechanism taking place inside her.

A first general remark on the relationship between commonsense psychology and the science of the mental is that the former incorporates in fact bits and pieces of "objective knowledge". It includes, beyond general rational principles and the famous "platitudes" concerning the relations between beliefs, desires and actions, empirical hypotheses about the workings of the mind and the possible causes for sub-optimal functioning. Commonsense psychology includes inter alia at least some kind of empirical explanation for *why* somebody is bright, arrogant, macho, deluded, lunatic etc. The kind of explanation used ranges from myth and tradition to vulgarized scientific results. Commonsense psychology is thus not ordinarily used as a complete body of knowledge, but rather as a field of inquiry open to extensions and enrichments from all kinds of sources. Of particular importance regarding our previous discussion of the role of deference to experts in justification, commonsense psychology includes recognition of its own incompleteness through various more or less deferential procedures that deserve careful study.[20] Even "simple-minded" people are ready to recognize that some types of behavior or some personality trait cannot be accounted for in ordinary terms. Reference is made to "conditions" or "natures" which are presented as in need of an explanation by some expert or through an ideally complete science of the mental. Nor is such a deferred qualification restricted to third-person attribution. It does involve first-person self-knowledge as well. This makes a view in which the project is to insulate commonsense psychological reasoning from empirical-scientific concerns difficult to defend in its own commonsensical terms.[21]

This remark introduces a way to respond to the third claim, i.e. the claim that there is a level of causation at the intentional level (characterized in subjective terms), over and above the level of events as characterized by physics and the neurosciences. Philosophers of mind like McDowell and Hornsby consider that no mechanism story needs to be told at the personal level, and that the personal level is all there is to explore when it comes to understanding content and rational justification. A main objection is that one can acknowledge that the philosopher's task is epistemological and logical rather than purely descriptive and psychological, while also recognizing that a philosopher needs to characterize the epistemological and logical roles of subpersonal states and events, to the extent that the latter turn out to have a causal role in rational reasoning and self-knowledge. Moreover, as we saw in the preceding section, a person is able to refer to her own subpersonal states through indexicals. She is thus able to bridge the gap, so to speak, between her higher-order states for which linguistic descriptions are available, and the subpersonal states that are represented in her language and in her thought through indexical/deferential expressions. For example, it seems impossible to deal adequately with the justification of memory reports without taking into account scientific explanations for illusory memories, nor with the justification of self-identity without bringing to bear scientific evidence concerning both the acquisition and the pathological disruption of self representation. The idea that there is one philosophically relevant source of intelligibility, having to do with the personal level of explanation, seems thus be defeated both by the *de facto* absence of boundaries between a person's beliefs (concerning herself, other agents, as well as the physical world), and

---

[20] See Sperber 1993, Recanati 2000.
[21] Such an incompleteness should not lure *philosophers* into accepting a double standard about the mind, with an exoteric level of commonsense retained in philosophical explanation and an esoteric level of scientific theory that would be the privilege of a few experts. The ultimate reason why a double standard is untenable is that, even if one rejects any *obligation* of using science, the notion of a reflective equilibrium in the various fields constituting knowledge forbids *flat contradiction* with science.

by the *de jure* necessity to strive for a coherent picture of the world, whether of the subjective or of the objective kind.

Admitting subpersonal explanation however implies a temptation for considering that the *only ontology* that needs to be taken into account is the subpersonal one. In other words, there is only one step from going subpersonal to falling into eliminativism. Dennett's early book *Content and consciousness*, for example, defends the view that two competing accounts should be offered for mental items. This would lead fragmenting mental predicates into two classes. For example, two predicates of awareness should be defined, on the following lines:

(1) A is aware$_1$ that p at time t if and only if p is the content of the input state of A's speech centre at time t.
(2) A is aware$_2$ that p at time t if and only if p is the content of an internal event in A at time t that is effective in directing current behavior (Dennett 1969, 118).

Awareness$_1$ would thus cover introspectible conscious states, whereas awareness$_2$ would include those brain states through which an organism represents its environment, and thus becomes able to control adequately its behavior.

Such definitions are supposed to "bridge the gap" between the personal and subpersonal levels of explanation. But do they? They may be taken rather to *expose* the gap: there is no way to identify (1) and (2) in any sensible way, because there is no person causally involved on the right side of the explanation in (2). According to Dennett, referring to personal level mental entities in a way misses its target.

> Starting from the position that thought, being what-is-reported, cannot be identified with anything in the sub-personal story, it would be poor philosophy to argue further that there must really be something, the thought, that is reported when it is true that I am reporting my thoughts [...] There is no entity in the perceiving machine, and by analogy, in the human brain, that would be well referred to by the expression 'that which is infallibly reported by the final output expression', and this is the very best of reasons for viewing this expression and its mate, 'thought', as non-referential. (Dennett 1969, 113)

Dennett thus denies that the first personal level has to involve an ontology of its own. There is only one level of causation, the subpersonal one, and the personal level, which is proper for philosophy, – on this Dennett agrees with McDowell and Hornsby – is also a subject matter *unsuited for causal purposes*. Some terms of the personal vocabulary may refer to actual entities at the subpersonal level; some of them however will fail to refer, for lack of a minimal matching between what is reported and what occurs subpersonally.

What is to be done with terms like "thought", or any other term (some philosophers would inscribe here: self, free will, or belief) that are found not to coincide with any item in the causal brain machinery? They are not deemed meaningless or nonsensical for that (they even may play major roles in communicating and influencing behavior). Dennett recommends a semantical procedure, which he calls 'fusion':

> Once we decide that a term is best viewed as non-referential, we fuse it in its proper contexts, as with 'sake' in the irreducible idiom 'for the sake of'. The contexts maintain their significance but are not subject for further analysis. (Dennett 1969, 14)

This procedure is meant to clarify the ontology of the mental; some mental terms may be retained because of their communicative value (like "for the sake of") although no attempt is done to use them referentially. In those cases, a commonsense psychological term will be found lacking reference, and shown meaningful only as part of a larger unit of analysis. (Example: "*sake*" in " for the sake of"; or maybe "belief", "commitment", etc.).

But the tension between the two poles does not seem really eased in the fusion. Let us distinguish two types of ways in which the commonsense views of the mental fare with causal-scientific analyses: they may contradict them, or they may more or less be found to supervene on specific informational processes. Thus there will be two kinds of revisions that will have to be made by a philosopher who wants to clarify a mental ontology to make it compatible with a fully rational epistemology. Let us call these two types parapersonal vs. subpersonal revisions. *Parapersonal revisions* will *remove* items previously taken to belong to a causally efficacious personal/intentional sphere to place it into the subpersonal, with a corresponding modification of the kind of control that the subjects may have on their actions, decisions or evaluations. For example, one might have to revise attributing to oneself certain kinds of intentions, and reinterpret the corresponding pieces of behavior as environmentally controlled. *Subpersonal revisions* will reciprocally confirm the causal validity of the personal-level purported entity (property, state, event) to the extent that it does supervene on a set of well-formed, dedicated subpersonal mechanisms.

Eliminativism only seems attractive when parapersonal revisions appear to be needed on a large scale, leaving a picture of the mental that is beyond recognition for an ordinary person. This solution is however a disaster for individual rationality, for there seems to be no ground left for a subject to know whether his beliefs are correct, his desires acceptable, his plans justified, whether the way he interprets others is warranted, and even whether he is an agent at all. Another possibility is to accept piecemeal revisions of the kind indicated above.

Conclusion

As philosophers, we want to account for the way in which a subject comes to a rational evaluation of a situation. In other words, the philosopher's essential task is epistemological rather than inherently descriptive. This task requires that we describe in an as objective and complete way as possible the cognitive tools on which knowledge can be attained, as well as the ways in which we may be misled by various psychiatric or neuropsychological problems. On the other hand, our main interest is in the conscious subject, the agent and thinker for the exclusive sake of which epistemological concerns can be raised meaningfully.

This dilemma imposes some kind of complex interplay between levels, of a very different kind from the double standard that the autonomy claim would encourage. The rule should be, in my view, that subpersonal mechanisms matter only when they belong to the subject's rational sphere. Part of the philosophical task consists in showing how they do. There seems to be no way available to carry out such a task without relying on the sciences of the mental, for they allow a subject to come to grip with the basic epistemological notions in a way that coheres with science and culture at large.

References

Davidson, D.: Actions, Reasons and Causes (1963), republished in: D. Davidson, *Essays on Actions and Events,* Oxford University Press, Oxford 1980, 3–19.
Davidson, D.: Mental Events (1970), republished in: D. Davidson, *Essays on Actions and Events,* Oxford University Press, Oxford 1980, 207–227.
Dennett, D.C.: *Content and Consciousness,* Routledge and Kegan Paul., London 1969.
Eilan, N.: Perceptual Intentionality, Attention and Consciousness. In: *Current Issues in Philosophy of Mind*, ed. by A. O'Hear, Cambridge University Press, Cambridge 1997, 182–202.
Goldman, A.I.: *Epistemology and Cognition,* Harvard University Press, Cambridge 1986.
Goldman, A.I.: *Knowledge in a Social World,* Oxford University Press, Oxford 1999.
Goodman, N.: *Fact, Fiction, Forecast,* Bobbs-Merrill, Indianapolis 1965.
Hatfield, G.: *The Natural and The Normative, Theories of Spatial perception from Kant to Helmholtz,* MIT Press, Cambridge 1990.
Hornsby, J.: Agency and Causal Explanation. In: *Mental Causation,* ed. by J. Heil and A. Mele, Clarendon Press, Oxford 1993, 161–188.

Hornsby, J.: *Simple Mindedness*, Harvard University Press, Cambridge 1997.
Jackson, F.: What Mary did not know, *Journal of Philosophy* 83 (1986), 291–5.
McDowell, J.: Functionalism and anomalous Monism (1985), republished in: J. McDowell, *Mind, Value and Reality*, Harvard University Press, Cambridge 1998, 325–340.
McDowell, J.: *Mind and World*, Harvard University Press, Cambridge 1994.
Nagel, T.: *The View form Nowhere*, Oxford University Press, Oxford 1986.
Putnam, H.: The Meaning of 'Meaning'. In H. Putnam, *Mind, Language and Reality, Philosophical Papers, Volume 2*, Cambridge University Press, Cambridge 1975, 215–271.
Rawls, J.: *A Theory of Justice*, Oxford University Press, Oxford 1971.
Recanati, F.: *Oratio Obliqua, Oratio recta; An Essay on Meta-representation*, MIT Press., Cambridge, Mass. 2000
Rey, G.: *Contemporary Philosophy of Mind*, Blackwell, Oxford 1997.
Rey, G.: A Plea for Substantive Philosophy of Mind. In: *Physicalism and Its Discontents*, ed. by C. Gillet and B. Loewer, Cambridge University Press, Cambridge 2001.
Shoemaker, S.: *The first-person perspective and other essays*, Cambridge University Press, Cambridge 1996.
Sperber, D.: Interpreting and explaining cultural representations. In: *Beyond boundaries: understanding, translation and anthropological discourse*, ed. by G. Palsson, Berg, Oxford 1993, 162–183.
Stich, S. P.: *The Fragmentation of Reason*, MIT Press, Cambridge 1990.

Pierre Jacob

Is Meaning Intrinsically Normative?[1]

Prima facie, meaning seems to be a normative property in the simple following sense: if something exemplifies a given meaning property, then some normative consequences follow. So, for example, if the French word 'cheval' means HORSE – if it is correctly used to refer to horses –, then it is a *mistake* to use it to refer to things that are not horses. Equivalently, one *ought* to use it to refer to horses and only to horses (provided some idealizations). Similarly, my concept HORSE – the thought constituent expressible by the French word 'cheval' – correctly applies to horses and only to horses. So my concept *ought* to be tokened to refer to horses and only to horses. Or else, I misapply it. The fact that it would be a *mistake* to use the word 'cheval' to refer to non-horses signals the fact that meaning is a normative property or that it has normative implications. So does the fact that one *ought* to use a word in certain circumstances and not in others. And furthermore this norm arises in virtue of the meaning of the word.

The question I want to ask is: Is meaning *intrinsically* normative? As I understand it, to claim [N] that meaning is intrinsically normative is to claim both [N1] that meaning is normative and [N2] that the normativity of meaning is *sui generis*, i.e., that it is irreducibly semantic. Hume is widely taken to have shown that it is a fallacy to derive a moral obligation from premises about matters of fact. Nor can one refute the ethical claim that one ought to keep one's promise by exhibiting unfulfilled promises. Almost a hundred years ago, Moore famously criticized what he called the "naturalistic fallacy", which he thought would undermine any attempt at providing a definition of the meaning of the word 'good' in purely descriptive non-normative naturalistic terms. Now, if [N] is correct – if meaning is intrinsically normative –, then presumably any naturalistic attempt at understanding

---

[1] Thanks to Fred Dretske, Wolfram Hinzen, Wolfgang Künne, Albert Newen, Armin Tatzel for comments at the GAP Conference and afterwards. Thanks to Ned Block, Tim Crane, Pascal Engel, Kati Farkas, Paul Horwich, Barry Loewer, Nenad Miscevic, Peter Railton, François Recanati, John Skorupski and Dan Sperber for conversations on this topic.

meaning properties in terms of non-semantic properties is bound to commit a version of the naturalistic fallacy.

1. Kripke's sceptical paradox and the thesis that meaning is intrinsically normative

The charge of a naturalistic fallacy that concerns me has been brilliantly made by Kripke in his famous (1982) book, *Wittgenstein on Rules and Private Language*. And it is based on thesis [N]. Let me briefly summarize Kripke's challenge as I understand it.

In his book, Kripke argues in favor of a certain thesis which he calls "the sceptical paradox". According to this thesis, no attribution of meaning to an expression of a natural language can be made true by any fact about the mental life and the history of a single speaker of the language. I know – or I think I know – the meaning of the French word 'chien'. I know that the word 'chien' in French applies to dogs. I have learnt its meaning on the basis of a finite amount of instances of application. What is it about me that makes it true that were I to apply the word 'chien' to something which would not be a dog I would misapply it? On account of what mental fact would my usage of the word constitute a mistake? If I am the speaker and if I use the French word 'chien', then no fact about me (about my mind or about my individual history) can make it true that by a token of the word 'chien', I mean to refer to dogs and only to dogs. (Incidentally, Kripke's thesis is stated in terms of the arithmetical predicate 'plus'. But the arithmetical meaning of the predicate is irrelevant.)

First of all, in the process of arguing for this sceptical and paradoxical thesis, Kripke appeals to considerations that have been made familiar by other philosophers such as Putnam (1975) and Burge (1979). However, Kripke's sceptical and paradoxical conclusion interestingly diverges from theirs. Their conclusion is an *externalist* conclusion. As Putnam famously put it, on his and Burge's view, "meaning ain't in the head". In other words, meaning or content is not an intrinsic property of an individual's brain: it supervenes on relations between an individual's brain and properties instantiated in his or her environment. It may even supervene on what other members of the individual's community may think.

Kripke's conclusion is that there are *no facts* about what words mean – no facts about meaning. Even though on the externalist view, meaning turns out to be an extrinsic property of an individual's brain, the externalist conclusion does not challenge the factual character of meaning attributions.

Meaning facts (or properties) may not be intrinsic to an individual's brain. Nonetheless they are or they may be respectable naturalistic facts. But Kripke's sceptical paradox does challenge the factuality of meaning because it claims that meaning attributions do not state or describe any fact; rather they express norms. Meaning attributions do not have truth-conditions. They are not aimed at stating facts, they do not have a fact-stating role. Meaning-ascriptions have assertibility conditions because meaning is intrinsically normative.

Secondly, Kripke offers a solution to the sceptical paradox which, he claims, was Wittgenstein's. He calls his solution a 'sceptical' solution by contrast with what he calls 'straight' solutions. Unlike 'straight' solutions, the 'sceptical' solution is not intended as a rebuttal of the sceptical paradoxical thesis: the solution does not consist in rejecting one of the steps leading to the paradoxical conclusion. Rather, in a Wittgensteinian spirit, the solution is to learn to live with the conclusion. Roughly, semantic norms governing an individual's use of an expression arise from the practices of his or her linguistic community in the following sense. What an individual means by his or her use of a word is a matter of agreeing with the uses of other members of his or her community. Meaning consists in a pattern of agreement between members of a community. This is what it takes to be part of a linguistic community: an individual belongs to a community if his or her uses of words coincide with the uses of others. So, to say of a person that he or she means addition by '+' is, as Hale (1997) puts it, to "acknowledge him or her as a fully-paid member of the community of adders, to convey that he or she can be relied upon not to come up with some bizarre answers".

In the sequel, I will disregard Kripke's 'sceptical solution' to the sceptical paradox. As I see it, the sceptical paradox is clearly a version of thesis [N], the thesis that meaning is intrinsically normative. If meaning is intrinsically normative in the sense that there are no facts about meaning, then entertaining the very idea that meaning properties might arise out of non-semantic properties or that the instantiation of non-semantic properties might explain (or account for) the instantiation of semantic properties is committing a naturalistic fallacy. Since the project of a naturalistic understanding of meaning is close to my heart, I do intend to reject thesis [N]. Given the way I construe it, if one wants to reject [N], one can either deny [N1], the thesis that semantic properties are normative, or one can can deny [N2], the thesis that the normativity of meaning is irreducible. I'll call the first strategy the *deflationary* strategy and the second the *reductionist* strategy. In this paper, I want to provide some rationale in favor of the reductionist strategy by exposing some of the difficulties that, according to me, lie ahead of the deflationary strategy.

In a nutshell, the deflationary strategy, as implemented by Horwich in his 1998 book, *Meaning*, involves three main ingredients: (i) the distinction between normative properties and normative consequences of non-normative properties; (ii) a pragmatic explanation of the normative consequences of meaning; and (iii) the lack of a distinction between semantic norms and other norms (e.g., ethical norms). However much I would have liked to embrace deflationism about the normativity of meaning, the goal of my paper is to explain why I cannot accept it.

2. The deflationary distinction between normative properties and normative consequences

Consider the following step in the reasoning leading to Kripke's sceptical paradox:

[C1] If the French word 'chien' refers to dogs or means DOG, then one *ought* to apply it to dogs and only to dogs.

Is conditional [C1] uncontroversial? Granted, it requires a little amount of idealization since French speakers do apply the word 'chien' not just to dogs but to *pictures* of dogs and *sculptures* of dogs as well. As a French speaker, it seems to me that whereas it *would* be incorrect to apply the word 'chien' to a picture of something which is not a dog, it is *not* incorrect to apply the word 'chien' to a picture of a dog which is a picture and therefore not a dog. Still it is, I think, uncontroversial that while it is correct to apply the word 'chien' to a picture of a dog, it is incorrect to apply it to a picture of something which is not a dog. So there is no doubt that some revised version of [C1] is correct. What would, I think, be controversial would be to conclude from [C1] that the meaning of the word 'chien' is *intrinsically* normative. The conclusion that the meaning of the word 'chien' is intrinsically normative could only follow from [C1] via the extra assumption [C2]:

[C2] Unless there are no semantic facts, meaning attributions cannot have normative consequences.

At this point, the deflationist rightly points out that [C2] is not plausible. The reason why [C2] ought to be rejected is that a number of prima facie non-normative properties clearly may have normative consequences. The instantiation of a non-normative property may be subject to normative assessment. With Dretske (2000), consider, for example, the relation expressed by the English verb 'kill'. On many occasions, if x and y are human and if *x* kills *y*, then some normative consequences follow. If *x* killed *y* intentionally and with no mitigating circumstances, then *x* ought to be sanctioned. Notice the contrast between the relations expressed respectively by the verb 'kill' and by the verb 'murder'. Whatever the circumstances, if *x* murdered *y*, then *x* ought to be sanctioned. Legal and moral norms are built into the very existence of murders. Legal and moral norms are constitutive of murders. The latter presuppose the former: in the absence of legal and moral norms, there would simply be no murder. Lack of legal and moral norms, however, would not be enough to prevent the killing relation from being instantiated. Unlike the murder relation, the killing relation can be characterized in natural descriptive terms. Similarly, meteorological properties and relations are presumably natural physical properties and relations. Although the instantiation of a storm, a flood or a hurricane is a physical process, nonetheless it can be subject to normative assessment. We can e.g., deplore it if it inteferes with our plans, our goals or our intentions.

According to the deflationist standpoint then, semantic properties are like the killing relation or like meteorological properties. According to deflationism, it is a fact that the French word 'cheval' refers to horses or means HORSE. Semantic properties are non-normative properties whose instantiation has normative consequences or implications. Notice, however, that prima facie there seems to be a difference between the way normative consequences arise from the instantiation of semantic properties and the way normative consequences arise from the instantiation of the killing relation or from the instantiation of meteorological properties. Whereas the instantiation of meterological properties may occasionally be subject to normative assessment, the instantiation of a semantic property *always* has normative implications. It does not seem as if the normative implications of meaning can sometimes be relaxed or loosened. In any case, given the assumption that meaning is not a normative property, it is incumbent upon the deflationist to account for the normative consequences of meaning.

3. A pragmatic explanation of the normative implications of semantic properties

Let us examine the deflationist explanation of the normative implications of meaning. What the deflationist has in mind, I think, is conditional [C3] which is a revised version of [C1]:

[C3] If the French word 'chien' refers to dogs or means DOG, then one *ought* to apply it to dogs and only to dogs *provided* one wants (or intends) to communicate with French speakers.

In other words, on the deflationary account, the normative consequences of meaning are contingent or conditional upon an individual's *intentions, desires* or *goals*.

At this stage, I want to make explicit a couple of assumptions on which my subsequent discussion will be predicated. On my view, any creature capable of engaging in intentional actions must be capable of entertaining two kinds of mental representations. It must be able to form beliefs and it must be able to form desires. As Anscombe and Searle have pointed out, beliefs and desires have opposite directions of fit. Beliefs have a mind-to-world direction of fit. Their job is to provide an accurate representation (or a correct picture) of how the world is. Now, unless they were motivationally inert, beliefs could not do their job: a creature whose beliefs would systematically be based on wishful thinking could not survive the test of natural selection. Goals, intentions and desires represent possible or impossible non-actual states of affairs. They have a world-to-mind direction of fit. They represent the world as it ought to be, not as it is. An intentional action is expected by the agent to bring the world in accordance with his or her desire. Unlike beliefs, goals, intentions and desires are motivational states: they are motivationally efficacious.

Now, I take it that truth is to beliefs or utterances what reference is to words or concepts. If meaning is normative, so are reference and truth. Deflationists about meaning deny that meaning is a normative property. Similarly, they deny that truth and reference are normative properties. Hence, they deny that, in Bernard Williams' (1970) words, "beliefs aim at truth". On their view, what is constitutive of beliefs is that they obey the principle of bivalence: beliefs ought not to be true simpliciter, they ought to be true *or* false. This is, according e.g., to Dretske (2000), enough to distinguish beliefs from other propositional attitudes, e.g., desires.

Just as it was incumbent upon the deflationist to account for the normative implications of meaning, it is incumbent upon him to account for the normative implications of truth. Why do we assess differently true beliefs and false ones? Again, the deflationary account of the normative implications of truth is pragmatic and it makes the normative consequences of truth conditional upon a creature's motivational states. Although beliefs do not aim at truth, we nonetheless generally prefer to hold true beliefs rather than false ones because true beliefs are more likely to promote practical success than false ones. Of two creatures, the one whose belief forming mechanisms are more reliable is the more likely to survive.[2] The pragmatic account of the normative consequences of truth could thus be captured by conditional [C4]:

[C4] If p is true (and sufficiently relevant), then one ought to believe that p provided that one intends to satisfy one's desires.

Presumably, the deflationist does not want to be saddled with the absurd view that if a proposition is true, then one ought to believe it provided that one intends to satisfy one's desires. Presumably, a person ought to believe only *relevant* truths provided he or she intends to satisfy his or her desires.[3] Conditional [C4] is expressed in terms of an individual's higher-order goal, intention or desire to satisfy his or her lower-order goals or desires. It makes the normative consequences of the truth of a relevant belief conditional upon the agent's higher-order desire to achieve practical success.

4. Criticism of the pragmatic explanation of the normative consequences of semantic properties

First, I want to consider the pragmatic explanation of the normative consequences of meaning. The deflationary view that the normative consequences of meaning are conditional upon an individual's goals or desires is plausible in the case of the meanings of words of public languages because ordinarily, one uses words of his or her language in order to communicate his or her thoughts to his or her conspecifics. So making a speech act by uttering words of a public language is an intentional action. And intentional actions depend on the agent's beliefs and desires.

But what about thoughts? Thoughts, just like words, have content. However, unlike uttering a word of a natural language, thinking or entertaining a thought is not – or at least, not always – an intentional action. It may but it need not be an intentional action. On my view, unlike my utterance of the word 'chien', my tokening of the concept DOG need not be an intentional action. Suppose I token my concept (or mental symbol) DOG upon hearing some dog bark in the neighborhood. My thinking about a dog involves my tokening of the concept DOG. And the tokening of my concept DOG may be automatically prompted or triggered by my processing an acoustic perceptual input. My tokening of my concept DOG or my thinking about dogs is not – not always – under the control of my goals, intentions and desires. If I

---

[2] The motivational state may be a personal or a sub-personal state.
[3] I take it that it would be strange to require of a person that she believes any truth. That is why I add 'relevant'.

cannot help thinking 'There is a dog in the street', then my entertaining that thought or belief is not an intentional action. Nonetheless, my concept DOG correctly applies to dogs and only dogs in virtue of its content.

I grant, however, that many beliefs may arise as a result of an intentional action. So when a mathematician believes (or knows) that a proposition is true because he just proved it or because he knows how to prove it, then his belief in the truth of the theorem is the outcome of an intentional action. He believes it because he proved it or because he grasped a proof. And he proved it because he decided, he wanted or he intended to prove it. Or he grasped a proof because he decided to learn or study a proof. Similarly, when a scientist comes to believe that a hypothesis is correct either because he has accumulated enough evidence in its favor or he has disproved a rival hypothesis, then his belief arises out of an intentional process. Following Dennett (1978) and Sperber (1997), I shall call such beliefs "reflective" beliefs because they typically involve linguistic communication which involves the grasp of communicative intentions which in turn relies on the metarepresentational ability to think about other people's thoughts.[4] Unlike "reflective" beliefs, however, what I call "intuitive" beliefs typically arise from basic cognitive processes such as perception, memory and rudimentary inferential mechanisms. I assume that, unlike "reflective" beliefs, a creature with no ability to form higher-order thoughts about thoughts can form "intuitive" beliefs.

Now, "intuitive" beliefs involve the intuitive application of concepts (e. g., the concept DOG). Conversely, the mastery of concepts involves knowledge of its conditions of application. Whether one wants to think of knowledge of the application of a concept as explicit or implicit, there are norms for the application of a concept: my concept DOG applies correctly in some circumstances, not in others. Possessing the concept DOG involves knowing in what circumstances it is correct to apply it. Deflationists deny that concepts have normative conditions of application. On their view, the conditions of application of a concept are not normative: it is merely a fact that the concept DOG applies to dogs and only to dogs. However, the conditions of application of a concept may have normative consequences that derive from an individual's desires. My point is that the normative consequences of the application of a concept cannot – not always – be conditional upon an individual's goals or desires. It cannot when the application of a concept is not an intentional action, i. e., something explainable by the agent's motivations. If a concept is a constituent of an "intuitive" belief, then the normative

---

[4] Dennett (1978) calls 'opinions' what I call reflective beliefs.

distinction between its correct application and its incorrect application cannot be conditional upon the individual's goals or desires.

Secondly, I want to consider a potential rebuttal from the deflationist. Suppose we accept the deflationst suggestion that beliefs do not aim at truth. Suppose rather that one ought to *prefer* true beliefs over false ones because, unlike false beliefs, true beliefs contribute to practical (or reproductive) success. Suppose also that correctly applying a concept contributes to forming true beliefs. Should one not conclude then that the norms for correct applications of a concept derive from one's preference for true beliefs over false ones? If so, then the fact that the application of a concept has normative consequences would indeed be conditional upon an agent's goals or desires.

But from the above two premises, what does follow is that one ought to prefer applying a concept correctly rather than incorrectly. It does not follow that the norms for correct applications of a concept derive from one's preference for true beliefs. It is one thing to hold a preference for applying concepts correctly. Norms for correct application are something else. If I prefer to form true beliefs over false ones, and given that my correct application of my concept DOG contributes to forming true beliefs about dogs, then it follows that I ought to prefer to apply correctly rather than incorrectly my concept DOG. But the fact that my concept DOG correctly applies to dogs and to nothing else does not depend on my preference for true beliefs. Even if I had a preference for false beliefs, my concept DOG would nonetheless apply correctly to dogs and incorrectly to anything else. The normative distinction between correct and incorrect application of a concept does not derive from one's preference for true beliefs.

Thirdly, I want to consider the deflationary view that truth is not a normative property of beliefs (or utterances). According to deflationism, beliefs do not aim at truth. According to the pragmatic account of the normative consequences of truth, beliefs must be true or false and we prefer true beliefs to false ones because true beliefs allow us to achieve practical success better than false ones. The reliability of belief-forming mechanisms enhances survival.[5] I have already offered reasons for rejecting the pragmatic account of the normative consequences of meaning and truth. Now, I want to question the deflationary view itself: I want to resist the claim that it is constitutive of beliefs to be true *or* false (or to obey the principle of bivalence), not to be true simpliciter. I claim that to believe that p is to believe that p is true, not to believe that p is true or false. Let me say why: if one discovers that one of one's beliefs is false, then one will either reject it or take it that

---

[5] Stich (1990) has argued that survival cannot depend only on the reliability of the belief forming mechanisms: there must be a trade-off between reliability and costs.

one ought to reject it. Now a false belief is a belief which is true or false. So if it were constitutive of beliefs to be true or false, then upon discovering that one of one's beliefs is false, then one would have no reason to reject it. One ought not to feel impelled to reject it. But I claim that one would – or one ought to – feel impelled to reject it. If I am right, then I think that, contrary to the deflationary view, in Williams' words, "beliefs *do* aim at truth".

I suppose that the deflationist might want to object to the above little argument in favor of the view that beliefs ought to be true – or aim at truth – by pointing out that if deflationism was correct, then indeed one ought to reject a false belief provided that one prefers to hold true beliefs rather than false ones. On the deflationist view, beliefs ought to be true or false. So, given that true beliefs, not false beliefs, are conducive to practical succcess, it would indeed follow that one ought to reject a false belief, on the assumption that one prefers to have beliefs that are conducive to practical success. But what if one prefers to have false beliefs? Presumably, if one did not prefer true beliefs, then one would not have any reason to reject a false belief. Hence: beliefs ought to be true or false, not just true. And one's preference for true beliefs must be independent from any intrinsic or constitutive property of beliefs.

The question raised by the deflationist rebuttal then is the following: What does it mean – what could it mean – to prefer *false* beliefs over true ones? Could one truly prefer false beliefs? I would like to distinguish two cases: one may have a *local* preference for false beliefs over true ones, and one may have a *global* preference for false beliefs. By local preference, I mean that one may have reasons to have, or it may be adaptive for one to have, *some* false beliefs among one's overall set of beliefs. Equivalently, one may no doubt prompt some one else to have *some* false beliefs. One may, for example, genuinely prefer to hold a subset of false beliefs if e.g., some true belief is too painful or if some subset of beliefs is too costly to form. But this local preference, I think, does not really threaten the claim that beliefs ought to be true – no more so than does the fact that many beliefs *are* in fact false. It is only, it seems to me, against the background of true beliefs that one may prefer to hold a subset of false beliefs, if e.g., either some true belief is too painful or too costly to entertain.

The real problem then has to do with one's *global* preference for false beliefs. If one had such a global preference for false beliefs, then one would (or ought to) reject any true belief and one would (or ought to) accept only false beliefs. The job of the belief-forming mechanism would be to get things wrong systematically. It is very hard, it seems to me, to make sense of such a global preference from either an evolutionary point of view or a (personal) psychological point of view. From an evolutionary point of view, I fail to see how a creature with a global preference for false beliefs could survive. A creature with a belief forming mechanism that would get things systematically wrong would be dead. From a psychological point of view, the problem seems to me to be that a global preference for false beliefs is threatened by a paradox which is reminiscent of the *liar*'s paradox. Presumably, a global preference for false beliefs would apply to higher-order beliefs about oneself (about one's lower-order beliefs, desires and other attitudes). So suppose that a person who claims to have a global preference for false beliefs were asked: "Is it *true* that you prefer to hold false beliefs? Do you truly believe that you prefer to have false beliefs?" What is this person going to answer? She can only falsely believe of herself that she prefers false beliefs. She cannot truly believe it. If she believes it, then she does not prefer to hold false beliefs. Conversely, if she does not believe that she prefers to hold false beliefs, then she believes it. She can only believe it if she does not believe it. So it cannot be right that she prefers to have false beliefs. This, I think, suggests that no creature can have a global preference for false beliefs. Only local preference for false beliefs makes sense. But, as I said, local preference for false beliefs does not really threaten the thesis that beliefs ought to be true any more than mistakes do.

5. Semantic and non-semantic norms

When an agent performs an intentional action – an action done for a reason –, the possibility arises of there being a *gap* between what the agent does and what he ought to do. If an agent does something for a reason, then his reason motivates his action. His reason is a motivating reason. Not all reasons for an action, however, are motivating reasons. In addition to motivating reasons, there are normative reasons for action. An agent's motivating reasons may, but they need not, coincide with his normative reasons. In other words, normative reasons and motivating reasons may part company. An agent may recognize a deontic or an ethical norm and fail to act in accordance with the norm. Recognition of an ethical norm is therefore consistent with having no desire to comply with it. I may recognize that I ought to do such-and-such and fail to do what the norm prescribes. Conversely, my motivating reason may conflict with some normative reason of which I am perfectly aware. Recognition of a norm without having a desire to comply with the norm simply lacks motivational force. Recognition of an ethical norm is therefore consistent with violation of the norm.

Let us call "valuing" the recognition of an ethical norm or of a normative reason. I think that the very possibility of a gap between recognition of an ethical norm and motivation suggests that valuing – recognition of an ethical norm – cannot consist in having a first-order ordinary desire. The question then arises whether recognition of an ethical norm – valuing – consists in having a belief or having a higher-order desire (a desire to form ordinary first-order desires). I will not try to adjudicate this dilemma here. In any case, as I already said, I assume that only ordinary first-order desires are genuine motivational states. So neither beliefs nor higher-order desires are, on my view, genuinely motivational states.

Now, consider the relation between truth and what I earlier called "intuitive" beliefs. There is simply no gap between recognition of truth and believing. It is neither open to me to refrain from believing what I take (or know) to be true, nor to believe what I take (or know) to be false. This is presumably what Moore's paradox taught us: I cannot consistently entertain the thought that it is raining but I do not believe it. Nor can I entertain the thought that it is not raining but I do believe it. Of course, I can accept a proposition for the sake of argument. But acceptance of a proposition for the sake of argument – as I already claimed – is not forming an "intuitive" belief. Arguably, the reason why there is no gap between truth and belief is that in the process whereby I recognize the truth of a proposition and I believe it, there is no room for motivation or for desire. And the reason why there is no room for motivation or for desire is that forming an "intuitive" belief is not an intentional action. I do not form an intuitive belief because I intend to or want to. Unlike ethical and deontic norms then, semantic norms are not norms of intentional action. Contrary to deflationism, I think that beliefs aim at truth. Beliefs ought to – their job or their function is to – be true. Contrary to deflationists, I think that truth is a normative property of beliefs.

6. Two objections

Before closing, let me consider two objections. The first objection consists in what seems to be a counterexample to the claim that semantic norms differ from other (e. g., ethical) norms in that they cannot always be willingly violated. It is an objection to the claim that in the case of semantic norms, there may be no gap between recognition of a norm and motivation. The second objection simply denies that what cannot be knowingly violated can be a norm at all.

First of all, there are cases where the "intuitive" belief-forming capacity seems to be at a loss. A stick seen in the water looks "broken". In spite of the fact that I know that unbroken sticks look broken when seen in the water, a stick seen in the water will still appear broken to me. In the famous Müller-

Lyer illusion, two equal segments with two different endings look unequal. Although I may know and therefore believe that two Müller-Lyer segments are equal, nonetheless the two equal segments will still look unequal to me. In such cases, the subject recognizes that visual appearances are deceptive. Although he recognizes that he ought to hold true a proposition, does he not lack the motivation to believe what he ought to?

I think not at all. Although the stick seen in the water seems broken to me, if I know that unbroken sticks seen in the water look broken, then I will discard the visual appearances and accept the belief that the stick, which looks broken when seen in the water, is in fact not broken. I will accept this "reflective" belief in order to minimize chaos in my overall picture of the world. Now, my choice is not infallible. I may be wrong: *broken* sticks too look broken when seen in the water. If I know that two Müller-Lyer segments are equal (either because I was told or because I measured them), then I will discard the visual appearances and judge them to be equal. So it is simply not true that I recognize a norm but I am not motivated to believe what I take to be true.

The last question I want to consider is the question whether it is constitutive of norms that they can be knowingly violated. I grant that the meaning of a word can be knowingly violated. Although I know that the French word for horses is 'cheval' and the French word for sheep is 'mouton', I can decide to apply the word 'mouton' to horses and the word 'cheval' to sheep. However, I deny that the norms for the correct application of a *concept* can be knowingly violated. I claim that although I can intentionally misapply the word 'mouton' to a horse, I cannot, upon hearing the sound produced by a galloping horse, intentionally misapply my concept SHEEP to categorize the auditory stimulus. I can make a mistake in perception. But I cannot intentionally misapply a concept. As I said, using a word of a public language for the purpose of communication is an intentional action and as such it depends upon one's goals, desires and intentions. But applying a concept as a result of processing a perceptual stimulus is not an intentional action and it does not depend upon one's goals, desires and intentions. Similarly, because forming an "intuitive" belief is not an intentional action, one cannot intentionally form a false "intuitive" belief. As far as "intuitive" beliefs are concerned, one cannot intentionally violate the norm of truth. Since all beliefs aim at truth and "intuitive" beliefs dot not arise out of intentional actions, one cannot intend to form a false "intuitive" belief. Now, the objection goes: what follows is not that semantic norms differ from other (e.g., ethical) norms. What follows is that what I call "semantic norms" are not norms after all.

According to the objection, nothing will be a norm unless it can both strike a person as a reason for action and at the same time lack motivational force. The issue raised by the objection is, I think, whether all norms do or not apply at the personal level – whether norms must be open to conscious personal inspection – or whether some norms may apply at the subpersonal level. In the remaining space, my goal will be modest: I will merely argue that the notion of a subpersonal norm is not incoherent. I will adduce two sorts of evidence in favor of this modest claim. I will appeal to the computational paradigm in cognitive science and to functional explanations in biology.

First of all, I want to reflect on the fact that the strong claim that all norms must apply at the personal level and be available for conscious inspection should be reminiscent of Searle's (1992) Connection Principle according to which genuine mental states – as opposed to merely physiological processes – must be accessible to consciousness. And it deserves, I think, the same response. Explanations in cognitive science are framed as computational explanations of the behavior of information-processing systems. I assume that not all information-processing systems are conscious systems. But all information-processing systems are physical systems. So they fall under physical laws and physical explanations. Computational explanations presuppose that not everything an information-processing system does can be usefully described by showing how it instantiates physical laws. Some of the behavior of an information-processing system is best explained as a set of computations. Since a little computing device is a physical device, its behavior falls under the laws of physics. If, however, it is capable of performing additions, then only a computational explanation may fully capture its arithmetical behavior. Now, my point is that a computational explanation presupposes norms of computation. Given a pair of natural numbers as input, there is a number which is their sum and which is such that the device *ought* to compute it as output. Norms for computing additions are built into the device. They are not accessible to the device for conscious personal inspection for the simple reason that the device is nonconscious. Nor could the normative implications of arithmetical computations be derivable from the device's motivational states since the device lacks motivational states. Cognitive science requires, it seems to me, that norms can apply at the subpersonal level and hence that they be unavailable for conscious inspection, let alone that they be knowingly violated.

Arguably, a computing device is an artefact. So norms of computations may have been built into the computing device by a human being with beliefs and desires. So the normative implications of arithmetical computations may after all depend upon a human being's motivational states. However, I do not think that any mistake I ever made in computing an addition could be explained as a failure to be motivated by an arithmetical norm which

I recognized. Nor do I think that arithmetical norms depend on motivations.

On the kind of teleosemantic reductionist view, which I hold, semantic and cognitive norms do not depend on motivations.[6] They derive from, and are built into, the semantic and cognitive functions which are, on my view, a species of biological functions. Like Millikan (1993) and Neander (1995), I think that, unlike physics and chemistry, biology is loaded with norms. If a planet of the Solar system were to stop gravitating towards the Sun, it would stop being a planet of the Solar system. If a chemical bond between two atoms within a molecule breaks down, then the whole molecule disintegrates or gives rise to another molecule. If, however, a biological organ stops performing its biological function, it does not ipso facto lose its identity. Why? Because a biological organ has a biological function. I accept Wright's (1973) etiological theory of functions according to which functions are selected effects, i.e., they are things which a device can do and which have been promoted by some selection process. It is the function of a mammal's heart to pump blood. A mammal's heart may fail to pump blood. If it does not pump blood, then it does not what it ought to do. If, however, it does not do its job, it is not thereby disqualified as a heart. A diseased heart may misfunction. But if it does, it is still a heart. The crucial point here is that the relevant biological notion of a function is a teleological notion, not a dispositional notion: if an organ (or a biological device) has a function in this teleological sense, then there are things that it is supposed to do or that it ought to do. In other words, there are biological norms and they arise from biological functions. Biological functions in turn arise from the physical process of natural selection at work in evolution.

In sum, my point is that not all norms depend on motivations. Norms of computations (or grammatical norms for that matter) and biological norms do not apply at the personal level. Nor are they available for conscious inspection. Nonetheless, I want to claim, they are norms. Furthermore, unlike ethical norms, they cannot, I claim, be knowingly violated because whether they are enforced does not depend upon any motivational state.

References

Burge, T.: Individualism and the Mental. In: *Midwest Studies in Philosophy, vol. IV*, ed. by P. French, T. Uehling, Jr. and H.K. Wettstein, University of Minnesota Press, Minneapolis 1979.

---

[6] See Jacob (1997).

Dennett, D.: How to Change Your Mind. In: D. Dennett, *Brainstorms*, Bradford Books Publishers, Inc., Mongtomery, Vt 1978.
Dretske, F.: Norms, History, and the Constitution of the Mental. In: F. Dretske, *Perception, Knowledge and Belief*, Cambridge University Press, Cambridge 2000.
Hale, B.: Rule-Following, Objectivity and Meaning. In: *A Companion to the Philosophy of Language*, ed. by B. Hale and C. Wright, Blackwell, Oxford 1997.
Horwich, P.: *Meaning*, Oxford University Press, Oxford 1998.
Jacob, P.: *What minds can do*, Cambridge University Press, Cambridge 1997.
Kripke, S.: *Wittgenstein on Following a Rule*, Blackwell, Oxford 1982.
Millikan, R.G.: *White Queen Psychology and Other Essays for Alice*, MIT Press, Cambridge, Mass. 1993.
Neander, K.: Misrepresenting and Malfunctioning, *Philosophical Studies* 79 (1995), 109–41.
Putnam, H.: The Meaning of 'Meaning'. In: H. Putnam, *Mind, Language and Reality, Philosophical Papers, Volume 2*, Cambridge University Press, Cambridge 1975, 215–271.
Searle, J.: *The Rediscovery of the Mind*, MIT Press, Cambridge, Mass. 1992.
Sperber, D.: Intuitive and Reflective Beliefs, *Mind and Language* 12 (1997), 67–83.
Stich, S.: *The Fragmentation of Reason*, MIT Press, Cambridge, Mass.1990.
Williams, B.: Deciding to Believe (1971). In: B. Williams, *Problems of the Self*, Cambridge University Press, Cambridge 1973.
Wright, L.: Functions. In: *Conceptual Issues in Evolutionary Biology*, ed. by E. Sober, MIT Press, Cambridge, Mass. 1973.

Manuel García-Carpintero

A Vindication of Sense-data[1]

1. In this paper I question the contemporary consensus against sense-data. I will argue that the consensus discards a straw man, and does not confront a stronger version of sense-data accounts. Here is, as I will show later, an example of this straw man, presented in an otherwise very insightful contribution to these issues: "Intentional approaches and sense-datum theories differ in at least two respects: intentional theories assert, and sense-datum theories deny, that mind-independent objects can be present to the mind in having perceptual experience; sense-datum theories assert, while intentional theories deny, that what is so present to the mind must actually exist" (M. Martin, "The Transparency of Experience", ms). Characterizations such as this, I will argue, provide (by a mere stroke of the pen) a measure of credit for what they call 'intentionalism', and a reciprocal measure of discredit for sense-data theories, which neither of them deserve.

I will proceed by examining the most influential contemporary views, briefly outlining the strongest arguments for and against them. My main point will be that there is a well-supported position, left unoccupied by the best known and most discussed contemporary proposals in the field, which posits sense-data. A full-fledged argument for the sense-data account would have to be much longer. This is why I limit the point I want to make here to the one just stated: to make apparent the real strength of the sense-data theory, and thus that contemporary discussions of the nature of phenomenal consciousness in perceptual states ignore it at their own risk. For this goal, the sketchy discussion that follows has, I hope, the level of perspicuity that is needed.

---

[1] Earlier drafts of this paper were presented at the LOGOS's seminar, Universitat de Barcelona, at Oxford University and at the 4th meeting of the *Gesellschaft für Analytische Philosophie: Argument und Analyse* held in Bielefeld. I would like to thank the audiences there for very useful suggestions, and in particular Martin Davies, José Antonio Díez, Josep Macià, Kevin Mulligan, and Manuel Pérez. Financial support was provided by the research projects BFF2001-3466, funded by the DGES, Spanish Government, and SGR2001-0018, Generalitat de Catalunya.

2. I start by indicating – trying not to beg any disputed question – what the main issue at stake is. Perception is a form of knowledge-acquisition, and hence perceptual states are intentional states. Intentional objects of perceptual states are, in central cases, instantiations by material, mind-independent objects or events of observable properties: shapes, spatial distances, temporal durations, forces like solidity and impenetrability, colors, sounds, and so on. Perceptual states are also paradigm conscious states, with phenomenal features characterizing what it is like for the subject to be in them. These phenomenal features are not features of perceptual states by themselves. They are rather features of *perceptual experiences* that, although being constitutive of perceptual states, in some cases (in illusions and hallucinations) could exist without constituting a perceptual state. For phenomenal features are modes of appearance, ways things seem to the perceiving subject; and in illusions and hallucinations some or all (respectively) aspects of what the subject is aware of appear to him as they would if he had been in a perceptual state instead. In what follows, the difference between illusion and hallucination will be irrelevant. We will be contrasting veridical perceptual experiences ('vpe' henceforth) with misleading perceptual experiences ('mpe' henceforth), focussing only, in the latter case, on those phenomenal features in virtue of which the experience is not constitutive of a perceptual state, but of an illusion or a hallucination.

Both observable and phenomenal features, qualities or characters involve types, instantiable repeatables. In natural language we use the same words for them. We count as 'red' or 'cramp' exemplars that we perceive, and also the sensations that we have when we merely hallucinate (an after-image, or what we feel in an amputated leg, caused in fact by a herniated disk). All the theories I will discuss provide explanations for this fact. However, they differ precisely in the explanations they provide. In some theories, we use the same expressions because instances of phenomenal and observable features are one and the same thing. In other theories this is not so. This goes to the heart of what I take to be the main issue at stake, which is to account for the constitutive nature of the phenomenal features of perceptual experiences. An assumption I will make (only marginally disputed) is that there might be perceptual experiences indistinguishable for the subject both when there actually exists a perceived instance of the relevant observable feature (in vpe), and when the subject is rather suffering an illusion or a hallucination (in mpe). The theories we will be critically examining are thus theories of the constitutive nature of a paradigm case of phenomenal consciousness: the phenomenal features of perceptual experiences.

3. The first kind of theory I want to consider is disjunctivist naïve realism (formerly called "the theory of appearing"), a view defended in one of its strongest and most discussed versions by McDowell (1982). The distinguishing trait of this theory is the claim that the phenomenal features of vpe are, in their constitutive natures, essentially different from those of mpe. The former are primitive relations between the subject and instances of observable properties; the latter are not. The phenomenal features of experience – what it is like for the subject to be aware of them – consist thus either in primitive relations with instances of observable properties, or in misleading appearances. Disjunctivists take a quietist Wittgensteinian attitude regarding the nature of the phenomenal features of mpe, studiously avoiding going beyond the negative claim.

The main consideration which defenders of this view marshal in its favor lies in its prima facie congruence with an important phenomenological datum, the diaphanousness of experience. This is the phenomenological fact that if we try to focus introspectively on the phenomenal features of an experience, what we focus on presents to us as instantiations of the observable features of material objects with which we are confronted in veridical experiences. This phenomenological datum is related to phenomenological descriptions of perceptual experiences as giving us "immediate" or "direct" access to the perceived objects, or as being "receptive" or "passive" (i.e., of something external to us which affects us, rather than of something which we make up).

The diaphanousness of experiences is, I take it, one of the important pieces of evidence that a constitutive account of them should capture. But against what is claimed for naïve realism, I do not think that it really captures the phenomenological fact of diaphanousness. The main reason is that the fact of diaphanousness applies also to mpe. When we focus on the phenomenal features of an experience we know to be hallucinatory, what we focus on still presents to us as instantiations of the observable features of material objects with which we are confronted in veridical experiences. Naïve realism explains diaphanousness in the case of vpe by claiming that their phenomenal features consist in the subject being related to instances of observable properties. This explanation cannot be extended to the diaphanousness of mpe. Naïve realism suggests rather that the diaphanousness of mpe is not the real thing, but merely apparent diaphanousness. According to naïve realism, in mpe there is not (what naïve realism takes to be) real diaphanousness (an actual instance of a phenomenal property being manifest to us), but it just happens that the subject has the erroneous impression of it. However, the fact of diaphanousness is just a phenomenological datum; as such, it cannot be distinguished as a real fact when it concerns vpe and a false illusion when it concerns mpe. Both vpe and mpe are diaphanous, or neither is; for, phenomenologically, they are on a par, and the fact at stake is nothing but a phenomenological fact.

Hence, a theory that accounted for diaphanousness better than naïve realism does would be a stronger contender in the field, *ceteris paribus*. Theories of this kind are to be found in the work of the opponents of disjunctivism – what McDowell aptly calls "highest common factor" theories.

4. The first such theory I want to consider is the contemporary intentionalism or representationalism defended by writers such as Dretske (1995), Harman (1989) and Tye (1995). According to this view, perceptual experiences themselves (not just the perceptual states to which they may give rise) have intentional contents, and the constitutive natures of their phenomenal features are to be analyzed in terms of these intentional contents. Disjunctivism does not necessarily deny the first conjunct in this description, but it does deny the second; for it takes the relevant relations to be primitive, i.e., non-analyzable. According to intentionalists, the possession of intentional content by experiences is to be analyzed in terms of externally constituted relations with externally constituted properties; the latter are the phenomenal features of experience, hence identical to observable properties of material things.

To appreciate the appraisal that follows, we should have in mind a more concrete elaboration of this rather abstract characterization of the representational relation and the allegedly represented phenomenal features, according to intentionalism. Let me appeal for this purpose to the teleological version of Dretske's informational semantics. Consider an experience, in which, among other things, an instantiation of a distance of about one meter is apparent to the subject. According to intentionalism, the experience has properties (perhaps neurological properties) such that there exists an indicator relation between instances of the distance of about one meter, and experiences with those properties: under normal conditions, the neurological properties are instantiated only if a distance of about one meter is instantiated. In virtue of the existence of that indicator relation, experiences with those neurological properties have been recruited (by a biologically provided psychological mechanism) to belong in a functional system. In this system, and under normal conditions, they cause beliefs also indicating the distance of about one meter, and, together with the appropriate intentions, behavior. (We could substitute 'proto-beliefs' and 'proto-intentions' for 'beliefs' and 'intentions' in the preceding description, if we felt that full-fledged beliefs require having more clearly conceptual contents than those merely constituted by informational relations.) The recruitment has taken place in virtue of the fact that the presence of an instance of the distance of about one meter has been instrumental in the satisfaction of the intentions leading to behavior together with those beliefs.

It should be clear from this outline that a phenomenal feature such as *distance of about one meter* is taken by intentionalism to be an observable property, instantiated (when conditions are normal) by a spatial relation between material objects or events. The experience is also supposed to have more intrinsic properties, in virtue of which the indicator relation obtains; but these properties are not taken to be apparent to the subject – they do not characterize what it is like for him to have the experience.

Let us first examine the superiority of this kind of view over naïve realism. Like naïve realism, intentionalism takes the phenomenal features of vpe to consist in relations between the perceiving subject and perceived instances of observable properties. Unlike naïve realism, however, intentionalism does not count this relation as constitutively primitive, but analyzes it in functional (causal-cum-teleological) terms. Such a causal analysis is allowed to intentionalism, because the object itself of a veridical perception (the instantiation of the observable property) is not involved in the constitutive nature of its having those phenomenal features. By having a veridical experience, according to intentionalism a subject is related to an instance of an observable property. But this is because for the experience to have one of its phenomenal features consists in that experiences like it nomically depend, under normal conditions, on instances of the relevant observable property (I overlook now the teleological element); and conditions *are* normal. Thus, although the observable property and the experience one of whose phenomenal features it is are constitutively related, intentionalism allows for the existence of a genuine causal relation, in the veridical case, between the perceived instance and the experience. This is not allowed to naïve realism; because, according to it, the particular perceived is constitutively involved in the phenomenal nature of the veridical experience, and therefore the experience cannot be said to be functionally (causal-cum-teleologically) dependent on it.

Intentionalism appeals to this functional dependence of the experience on the perceived instance in veridical cases, to explain diaphanousness. The proposal goes beyond mere congruence with the phenomenological datum; it *accounts* for it. Our impression that, when we try to introspectively focus on phenomenal features of experience, we in fact focus on instances of observable properties is explained by the fact that the phenomenal features are constituted by the observable features, in the indicated manner. What is more important, intentionalism is not implausibly forced to say that, in the case of mpe, diaphanousness is the mere appearance of diaphanousness. Intentionalism can attribute the same phenomenal features to vpe and mpe; for, as we have seen, the relation with the perceived object is not a brute constitutive part of the phenomenal features of an experience. If conditions are not normal, an experience can misleadingly represent the same as it would if conditions had been normal. The represented instance of an observable feature is in that case a *merely* intentional object. (A merely intentional object is as much an object according to intentionalism as a fake Velázquez is a Velázquez.) Even when we focus on the phenomenal features of experiences that we know to be misleading, it is to be expected, according to intentionalism, that what we seem to focus on are just instances of observable properties. For it is (merely intentional, in that case) instances of observable properties which still constitute their phenomenal features. In sum, intentionalism analyzes the constitutive nature of phenomenal features by ascribing to them a specific functional role, as observable inputs in a specification of the functional nature of the experiences that instantiate them. The account then uses this functional claim to provide a more plausible account of diaphanousness than the one provided by disjunctivist naïve realism.

A related point could be made in terms of the epistemic role intentionalists typically attribute to experiences and their phenomenal features, against the claims of disjunctivists. A well-known tenet of contemporary epistemology, forcefully emphasized by McDowell (1995) and Williamson (1995) among others, is that repeated failures to find adequate reductive analyses of knowledge in terms of non-factive doxastic states suggest that there are none. Knowledge only allows for non-reductive philosophical explications. Applied to the case of perception, the point will be that a reductive analysis of perception in terms of a non-factive state (perceptual experience) and something more is not to be expected. Disjunctivists advertise their views in terms of the congruence of their main tenet with this; for they analyze perceptual states as ineliminably involving already factive vpe, constituted by "the perceived object making itself manifest" to the subject.

However, intentionalism also accounts for the point, in a different way; this is an epistemological dimension of the intentionalist's explanation of diaphanouness. Intentionalism ascribes a common intentional content to vpe and mpe, and thus common phenomenal features. The explanation, however, gives priority to the intentional content and the phenomenal features of vpe; mpe have content, and phenomenal features, only by being deviant cases of vpe. Intentionalism thus accounts for the epistemological point, in that it takes mere belief to be explicated relative to knowledge (or proto-knowledge) – as a deviant case of it – instead of being the other way around. This is the epistemological side of the explanation of diaphanousness provided by intentionalism. The phenomenal features of experience on which we focus correctly appear to us as the observable features we sometimes perceive, because, in explanatorily ineliminable paradigm cases, experiences provide genuine information about the observable traits of a mind-independent world.

A final dimension of the diaphanousness issue has to do with the singularity of experience. Perceptual experience appears to us to present concrete particulars. Once again, disjunctivists contend that their main tenet is in agreement with this point. Disjunctivists suggest that, in opposition to the point, intentionalism characterizes the phenomenal objects of experiences as if experiences referred to them merely by description, and is in that respect less congruent with the impression of singularity. But this is not a convincing consideration either. Reichenbachian accounts of natural language expressions like indexicals and proper names (see García-Carpintero 2000) ascribe to them genuinely singular contents, while positing a common descriptive factor to referring and non-referring terms (in appropriate contexts). These models could be invoked to elaborate on the representational relation posited by intentionalism, capturing therefore the impression of singularity. As in the ontological and epistemological cases, intentionalism provides in fact a better explanation than disjunctivism of this semantic side of diaphanousness. For the impression of singularity, like the impression of factivity, is there *also* in the case of mpe; but disjunctivist naïve realism lacks the resources to properly account for them in those cases.

I think that these considerations concerning diaphanousness give a decisive explanatory advantage to intentionalism over disjunctivist naïve realism. There is one more consideration. By itself it would not be sufficiently convincing, but it acquires its full power when placed after the preceding discussion. Intentionalism contends that vpe and mpe can fully share their phenomenal features; they can be indiscriminable for their subjects, because they can be identical in their constitutive natures. Intentionalism achieves this by analyzing phenomenal features in terms of the functional roles of experiences vis-à-vis observable features of perceived objects, identified as the phenomenal features themselves. According to intentionalism, a commonality in phenomenal features (a commonality in what it is like for the subject) is a commonality in functional (causal-cum-teleological) role; and this (in its ontological, epistemological and semantic sides) is what accounts for diaphanousness. A commonality in phenomenal features is a commonality in an apparent causal role, in a causal role "made manifest" to the experiencing subject.

Now, if we add to this the usual a posteriori considerations in favor of physicalism – of a common physical basis for every common causal role discerned at higher levels of explanation – intentionalism leads us to expect a common physical basis for vpe and mpe. Therefore, if neurology confirms this expectation, intentionalism receives additional confirmation vis-à-vis disjunctivism. For disjunctivism, in ascribing a very different constitutive nature to the phenomenal features of vpe and mpe, does not give us any reason for that expectation; quite the opposite. Notice that it is not just the fact that, in all probability, vpe and mpe might well have a common neurological basis that I mention as providing support for intentionalism. It is this (plus independent considerations in favor of physicalism), but only together with the fact that it is predicted by the philosophical account provided by intentionalism, independently supported.

Robinson (1985, 1990) invokes against disjunctivism the point that vpe and mpe might have a common neurological basis. Langsam (1997) plausibly rejoins that, according to disjunctivism, vpe have relational natures, and there is no reason to expect that a relational state and a non-relational one (even if somehow indistinguishable from it) should have a common physical cause or basis. This rejoinder is well taken as a reply to Robinson's point, when it is not derived from an independent argument, based only on relevant philosophical considerations, for the existence of causal commonalities to vpe and mpe. But I do not think that Langsam's rejoinder answers the present version of the argument. If there were no philosophical reasons to ascribe to the phenomenal features of some vpe and some mpe a common constitutive nature, outflanking reasons to ascribe them different constitutive natures, physical commonalities between them would give no edge to a philosophical account of their natures. However, we have seen that those reasons exist.

I have dwelt upon the advantages of intentionalism over disjunctivism for the good reason that I take all that have been said so far to be more or less true. However, I think that intentionalism is false. So far, I have only presented its most appealing side. I have characterized it as the view that the phenomenal features of phenomenal experiences are constituted by their intentional contents, in their turn consisting in externally constituted relations with externally constituted properties. But this does not fully distinguish the contemporary view defended by writers such as Dretske, Harman or Tye. Although we have presented the view in modern terms alien to philosophers like Descartes or Locke, they might be prepared to accept what we have been discussing as intentionalism so far. Russell, I think, would have been prepared to do so during the short period (around 1915) when he invoked sense-data to provide a representative account of perception. Be that as it may, what really distinguishes the views of writers like those I have mentioned is the additional claim that there is nothing else to the constitutive natures of the phenomenal features of perceptual experiences than what has been attributed to them so far. This, I think, is wrong. In any case, there are good reasons to doubt it; and there is a view that, while accepting all the points we have made so far on behalf of intentionalism, should not be objected to on the basis of *those* reasons. This is the sense-data theory.

5. Before introducing it, however, I will round off my critical discussion of contemporary positions by examining the main rival of the sort of intentionalism we have been discussing, which also counts as a "highest common factor" view of the phenomenal features of perceptual experience. This is the *phenomenism* of Block (1995), Chalmers (1996) and others. Phenomenism differs from intentionalism mainly in that, while instances of phenomenal properties are according to intentionalism *material*, they are rather *subjective* for phenomenists. According to intentionalism, actual (i.e., not merely intentional) instances of phenomenal features are material entities by two clear-cut criteria. Firstly, although they are as a matter of fact relata of an experiential state of a subject, they are either material events, or constitutive of the history of material objects, which could have existed without any subject being aware of them. Secondly, the very same instances of phenomenal features might be relata of experiential states of more than one subject, if more than one subject has experiences with them as contents.

According to phenomenism, however, instances of phenomenal features are straightforwardly subjective, in that they do not satisfy either of those two criteria. Phenomenal features themselves (the types, not their instances) are not observable properties with which experiences are related, but more intrinsic properties of experiences, of which the subject is aware. Phenomenists adopt an adverbialist attitude regarding the logic of the relation between experiences and their phenomenal features, i.e., they do not think of it in act-object terms. To experience is not for them to be in a relation with instances of phenomenal features; rather, to experience is a determinable, of which phenomenal features provide adverbial determinations (modes). Thus, instances of phenomenal features are for phenomenists necessarily instances of experiences, and thus are constitutive of the mental history of a conscious subject. Hence, they are not material by the first criterion: they could not have existed without a conscious subject thereby existing. Secondly, a given instance of a phenomenal property is, according to phenomenism, constitutive of just one subject, by the same reason that no two subjects could share two token-experiences. Such an instance cannot thus constitute the experiences of more than one subject, nor be material relative to the second straightforward criterion above. (No problematic form of privacy is involved here; notice that we are just discussing facts concerning instances of phenomenal features, not their types.) Henceforth, I will place expressions for phenomenal qualities inside a peculiar form of quotation mark (like this: ^{s}toothache^s) to distinguish the subjectively instantiated characters posited by phenomenism from the material observable features to which intentionalists reduce them.

There are two main reasons against contemporary intentionalism and in favor of some form of phenomenism, which I think we should take very seriously. Firstly, intentionalism requires that all observable (i. e., phenomenal) properties are (almost) primary properties; but there is no reason to think that this is the case, still less as a result of essentially a priori considerations. A correct philosophical explication of observable properties should leave open, for empirical resolution, the possibility that some of them be secondary properties. Secondly, intentionalism makes "inverted spectrum" situations impossible, again as a matter of a priori considerations; once again this seems wrong, even if it turns out to be empirically correct. I will elaborate on these related points.

A primary property is a property that has a fully objective nature; it has a nature that does not involve the mental states of subjects, and whose precise characterization can only be justified, if at all, on the basis of empirical research. I do not think that intentionalists need to accept that phenomenal features are primary properties in this demanding sense, for reasons to be given presently. However, they cannot accept that phenomenal features are secondary properties, if we define them not just as non-primary properties, but as dispositions in material things to cause experiences with specific phenomenal properties, instances of which are subjective by the two criteria discussed above. Let us refer to secondary properties thus understood as 'sensory properties'. In the intentionalist framework, to consider some phenomenal features sensory would be indulging in a vicious form of circularity.

According to the intentionalist account that we presented earlier, perceptual experiences, in virtue of having phenomenal features, are essentially recognitional capacities for the observable qualities that are their phenomenal features. The reason is that a recognitional capacity for a property is the capacity to come to know in normal circumstances that an instance of the property is present, without conscious inference, as a causal result of previous interactions with instances of the property. Phenomenal qualities (observable properties) are thus for intentionalists essentially recognizable properties. The subject of experiences with those features, as a result of having them, is able to come to know the presence of their instances in normal circumstances, without conscious inference, and as a result of having been in contact with instances of them. This implies, I think, that observable properties cannot be fully objective primary properties for the intentionalist. The reason is that representations of recognizable properties are vague – like the example used earlier to illustrate the intentionalist account, *distance of about one meter*. Now, this vagueness is to be accounted for, I think, by taking the "property" to involve in its nature the fact that it is the object of a recognitional capacity of a given subject. But I do not think that a refutation of intentionalism follows merely from this. For we can give an account of these vague recognizable "properties" along supervaluationist lines, taking them to be indeterminately constituted by a number of fully objective precise primary properties. Intentionalists can then plausibly contend that phenomenal features sufficiently approximate fully objective primary properties.

The problem, however, is that it is not plausible to believe that something like this applies to all phenomenal features. Intentionalism must apply also to phenomenal features such as pains and orgasms. Against what some phenomenists have claimed, I do not find it wrong to say that, by having experiences with those phenomenal characters, we are also in states presenting instances of observable qualities to us (properties of parts of our bodies, in these cases). What I do think unwarranted is the assumption that the properties in question are even the kind of approximations to fully objective primary properties considered in the previous paragraph. The only unity behind the variegated conditions of our bodies we recognize in normal conditions by having experiences with phenomenal features such as pains might well lie in that all of them cause, in normal conditions, experiences with a feature of which we are aware. This feature cannot then be analyzed without vicious circularity along intentionalist lines. The same applies perhaps to tastes, smells, colors and sounds. This point is elegantly made by Perkins (1983), in one of the few contemporary defenses of sense-data. Even if the intentionalist assumption turned out to be empirically correct for all such cases, to make the assumption as a matter of philosophical theorizing seems by itself wrong.

As Shoemaker (1990) indicates, this difficulty for contemporary intentionalism supports a phenomenist view of phenomenal features incompatible with it, in which instances of phenomenal properties are not material (in the sense previously explicated) but subjective. The same conclusion follows from the well-known inverted-spectrum considerations, also elaborated by Shoemaker (1984), which I will not develop here. They too seem to require, for some phenomenal features at least, that we count their instances as subjective by the two criteria above.

I have dwelt upon the reasons for phenomenism once again because I take them to be essentially correct. But I do not think that phenomenism is true. It differs from a sense-data theory on two counts. Firstly, in the adverbialist logic that it applies to the relation between phenomenal features and experiences. Secondly, in reducing the phenomenal features to their subjective sides, leaving out any representational matters in its account of the constitutive nature of phenomenal features. Writers like Block (1995) and Chalmers (1996) separate the "psychological" properties of states such as experiences, to be understood along intentionalist lines, from the truly phenomenal properties, which according to them have nothing to do with representational matters. Both things are wrong, in my view. The well-known arguments of Jackson (1977), against an adverbialist rendering of the relation between experience and phenomenal character, are in my view still decisive; I will not pursue this matter here.[2] I cannot go into the problems caused by the split of phenomenal and representational features.[3] For present purposes, it is enough to say that phenomenism appears to be incompatible with the diaphanousness of experience. Any account that, while preserving the improvements of phenomenism over intentionalism, accounts for diaphanousness in the manner that intentionalism does would have a clear explanatory advantage.

6. Such is, in my view, a sense-data account; let us see first how such an account characterizes the constitutive nature of phenomenal features. According to a sense-data theory, there are two different sides to the phenomenal features of perceptual experiences – to what it is like for the subject to have them.[4] This is the distinction between the *material* and the *objective* way of taking ideas, which Descartes draws in the *Preface* to the *Meditations*.[5] As an illustration of this double role that sense-data theories ascribe to phenomenal features, suppose that I am going to have my room painted. In order to indicate what color will be used, the painter gives me a picture of a similar room painted in that color. There are two different instances of the color to be considered, when we want to characterize what is involved in the comprehension of the picture. There is the one instantiated by the picture, and there is the instance to be instantiated by the room. The first plays a representing role, the second the role of the represented content. The representing is in this case partly iconic; it takes place in part on the basis of the fact that the two colors are (relevantly) indistinguishable to the customer. This is not all that there is to the representing relation, however; the communicative intentions with which the painter hands over the picture also play a crucial role. Notice also that it is not necessary that the two colors are, to all effects,

---

[2] I elaborate on this in García-Carpintero, forthcoming g-a.
[3] I develop them in García-Carpintero, forthcoming g-b.
[4] For a recent proposal along these lines, see Perkins (1983), ch. 8.
[5] "There is an ambiguity in the word 'idea'. 'Idea' can be taken materially, as an operation of the intellect ... Alternatively, it can be taken objectively, as the thing represented by that operation" (J. Cottingham, translation and edition, Cambridge U.P., 1996).

the same property. They can differ, even in matters constitutive of their nature; they certainly can be differently constituted physically. What matters only is that they are similar enough to play their role. Now, it seems clear that, in such a case, to properly understand the picture requires awareness of the two colors at stake, the one whose instance plays the representing role, and the one which is represented as instantiated by the room. (Even if the attention of the customer is so engaged by the color that his room is going to have that he attentionally bypasses the color of the picture.) The two, in their two different roles, characterize the way the situation appears to the understanding subject.

Sense-data theories contend similarly that the phenomenal features of an experience are constituted by two potentially different sets of properties. There is, first, a ^{s}red^s-instance, say, which does the representing. This is subjective, by the two criteria in § 5. Its relation to the experience is not to be interpreted under an adverbialist logic, but in an act-object manner. It will not be accurate to say that the subject is *perceiving* an instance of ^{s}redness^s, for reasons given by Shoemaker (1994). Instances of ^{s}redness^s, in contrast with instances of redness, are such that it is enough for the subject to be aware of them that they are instantiated and the subject does not have his attention fully occupied elsewhere. This awareness is therefore too easy to be properly counted as an act of perception, which is typically harder to achieve, and more liable to failure due to contingencies outside the control of the conscious subject. I will instead say that the subject is consciously aware of such an instance. This does not exhaust what it is like for the subject to have the experience. There is also a material intentional instance of redness, apparent for the subject whenever he is aware of an instance of ^{s}redness^s. Another way of making the point is this.[6] Perceptions are representational states involving genuine Fregean reference to objective, mind-independent particulars (instances of phenomenal qualities, in their objective guises). They require modes of presentation involving properties (phenomenal features in their material guises) differing from the properties that the referred particulars are represented as having. Conscious awareness of the representing instances, on the other hand, only architectonically requires modes of presentation. But these modes of presentation do not involve properties differing from the property which the instance is experienced as having. In conscious awareness of the material guises of phenomenal features, the mode of presentation is the property-instance itself.

The representational relation determining the intentional object, as in the previous illustration, is partly iconic. As in the previous example, this does not require that redness and ^{s}redness^s be the same property. To be

---

[6] Close to Loar's (1997).

sure, in many respects they are not. They are very differently constituted physically, from which all kinds of differences in causal role result; redness is constituted by a disposition of material surfaces to reflect light in differential ways, ^{s}redness^s by neurophysiological states that do not constitute such dispositions. Iconicity in the painter's sample case consists in that a normal subject cannot discriminate chromatically the actual representing instance of redness from the actual color of the wall (assuming that the representation proves to be true). Analogously, the iconicity in the relation between the material and objective guises of qualia consists in this: experiencing subjects cannot typically discriminate situations in which an actual instance of redness that they perceive is present from situations such that only an actual instance of ^{s}redness^s of which they are aware is present, the alleged instance of redness being merely intentional.

As in the previous illustrative example, iconicity is not enough to account for the representational relation; and communicative intentions are in this case obviously out of the question. What is needed in addition is something along the lines of the Dretskian informational account. Both the nature of the iconicity at stake, and the nature of the causal-cum-teleological dependence of the subjective side of phenomenal features on their objective side are in fact slightly more complicated than so far suggested. For the sake of making the account more realistic and more plausible, I will say something more on this additional complexity to conclude my sketch of the sense-data account.

The sense-data theory shares with intentionalism its positive tenet, the view that phenomenal features of perceptual experiences are (in part) constituted by observable properties of material objects, with respect to which experiences have a certain functional role. Like the intentionalist account, the sense-data theory also characterizes an experience with a given phenomenal feature as involving a certain recognitional capacity vis-à-vis an observable property. To have a red sense-datum is thus to have an ability to recognize red surfaces, under appropriate circumstances, in an iconic way which involves consciously recognizing an actual instance of ^{s}red^s that would be indistinguishable if no actual instance of red were present. Now, to have the ability to recognize instances of a type is to have the ability to identify (different instances of) the type; and to have the ability to identify a type is to have the ability to discriminate instances of it from non-instances, i.e., from instances of incompatible types. In fact, by having perceptual experiences with phenomenal features we are not just able to identify qualities, thus discriminating them from other qualities. As Shoemaker (1975a) and Clark (1993) emphasize (following earlier theories of qualia, the one by Goodman (1977) outstanding among them), we are also able to order them along different dimensions of phenomenal likeness. We cannot just identify colors, and discriminate them from other colors; we are also able to order them, according to different dimensions of likeness such as hue, saturation and brightness. We are also able to order pains in terms of temporal, spatial and intensity relations, colors in terms of both temporal and spatial relations, and so on.

This is not a contingent aspect of our phenomenal fields. In my view, these facts should be taken into account in the specification of the functional (causal-cum-teleological) dependence relating the subjective and the material sides of phenomenal features. Redness is not just such that, under normal conditions, instances of it cause instances of ˢrednessˢ, more or less as in the Dretskian account outlined in §4 – except, of course, in that here the two terms of the indicator relation are phenomenal features. Under normal circumstances, orderly variations of the properties constituting the perceived scene in the different phenomenally discernible dimensions (say, the chromatically specific saturation, hue and brightness, but also the temporal and spatial relations that are not specific to any particular sense) would have caused correspondingly orderly variations in sensory properties. This is in my view the proper way of characterizing the functional dependence of appearances on the perceived scene, so as to avoid Lewis' (1980) reciprocal problems of veridical hallucination and prosthetic vision. It requires not only that the observable properties of material objects have subjectively instantiated correlates, but also that the observable relations involving them do.

Phenomenists incur in a telling neglect. In presenting their views, they mention phenomenal features such as pains or colors (hues). This is understandable, because it is with respect to them that we can most easily elaborate on the possibility of sensory properties and inverted spectrum scenarios, which pose the main problems for intentionalism. However, it should be clear that, to the extent that we accept the existence of (subjectively instantiated) ˢrednessˢ or ˢtoothacheˢ, we must also accept the existence of things like ˢduration of about ten secondsˢ, ˢcircularityˢ, or ˢbeing more painful to about such a degreeˢ. For no instance of ˢtoothacheˢ is instantiated without instantiating also some duration, spatial location and some comparative degree of painfulness, and no instance of ˢrednessˢ is instantiated without instantiating temporal, spatial, and specifically chromatic relations. Now, the phenomenists' claim that "phenomenal" and "psychological" consciousness are constitutively unrelated is already intuitively doubtful regarding pains and colors (on account of its implausible consequences for the causal role of conscious states, and for the nature of introspective knowledge). But it is *prima facie* absurd when it comes to qualities such as ˢcircularityˢ. Stories trying to make clear the possibility of sensory properties, or inverted spectrum scenarios, always assume that phenomenal features such as those correspond to (sufficiently objective) observable properties, and also that they are not inverted.[7]

7. This cursory presentation of the nature of the relation between the material and the subjective guises of phenomenal features in the sense-data account will serve as a basis for the introduction of a new element of the global argument for sense-data. The phenomenological datum of diaphanousness has had so far a decisive role in deciding between theories of the constitutive nature of perceptual experience. I have invoked considerations concerning diaphanousness to reject both disjunctivist naïve realism and phenomenism, leaving us with intentionalism and the sense-data theory. Now, the argument against intentionalism in §5 was based on its difficulty in accounting for the possibility of sensory properties and inverted-spectrum scenarios. I will argue now that these difficulties can be seen, illuminatingly, as inadequacies in accounting for another diaphanousness intuition.

Diaphanousness, as we have discussed it so far, has to do with the tokens with which we seem to be confronted when we focus on the phenomenal features of our experiences: they present to us as instances of manifest properties of material objects and events. There is, however, also a side of the phenomenological datum of diaphanousness that has to do with the types themselves, not their instances. I have so far emphasized the token side, because the dividing line between disjunctivism and intentionalism lies in whether or not primitive relations with *instances* of observable properties are constitutive of the phenomenal features of veridical experiences. But there is also a type side to diaphanousness, as I say. This is the fact that, if we focus on the phenomenal features of our experiences, the *types* with which we appear to be confronted present to us as objective, mind-independent features of external objects. Note that 'objective' is now predicated of types, while the criteria used before to characterize materiality and subjectivity had to do with tokens. For present purposes, it is enough to say that types (kinds, and the properties constituting them) are objective if they are *primary*, this understood along the lines used earlier to distinguish primary and sensory properties.

What I want to suggest now is that the way intentionalism incorporates this type-side of the diaphanousness datum constitutes a mistake of the same kind as the one made by disjunctivism in trying to incorporate the token-side of diaphanousness. To the extent that intentionalism improves on disjunctivism,

---

[7] The view I am defending has close relationships with a claim that Shoemaker has been making against phenomenists since his 1975b, namely, that while particular phenomenal qualities cannot be functionally analyzed, phenomenal consciousness in general can.

in providing a better account of the token-side of diaphanousness, the sense-data theory improves on intentionalism in providing a better account of the type-side of diaphanousness. Disjunctivism attempts to account for the token-side of diaphanousness by contending that the concrete perceived instances are *unanalyzably* constitutive of the phenomenal features of vpe. The problem with this was that mpe are as phenomenologically diaphanous as vpe. Similarly, intentionalism attempts to account for the type-side of diaphanousness by contending that objective observable properties are *unanalyzably* constitutive of phenomenal features. This, I will now try to show, puts intentionalism with respect to types in a similar quandary as that of disjunctivism regarding token. We already saw that *objective* and *observable* do not go happily together, on account of the vagueness that appears to be an inevitable side of observability; but I declined to mount an objection to intentionalism on this basis. The problem for intentionalism lies rather, I said, in the possibility of sensory properties (and, relatedly in my view, inverted-spectrum scenarios). I want to show that the sense-data theory's advantageous treatment of these possibilities lies in the fact that it provides a better account than intentionalism of the type-side of diaphanousness.

The sense-data account agrees with intentionalism that some phenomenal features constitutively involve (sufficiently) objective observable properties. But the sense-data theory does not take the relation between phenomenal features and experiences as primitive at the first-personal level of philosophical explication. It provides an analysis at that level not available to intentionalism, by ascribing a subjective guise to phenomenal features in addition to their material guise. The analysis is the one sketched at the end of § 6, appealing to an isomorphy between the material and the subjective guises of phenomenal features. No analysis of this kind is available to intentionalism; for it is essentially given by identifying qualia in part with the subjectively instantiated phenomenal properties of phenomenism, instead of merely explaining the indicator relation in terms of neurological properties of experiences of which the conscious subject as such is not aware. Thanks essentially to this, the sense-data theory is in a position to provide a better account of the type-side of diaphanousness. For, in explicating sensory properties as dispositions in objects to cause the subjective side of some phenomenal qualities, it allows for the fact that, in experiencing qualia whose material sides are merely sensory properties, there is still a *phenomenal* unity to what is experienced. Intentionalism can also explicate sensory properties as dispositions to cause the neurological properties that have indicator properties; but these properties are not themselves, according to the intentionalist account, phenomenal qualities. They do not provide for any real commonalities in that which is *phenomenally* experienced for phenomenal states involving sensory properties, if there are any. At the level of types intentionalism appears to be forced to take a disjunctivist view with respect to sensory properties. Phenomenal states either unanalyzably represent real, objective phenomenal properties, or they do not; a philosophical explication of the nature of phenomenal qualities, has nothing more to say.

To make the analogy clearer, let us use 'veridical' in a new sense, to qualify now those phenomenal *qualities* by instantiating which we do have access to (sufficiently) objective observable properties, and 'misleading' to qualify those by instantiating which we only have access to sensory properties. The latter are properties not needed for an accurate description of the mind-independent material world; in my account, they are just objectively variegated dispositions in material objects to cause the subjective aspects of phenomenal features. The sense-data account accepts that some phenomenal features of experiences constitutively involve relations with objective observable properties. With respect to the relation between veridical phenomenal features and misleading phenomenal features it takes a stand analogous to the one taken by intentionalism with respect to the relation between vpe and mpe. The account has it thus that misleading phenomenal qualities are ontologically derivative cases vis-à-vis veridical phenomenal qualities. But it differs from intentionalism in providing *an analysis* of the relation with objective observable properties constitutive of veridical phenomenal features, in terms of properties (the subjective guises of qualia) lying as much at the first-personal level of description as the phenomenal properties of intentionalism are. By relying on the analysis, the sense-data theory can account for the fact that type-diaphanousness is as much a datum concerning misleading phenomenal qualities as it is one concerning veridical phenomenal features. It explains in the same terms the type-diaphanousness of phenomenal features whose material aspects are objective observable properties, and that of those whose material aspects are in actual fact only sensory observable properties.

According to the sense-data theory, phenomenal features that do not involve objective observable properties, and therefore do not constitute recognitional capacities for objective properties (sufficiently so in any case, modulo vagueness), are to be taken as derivative cases with respect to the former. What does this derivativeness come to? In opposition to phenomenism, the sense-data theory shares with intentionalism the view that, in explanatorily fundamental cases, the phenomenal features of perceptual experiences are constituted by mind-independent instances of objective properties, which the subject of experience perceives by having the experience. In contrast to intentionalism, it allows that phenomenal features have a subjective side, subjectively instantiated qualities of which the subject is aware. But the sense-data theory insists that in some cases those subjectively instantiated qualities have the functional role of equipping their subjects with information concerning not just materially instantiated types, but objective, mind-independent ones, by making them consciously available to the subject. This is to say that it is a constitutive and irreducible aspect of some phenomenal features of perceptual experiences that by instantiating them the subject has knowledge of the mind-independent character of the material world.

Let us thus assume, for illustrative purposes and as seems plausible, that phenomenal features such as the duration, location and intensity of toothaches are among those whose materially instantiated side is (sufficiently) objective. They are materially instantiated scientifically identifiable kinds, with respect to which experiences with a subjectively instantiated side have the kind of functional-cum-teleological role earlier outlined. Now, relational qualities like those we have mentioned (temporal duration, spatial location, intensity) are always necessarily instantiated together with other equally objective properties, like forces and their structural bases. We can make sense of the possibility that there is no way of identifying the normal circumstances associated with the functional role of the relevant experiences, so that by instantiating ^{s}toothache^s, the subject can be said to recognize an *objective* type. Perhaps the only type we can isolate in that way is too disjunctive a condition of the subject's body for it to be an objective type, a type acknowledged as such in any true account of the material world. But it can still be considered a sensory property, a disposition in the subject's body to produce under given circumstances determinate subjective qualities, of which the subject is aware. This possibility is allowed by the fact that the account makes available to us the relevant subjective response.[8] It is in this sense that the present sense-data account makes phenomenal features whose materially instantiated sides are merely sensory properties secondary with respect to veridical ones.

Let me sum up. Token-diaphanousness is as much a phenomenological given for vpe as for mpe. An account of token-diaphanousness that relies on a "highest common factor" to vpe and mpe improves on the disjunctivist account, which considers diaphanousness as unreal in the case of mpe. Any theory including the intentionalist explication of phenomenal features will account for token-diaphanousness by ascribing common intentional instances of observable phenomenal features to vpe and indistinguishable mpe, together with a common derivativeness to merely intentional instances vis-à-vis actual ones. This account improves on disjunctivism, for it applies

---

[8] The fact that some other sensory responses, with which the relevant one is necessarily coinstantiated, *do constitute* recognitional capacities for fully objective properties is also a necessary requirement to allow for that possibility, as I have insisted.

in the same terms to vpe and corresponding mpe. Now, there is also a phenomenological datum of type-diaphanousness, indistinguishably present when we experience veridical and misleading features (features involving, respectively, primary and sensory properties). This is acknowledged even by philosophers who nonetheless contend that some observable properties are sensory, like Locke. A theory that can explain that there will be a common appearance, at the proper phenomenal level, that a unitary type is being phenomenally accessed both when the observable property is primary and when it is merely sensory, explains the datum better than intentionalism does. For, given its reductivist goals, the intentionalist account of phenomenal features can at the most account for sensory properties as objectively variegated dispositions to cause common neurological states. However, these common neurological states are not, according to intentionalism, phenomenal features themselves.

8. The theory of the constitutive nature of phenomenal features that I have outlined is problematic; a fully-fledged defense would require much more than I have provided here.[9] But I think I have shown that characterizations of the sense-data theory like the one by Martin mentioned at the outset present a straw man. Martin said: "Intentional approaches and sense-datum theories differ in at least two respects: intentional theories assert, and sense-datum theories deny, that mind-independent objects can be present to the mind in having perceptual experience; sense-datum theories assert, while intentional theories deny, that what is so present to the mind must actually exist". Sense-data theories may share with intentionalism the view that mind-independent objects can be fully present to the mind, and also the view that something which does not actually exist (a merely intentional object) can be present to the mind. What I take issue with in Martin's claim is its traditional intimation that, in contrast to intentionalism, sense-data theories cannot account for diaphanousness; that they posit a "veil" between the subject and the external world. I have argued that sense-data theories provide as acceptable an account of the fact of diaphanousness as intentionalism does, and indeed improve on intentionalism on this count.

No objectionable veil is thus posited by the sense-data theory defended here. Similarly, no "sense-datum fallacy" is involved in the preceding argument for sense-data. I have not argued for the existence of an actual instance of ^{s}redness^s from the existence of an appearance of redness. The argument I have outlined is rather a straightforward case of inference to the best explanation. At least in some places, it even appealed to empirical data

---

[9] More elaboration is given in García-Carpintero, forthcoming g-a

(or, at least, to empirical data that it is plausible to think will be forthcoming); namely, data regarding the existence of a common neurological factor to vpe and mpe. Compelling objections to the present sense-data theory are not going to be so easy as usually thought. I think this makes the case I announced at the outset: the contemporary consensus against sense-data has no rational justification.

Let me conclude by taking up a possible objection to the sense-data theory, which I have been neglecting so far. The crucial feature of the sense-data account lies in its ascribing a double role to phenomenal character: each so-called quale involves a subjectively instantiated property of the experience, and a materially instantiated, typically objective observable character. Now, it can be objected that this is phenomenologically implausible, that qualia (the phenomenal characters of our perceptual experiences) do not seem to have this double character. To this I would like to give a Wittgensteinian rejoinder. Confronted with the remark that the Earth does not appear to us to move around the Sun, Wittgenstein apparently asked, How should it be, for the Earth to appear to us to move around the Sun? The remark presupposes that there should be a telling difference in the appearances corresponding to the two states of affairs, the Earth moves around the Sun, the Sun moves around the Earth; but once we reflect on it, we can see this presumption to be ungrounded. It is only to be expected that both states of affairs give rise to the same appearances; to discriminate between them is a more theoretical affair.

I would retort in an analogous manner to the remark that phenomenal features do not appear to us to have the double character here ascribed to them: how should it be, for phenomenal features to appear to us as having that double character? The objector is assuming that the facts about such an issue as the ontological nature of phenomenal features should phenomenally strike us one way or another; but there is no reason for that to be so. Whether or not the theory whose merit I have tried to bring forward is correct is not to be decided just on the basis of facts regarding how things appear to us in having perceptual experiences. The matter is to be decided on the basis of additional theoretical considerations. And I think I have shown that it is not easy to decide against sense-data on the basis of this kind of consideration.

References

Block, N.: On a Confusion about a Function of Consciousness, *Behavioral and Brain Sciences* 18 (1995), 227–247.
Chalmers, D.: *The Conscious Mind*, Oxford University Press, Oxford 1996.
Clark, A.: *Sensory Qualities*, Clarendon Press, Oxford 1993.
Dretske, F.: *Naturalizing the Mind*, MIT Press, Cambridge, Mass. 1995.

García-Carpintero, M.: A Presuppositional Account of Reference-Fixing, *Journal of Philosophy* XCVII (2000), 109–147.
García-Carpintero, M.: Sense-data: the Sensible Approach, *Grazer Philosophische Studien*, 2002 (forthcoming g-a).
García-Carpintero, M.: Qualia that it Is Right to Quine, *Philosophy and Phenomenological Research* (forthcoming g-b).
Goodman, N.: *The Structure of Appearance*, Kluwer, Dordrecht 1977.
Grice, H. P.: The Causal Theory of Perception, *Proceedings of the Aristotelian Society* 35 (1961). Also in: H.P. Grice, *Studies in The Ways of Words*, Harvard U.P., Cambridge, Mass. 1989, 224–248, from where I quote.
Jackson, F.: *Perception. A Representative Theory*, Cambridge U.P., Cambridge 1977.
Harman, G.: The Intrinsic Quality of Experience. In: *Philosophical Perspectives, 4: Philosophy of Mind and Action Theory*, ed. by J. Tomberlin, Ridgeview Pub. Co., Atascadero, California 1989, 31–52.
Langsam, H.: The Theory of Appearing Defended, *Philosophical Studies* 87 (1997), 33–59.
Lewis, D.: Veridical Hallucination and Prosthetic Vision, *Australasian Journal of Philosophy*, 58 (1980). Also in: D. Lewis, *Philosophical Papers vol. 2*, Oxford U. P., Oxford 1986, 273–290.
Loar, B.: Phenomenal States. In: *The Nature of Consciousness*, ed. by N. Block, O. Flanagan & G. Guzeldere, MIT Press, Cambridge, Mass. 1997, 597–616.
McDowell, J.: Criteria, Defeasibility and Knowledge, *Proceedings of the British Academy* 68 (1982), 455–79.
McDowell, J.: *Mind and World*, Harvard U.P., Cambridge, Mass. 1994.
McDowell, J.: Knowledge and the Internal, *Philosophy and Phenomenological Research* 55 (1995), 877–93.
Perkins, M.: *Sensing the World*, Hackett, Indianapolis 1983.
Robinson, H.: The General Form of the Argument for Berkeleian Idealism. In: *Essays on Berkeley*, ed. by J. Foster and H. Robinson, Clarendon Press, Oxford 1985, 163–186.
Robinson, H.: The Objects of Perceptual Experience II, *Proceedings of the Aristotelian Society*, Supplementary Volume 64 (1990), 151–66.
Sellars, W.: Empiricism and the Philosophy of Mind. In: W. Sellars, *Science, Perception and Reality*, Routledge and Kegan Paul, London 1963, 127–196.
Shoemaker, S.: Phenomenal Similarity, *Crítica* 7 (1975a), 3–34.
Shoemaker, S.: Functionalism and Qualia, *Philosophical Studies* 27 (1975b), 291–315.
Shoemaker, S.: The Inverted Spectrum. In: S. Shoemaker, *Identity, Cause and Mind*, Cambridge University Press, Cambridge 1984.
Shoemaker, S.: Qualities and Qualia: What's in the Mind, *Philosophy and Phenomenological Research* 50 (1990), Supplement, 109–31.
Shoemaker, S.: Self-Knowledge and 'Inner Sense', *Philosophy and Phenomenological Research* 54 (1994), 249–315.
Tye, M.: *Ten Problems of Consciousness*, MIT Press, Cambridge, Mass. 1995.
Williamson, T.: Is Knowing a State of Mind?, *Mind* 104 (1995), 533–65.

E. J. Lowe

A Defence of the Four-Category Ontology

Abstract

By 'the four-category ontology', I mean the ontological theory which holds that there are four basic and irreducible categories of entities, namely, (1) particular substances (or objects), (2) particular property- and relation-instances (or tropes), (3) substantial universals (or kinds) and (4) properties and relations (or non-substantial universals). Various other philosophers maintain that one or more of these categories are redundant or empty. For instance, C. B. Martin accepts categories (1) and (2), but not categories (3) and (4). D. M. Armstrong accepts categories (1) and (4), but not categories (2) and (3) (though he also denies that categories (1) and (4) are ontologically basic, holding instead that states of affairs have this status). Keith Campbell favours a one-category ontology which admits as basic only category (2). Some philosophers hold that particular substances or objects are bundles of tropes, and others that they are bundles of universals. Again, some philosophers hold that talk of universals can be replaced by talk of resemblance classes of tropes, while others hold that it can be replaced by talk of resemblance classes of objects. And so on. The four-category ontology will be considered extravagant by any of these philosophers, although different philosophers will give different reasons for thinking it to be so. However, I argue in the present paper that only the four-category ontology can adequately accommodate and account for all of the following metaphysical features of reality: the relationship between object and property, the distinction between the dispositional and the occurrent, the status of natural laws, the nature of natural necessity, and the possibility of empirical knowledge.

There are many ways of constructing a system of ontological categories and little agreement as to what, exactly, we should understand by the expression 'ontological category'. As I understand this expression, an ontological category is a *kind of being*, that is, a kind of entities, membership of which is determined by certain distinctive existence- and identity-conditions whose nature is determinable *a priori*. Such a kind, then, is not to be confused with so-called 'natural' kinds, referred to by specific sortal terms such as 'tiger' or 'gold'. For, although the members of such natural kinds will, of course, be entities belonging to appropriate ontological categories – as, for example, a tiger is a *living organism* and a portion of gold is a *quantity of matter or stuff* – the nature of such kinds is determinable only *a posteriori*, by scientific observation and experimentation. Ontological categorisation, as I understand it, operates at a higher level of abstraction than does scientific taxonomising, and the latter presupposes the former.[1] But some ontological categories are more basic than others, so that such categories can be organised into a hierarchy, perhaps in more ways than one. Thus, the category of *living organism*, to which an individual tiger belongs, is a sub-category of the higher-level category of *individual substance* or *particular 'object'* (in one sense of that dangerously ambiguous term). The basic categories of an ontological system are those occupying the highest level and are at the same time those by reference to which the existence- and identity-conditions definitive of the lower-level categories are specified. For instance, what makes living organisms different, in respect of their existence- and identity-conditions, from certain other categories of individual substance, is that they may survive a systematic change of their constituent matter, provided that they continue to exemplify a specific form appropriate to their natural kind.

My concern in this paper is to defend a certain position regarding what *basic* ontological categories we should recognise. The position in question seems to be implicit in what is perhaps the first treatise ever devoted explicitly and wholly to our subject, Aristotle's *Categories*.[2] It is that the basic categories are four in number, two of them being categories of particular and two being corresponding categories of universal. The terms 'particular' and 'universal' themselves, we may say, do not strictly denote categories, however, because they are *transcategorial*, applying as they do to entities belonging to different basic categories.

The first category and in a certain sense the most fundamental – even though in another sense all four of our categories are equally 'basic' – is the category of *individual substance* or *particular 'object'*, which I have already mentioned. Corresponding to this category of particular, there is a basic category of universal, namely, the category of *substantial universal* or *substantial kind*, the correspondence consisting in the fact that each individual substance necessary instantiates – is a particular instance of –

---

[1] See further my *The Possibility of Metaphysics: Substance, Identity, and Time* (Oxford: Clarendon Press, 1998), Ch. 8.

[2] See the *Categories*, Ch. 2, in *Aristotle's Categories and De Interpretatione*, trans. J. L. Ackrill (Oxford: Clarendon Press, 1963).

some substantial kind. The natural kinds *tiger* and *gold*, cited earlier, are examples of substantial universals or, as I shall henceforth briefly refer to them, *kinds* (on the understanding, of course, that by such a 'kind' I do not mean an ontological category, for reasons already given). The other basic category of universal is the category of *properties and relations*, or (as I also call them) *non-substantial universals*, examples of these being the properties redness and squareness and the spatial relation of betweenness. Obviously, the distinction between the two basic categories of universal is reflected in language in the distinction between substantival general terms on the one hand and adjectival and relational general terms on the other. This leaves one further basic category, which is the category of particular corresponding to the category of non-substantial universals – the category whose members are particular instances of properties and relations, that is, *property- and relation-instances* or, as they are sometimes called, *tropes*.[3] My own preferred term for (monadic) property-instances is *modes*, though they have also been variously called individual accidents, particular qualities and abstract particulars.

We need to be clear about exactly how items in these four categories are related to one another. I have already remarked that the relationship between an individual substance and its kind is one of *instantiation*, as is the relationship between a property- or relation-instance – a trope – and the corresponding non-substantial universal.[4] A particular tiger is an instance of the kind *tiger*, and a particular redness – say of a certain individual flower – is an instance of the non-substantial universal or property *redness*. But this still leaves certain other crucial relationships between members of the different basic categories undescribed. Most importantly, there is the relationship between a property- or relation-instance and the individual substance or substances to which that instance belongs or which that instance relates. I call this the relationship of *characterisation*. A particular redness *characterises* the individual substance whose redness it is and a particular betweenness *characterises* the three individual substances (taken in a certain order) which it relates. (Here I leave aside the question of whether points of space exist as relata of betweenness relations and, if so, whether they qualify as 'individual substances'.) Paralleling this relationship at the level of particulars is a corresponding relationship at the level of universals. For, just as we may say that a particular redness characterises a certain individual substance, such as a particular flower, so we may say that the property or non-substantial universal *redness* characterises a certain substantial universal or kind, such as the natural kind *tomato*. Speaking

---

[3] See further Keith Campbell, *Abstract Particulars* (Oxford: Blackwell, 1990).
[4] For more on instantiation, see my *Kinds of Being: A Study of Individuation, Identity and the Logic of Sortal Terms* (Oxford: Blackwell, 1989), Ch. 3.

quite generally, then, and prescinding from the distinction between universals and particulars, we may say that characterisation is a relationship between property- or relation-like entities on the one hand and substantial entities on the other. We may summarise our proposals so far in the form of the following diagram:

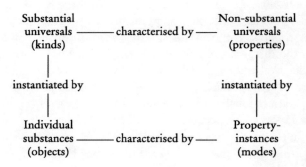

It will be clear from this diagram that one important species of relationship between entities of different basic categories has yet to be given a name by us. This is the relationship between an individual substance and some non-substantial universal to which it is indirectly related either via one of its property- or relation-instances or via its substantial kind. I propose to call this sort of relationship *exemplification*. Thus, in the present system of ontology, it is vital to distinguish clearly between instantiation, characterisation, and exemplification. An individual ripe tomato *instantiates* the kind *tomato*, is *characterised* by a particular redness, and *exemplifies* the non-substantial universal or property *redness*. The tomato's particular redness, by contrast, *instantiates* the property *redness*. And the kind *tomato* is *characterised* by the property *redness*.

The ontological system that I have been describing will certainly strike some metaphysicians as being unnecessarily complex, with many redundant features. Do we really need four basic ontological categories and (at least) three different kinds of relationship between members of those categories – instantiation, characterisation, and exemplification? Some philosophers, for example, while happy to countenance the existence of universals, may think it extravagant to include in our ontology property- and relation-instances, in our sense, in addition to both individual substances and non-substantial universals.[5] Why not say, as some philosophers do, that non-substantial universals such as *redness* are instantiated by individual substances, that is,

---

[5] See, for example, D. M. Armstrong, *A World of States of Affairs* (Cambridge: Cambridge University Press, 1997).

that things such as an individual tomato or an individual flower are the particular instances of such a universal, rather than the supposed particular 'rednesses' of such individual substances? From our point of view, this is to obliterate the distinction between instantiation and exemplification, but some may say that this is a welcome economy.

I have various responses to philosophers of this persuasion. For one, consider the fact that we can, it seems clear, *perceive* at least some of the properties of individual substances, such as an individual tomato's redness. But perception, it would seem, is necessarily of particulars, since only particulars can enter into causal relations or literally possess causal powers – and perception necessarily involves a causal relation between the perceiver and what is perceived. Moreover, not only can we perceive at least some of the properties of individual substances, we can also perceive them undergo *changes* in their properties. When I see a leaf change from green to brown as it is burnt by a flame, I seem to see its former greenness go out of existence and its new brownness come into existence. But neither greenness nor brownness the *universals* are affected by such changes: they both exist before and after the leaf is burnt. So, it seems, it must be the leaf's *particular* greenness and brownness that I see ceasing and beginning to exist respectively. To this it may be replied that what I see is not a particular greenness ceasing to exist and a particular brownness beginning to exist, but just greenness and brownness – the universals – beginning and ceasing to be *exemplified* by the leaf. However, the change that I see is *in the leaf itself*, not in its relationship to something universal that is unchanging. Furthermore, we may ask *in virtue of what* it is that the leaf now exemplifies brownness where it formerly exemplified greenness. Surely, it is in virtue of how the leaf now is, in all its particularity – that is, it is in virtue of the *particular* characteristics of the leaf, one of which is its particular colour, that is, its particular brownness.

Those who believe in properties as universals only, not as particulars, are apt to say that universals are 'wholly present' in the various individual substances which exemplify them – for instance, that the very same universal redness is 'wholly present' in two different tomatoes which exactly match one another in hue.[6] And by this they mean to imply that a universal can be wholly – that is, *all* of it can be – in two different places at the same time. They tell us not to worry that this seems to make no sense, assuring us that we have this impression only because we are mistakenly tempted to assimilate the spatiotemporal location of universals to that of particulars, which, indeed, cannot be wholly in two different places at once. But, none the less, I am far

---

[6] See, for example, D. M. Armstrong, *Universals: An Opinionated Introduction* (Boulder, CO: Westview Press, 1989), pp. 98–9.

from convinced that it does make sense to say that *anything*, be it universal or particular, can be wholly in two different places at once. This is because the relation of *being wholly in the same place as* appears to be an equivalence relation and therefore a symmetrical and transitive relation, which poses the following difficulty. Suppose that tomatoes A and B exemplify exactly the same shade of redness and that this universal is both wholly in the same place as A and wholly in the same place as B. Then it seems to follow, given the symmetry and transitivity of the relation *being wholly in the same place as*, that tomato A is wholly in the same place as tomato B – which we know to be necessarily false, given the non-identity of A and B.

To this it may be replied, perhaps, that the relation *being wholly in the same place as* is not in fact a symmetrical relation, so the fact that the universal in question is wholly in the same place as tomato A does not imply that tomato A is wholly in the same place as the universal. Indeed, it may be urged that tomato A plainly is *not* wholly in the same place as the universal, because the universal, unlike tomato A, is also wholly in the same place as tomato B. But this response strikes me as being both unprincipled and question-begging. Certainly, according to the theorists whose view is under scrutiny, *all* of the tomato is in a place where *all* of the universal is located. (I ignore here the quite separate issue of whether persisting things like tomatoes should be deemed to have 'temporal' parts.) If this doesn't mean that tomato A is wholly in the same place as the universal – that they are wholly co-located – then it is altogether obscure to me what 'being wholly in the same place as' can possibly mean. But if tomato A is wholly in the same place as the universal and the universal is wholly in the same place as tomato B, then it seems to me to follow, ineluctably, that tomato A is wholly in the same place as tomato B – and this is absurd.

At the very least, I think we can say that those who speak of universals being 'wholly present' in many different places at once owe us a much more perspicuous account of what they could possibly mean by saying this. My own suspicion is that what such theorists are doing, when they say this, is precisely conflating a non-substantial universal with its particular property-instances. For what are in many different places at once, I should say, are the various particular property-instances, although these are united by the fact that they are all instances of exactly the same universal. But the universal itself cannot, I think, properly be said to have a location at all, much less many locations. This, however, does not make it some queer sort of 'Platonic' entity, inhabiting an 'ideal' realm somehow isolated from the world of things in space and time. The universal doesn't have to exist 'elsewhere', just because it doesn't have a location in space: it just has to *exist*, but without any spatial determination to its manner of existing. We can still say, indeed, that its manner of existing is, in a perfectly good sense, 'immanent' (rather than 'transcendent'), inasmuch as it exists only 'in' or 'through' its particular instances, precisely insofar as they instantiate it.[7] We can insist, thus, that there can be no *uninstantiated* universals and that particulars enjoy a kind of ontological priority over universals, just as Aristotle believed.

So far, I have been defending the four-category ontology against those who favour including universals, but not property-instances, in our ontology. But, of course, there are other philosophers who are happy to include property-instances but are opposed to including universals. Against these philosophers, I have another set of objections. But first I should defend my view that universals fall into two distinct basic categories, the substantial and the non-substantial, which many philosophers may dismiss as being overly reliant upon a superficial grammatical distinction. In point of fact, I do not at all think that metaphysics should be conducted entirely through the filter of language, as though syntax and semantics were our only guides in matters metaphysical – although it should hardly be surprising if natural language does reflect in its structure certain structural features of the reality which it has evolved to express.[8] The distinction between the substantial and the non-substantial must, however, be simultaneously defended at two different levels – at the level of particulars and at the level of universals. On the one hand, we must defend the ontological status of individual substances as basic entities against those who would represent them as being, or reduce them to, 'bundles' of 'compresent' property-instances or tropes.[9] On the other hand, we must defend the ontological irreducibility of substantial kinds against those who would reduce them to complexes of co-exemplified non-substantial universals.[10] Let me turn to this second strand of the project first.

It cannot be denied that there is an intimate relationship between a substantial universal, such as the natural kind *gold*, and certain non-substantial universals that are typically exemplified by individual substances of that kind – a golden colour, a certain melting point, a certain density, malleability, ductility, solubility in *aqua regia*, and so forth. But we plainly cannot say that an individual substance necessarily instantiates the kind *gold* if and only

---

[7] See further my 'Abstraction, Properties, and Immanent Realism', in Tom Rockmore (ed.), *Proceedings of the Twentieth World Congress of Philosophy, Volume II: Metaphysics* (Bowling Green, OH: Philosophy Documentation Center, 1999), pp. 195–205.

[8] See further my *The Possibility of Metaphysics*, Ch. 1.

[9] See, for example, Campbell, *Abstract Particulars*, and Peter Simons, 'Particulars in Particular Clothing: Three Trope Theories of Substance', *Philosophy and Phenomenological Research* 54 (1994), pp. 553–75.

[10] See, for example, Armstrong, *A World of States of Affairs*, pp. 65–8.

if it exemplifies all of these typical properties, for any substantial universal like this may have untypical individual exemplars.[11] It may also be that gold has a 'scientific essence', consisting in its being constituted by atoms possessing an atomic number of 79, in which case the predicates 'is gold' and 'is constituted by atoms possessing an atomic number of 79' would appear to be, of metaphysical necessity, co-extensive. However, 'is gold', in this context, means 'is made of gold', and 'gold' as a substantival general term must be distinguished from the predicative expression 'made of gold', or 'golden'. The substantival general term refers to a kind of stuff, which as a matter of natural law is characterised by many non-substantial universals, such as those cited a moment ago. But there is, in principle, no finite limit to the number of such characteristics nomically tied to the nature of gold: 'gold', used as a substantival general term, is not a way of denominating the totality of such characteristics, but rather a way of referring to what it is – a kind of substance – that *bears* those characteristics, as a matter of natural necessity. However, a fuller defence of this position will only become possible when, in due course, I say more about the nature of natural laws and natural necessity.

At the level of particulars, as opposed to that of universals, a defence of the distinction between the substantial and the non-substantial means defending the ontological irreducibility of the category of individual substance both against those who, as mentioned earlier, try to reduce individual substances to bundles of compresent tropes and against those who, even more implausibly, try to reduce them to bundles of co-exemplified universals. The latter strategy is defeated, not least, by its commitment to an implausibly strong version of Leibniz's principle of the identity of indiscernibles, so I shall ignore it from now on. The former strategy is not subject to this defect, but is still, I believe, fatally flawed, its basic problem being that it can provide no adquate account of the existence- and identity-conditions of tropes or, as we have been calling them, property-instances.[12] Property-instances are ontologically dependent entities, depending for their existence and identity upon the individual substances which they characterise, or to which they 'belong'. A particular redness or squareness can, ultimately, be identified as the particular property-instance that it is only by reference to the individual substance which it characterises. This is not an epistemic point but a metaphysical one: it concerns individuation in the metaphysical rather than in the cognitive sense – that is, individuation as a determination relation between entities rather than

---

[11] On this point and others made in this paragraph of the present paper, see further my *Kinds of Being*, Ch. 8.
[12] See further my *The Possibility of Metaphysics*, pp. 205 ff.

individuation as a kind of cognitive achievement. And this is the reason why it makes no sense to suppose that particular property-instances could exist free-floating and unattached to any individual substance or migrate from one individual substance to another.

Of course, one reason why some philosophers believe that what we have been calling 'individual substances' are reducible to, or consist in, bundles of compresent tropes is that they think – erroneously, as I consider – that to deny this commits one to an indefensible doctrine of 'bare particularity' or to the notion of a propertyless 'substratum' that somehow 'supports' and 'unites' the properties of a single object. Their mistake is to think that we can only deny that an individual substance, or particular 'object', is the sum of its particular properties or tropes by contending, instead, that it somehow consists of these properties *plus* an extra non-qualitative ingredient, its 'substratum' or 'bare particular'. Not so. The underlying error is to think that an individual substance is any kind of *complex* at all, at least insofar as it is propertied in various ways. Individual substances may be complex in the sense of being *composite*, that is, in the sense of being composed of lesser substantial parts, as, for example, a living organism is composed of individual cells. But an individual substance's (particular) *properties* – its modes, as I prefer to call them – are not items of which it is *composed*.

There is, I think, an implicit conflation between parts and properties in the trope-bundle view of objects.[13] An individual substance has many properties – perhaps even infinitely many (if we include relational properties) – and in this sense is multifaceted: but this does not amount to any sort of ontological complexity in its constitution. *Of course* an individual substance's properties need no 'substratum' to 'support' them, if by such a substratum we mean some entity which somehow lacks properties 'of its own' and is some sort of non-qualitative ingredient of the individual substance. But the properties do indeed need 'support', in the sense that they are ontologically dependent entities which can only exist as the properties of that very individual substance. However, it is the individual substance *itself* which provides their 'support' in this entirely legitimate sense, and this it can do without the spurious aid of some mysterious 'substratum'.[14] There is no mystery here

---

[13] Compare C. B. Martin, 'Substance Substantiated', *Australasian Journal of Philosophy* 58 (1980), pp. 3–10. Martin has a two-category ontology of particular properties and particular substances. I endorse his recognition of this irreducible distinction, but disagree with some aspects of his conception of particular substances: see my 'Locke, Martin and Substance', *Philosophical Quarterly* 50 (2000), pp. 499–514.

[14] See further my 'Locke, Martin and Substance'.

as to *how* individual substances can perform this 'supporting' role, for once we recognise the category of individual substance as basic and irreducible and the category of property-instance as correlative with it, we can see that their having such a role is part of their essential nature. Explanation – even metaphysical explanation – must reach bedrock somewhere, and this, according to the four-category ontology, is one place where bedrock is reached. The idea that some more fundamental explanation is somehow available, if only we can probe reality more deeply, is, I think, just an illusion born of some of the confusions mentioned above.

The stage at which my defence of the four-category ontology has now reached is this. I have defended the inclusion of property-instances in our ontology. I have also defended the distinction between the substantial and the non-substantial, both at the level of universals and at the level of particulars. This means that I have thereby defended the inclusion of individual substances in our ontology as forming a basic and irreducible category of particulars additional to, and correlative with, the category of property-instances (in which I also include, by implication, relation-instances). But although I have defended the distinction between substantial and non-substantial universals against those supporters of universals who would reduce these two categories to one, I have said nothing yet explicitly to defend the four-category ontology against those who deny the existence of universals altogether. Here my main argument makes common cause with certain other defenders of universals who differ from me in not recognising the distinction between substantial and non-substantial universals as fundamental: but I believe that recognising that distinction helps to strengthen this argument against the opponents of universals in some important ways. I should say at once that I do not have in mind here any species of 'one over many' argument, to the effect that varieties of particularism such as resemblance nominalism cannot adequately account for the meaning we attach to general terms or our ability to classify particulars – arguments which appeal at least partly to semantic or psychological considerations rather than to purely metaphysical ones.

The argument that I have in mind is one which contends that the ontological status of natural laws can only be properly understood if one acknowledges the existence of universals. The gist of this argument is that an opponent of universals can at best represent natural laws as consisting merely in universal constant conjunctions amongst particulars, which reduces those laws to nothing more than cosmic coincidences or accidents. The remedy, it is then proposed, is to regard natural laws as consisting in relations between *universals* rather than in constant conjunctions amongst particulars and, more specifically, as involving a 'second-order' relation of 'necessitation' between universals.[15] Thus, in the simplest sort of case, it is proposed that the form of a law is something like '*F*-ness necessitates *G*-ness'. It is then further claimed that although '*F*-ness necessitates *G*-ness' entails the corresponding constant conjunction amongst particulars, namely, 'For any (individual) *x*, if *x* is *F*, then *x* is *G*', the reverse entailment does not hold, so that the law is stronger than the constant conjunction and *explains* it, thus differentiating such a conjunction which is backed by a law from one which is a mere cosmic coincidence – a differentiation which the opponent of universals is unable to make or explain.

All of this is familiar territory, as is the objection raised in some quarters that the supposed entailment of 'For any *x*, if *x* is *F*, then *x* is *G*' by '*F*-ness necessitates *G*-ness' is unexplained and mysterious.[16] To this I would add the objection that laws do *not*, in fact, entail constant conjunctions amongst particulars in any case, because laws – apart, perhaps, from certain fundamental physical laws – admit of exceptions which arise from the possibility of interfering factors in the course of nature, an example being the possible deviation of planets from their elliptical orbits as specified by Kepler's laws of planetary motion.[17] Laws, in my view, determine *tendencies* amongst the particulars to which they apply, not their actual behaviour, which is a resultant of many complex interactions implicating a multiplicity of laws.

However, this is not the main source of my dissatisfaction with the view that laws have the form, in the simplest sort of case, '*F*-ness necessitates *G*-ness'. For, although I certainly agree that the key to understanding the ontological status of laws is to recognise them as involving universals rather than particulars, I consider that we can only understand laws properly if we recognise as ontologically fundamental the distinction between substantial and non-substantial universals. Looking back at the diagram introduced earlier, we can see directly from that in what way a law involves universals. A law simply consists – in the simplest sort of case – in some substantial universal or kind being characterised by some non-substantial universal or property, or in two or more kinds being characterised by a relational universal. Our very statements of law in everyday and scientific language tell us this, if only we are prepared to take them at their literal face value. We say, for example, 'Rubber stretches', 'Gold is ductile', 'Water dissolves common salt', 'Planets

---

[15] See, especially, D. M. Armstrong, *What Is a Law of Nature?* (Cambridge: Cambridge University Press, 1983).

[16] For this complaint, see Bas van Fraassen, *Laws and Symmetry* (Oxford: Clarendon Press, 1989), Ch. 5.

[17] See again my *Kinds of Being*, Ch. 8, and also my 'What *is* the "Problem of Induction"?', *Philosophy* 62 (1987), pp. 325–40.

move in elliptical orbits', 'Electrons carry unit negative charge' and 'Protons and electrons repel each other'. These are all statements of natural law and each can be understood, in terms of the ontological system represented in our diagram, as saying that one or more substantial kinds is or are characterised by some property or relation. There is no need, then, to think of the univerals involved in a law as being linked by some mysterious 'second-order' relation of 'necessitation', for they are in fact linked quite simply by the familiar characterising tie which links substantial entities quite generally, whether universal or particular, to non-substantial entities. The basic form of a law is not 'F-ness necessitates G-ness', but 'Ks are F', or 'Ks are R-related to Js', where 'K' and 'J' denote substantial universals, 'F' denotes a property and 'R' denotes a relation – that is, where 'F' and 'R' denote non-substantial universals.

Lest it be complained that the 'characterising tie' invoked here is itself mysterious or problematic, I hasten to point out that this is not an objection which can be levelled against me by those philosophers who accept universals but merely dispute my differentiation of them into substantial and non-substantial universals – that is to say, the kind of philosophers who support the view that laws have the form 'F-ness necessitates G-ness'. For these philosophers too are committed to the existence of some sort of characterising tie, either directly between individual substances and universals or between individual substances and property-instances. Nor do I, in any case, accept that the notion of the characterising tie, properly understood, is inherently mysterious or problematic. The key to understanding it is not to regard this 'tie' as a genuine *relation*, for once we do that we are doomed to set out upon the sort of regress made famous by Bradley. Rather, we need to appreciate – adapting Frege's terminology to a slightly different purpose – the essential 'unsaturatedness' of non-substantial entities as being what makes such entities necessarily 'tied' to substantial ones.[18] This is why, earlier, I described characterisation, along with its relatives instantiation and exemplification, as 'relationships' rather than as 'relations'. What we are concerned with here are certain species of metaphysical dependency, not *relational universals* in the sense in which these are members of one of our fundamental ontological categories of *being* or *entity*.

With this account of the ontological status of natural laws in place, the four-category ontology now delivers a further important insight which confirms its fruitfulness as a metaphysical hypothesis. This is that it enables us to understand in a fresh way the much-bedevilled distinction between the dispositional and the occurrent, or 'categorical', features of objects – though

---

[18] See further my 'Locke, Martin and Substance'.

I shall avoid the expression 'categorical' as potentially misleading, especially in the context of the present paper. Some philosophers have regarded this as a distinction between types of *property*, but that seems to me to be a serious mistake. Others have held that it is a distinction between different 'aspects' which every property possesses, which is a more sustainable view but still, I think, mistaken.[19] I prefer to start with a distinction between dispositional and occurrent *predication*, a distinction which is reflected in language but which at bottom, I believe, rests on an ontological distinction – one that is immediately apparent from the diagram presented earlier.[20] It will be observed from that diagram that there are two fundamentally different ways in which an individual substance can be related ontologically to – that is, in which it can *exemplify* – a non-substantial universal. One way is for the individual substance to be characterised by a property-instance which instantiates the non-substantial universal in question. The other way is for the individual substance to instantiate a substantial universal or kind which is characterised by the non-substantial universal in question. These two ways correspond, I contend, to occurrent and dispositional predication respectively, in the sense that these forms of predication can be understood as having as their respective truth-makers the two types of circumstance just described.

Consider, for example, a dispositional predication such as 'This object is soluble in water' or, as we might also put it, 'This object *dissolves* in water', and contrast this statement with the corresponding occurrent predication, 'This object *is dissolving* in water'. Many fruitless attempts have been made to explain or analyse such a dispositional predication, sometimes by reducing it to some sort of conditional statement involving only occurrent predication, along the lines of 'If this object were to be immersed in water, then it would be dissolving in water'. These attempts have all foundered on various obstacles and, although some philosophers still desperately try to remedy their defects, it should be clear by now that the strategy is doomed to failure.[21] However, the four-category ontology offers a simple explanation of the distinction that underlies the difference between these two types of predication, the

---

[19] For this view, see C. B. Martin's contributions to D. M. Armstrong, C. B. Martin and U. T. Place, *Dispositions: A Debate*, ed. Tim Crane (London: Routledge, 1996). See also C. B. Martin and John Heil, 'The Ontological Turn', *Midwest Studies in Philosophy* XXIII (1999), pp. 34–60.

[20] For an early version of the theory of dispositions about to be described, see my 'Laws, Dispositions and Sortal Logic', *American Philosophical Quarterly* 19 (1982), pp. 41–50, and my *Kinds of Being*, Ch. 9.

[21] See, especially, C. B. Martin, 'Dispositions and Conditionals', *Philosophical Quarterly* 44 (1994), pp. 1–8. This paper has already generated a considerable literature but, to my mind, no satisfactory response in defence of a conditional analysis of disposition statements.

dispositional and the occurrent. To say of an object that it is disposed to dissolve in water, according to my proposal, is effectively to say that the object instantiates some kind (that is, some substantial universal), K, such that water dissolves K – where, of course, 'Water dissolves K' expresses a natural law, as explained earlier. An example of such a law would be the previously cited law, 'Water dissolves common salt'. And, as was also explained earlier, laws only determine the *tendencies* of individual substances, not their *actual* behaviour, which has a multiplicity of determinants, including the actual behaviours of many other individual substances. The other half of the proposal is that the corresponding *occurrent* predication, in which it is said that the object is (actually) dissolving in water, effectively says of the object that it possesses a (relational) *property-instance* of the non-substantial universal *being dissolved by water*. Similarly, to say of a particular piece of rubber that it *is stretching* is to say that it possesses an instance of the very same non-substantial universal that, in virtue of the law 'Rubber stretches', characterises the substantial universal or kind *rubber*: whereas to say that the piece of rubber *stretches* – in other words, that it is elastic – is to say that it instantiates *some* kind which is characterised by the non-substantial universal in question.

A full defence of this theory would be out of place here. But what should be clear, at any rate, is that if the ontology is as our diagram depicts it, then these two modes of predication ought to be available, just as we apparently find them in fact to be. So the theory predicts and explains the existing linguistic phenomena, which is to its credit – whereas no rival theory has, I believe, come anywhere near to achieving the same result. Other theories have so far left the distinction between the dispositional and the occurrent altogether mysterious and obscure.

Let me now sum up some of the advantages of the four-category ontology over its various more parsimonious rivals. Its advantages over a one-category ontology of property- and relation-instances (a pure trope ontology) are (1) that it can provide, as this rival cannot, an adequate account of the existence- and identity-conditions of property- and relation-instances, (2) that it has a superior account of the ontological status of natural laws, and (3) that it offers a principled understanding of the distinction between the dispositional and the occurrent. Its advantages over a two-category ontology of individual substances and property- and relation-instances are the second and third of the aforementioned advantages. And its advantages over a two-category ontology of individual substances and non-substantial universals is the third of the aforementioned advantages, together with (4) the advantage of providing a superior account of our empirical acquaintance with the properties and relations of individual substances, which avoids mysterious talk of the 'multiple location' of universals. These advantages may be summed up in the following table.[22]

	Trope individuation	Analysis of laws	Analysis of dispositions	Property perception
Tropes alone	No	No	No	Yes
Tropes plus objects	Yes	No	No	Yes
Objects plus universals	N/A	Yes	No	No
Four-category ontology	Yes	Yes	Yes	Yes

References

Aristotle: *Categories and De Interpretatione*, trans. J. L. Ackrill, Clarendon Press, Oxford 1963.
Armstrong, D.M.: *What Is a Law of Nature?*, Cambridge University Press, Cambridge 1983.
Armstrong, D.M.: *Universals: An Opinionated Introduction*, Westview Press, Boulder 1989.
Armstrong, D.M.: *A World of States of Affairs*, Cambridge University Press, Cambridge 1997.
Armstrong, D.M., Martin C.B., Place, U.T.: *Dispositions: A Debate*, ed. by T. Crane, Routledge, London 1996.
Campbell, K.: *Abstract Particulars*, Blackwell, Oxford 1990.
Lowe, E.J.: Laws, Dispositions and Sortal Logic, *American Philosophical Quarterly* 19 (1982), 41–50.
Lowe, E.J.: What is the "Problem of Induction"?, *Philosophy* 62 (1987), 325–40.
Lowe, E.J.: *Kinds of Being: A Study of Individuation, Identity and the Logic of Sortal Terms*, Blackwell, Oxford 1989.
Lowe, E.J.: *The Possibility of Metaphysics: Substance, Identity, and Time*, Clarendon Press, Oxford 1998.
Lowe, E.J.: Abstraction, Properties, and Immanent Realism. In: *Proceedings of the Twentieth World Congress of Philosophy, Volume II: Metaphysics*, ed. by T. Rockmore, Philosophy Documentation Center, Bowling Green 1999, 195–205.

---

[22] I am very grateful for comments received when this paper was delivered at the GAP Congress held in Bielefeld in September 2000.

Lowe, E.J.: Locke, Martin and Substance, *Philosophical Quarterly* 50 (2000), 499–514.
Martin, C.B.: Substance Substantiated, *Australasian Journal of Philosophy* 58 (1980), 3–10.
Martin, C.B.: Dispositions and Conditionals, *Philosophical Quarterly* 44 (1994), 1–8.
Martin, C.B. and Heil, J.: The Ontological Turn, *Midwest Studies in Philosophy* XXIII (1999), 34–60.
Simons, P.: Particulars in Particular Clothing: Three Trope Theories of Substance, *Philosophy and Phenomenological Research* 54 (1994), 553–75.
van Fraassen, B.: *Laws and Symmetry*, Clarendon Press, Oxford 1989.

Uwe Meixner

How to Reconcile Non-Physical Causation with the Physical Conservation Laws

Abstract

It is widely assumed (especially in the philosophy of mind) that the non-physical causation of physical events (by non-physical substances or non-physical mental events) is incompatible with physics. The paper clarifies in what sense there is such an incompatibility. The paper shows that there is no incompatibility of non-physical causation of the physical with the physical laws, that is, with physics properly speaking, by describing a physically consistent and even plausible situation of non-physical causation of the physical. In the very same situation, however, the Strong and also the Weak Principle of Causal Closure of the physical world are violated. But, it is argued, this violation does not show an incompatibility of the non-physical causation of the physical with physics, but only with the metaphysical "Überbau" of physics, physicalism; physics and physicalism should be carefully distinguished, just as physics and metaphysics. Nevertheless, in the appendix of the paper an attractive way of preserving the Weak Principle of Causal Closure while admitting non-physical causation of the physical is also explored.

There are two types of non-physical causation: causation by non-physical events, for example physically non-reducible mental events, and causation by non-physical agents, for example Cartesian substances, *res cogitantes*. *Since* non-physical causation of physical events is widely assumed to be irreconcilable with the physical conservation laws, in particular with the law of the conservation of energy, and *since* the physical conservation laws are very well confirmed items of physics, the only ontological status that remains for non-physical entities, like non-physical events and non-physical substances, is widely regarded to be, at least with respect to the physical world, a causally totally inefficacious one. And this, in the eyes of most philosophers, is a very uncomfortable ontological status indeed, since, according to them, it suggests or even implies non-existence.

I will not here discuss whether physical inefficaciousness is ontologically negative, although I do believe that the opinion that it is is unwarranted. Rather, I will focus on the basic assumption of naturalistically minded philosophers that non-physical causation of the physical is irreconcilable with the physical conservation laws. This assumption is false, or to phrase it more carefully: there is a plausible general view of causation according to which non-physical causation of the physical is reconcilable with the physical conservation laws. That does not yet mean that non-physical causation of the physical does in fact occur, without any detriment to the conservation laws; but I will also attempt to make plausible that it does in fact so occur.

Sometimes (and even mostly) when philosophers speak of non-physical causation of the physical being irreconcilable with *physics*, they actually have in mind something else than an alleged irreconcilability with the physical conservation laws: they mean that non-physical causation of the physical is irreconcilable with the so-called *Principle of Causal Closure of the Physical World*. Now, that Principle, which actually has two different versions, as we shall presently see, has to be distinguished carefully from the physical conservation laws. Indeed, it is logically independent from them in both versions:

PCC1   Everything that is physical and that has a cause also has a physical cause.
In symbols: $\forall x(\Phi x \wedge \exists y Cyx \supset \exists z(\Phi z \wedge Czx))$.

PCC2   Everything that is a cause of something that is physical is physical.
In symbols: $\forall y \forall x(Cyx \wedge \Phi x \supset \Phi y)$.

These are the two versions of the Principle of Causal Closure (I henceforth omit the tag "of the Physical World").[1] They are not always carefully distinguished (not for example by Peter Bieri and by Ansgar Beckermann, when they discuss the difficulties of mental causation in *Analytische Philosophie des Geistes*, p. 5f, and *Analytische Einführung in die Philosophie des Geistes*, p. 115f); but they should be so distinguished since they are very different. PCC2 is the *strong version* of the Principle of Causal Closure; PCC1 is the *weak version* of the Principle: PCC1 follows logically from PCC2, but

---

[1] Other formulations of the Principle of Causal Closure have been proposed. Jonathan Lowe, for example, proposes a temporalized version of PCC1 as "the *strong* ... principle of the causal closure of the physical": "At every time at which a physical state has a cause, it has a fully sufficient physical cause"; and he proposes PCC1 without the condition "and that has a cause" (see PPC below) as "the ... *weak* principle of the causal closure of the physical": "Every physical state has a fully sufficient physical cause" (see *An Introduction to the Philosophy of Mind*, p. 27, p. 30). I do not find his terminology quite appropriate here.

not vice versa. PCC1 allows non-physical causal overdetermination of the physical,[2] PCC2 does not. PCC1 appears to be well-confirmed; PCC2, in contrast, is confirmed only to the extent that PCC1, its logical consequence, is confirmed. Indeed, there are prima facie counterinstances to PCC2 (derived from the straightforward – physicalists say "naïve" – construal of mental causation), and that leaves PCC2 more or less a metaphysical postulate: not something one arrives at, but something one presupposes from the very beginning. As such PCC2 is definitely not a part of the empirical science of physics, but at most a *regulative principle* for it in Kant's sense. More likely, it is *merely* a part of the metaphysical position of *physicalism*. I will further substantiate these claims in what follows.

Non-physical causation of the physical, as I will argue, is reconcilable with the physical conservation laws. It is *in addition* reconcilable with the Weak Principle of Causal Closure if we do not exclude causal overdetermination, that is, the occurrence of two or more *sufficient* causes for one and the same effect. Causal overdetermination, and in particular its psycho-physical variety, may be un-esthetical or un-economical, but that can be no ground for the ontological claim that it does not occur; much less can it be excluded on the mere ground that it would be at best "extremely odd," as Eugene Mills points out against Jaegwon Kim.[3] The denial of causal overdetermination must be argued for differently (that is, it must be *argued* for), and it is very difficult to do this in a non-circular fashion, since there is good prima facie evidence for the occurrence of causal overdeterminations. For example, given transitivity of causation, any causal chain of more than one sufficient cause constitutes a case of causal overdetermination. It may be harder to find overdeterminations by *independent* causes – as long as one forgets the one *glaring* prima facie example: independent mental and neurophysiological causation of the same effect (a certain behavior, for example). The task is to dislodge the intuition that *such* causal overdeterminations do in fact occur (which cannot be done by assuming dogmatically that they do not, or rather: *must not*, occur).[4]

Note that there is no apparent problem at all, not even the problem of causal overdetermination, in reconciling the Weak Principle of Causal Closure with the non-physical causation of physical events if "cause" is taken to mean

---

[2] This is noted by Eugene Mills, since his principle of "physical closure" is no other than PCC1 (see his "Interactionism and Overdetermination", p. 105f). Mills does not draw into consideration any other version of the Principle of Causal Closure.

[3] See Kim, *Supervenience and Mind*, p. 247, and Mills, "Interactionism and Overdetermination," p. 106, p. 113f).

[4] *Systematic* causal overdetermination can be used to reconcile prominent psychophysical intuitions in the philosophy of mind that are widely held to be irreconcilable. See for this the Appendix, (2).

sine-qua-non cause, and not *sufficient cause* (what "cause" is here taken to mean).[5] Deplorably, many philosophers, even many who call themselves "analytic philosophers," do not bother at all to specify, even roughly, what concept of causation they have in mind when they confidently assert that non-physical causation of the physical is irreconcilable with physics.

Non-physical causation of the physical remains, however, irreconcilable with the Strong Principle of Causal Closure, no matter how causation is explicated. But as long as non-physical causation of the physical is reconcilable with the physical conservation laws that should only be of secondary interest *to physicists*. And as philosophers, we are obliged to honor physics, we are not obliged to honor physicalism. From the point of view of physics, it would even be of secondary interest if the Weak Principle of Causal Closure is violated while the conservation laws are left intact. Physics already had to jettison a lot of quasi-metaphysical baggage in the last one hundred years, among them the time-honored *Physical Principle of Causation*:

PPC   Every physical event has a physical cause.
In symbols: $\forall x(\Phi x \wedge Ex \supset \exists y(\Phi y \wedge Cyx))$.

PPC is stronger than PCC1 (in view of the fact that $\exists y Cyx$ – "x has a cause" – is taken to analytically imply Ex – "x is an event"), and physics (or at least the majority of physicists) has already given up PPC: it is ready to face standard physical events that have no physical cause (for example, certain events of radioactive decay, or, for that matter, even the Big Bang).[6] Given this situation, it would really be no great matter any more for physicists qua physicists (and not qua metaphysicians) if they gave up PCC1, too, and consequently, to the

---

[5] Jonathan Lowe distinguishes (without further explanation, but apparently in the tradition of Mackie's INUS-conditions) *cause* from *fully sufficient cause* (which is made up of *causes*) and has a conception of causal overdetermination according to which a case of both "mental state M is a cause of P" and "P has a fully sufficient physical cause" being true does not constitute a case of causal overdetermination, even if M is supposed to be a non-physical state. (See *An Introduction to the Philosophy of Mind*, p. 27f, p. 30f). Yet, in the supposed circumstances, since P has a fully sufficient physical cause, M, being non-physical, is clearly no part of that cause and clearly not necessary for causing P, and hence every fully sufficient cause *that involves* M is, quite obviously, causally overdetermining P. And why shouldn't there be *some* fully sufficient cause of P *involving* M, since M is after all supposed to be a cause of P? So we do have a case of causal overdetermination of P after all, and one for which M is responsible.

[6] For David Chalmers, PPC expresses the causal closure of the physical world, and surprisingly he thinks PPC is very well confirmed: "The best evidence of contemporary science tells us that the physical world is more or less causally closed: for every physical event, there is a physical sufficient cause." (*The Conscious Mind*, p. 125.) Jonathan Lowe, too, is ready to defend PPC (his *"weak* principle of the causal closure of the physical"): see *An Introduction to the Philosophy of Mind*, p. 30. As should be clear by now, taking this stance is not recommendable: it contradicts what most believe to be our best *physics*.

extent they actually believed in it, PCC2. I do, of course, not deny that giving up PCC1 and PCC2 would be a really great matter for *some philosophers*.

Consider now some situation of *physical indeterminism* such as physics finds acceptable today. At a certain point in time the laws of physics – that is, as far as we know, the laws of nature – and the course of physical events up to that point in time are not sufficient for determinining how things will physically go on. There are two or more nomologically possible continuations of the physical past and present, two or more nomologically possible immediate physical futures. How will this situation be resolved? I will consider the a priori possible general ways of resolving this situation in turn:

(1) The physical world simply stops: none of its nomologically possible immediate futures becomes real. – This simply isn't the case: the physical world goes on (in fact, the laws of physics may require that it go on *in some way or other*). Or as Shakespeare has expressed it: "Come what come may / Time and the hour runs through the roughest day." (*Macbeth*, I, 3.)

(2) The physical world branches: all, or at least several, of its nomologically possible immediate futures become real. – This means that we get a plurality of physical worlds, not a plurality of merely possible worlds, but a plurality of *real* worlds, that is, a plurality of real spacetimes, existing side by side without any possibility of physical exchange beyond the branching point. Whoever is ready to jump into this metaphysical abyss may do so, I shall not. Let me just add that it is one of the more bizarre features of contemporary physicalism that most physicalists consider the idea of pure possibilia, and in particular: of merely possible worlds, an extravagant metaphysical fancy not worth their serious attention, but that some physicalists, if faced with certain difficulties for their position, are resolutely ready to embrace a plurality of *real worlds*.[7]

(3) The physical world continues in precisely one way: exactly one of its nomologically possible immediate futures becomes real. This, surely, is the most plausible resolution of a situation of physical indeterminism. But merely stating it is not enough. The plausibility of this third resolution disguises a disturbing question: Given that the physical world could have continued in this or another nomologically possible way, *why* did it continue in precisely *this* way, and not the other?

---

[7] Such a difficulty is the difficulty of explaining the "fine-tuning" of the universe. See Bernulf Kanitscheider, *Im Innern der Natur*, p. 126f. I do not wish to suggest, however, that the idea of a plurality of real worlds resulting from a situation of physical indeterminism is intrinsically connected to physicalism. It is not.

This is a demand for *explanation*, and we now have to consider in which way an explanation way be forthcoming. But there is one thing that is already clear even now: Howsoever the real immediate physical future after a situation of physical indeterminism is to be explained, none of the possible explanations can be in conflict with the physical conservation laws. Those laws are preserved *after* the moment of indeterminism just as they were preserved up to and including the moment of indeterminism, since the possible immediate physical future which becomes real is a *nomologically possible* immediate future, that is, an immediate physical future which is compatible with the totality of physical laws, and therefore, in particular, compatible with the physical conservation laws. *No physical fact after an indeterministic situation contradicts physical laws*; this fact, call it "the compatibility fact," is implicit in the very description of a situation of physical indeterminism. Now: any explanation of the real immediate physical future after such an indeterministic situation has to respect the compatibility fact. Therefore: any such explanation will be compatible with the physical conservation laws.

And here is the best way, I submit, to make some headway in obtaining an explanation of the immediate real physical future after an indeterministic situation. Given a situation of physical indeterminism after which the physical world, as it always does, goes on in a single manner, let e^* be the totality of (real) physical events immediately after the indeterministic situation. What is the (or a) cause of this event? If we mean, as I think we should, by "cause" *actualized sufficient cause*, the (or a) cause of e^* cannot be a physical event or anything physical (e.g., particles, electromagnetic fields, etc.), since not even the totality of all events that have happened before e^*, and therefore not the totality of their physical constituents (e.g., actual particles, electromagnetic fields, etc.),[8] could determine the happening of e^*. Therefore: if e^* has a cause at all, it must be a non-physical cause. But according to the *General Principle of Causation*,

GPC Every event has a cause,
in symbols: $\forall x(Ex \supset \exists y Cyx)$,

---

[8] In my view, there are no physical objects that are not constituents or parts of physical events, and I do not believe in an independent causality of the, if I may say so, *non-eventy* constituents of physical events (these views are corollaries of the metaphysical theory I expound in my book *Ereignis und Substanz*). In other words, the causal influence of non-eventy physical objects is completely reducible to the casual influence of the events of which these objects are constituents. Therefore, if the totality of all physical events before e^* is not sufficient for determining e^*, then neither is the totality of all the physical constituents of these events. This leaves us with no physical cause for e^*.

e^* must have a cause. Therefore: e^* has a non-physical cause,[9] and e^* having a non-physical cause points us towards a certain kind of explanation of the immediate real physical future after an indeterministic situation: such an explanation had best be a *causal and non-physical* one.

The argument that has just been deployed, call it "the C-Argument," is based on certain assumptions: (1) on the assumption of the occurrence of a situation of physical indeterminism with several nomologically possible continuations into the future, but with a single real continuation; (2) on the assumption of a certain conception of causation; (3) on the assumption of the General Principle of Causation. But these assumptions are certainly *compossible*. Therefore the C-Argument establishes the *compatibility* of non-physical causation of the physical with the physical conservation laws. If the assumptions of the C-Argument are not only compossible, but also *complausible*, then the argument establishes something more: namely, the *plausibility* of non-physical causation of the physical in accordance with the physical conservation laws.

Are the assumptions (1) to (3) complausible? This, in their particular case, is really a matter merely of their separate plausibility: if each of them is plausible, then, in their case, they are also plausible together. What about the plausibility of each of the three assumptions?

I start with the General Principle of Causation, since most philosophers nowadays may find this principle implausible. Logical carelessness is one of the vices of philosophers, and therefore many of them apparently confuse PPC – the *Physical* Principle of Causation – with GPC – the *General* Principle of Causation. There is indeed evidence in physics against PPC, but that evidence leaves GPC unscathed.

But perhaps something more than logical carelessness is, after all, involved here. Given that there is a physical event that has *no physical cause*, in contradiction to PPC, how could one derive from this that there is an event that has *no cause at all*, in contradiction to GPC? Answer: By assuming that if there is no physical cause, then there is no cause at all, or in other words:

PCP1   Everything that has a cause also has a physical cause.
In symbols: $\forall x(\exists y Cyx \supset \exists z(\Phi z \wedge Czx))$.

Or by assuming the logically stronger

---

[9] A similar, but more specialized argument can be constructed with respect to the Big Bang: The Big Bang is a physical event that, as science is ready to concede, has no physical cause. But GPC demands its having a cause. Hence the Big Bang has a non-physical cause, and obviously (since there is no time before the Big Bang) without hurting the physical conservation laws.

PCP2   Everything that causes something is physical.
In symbols: $\forall y \forall x(Cyx \supset \Phi y)$.

PCC1 and PCC2 are obvious logical consequences of PCP1 and PCP2, respectively. I call PCP1 the *Weak Principle of Causal Physicalism*, PCP2 the *Strong Principle of Causal Physicalism*. These latter principles bear their metaphysical character on their faces. They can never be confirmed within physics, since physics treats only of the physical. Thus, what could *at most* be confirmed within physics are PCC1 and PCC2, the respective logical weakenings of PCP1 and PCP2. However, we have already seen that even PCC1 and PCC2 – PCC2 more so than PCC1 – are much less principles of physics than principles of *physicalism*, of the metaphysical "Überbau" of physics.

Given metaphysical neutrality, there is no reason to assume PCP2 or PCP1, and therefore the statement stands: that physical evidence against PPC leaves GPC unscathed. But given metaphysical neutrality, there is indeed every reason to assume GPC. This latter principle is *not* a biased metaphysical principle; it is something that every philosopher of any metaphysical persuasion can accept. And being a philosopher, he or she rationally ought to accept it, since GPC asserts part of what is the objective basis for a rational view of the world.[10] In case the reader is not convinced (as is likely),[11] let me add that for establishing an instance of the non-physical causation of the physical it is indeed not even necessary to assume GPC, but only necessary to assume that *in some* (not necessarily *in every*) situation of physical indeterminism there is a cause of whatever happens immediately after it. It does not seem plausible to deny this latter assumption, although, of course, one *can* deny it; the denial, however, seems gratuitous, or – alternatively – *ad hoc*.[12]

What about the second assumption of the C-Argument, the particular conception of causation made use of in it? This conception was that of causation as *sufficient causation*. There were no further restrictions on the

---

[10] As such, GPC is coeval with philosophy itself. Since the time of antiquity it was often asserted in the form of the principle "Nothing comes of nothing."

[11] The reason for such skepticism may well be that GPC apparently enables a cosmological argument for the existence of God. Cf. footnote 9. But aside from the fact that GPC *does not* lead straight from the Big Bang to the existence of God, one should consider that a principle may indeed be effectively refuted by a *reductio ad absurdum*, but certainly not by a *reductio ad deum*.

[12] One can also plead *ignorance* with respect to the assumption. This is legitimate (even though somewhat unsatisfactory philosophically) as long as it does not turn out that the only reason for taking this stance is the wish to escape the conclusion that there is non-physical causation of the physical.

concept of causation, except that causes have to be already *actualized* (this in order to exclude backward causation by *future* physical causes) and (in parentheses) that what is caused is always an event; in particular, and appropriately so, there was no legislation on the question of what categories of entities can be causes.

Sufficient causation with actualized causes and with events as effects is as respectable a conception of causation as sine-qua-non or probabilistic causation or any other conception of causation, and, more importantly, it seems to be essentially the conception that is meant when non-physical causation of the physical is held to be irreconcilable with the physical conservation laws.[13] Now, it would be a blatant *petitio principii* if a proponent of that position considered causation to be intrinsically connected to the transmission of energy or impulse in the physical sense, or even to *be* such transmission.[14] Non-physical causation *in that sense* of the physical, that is, causation of something physical by something non-physical that nevertheless inexorably involves transmission of, say, energy in the physical sense, is of course irreconcilable with the physical conservation laws, no doubt about that (at least no doubt I care to go into here). But this *physicalistic* conception of causation is also at issue in the whole question, and indeed the C-Argument *also* leads to the conclusion, on minimal assumptions, that the physicalistic conception of causation as involving transmission of a conserved physical quantity is simply not adequate.

But are those assumptions all that minimal? How about the first assumption of the C-Argument, the occurrence of a situation of physical indeterminism with several nomologically possible continuations into the future, but with a single real continuation? I have already argued for the *singleness* of real continuation after a situation of physical indeterminism. This leaves us with the question of the occurrence of situations of physical indeterminism. But it is received opinion among physicists that such situations do occur, and philosophers had better not deny this.

In fact, physicalist philosophers usually do not deny the occurrence of situations of physical indeterminism, they usually do not want to revert to 19th-century determinism. For this would all too clearly reveal the metaphys-

---

[13] If causes are merely supposed to be probabilistic or sine-qua-non causes, why then, after all, might there not be probabilistic or sine-qua-non *non-physical* causes of a certain physical effect in addition to the probabilistic or sine-qua-non *physical* causes of it (considering, in particular, that causal overdetermination cannot be a problem then)?

[14] Views identical or close to this have been held, notably, by W. V. O. Quine (see *The Roots of Reference*, p. 7), D. Fair, P. Dowe, and W. Salmon. The idea has recently been brought forward again by M. Kistler. (See References for bibliographical data.)

ical nature of their position. Rather, physicalists[15] usually deny the *relevance* of indeterministic situations, which they regard as being confined to the microphysical world, for the question of *free human agency*. The denial is not reasonable, in particular if at the same time, as is usually done, the basic laws of physics are supposed to explain not only microphysical phenomena but also macrophysical ones. This clearly implies that what happens on the microscopic scale is after all held *to be relevant* for what happens on the macroscopic scale. And why should only (nomologically) explainable (that is, determined) microphysical events *be relevant* for macrophysics, and not also *unexplainable*? Why, in other words, should microscopic indeterminism never magnify itself into macroscopic indeterminism?

The question of free human agency brings us to the final considerations in this paper: What does the C-Argument, which has now been shown to rest on complausible assumptions, mean for non-physical agent and mental causation of the physical, in particular if we focus our attention on the human sphere?

The C-Argument has the conclusion that a certain physical event e^* has a non-physical (sufficient) cause, without there being any violation of the physical conservation laws. This cannot mean that that cause is *entirely non-physical*, it can only mean that that cause is *not entirely physical*, *if* we consider physical events that went before e^* to be not only relevant circumstances for the causation of e^*, but also parts of its non-physical cause. *If*, however, all the physical events that went before e^* are merely relevant circumstances for the causation of e^*, then indeed the non-physical cause of e^* could be *entirely non-physical*. Moreover, since e^*, however short, is a complete section of the course of the physical world, e^* is a big event, and therefore, prima facie, it is more likely than not that its non-physical cause is, in some sense, big too. And therefore, if for example the cause is to be a non-physical agent, then that agent is more likely to be a large group of non-physical substances, acting together, than a single non-physical substance, acting alone. However, if the difference between e^* and the course of events that has gone immediately before is small, then the reality of e^*, if due to the action of a non-physical agent, could after all be due to a *single* non-physical substance.

Yet, all of this is speculation, the offering of possibilities on conditions. The C-argument is silent about the composition and nature of the non-physical cause of e^*. It leaves many open questions, and this makes it difficult to apply to the human sphere. But suppose we hold that human beings are in a certain sense non-physical substances (*entirely non-physical* or *not entirely physical*?)

---

[15] And also, at least tentatively, some non-physicalists. Cf. Jonathan Lowe, *An Introduction to the Philosophy of Mind*, p. 30.

that each have one, in a certain sense, non-physical mental life, as so many people have believed in the course of the last 2500 years.[16] This view is not shown to be correct by the C-argument (far from it), but it is certainly *corroborated* by that argument, since the C-argument shows that a certain intuition which is intimately connected to the mentioned view is logically, scientifically and philosophically *coherent*. This is the intuition that the course of human history, with all its glories and terrible crimes, *is not*, not even as far as its purely physical side is concerned, purely due to physical causes, and *is not*, where physical causes give out, purely due to absolute chance, but is more often than not *causally due* to non-physical human substances making decisions on the basis of their non-physical mental lives.

Appendix

(1) General principles of causation and their logical relations

Weak Principle of Causal Closure (of the Physical World)
PCC1   Everything that is physical and that has a cause also has a physical cause.
In symbols: $\forall x(\Phi x \wedge \exists y Cyx \supset \exists z(\Phi z \wedge Czx))$.

Strong Principle of Causal Closure
PCC2   Everything that is a cause of something that is physical is physical.
In symbols: $\forall y \forall x(Cyx \wedge \Phi x \supset \Phi y)$.

Physical Principle of Causation
PPC   Every physical event has a physical cause.
In symbols: $\forall x(\Phi x \wedge Ex \supset \exists y(\Phi y \wedge Cyx))$.

General Principle of Causation
GPC   Every event has a cause.
In symbols: $\forall x(Ex \supset \exists y Cyx)$.

Weak Principle of Causal Physicalism
PCP1   Everything that has a cause also has a physical cause.
In symbols: $\forall x(\exists y Cyx \supset \exists z(\Phi z \wedge Czx))$.

Strong Principle of Causal Physicalism
PCP2   Everything that causes something is physical.
In symbols: $\forall y \forall x(Cyx \supset \Phi y)$.

---

[16] And as I have argued in *Ereignis und Substanz*.

GPC does not logically imply, nor is logically implied by, any of the other five principles of causation listed above: it is quite on its own. But for the other five we have:

$$\begin{array}{ccc} \text{PCP2} & \to & \text{PCC2} \\ \downarrow & & \downarrow \\ \text{PCP1} & \to & \text{PCC1} \leftarrow \text{PPC} \end{array}$$

(2) A reconciliation of psychophysical intuitions on the basis of systematic causal overdetermination

The following[17] is for those readers who are not *a priori* afraid of causal overdetermination (it may be helpful for the timid to give the thing a *neutral* name: *multiple causal determination*). (Before beginning, I hasten to say that, in what follows, all quantifiers will be restricted to the entities that are left in the world if we subtract from it all disembodied spirits that may perhaps be found in it. Without that restriction, some of the principles posited might appear to be *too general*.)

Definition 1

Let F and G be properties, x an individual, t a moment of time:
F is at t in x a causal representative of $G := x$ has F at t, and x has G at t, and $\forall p$(that x has F at t causes p iff that x has G at t causes p) and $\forall p(p$ causes that x has F at t iff p causes that x has G at t).[18]

The above defined time- and individual-dependent relation between properties – the relation of *causal representation* for properties – is symmetric and transitive, and, moreover, reflexive with respect to all properties F, individuals x and times t such that x has F at t.

Principle 1a

For all Ψ-properties G, all individuals x, all times t: if x has G at t, then there is a Φ-property F such that F is at t in x a causal representative of G (or equivalently: ... such that G is a t in x a causal representative of F).

Principle 1a states that any mental (or psychical: Ψ-)property, whenever it is instantiated (no matter in which individual or at what time), is, in that instance, causally represented by a physical (or Φ-)property. *Principle 1a* is

---

[17] It is close in sentiment to ideas Eugene Mills defends in "Interactionism and Overdetermination." The details are rather different.
[18] In what follows, "p", "q" and "r" are variables for states of affairs.

already to a very high degree empirically confirmed, and cognitive science and neurophysiology are working strenuously to confirm it even better.

Now, *Principle 1b*, following below, is closely related to *Principle 1a* (and like the latter it is very well confirmed). The only major difference is that *Principle 1b* concerns states of affairs instead of properties. But before stating it, we need another definition (which is closely related to *Definition 1*):

Definition 2
Let p and q be states of affairs:
p is a causal representative of $q := p$ obtains, and q obtains, and $\forall r(p$ causes r iff q causes $r)$ and $\forall r(r$ causes p iff r causes $q)$.

Definition 2 gives us a symmetric and transitive relation of causal representation between state of affairs; it is, moreover, reflexive with respect to all obtaining states of affairs. And we are all set to posit

Principle 1b
For every obtaining Ψ-state of affairs q: there is a Φ-state of affairs p such that p is a causal representative of q.

Note that if a Ψ-state of affairs q and a Φ-state of affairs p are causal representatives of each other, then they are indeed closely related to each other. *But* that relation cannot be equivalent to causation. We cannot but conclude that it is neither the case that q causes p, nor the case that p causes q, for otherwise either p or q would cause itself (according to *Definition 2*, since p and q are causal representatives of each other), and that is absurd.

Further we have

Principle 2a
No Ψ-property is a Φ-property.

Principle 2a is the expression of a deeply entrenched dualistic intuition (the one that is denied by the so-called type-identity theory, which nowadays even hard-core physicalists find somewhat hard to believe). *Principle 2a*, just like *Principle 1a*, has a counterpart for states of affairs, which is, however, from the epistemological point of view not entirely its equal (because states of affairs are, in a way, *tokens*, and many people find so-called token-identity theories so much more plausible than type-identity theories):

Principle 2b
No Ψ-state of affairs is a Φ-state of affairs.

Nevertheless, strong common sense intuitions also support *Principle 2b*, common sense being dualistic in sentiment. Continuing, we also have:

Principle 3
There are Ψ-states of affairs p and Φ-states of affairs q such that p causes q.

Principle 3 affirms the existence of the causation of physical states of affairs by mental (psychical) states of affairs.[19] *Principle 3*, too, is the expression of a deeply entrenched intuition, one that interactionist dualists and (non-eliminativist) physicalists (hence the majority of philosophers) share, an intuition that is apparently confirmed by experience at every turn. Finally we posit

Principle 4
Every Φ-state of affairs that is caused at all is caused by a Φ-state of affairs.

Principle 4 simply is the Weak Principle of Causal Closure *intended for states of affairs as effects and causes*. (PCC1, on the other hand, taken as we left it, is the Weak Principle of Causal Closure *intended for events as effects. Merely* given that some physical events have causes, PCC1 is *compatible* with assuming that some *or even all* of these causes are not events. But merely given that some physical states of affairs have causes, *Principle 4* is compatible *only* with assuming that *some* of these causes are not states of affairs.)

What is remarkable about the above six principles is that there is *no* logical contradiction in their conjunction, that each of them is plausible in itself, and that, taken together, they give a rather a satisfactory picture of the relationship between mental and physical entities, one that reconciles the demands of science and of common sense: Common sense assumes, in accordance with *Principle 3*, that some mental state of affairs q – for example, that Jim feels ashamed at t_0 – causes a physical state of affairs p – for example, that blood rushes to Jim's cheeks at t_1. Science demands, following *Principle 4*, that p also have a physical cause (let us *here* neither question that science demands this, nor question that the demand is in every case in fact fulfilled, even though we have seen above that physics might dissociate itself even from the Weak Principle of Causal Closure, and even though we have argued above for the occurrence of violations of even the Weak Principle of Causal Closure). But *Principle 1b* already provides for the required physical cause. According to it, there must be a physical state of affairs r which is a causal representative of q – which state of affairs r, therefore, causes p, since q causes p.[20] Hence science, as far as the relation of the mental to the physical is concerned, may

---

[19] Note that if F is a Ψ-property (alternatively: Φ-property), then *that x has F at t* is here taken to be a Ψ-state of affairs (alternatively: Φ-state of affairs). This allows it to easily generate prima facie examples for the causation of physical states of affairs by mental ones.

[20] In fact, *Principle 1b* alone suffices to prove the following corollary of *Principle 4*: Every Φ-state of affairs *that is caused by a Ψ-state of affairs* is also caused by a Φ-state of affairs.

as well follow *Principle 1b* instead of *Principle 4*. Guided by *Principle 1b*, it becomes the task of science to *specify* (actually *find*) some such physical state of affairs r whose existence as a causal representative of q is already predicted by *Principle 1b* (and actual scientific practice shows that this task is taken up, and that it is worthwhile to take it up, since the prospects of completing it are promising). Here *Principle 1a* is helpful: Given (as assumed) that q is the state of affairs that Jim feels ashamed at t_0 and that this state of affairs obtains, Jim has at t_0 the mental property *of feeling ashamed*, and therefore, according to *Principle 1a*, there must be a physical property F such that F is at t_0 in Jim a causal representative of that property of feeling ashamed. Science merely needs to specify F,[21] for then it has automatically given a full specification of a physical state of affairs r that is a causal representative of the mental state of affairs q: because, clearly, r can be taken to be the state of affairs that Jim has F at t_0.

There may indeed be a *unique* way of specifying F. For the following additional principle seems to be highly plausible (it has never been refuted):

Principle 5
For all Φ-properties F and F', Ψ-properties G, individuals x and moments of time t: if F is at t in x a causal representative of G, and F' is at t in x also a causal representative of G, then $F = F'$.

Principle 5 makes it possible to speak of *the* physical property which is a causal representative of G in x at t, if x has a Ψ-property G at t. We can abbreviate the definite description just used by "$\varphi_{G,x,t}$", and thus can formulate the following psychophysical law (as a corollary of *Principles 1a* and *5*):

For all Ψ-properties G, all individuals x, all times t: if x has G at t, then x has $\varphi_{G,x,t}$ at t.

In other words, there is no instance of a mental property which is not also an instance of the physical causal representative, relative to the instance, of that property. In this (new) sense mental properties can be said to *depend* on physical ones.

In view of the rather satisfactory epistemological situation created by the seven principles now stated – a situation which serves common sense and science alike, *preserving* common sense and *furthering* the progress of science – why should one want to give up any one of the principles stated

---

[21] It is worth remarking that if Jim is again ashamed at t_2, one of the physical properties which are *at* t_2 in Jim causal representatives of the property of feeling ashamed *may*, but *need not* be one of the physical properties that are *at* t_0 in Jim causal representatives of the property of feeling ashamed.

above, especially in view of the fact that none of them is contradicted or disconfirmed by experience?[22] The only "reason" seems to be a *mere dislike* of causal overdetermination, or a *mere dislike* of dualism. But mere dislikes are no reasons.

References

Beckermann, A.: *Analytische Einführung in die Philosophie des Geistes*, de Gruyter, Berlin 1999.
Bieri, P.: *Analytische Philosophie des Geistes*, Beltz/Athenäum, Weinheim ³1997.
Chalmers, D.: *The Conscious Mind. In Search of a Fundamental Theory*, Oxford University Press, New York/Oxford 1997.
Dowe, P.: Wesley Salmon's Process Theory of Causality and the Conserved Quantity Theory, *Philosophy of Science* 59 (1992), 195–216.
Fair, D.: Causation and the Flow of Energy, *Erkenntnis* 14 (1979), 219–250.
Kanitscheider, B.: *Im Innern der Natur. Philosophie und moderne Physik*, Wissenschaftliche Buchgesellschaft, Darmstadt 1996.
Kim, J.: *Supervenience and Mind: Selected Philosophical Essays*, Cambridge University Press, Cambridge 1993.
Kistler, M.: Reducing Causality to Transmission, *Erkenntnis* 48 (1998), 1–24.
Lowe, J.: *An Introduction to the Philosophy of Mind*, Cambridge University Press, Cambridge 2000.
Meixner, U.: *Ereignis und Substanz*, Schöningh, Paderborn 1997.
Mills, E.: Interactionism and Overdetermination, *American Philosophical Quarterly* 33 (1996), 105–117.
Quine, W. V. O.: *The Roots of Reference*, Open Court, La Salle, Illinois 1973.
Salmon, W.: Causality Without Counterfactuals, *Philosophy of Science* 61 (1994), 297–312.

---

[22] *Principle 4* and *PCC1* is a subtle case. There is empirical evidence that some physical events / (obtaining) states of affairs have no physical cause. But this, by itself, does not disconfirm these two principles: we need empirical evidence that some physical events / states of affairs *that have a cause* have no physical cause. No such empirical evidence is forthcoming. One reason for this is that there is no evidence for causation by mental states of affairs / events *without* a physical representation of it, and lots of evidence for such causation *with* a physical representation; precisely this fact of the matter makes the (relevant version of) *Principle 1b* empirically well-confirmed. We frequently *do* have the feeling that *we* (and not our body or parts of it, or current conditions of them, nor our current mental life or parts of it or facts about it) cause a physical event / state of affairs that is otherwise entirely undetermined; but this feeling is surely not empirical evidence in the strict sense, its importance for our self-understanding as *freely acting* human beings notwithstanding. Given that some physical events / (obtaining) states of affairs have no physical cause, it may, indeed, be *plausible* that some physical events / states of affairs *that have a cause* have no physical cause. But this plausibility is best seen as supported by the (relevant version of the) General Principle of Causation, which for all its metaphysical neutrality is a *metaphysical* principle nonetheless.

Teil III
Ethik und Politische Philosophie

Günther Patzig

Gibt es Grenzen der Redefreiheit?

Als ich von den Organisatoren dieses Kongresses die ehrenvolle Einladung bekam, den Eröffnungsvortrag zum 4. GAP-Kongress zu halten, stellten sie mir freundlicherweise die Wahl des Themas frei. Ich überlegte daraufhin, welches der von mir zur Zeit behandelten Themen sich für diese besondere Gelegenheit wohl am ehesten eignen könnte: noch einmal etwas über rationale Begründungsansätze für moralische Normen? Oder neue kritische Betrachtungen der verbreiteten relativistischen und historisierenden Positionen in der Wissenschaftsphilosophie? Oder Argumente gegen die Auffassungen vom richtigen Umgang mit klassischen philosophischen Texten, wie sie etwa bei H. G. Gadamer, R. Rorty und den „Dekonstruktivisten" vertreten werden?

Diese Überlegungen wurden im Januar dieses Jahres[1] durch die Nachricht beendet, daß Dieter Birnbacher, dessen Texte zur Bioethik nicht nur nach meinem Urteil Muster einer wohlabgewogenen, vorurteilsfreien Argumentation in diesem heiklen Gebiet sind, von den Veranstaltern einer Berliner Tagung der Adenauer-Stiftung zu Behindertenfragen als Hauptreferent eingeladen, plötzlich wieder ausgeladen worden war, nach der Demarche eines offensichtlich einflußreichen Bundestagsabgeordneten der CDU, des Herrn Hubert Hüppe. Auf Berichte und Leserbriefe zu dem Vorfall in der FAZ (28.1. und 10.2.2000) antwortete Herr Hüppe in einem „Dieter Birnbachers unverhohlener Tabubruch" betitelten Leserbrief in der FAZ. Der „Tabubruch" Birnbachers soll darin bestehen, daß er Überlegungen vorgetragen hat, die sich auf die Akzeptabilität der Zulassung von Schwangerschaftsabbrüchen im Falle schwerer genetischer Defekte des Embryos beziehen. Diese Überlegungen stehen freilich in einer gewissen Spannung, zwar nicht zu der Lebensschutz- und Freiheitsgarantie des Grundgesetzartikels 2, Absatz II, wohl aber zu der extensiven Auslegung des Begriffs der Person, die das Bundesverfassungsgericht vertritt, nach der schon die befruchtete menschliche Eizelle den vollen Schutz der Verfassung genießt. Nach der Auffassung von Hüppe ist es

---
[1] Januar 2000.

offenbar schon unzulässig, kritische Betrachtungen über die Rechtsprechung des Bundesverfassungsgerichts öffentlich vorzutragen.

Das erinnerte an die skandalösen Kampagnen 1989/90 gegen Vorträge von P. Singer und H. Kuhse an deutschen Universitäten und die zwangsweise Absetzung von Lehrveranstaltungen, die sich mit Texten von Singer befassen sollten. Er erinnerte auch an die beschämenden Vorgänge in Trier und Göttingen 1997 und 1998, als Norbert Hoerster, unter grober Mißdeutung und Verzerrung seiner Auffassungen und mit der Unterstellung, er wolle die eugenischen Programme der Nationalsozialisten wiederbeleben, an Vortrag und Diskussion gehindert wurde. Bei den Göttinger „Vorkommnissen" 1998 spielte die „Akademie für Ethik in der Medizin" leider keine rühmliche Rolle. Jedoch hat sie verdienstlicher Weise diese Vorgänge zum Anlaß genommen, im April diesen Jahres in Düsseldorf eine Tagung zum Thema „Toleranz – Grenzen der Toleranz", unter Herrn Birnbachers Leitung, zu veranstalten. Die mir bekannt gewordenen Pressereaktionen auf diese Tagung (FAZ 5.5.2000, Deutsches Ärzteblatt 97, H. 21, 26.5.2000, S. A 1485/6) waren ambivalent, traten jedenfalls nicht entschieden für die unbeschränkte Freiheit der wissenschaftlichen Diskussion, auch in der Bioethik, ein.

Unter diesen Umständen scheint es mir sinnvoll, auch im Rahmen dieses Kongresses über „Argument und Analyse" noch einmal prinzipielle Fragen zu stellen und besonders die Argumente der Vertreter der Einschränkungsthese zu analysieren, wobei ich den Argumenten Anselm W. Müllers schon deshalb besondere Aufmerksamkeit widmen möchte, weil er sich in origineller Weise auf Thesen Wittgensteins in „Über Gewißheit" stützt.

Nun zur Sache: Es scheint mir mißverständlich, Meinungsfreiheit bzw. Redefreiheit, die von unserer Verfassung in Artikel 5, Absatz II als allgemeine Meinungsfreiheit und in Abs. III – als Freiheit der Wissenschaft, Forschung und Lehre noch einmal gesondert – als *Grundrechte* gesichert sind, so wie im Titel der Düsseldorfer Tagung vom April 2000 mit dem Begriff der „Toleranz" in Zusammenhang zu bringen. Toleranz „πολλαχῶς λέγεται", wie Aristoteles sagen würde. Gemeint kann etwa sein, daß man eine Ansicht toleriert, weil man sie für so absurd hält, daß sie schon von selbst wieder aussterben wird. Das wäre Toleranz aus Gleichgültigkeit. Historisch bedeutsamer ist vor allem eine Toleranz, die zwar eine Auffassung, Weltanschauung, Religion für verkehrt, schädlich oder gefährlich ansieht, aber aus übergeordneten Gründen, z. B. Freiheitsliebe, darauf verzichtet, mit Gewalt gegen sie vorzugehen. (Das war die Toleranz, die John Locke vor allem im Blick hatte.) Eine wichtige Komponente auch dieses Gebrauchs ist die Meinung, die tolerierte Überzeugung sei sichtlich falsch, die tolerierte Handlungsweise offenbar kritikwürdig. Das hatte wohl Goethe im Blick, als er sagte: „Toleranz sollte eigentlich nur eine vorübergehende Gesinnung sein: sie muß zur Anerkennung führen. Dulden heißt beleidigen."[2]

Toleranz im vollen Sinne des Worts schließt Respekt ein, Respekt vor einer Auffassung oder Handlungsweise, die man sich zwar selbst nicht zu eigen machen kann, von der man aber unterstellt, daß ihre Vertreter von Gründen geleitet werden, die man nicht ohne weiteres von der Hand weisen kann. Es gibt auch noch eine andere, respektvolle, Art von Toleranz im praktischen Bereich, die dort vorliegt, wo jemand ein Verhalten akzeptiert, obwohl er es rechtlich unterbinden könnte. So kann man, um ein triviales Beispiel zu nennen, tolerieren, daß der Nachbar in der Mittagszeit mit seinem Motormäher den Rasen schneidet.

Wozu jemand ein Recht hat, das toleriert man nicht, sondern man akzeptiert oder respektiert es. Wenn es um Rede- und Meinungsfreiheit geht: Man braucht nicht zu akzeptieren was einer sagt, aber man hat zu akzeptieren, daß er es sagt. Es gibt natürlich auch Grenzen und Einschränkungen von Grundrechten, einmal dort, wo sie mit anderen Grundrechten in Konflikt kommen, aber auch dort, wo ein Gesetzesvorbehalt ausdrücklich in das Grundrecht eingearbeitet ist, wie im Fall des Artikels 5 (Meinungfreiheit) unseres Grundgesetzes, wo im Absatz II „die allgemeinen Gesetze", die „gesetzlichen Regelungen zum Schutze der Jugend" und das „Recht der persönlichen Ehre" als Einschränkungsgründe genannt werden. Dabei, so die Kommentare, haben die Verfassungsgeber vor allem an die Freiheit von Presse, Rundfunk und Film gedacht (Fernsehen war damals, im Mai 1949, noch nicht aktuell).

Rechtlich scheint die Frage also eindeutig geregelt: Zu den brisanten Fragen der Bioethik, also etwa den Fragen der Euthanasie, der Präimplantationsdiagnostik, der Organtransplantation und der Frage der Bestimmung des Todeszeitpunkts, der Verteilungsgerechtigkeit, der Gentherapie und der Forschung an Embryonen hat jeder, angesichts der großen Bedeutung einer sinnvollen Regelung dieser Fragen für die Mitglieder der Gesellschaft, das Recht, seine Meinung zu diesen Problemkomplexen vorzutragen (insbesondere vor denen, die sich für diese seine Meinung interessieren!). Erst recht gilt das für jeden, der sich im Rahmen wissenschaftlicher Diskussionen zu solchen Themen äußern will oder soll. Die z. T. leider erfolgreichen Versuche, Teilnehmer an Diskussionen durch Aufruf zum Boykott, durch Drohung und durch tatsächliche Gewaltanwendung zum Schweigen zu bringen, sind eindeutig grundgesetzwidrig und überdies schädlich für die Allgemeinheit, weil auf diese Weise Vertreter von Auffassungen aus der Diskussion „ausgegrenzt" werden (wie man jetzt gern sagt), die wichtige Gesichtspunkte zur Debatte

---

[2] Sprüche in Prosa (Hrsg. H. Fricke), Goethes sämtliche Werke, Deutscher Klassiker Verlag, Frankfurt a.M. 1995, S. 249.

beisteuern könnten, deren Unkenntnis zu einseitigen und undurchdachten gesetzlichen Regelungen führen kann. So wäre es fast z.B. beim Transplantationsgesetz (1995) gegangen, und so ist es, jedenfalls nach meinem Urteil, beim sogenannten „Embryonenschutzgesetz" von 1991 schon geschehen, dessen rigide Verbote nach z.Zt. „herrschender Meinung" unter den Juristen z.B. die in manchen Fällen sehr sinnvolle Präimplantationsdiagnostik ausschließen.

Obwohl klar ist, daß der Versuch, mit verbreiteten Auffassungen unvereinbare Ansichten aus der Diskussion auszuschließen, gegen Grundrechte unserer Verfassung verstößt, haben diejenigen, die solche Versuche bisher unternommen haben, doch mit ihren Vorwürfen, Warnungen und Unterstellungen viel Erfolg gehabt. Das „Kinsauer Manifest"[3] ist von vielen Wissenschaftlern und Ärzten unterschrieben oder mit Zustimmung aufgenommen worden, deren Sachkompetenz und Integrität außer Zweifel stehen. Es ist den Verfassern dieses Manifests und den mit ihnen sympathisierenden Medienvertretern gelungen, eine Welle von Befürchtungen auszulösen, die klarem Denken abträglich war. Dabei sind, wie in der Bioethik häufig, in diesem Falle aber exemplarisch, zwei „Topoi", wie Aristoteles sagen würde, besonders in Anspruch genommen worden: Der erste Topos ist das „Argument der schiefen Ebene" (Slippery-Slope-Argument), das man in unserem Land auch das „Dammbruch-Argument" nennt: Wer jetzt z.B. dafür plädiert, das Strafrecht im Bereich des § 216, der die Tötung auf Verlangen unter Strafe stellt, soweit zu lockern, daß Ärzte schwer leidende und unheilbare Patienten *auf deren ausdrücklichen, ernstlichen und nachvollziehbaren Wunsch hin* töten dürfen (wofür sich bei Befragungen regelmäßig mehr als 70% der befragten Mitglieder der Bevölkerung ausgesprochen haben), verletzt nach Auffassung der meist selbsternannten Deichgrafen „Sicherungen, mit denen die Sintflut eines moralischen Abstiegs von unserer Welt ferngehalten werden kann".[4]

Wenn erst einmal diese Hemmschwelle gefallen ist, die den Arzt, dessen Berufung es ist, Leben zu erhalten, davon abhält, Leben, das dem Patienten zur unerträglichen Last geworden ist, auf dessen ausdrücklichen und nachvollziehbaren Wunsch hin zu beenden, dann werden, so die Argumentation, die Ärzte in Fällen, in denen sie es für angezeigt halten, auch ohne solche Einwilligung Patienten töten, oder es werden Patienten unter Druck z.B. von Seiten der Angehörigen um eine solche Sterbehilfe bitten, obwohl sie diese nicht wirklich wünschen. Es werden dann, wieder einen Schritt weiter, entsprechende Tötungshandlungen nicht nur vollzogen, um dem Patienten weiteres sinnloses Leiden zu ersparen, sondern auch aus Gründen der

---

[3] Kinsauer Manifest in: Rest, F., Das kontrollierte Töten, Gütersloh 1992, S. 171–176.
[4] Adolf Laufs, Arztrecht 5. Aufl., München 1993, S. 175.

Mühe und der Kosten, die seine weitere Pflege, besonders auf der Intensivstation, fordert. Ist erst diese Stufe des moralischen Abstiegs erreicht, dann ist eine Entwicklung nicht mehr aufzuhalten, an deren Ende jeder Kranke und Schwache, im Arbeitsprozess nicht mehr Einsatzfähige, auch wenn er gerne weiterleben würde, dem gewaltsamen Zugriff der ärztlichen Exekutoren ausgesetzt sein wird. Als auf ein abschreckendes Beispiel wird meistens auf die Euthanasie-Politik der nationalsozialistischen Regierung verwiesen. Dabei wird vernachlässigt, daß selbst die Nationalsozialisten diese Aktion sorgfältig geheim hielten, daß, als etwas davon bekannt wurde, z.B. durch den bewundernswerten Kardinal Galen in Münster 1941, offene Empörung ausbrach und die Aktion zunächst einmal eingestellt wurde (allerdings wurde sie im geheimen fortgesetzt).

Grundsätzlich gilt: Wer mit einem Dammbruch-Argument gegen eine vorgeschlagene Änderung strafrechtlicher und moralischer Rahmenbedingungen vorgehen will, hat die Verpflichtung, nicht bloß ein abschreckendes Szenario in der Zukunft zu beschwören, dessen Eintreten man *sich vorstellen* könnte. Er muß zeigen, daß es *wahrscheinlich* ist, daß aus der vorgeschlagenen Änderung A sich eine zunächst ungewollte Folgerung B ergibt, und die Entwicklung über die Stadien B, C usw. zu N, dem gefürchteten Endstadium, führen wird. Außerdem muß er zeigen, daß es unwahrscheinlich ist, daß, wenn erst einmal klar geworden ist, daß die befürchtete Entwicklung sich tatsächlich anbahnt, entsprechende Gegenmaßnahmen noch greifen werden.[5]

Im Fall der Sterbehilfe wollen die entschiedenen Gegner jeder neuen Regelung denen, die die Freigabe der aktiven Sterbehilfe unter den entsprechenden rechtlichen Sicherungen befürworten, das Rederecht verweigern und halten sogar Gewaltanwendung gegen Vertreter solcher bioethischer Ansichten für zulässig, ja sogar für ein „begrüßenswertes Zeichen geistiger Gesundheit" (so wörtlich R. Spaemann).[6]

Unter solchen Bedingungen kann man sich kaum darüber wundern (damit komme ich zum *zweiten* „Topos"), daß den Befürwortern einer rechtlichen Neuregelung der aktiven Sterbehilfe unterstellt wird, sie träten nicht nur gleichsam fahrlässig eine medizin-ethische Lawine los, sondern sie *wollten* eigentlich eine Gesellschaft, in der Schwache und Kranke nach nationalsozialistischem Vorbild „ausgemerzt" werden, eine sogenannte „Stromliniengesellschaft", und sie benutzten die vorgeschobene Forderung nach Freigabe

---

[5] Vgl. das vorzügliche Buch von Barbara Guckes, „Das Argument der schiefen Ebene", G. Fischer Verlag, Stuttgart 1997.
[6] Robert Spaemann, Die Herausforderung des ärztlichen Berufsethos durch die medizinische Wissenschaft, in: Medizinische Klinik, S. 595–600, hier S. 599.

aktiver Sterbehilfe für schwerleidende Kranke im Endstadium unheilbarer Krankheiten nur als „Einstiegsdroge" (so wörtlich das „Kinsauer Manifest").

Versucht man sich klar zu machen, warum sonst klar denkende und philosophisch hervorragend begabte und geschulte Köpfe, wie z. B. R. Spaemann, so etwas schreiben, gerät man in schwieriges Fahrwasser. Einer der neben Spaemann wichtigsten Wortführer gegen die aktive Sterbehilfe, Klaus Dörner, ist freilich auf die Logik schlecht zu sprechen, die er in diesem Zusammenhang als „schlagende, zwingende, umwerfende, tödliche Logik" bezeichnet, so daß für ihn eine Theorie im Bereich der Medizinethik schon deshalb ausscheiden muß, weil sie sich dem „rein rationalen und klaren Denken verschrieben hat".[7]

Natürlich: In solchen Fragen ist mit konsequentem Denken allein nicht allzuviel getan; Empathie und Sympathie, also Emotionen, müssen mitwirken. Ganz ohne Denken geht es aber auch nicht, und ob ein unklares und nicht-rationales Denken in solchen schwierigen Fragen weiter hilft, dürfte zweifelhaft sein. Wie schon Norbert Hoerster in seinem Buch „Sterbehilfe im säkularen Staat"[8] wahrscheinlich gemacht hat, kann man die Leidenschaft, mit der Gegner jeder Legalisierung aktiver Sterbehilfe gegen deren Befürworter vorgehen, wohl nur erklären, wenn man weltanschaulich-religiöse Grundauffassungen einbezieht, die hier nach Meinung der Euthanasie-Gegner (und wohl auch der Befürworter) ins Spiel kommen. Besonders deutlich wird das bei Robert Spaemann, der einen Sinn des Leidens darin sieht, „die Flucht des Leidenden zu Gott zu bewirken, indem ihm alle anderen Befriedigungsmöglichkeiten genommen worden sind". Die Befürworter der Sterbehilfe, so Spaemann, folgten der „grausamen Logik des Hedonismus" und dem Motto „Wenn das Leiden nicht verschwindet, muß der Leidende sterben!" Leiden wird also als etwas Wertvolles angesehen. Es scheint mir geradezu unmenschlich, den Ausdruck „Hedonismus" im Zusammenhang mit den Qualen mancher Sterbender zu verwenden; und die Behauptung, daß nach Auffassung der Freigabe-Befürworter der Leidende sterben muß, wenn sein Leiden nicht mehr medizinisch beherrscht werden kann, geht insofern fehl, als ja davon nicht die Rede ist, daß jemand getötet werden dürfen soll, der nicht ausdrücklich darum bittet.

In einer Veröffentlichung des apostolischen Stuhls, Bonn 1980, einer „Erklärung der Kongregation für die Glaubenslehre zur Euthanasie", S. 9ff., heißt es[9], die „intensive Anwendung schmerzstillender Mittel sei nicht pro-

---

[7] In seiner Rezension von H.H. Attrott u. H. Pohlmeier (Hrsg.): Sterbehilfe in der Gegenwart, 1990 in: Suizidprophylaxe, S. 157–161, 1991.
[8] Norbert Hoerster, „Sterbehilfe im säkularen Staat", Frankfurt a.M. 1998, S. 154–166.
[9] Ich zitiere auch hier nach Hoerster.

blemlos". Der Schmerz könne „zumal in der Sterbestunde, eine besondere Bedeutung im Heilsplan Gottes" haben. So erhalte der Mensch „Anteil am Leiden Christi"; außerdem könne er sich ohne Narkotika besser „auf die Begegnung mit Christus ... vorbereiten".

Solche Verklärung des Leidens dürfte wohl nur noch einer kleinen Minderheit, auch unter Christen in unserer Gesellschaft, aus dem Herzen gesprochen sein. Mit dem Argument der Gottgesandtheit der Leiden, auch als Strafe, ist noch im 19. Jahrhundert von Vertretern der Kirche in England gegen die Operationsnarkose argumentiert worden, mit entsprechenden Argumenten wurde im 18. Jahrhundert auch gegen Blitzableiter und Feuerversicherungen gepredigt. (Heute sieht man sogar auf Kirchtürmen Blitzableiter!) Gegen die Bereitschaft von einzelnen religiös bestimmten Menschen, auch schwerste Leiden am Ende ihres Lebens bewußt zu durchleben, kann man nichts einwenden. Es wird ja auch durch eine Sterbehilfe-Regelung, wie sie etwa von Hoerster vorgeschlagen wird, niemand genötigt, von der damit sich öffnenden Möglichkeit Gebrauch zu machen. Das *Abwehrrecht* des Individuums gegen ein staatliches Verbot in Hinblick auf eine Vereinbarung über eventuelle Sterbehilfe mit einem behandelnden Arzt ist nicht als *Anspruchsrecht* zu verstehen: Kein Arzt, der aktive Sterbehilfe aus moralischen Gründen ablehnt, kann verpflichtet sein, sie einem Patienten auf dessen Wunsch zu gewähren. Eine Pflicht könnte nur auf Seiten der ärztlichen Standesorganisationen bestehen, prospektiven Patienten solche Ärzte zu benennen, die im Eventualfalle zu rechtlich zugelassener Sterbehilfe bereit wären.

Während die bisher genannten Autoren, die den Andersdenkenden das Rederecht absprechen, sich vor allem an den Problemen der aktiven Sterbehilfe orientiert haben, ist der Autor, mit dessen Position ich mich nun auseinandersetzen möchte, Anselm W. Müller, mehr auf das Problem der sogenannten Früheuthanasie konzentriert, und sein Hauptgegner ist P. Singer.[10]

Mir scheint auch die von Anselm Müller vertretene Auffassung nicht haltbar; jedoch ist seine These, daß man über grundlegende Überzeugungen wie in der Wissenschaft so auch in der Moral keine Diskussion zu ihrer *Begründung* oder *Widerlegung* führen kann und daher nur Werbung bzw. Abwehr möglich bleiben, immerhin interessant genug, um näher besprochen zu werden. Nach Müllers Auffassung würden öffentliche Vorträge über solche Materien als *Propaganda* eingestuft werden müssen, und die Unterbindung

---

[10] Ich beziehe mich auf seinen Aufsatz mit dem Titel „Totale Toleranz in Sachen Singer?", abgedruckt im Diskussionsteil der Zeitschrift für Philosophische Forschung Bd. 51, Heft 3, 1997, S. 448–470, und auf das Buch „Tötung auf Verlangen – Wohltat oder Untat?", Kohlhammer-Verlag Stuttgart, ebenfalls 1997.

solcher Veranstaltungen wäre dann eine Form der Abwehr solcher Werbung. Übrigens räumt Anselm Müller, wenn auch etwas verklausuliert, ein, daß *gewaltsame Aktionen* wie Pfeifkonzerte während akademischer Veranstaltungen und Anwendung physischer Gewalt wohl fast von jedem und jedenfalls von ihm mißbilligt werden.[11] Etwas anderes sei es freilich, das Zustandekommen solcher Veranstaltungen z. B. schon im Vorfeld zu verhindern.

Das Beispiel, an dem Anselm Müller sich orientiert, sind Singers Ansichten zur Früheuthanasie, d. h. seine These, daß Neugeborene noch keine Personen sind, die ein Interesse an ihrem eigenen Leben und seiner Fortsetzung haben könnten, und daher die Eltern das Recht haben sollten, im Falle schwerster Behinderung des Neugeborenen, die sowohl für das Neugeborene selbst als auch für seine Eltern schwere Belastungen mit sich bringen würde, das Neugeborene töten zu lassen.

Hier bin auch ich selbst anderer Ansicht als Singer. Mir scheint, daß eine Tötung von Neugeborenen nur in den Fällen gerechtfertigt sein kann, in denen auch bei Erwachsenen eine Sterbehilfe gerechtfertigt wäre, und daß nur das unzumutbare Leiden des Neugeborenen, nicht die Belastung der Eltern und Dritter die Basis einer solchen Rechtfertigung sein könnte. Aber wenn ich hier auch, anders als bei der aktiven Sterbehilfe, die Auffassung Singers ablehne, halte ich es doch für selbstverständlich, daß er und alle, die seine Meinung teilen, wie z. B. Frau Kuhse, ihre Auffassungen öffentlich vortragen, begründen und natürlich auch öffentlicher Kritik müssen aussetzen können. Unhaltbar scheint mir die Behauptung von Müller, merkwürdig sei das Befremden von Kuhse und Singer darüber, daß andere sie daran hindern wollten, für ihre Auffassungen öffentlich einzutreten; denn sie verhielten sich damit nicht anders als z. B. ein monarchistischer Revisionist, der Kränkung und Ressentiment darüber empfindet, daß die Verfassung der Bundesrepublik Deutschland seine Partei nicht zuläßt.[12] Sieht er, Anselm Müller, nicht den wichtigen Unterschied zwischen einer Beschwerde darüber, daß eine Verfassung eine bestimmte Parteigründung ausschließt, und einer Klage darüber, daß ein von der Verfassung ausdrücklich als Grundrecht eingestuftes Rederecht von einzelnen Individuen aus was immer für Motiven massiv mißachtet wird?

Wie kommt nun ein respektabler Philosoph wie Anselm Müller zu solchen erstaunlichen Thesen?

Werfen wir einen Blick auf seinen Gedankengang: Er extrahiert zunächst aus Äußerungen von Kuhse und Singer und der „Erklärung von Mitgliedern der Allgemeinen Gesellschaft für Philosophie in Deutschland" (die 1989 von

---

[11] Zeitschrift für Philosophische Forschung 51, 1997, S. 465.
[12] a. a. O., S. 462–463.

180 Philosophen unterschrieben wurde, aber von den maßgebenden Zeitungen nicht abgedruckt worden ist, und erst 1991 im Druck erscheinen konnte)[13] vier Grundsätze:

1.) Argumente, die für die Zulassung einer bisher verbotenen Praxis vorgelegt werden, sollten durch Gegenargumente, und nichts sonst, bekämpft werden.
2.) Eine Unterscheidung zwischen öffentlichen und fachinternen Debatten spielt für das Recht auf Meinungsäußerung und insbesondere für die akademische Freiheit (besser wäre wohl „Wissenschaftsfreiheit", G. P.) keine Rolle.
3.) Eine öffentliche Euthanasie-Debatte kann und soll man unabhängig von der je eigenen Stellungnahme zur Sache selbst bejahen und fördern.
4.) Die Kundgabe einer moralphilosophischen Äußerung ist als solche moralisch neutral.

Gegen diese vier Grundsätze führt nun Müller in seinem Aufsatz folgende Gegenargumente an: Zum ersten Grundsatz: Moralische Überzeugungen sind jedenfalls zum Teil von der Art, daß sie *ursprüngliche Überzeugungen* und daher weder einer Begründung noch einer Widerlegung fähig sind. „Für die überwiegende Mehrheit des Publikums" läßt „die eigene Position weder Begründung noch Widerlegung zu". Aus dieser Perspektive sei es „keineswegs irrational [...], für diese Position und gegen ihre Konkurrenten auf Wegen einzutreten, wie sie der Auseinandersetzung um Fundamente einer Lebensform zu Gebote stehen".[14] Das klingt, jedenfalls für mich, einigermaßen bedrohlich. Anselm Müller beruft sich hier auf Wittgenstein und dessen Schrift „Über Gewißheit"[15], deren Hauptthese darin liegt, daß es für jede Gemeinschaft gewisse Voraussetzungen *gemeinsamer Lebensformen* gibt, die ihrerseits nicht in Frage gestellt werden können. Solche Gewißheiten sind der Diskussion entzogen; wer sie anzweifelt, ist oder gilt insofern als verrückt.

Die Auffassung, daß solche Vorstellungen gewiß und unbezweifelbar sind, *weil* sie die Grundlage unserer wissenschaftlichen Verfahren und unseres praktischen Handelns bilden, scheint mir unhaltbar. Es ist zwar so, daß wir weder in der Wissenschaft noch in unserem praktischen Leben *alles gleichzeitig* in Frage stellen können; aber wir können jederzeit das Netz der Voraussetzungen ändern, wenn wir das für zweckmäßig oder geboten halten und durch neue Erfahrungen an den alten Voraussetzungen irre geworden

---

[13] In: Rainer Hegselmann und Reinhard Merkel (Hrsg.): Zur Debatte über Euthanasie, Frankfurt am Main 1991, S. 327–330.
[14] a.a.O., S. 457.
[15] Ludwig Wittgenstein, Über Gewißheit, Frankfurt am Main 1970.

sind. Wie willkürlich Wittgenstein seine „unbezweifelbaren" Gewißheiten ausgewählt hat, sieht man deutlich im § 286 seiner Schrift „Über Gewißheit", wo es heißt: „Wir alle glauben, es sei unmöglich, auf den Mond zu kommen; aber es könnte Leute geben, die glauben, es sei möglich .... Sie sind im Irrtum, und wir wissen es".[16] Geschrieben hat Wittgenstein das wohl 1950; als das Buch 1969 zuerst herauskam, landete peinlicherweise am 20. Juli desselben Jahres der erste Astronaut auf dem Mond (freilich befand sich Wittgenstein mit seiner Meinung in guter Gesellschaft: auch Kant war ja der Ansicht, es werde nie ein Mensch auf den Mond gelangen können).

Die Vorstellung, daß, à la Wittgenstein, auch unsere moralischen Überzeugungen eine nicht hinterfragbare Basis haben müssen, scheint etwas Weltfremdes zu haben. Die moralischen Überzeugungen, auch die, die wir jeweils für fundamental halten, sind deutlich dem Wandel unterworfen. Man denke an die inzwischen aufgelösten Vorstellungen von der gottgewollten Ständegliederung der Gesellschaft, der alles überragenden Stellung der Verpflichtungen gegenüber dem Vaterland; man denke an die sogenannte sexuelle Revolution, die Revision der moralischen Verurteilung der Homosexualität, die Ablehnung der Todesstrafe, die gesteigerte Sensibilität gegenüber den Leiden der Tiere, das Bewußtsein ökologischer Verpflichtungen gegenüber den nachfolgenden Generationen usw. Statt einer solchen, von den Mitgliedern der Gesellschaft mit Klauen und Zähnen verteidigten moralischen Zitadelle (zu der, jedenfalls nach den Umfragen, z. B. das Verbot der aktiven Sterbehilfe offensichtlich nicht gehört) sehen wir einen ständigen Wandel und Pluralität, ohne daß unsere Gesellschaft deshalb in Überlebensschwierigkeiten geriete. Darauf hat der pluralistische moralphilosophische Diskurs durchaus Einfluß ausgeübt, und zwar nach meiner Meinung einen positiven Einfluß, wenn ich auch nicht der Meinung bin, daß *jede* Veränderung der moralischen Tradition eine Verbesserung ist.

In den meisten dieser Fälle stand vor der späteren Veränderung der moralischen oder sogar strafrechtlichen Normen eine lange und meist heftige Auseinandersetzung, in der die Anhänger des status quo für den Fall der Änderung bestehender Normen regelmäßig den Zusammenbruch der bestehenden Gesellschaft oder wenigstens einiger ihrer wichtigsten Institutionen voraussagten.

So begründete z. B. der Regierungsentwurf eines neuen westdeutschen Strafgesetzbuches noch 1962 die strikte Ablehnung der Forderung nach Streichung strafrechtlicher Sanktionen gegen homosexuelles Verhalten (im Einverständnis unter Erwachsenen) wie folgt: „Wo die gleichgeschlechtliche Unzucht um sich gegriffen und großen Umfang angenommen hat, war die

---

[16] a.a.O. S. 76.

Entartung (Hervorhebung v. Vf.) des Volkes und der Verfall seiner sittlichen Kräfte die Folge". Die Rechtsordnung habe die Aufgabe, „durch die sittenbildende Kraft der Strafgesetze einen Damm gegen die Ausbreitung eines lasterhaften Treibens zu errichten, das, wenn es um sich griffe, eine schwere Gefahr für eine gesunde und natürliche Lebensordnung im Volke bedeuten würde". (Dieser Text von 1962 würde doch eher etwa ins Jahr 1935 passen!)

Zum Nachweis, wie verbreitet auch außerhalb Deutschlands solche Auffassungen waren, z. T. noch sind, kann man den bedeutenden englischen Richter Lord Devlin zitieren:

> There is disintegration when no common morality is observed, and history shows that the loosening of moral bonds is often the first stage of disintegration, so that society is justified in taking the same steps to preserve its moral code as it does to preserve its government and other essential institutions.[17]

Seit im Jahre 1973 die Sanktionen des Strafrechts in der Bundesrepublik gegenüber Homosexuellen entfallen sind, ist es um die vorausgesagten katastrophalen Folgen still geworden. Man hat zur Kenntnis genommen, daß die Zahl homosexuell orientierter Individuen nach Abschaffung der Strafandrohung nicht erkennbar zugenommen hat, daß aber erfreulicherweise viele Homosexuelle von der Last ständiger Furcht vor strafrechtlicher Verfolgung und, damit zusammenhängend, eventueller Erpressung befreit wurden.

Entsprechend verlief auch die Diskussion um die vorgeschlagene Streichung des § 172 StGB, der die Möglichkeit vorsah, auf Antrag des betrogenen Ehepartners in wegen Ehebruchs geschiedenen Ehen die beteiligten Personen mit Gefängnis zu bestrafen. Die Abschaffung dieses „Racheparagraphen" wurde weithin gedeutet als ein Zeichen dafür, daß der Staat seine schützende Hand von der Ehe zurückzuziehen gedenke, ja, daß eine solche Lockerung der Sanktionen gegen den Ehebruch als eine staatliche Aufforderung oder doch Ermutigung zum Ehebruch aufgefaßt werden und so dem Sittenverfall Tür und Tor öffnen würde. Auch hier ist später, nach Abschaffung der Strafandrohung, die Diskussion bald verstummt. Zwar stieg die Zahl der Ehescheidungen bedauerlicherweise weiter an, aber als Ursache wird nicht der Wegfall der Strafandrohung für Ehebrecher, sondern der allgemeine soziale Wandel angesehen, z. B. der immer höhere Anteil der Frauen, die sich (und ihre Kinder) aufgrund eigener Berufstätigkeit notfalls selbst ernähren können und daher auch nicht mehr bereit sind, in einer für sie unbefriedigenden Ehe unter allen Umständen auszuharren.

---

[17] Patrick Devlin, „The Enforcement of Morals", Oxford 1965, S. 13. Kritisch und überzeugend dazu: H.L.A. Hart, „Law, Liberty and Morality", Oxford 1963.

Neben den apokalyptischen Erwartungen hinsichtlich der Wirkungen fast jeder wichtigen moralischen und juristischen Regeländerung wirkte hier wohl, bewußt oder nicht bewußt, die Meinung mit, Gott selbst habe die jeweils umstrittene rechtliche und soziale Ordnung gesetzt und stehe hinter ihr. So wurden die Sachdiskussionen über eine begründbare oder nicht begründbare moralische bzw. juristische Norm zu einer Auseinandersetzung zwischen Gottesfreunden auf der einen Seite und Gottlosen oder Gottesfeinden auf der anderen. Und wer sich in einer Streitfrage auf der Seite Gottes wähnt, pflegt, wie die Geschichte lehrt, in der Wahl seiner Worte und der Verfahrensweisen gegen seine Gegner nicht wählerisch zu sein.

Nun noch kurz zu den drei weiteren der oben genannten vier Grundsätze: Anselm Müller will den Unterschied zwischen *Fachdiskussion* und *öffentlicher Diskussion* bei Fragen der Redefreiheit beachtet sehen. Er führt dazu an, daß Laien meist nicht über das nötige Rüstzeug verfügen, um falsche Argumente zu durchschauen; sie könnten durch bloße demagogische Tricks zur Aufgabe ihrer triftigen moralischen Überzeugungen *überredet*, nicht von der Zweckmäßigkeit der vorgeschlagenen Veränderungen *überzeugt* werden. Bei Fachleuten sei dieser Effekt nicht ebenso zu befürchten. Andererseits sagt er auch: „Die Moral ist Jedermanns Sache".[18] Wird da nicht eine Schranke zwischen Fachleuten und Laien errichtet, und den Laien die Kompetenz zu eigener moralischer Urteilsbildung abgesprochen? Ich halte es nicht für unfair, wenn ich sage, daß mich diese Auffassung doch etwas an den „Index librorum prohibitorum" erinnert, der, wenn ich recht unterrichtet bin, vom Zweiten Vatikanischen Konzil abgeschafft worden ist. Ich sehe in der Auffassung Müllers eine deutlich paternalistische Komponente. Anselm Müller entscheidet doch wohl, welche moralischen Normen als „selbstverständliche Elemente in eine gemeinsamen Lebensform verwoben sind"[19], und er entscheidet auch darüber, wer zur Diskussion dieser Normen zugelassen wird.

Gegen den dritten Grundsatz, daß man, gleichgültig wie man nun zu dem Vorschlag einer Änderung stehen möchte, doch jedenfalls eine öffentliche Diskussion solcher Streitfragen begrüßen sollte, wendet Anselm Müller ein, daß ein Gegner solcher Neuerungen gute Gründe habe, die auch moralisch qualifiziert seien, eine öffentliche Diskussion hierüber abzulehnen, weil er wisse, daß es sich um Grundüberzeugungen handele, die nicht durch Argumente gesichert oder widerlegt werden können, und außerdem die Tatsache ernst nimmt, daß Menschen *der Versuchung ausgesetzt* sind, eine ihnen unbequeme moralische Pflicht, revolutionären Vorschlägen folgend, aufzuheben, um sich der Mühen zu entledigen, die die Erfüllung dieser Pflicht von ihnen verlangen

---

[18] Anselm Müller: Tötung auf Verlangen, S. 10.
[19] a.a.O., S. 19.

könnte. Auch hier kommt, so möchte ich sagen, eine sehr pessimistische Auffassung von der menschlichen Natur ins Spiel, die ich für unbegründet halte.

Ganz und gar durcheinander gerät, so meine ich, bei Müller die Argumentation hinsichtlich des vierten Punkts. Aus der „Erklärung der 180 Philosophen" leitet Müller ab, daß nach der Auffassung dieser Philosophen die *Vertretung einer moralphilosphischen Meinung* in jedem Falle moralisch unbedenklich, höchstens die *Realisierung* einer solchen Auffassung bedenklich sein könne. Dem gegenüber konstatiert Müller, daß „die Kundgabe einer moralphilosophischen Auffassung selbst [...] moralisch bewertbares Verhalten" sei. Daher sei jemand, der eine bestimmte Verhaltensorientierung für schlecht hält, „nur konsequent, wenn er auch deren Empfehlung für schlecht hält und sie daher nicht [...] toleriert".[20] Zunächst: Die Vertreter der „Erklärung" sagen selbst: „Unser Wissen um die verbrecherische nationalsozialistische „Euthanasie"-Praxis erlegt einer jeden Diskussion des gesamten Themenbereichs eine besondere Sorgfaltspflicht auf. Diese besondere Verpflichtung erkennen wir nachdrücklich an".[21] Kaum jemand wird bestreiten, daß die „Kundgabe einer moralphilosophischen Auffassung" selbst ein moralisch bewertbares Verhalten ist. Aber die Sache liegt nicht so, wie Anselm Müller sagt: Meine moralische Ablehnung einer Auffassung als solcher ist nicht ohne weiteres Grund für eine moralische Ablehnung dessen, der eine solche Auffassung vertritt: Wenn er die von mir abgelehnte Auffassung bona fide, nach bestem Wissen und Gewissen vorträgt, so ist diese Äußerung seiner Meinung moralisch einwandfrei, und niemand hat das Recht, ihn für diese seine nach bestem Wissen und Gewissen vorgetragene Ansicht moralisch zu tadeln. Es kommt dabei also vor allem auf die Echtheit einer Überzeugung an. Wenn jemand den Utilitarismus oder den Kohärentismus oder den Kommunitarismus als moralische Theorie empfiehlt und ich der Meinung bin, die von ihm vertretene Theorie sei falsch und würde, praktiziert, zu vielleicht sogar verhängnisvollen Ergebnissen führen, werde ich doch die Vertretung solcher Ansichten nicht schon deshalb, weil ich diese Theorie ablehne, für moralisch schlecht halten. Daher habe ich keinen vernünftigen Grund, ihn an der Verbreitung seiner Auffassung zu hindern. Hinzu kommt, daß ich in den meisten Fällen ohnehin kein Recht hätte, jemanden daran zu hindern, etwas zu tun, was von mir moralisch mißbilligt wird.[22]

---

[20] Vgl. Anm. 10, S. 467.
[21] „Zur Debatte über Euthanasie", hrsg. von R. Hegselmann u. R. Merkel 1991, S. 320.
[22] Ich will nicht ausschließen, daß es in Extremfällen erlaubt sein kann, jemand an der öffentlichen Äußerung seiner moralischen Auffassungen zu hindern, so etwa bei rassistischen und anderen gemeingefährlichen Ideologien. Aber das sollte dann, wie im Fall der „Auschwitz-Lüge" durch

Die von Anselm Müller vertretene Auffassung von Moral (in Anlehnung an Wittgensteins Ideen über „Gewißheit") erweckt den Eindruck, als lebten wir gleichsam auf ein für alle Mal akzeptierten moralischen Fundamenten, die für das Gemeinschaftsleben gültige Verhaltensformen oder -normen sind; daher müßten wir mit aller Kraft bestrebt sein, unsere Insel gegen die Sturmflut anderer Ideen zu verteidigen, um das Wegbrechen unserer Lebensgrundlagen zu verhindern. Dabei wäre jedes Mittel recht, auch die Unterdrückung aller abweichender moralischer Auffassungen oder wenigstens Diskussionsverweigerung und schneidende, unbegründete Ablehnung.

Mir scheint demgegenüber eine Auffassung akzeptabler, die zwar anerkennt, daß wir einen großen Teil unserer moralischen Standards ohne vorherige rationale Prüfung übernommen haben, aber uns eben deshalb empfiehlt, uns darum zu bemühen, das moralische Normensystem, das unser Leben steuert, unter dem Gesichtspunkt vernünftiger Begründbarkeit ständiger Verbesserung unter Rationalitätsgesichtspunkten zu unterziehen. Dabei geht es nicht nur darum, nicht mehr gut begründbare moralische Traditionen und Vorstellungen abzubauen, sondern durchaus auch neue Verpflichtungen einzuführen, von denen ich schon einige genannt habe: Gleichberechtigung der Geschlechter, Chancengleichheit in Bildungsfragen, ökologische Verpflichtungen, Völkerverständigung. Es scheint mir nicht zweifelhaft, daß das zweite Konzept für eine günstige Entwicklung der menschlichen Gesellschaften fruchtbarer ist. Ich meine auch, daß diese Auffassung von der Mehrheit der Bürger unseres Landes geteilt wird. Der hohe Rang, den unsere Verfassung der Freiheit der Diskussion – insbesondere der wissenschaftlichen Diskussion – einräumt, ist davon ein klarer Ausdruck.*

Literatur

Birnbacher, D. (Hrsg.): *Bioethik als Tabu? Die Toleranz und ihre Grenzen*, LIT-Verlag, Münster u. a. 2000.
Bleckmann, A.: *Staatsrecht II – Die Grundrechte*, 3. Aufl. Köln 1989.
Devlin, P.: *The Enforcement of Morals*, Oxford 1965.
Goethe, J. W. von: *Sprüche in Prosa* (Hrsg. H. Fricke), Goethes sämtliche Werke, Deutscher Klassiker Verlag, Frankfurt/Main 1995.
Grundgesetz der Bundesrepublik Deutschland von 1949, Art. 5, I u. III
Guckes, B.: *Das Argument der Schiefen Ebene*, Fischer, Stuttgart 1997.

---

gesetzliche Vorschriften geregelt werden. Es kann nicht hingenommen werden, daß einzelne oder kleine Gruppen darüber entscheiden, wessen Auffassungen sie nicht zu öffentlicher Diskussion zulassen wollen.

* Eine frühere Fassung dieses Textes ist erschienen in D. Birnbacher (Hrsg.): Bioethik als Tabu? Die Toleranz und ihre Grenzen. LIT-Verlag Münster u. a. 2000, S. 11–22.

Hart, H.L.A.: *Law, Liberty and Morality*, Oxford 1963.
Hegselmann, R., Merkel, R. (Hrsg.): *Zur Debatte über Euthanasie*, stw 943, Suhrkamp, Frankfurt/Main 1991.
Hoerster, N.: *Sterbehilfe im säkularen Staat*, stw 924, Suhrkamp, Frankfurt/Main 1998.
Laufs, A.: *Arztrecht*, 5. Aufl., München 1993.
Müller, A.: *Tötung auf Verlangen – Wohltat oder Untat?*, Kohlhammer, Stuttgart 1997.
Müller, A.: Totale Toleranz in Sachen Singer?, *Zeitschrift für Philosophische Forschung* 51 (1997), 448–470.
Rest, F.: *Das kontrollierte Töten*, Gütersloh 1992
Schöne-Seifert, B., Rippe, K.P.: Silencing the Singer, *Hastings-Center-Report*, 1991, 20–27.
Spaemann, R.: Die Herausforderung des ärztlichen Berufsethos durch die medizinische Wissenschaft. In: *Medizinische Klinik*, 595–600.
Wittgenstein, L.: *Über Gewißheit*, Frankfurt/Main 1970.

Peter Railton

Kant Meets Aristotle where Reason Meets Appetite

Abstract

The Aristotelian picture of practical reason as matter of combining thought and motivation in a principled way to yield directed movement remains compelling, yet poses deep puzzles. Two central puzzles are discussed here. First, we must be able to see how ideas and deliberation (which are *logon*) could be combined in a principled way with appetite (which is *alogon*) to generate some sort of thought-directed motivation, "appetitive intellect or intellectual appetition", as Aristotle calls it. Second, we must be able to see how "appetitive intellect" could yield action that could be considered *morally* (or, more generally, *normatively*) guided, that is, "non-hypothetically" or "independent of antecedent inclination". Kant's theory of desire, which has been little discussed, presents us with the materials to begin to solve these puzzles. For Kant, a desire is appetition *through* an idea, and he applies this notion to practical reason both of a prudential and a moral character.

1. Aristotle's Puzzles

Rational people are supposed to be guided by something that deserves the name *practical reason*. In its more explicit moments, practical reason is supposed to take the form of *practical deliberation*. On the view classically articulated by Aristotle, practical deliberation – unlike theoretical reasoning – concludes not in a belief or a judgment, but in an action, or at least an attempt to act: "the final step is the starting-point of action" (Aristotle, *De anima* 433a16).[1]

We normally think of reasoning as operating with *propositions* for premises and conclusions. What would it be like to construct a piece of reasoning with something like an action or an attempt to act as its conclusion? Surely, this would not be a typical deductive inference of the sort found in logic texts.

---

[1] Aristotle, *De Anima*, trans. by D. W. Hamlyn (Oxford: Clarendon, 1993).

After all, it is a quite general feature of valid reasoning that there can be nothing in the conclusion that is not already contained in the premises. If we think of an act as Aristotle does – a "principled" fusion of thought and motivation to yield directed movement – then *thought* and *motivation* must somehow be present among the "premises" of practical deliberation, and *activity* be present in the "conclusion". This indeed appears to be Aristotle's view:

> ... it is reasonable that these two appear the sources of movement, desire and practical thought. For the object of desire produces movement, and, because of this, thought produces movement .... [T]he intellect does not appear to produce movement without desire (for *boulesis* is a form of desire, and when one is moved in accordance with reasoning, one is moved in accordance with *boulesis* too) .... (Aristotle, *De anima* 433a17–25)[2]
>
> Now the origin of action (the efficient, not the final cause) is choice, and the origin of choice is appetition and purposive reasoning. ... Hence choice is either appetitive intellect or intellectual appetition; and man is a principle of this kind. (Aristotle, *Nicomachean Ethics* 1139a32–b5)[3]

Appetition, Aristotle tells us, is not a cognition – it belongs to the part of the soul that is *alogon* (sometimes rendered "nonrational" or "irrational"). Reasoning and intellect, by contrast, belong to the part of the soul that is *logon* (sometimes rendered "rational") (cf. Aristotle, *Nicomachean Ethics* 1102a28). But then "intellectual appetition" or "appetitive intellect" sounds like oil and water. How can appetite and intellect combine via practical deliberation into action – and in a principled way? Oil and water can be *mixed* together by

---

[2] Hamlyn gives 'wish' as the translation of *boulesis*, following standard practice. However, I prefer to keep the Greek term here, since the English 'wish' strikes me as insufficiently close to the tasks of practical reason to be a suitable rendering. The root of the term in ancient Greek seems to have more to do with notions of action-oriented deliberation, as in an legislative assembly, or advice, as given by a counsel (see Lidell & Scott). A better translation might be 'want' – not in the sense of a faculty, but in the sense of a *volonté*: what the assembly or counsel *wants to bring about or see happen* through the activity of government. Wanting is distinguished both from *liking* (I can *want* very much to do exercises, or bring an activity to completion, that I don't particularly *like*, or even dislike) and from *wishing* (*wanting* characteristically expresses itself in action, whereas mere *wish* characteristically does not). A contemporary native speaker of Greek, trained as a moral philosopher, tells me that 'will' is a close approximation of the modern sense of the term, which also suggests activity and *volonté*. Defradas' translation of the *Nicomachean Ethics* (*Ethique à Nicomaque*, Paris: Agora, 1992) gives *volonté* as the translation of *boulesis*, even in such passages as those at Aristotle, *Nicomachean Ethics* 1111b, thought to support the 'wish' translation (in French, *souhaite* rather than *volonté*), as do the standard French-Ancient Greek lexicons in general (e.g., Hachette, Hatier).

[3] Aristotle, *Nicomachean Ethics*, trans. by J. A. K. Thomson, rev. by J. Tredennick (London: Penguin, 1976). Line references to the original are approximate.

mere shaking, but this sort of emulsion is the very opposite of a chemically "prinicipled" combination – neither really engages the other, and with time the two elements will simply reseparate. Yet choice is a principled fusion, "a deliberate appetition of things that lie in our power" (Aristotle, *Nicomachean Ethics* 1113a10).

Aristotle here sets various puzzles for us, two of which will be the primary concerns of this paper. First, if practical deliberation is to be a form of valid reasoning, it must contain an element of desire – not simply a claim about what "is desirable" (or "good"), but an *actual* desire, an appetitive state of the organism capable of producing movement – among what are in effect its "premises". Since appetite is *alogon*, it cannot be the product of *logos* as such; practical deliberation *presupposes* and *brings to bear* desire rather than deriving or originating it (Aristotle, *Nicomachean Ethics* 1112b). Given this presupposed motivational state, how can deliberative intellect, reasoning, work with it to give it a definite, practical form in choice and action? This is a perfectly general puzzle about action, and quite familiar to modern philosophy, where the view that action combines belief, seen as a "cognitive" state, and desire, seen as a "non-cognitive" state, remains widespread despite various criticisms.

A second puzzle concerns those acts said to be *normatively regulated* in the peculiar way that moral action is often supposed to be – i.e., governed by principles that are *categorical* or *independent of antecedent inclination*. If Aristotle is right, then all rational action presupposes desire, yet action done from a sense of duty is commonly *contrasted* with action done from desire. Unless Aristotle is wrong, how could moral reasoning ever be practical, or rational action ever dutiful?

The beginnings of a solution to both puzzles can, I believe, be found in the work of a philosopher often seen as the arch-defender *both* of the opposition between duty and desire, and of the allegiance of morality and practical reason – Kant.

2. Kant's Solutions, Part I: The Theory of Desire

Kant's œuvre might appear a strange place to look a theory of desire, yet in his much-delayed *Metaphysics of Morals* (in a section entitled "On the Relation of the Faculties of the Human Mind to Moral Laws"), Kant spells out a compelling model of desire and its relation to normatively-regulated action, making good on a number of remarks about desire and reason scattered through his earlier works. One would expect Kant to offer, as the source of a motivational force sufficient to yield action yet capable of operating even directly in the face of antecedent inclination, the *will*. And he does. However, far from contrasting will with desire, Kant locates the will in a most Aristotelian place, namely, the "faculty of desire according to concepts" (Kant, *The Metaphysics of Morals* 213).[4]

> The faculty of desire whose inner determining ground, and hence even what pleases it [*selbst das Belieben*], lies within the subject's reason is called the *will* [*Wille*]. (Kant, *The Metaphysics of Morals* 213)

But how can desire have a concept as a "determining ground"? Moreover, the force of will is often contrasted with the force of pleasure and inclination, as when we speak of "will power" in the face of temptation. If will is a "faculty of desire", then "will power" is a matter of being able to have *strong desires*. But how could a strong desire (*Begierde*) be somehow different in kind from "inclination" (*Neigung*)? And what would it mean for that which "pleases" a faculty of desire to "lie within the subject's reason" rather than, as Kant puts it, "in the object of desire" as such (Kant, *The Metaphysics of Morals* 213)?

We can begin to untangle these seeming mysteries by indicating how Kant conceives the structure of desire, and therefore how he analyzes the structure of a putative "faculty of desire". Desire is always allied to pleasure and displeasure (Kant, *The Metaphysics of Morals* 211), which are themselves intrinsically motivating states, incapable of further analysis (Kant, *The Metaphysics of Morals* 212), and presumably are shared with many nonrational species. Is "desire in accordance with concepts" like finding pleasure in contemplating a concept, then? No – pleasant daydreaming is not "practical pleasure" (Kant, *The Metaphysics of Morals* 212) or true action-guiding desire, a point Aristotle would be happy to agree upon. Daydreaming is a "contemplative pleasure or *inactive delight*", which therefore does not depend upon any thought that the object contemplated is actually attainable (Kant, *The Metaphysics of Morals* 212). Desire, by contrast, yields *frustration* and *disappointment* ("practical displeasure") when its objects are not, or cannot, be had. So this is the first point about desire: what is to "accord with concepts" is a practical upshot.

---

[4] Immanuel Kant, *The Metaphysics of Morals*, trans. by M. J. Gregor. As printed in *Immanuel Kant: Practical Philosophy*, ed. by M. J. Gregor (Cambridge: Cambridge University Press, 1996). See also his remark in the third *Critique* that "to will something, and to have a liking for its existence, i.e. to take an interest in it, are identical" (*The Critique of Judgment*, trans. W. S. Pluhar [Indianapolis: Hackett, 1987], 209). Other Kant references occurring in the text are to the *Groundwork of the Metaphysics of Morals*, trans. by M. J. Gregor, *ibid*. Page numbers are from the Academy edition of Kant's work.

Next, though always associated with desire, pleasure and displeasure are not always the *origin* of desire, which is why "what pleases" need not always lie in the "object" as such:

> *Second*, pleasure or displeasure in an object of desire does not always precede the desire and need not always be regarded as the cause of desire but can also be regarded as the effect of it. (Kant, *The Metaphysics of Morals* 211)

Desire sometimes fixes on a particular object in view of the pleasure it produces or promises. Eating tasty food tends to please, and eating when hungry to please even more – "hunger is the best sauce", Kant reminds us (Kant, *The Critique of Judgment* 210). But not all desires are grounded in this way in pleasant sensation – we might desire something that *in itself* has no particular experienced or anticipated sensory character or hedonic quality, say, keeping an appointment with a new person in a new location. However, once desire has fixed on an object, we will tend to experience some satisfaction ("practical pleasure") in seeing ourselves to be making progress toward attaining that object ("Good, I'm a bit ahead of schedule"), and also some dissatisfaction or restless frustration ("practical displeasure") when we cannot ("Blasted traffic, this bus is barely moving!").

Consider even eating. If, as a result of illness, one has no appetite, eating can become a chore, even actively distasteful. Yet one might very much want to eat in order to avoid excessive weight loss, in accord with what one's doctor has recommended. So one "chokes down" one's food. The desire to sustain normal weight is not a direct appetite for food, and certainly does make food gustatorily gratifying. Yet, given this desire, there will be a kind of practical, non-gustatory satisfaction to be found in managing to eat, and a frustration with oneself in trying but failing. Here, then, we see how a *desire* (to follow doctor's advice and eat regularly) can oppose a distaste-based *inclination* (the distastefulness of eating and inclination to stop), if one has sufficient *will*, i.e., a sufficiently strong "faculty of desire in accordance with concepts":

> ... the will, as the power of desire, is one of the many natural causes in the world, namely, the one that acts in accordance with concepts .... (Kant, *The Critique of Judgment* 172)

We know that someone possesses a genuine desire to succeed at a task or in an activity (and not a mere *wish* that he were more successful) by the force and character of his frustration with – and motivation to overcome – obstacles or personal disinclinations in accomplishing it.

Thus we arrive at Kant's basic schema for desire. Whereas in contemplation, we may *appreciate* an end or a state that we represent to ourselves; in desire, we are moved to become a *cause* of it:

The *faculty of desire* is the faculty to be, by means of one's representations, the cause of the objects of those representations. (Kant, *The Metaphysics of Morals* 211)

So desire is not *mere* appetite – it is appetite *through* an idea or concept, a representation that can be "*sense-free*" (Kant, *The Metaphysics of Morals* 213). Even the ideas of *food* and *eating* are themselves without taste, texture, or alluring smell. Animals can use sensation to seek food, and can eat with appetite and pleasure, but lack (we suppose) any concepts, and so are incapable of the sort of desire to eat that our recovering patient possesses. They therefore are unequipped for practical reason, wherein – astonishingly – "thought produces movement" (Aristotle, *De anima* 433a1).

3. Building up to Desire

Let us take this step-by-step. Consider first a very elementary fish.[5] When deprived of food for several hours, it enters into a physiological condition in which it characteristically perks up when food is introduced into its tank, and expends a considerable amount of energy following any sensory trail to food, whereupon it stops and eats vigorously. There seems no harm in saying it is hungry, i.e., has the *appetite* of hunger. Since, when hungry, it will follow a sensory trail to food, we can say it is capable of *appetitive pursuit*, "guided by sensation of the object of appetite" (see fig. 1).

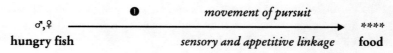

Figure 1: Animal guided directly by sensation and appetite

Appetitive pursuit can be *intelligent*. Were some alternative, equally recognizable foodstuff suddenly introduced much closer to it, at ●, the fish would deflect its course and eat there. But appetitive pursuit, even using senses and brain, is not yet Aristotle's "intellectual appetition". For the fish guides its motion entirely by "following its nose", not by "following its ideas" or "practical reasoning". The issue is not whether the fish constructs a practical syllogism – we ourselves seldom do so, even when acting in ways we

---

[5] More elementary, perhaps, than any actual fish, as will emerge below.

commonsensically call practically rational. Rather, in this simple fish, there simply is no role, even implicit, for any *idea* or *concept* of food in explaining its pursuit.

Contrast the behavior of a traveler just arriving in a new city, finding herself alone in her hotel room with her bags still full and her stomach empty around seven in the evening. She doesn't feel hungry – plane travel deadens her appetite – but she sees that it's about time for dinner, and knows that she soon will be ravenous. She's also tired and needs to work. The hotel restaurant? No, the thought of that holds little charm – she'd like to have a decent meal. She's heard from a friend that this city has excellent Vietnamese food, but that most of the restaurants calling themselves 'Vietnamese' actually serve an inauthentic variant of Chinese cuisine meant to please tourists. She's not certain that she's ever tasted *authentic* Vietnamese food, and so has only an indistinct idea of what it is like, but she is very eager to seize this opportunity to try it.

A few minutes later, we find her actively hungry and seeking for food, but she isn't "following her nose" down a sensory trail. Rather, she is sitting on the edge of the bed and studying an ill-smelling yellow book. What explains this behavior? Surely neither the yellow book nor reading is "the object of her appetite" – why doesn't she move toward food as the hungry fish is intelligent enough to do? "Well, she is moving toward food, but in a rather indirect way. Her friend mentioned to her the name of an authentic Vietnamese restaurant in town, but she can't find the scrap of paper on which she wrote it down, so now she's scanning the restaurant listings in the *Yellow Pages* hoping that one name will click."

She is indeed acting to "be the cause of the object of her appetite", but she is doing so by acting to "be the cause of the object of her representation" – namely, actively seeking a dinner that accords with a certain concept, "authentic Vietnamese cuisine". She is not doing so thanks to any direct sensation of such an object – there is not the least *sensory trace* of authentic Vietnamese food available in her room, and she in any event has no ability to detect authentic Vietnamese food by its scent. Yet there may well be *"sense-free" information* in her room about the availability of authentic Vietnamese food, and she has turned to that in order to guide her pursuit. Mere nutritive stuff is not the object of her pursuit; neither is pleasant-tasting but inauthentic Vietnamese food. Her appetitive pursuit is therefore not being guided by a sensation of food, nor even by the pleasure of direct liking for a particular kind of food. She does not know whether she likes such food or not, and even suspects she'd enjoy the inauthentic cuisine's *taste* rather more – it is, after all, prepared to cater to a palate just like hers. So we say that she likes the *idea* of tasting authentic Vietnamese food.

Though true, however, this is not yet the whole story. After all, I like the idea of being in the Olympics, and can contemplate it happily in daydreaming – enjoying this "inactive delight" without lifting a finger to begin training or suffering any pains on its behalf. Our traveler is not merely daydreaming about authentic Vietnamese food, but rather has an active, focused motivation to seek it – an appetite that bestirs her to action. We see the direct motivating force of this appetite in the effort she is expending to seek it, postponing eating to consult a book, and perhaps even to hire a cab and travel some distance – tired and hungry as she is, spending money and using up precious worktime. She has a desire, not just a wish, as Kant would insist:

> I have been reproached ... (Preface to the *Kritik der praktischen Vernunft*, p. 16) ... for defining the power of desire as the *power of being the cause, through one's representations, of the actuality of the objects of these presentations*. The criticism was that, after all, mere wishes are desires too, and yet we all know that they alone do not enable us to produce their object. ... [Yet] In such fanciful desires we are indeed aware that our presentations are insufficient (or even unfit) to be the *cause* of their objects. (Kant, *The Critique of Judgment* 177n)

Though a "*wish*" always suggests to us, perhaps vicariously, the idea of active striving (Kant, *The Critique of Judgment* 177n), still, such "fanciful desires" do not play the active role in guiding action that desire itself does.

Desire, then, with its characteristic *combination* of idea and appetite, shows its "signature" in an agent's practical pleasures and displeasures. Unlike a daydreamer without active appetite, or someone with an active appetite not mediated by the idea of authentic Vietnamese food, our traveler would be frustrated and a bit put out with herself if she could not succeed in finding a meal which answers to the concept of authentic Vietnamese cuisine, even if the inauthentic dinner turned out to be quite satisfying. Thus, she would experience "practical displeasure" if she sat down at a self-proclaimed Vietnamese restaurant only to realize (too late!) that it definitely belongs in the tourist category, and even if she finds the hybrid food they serve quite tasty and satisfying. By contrast, she will experience a "practical pleasure" of satisfaction and even perhaps some small pride, if, having sat down, she discovers to her surprise the missing scrap of paper on which she had written her friend's recommendation, and the name thereon precisely matches the one atop the menu now in her hands – even though the food is yet untasted, and even if the food turns out to a bit odd and not to her liking after all.

We need to be careful not to say that the "sense-free" *idea* of authentic Vietnamese food is itself the *object* of her desire. She can easily have access to that idea in her room, or while eating hotel-restaurant chicken downstairs. Instead we see her pursuing a gustatory *reality* lying at some distance from

Kant Meets Aristotle where Reason Meets Appetite   283

the hotel. But she acts toward this object *through* that idea, and therefore her activity can be guided or regulated correspondingly. As Kant puts it, in desire, "the concept ... gives the rule to the will's causality" (Kant, *The Critique of Judgment* 172). (See fig. 2.)

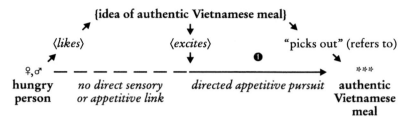

Figure 2: Individual guided by desire[6]

Since her appetitive pursuit is mediated by the idea of authentic Vietnamese cuisine, if some alternative foodstuff, more familiar to (and well-liked by) her were to appear at ❶, she still would not deflect her search for "authentic Vietnamese food".

Desire, like language, thus reaches toward a referent or object (the "object of the intentional attitude") through an image, meaning, or intension. Practical deliberation and action take place "through concepts", just as theoretical reasoning and assertion do. Aristotle writes:

> ... brutes have sensation, but no share in action. Pursuit and avoidance in the sphere of appetition correspond exactly to affirmation and negation in the sphere of intellect; [...] choice is deliberative appetition [...]. (Aristotle, *Nicomachean Ethics* 1113a20)

Our hungry hotel guest deliberatively shapes the playing out of her appetite as she works her way through a complex, directed course of action. In doing so, she brings to bear background knowledge ("I'll have to be careful – the best places sometimes aren't listed in the *Yellow Pages*" or "Whatever it's

---

[6] In this figure, the items in angle braces are "mental operations". Now, where is the *desire* in figure 2? Is it liking the idea of an authentic Vietnamese meal? No, one could like that idea without being hungry or interested in eating. Is it in the exciting of appetite? No, since appetite can be excited (as in fig. 1) without a role for concepts or for "desire", properly speaking. A delectable scent can excite one's appetite directly, without the help of any concepts. The desire in figure 2 in fact is the entire *structure* combining idea and motivation in just this relationship – a desire is tendency toward appetitive seeking of an object that answers to (i.e., is "picked out" by) an idea or concept to which one is attracted. Desires may be dispositional or active.

called, it probably isn't this one with the big display ad saying 'Ask about our exotic drink pitcher specials! Ladies half price Thursday nights!'"), strategies ("Here's a neighborhood that lists a number of places, I'll go there and have a look"), and on-going experience (walking along, she shuns one place that "seems too empty at this hour" but stops in front of another because "the clientele looks right, and the specials are posted in what looks like Vietnamese script"). She is deploying a well-developed, skillful faculty of being, "by means of one's representations, the cause of the objects of these representations". To carry it off, she is thinking constantly, and to considerable extent overcoming inclination – controlling her hunger in order to have the patience, energy, and concentration to carry out her deliberation and indirect searching (see fig. 3).

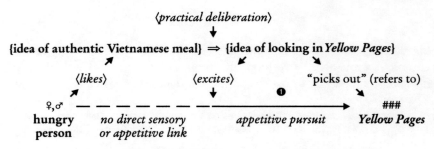

Figure 3: Individual guided by desire and deliberation

Despite her hunger and impatience, our desire-guided hotel guest will stop at the hotel lobby to look for the *Yellow Pages* if she could find no copy in her room – and she'll be pleased to spot one there, or frustrated if she can't. And even if the copy she spots is located at a pay-phone just opposite the hotel restaurant, ⓿, which looks surprisingly pleasant and where she sees her favorite fish featured on tonight's menu, she will still eschew the restaurant and consult the ragged, unappetizing *Yellow Pages*.

Of course, talk of "ideas", "deliberation", and "choice" should not entirely dominate our thinking about the role of desire in action. For while it is characteristic of acting on desire that it involves an idea of some kind, and thus makes a place for deliberation and linguistically-encoded information to enter into the engagement and operation of motivation, action on desire is possible without explicit linguistic formulation and active deliberation. Not only does habit and familiar practice predominate in this, as in most spheres of life, but often the conception of the object of appetite or of the paths to it are at best vague images or ill-articulated thoughts that we can recover reflectively only with some difficulty. We would be very slow and poor actors – if indeed we could ever get started acting in the first place! – if all action required explicit formulation of a linguistically-encoded thought and a conscious, deliberative process of application in reasoning and action.

We therefore need to be wary of accounts of desire that go beyond imputing to it a cognitive element, and go on to claim that desire is constituted by something like a "judgment of desirability". Just as we often learn what we have believed all along only by discovering that some event or action does or does not surprise us, we often learn what we have desired all along only by discovering that some event or action frustrates or pleases us. And just as we may, if exposed to a suitably vivid stereotype, acquire a belief that we would not judge to be credible were we to be more self-conscious and self-critical, we may, if exposed to a suitably vivid and "compelling" image in advertising, acquire a desire for an object or activity that we would not judge to be desirable were we to be more self-conscious and more self-critical. Yet these "unauthorized" acquired beliefs and desires will nonetheless shape our thought and action.

We should resist as well the thought that a *merely* cognitive "judgment of desirability", unbacked by appetite, could suffice explain action. As Aristotle and Kant agree, all action, however elevated and judgmental the idea through which it takes place, operates through a motivational system that has a characteristic appetitive element, a signature connection to activity and "practical pleasure and displeasure" – the satisfaction arising from seemingly successful pursuit of an object, the frustration arising from seeming unsuccess at same. Aristotle writes "every feeling and every action is always accompanied by pleasure or pain", and:

> The pleasure or pain that accompanies people's acts should be taken as a sign of their dispositions. (Aristotle, *Nicomachean Ethics* 1104b8)

To yield a disposition to act, a judgment of desirability must mobilize appetite, and this, indeed, is the function of the "faculty of desire" in Kant.

Desire is a *redeployment* of appetition and appetitive pursuit in a concept-mediated mental economy. In animals, as in us, appetite can be directly stimulated by experience, and will arouse activity, direct attention, supply energy for movement, selectively sharpen sensation, orient and prepare response in myriad ways, shaping receptivity, pains, and pleasures. It supplies a force capable of moving the organism, which Aristotle claims all genuinely practical deliberation must presuppose and engage (cf. Aristotle, *Nicomachean Ethics* 1113a36). In humans, concept-mediated redeployment of appetite supplements but does not *supplant* more direct appetition and appetitive pursuit, which continues to operate alongside desire. I may be busy acting in light of an idea and through complex deliberation, but appetites of which I might not even be reflectively aware will all the while be selectively shaping my activity, focusing what I do and even what I notice or think quite without my prior permission. Appetite continues to *incline* me in it own right even when desire acts as well to *guide* me. Indeed, I learn something about my own inclinations by noticing not only what *attracts* me, but what *distracts* me – where I find my mind wandering and my effort going despite attempts to keep them elsewhere.

This mention of distraction should also remind us that bringing intellect to bear on appetite and action is not always for the true and the good, or the well-considered. Appetite, as a non-representational state in itself, can be neither true nor false, moral or immoral. Yet human appetites are linked to internal states and perception in myriad ways through a long history of natural selection. Desire by its nature makes thought bear on, or be manifest in, activity. It therefore enables me to be guided by falsity as well as truth, by immoral as well as moral aims and intents, by confused, grandiose, dangerous, unprecedented notions as well as practical, efficient, time-tested ones. Desire can make me a sage or a sucker, since it generates strong *incentives* to act by linking an attraction to a notion or image given by intellect and imagination to sure-fire, intrinsic organismic motivators, pleasure and pain. I can be thrilled to acquire that which is terribly bad for me, or acutely frustrated to be denied it – desire permits me to find practical pleasures and pains in pursuing quite misguided ideas. Aristotle writes:

> Pleasure and pain are also the standards by which – to a greater or lesser extent – we regulate our actions. Since to feel pleasure or pain rightly or wrongly has no little effect upon conduct, it follows that our whole inquiry must be concerned with these sensations. (Aristotle, *Nicomachean Ethics* 1105a3–5)

4. Kant's Solutions, Part II: Duty and Desire

If we accept Kant's account of the nature of desire, we can say that *if* the idea through which I am led into an appetitive pursuit is an idea of sort S, *then* I can be said to act "for the sake of S", even though practical pleasure and pain always accompany and shape the process. That is, you need not describe me as "acting for the sake of pleasure" rather than "for the sake of S", even though my practical pleasures and pains provide a crucial "incentive" for my activity – for they are the *result* of my desire for S, not what initially shaped it or selected its object.

Here's a picture. Think of the idea that something is S as functioning for me like a *switch* or a *valve* in "turning on" appetitive pursuit, in much the same way that, for the fish in figure 1, the sensation of food functions to "turn on" its appetitive pursuit of the sensory trial.[7] Once the appetitive pursuit mechanism has been "switched on", my conduct, like the fishe's, will partly be "steered" by pleasures and pains – frustration tells me to try something else, success rewards persistence. The incentive is, importantly, not merely "consummatory" (realized when the object is actually attained), but operates all along the way, encouraging or discouraging – "Great! Here's an up-to-date *Yellow Pages*" or "Rats! Still nothing and I've already walked halfway down this block. I'd better head back to the main street." In Kant's sense, this is an "interest":

> Every determination of choice proceeds *from* the representation of a possible action *to* the deed through the feeling of pleasure or displeasure, taking an interest in the action or its effect. (Kant, *The Metaphysics of Morals* 399)

Such an "interest" is far from being a "natural appetite" or "inclination". It arises only in the wake of a settling upon an idea, which need not involve any pleasant experience, and it attaches to a choice whether that choice will in the end prove pleasant or not.

> So if a pleasure necessarily precedes a desire, the practical pleasure must be called an interest of inclination. But if a pleasure can only follow upon an antecedent determination of the faculty of desire it is an intellectual pleasure, and the interest in the object must be called an interest of reason .... [W]here a merely pure interest of reason must be assumed no interest of inclination can be substituted for it .... (Kant, *The Metaphysics of Morals* 211–212)

The very possibility of *normative guidance*, for Kant, depends upon the possibility of these "interests of reason" – otherwise we'd be prisoners of what is pleasant or unpleasant in directing our lives. To be sure, we need not be guided by immediate pleasures and pains. A repeated pattern of pleasure or displeasure in connection with a given object or activity can yield a kind of conditioned learning, which Kant deems a form of "habitual desire" or "inclination" (Kant, *The Metaphysics of Morals* 212). Relatively simple animals are capable of this sort of "stimulus conditioning" via associated pleasures and pains, and indeed the "operant conditioning" of behavioral animal psychologists is founded upon it. Simple animals are also capable of acting on "stereotyped cues" without any history of reward or punishment. What they lack, however, is a capacity to be guided in appetitive pursuit by a

---

[7] This may in fact be quite realistic psychologically. Recent work on the neurophysiology of conditioning with food rewards shows that the non-gustatory conditioned stimulus directly triggers the same activity-initiating "signature" in the brain as direct sensation of the original, gustatory stimulus of food itself. See W. Schultz, et al., "A Neural Substrate of Prediction and Reward", *Science*, 275 (1997): 1593–1599 and W. Schultz, "Predictive Reward Signal of Dopamine Neurons", *Journal of Neurophysiology* 80 (1998): 1–27.

non-stereotyped, non-sensory concept or rule, free of an associated history of reward and punishment.

This sort of capacity can be seen at work in humans in the most familiar sort of practical reasoning – means/end reasoning. If our traveler is to consult the *Yellow Pages*, it must be possible for her deliberation ("Now, how would I jog my memory about this restaurant recommendation?") to *transfer* the "interest" in one idea ("an authentic Vietnamese meal") to a logically-independent idea that nonetheless presents a *means* to the realization of the first ("looking in the *Yellow Pages*") – and without any history of "positive reinforcement" to cement the connection. Is one tempted to say that the traveler has been "reinforced" in the past when consulting the *Yellow Pages* in similar circumstances? Perhaps, but then suppose that the *Yellow Pages* she finds in the lobby is badly out-of-date. Knowing that restaurants come and go, she realizes that she "needs a new idea" to jog her memory or help her find an alternative. She soon gets such an idea when she sees a new-fangled device standing nearby, labeled "Electronic Concierge". She must now switch off her motivation to consult the *Yellow Pages*, and switch on a motivation to get this unknown bit of machinery to work. More than that. She actively *dislikes* this sort of device, and even the whole idea of "Electronic Concierges". Her past experience with things like this has been far from "reinforcing" – last time she tried an "electronic locator" she grew so frustrated that she vowed, "Never again!" Yet for now she sees no better alternative, so she overcomes her aversion to go over to it, and even is pleased when she spies a red icon on the touch-screen saying "Begin". She is pleased, too, as she begins to navigate her way successfully through a sequence of computer menus and reaches a listing of "Asian Restaurants". She then is frustrated when the listing seems bizarrely short for a city known for its sizeable Asian population, so she now must be motivated to retrace her electronic steps. She's strongly tempted to give this "Electronic Concierge" a swift kick and leave, but instead she doggedly scrolls back through the menus ("Maybe I accidentally confined the search to a particular price range?"). And on it goes.

Think, then, of the "faculty of desire" as Kant appears to: a developed ability to "regulate" or give a "rule" to the flow of motivation, through an intellectual process of working with mental representations by following "lines of reasoning", "using imagination to come up with alternatives", and "using experience to help cull them". The ideas arrived at need not themselves be objects of direct liking ("antecedent appetite") or conditioned liking ("habitual inclination"), and may even be quite aversive in their own right ("Approach a stranger and ask which street this is"). But somehow their deliberative connection to a "guiding thought" must make them, immediately, attractive enough to excite appetite on their behalf, releasing motivational force even in the face of contrary inclination. They must become sources of "derived" or (as Thomas Nagel might say?[8]) "motivated desire" if we are to be practically rational.

Is this process of triggering or "switching" motivation and activity in the "faculty of desire" confined to instrumental thought? Kant gives us an example of the faculty of desire at work in the most sublime accomplishment of practical reasoning, *acting dutifully*. In order to act dutifully, Kant claims, we must possess "moral feeling".

> *Moral feeling*. This is the susceptibility to feel pleasure or displeasure merely from being aware that are our actions are consistent with or contrary to the law of duty. Every determination of choice proceeds *from the representation of a possible action to* the deed, through the feeling of pleasure or displeasure, taking an interest in the action or its effect. The state of *feeling* here (the way in which inner sense is affected) is either *pathological* or *moral*. – The former is that feeling which precedes the representation of the law; the latter, that which can only follow upon it. (Kant, *The Metaphysics of Morals* 399)

By now we recognize this moral feeling as a Kantian *desire*. But how can desire, which involves "feeling" and seems so involuntary, be the basis of duty, which is supposed to be voluntary and subject to the "will"? Doesn't *ought* imply *can*? – It does, and thus moral feeling must be *presupposed* in moral agents as a precondition of any practical sense of duty. We cannot be responsive to duty without it, and therefore could not have a duty to acquire it *de novo*:

> Since any consciousness of obligation depends upon moral feeling … there can be no duty to have moral feeling or acquire it; instead, every human being (as a moral being) has it in him originally. Obligation with regard to moral feeling can be only to *cultivate* it and to strengthen it … . No human being is entirely without moral feeling, for were he completely lacking in receptivity to it he would be morally dead … . (Kant, *The Metaphysics of Morals* 399–400)

Because this "receptivity" belongs to the "faculty of desire", it can be *at the same time* "on the side of feeling" (Kant, *The Metaphysics of Morals* 399) and a matter of "will" subject to reason. For although we cannot will ourselves via concepts to have a desire, we can, given a desire, excite appetite on behalf of the concept it contains. "Action through moral desire" *is* "action through moral concepts" or "action for the sake of a realizing a moral concept" – it is neither "brutish" nor "merely conditioned" nor "grounded in inclination".

---

[8] Thomas Nagel, *The Possibility of Altruism* (Princeton: Princeton University Press, 1978), 29–30.

Consider an act such as giving assistance to a stranger, apparently an impoverished foreigner, who looks desperately lost on a street corner, despite the fact that you are rushing home, already late for preparing your family's dinner. Now, you might be the kind of person who finds direct pleasure in helping someone, in "coming to the rescue". Well, now you're inclined both to stop and to run home to feed the kids. Perhaps, however, this stranger before is much more salient, more compelling. As a highly sympathetic person, you are distressed by the evident distress of this individual, and that pain arrests your motion. His surprised and grateful look when you stop and head over forthrightly to help him is actively gratifying for you, rewarding your approach.

> *Sympathetic joy* and *sadness* (*sympathia moralis*) are sensible feelings of pleasure or displeasure (which are therefore to be called "aesthetic") at another's state of joy or pain (shared feeling, sympathetic feeling). Nature has already implanted in human beings receptivity to this feeling. (Kant, *The Metaphysics of Morals* 456)

Here, though, we find not will and desire, but *sensation* and *inclination* – feelings of pleasure or displeasure that guide your response without the intermediation of any moral concepts. The operation of this feeling is non-voluntary, belonging to your sympathetic humanity. We find it sympathetic, too, contemplating you. Very pleasing – and no act of will or dutifulness in sight:

> ... humanity can be located either in the *capacity* and the *will* to *share in others' feelings* (*humanitas practica*) or merely in the *receptivity*, given by nature itself, to the feeling of joy and sadness in common with others (*humanitas aesthetica*). The first is *free* ... it is based on practical reason. The second is *unfree* ... it can be called *communicable* (since it is like receptivity to warmth or contagious diseases) .... There is obligation only to the first. (Kant, *The Metaphysics of Morals* 456–457)

A receptivity, "given by nature itself" and involving "feeling", will be unfree and non-rational if it is mere inclination, even sympathetic inclination; but a natural receptivity in the form of desire predisposes us to be "given a rule" by concepts, to oppose mere inclination, and thus to make us into beings capable of recognizing and being guided by moral law.

> There are certain moral endowments such that anyone lacking them could have no duty to acquire them. – They are *moral feeling*, *conscience*, *love* of one's neighbor, and *respect* for oneself (*self-esteem*). There is no obligation to have these because they lie at the basis of morality, as *subjective* conditions of receptiveness to the concept of duty, not as objective conditions of morality. All of them are natural predispositions of the mind (*praedispositio*) for being affected by the concepts of duty, antecedent predispositions on the side of *feeling*. (Kant, *The Metaphysics of Morals* 399)

Suppose, then, you were not so sympathetic. Indeed, suppose that you are averse to this odd-looking and hopeless-seeming foreigner, strongly inclined to walk by. You are averse, too, to facing the gathering impatience of your family at home if you stop. Yet you summon to mind an idea of this person as someone just like you. You ask what this situation means to that person, what it would mean to you. Once you have thought of it that way, you find you cannot like the *idea* of yourself passing him by in this situation. You recall how things looked to you when you last needed help in a comparable situation, and cannot see why this case is any different. You stop and approach him, forcing a smile. Why? Not from inclination, surely, but from desire.

Desire, of course, suits us for being "given a rule" by concepts other than moral ones. A desire for an authentic Vietnamese meal can lead our traveler to overcome hunger and aversion to interrogate the "Electronic Concierge". The desire that constitutes "moral feeling" furnishes the subjective wherewithal to mobilize motivation to oppose difficulty, fear, and lack of sympathy with this odd-seeming and penniless foreigner and to resist walking away. But what of *respect* for the moral law? Shouldn't that enter? It does:

> Respect for the law, which in its subjective aspect is called moral feeling, is identical with consciousness of one's duty. (Kant, *The Metaphysics of Morals* 464)

In a famous footnote in the *Groundwork*, Kant asks for our patience.

> It could be objected that I only seek refuge, behind the word *respect*, in an obscure feeling, instead of distinctly resolving the question by means of a concept of reason. But though respect is a feeling, it is not one *received* by means of influence ... and therefore [is] specifically different from all feelings of the ... kind [that] can be reduced to inclination or fear. (Kant, *Groundwork of the Metaphysics of Morals* 401n)

We now see that in the fullness of his story about desire, Kant does show how it is possible for an act for which we had no antecedent inclination – indeed, to which we are in some measure averse – nonetheless to become an object of appetite ("feeling") *through* an idea of it that is given not by pleasure or dread, but by thought and rules ("practical reason"). To have this desire is to meet the subjective condition for "respect for the moral law" – one has a direct dislike (not arising from the prospect of pleasure or reward) of the idea of action that does not accord with the conception of things embodied in the moral law, and this triggers a motivation to avoid it and pursue another, one which *can* be squared with moral concepts.

> Respect (*reverentia*) is, again, something merely subjective, a feeling of a special kind, not a judgment about an object that it would be a duty to bring about or promote. For, such a duty, regarded as a duty, could be represented to us only through the *respect* we have for it. A duty to have respect would thus amount to being put under obligation to duties. (Kant, *The Metaphysics of Morals* 402)

To be sure, not every thought or rule counts as moral – the pursuit of an authentic Vietnamese meal is not a moral quest. Practical reasoning needs specifically moral thoughts and rules if it is to deploy desire morally. Happily, given the will (i.e., desire) to use it, there is at least a *test* for whether our reasoning has such a character: the test of the categorical imperative.

> Inexperienced in the course of the world, incapable of being prepared for whatever might come to pass in it, I ask myself only: can you also will that your maxim become a universal law? ... Here it would be easy to show how common human reason, with this compass in hand, knows very well how to distinguish in every case that comes up what is good and what is evil, what is in conformity with duty or contrary to duty .... (Kant, *Groundwork of the Metaphysics of Morals* 403–404)

Dutiful motivation and a "good will" – motivation that is *normatively regulated morally* in the strict sense that it mobilizes appetite for an act through specially moral ideas, even in the absence of antecedent inclination for that act – is thus possible thanks to "moral feeling". Subjecting oneself to a moral *ought* is not contrary to human motivational nature because we "originally" possess the capacity for "moral feeling", and, as a desire, it can if strengthened provide the needed incentive to duty in the face of inclination without further, "external" incentive. This is an *appropriate* incentive that does not destroy the dignity of the act, and allows moral concepts to be practical.

5. Conclusion

When Kant inquires, at the beginning of the *Groundwork*, into the question why nature has "assigned reason to will as its governor" (Kant, *Groundwork of the Metaphysics of Morals* 395) the reader naturally assumes that we are a long way from such things as desire and appetite. But we now see that for reason to operate through will is precisely for it to find a place *within* the territory of desire and appetite. Reason is not the *source* of the motivational force of will. Rather it functions as a "governor", "regulator", "compass", or, as we put it, a "switch", for regulating the flow of motivation. As Aristotle puts it:

> choice is deliberative appetition, it follows that if the choice is to be a good one, both the reasoning must be true and the desire right; and the desire must pursue the same things that the reasoning asserts. We are here speaking of intellect and truth in a practical sense ... the function of practical intellect is to arrive at the truth the corresponds to right appetition. (*Nicomachean Ethics* 1139a21–28)

Kant's "moral feeling" does not replace or degrade guidance by reason.[9] Nor is it a mysterious "moral sense" that replaces moral thought and tells us what to choose like some sort of "affective compass" or "intuition":

> It is inappropriate to call this feeling a moral *sense*, for by the word "sense" is usually understood a theoretical capacity for perception directed toward an object, whereas moral feeling (like pleasure and displeasure in general) is something merely subjective, which yields no cognition. (Kant, *The Metaphysics of Morals* 400)

The moral feeling is a disposition to mobilize appetite *on behalf of* a "mere cognition", but does itself constitute special kind of knowledge. It permits us to take an "interest of reason" in the reading of a "cognitive compass" – the categorical imperative – so that action through moral concepts can be motivated and even satisfying in the face of greatest difficulty or aversion. Acting well thus is, as Aristotle claimed, a matter of exercising, developing, maturing, strengthening, and attuning desire as well as thought.

Does anything like this actually happen? Well, do we ever pursue an authentic Vietnamese meal in a strange city, guided by just that idea and through the application of practical reasoning, even in the face of inclination and fatigue? And do we ever find acting dutifully in the face of fear and difficulty deeply satisfying? I certainly hope so.

References

Aristotle: *De Anima* (trans. by D. W. Hamlyn), Clarendon, Oxford 1993.
Aristotle: *Nicomachean Ethics* (trans. by J. A. K. Thomson), rev. by J. Tredennick, Penguin, London 1976.
Kant, I.: *The Metaphysics of Morals* (trans. by M. J. Gregor). In: *Immanuel Kant: Practical Philosophy*, ed. by M. J. Gregor, Cambridge University Press, Cambridge 1996.
Kant, I.: *The Critique of Judgment* (trans. by W. S. Pluhar), Hackett, Indianapolis 1987.
Kant, I.: *Groundwork of the Metaphysics of Morals* (trans. by M. J. Gregor). In: *Immanuel Kant: Practical Philosophy*, ed. by M. J. Gregor, Cambridge University Press, Cambridge 1996.
Nagel, T.: *The Possibility of Altruism*, Princeton University Press, Princeton 1978.
Schultz, W. et al.: A Neural Substrate of Prediction and Reward, *Science* 275 (1997), 1593–1599.
Schultz, W.: Predictive Reward Signal of Dopamine Neurons, *Journal of Neurophysiology* 80 (1998), 1–27.

---

[9] Here I hope to mitigate Nagel's worry that, in introducing respect as a "feeling", Kant has "compromised" the purity of his defense of action on moral principles. Compare Nagel, p. 11.

Georg Meggle

NATO-Moral & Kosovo-Krieg

Ein ethischer Kommentar ex post.[1]

Abstract

Im Frühjahr 1999 führte die NATO (Deutschland inklusive) Krieg gegen Jugoslawien/Serbien. In diesem Krieg konnten sich die NATO-High-Tech-‚Luftschläge' auf zwei Instrumente von größter Wirksamkeit stützen: *Begriffsstrategie* (z.B. „Humanitäre Intervention" statt „Krieg") und *Moral* („Nie wieder Auschwitz. Völkermord verlangt militärisches Eingreifen."). Bezüglich beider Instrumente gelten Philosophien, speziell analytische, als Experten. Also: Wie beurteile ich den Gebrauch bzw. Mißbrauch dieser Instrumente durch die NATO (und die Mehrheit der deutschen Bevölkerung) heute, ex post? Insbesondere: (i) Lassen sich Humanitäre Kriegs-Interventionen moralisch rechtfertigen? Und: (ii) Erfüllten die NATO-Bombardierungen die relevanten Rechtfertigungs-Kriterien? Meine Positionen: Ja zu (i), Nein zu (ii).

Was den circa 37 000 sogenannten Luftschlägen der NATO gegen Jugoslawien (Serbien und Montenegro) im Frühjahr '99 in den meisten NATO-Ländern breite Zustimmung verschaffte, war deren schon allein mit ihrer Benennung zum Ausdruck gebrachte (echte bzw. angebliche) Zielsetzung: Das Ganze war, so hieß es, kein Krieg; es war eine Humanitäre Intervention. Als Problem

---

[1] Dies ist der stark gekürzte Text meines Vortrags *NATO's Gappy Morals*, den ich auf dem GAP4-Kongress gehalten habe – und mit dem ich meine Reflexionen zum Kosovo-Krieg fortsetze, die ich im Mai 1999 mit dem Vortrag „Ist dieser Krieg gut? Ein ethischer Kommentar" begonnen hatte. (Erschienen in Reinhard Merkel (Hrsg.), *Der Kosovo-Krieg und das Völkerrecht*, Frankfurt/M. (edition Suhrkamp), 2000.) Mit diesem GAP4-Vortrag ist mein Nachdenken über diesen Krieg – und all die mit ihm verbundenen Moralaxiome und deren Implementierungen – nicht zu Ende. Auch wenn mir erst durch diesen Krieg vieles klar geworden ist – allzu viel ist mir noch viel zu unklar. Für Kritik und Anregung wäre ich daher dankbar.
Die ungekürzte Fassung dieses Vortrags steht im Netz: http://www.uni-leipzig.de/~philos/meggle//publ-o.htm

wurde allenfalls das fehlende Mandat durch die UN angesehen. Doch sogar diesen Mangel hefteten sich die dezidiertesten Interventions-Proponenten auf die eigenen Fahnen: als überfälligen Sieg der *Moral* über das bloße *Recht*, als Sieg der *Menschenrechte* über das *Völkerrecht*. So die eine Seite.

Andere sahen und sehen diesen ersten NATO-Krieg anders: als *Rückfall in die Barbarei*, in die seit dem Westfälischen Frieden zwar nie wirklich vermiedene (im Gegenteil: gerade im 20. Jahrhundert ins Extrem gesteigerte), aber zumindest von den sogenannten zivilisierten Staaten seitdem immerhin doch zu vermeiden versuchte *vor-völkerrechtliche Barbarei*.

Moral – das war schon immer das wirksamste Rechtfertigungsmittel von Kriegen. Und somit sicher eines der wichtigsten Kriegs-Instrumentarien selbst.

Was geht das die Ethik an? Es gibt wenige Fälle, an denen sich die praktische Relevanz der Ethik (als gleichermaßen grundlagen-theoretischer wie kritisch-applikativ interessierter philosophischer Disziplin) deutlicher zeigen würde. Die Moral ist *die* kriegsentscheidende Software. Marschflugkörper kann man stoppen. Das Moral-Programm, wenn es erst einmal läuft, kaum. Wie steht es mit dem Moral-Programm der NATO im Kosovokrieg?

Die folgenden Gedanken setzen meinen Vortrag „Ist dieser Krieg gut?" aus den letzten Kriegswochen des Frühsommers von 1999 fort. Das erste Modul des heutigen Vortrags ist der hier stark geraffte Kern aus jenem '99er Vortrag.

1. Notwehr & Nothilfe

1.1 Nehmen wir den üblichen Einstieg, den, der über Notwehr und Nothilfe führt. Wenn mir jemand ans Leben will, dann darf ich mich, wenn ich seinen Angriff auf mein Leben nicht anders abwehren kann, auch dadurch zur Wehr setzen, daß, ehe er mich tötet, ich ihn töte. Ich darf, aber ich muß nicht. Vielleicht ist mir mein Leben nicht so viel wert, daß ich, um es zu retten, selbst zum Töten bereit bin. Notwehr ist ein Recht, keine Pflicht.

Bei Nothilfe hingegen geht es nicht um mein Leben, sondern um das von mindestens einem andern. Ein Killer will einem wehrlosen Kind ans Leben. Darf ich, um das Leben des Kindes zu retten, meinerseits dem Killer, falls es denn sein muß, ans Leben? Aber sicher! Und hier ist das vielleicht sogar meine Pflicht. Ich darf auf mein Leben verzichten; aber vielleicht nicht darauf, das des Kindes zu retten. Auf Notwehr haben wir ein Recht, zur Nothilfe können wir sogar verpflichtet sein. Der Spielraum der Aktionen, die mir bei einem Nothilfe-Einsatz geboten bzw. zuzumuten sind, ist freilich nicht unbegrenzt. Er hängt zum einen daran, wie viel für mich bei meinem Einsatz selbst auf dem Spiel steht; zum anderen daran, ob ich – z.B. als Polizist oder Rettungsschwimmer bei der Wasserwacht – zu bestimmten Einsätzen in einem besonderen Maße verpflichtet bin. Zudem sind wie in der Notwehr selbst auch bei der Nothilfe nicht alle mir möglichen Aktionen erlaubt. Was diese Grenzen des Erlaubten sind – dazu gleich mehr.

1.2 Dieser Einstieg per Notwehr und Nothilfe wird fast immer gewählt, wenn es um die moralische Rechtfertigung von Tötungslizenzen oder gar Tötungsverpflichtungen geht. Auch dann, wenn es um Krieg geht. Denn: auch Staaten sind Individuen. Und jedes Individuum, egal ob Einzelmensch oder Menschenkollektiv, darf seine Existenz verteidigen – auch wenn dies vielleicht das Ende des Angreifers bedeutet. Verteidigungskriege sind nichts anderes als Fälle von Staats-Notwehr; und Beistandskriege – egal ob innerhalb oder außerhalb von Verteidigungs-Bündnissen – sind nichts anderes als Nothilfefälle. Und eben damit sind sie, so das Hauptargument, auch moralisch gerechtfertigt. Diese Kriege bezeichnet man daher, was das Recht zum Kriegseintritt (das *jus ad bellum*) angeht, auch als in dieser Hinsicht „gerechte Kriege". So weit, so gut. Vielleicht.

1.3 Aber jetzt gibt es ein Problem. Staaten bestehen selber aus Individuen bzw. eben aus Gruppen von Individuen. Hauptzweck des Staates sei zwar, so heißt es, der Schutz seiner Bürger. Aber nicht jeder Staat dient diesem Zweck auch tatsächlich. Was ist, wenn sich der Staats-Apparat selber gegen seine eigenen Bürger, meist natürlich gegen einzelne Gruppen derselben, wendet? Besitzen dann auch diese, wenn es um ihre Existenz geht, ebenfalls ein Recht auf Notwehr? Selbstverständlich. Das ist das berühmte Widerstandsrecht. Es ist ein moralisches Recht, welches die derart bedrohte Gruppe gegenüber dem eigenen Staat auch dann hat, wenn dieser in seinen Gesetzen kein solches Recht vorsieht oder ein solches Recht sogar strikt negiert. Also haben Dritte auch in diesem Fall, falls die bedrohte Gruppe zur Selbsthilfe nicht in der Lage ist, das Recht zur Nothilfe.

1.4 Gruppen – z.B. Parteien, Volks-, Religions-, oder sonstige Gruppen – werden aber nicht nur von Staaten, sondern auch von anderen Gruppen bedroht. Gegen solche Bedrohungen ist zunächst der jeweilige Staat mit seinem Hauptzweck, mit seiner Beschützerrolle, gefragt. Mit der ist es aber oft nicht so weit her; zudem kommen mitunter Repression, Vertreibung oder Vernichtung der einen Gruppe durch mindestens eine andere Gruppe den Herrschenden gerade recht bzw. werden von diesen nicht nur gedeckt, vielmehr forciert, mitunter auch initiiert. Auch hier gilt: Insoweit der Staat versagt, dürfen auch hier Dritte bei nicht hinreichender Notwehrmöglichkeit von Seiten der Bedrohten selber Hilfe substituieren.

1.5   Frage an Sie: Ging bei Ihnen die Notwehr- und Nothilfe-Legitimierung bis hierher glatt durch? Dann haben Sie eine kritische Grenze bereits überschritten: nämlich die des betreffenden Staates. Wer dem Prinzip zustimmt, daß wir einer bedrohten Population auch auf dem Gebiet eines anderen Staates zu Hilfe kommen dürfen, für den ist offensichtlich die Hilfeleistung als solche wichtiger – wichtiger als die Frage, ob diese Hilfe von diesseits oder jenseits der jeweiligen Staatsgrenze kommt.

Und so sollte es auch sein. Hätte etwa, wenn Hitler keine Eroberungskriege geführt und die KZ's ausschließlich auf deutschem Boden gestanden hätten, der Rest der Welt angesichts einer derart lokal begrenzten Vernichtungspolitik tatenlos zusehen sollen? Nun, vielleicht hätte die Welt das getan. Aber nie und nimmer hätte sie das tun dürfen. (Und an dieser Stelle kommt jetzt der Satz, der bei meinem '99er Vortrag einige sehr getroffen hat. Er lautet:) Das ist der Punkt, an dem Pazifismus zum Verbrechen wird. „Nie wieder Auschwitz!" kann tatsächlich stärker wiegen als „Nie wieder Krieg". Wenn man ein zweites Auschwitz verhindern kann, dann muß man es auch verhindern – egal, wo es liegt. Die Generalisierung: Menschenrechtsverletzungen sind keine Ländersache. Gegenüber der Verletzung von Menschenrechten ist das Verletzen von Grenzen eher das geringere Übel, bei Verletzungen von der Dimension von Auschwitz überhaupt keines. Staatssouveränität ist nicht das höchste Gut.

2.   Humanitäre Interventions-Axiome

2.1   Die Quintessenz ist: Auch Interventionen durch Drittstaaten lassen sich somit rechtfertigen, jedenfalls solche, die wirklich entsprechende Nothilfe-Interventionen sind. Solche Interventionen werden, zumindest von denen, die sie durchführen, auch als Humanitäre Interventionen bezeichnet.[2] Schließen wir uns diesem Sprachgebrauch an, dann ist die Quintessenz des soeben durchgezogenen Nothilfe-Einstiegs nichts anderes als:

---

[2] Damit auch ja klar ist, daß es hier nicht bloß um sanitäre Hilfseinsätze geht, sollte man die Dinge beim Namen nennen – und so expliziter von *Humanitären Kriegs-Interventionen* sprechen. Diese sind durch die folgenden Bedingungen charakterisiert:

1: *Ziel* des Intervenierenden X ist die Verhinderung, Beendigung oder zumindest Verringerung von massiven und systematischen Menschenrechtsverletzungen (begangen an Mitgliedern der Gruppe Z) auf dem Gebiet des Staates Y.
2: *Akteur* X: ein Staat oder Gruppe von Staaten (z.B.: NATO).
3: *Aktion*: Militäreinsatz mit Kampfauftrag
4: *Fremstaatenklausel*: Intervenierter Staat Y $\neq$ X.

> ⊕ ZENTRAL Humanitäre Kriegs-Interventionen können moralisch gerechtfertigt sein.

Es ist *das* Zentrale Axiom aller Interventionisten. Was kein Wunder ist: „Interventionisten" heißen genau die, die eben dieses Axiom unterschreiben. Ich bin einer. Denn trotz vieler Wenn und Aber halte ich den ganzen bisherigen Begründungsgang im groben für richtig.

Eine interventionistische Philosophie vertreten auch die USA und damit auch die NATO. Aber auch andere Staaten und Organisationen. Auch die UNO.

2.2 Die Differenzen zwischen USA, NATO etc. vs. UNO betreffen allenfalls die Frage, ob auch noch die zwei folgenden Interventions-Axiome gelten sollen, die zusammen den starken Interventionismus charakterisieren:

> ⊕ MR Menschen-Rechte können mehr zählen als Souveränitäts-Rechte von Staaten.
> ⊕ NO UN Humanitäre Kriegs-Interventionen dürfen notfalls auch ohne UN-Mandat / Votum des Sicherheitsrates begonnen werden.

Wie mein obiger Nothilfe-Begründungs-Crashcourse schon klarmachte, bin auch ich ein *starker Interventionist*.

2.3 Diese Axiome gehören, wie gesagt, zum Kern der moralischen NATO-Software. Diese Software wurde auch bei der NATO-Intervention im Kosovokrieg implementiert. *War und ist damit dieser Krieg bereits moralisch legitimiert?*

3. Humanitäre Kriegs-Interventionen – moralische Kriterien

Nein. Diese Axiome sind kein Blankoscheck. Auch für Humanitäre Kriegs-Interventionen gelten die Beschränkungen, die für Nothilfe generell einschlägig sind. Jede moralische Beurteilung von Humanitären Interventionen hängt wesentlich daran, ob *mindestens* diese generellen Nothilfe-Auflagen beachtet sind. Damit eine Humanitäre Intervention rechtfertigbar ist, muß nicht nur das Kriterium des *ius ad bellum* erfüllt, bei dieser Art von Krieg also die entsprechende *Notlage* als Interventionsgrund tatsächlich gegeben sein. Es müssen auch die Kriterien für die Rechtfertigbarkeit der speziellen

Ausführung der Nothilfe erfüllt sein. Wiederum mit den klassischen Worten: Es müssen auch die für diese Art von Krieg einschlägigen Kriterien des *ius in bello* erfüllt sein.

Die Liste der zu beachtenden Kriterien für die moralische Legimität einer Humanitären Kriegs-Intervention (kurz: einer HKI) ist diese.[3]

Eine HKI ist nur dann erlaubt / gerechtfertigt, wenn

(i) (a) es um die Beendigung etc. massiver Verbrechen gegen die Menschlichkeit geht ($\geq$ „KD");
(b) dies nicht anders erreichbar ist;
(ii) die Art der Intervention
(a) dem Interventions-Ziel dienlich ist;
(b) die Gefährdung Dritter möglichst gering hält;
(c) die Schädigung bzw. Gefährdung der Intervenierenden selber möglichst gering hält;
(d) das Interventions-Ziel mit der geringstmöglichen Schädigung des Interventions-Verursachers erreichen läßt;
(iii) die Intervention nicht ihrerseits massive Verbrechen gegen die Menschlichkeit involviert;
(?-iv-?) die Intervention (a) vom Völkerrecht – und (b) insbesondere durch einen Beschluß des UN-Sicherheitsrates gedeckt ist.

Die Forderung (iii) ist nur der Deutlichkeit wegen aufgenommen; sie dürfte aus den anderen, speziell aus (ii) (b) und (d), ohnehin schon folgen. Die Forderung (?-iv-?) trägt die beiden Fragezeichen zu Recht. Sie steht im Widerspruch zu dem starken Interventionismus-Axiom ⊕ NO UN.

Jetzt gehe ich vor allem auf die Kriterien ein, die in meinem '99er Vortrag zu kurz gekommen waren; also insbesondere auf (i) und (ii) (a) und (b).[4]

---

[3] Zur *Begründung* dieser Forderungen siehe meinen '99er Vortrag. Die Liste ergibt sich aus der entsprechenden Liste für Nothilfe im allgemeinen – mit Ausnahme der Forderung (ii) (b): Drittschädigungen bzw. Gefährdungen sind nach § 32 II.2. Alt. STGB strikt verboten.

[4] Die Kriterien (ii) (c) und (d) bedürfen ohnehin keiner langen Diskussion. Es sind die Kriterien, die von der NATO im Kosovokrieg fast perfekt erfüllt worden waren. Der 1. NATO-Krieg war zugleich der erste Krieg der Weltgeschichte mit Null Verlusten auf Seiten des Angreifers (sofern sich „Verlust" hier ausschließlich auf „Verlust von Menschenleben im direkten Kampfeinsatz" bezieht); und auch die Verluste des jugoslawischen Militärs waren, an Leben wie an Gerät, unglaublich gering. (Das wirft die Frage auf, gegen wen diese Intervention primär gerichtet war.)

4. Kriterium (i)

Um moralisch gerechtfertigt werden zu können, müssen Humanitäre Interventionen – in direkter Parallele zum allgemeinen Nothilfe-Fall – ihrem Selbstverständnis als Nothilfe-Fälle auch tatsächlich entsprechen. Es muß bei der Gruppe, zu deren Schutz die Intervention unternommen werden soll, also tatsächlich eine Notstands-Lage vorliegen.

4.1 Die in der einschlägigen Literatur genannten Kriterien variieren extrem. Was zum Teil einfach daran liegt, daß dort die von mir so genannten Humanitären Interventions-Kriege nur selten scharf bestimmt und so gut wie nie bei ihrem Namen genannt werden. *Communis opinio* ist, daß es bei den einschlägigen Notstands-Interventions-Anlässen um *Verstöße gegen die Menschenrechte* gehen soll. Im Zuge der Globalisierung sollen, so heißt es, Humanitäre Interventionen zu einem mit zunehmender Schärfe zu schmiedenden Instrument einer universalen Menschenrechtspolitik entwickelt werden.

4.2 Erkannt wird jedoch in der Regel, daß nicht *jeder* Verstoß gegen die Menschenrechte schon einen zulässigen Interventionsanlaß abgeben kann. Auch nicht solche, die ein Land systematisch begeht. Andernfalls dürfte man einen Humanitären Interventions-Krieg z.B. auch gegen die USA führen. Eine Menschenrechtverletzung ist auch, so jedenfalls *Amnesty International*, die dort praktizierte Todesstrafe. Auch wir wären bedroht: Denn bei vielen Menschen in den noch nicht verwestlichten Ländern weckt die Tatsache, daß in unserer Gesellschaft gerade die Mitmenschen, denen wir am meisten verdanken, zu Hunderttausenden ‚in speziellen Isolationsanstalten kaserniert werden', sobald sie älter als 80 und der Pflege bedürftig sind, nur Unverständnis und Abscheu. Auch die für einen Interventionsgrund sehr oft verwendete Formel von einem „Grund für den Abscheu der Menschen" dürfte daher nicht so recht glücklich sein. Auch nicht für uns. Und ich unterstelle, daß die gesuchte Definition keine kulturrelative sein soll.

4.3 Die weitaus meisten Staaten der Erde zu Interventions-Verursachern erklärend und damit wohl ebenfalls unbrauchbar dürfte auch die folgende Bestimmung aus einem der meistzitierten derzeitigen Humanitären-Interventions-Theorie-Klassiker sein: Danach ist ein Interventionsgrund: [a situation, inviting] „transboundary [forcible] ... help, provided by governments to individuals in another state who are being denied basic human rights and who themselves would be rationally willing to revolt against their oppressive governments" (Tesón 1997, S. 5).

Die Frage ist: Wie schwer müssen denn Menschenrechtsverletzungen sein, damit sie eine Intervention rechtfertigen?

4.4 In meinem '99er Kriegs-Beitrag hatte ich mich gegenüber dieser Frage einfach aus der Affäre gezogen. Die „*Kosovo-Dimension*" reicht, war meine Antwort. Darunter hatte ich die Größenordnung jener Verbrechen gegen die Menschlichkeit verstanden, „von der wir glauben gemacht wurden, daß sie die NATO in der Kosovo-Krise zum Eingreifen bewogen haben: also all die Massaker, planmäßigen Vergewaltigungen, massenhaften Vertreibungen usw., die von den USA und anderen Staaten als Interventionsgrund angeführt worden sind. Nennen wir die Dimension dieser Verbrechensberichte i.f. kurz die „Kosovo-Dimension" („KD")". (Genau auf diese Dimension bezieht sich die Abkürzung in der Forderung (i) (a).)

Eine HKI ist nur dann erlaubt/gerechtfertigt, wenn

(i) (a) es um die Beendigung etc. massiver Verbrechen gegen die Menschlichkeit ($\geq$ „KD") geht.

4.5 Ich glaube, daß sich mit der gleichen „Die Kosovo-Dimension reicht"-Lösung im letzten Jahr auch viele andere Interventionisten aus der Affäre gezogen haben. Heute geht das nicht mehr. Inzwischen sind einige Fragen fällig. Erstens: Fragen von allgemeiner Bedeutung. Und dann Fragen zu den Tatsachen. Zu den allgemeinen Fragen – zu einigen allgemeineren Fragen – zuerst:

Bei diesen geht es nicht darum, ob die so definierte „Kosovo-Dimension" den Tatsachen entsprach. Das sei jetzt einfach unterstellt. Die wichtigsten beiden Fragen von genereller Interventions-Bewertungs-Relevanz sind dann diese:

(α) Ist die (i) (a) Bedingung nicht *zu stark*? Müssen massive Verbrechen wirklich erst diese „Kosovo-Dimension" angenommen haben, ehe interveniert werden darf?

Und umgekehrt:

(β) Kam die Interventions-Bereitschaft der NATO (und vieler von uns) nicht zu früh? War selbst mit der „Kosovo-Dimension" die kritische Schwelle für das Geboten/Erlaubtsein einer HKI noch nicht erreicht? Mit anderen Worten: Ist die (i) (a) Bedingung nicht *zu schwach*?

Das sind Fragen, die schon als Fragen, wenn sie klar und deutlich gestellt werden, Qual bereiten. Daher werden sie auch so gut wie nie gestellt. Trotzdem *müssen* sie gestellt werden. Wie die Antwort aussieht, davon hängt das Leben von Tausenden ab. Und zwar bei allen involvierten Parteien. (Bei *allen*, falls nicht gerade die NATO High-Tech-interveniert). Darf man sich um die Klärung dieser Fragen einfach drücken? Genau ab wann sind Menschenrechtsverletzungen so schlimm, daß eine Intervention als *ultima ratio* geboten ist?[5]

4.6 Dieser Frage weichen nicht nur Analytiker und andere guten Philosophen bisher aus. Auch die, die über Krieg und Nicht-Krieg entscheiden bzw. diese Kriegs-Entscheidungen mittragen.

Wie sich solches Ausweichen am leichtesten rhetorisch kaschiert, ist bekannt. Man beantwortet statt der schwierigen Frage eine sehr viel leichtere; und gibt auf diese dann die stärkstmögliche Antwort, die sich überhaupt denken läßt. Die Frage, um die es wirklich geht, ist, ich wiederhole: Wie schlimm müssen Verbrechen sein, damit, als *ultima ratio*, Krieg geboten ist? *Die* ultimative Antwort von 1999 war „Auschwitz". Als Paradigma für einen Humanitären Worst Case, in dem die Kriegsfrage dann ohnehin keine echte mehr ist, wäre diese Antwort richtig gewesen. (Genau so hatte ich ja in meinem ersten Begründungs-Schnelldurchgang selbst argumentiert – siehe § 1 oben.) Aber als Schwellen-Rechtfertigung für den NATO-Angriff? Dann hätte dieser Angriff mit Sicherheit *nicht* stattfinden dürfen. Doch so war dieses Musterbeispiel einer Auschwitz-Instrumentalisierung gerade *nicht* gemeint.

4.7 Als Paradigmen für gerechtfertigte Humanitäre Kriegs-Interventionen gelten inzwischen u.a. die zwei folgenden: Indiens '71-er Intervention im damaligen Ost-Pakistan (zur Beendigung des Völkermords an den Bengalis); und die von Tansania in Uganda in 1979, die den Schlächtereien von Idi Amin ein Ende setzten. Beide Beispiele gehen aber, was die Größenordnungen der vorangegangenen Massaker angeht, selbst über das Maximum der „Kosovo-Dimensions"-Opfer jeweils über das Hundertfache hinaus. Die Indien-Ostpakistan Intervention ist nebenbei auch das Paradigma einer auch *ohne* UN-Mandat rechtfertigbaren Humanitären Intervention. Der Staat, der gegen diese Intervention wegen des in *diesem* Fall fehlenden UN-Mandats am schärfsten protestiert hatte, waren die USA.

---

[5] Kritische LeserInnen werden bemerken, daß ich an dieser Stelle von „erlaubt" zu „geboten" übergegangen bin. Wie das? Nun, mithilfe des von mir in der nicht-gekürzten Fassung (dort § 5.7) vertretenen Prinzips, wonach Humanitäre Kriegs-Interventionen *genau dann* moralisch *erlaubt* sind, wenn sie auch moralisch *geboten* sind. Da Erlaubnis aus Gebotensein ohnehin folgt, ist der entscheidende Übergangsschritt dieser: Eine HKI ist nur dann moralisch *erlaubt*, wenn die Menschenrechtsverletzungen, die sie beenden soll, derart schlimm sind, daß auf sie mit einer HKI zu reagieren auch moralisch *geboten* ist.

4.8   Wir werden uns noch lange quälen müssen, ehe sich auf unsere offene Frage – genau ab wann Humanitäre Kriegs-Interventionen o.k. sind – Antworten finden, die über *ad hoc* Antworten hinausgehen. Es geht um nichts weniger als um eine Skalierung unterschiedlich schwerer Arten von Menschenrechtsverletzungen: die Hölle des Holocaust, der Völkermord an den Armeniern, Vertreibungen, Vergewaltigungslager, Folterungen, Srebrenica, Kinderverschleppungen, Verstümmelungen … – die schier endlose Liste all dessen, wozu Menschen fähig sind.

4.9   Mit einer solchen Skalierung der Negativ-Potentiale der Gattung Homo Sapiens wäre aber eine weitere Frage noch nicht einmal gestellt – die nach der Skalierung der Interventions-Pflichtigkeit. Von welchen Faktoren soll das Ranking der unterschiedlich starken Interventions-Pflichtigen abhängen?. Wen trifft ceteris paribus (also z.B.: bei gleichem Militärpotential) die Verpflichtung zum Eingreifen am ersten? Die, die am nächsten dran sind? Räumlich am nächsten dran? Oder als Mitglieder der gleichen Kultur? Der gleichen Religion? Der gleichen Sprache? Oder kommen, um weitere Eskalierungen zu minimieren, nur gemischte Interventionstruppen in Frage? Und sollen in solche Rettungsfeldzüge nur Freiwillige oder auch Zwangsrekrutierte geschickt werden? Oder sind für diese Humanitären Zwecke nur die besten Killer, Söldner etwa, gerade gut genug?

4.10   Und am allerwichtigsten: Wer entscheidet das alles? Wie sehen, wenn es um die Durchsetzung universaler Menschenrechtsfragen mittels Militärgewalt geht, die zulässigen Entscheidungsverfahren aus? Liegt die Beantwortung all dieser Fragen nur im Ermessen von Washington, Moskau und Peking? Bei den Staaten-Organisationen der verschiedenen Kontinente, der OSZE z.B.?

4.11   Und was ist zu tun, damit in die so konzipierte moralisch/geistige Software für diese „Kriege für die Menschenrechte" nicht genau das eingebaut ist, was deren universalistischem Grundgedanken wirklich absolut widerspräche: genau der Chip, der den großen wechselseitigen Humanitären Interventions-Krieg auslöst, den ohnehin bereits prognostizierten Krieg der Kulturen?

Diese Fragen und ähnliche werden in den kommenden Jahrzehnten auch die Philosophen beschäftigen, falls es zutrifft, daß Humanitäre Menschenrechts-Kriege die Strategie der Zukunft sein werden. Und danach sieht alles aus. Es wird zunehmend Bedarf an Humanitären Interventions-Experten geben.

5. Die „Kosovo-Dimension" versus die Kosovo-Dimension

Zurück zur Vergangenheit. War die Humanitäre NATO-Intervention vom Frühjahr 1999 moralisch o.k.? Wir sind, was diese Frage angeht, immer noch beim ersten Schritt: Beim ersten Kriterium, bei der Humanitären-Interventions-Präsupposition (i) (a). Und bei diesem Schritt, wenn wir ehrlich sind, keinen Schritt weiter.

Fragen wir uns also nochmal: Angenommen, es hätte wirklich keine Alternative gegeben: War dann angesichts der Kosovo-Dimension die NATO-Intervention wirklich geboten?

5.1 Um mit dieser Frage etwas anfangen zu können, muß man eines schon wissen: Wie groß war „die Kosovo-Dimension"? Was gehörte alles zu ihr? Was gab, sofern diese Dimension wirklich den Ausschlag gegeben hatte, den Ausschlag dafür, daß der ehemalige spanische anti-NATO-Aktivist Javier Solana am 24. März 1999 im Auftrag von Clinton als NATO-Generalsekretär grünes Licht für den Angriff auf Jugoslawien gab?

Diese Frage mag nicht leicht zu beantworten sein. Aus der langen Liste meiner Fragen ist sie aber noch eine der leichtesten. Dabei zählt jetzt, wie eben gesagt, nicht alles, was hier ausschlaggebend gewesen sein mag: nur der für die Bestimmung der damaligen „Kosovo-Dimension" relevante Humanitäre Aspekt. Also die Hauptmessage der uns alle damals (wie heute immer noch) mit Entsetzen erfüllenden Berichte. *Diese* Dimension ist leicht verifizierbar. Die Berichte gibt es ja noch.

5.2 Gegeben, diese Berichte trafen zu. Waren wir dann wirklich zum Eingreifen verpflichtet? „Wir dürfen nicht einfach zuschauen" – das versteht sich bei solchen Humanitären Katastrophen von selbst. Aber das rechtfertigt noch lange nicht Krieg. Um aber der alten Frage nicht wie allenthalben üblich per Themenwechsel auszuweichen, noch einmal die Frage: Ist diese „Kosovo-Dimension" auch noch aus heutiger Sicht, mit etwas größerer Distanz zu dem ganzen Geschehen, eine Dimension, die Humanitäre Interventionen rechtfertigen würde? Per Universalisierbarkeitspostulat also etwas, was zu tun ceteris paribus auch in anderen Fällen von gleicher Dimension etwas Gebotenes ist?

Angenommen, dem wäre so. Dann hätte das Folgen. Unter diesen, um nur eine der schwächsten zu nennen, zum Beispiel diese. Wir wären in allen Fällen, in denen, *1.*, die „Kosovo-Dimension" ebenfalls erreicht bzw. sogar deutlich übertroffen wird, wir, *2.*, zum Eingreifen nicht weniger in der Lage wären, dieses Eingreifen, *3.*, einer Humanitären *Kriegs*-Intervention, ja überhaupt eines Militäreinsatzes, überhaupt nicht bedürfte, und, *4.*, alle anderen Nothilfe-Legitimations-Bedingungen (vielleicht mit Ausnahme von

(ii) (d)) ohnehin mit Leichtigkeit erfüllt wären – ja, was wären wir in so einem Fall? Zum allermindesten doch dies: unter Begründungszwang. Solche Fälle sind nicht bloß hypothetisch. Stichwort: Türkisch Kurdistan. Was sind hier die *Argumente*? Und hielten diese Argumente einer näheren *Analyse* stand?

Hier geht es nicht um die Frage nach möglichen Erklärungen. Von denen liegen einige ziemlich nahe. Es geht um die Begründung dafür, warum bestimmte Unterschiede zwischen diesen beiden Fällen *moralisch* relevant sind. Wo ist eine solche Begründung?

5.3   Eine der vielen Erklärungen ist trivial: Gegen die Türkei kann die NATO schon *begrifflicherweise* nicht Humanitär-Kriegs-intervenieren. Das folgt aus der interventionistischen Fremdstaatenklausel. Aber wäre das nicht ein weiteres Argument *für* das Initiieren von pro-kurdischen Human-Interventionen? Von Interventionen, die, wie gesagt, 1. (über die Jahre hinweg) mindestens „Kosovo-Dimensions"-relevant-nötig, 2. unvergleichlich leichter durchführbar, 3. überhaupt keine Militär-Aktionen unsererseits involvierend und 4. sämtliche Nothilfe-Legitimationsansprüche optimal erfüllen würden.

Ähnliche Stichworte gäbe es viele. Ein Federstrich von Clinton zur Lockerung des Wirtschafts-Boykotts gegen Irak – und etwa 300 000 Kinder wären am Leben geblieben.

5.4   Dieses Inkonsistenz-Argument spricht nicht per se gegen die Legitimität der NATO-Intervention des letzten Jahres. *Wenn* an 3 Orten eine Intervention wirklich geboten ist, dann ist es immer noch besser, an einem der Orte wird interveniert als an keinem. Aber das wirft ein neues Begründungsproblem auf: Was sprach *ex ante* dafür, gerade dort zu intervenieren, wo diese Intervention am riskantesten ist? Wie sehen wir das jetzt *ex post*? Welche Regel ist es, die diese Unterschiede legitimiert? Sind Interventionen desto moralischer, je riskanter sie sind – für alle riskanter bis hin zur Gefährdung des Weltfriedens? Haben *Kriegs*-Interventionen wirklich generell Vorrang?

Klar, wir sind nicht doof. Wir wissen, daß in der internationalen Politik außer Moral noch vieles andere eine Rolle spielt. Wirtschaftsinteressen, Supermacht-Ambitionen und -Zwänge, exakt getimete Affären-Entlastung und tausenderlei mehr. Die einzig entscheidende Frage ist aber: Dürften all diese Dinge zusammen *den* Unterschied ausmachen? *Den* moralischen Unterschied, der zwischen Federstrich und 37 000 Bombenattacken liegt?

5.5   Wie schlimm war die „Kosovo-Dimension"? Hält diese Dimension als Kriegs-Interventions-Auslöser auch heute noch unserer moralischen Analyse stand? Die „Kosovo-Dimension" – das hieß dabei stets: die Dimension, von der wir über die Medien *glauben* gemacht wurden, dass sie die tatsächliche ist.

War sie das? Das ist für die *ex post* Beurteilung der NATO-Intervention gewiss keine unwichtige Frage. Wie verifiziert man sie? Über welche Kanäle bekommt man das raus? (CNN, ZDF, TV Belgrad, UCK-Sender, das Zet-Net, Human Rights Watch?) Wer hier anfängt, merkt schnell: Unsere ganzen philosophischen Probleme mit Veri- und Falsifikation, Hypothesentest, Kohärenz-Präsumptionen und was sonst – all diese eher an der Scientific Community orientierten Probleme sind ein Klacks gegenüber denen, auf die man trifft, wenn man „die Wahrheit" über die tatsächlichen Dimensionen unserer wirklichen Welt herausbekommen möchte. Probleme also, die auch für mich jetzt zu groß sind.

Aber in einem stimmen doch die allermeisten der Quellen, die ernster zu nehmen naheliegt, überein. Was allein die Zahl der Toten angeht, war die *reale Kosovo-Dimension* in etwa 1/10 der *Medien-„Kosovo-Dimension"*. Das legt zumindest einen Rat nahe: Lasst uns, wenn wir wieder auf eine Humanitäre Kriegs-Intervention zusteuern, um mindestens das 3-fache skeptischer sein als im Frühjahr '99. Aber alle Erfahrung lehrt: Ein solcher Ratschlag wurde noch nie befolgt.

Wie steht es mit dem Kriterium (i) (b): Gab es Alternativen? Erlaubte Alternativen zu was? Zum Bombenkrieg? Sicher. Zu einer militärischen Intervention überhaupt? Ich weiß es nicht.

6. Kriterium (ii)

Eine HKI ist nur dann erlaubt/gerechtfertigt, wenn

(ii) die Art der Intervention (a) dem Interventions-Ziel dienlich ist.

6.1 *Dem* Interventions-Ziel? Jede Aktion kann viele Ziele haben. Und die betreffende Aktion kann zur Erreichung des einen Ziels dienlich sein, zur Erreichung anderer Ziele nicht. Das gilt auch für Interventionen, egal, ob Humanitär oder nicht. *Das* Ziel einer Aktion gibt es gewöhnlich nicht; es sei denn, man meint damit: entweder das Gesamtziel der Aktion, d.h. die Summe aller Ziele; oder das primäre Ziel, also das, dessentwegen der Akteur die Handlung überhaupt unternimmt, wobei die anderen Ziele dann ihrerseits nur Mittel zur Erreichung dieses Primärzieles sind.

6.2 War der Humanitäre NATO-Luftkrieg gegen Jugoslawien seinem (zumindest so erklärten) Humanitären Ziel dienlich? Wurde mittels der 78 Tage bzw. Nächte dauernden Bombardierung Jugoslawiens die „Kosovo-Dimension" minimiert?

Nein. Was das Humanitäre Ziel der Intervention betrifft, waren die Humanitären Bomben *kontraproduktiv*. Und zwar aus zwei Gründen:

Erstens: Ohne die Bombardierungen hätte es die Flüchtlingsströme in *der* Größenordnung, die wir als *die* „Kosovo-Dimension" zu lesen bekamen, also mit den *zuletzt, nach* den Bombardierungen bis über eine Million reichenden Flüchtlingsströmen gar nicht gegeben; für Hunderttausende Kosovaner waren die beginnenden *Bombardierungen selbst die Ursache* der Flucht aus ihren Siedlungen und über die Grenzen; und erst *mit* dem Beginn dieser Bombardierungen (genauer: mit Beginn des Abzugs der OSZE-Beobachter und der Ankündigung dieser Bombardierungen) eskalierten die serbischen Übergriffe – was wiederum nicht nur voraussehbar war; genau diese Eskalation war von den Spitzen-„Experten" vorausgesagt worden: z.B. von dem in Oxford mit Auszeichnung in Philosophie promovierten amerikanischen Oberkommandieren Wesley Clark. Die NATO schüttete mit der Bombardierung Jugoslawiens Öl auf das im Kosovo keineswegs nur von den Serben geschürte Feuer.

6.3 Zweitens: Die Bombardierungen haben nicht nur direkt zur Eskalation der gegen die albanische Bevölkerung gerichteten Säuberungen beigetragen und damit die Vertreibungen erhöht statt gemindert, sie haben *mitbewirkt, was* durch die Intervention angeblich doch *verhindert werden sollte*: weitere ethnische Säuberungen. Heute, dank der Bombardierungen und dem so herbeigebombten Sieg der UCK *ist* der Kosovo weitestgehend ethnisch gesäubert. Nur eben anders herum. Daß mit dem Bombardement weitere Menschenrechtsverletzungen verhindert wurden, ist falsch.

6.4 Heute berichten die damaligen NATO-Strategen stolz, daß inzwischen von den albanischen Kosovo-Flüchtlingen und Vertriebenen die meisten doch wieder in ihre Heimat zurückkehren hätten können. Das ist richtig. Aber kein Argument für die Rechtfertigbarkeit (via Notwendigkeit bzw. Ziel-Dienlichkeit) der Bombardierungen. Die Geflüchteten und Vertriebenen sind nicht in ihre Heimat zurückbombardiert worden; die *Einstellung* der Bombardierungen, nicht die Bombardierungen selbst haben die Rückkehr ermöglicht.

Als Schutz vor Morden und Vertreibungen waren die Bombardierungen nicht nur das schlechteste denkbare Mittel; sie waren zur Erreichung dieses Schutzes überhaupt kein taugliches Mittel.

6.5 Diese Einschätzung enthält viele Prämissen, für die ich nicht einstehen kann. Zu viel hängt an den Unsicherheiten bezüglich der *faktischen*, nicht der *medialen* Kosovo-Dimension. Und mindestens so viel an dem, wovon bisher noch mit keinem Wort die Rede war: den Ursachen und den geschichtlichen, religiösen, sozialen Hintergründen des ganzen Geschehens. Betrachten Sie ob dieser ganzen Prämissen meiner Einschätzung diese also nur als so etwas wie meine persönliche Meinung. Aber lassen Sie mich's bitte wissen, wenn sie gute Gründe für eine andere haben.

Von meiner Einschätzung her komme ich freilich zu einem eindeutigen Schluß. Der NATO-Krieg verstieß gegen das Kriterium (ii) (a) – und war insofern, als eben dies auch ex ante den Intervenierenden klar sein mußte, weder ex ante erlaubt, noch ist er in Anbetracht der dann auch tatsächlich bewirkten Verschlimmerung der Situation ex post zu rechtfertigen.

6.6 Diese Einschätzung macht dann den weiteren Verstoß gegen die Regeln der gerechten Kriegsführung, den gegen (ii) (b), umso gravierender.

Die NATO-Bombardierungen trafen nicht nur den Kosovo, sie trafen ganz Rest-Jugoslawien.

Getroffen wurde nicht nur die *militärische* Infrastruktur – die am allerwenigsten; die Angriffe zielten primär auf die Zerstörung der Infrastruktur *des Landes* ab. Dieses Ziel wurde sehr weitgehend erreicht. Zu welchem Zweck? Wenn ich jemandes Gewaltbereitschaft vermindern möchte, erreiche ich das ausgerechnet dadurch, daß ich seine Lebens-Basis zerstöre? Ich frage nochmal: Zu welchem Zweck? Zu welchem Zweck wohlgemerkt, der mit dem angeblich primären Humanitären Interventionsziel in eine einsichtige Verbindung zu bringen wäre? Und zu welchem Zweck, dessen notwendige Erreichung dann auch den „Kollateralschaden" von über 500 Toten, darunter ca. 80 Kinder, als in Kauf zu nehmende – weil unvermeidbare – Nebenwirkung erscheinen lassen könnte? So angestrengt ich suche: Einen solchen Zweck finde ich nicht. Kann mich hier jemand eines Besseren belehren?

6.7 Humanitäre Interventionen sind Nothilfe-Fälle. Das war der Einstieg, der uns, falls Sie mir gefolgt sein sollten, zu Interventionisten gemacht hat.[6] Nach diesem Einstieg, wenn sich dieser wirklich strikt an unserem Ausgangspunkt (Notwehr und Nothilfe) orientieren würde, bräuchten wir uns bei dem Kriterium (ii) (b) nicht lange aufhalten. Wer nämlich bei normaler Notwehr bzw. Nothilfe nicht geschädigt werden darf, das sagt das auf solche Fälle begrenzte Strafrecht recht klar: Die Notwehr bzw. -Hilfe darf sich nur gegen den *Angreifer* richten, nicht gegen die *Rechtsgüter Dritter*. Der gezielte Todesschuß gegen den Geiselnehmer mag, wenn das denn wirklich die letzte Rettungsmöglichkeit ist, strafrechtlich o.k. sein; er ist es nicht mehr, sobald durch diesen Schuß auch nur *eine* unschuldige Person gefährdet ist.[7]

---

[6] Teile der nächsten §§ sind wieder meinem „Ist dieser Krieg gut?"-Vortrag entnommen.
[7] Zu diesem Punkt siehe vor allem den Artikel von Reinhard Merkel in Merkel 2000.

6.8   Dieses Verbot ist im Rahmen des Strafrechts völlig in Ordnung. Bei einer moralischen Überlegung, und bei einer solchen sind wir ja, wird man dieses Verbot aber nicht unter allen Umständen durchhalten können. Und jetzt müßte man in eben solche Abwägungen eintreten, wie sie in jedem Proseminar pro oder contra Utilitarismus durchgespielt werden. Angenommen, so eine der gängigsten Übungen, ein Geiselnehmer hat 20 Geiseln in seiner Gewalt; und angenommen, wir wären uns alle absolut dessen sicher, daß er sich, nachdem seine Forderungen nicht erfüllt worden sind, in den nächsten Sekunden mit allen Geiseln zusammen in die Luft sprengen wird. Sollte da der GSG-9-Scharfschütze, der den Gangster bereits im Visier hat, wirklich nicht auch dann abdrücken dürfen, wenn er *nicht* mit völliger Sicherheit ausschließen kann, daß durch seinen Schuß ein soeben plötzlich aufgetauchter und seine Visierlinie kreuzender unbeteiligter Passant in die Gefahr kommt, getroffen zu werden? Und wenn Sie jetzt zögern, täten Sie das auch noch bei 50 Geiseln? Auch bei 200? Auch bei 1000? Solche Reflexionsspiele sind schrecklich. Aber der Witz von Ethik ist nicht der, daß sie Spaß macht.

6.9   Die Kosovo-Dimension, egal wie eng oder weit diese wirklich war, übersteigt alle Bankräuber-Szenarien. Wer angesichts dieser Dimension eine Humanitäre Kriegs-Intervention auch nur als prima facie in Betracht kommend akzeptiert, der hat die Entscheidung bereits getroffen. Er überschreitet aus moralischen Gründen den Bereich des (in den verwandten Kontexten) strafrechtlich Zulässigen. Wir kommen hier also in ein Gebiet, in dem, was *strafrechtlich verboten* ist, *moralisch erlaubt*, ja vielleicht sogar *moralisch geboten* ist. Militärische Interventionen ohne Gefährdung sogenannter Unschuldiger gibt es nicht. Militärische Interventionen auch mit noch so Humanitären Absichten sind da keine Ausnahme. Man kann nicht Humanitäre Kriegs-Interventionen billigen – und die Gefährdung Dritter ausschließen.

6.10   Was freilich nicht heißt, daß, was die Gefährung Dritter angeht, damit der Damm gebrochen und mit dem Verbot dieser Gefährdung umso lockerer umgegangen werden kann je größer der Schrecken ist, den die Humanitäre Intervention zu bekämpfen hat. Wie weit trotzdem ein Zusammenhang zwischen notwendiger Bekämpfung des Interventions-Verursachers und Dritt-Gefährdung gehen darf, auch dieser qualvollen Frage werden sich Interventions-Ethiker zu stellen haben. Menschen als auf die angreifenden Panzer gebundene Schutzschilder, Fabrikarbeiter, die in den kriegswichtigen Betrieben arbeiten usw. – das wäre die Art der für diese Frage genauer zu betrachtenden Fälle.

6.11   Für den 1. NATO-Krieg brauchen wir *diese* Diskussion jedoch nicht. Jedenfalls nicht, wenn man die Einschätzung teilt, daß die Bombardierungen kein ihrem Humanitären Zweck dienliches Mittel waren. Denn dann bestand für die, wie es hieß, angefallenen Kollateralschäden keine Notwendigkeit.

6.12   Mein Schluß ist dieser: Selbst wenn die tatsächliche Kosovo-Dimension der von uns zumindest im Frühjahr '99 als ein guter Interventionsgrund akzeptierten medialen „Kosovo-Dimension" entsprochen hätte – die *causa iusta* also tatsächlich gegeben gewesen wäre, dieser *causa* die *intentio* der Intervenierenden sogar entsprochen und zudem wirklich keine andere Alternative bestanden hätte, selbst unter all diesen Unterstellungen verstieß die Art und Weise der Intervention gegen zentale Regeln des *ius in bello* – und ist somit moralisch zu verurteilen.

Literatur

Merkel, R. (Hrsg.): *Der Kosovo-Krieg und das Völkerrecht*, edition Suhrkamp, Frankfurt/M. 2000.

Tesón, F. R.: *Humanitarian Intervention: An Inquiry into Law and Morality*, Irvington-on-Hudson, NY 1997[2].

Dietmar von der Pfordten

Politisches Handeln

Jede Politische Philosophie muß zunächst ihren Gegenstand bestimmen. Wer etwa politisches Handeln als gerecht oder ungerecht bewerten will, muß erst einmal entscheiden, welches Handeln überhaupt als politisches Handeln anzusehen ist. Wie die allgemeine Ethik eine allgemeine Handlungstheorie, erfordert die Politische Ethik eine Theorie politischen Handelns und Entscheidens.

Zwar wird man annehmen können, daß verschiedene Theorien der Politischen Ethik unterschiedlich umfängliche politische Handlungen in einer Gesellschaft legitimieren. Eine libertäre Theorie führt zu einem Minimalstaat, der sich auf Polizei, Gerichte und Militär beschränkt,[1] eine sozialistische Theorie zu einem umfassenden, alle gesellschaftlichen Bereiche durchdringenden Wohlfahrtsstaat. Man kann also mit der handlungstheoretischen Bestimmung der Merkmale politischen Entscheidens nicht auch die ethische Frage nach gerechtem politischem Handeln beantworten. Aber man kann im Rahmen einer Handlungstheorie des Politischen zumindest hoffen, einige Strukturmerkmale politischen Handelns herauszuarbeiten, die dann zum Ausgangspunkt ethischer Rechtfertigung und Kritik werden können.

Eine derartige Handlungstheorie der Politik sollte dabei nicht versuchen, nach einem „Wesen" des Politischen zu fahnden, etwa im Sinne von Carl Schmitts Bestimmung des „Begriffs des Politischen" als Unterscheidung von Freund und Feind.[2] Wesensbestimmungen setzen starke ontologische und erkenntnistheoretische Annahmen voraus, die bereits einer allgemeinen philosophischen Skepsis zum Opfer fallen. Sie verbieten sich für politisches Handeln erst recht, denn politisches Handeln muß als ein kontingentes, durch soziale Zuschreibung von Menschen konstituiertes Phänomen verstanden werden. Man wird deshalb allenfalls die schwächere erkenntnis- und sprachphilosophische Prämisse zu Grunde legen können, daß es sinnvoll

---

[1] Vgl. Robert Nozick, Anarchy, State and Utopia, New York 1974, S. 119.
[2] Carl Schmitt, Der Begriff des Politischen, Nachdruck der 1963 erschienenen Auflage, Berlin 1987, S. 26.

ist, zwischen divergenten sozialen Phänomenen zu unterscheiden und sie verschieden zu bezeichnen. Derartige Unterscheidungen sind besser oder schlechter begründet, ohne damit ein „Wesen" des Politischen treffen zu können und ohne ausschließen zu können, daß sinnvollere Unterscheidungen zu finden sind.

Man mag zweifeln, ob das Phänomen des Politischen statt durch die Frage nach „politischem Handeln" nicht besser durch die Frage nach „politischen Institutionen" zu bestimmen wäre.[3] Es dürfte kaum kontrovers sein, daß das Phänomen des Politischen als institutionelle Struktur zu beschreiben ist, wenn man unter Institution ein durch Konventionen konstituiertes gemeinsames soziales Handeln versteht.[4] Die Grenze zwischen einer Handlungstheorie und einer Sozialontologie des Politischen ist insofern fließend. Der Begriff der Handlung erscheint allerdings gegenüber dem Begriff der Institution basaler und verdeutlicht den intentionalen Charakter der Bausteine, auf denen die Zuschreibung politischer Phänomene aufruht, besser. Man gerät nicht in die Gefahr, das Politische als Schicksal oder überindividuelle Struktur zu fassen und damit gewollt oder ungewollt menschlicher Gestaltung zu entziehen.

Die Frage nach dem Spezifikum politischen Handelns hängt selbstredend mit der Frage nach der Struktur des Staates zusammen. Aber dieser Zusammenhang muß genauer gefaßt werden. Man kann wohl mit dem allgemeinen Sprachgebrauch und der Mehrheit der Theoretiker[5] davon ausgehen, daß jeder Staat auch als politische Gemeinschaft zu qualifizieren ist, nicht jede politische Gemeinschaft aber als Staat. Dann ist die Bestimmung der Merkmale politischen Handelns grundlegender. Um die Merkmale des Staates aufzusuchen, muß man über das politische Handeln bereits Klarheit gewonnen haben. Die Frage nach der Struktur politischen Handelns gewinnt angesichts der Verfallserscheinungen der klassischen Staaten[6] und der Konsti-

---

[3] Vgl. Neil MacCormick/Ota Weinberger, Grundlagen des Institutionalistischen Rechtspositivismus, Berlin 1985; Ota Weinberger, Das philosophische Framework der Handlungs- und Institutionentheorie, in: Rechtstheorie 31 (2000), S. 47–66.

[4] Vgl. zu einem derartigen Verständnis z.B. Raimo Tuomela/Wolfgang Balzer, Collective Acceptance and Collective Social Notions, in: Synthese 117 (1999), S. 176. Tuomela und Balzer verweisen auf engere Begriffe der „Institution", etwa den soziologischen Begriff eines normativen Einflusses, der durch ein hierarchisch strukturiertes System der Ausübung von Macht bewirkt wird oder den spieltheoretischen Begriff des Gleichgewichtspunkts in einem iterierten Spiel.

[5] Vgl. z.B. Max Weber, Wirtschaft und Gesellschaft, 5. Aufl. Tübingen 1985, Kap. 1, § 17, S. 29; Carl Schmitt (Fn. 2), Der Begriff des Politischen, S. 20.

[6] Vgl. Dieter Grimm, Wachsende Staatsaufgaben – sinkende Steuerungsfähigkeit des Rechts, Baden-Baden 1990; Oliver Lepsius, Steuerungsdiskussion, Systemtheorie und Parlamentarismuskritik, Tübingen 1999.

tution neuer supranationaler Gebilde wie der Europäischen Union überdies auch praktische Bedeutung.

In der Politischen Philosophie findet sich kaum eine klare Kennzeichnung politischen Handelns bzw. Entscheidens. Man wird eher bei Konservativen, etwa bei dem schon erwähnten Carl Schmitt,[7] fündig als auf der Linken. Das hat vermutlich folgenden Grund: Während Hobbes und Locke noch relativ deutlich zwischen Politik im Sinne von souveräner Regierung und Gesellschaft im Sinne sozialen Zusammenlebens unterschieden,[8] haben Rousseau, aber auch die Utilitaristen diese Unterscheidung systematisch verwischt. Während bei Hobbes und Locke der Vertrag zur Rechtfertigung politischer Herrschaft diente, wird er erst bei Rousseau zum „Gesellschafts"-Vertrag, zum Vertrag, der die Gesellschaft konstituiert. Der Mensch wird für Rousseau überhaupt erst durch den Gesellschaftsvertrag vom nackten Wilden zum sozialen und vernünftigen Wesen.[9] Politik und Gesellschaft fließen ineinander. Der Utilitarismus verficht dagegen das Ziel der Glücksmaximierung für alle Bereiche des Lebens. Deshalb verliert für ihn die Unterscheidung zwischen einer politischen und einer gesellschaftlichen Sphäre ebenfalls an Bedeutung.

Auch bei John Rawls findet sich keine wirklich klare Abgrenzung politischer Handlungen von anderen sozialen Handlungen. An einer wichtigen Stelle bestimmt er als Gegenstand seiner Gerechtigkeitstheorie: „For us the primary subject of justice is the basic structure of society, or more exactly, the way in which the major social institutions distribute fundamental rights and duties and determine the division of advantages from social cooperation. By major institutions I understand the political constitution and the principal economic and social arrangements."[10] Rawls Theorie einer Verteilung „sozialer Grundgüter" legt im übrigen eine Verschmelzung von politischen Entscheidungen und gesellschaftlichen Realisationen nahe, so daß zwischen Politik und Gesellschaft kaum unterschieden werden kann. Rawls ist gerade

---

[7] Vgl. Carl Schmitt (Fn. 2), Der Begriff des Politischen.
[8] Thomas Hobbes, Leviathan, hg. von Richard Tuck, Cambridge 1991, Kap. 17 a. E., S. 120f.: Das politische Gemeinwesen wird als „civitas" bezeichnet und definiert als „one Person, of whose Acts a great Multitude, by mutuall Covenants one with another, have made themselves every one the Author". In Kapitel 22 werden politische Vereinigungen klar von privaten abgegrenzt. Politische Vereinigungen sind solche, die mit Autorität des Souveräns errichtet wurden. John Locke, Two Treatises of Government, hg. von Peter Laslett, Cambridge 1960, Kap. 1, § 3: „Political Power then I take to be a Right of making Laws with Penalties of Death, and consequently all less Penalties, for the Regulating and Preserving of Property, and of employing the force of the Community, in the Execution of such Laws, and in the defence of the Common-wealth from Foreign Injury, and all this only for the Publick Good".
[9] Vgl. Jean-Jacques Rousseau, Du Contrat Social, Paris 1992, I 8, S. 43.
[10] John Rawls, A Theory of Justice, Oxford 1972, S. 7.

an diesem Punkt noch stark utilitaristisch beeinflußt, während eine weniger auf die Konsequenzen als auf die Handlung bzw. Entscheidung bedachte Theorie zu einer schärferen Abgrenzung politischen Handelns und Entscheidens kommen müßte. Trotz dieser stärkeren Relevanz der Frage nach einer politischen Handlungstheorie für nichtutilitaristische Konzepte, erscheint sie von theorieübergreifendem Interesse.

1. Max Webers Bestimmung des politischen Verbandes

Die differenzierteste Bestimmung politischen Handelns findet sich soweit ersichtlich nach wie vor bei Max Weber: „Politischer Verband soll ein Herrschaftsverband dann und insoweit heißen, als sein Bestand und die Geltung seiner Ordnungen innerhalb eines angebbaren geographischen Gebiets kontinuierlich durch die Anwendung und Androhung physischen Zwangs seitens des Verwaltungsstabs garantiert werden."[11] Dabei ist ein Herrschaftsverband dadurch gekennzeichnet, daß seine Mitglieder „kraft geltender Ordnung Herrschaftsbeziehungen unterworfen sind."[12] „Herrschaft" ist wiederum die „Chance, für einen Befehl bestimmten Inhalts bei angebbaren Personen Gehorsam zu finden."[13] Und „Verband soll eine nach außen regulierend beschränkte oder geschlossene soziale Beziehung dann heißen, wenn die Innehaltung ihrer Ordnung garantiert wird durch das eigens auf deren Durchführung eingestellte Verhalten bestimmter Menschen, eines Leiters und, eventuell, eines Verwaltungsstabes."[14] Die soziale Beziehung ist wiederum dadurch gekennzeichnet, daß „ein seinem Sinngehalt nach aufeinander gegenseitig eingestelltes und dadurch orientiertes Sichverhalten mehrerer"[15] besteht. Sie erfordert die Chance, daß in einer sinnhaft angebbaren Weise sozial gehandelt wird. Soziales Handeln bedeutet schließlich, sich am vergangenen, gegenwärtigen oder künftig erwarteten Verhalten anderer zu orientieren.[16]

Man erhält auf diese Weise folgende Stufung von Merkmalen, die jeweils als einzelne notwendig aber nicht hinreichend sind, um ein Phänomen als politisch zu qualifizieren. Erst wenn sämtliche Merkmale erfüllt sind – so

---

[11] Max Weber (Fn. 5), Wirtschaft und Gesellschaft, § 17, S. 29.
[12] Max Weber (Fn. 5), Wirtschaft und Gesellschaft, § 16, S. 29.
[13] Max Weber (Fn. 5), Wirtschaft und Gesellschaft, § 16, S. 28.
[14] Max Weber (Fn. 5), Wirtschaft und Gesellschaft, § 12, S. 26.
[15] Max Weber (Fn. 5), Wirtschaft und Gesellschaft, § 3, S. 12.
[16] Vgl. Max Weber (Fn. 5), Wirtschaft und Gesellschaft, § 1, S. 11.

kann man Weber verstehen – läßt sich ein Phänomen als politisches Handeln bzw. politische Gemeinschaft oder politische Tatsache interpretieren:

Typ der Handlung	Beispiele	Abgrenzung gegen vorherige Stufe
1) Einfaches, individuelles Handeln	Individuelles Gebet; Aufspannen eines Regenschirms	
2) Soziales Handeln	Rache für frühere Angriffe; Versuch, dem anderen auszuweichen; Schimpfen	Orientieren des eigenen Verhaltens am vergangenen, gegenwärtigen oder künftigen Verhalten anderer.
3) Soziale Beziehung	Freundschaft, Feindschaft, Marktaustausch	Seinem Sinngehalt nach aufeinander gegenseitig eingestelltes und dadurch orientiertes Sichverhalten mehrerer.
4) Verband	Kirche, Verein, Familie jeweils mit Leiter	Eine nach außen regulierend beschränkte oder geschlossene soziale Beziehung, wenn die Innehaltung ihrer Ordnung durch das eigens auf deren Durchführung eingestellte Verhalten bestimmter Menschen garantiert wird: eines Leiters und evtl. eines Verwaltungsstabs.
5) Herrschaftsverband	Familie mit Hausvater	Falls die Mitglieder kraft geltender Ordnung Herrschaftsbeziehungen unterworfen sind. Herrschaft ist die Chance, für einen Befehl bei anderen Gehorsam zu finden.
6) Politischer Verband	Dorfgemeinden, Verbände von Zünften, Staaten	Herrschaftsverband, sofern sein Bestand und die Geltung seiner Ordnungen innerhalb eines angebbaren geographischen Gebiets kontinuierlich durch die Anwendung und Androhung physischen Zwangs seitens des Verwaltungsstabs garantiert werden.

Eine derartige Kaskade von Begriffsbestimmungen erscheint methodisch der richtige Weg, um ein komplexes Phänomen wie politisches Handeln zu analysieren. Denn auf diese Weise wird der Zusammenhang politischen Handelns mit einfacheren Handlungsformen und schließlich mit bloßem menschlichen Verhalten als natürlicher Tatsache expliziert. Man wird mit Weber, Searle und anderen Autoren annehmen dürfen, daß allem politischen wie sonstigem sozialem Handeln einfache Handlungen von Individuen zugrunde liegen (methodischer Individualismus).[17] Einfaches individuelles Handeln setzt gegenüber bloßem Verhalten als natürlicher Tatsache Handlungsintentionen voraus.[18]

Die Kaskadenbildung zur Bestimmung komplexer sozialer Begriffe ist dabei in der ontologischen bzw. erkenntnistheoretischen Auseinandersetzung zwischen Realismus und Antirealismus neutral. Die einzelnen Merkmale können sowohl als Eigenschaften der Realität als auch als bloße Begriffs- bzw. Wortdifferenzierungen aufgefaßt werden. Die Kaskadenbildung wäre sogar mit einer dritten vermittelnden Alternative zwischen Realismus und Antirealismus kompatibel: der Vorstellung eines Kontinuums unserer Wirklichkeitswahrnehmung zwischen weniger durch den Erkennenden bestimmten und mehr durch den Erkennenden bestimmten Phänomenen. Natürliches Verhalten und abgeschwächt einfaches Handeln wären dann stärker betrachterunabhängig, während mit jeder weiteren Merkmalsstufe die Betrachterabhängigkeit zunähme.

Fraglich ist nun, ob die einzelnen inhaltlichen Bestimmungen von Max Webers Kaskade überzeugen können. Zwischen der Ebene der sozialen Beziehung und der des Verbandes fehlen offensichtlich Gemeinschaften, die von ihren Mitgliedern als Gemeinschaften wahrgenommen werden, ohne daß die Ordnung der Gemeinschaft durch einen Verwalter oder Verwaltungsstab garantiert wird. Beispiele wären Gesprächskreise, Bürgerinitiativen, Fanclubs, Skatrunden, Bands, Musiktrios, Fahrgemeinschaften, Wohngemeinschaften, Familien ohne Familienoberhaupt etc. Derartige Gemeinschaften gehen über bloßes wechselseitig aufeinander eingestelltes Sichverhalten im Sinne der Weberschen Bestimmung sozialer Beziehungen hinaus. Sie schließen nach John Searle ursprüngliche Wir-Intentionen der Beteiligten ein, die sich nicht auf deren wechselseitige Ich-Intentionen reduzieren lassen.[19] Die Annahme

---

[17] Vgl. Max Weber (Fn. 5), Wirtschaft und Gesellschaft, § 1, S. 1; John Searle, The Construction of Social Reality, Harmondsworth 1995, S. 121; Robert Nozick (Fn. 1), Anarchy, State and Utopia; John Rawls (Fn. 10), A Theory of Justice.

[18] Max Weber (Fn. 5), Wirtschaft und Gesellschaft, § 1, S. 1; Julian Nida-Rümelin, Kritik des Konsequentialismus, München 1993, S. 29ff.

[19] Vgl. John Searle, Collective Intentions and Actions, in: Cohen/Morgan/Pollack (Hg.), Intentions in Communication, Cambridge 1990, S. 401–415; ders. (Fn. 17), The Construction of

derartiger Wir-Intentionen verläßt dabei das Paradigma des methodischen Individualismus nicht, denn die Wir-Intentionen bleiben Intentionen der einzelnen Handelnden. Sie sind nur – anders als Ich-Intentionen – auf ein gemeinschaftliches Handeln bezogen. Dabei sollen aber nach Searle nicht nur Gemeinschaften, die nach den Vorstellungen der Beteiligten über bestimmte aktuelle Handlungen hinaus reichen, wie Skatrunden, Gesprächskreise und Bands, durch derartige Wir-Intentionen konstituiert werden, sondern bereits die dritte Stufe der Weberschen Kaskade, also bloße wechselseitige soziale Beziehungen, etwa zwei Preisboxer in einem Kampf oder zwei gegnerische Anwälte in einem Prozeß.[20] Die Preisboxer müssen nach Searle auf einer höheren Ebene kollektive Intentionalität aufweisen und kooperieren, um den Kampf durchführen und sich wechselseitig Schläge versetzen zu können. Insofern unterscheidet sich der Boxkampf von der bloßen Attacke gegenüber einem anderen auf der Straße. Man wird kaum bezweifeln können, daß entsprechende soziale Beziehungen neben einer Ich-Intention auch eine Wir-Intention voraussetzen. Aber diese Wir-Intention bleibt im Gegensatz zur Bildung von Gemeinschaften wie Gesprächskreisen oder Skatrunden von vornherein auf die Durchführung der aktualen Handlung beschränkt. Die Boxer würden sagen „wir boxen gegeneinander", aber nicht „wir boxen gegeneinander und bilden dabei ein Team/eine Gemeinschaft". Die Mitglieder eines Gesprächskreises würden dagegen sagen: „Wir diskutieren miteinander und bilden einen Gesprächskreis". Im einen Fall bleibt die gemeinsame Handlung Episode, im anderen Fall ist sie ein Element im Rahmen der Bildung einer Gemeinschaft. Man wird deshalb zwischen handlungsbezogenen und gemeinschaftsbezogenen Wir-Intentionen unterscheiden müssen. Searle trifft eine ähnliche Unterscheidung, spezifiziert sie aber nicht für die Wir-Intentionen, sondern bildet – wie noch erläutert wird – innerhalb der kollektiven Intentionalität die Untergruppe der Statusfunktionen bzw. institutionellen Fakten.

Gegen das Konzept der Wir-Intentionen hat Ulrich Batzer u.a. folgenden generellen Einwand erhoben:[21] Searles Konzeption der kollektiven Intentionen werde dem Umstand nicht gerecht, daß jede einzelne unserer Handlungen je nach ihrer Verknüpfung mit anderen Handlungen Teil eines sehr unterschiedlichen Gemeinschaftshandelns sein könne. Entscheidend für

---

Social Reality, S. 23 ff. Raimo Tuomela, The Importance of Us, Stanford 1995. Zustimmend: Ota Weinberger (Fn. 3), Das philosophische Framework der Handlungs- und Institutionentheorie, S. 63. Vgl. zu einer Kritik: Ulrich Baltzer, Gemeinschaftshandeln. Ontologische Grundlagen einer Ethik sozialen Handelns, Freiburg/München 1999, S. 66 ff.

[20] Vgl. John Searle (Fn. 17), The Construction of Social Reality, S. 24.
[21] Vgl. Ulrich Baltzer (Fn. 19), Gemeinschaftshandeln, S. 71.

die Bestimmung des Gemeinschaftshandelns seien die Anschlußhandlungen anderer Personen. Dem muß aber entgegengehalten werden, daß klar zwischen den sozialontologischen Fakten und der Erkenntnis dieser Fakten differenziert werden muß. Zur Erkenntnis, welche Wir-Intentionen ein Akteur im Einzelfall hat, ist es sinnvoll wie beim pragmatischen Verständnis von Sprechakten Anschlußhandlungen anderer zu berücksichtigen. Diese Anschlußhandlungen anderer sind allerdings schon auf der erkenntnistheoretischen Ebene nicht die einzige Erkenntnisquelle, denn man kann auch andere Handlungen des Akteurs selbst auswerten oder ihn um verbale Aufklärung bitten. Die Anschlußhandlung anderer kann auf der ontologischen Ebene an der ursprünglichen Handlungsintention des Akteurs als sozialontologischem Faktum nichts ändern.

Nun zurück zur Konzeption Max Webers. Max Weber benennt als Unterfälle der sozialen Beziehungen zwar die „Vergemeinschaftung" und die „Vergesellschaftung". Diese werden aber nicht über Gemeinschaftsannahmen der beteiligten Mitglieder definiert, sondern über bestimmte akteursbezogene Qualifizierungen der wechselseitigen Einstellung im Rahmen des sozialen Handelns. In Anlehnung an die Terminologie von Tönnies [22] bestimmt Weber die „Vergemeinschaftung" als „subjektiv gefühlte Zusammengehörigkeit der Beteiligten", während die Vergesellschaftung auf rationalem Interessenausgleich oder entsprechend motivierter Interessenverbindung beruht.[23] Eine „vergemeinschaftende" soziale Beziehung wäre also im Sinne Webers bereits eine Freundschaft, eine „vergesellschaftende" der ökonomische Güteraustausch. In derartigen Fällen ist aber nicht die Entwicklung einer Gemeinschaft mit gemeinschaftsbezogener Wir-Intention nötig.

Gemeinschaften, bei denen die Mitglieder derartige gemeinschaftsbezogene Wir-Intentionen entfalten, manifestieren sich regelmäßig in verschiedenen äußeren Handlungen, etwa einem eigenen Namen, gemeinsamen Erkennungszeichen, einem regelmäßigen Treffpunkt, Kleidungs- und Verhaltensähnlichkeiten etc. Nicht nötig ist für derartige Gemeinschaften die Bestellung eines „Leiters".

Im Hinblick auf politische Gemeinschaften stellt sich die Frage, ob die Notwendigkeit eines derartigen „Leiters" anzunehmen ist. Bevor der Frage nach der Plausibilität dieser und der weiteren Stufen der Weberschen Kaskade nachgegangen wird, soll aber noch ein zweites Stufungsmodell entfaltet werden, von dem schon einzelne Elemente erwähnt wurden: das von John Searle.

---

[22] Ferdinand Tönnies, Gemeinschaft und Gesellschaft, 3. Aufl. Darmstadt 1991.
[23] Max Weber, Wirtschaft und Gesellschaft, (Fn. 5), Kap. I § 9, S. 21.

2. Das Modell sozialer Konstruktion von John Searle

John Searle hat eine der Weberschen Kaskade methodisch sehr ähnliche,[24] wenngleich inhaltlich zum Teil divergierende Stufung vorgeschlagen.[25] Diese Kaskade beginnt auf einer ersten Stufe mit Fakten. Dann folgen auf einer zweiten Stufe mentale Fakten, nicht Handlungen. Da die sozialen Fakten der vierten Stufe aber auf individuelle Intentionen als Teilbereich der mentalen Fakten (3. Stufe) zurückgeführt werden, ist die Basis für die soziale Stufung dem Weberschen Ausgangspunkt bei intentionalen (sinnhaften) Handlungen vergleichbar, wenn auch breiter, da auf das Mentale gestützt. Auf der fünften Stufe tritt nach Searle zu den kollektiven Intentionen eine funktionale Handlungsbestimmung hinzu.[26] Beispiel hierfür wäre ein Schraubenzieher. Die sechste und letzte Stufe der institutionellen Fakten ist schließlich durch eine Realisation der sozialen Funktion allein durch gemeinsame Akzeptanz gekennzeichnet. Beispiele wären Geld, Gerichte, Parlamente etc.

Typ des Faktums	*Beispiele*	*Abgrenzung gegen vorherige Stufe*
1) Fakten	Schnee auf dem Mt. Everest	
2) Mentale Fakten	Schmerzgefühl	Mentale Konstitution
3) Intentionale Fakten	Ich will ein Glas Wasser.	Intentionale Gerichtetheit
4) Soziale = kollektiv intentionale Fakten	Hyänen jagen einen Löwen.	Kollektive Intentionalität
5) Handlungsfunktionale soziale Fakten	Dies ist ein Schraubenzieher.	Kollektive handlungsbezogene Funktionszuweisung
6) Statusfunktionen = Institutionelle Fakten	Geld, Sprache, Gerichte, Regierung	Funktionen werden ausschließlich im Wege der kollektiven Akzeptanz wahrgenommen.

---

[24] John Searle (Fn. 17), The Construction of Social Reality. Searle meint auf S. XII, Weber habe nicht die entsprechenden Werkzeuge zur Entwicklung einer vergleichbaren Theorie besessen und beachtet Webers Theorie deshalb nicht weiter. Er unterschätzt aber meiner Ansicht nach die Ähnlichkeit beider Vorschläge. Vgl. zu einer Kritik der Konzeption von Searle die Diskussion in der Zeitschrift Philosophy and Phenomenological Research LVII (1997), S. 429 ff.

[25] John Searle (Fn. 17), The Construction of Social Reality, S. 121 für die Übersicht. Die Stufung wird im Verlauf des gesamten Buches entfaltet, v. a. in den Kapiteln 1 und 2.

[26] Ich vereinfache das Modell an dieser Stelle etwas, um die für politische Handlungen wesentlichen Bestimmungen herauszupräparieren. Die Zuschreibung von Funktionen kann sich nach Searle nicht nur auf soziale Fakten beziehen, sondern auch auf physikalische oder individuell intentionale Fakten. Vgl. John Searle (Fn. 17), The Construction of Social Reality, S. 121–123.

Politische Institutionen rechnet Searle der sechsten Stufe seiner Kaskade, also den institutionellen Fakten, zu – allerdings ohne sie näher zu spezifizieren.[27] Diese sechste Searlsche Stufe entspricht etwa der oben zwischen die Weberschen Stufen der sozialen Beziehung (3) und des Verbandes (4) eingeschobenen Stufe der einfachen Gemeinschaft. Searles sechste Stufe der institutionellen Fakten ist also wesentlich umfassender und damit unspezifischer ausgestaltet als Webers letzte Stufe des politischen Verbandes. Sie umfaßt auch institutionelle Fakten, wie die Akzeptanz von Geld, die man nicht notwendig als politisch ansehen würde.[28] Searles dritte Stufe der intentionalen Fakten entspricht in etwa Webers erster Stufe der einfachen Handlung, ist allerdings ebenfalls weiter, weil es Intentionen geben kann, die sich nicht in Handlungen realisieren, während Handlungen notwendig Intentionen voraussetzen. Webers zweite Stufe des sozialen Handelns findet bei Searle keine Entsprechung. Webers dritte Stufe der sozialen Beziehung korrespondiert dagegen mit Searles vierter Stufe der sozialen Institutionen. Aber auch hier ist Searles Bestimmung weiter. Während bei Weber tatsächliche Handlungen stattfinden müssen, genügt bei Searle die gemeinsame Intention. In der Realität dürfte jedoch kein Unterschied zwischen beiden Auffassungen bestehen. Denn es ist kaum vorstellbar, wie eine soziale Tatsache ohne eine wenigstens rudimentäre Form gemeinschaftlichen, gegenüber den anderen Teilnehmern äußerlich erkennbaren Handelns entstehen sollte. Dies gesteht Searle auch zu.[29] Es gilt auch für politisches Handeln. Um die Handlungsgrundlage sozialer Phänomene deutlich zu machen, verdient deshalb die engere Webersche Bezeichnung der „Handlung" gegenüber der Searleschen Bezeichnung des „Faktums" den Vorzug – zumindest so lange bis die Stufe einer sozialen Gemeinschaft erreicht ist.

---

[27] Searle behaupte auf S. 124 zwar, daß eine weitere Unterscheidung in linguistische, ökonomische, politische, religiöse Fakten möglich sei, spricht aber nur von einer Unterscheidung by „subject matter".
[28] Allerdings kann eine politische Gemeinschaft die Bildung einer derartigen Institution – wie beim Geld mit Zentralbanken fast überall geschehen – natürlich an sich ziehen.
[29] John Searle (Fn. 17), The Construction of Social Reality, S. 57: „What we think of as social *objects*, such as governments, money, and universities, are in fact just placeholders for patterns of *activities*. I hope it is clear that the whole operation of agentive functions and collective intentionality is a matter of ongoing activities and the creation of the possibility of more ongoing activities."

3. Kritik der Weberschen Stufen 4–6 zur Bestimmung politischen Handelns

Im folgenden sollen nun die Stufen 4–6 der Weberschen Kaskade diskutiert und kritisiert werden:

a) Die Bildung eines Verbands soll nach Weber als nach außen regulierend beschränkte oder geschlossene soziale Beziehung verstanden werden, wenn die Innehaltung ihrer Ordnung durch das eigens auf deren Durchführung eingestellte Verhalten bestimmter Menschen garantiert wird: eines Leiters und, eventuell, eines Verwaltungsstabes.

Die oben in die Webersche Kaskade eingeschobene Stufe einfacher Gemeinschaften mit Wir-Intentionen der Mitglieder, jedoch ohne Leiter, wie Gesprächskreise, Bands, Wohngemeinschaften impliziert nicht, daß derartigen Gemeinschaften nicht auch ein Leiter zugeschrieben werden kann. Gesprächskreise können einen Organisator und Diskussionsführer haben, Bands einen Bandleader, Wohngemeinschaften einen Sprecher. Dann sind sie nicht mehr auf der oben in die Webersche Kaskade eingeschobenen Stufe einfacher Gemeinschaften anzusiedeln, sondern werden zu einem Verband im Sinne Webers.

Allerdings stellen sich in unserem Zusammenhang zwei Fragen: Ist die „Leiterfunktion" durch die „Einhaltung der Ordnung der Gemeinschaft" hinreichend beschrieben? Muß man auch für politische Gemeinschaften eine derartige „Leiterfunktion" annehmen?

Die Einhaltung der Ordnung der Gemeinschaft wird zwar regelmäßig eine zentrale Funktion eines derartigen Leiters sein. Denkbar sind aber noch andere Funktionen: etwa die Durchführung der Zwecke der Gemeinschaft, die zwar in vielen Fällen die Erhaltung oder Verbesserung der Gemeinschaftsordnung voraussetzt, nicht aber notwendig. Wenn etwa der Leiter einer Bürgerinitiative gegenüber den zuständigen Behörden Protest anmeldet, so dient das nicht der Erhaltung der internen Ordnung. Eine weitere Funktion wäre die Vertretung der Gemeinschaft nach außen, etwa wenn Anfragen kommen oder neue Mitglieder beitreten wollen. All diesen funktionalen Handlungen für die Gemeinschaft liegt die Annahme der Repräsentation der Gemeinschaft zu Grunde. Max Weber spricht bei den Qualifizierungen verschiedener sozialer Beziehungen auch davon, daß es solche geben kann, bei denen das Handeln aller oder einiger allen Beteiligten „zugerechnet" werden kann.[30] Dieses Merkmal wird aber nicht zum entscheidenden Kennzeichen der Verbandsbildung. Weber erwähnt nur, daß der Verwal-

---

[30] Max Weber (Fn. 5), Wirtschaft und Gesellschaft, Kap. I, § 11, S. 25.

tungsstab eines Verbands gegebenenfalls normalerweise „Vertretungsgewalt" habe.[31] Die Leitungsfunktion ist primär und die Vertretungsfunktion dient ihrer Realisation. Damit bleibt aber unerklärt, warum ein Leiter als Leiter einer Gemeinschaft anzusehen sein soll. Dies ist nur verständlich, wenn sein Handeln als Handeln *für* die Gemeinschaft zu interpretieren ist. Dies setzt aber wiederum notwendig eine Repräsentationsannahme voraus. Bevor diese Repräsentationsannahme näher analysiert wird, sollen aber noch die Stufen 5 und 6 der Weberschen Kaskade zur Bestimmung des politischen Verbandes diskutiert werden.

b) Ein Verband soll nach Max Weber insoweit, als seine Mitglieder als solche kraft geltender Ordnung Herrschaftsbeziehungen unterworfen sind, Herrschaftsverband heißen.[32] Herrschaft ist die Chance, für einen Befehl bestimmten Inhalts bei angebbaren Personen Gehorsam zu finden.

Diese Festlegung des Politischen auf die Ausübung von Herrschaft ist in mehrfacher Hinsicht problematisch. Man wird zwar nicht bestreiten können, daß politische Repräsentanten in Einzelfällen auch gegen den aktuellen Willen der Betroffenen handeln. Dabei bleiben sie aber immer auch Repräsentant desjenigen, gegen dessen aktuellen Willen sie handeln. D.h. sie handeln in jedem Einzelfall auch für den Betroffenen. Damit verträgt sich der Begriff eines Befehls kaum, denn ein Befehlender befiehlt aus eigener Machtvollkommenheit und nicht als Repräsentant desjenigen, dem befohlen wird. Der Arbeitgeber mag seinem Arbeitnehmer befehlen oder der Bauer seinem Knecht oder der Offizier dem Soldaten. Aber in diesen Verhältnissen stehen die Beteiligten nicht in einer Gemeinschaft mit Repräsentationscharakter wie sie politische Gemeinschaften darstellen.

c) Politischer Verband ist für Max Weber schließlich „ein Herrschaftsverband dann und insoweit, als sein Bestand und die Geltung seiner Ordnungen innerhalb eines angebbaren geographischen Gebiets kontinuierlich durch die Anwendung und Androhung physischen Zwangs seitens des Verwaltungsstabs garantiert werden."[33] Zu der Kennzeichnung als Herrschaftsverband treten für den politischen Verband also noch zwei Merkmale hinzu: das Territorium und die Androhung physischen Zwangs. Beides ist jedoch zweifelhaft. Während man für einen Staat als spezifischen Typ eines politischen Verbandes im Einklang mit Georg Jellineks Dreielementenlehre[34] ohne weiteres die Zuordnung eines Territoriums anerkennen kann, wird man für

---

[31] Max Weber (Fn. 5), Wirtschaft und Gesellschaft, Kap. I, § 12, S. 26.
[32] Max Weber (Fn. 5), Wirtschaft und Gesellschaft, Kap. I, § 16, S. 29.
[33] Max Weber (Fn. 5), Wirtschaft und Gesellschaft, Kap. I, § 17, S. 29.
[34] Vgl. Georg Jellinek, Allgemeine Staatslehre, 3. Aufl. Darmstadt 1959, S. 394 ff.

eine politische Gemeinschaft anders entscheiden müssen. Es spricht nichts dagegen, auch repräsentatives Handeln für Nomadenstämme ohne festes Gebiet als politisches Handeln anzusehen. Umgekehrt können auch nichtpolitische Gemeinschaften ihre Ordnung mit Bezug zu einem Territorium etablieren, etwa Religionsgemeinschaften oder Unternehmen. Das Merkmal des Territoriums ist also weder notwendig noch hinreichend, um politische Gemeinschaften von anderen Gemeinschaften mit Repräsentationscharakter abzugrenzen.

Gleiches gilt für die kontinuierliche Anwendung und Androhung physischen Zwangs. Diese Anwendung und Androhung geschieht auch in anderen Gemeinschaften, etwa Familien oder Banden. Umgekehrt ist es nicht von vornherein ausgeschlossen, daß eine politische Gemeinschaft aus sehr friedliebenden Bürgern besteht und in einer sehr friedliebenden Umgebung situiert ist, so daß die Anwendung und Androhung physischen Zwangs nicht notwendig ist. Auch die Anwendung und Androhung physischen Zwangs erscheint also zur Bestimmung politischen Handelns weder notwendig noch hinreichend. Damit soll nicht geleugnet werden, daß politische Gemeinschaften in der Gegenwart und jüngeren Vergangenheit sehr häufig ihre Ordnung auf einem bestimmten Territorium mit Hilfe von Zwang stabilisiert haben. Für eine empirische Soziologie politischen Handelns, wie sie Max Weber entworfen hat, sind die beiden Merkmale also unverzichtbar. Die Politische Philosophie kann sich dagegen auf die schmalere Basis notwendiger und hinreichender Begriffsmerkmale beschränken. Dazu sollen in Abgrenzung gegenüber anderen nichtpolitischen Gemeinschaften nachfolgend zwei vorgeschlagen werden.

4. Handeln für eine Gemeinschaft: Repräsentation

Politisches Handeln ist mehr als bloßes gemeinschaftliches Handeln oder Handeln im Rahmen einer Gemeinschaft. Politisches Handeln erfordert – wie anderes Handeln *für* eine Gemeinschaft – die Zuschreibung von Repräsentation. Wer den repräsentativen Charakter der Politik mißachtet, kann über ihre zentralen Begriffe, wie Legalität, Legitimität und Souveränität, keine Klarheit gewinnen. Allerdings darf der Begriff der „Repräsentation" dabei nicht wie in der weithin üblichen Unterscheidung in direkte und repräsentative Demokratie verstanden werden. Denn im Rahmen dieser Unterscheidung schrumpft der Repräsentationsbegriff zum bloßen Alternativmechanismus demokratischer Willensbildung. Als Gegenbegriff zur direkten Demokratie wird er auf eine bestimmte Teilklasse einer spezifischen Regierungsform eingeschränkt.

Dies birgt die Gefahr, die Grundstruktur des Phänomens Politik zu verschleiern. Denn: Nicht nur die repräsentative Demokratie ist repräsentativ. Auch die direkte Demokratie ist es in einem bestimmten Sinne – ja sogar jede Form politischer Herrschaft, selbst die Diktatur.

Mit dem Verständnis der Politik als gedanklicher Konstruktion der Realität in Form der Wir-Intentionen zu einer Gemeinschaft ist noch nicht erklärt, warum Politik wesentlich durch eine ganz spezifische derartige Konstruktion gekennzeichnet ist: durch Repräsentation. Denn wir definieren auch nichtpolitische Personen und Sozialhandlungen mit Hilfe gedanklicher Annahmen und Konstrukte: Menschen werden auf diese Weise zu Schauspielern, Rechtsanwälten, Fußballspielern, Priestern etc. Einfaches Handeln wird zu gemeinschaftlichem Handeln bzw. Handeln in Gemeinschaft etwa zum Einkaufen, Gespräche führen oder Handballspielen.

Die Politik unterscheidet sich von derartigen gedanklichen Konstrukten durch ein Spezifikum: Wir gehen davon aus, *daß politische Entscheidungen unsere eigenen Entscheidungen bewußt und gewollt ersetzen, einschränken oder zumindest ergänzen*. Wenn das Parlament ein Steuergesetz beschließt, so bestimmt es, was mit einem Teil unseres Geldes gemacht werden soll. Wenn das Kabinett eine Straßenverkehrsverordnung erläßt, so schränkt es unser Handeln im Verkehr ein. Politik ist also die gedankliche Konstruktion von Handlungen, die über bloßes soziales und gemeinschaftliches Handeln hinausgehen, indem sie unsere einfachen, individuellen Handlungen ersetzen, einschränken oder ergänzen. Das bedeutet: Politik ist wesentlich *Repräsentation* – wobei der Begriff der Repräsentation weit gefaßt wird: d. h. einschließlich aller Handlungen, die auf die Konstitution der Repräsentation hinzielen, also der politische Prozeß der Interessenformulierung, der Wahl, der Machterringung etc. Dabei nimmt an der Peripherie politischer Entscheidungen der Repräsentationscharakter ab und die darunter liegende Basis des gemeinschaftlichen Handelns tritt wieder stärker zu Tage, etwa im Falle des Wählens, Steuerzahlens oder Nutzens öffentlicher Einrichtungen. Besonders stark wird der Repräsentationscharakter im Zentrum politischer Entscheidungen, also dem Zentrum politischer Macht.

Die Annahme einer Repräsentation setzt dabei notwendig eine zweifache Akzeptanz voraus: Der Repräsentierende – also der Politiker – muß die Repräsentation intendieren. Darüber hinaus müssen aber auch die Mitglieder der repräsentierten Gemeinschaft von der Repräsentation ausgehen. Dabei ist natürlich fraglich, wie hoch der Prozentsatz der Akzeptanz bei den Mitgliedern zu sein hat. Man wird jedenfalls eine klare Mehrheit erwarten. Diese Repräsentationsannahmen der Beteiligten müssen schließlich für einen dritten unbeteiligten Beobachter zumindest nachvollziehbar sein.

Die Bestimmung der Politik als Repräsentation gilt auch für den Zwang eines Diktators. Auch ein Diktator repräsentiert die Gruppe von Menschen die er beherrscht, weil er ihre Entscheidungen ersetzt, einschränkt oder ergänzt. Hitlers Entscheidungen muß man deshalb – auch wenn sich alles in einem dagegen sträubt – aus einer deskriptiv-interpretatorischen Perspektive – als politische Repräsentation der Deutschen ansehen. Hitler wollte die Deutschen repräsentieren und eine Mehrheit hat dies akzeptiert. Allerdings impliziert diese *faktische* Repräsentation natürlich keine *normative* Repräsentation. Jegliche faktische Repräsentation muß klar von einer etwaigen *legalen* oder gar *ethisch legitimen* Repräsentation unterschieden werden. Das bedeutet: Auch wenn man zugestehen muß, daß die Entscheidung eines Diktators, wie Hitler, die ihm unterworfenen Menschen faktisch repräsentiert, ist diese Repräsentation noch lange nicht *legal*, d.h. den Gesetzen gehorchend, oder gar *ethisch legitim*, d.h. gerecht und gerechtfertigt. Ein großer Teil der politischen Entscheidungen in Geschichte und Gegenwart waren illegal und illegitim. Trotzdem wird man nicht umhin können, ihren repräsentativen Charakter anzuerkennen. Man muß vielmehr noch einen Schritt weitergehen und realisieren, daß erst die Anerkennung einer Entscheidung als repräsentierend die Frage nach ihrer normativen Legalität und Legitimität in einer gehaltvollen, nichttrivialen Weise auslöst. Denn gerade die Ersetzung der eigenen Handlung durch den Repräsentanten macht die Repräsentation gegenüber dem Repräsentierten rechtfertigungsbedürftig.

Das völkerrechtliche Verständnis von Politik spiegelt den hier vorgeschlagenen weiten Begriff von Repräsentation wieder. Im Völkerrecht wird auch eine diktatorische Regierung als Repräsentant des von ihr regierten Staates anerkannt.

Aber was wäre mit einer idealen direkten Demokratie, also einer Demokratie in der alle Entscheidungen immer direkt von allen Bürgern getroffen werden? Wäre auch sie als repräsentative Politikform in dem bisher erläuterten weiten Sinne zu qualifizieren? Man sollte sich klarmachen, daß real existierende direkte Demokratien in Geschichte und Gegenwart weit hinter dem Idealbild einer permanenten und vollständigen direkten Demokratie zurückgeblieben sind und zurückbleiben. Auch in der attischen Demokratie wurde nur ein gewisser Teil der politischen Entscheidungen von allen Bürgern getroffen. Die Ausführung lag in den Händen von repräsentierenden politischen Organen. Ähnliches gilt in der Gegenwart für die Schweiz. Aber selbst wenn eine permanente und vollständige direkte Demokratie realisierbar wäre, hätte die politische Handlung aller versammelten Bürger ebenfalls repräsentativen Charakter. Auch wenn im Rahmen einer derartigen Versammlung jeder einzelne beteiligt wird, ist die Handlung doch eine andere als wenn er selbst handelt. Denn wenn alle beteiligt sind, so kann er nicht wie bei einer Einzelentscheidung in jedem Fall seinen Willen verwirklichen. Die anderen haben entweder ein Vetorecht oder müssen dem einzelnen zumindest die alleinige Entscheidungsgewalt übertragen. Das bedeutet: Jede kollektive Entscheidung repräsentiert die jeweiligen Teilnehmer in ihren möglichen Einzelhandlungen. Auch eine fiktive permanente und vollständige direkte Demokratie wäre demnach in diesem Sinne immer und notwendig repräsentativ, sofern die Entscheidung in irgend einer Weise normativ fortwirkt, d.h. eine zeitliche Dimension in die Zukunft haben soll. Einfaches gemeinschaftliches Handeln ersetzt dagegen anders als politisches Handeln nicht die individuelle Handlung. Die Probe aufs Exempel ist leicht zu machen: Wenn der einzelne seinen Beitrag zum Handeln einer einfachen Gemeinschaft zurückzieht, dann bricht die Gemeinschaftshandlung zusammen – zumindest für ihn, möglicherweise aber sogar für alle, wenn sein Beitrag zum Gemeinschaftshandeln notwendig für die Ausführung war, z.B. wenn vier Personen ein Klavier transportieren wollen. Anders bei politischem Handeln. Die repräsentierende Gemeinschaft ist derart institutionalisiert, daß einzelne Beiträge einfacher Mitglieder ersetzt werden können, da ja die Repräsentanten für jeden einzelnen handeln. Die repräsentierende Gemeinschaft bricht nicht zusammen, wenn einer sein Handeln zurückzieht.

Politische Organe, die die politische Gemeinschaft in einem engeren Sinne repräsentieren, tun dies in *doppelter Weise*. Sie repräsentieren zum einen die politische Gemeinschaft als Ganzes, zum anderen deren Repräsentation des Handelns des einzelnen. Auf diese Weise läßt sich auch die Unterscheidung zwischen Sozialvertrag und Herrschaftsvertrag in den politischen Vertragstheorien erklären. Jeder der beiden Vertragstypen formuliert ein Modell für eine der beiden Repräsentationsbeziehungen.

Sucht man nach Vertretern für diese Kennzeichnung der Politik als repräsentativ so stößt man auf den Nestor der neuzeitlichen politischen Philosophie: Thomas Hobbes. Hobbes hat in dem wenig beachteten 16. Kapitel seines „Leviathan" mit dem Titel „Von Personen, Autoren und der Vertretung von Dingen", das als letztes Kapitel vor dem 2. Teil zum Staat den 1. Teil zum Menschen abschließt, den repräsentativen Charakter politischer Herrschaft klar herausgestellt: „A Multitude of men, are made *One* Person, when they are by one man, or one Person, Represented; so that it be done with the consent of every one of that Multitude in particular."[35]

Es gab in der politischen Philosophie häufig Versuche, den repräsentativen Charakter politischer Entscheidungen zu überwinden und eine Identität zwischen politischem Entscheider und repräsentiertem Volk zu konstruieren,

---

[35] Thomas Hobbes (Fn. 8), Leviathan, Kap. 16, S. 114.

etwa durch Rousseau oder Carl Schmitt.³⁶ Volk und Herrscher sollten im Idealfall identisch werden. Das Programm einer derartigen Identität von Volk und Herrscher ist häufig als utopisch qualifiziert worden. Aber diese Qualifikation ist zu schwach. Denn sie mißachtet die Grundstruktur des Politischen. Die Identität von Regierten und Regierenden ist nicht utopisch im Sinne eines οὐκ τόπος, eines „Nichtortes" der möglichen Realisierung aufgrund äußerer Umstände. Sie ist selbstwidersprüchlich und deshalb „unpolitisch", weil sie die Bedingungsstruktur des Politischen aufhebt. Identisch kann allenfalls der einzelne mit sich selbst sein (und selbst dies wird in der heutigen Philosophie des Geistes angezweifelt). Wird er Teil einer Gruppe, so impliziert das eine grundsätzlich unaufhebbare strukturelle Nichtidentität mit sich selbst und seinen Entscheidungen als einzelner. Deshalb konnte Rousseau auch nicht erklären, wie die volonté générale gebildet werden soll, ohne auf die volonté de tous zurückzugreifen.³⁷

Man muß angesichts dieser Nichtidentität mit sich selbst in der Gruppe nun aber nicht in Verzweiflung über die ausweglose Entfremdung des einzelnen fallen. Jede Gruppenpartizipation bedeutet eine partielle Entfremdung von sich selbst. Aber sie bietet auch Chancen: In der Gruppe eröffnen sich neue Handlungsalternativen, neue Formen gemeinsamen Lebens und nicht zuletzt eine neue Möglichkeit der Selbstfindung. Die Teilnahme an einer politischen Gemeinschaft bedeutet also jenseits aller kollektiven Entscheidungen immer auch: partielle Selbstentfremdung, verbunden mit der Chance neuer Handlungsalternativen, neuer Gemeinschaftsformen und neuer Wege der Selbstfindung.

5. Handeln für die politische Gemeinschaft

Das Merkmal der Repräsentation ist notwendig, um politisches Handeln von nichtpolitischem zu unterscheiden. Aber es ist als Differenzierungskriterium nicht hinreichend, denn Repräsentation findet sich auch in nichtpolitischen

---

³⁶ Jean-Jacques Rousseau (Fn. 9), Du Contrat Social, S. 40: „A l'instant, au lieu de la personne particulière de chaque contractant, cet acte d'association produit un corps moral et collectif composé d'autant de membres que l'assemblée a de voix, lequel reçoit de ce même acte son unité, son *moi* commun, sa vie et sa volonté. Cette personne publique qui se forme ainsi par l'union de toutes les autres prenait autrefois le nom de *Cité*." Carl Schmitt, Verfassungslehre, 8. Aufl. Berlin 1993, S. 206, 235. Schmitt betont aber an dieser Stelle und auf S. 276 f., daß kein Staat auf alle Strukturelemente der Repräsentation verzichten kann.

³⁷ Jean-Jacques Rousseau (Fn. 9), Du Contrat Social, S. 54: „Il y a souvent bien de la diférence entre la volonté de tous et la volonté générale; celle-ci ne regarde qu'à n'est qu'uni somme de volontés particulières: mais ôtez de ces mêmes volontés les plus et les moins qui s'entredétruisent, reste pour somme des différences la volonté générale."

Gemeinschaften: Der Vorstand und die Aktionärsversammlung repräsentieren das Unternehmen, der Vereinsvorsitzende und die Mitgliederversammlung den Verein, der Papst und der Klerus die Katholische Kirche etc. Mit anderen Worten: Nur eine *bestimmte* Form der Repräsentation kann als politische angesehen werden.

Folgt man der klassischen Dreielementelehre des Staates, so wären Staatsgebiet, Staatsvolk und Staatsgewalt als Repräsentationsobjekte notwendig. Aber auch auf kommunaler Ebene wird repräsentiert. Und auch internationale Organisationen handeln politisch. Der Begriff des Staatsvolks enthält allerdings einen zutreffenden Kern: Wenn politisches Handeln immer nur politisches Handeln ist, weil es Individuen (wenn vielleicht auch nicht ausschließlich) repräsentiert, dann ergibt sich notwendig eine Gruppe von Repräsentierten und – wenn man einen Weltstaat einmal außer acht läßt – von Nichtrepräsentierten. Die Gruppe der Repräsentierten bildet die politische Gemeinschaft.

Auf einem Territorium können verschiedene politische Gemeinschaften agieren. Allerdings setzt dies eine funktionale Segmentierung voraus. Das bedeutet: Eine Person kann einer Gemeinde, einem Landkreis, einem Bundesland, einem Staat, der Europäischen Gemeinschaft und vielleicht in Zukunft einer politischen Weltgemeinschaft als Mitglied angehören. Voraussetzung ist allerdings, daß festgelegt ist, welche Gemeinschaft für welche Sachentscheidung zuständig ist.

Für die Zurechnung von repräsentierendem Handeln als politisch genügt dabei nicht nur die einfache Zuständigkeit für eine bestimmte Sachentscheidung, denn auch die Organe von Unternehmen, Vereinen und Kirchen weisen eine derartige Sachzuständigkeit auf. Das differenzierende Merkmal politischen Handelns ist vielmehr, *daß die Möglichkeit der Letztentscheidung in handlungs- und nicht nur gedankenrelevanten Angelegenheiten mit einer gewissen Aussicht auf Erfolg in Anspruch genommen wird, wobei auch der Prozeß, der auf derartige Entscheidungen hinzielt, miteinzubeziehen ist.*

Gegen dieses Abgrenzungsmerkmal ließe sich einwenden, daß ja auch Privatpersonen oder Privatgemeinschaften letzte Sachentscheidungen auf bestimmten Gebieten treffen. So handeln die Eltern – sofern sie das Sorgerecht innehaben – für ihre minderjährigen Kinder und entscheiden z.B. ob sie einen Kindergarten besuchen oder nicht. Oder der Vorstand eines Unternehmens fällt die letzte Entscheidung über eine Investition. Das Abgrenzungsmerkmal behauptet aber nicht, daß die politische Gemeinschaft *jede* letzte Entscheidung *realiter* trifft. Behauptet wird nur die *Möglichkeit* der politischen Gemeinschaft, jede letzte Entscheidung an sich zu ziehen. Die politische Gemeinschaft beansprucht also in den Augen ihrer Repräsentanten und Mitglieder, aber auch dritter Beobachter, die Definitionskompetenz, wer die letzte Entscheidung in einer Angelegenheit trifft. So hat etwa der deutsche Gesetzgeber den Eltern das Recht eingeräumt, für ihre Kinder letzte Entscheidungen zu treffen. Aber er hat gleichzeitig mit der allgemeinen Schulpflicht, im Hinblick auf den Schulbesuch die letzte Entscheidung für sich in Anspruch genommen. Die Möglichkeit, die Letztentscheidung an sich zu ziehen, besteht aber nicht nur generell wegen der Kompetenz zur Gesetzesänderung, sondern auch im Einzelfall: Wenn die elterliche Entscheidung das Wohl des Kindes verletzt, die Eltern z.B. eine lebensrettende medizinische Behandlung verweigern, kann das Vormundschaftsgericht die Letztentscheidung an sich ziehen und die Entscheidung der Eltern ersetzen (§ 1666 BGB).

Ganz ähnlich ist die Situation beim Beispiel der Investitionsentscheidung eines Unternehmens. Im Rahmen der in der Bundesrepublik institutionalisierten sozialen Marktwirtschaft ist die Freiheit der Unternehmen, über ihre Investitionen selbst zu entscheiden, gewährleistet. Die Organe der Bundesrepublik Deutschland nehmen aber die Möglichkeit mit Aussicht auf Erfolg in Anspruch, die Letztentscheidung an sich zu ziehen. Sollte etwa ein Unternehmen die Produktion von Waffen planen, die in ihrer Explosionskraft Kernwaffen vergleichbar sind, so könnte der Bundestag zur Verhinderung außenpolitischer Störungen oder aus sonstigen Gründen ein Verbotsgesetz erlassen. Eine vergleichbare Möglichkeit die letzte Entscheidung zu übernehmen, haben private Gemeinschaften (Unternehmen, Vereine etc.) gegenüber den politischen Gemeinschaften nicht.

Wir haben mit der Begriffsbestimmung politischen Handelns als Letztentscheidungsmöglichkeit nicht nur eine Schwundstufe des Begriffs der Staatsgewalt, sondern auch des Begriffs der Souveränität vor uns. Souveränität bedeutet, daß die politische Gemeinschaft für *alle* Sachfragen die Letztentscheidungsmöglichkeit sowohl nach innen als auch nach außen in Anspruch nimmt. Der hier vorgeschlagene Begriff politischen Handelns ist dagegen wesentlich schwächer. Es wird nicht gefordert, daß die Letztentscheidungsmöglichkeit von der politischen Gemeinschaft für *alle* Sachfragen in Anspruch genommen wird. Es genügt, daß dies für *eine* Sachfrage geschieht. Deshalb können auch innerhalb einer politischen Gemeinschaft wie der Bundesrepublik Deutschland andere politische Gemeinschaften bestehen. Die Bundesrepublik Deutschland nimmt gemäß Art. 20 I und Art. 28 GG die Möglichkeit zu bestimmten letzten Sachentscheidungen zu Gunsten der Länder und Gemeinden nicht in Anspruch. Auch die Länder und Gemeinden werden also in Deutschland als ursprüngliche und unabgeleitete politische Gemeinschaften verstanden und das repräsentierende Handeln ihrer Organe und Bürger ist ursprüngliches und unabgeleitetes politisches Handeln. Die Gemeinden haben etwa die Möglichkeit zur Letztentscheidung in Angelegenheiten der örtlichen Gemeinschaft. Eine Gemeinde kann z.B. über den

Bau eines Schwimmbades auf ihrem Gemeindegebiet die letzte Entscheidung treffen, ohne daß die Bundesrepublik für sich die Möglichkeit zur Revision dieser Entscheidung in Anspruch nimmt.

Treffen dagegen Behörden der Bundesrepublik Deutschland eine Entscheidung, die von höheren Behörden revidiert werden kann, etwa ein Arbeitsamt die Bewilligung von Arbeitslosengeld, so wird das Arbeitsamt zwar repräsentierend für die politische Gemeinschaft tätig, aber die Letztentscheidungsmöglichkeit fehlt. Als Teil der Behördenhierarchie einer politischen Gemeinschaft, die in dieser Frage die Letztentscheidungsmöglichkeit für sich in Anspruch nimmt, ist die Entscheidung des Arbeitsamts aber trotzdem eine politische Entscheidung.

Supranationale Organisationen wie die Europäische Union, werden zu politischen Gemeinschaften sobald die Mitgliedsstaaten deren Möglichkeit zur Letztentscheidung zumindest für einzelne Sachfragen anerkennen und somit auf ihre eigene Letztentscheidungsmöglichkeit in einzelnen Angelegenheiten verzichten.

Auch die freie Wahl durch den einzelnen Bürger ist eine politische Handlung, da er insofern als Teil der Wählerschaft und damit einfach repräsentierend für die politische Gemeinschaft letztentscheidend tätig wird, wobei niemand die Möglichkeit in Anspruch nimmt, die Wahlentscheidung des Bürgers zu revidieren.

Die Qualifikation der politischen Meinungsbildung in Parteien und Bürgerinitiativen hängt dagegen von der Ausgestaltung ihrer Partizipation am politischen Handeln der fraglichen politischen Gemeinschaft ab. Wenn die politische Willensbildung als private Meinungsbildung definiert wird, so handelt es sich nicht um politisches Handeln im obigen engeren Sinne. Wenn dagegen in einem offenen politischen Gemeinwesen die vorparlamentarische Meinungsbildung als Teil des politischen Willensbildungsprozesses angesehen wird, so mag auch dies als Teil des politischen Handelns der politischen Gemeinschaft in einem weiteren Sinne gelten. Die Grenzen des Begriffs der Politik hängen deshalb in seinen Randbereichen auch von den kontingenten Annahmen in einzelnen politischen Gemeinschaften ab.

Im Hinblick auf die Sachfragen, die der Letztentscheidungsmöglichkeit politischer Gemeinschaften unterworfen sind, wurde im Rahmen der obigen Bestimmung des Abgrenzungsmerkmals für politisches Handeln eine kleine Einschränkung vorgenommen. In Frage kommen nur handlungsrelevante Angelegenheiten, also äußeres Handeln. Gedanken sind der Repräsentation und damit dem politischen Handeln per definitionem entzogen. Politische Gemeinschaften haben allerdings in Geschichte und Gegenwart immer wieder versucht, auch für das Denken der einzelnen Menschen die Letztentscheidungsmöglichkeit an sich zu ziehen. Aber mehr als eine Beeinflussung des

Mentalen ist nicht möglich. Denn wenn jemand anderes anstelle des Betroffenen denkt, so ist es per definitionem nicht der Gedanke des Betroffenen. Das gleiche gilt für andere mentale Zustände wie Gefühle etc.

Im Hinblick auf mentale Zustände ist zwar keine Repräsentation möglich, aber eine Form der Gemeinschaftsbildung. Die Wir-Intentionen können sich z.B. auf bestimmte religiöse Inhalte richten. Die Gemeinschaften sind dann religiöse Gemeinschaften. Sie unterscheiden sich von anderen Gemeinschaften, die sich auf äußeres Handeln beziehen dadurch, daß das Politische den Kern ihrer Gemeinschaftsbildung nicht unter den Vorbehalt der Letztentscheidungsmöglichkeit stellen kann. Dies gilt auch im Falle einer religiösen politischen Gemeinschaft, wie etwa dem Oströmischen Reich. In einem derartigen Fall koinzidiert zwar das religiöse und das politische Element der Gemeinschaftsbildung. Aber die zusätzlichen über die bloße Gemeinschaftsbildung hinausgehenden politischen Merkmale der Repräsentation und Letztentscheidungsmöglichkeit kann die Politik nicht vollständig auf das religiöse Denken der Bürger erstrecken.

Zu betonen ist noch einmal, daß die Qualifikation eines Handelns als politisches Handeln dieses weder als legal noch als legitim auszeichnet. Legal ist eine politische Entscheidung, wenn sie den selbst gesetzten Regeln der politischen Gemeinschaft entspricht, legitim wenn sie jenseits dieser selbst gesetzten Regeln gerecht ist. Wegen ihres Repräsentationscharakters kann eine politische Entscheidung letzteres aber in zweifacher Weise sein: einmal gegenüber denjenigen, die Teil der politischen Gemeinschaft sind und repräsentiert werden und einmal gegenüber denjenigen, die nicht Teil der politischen Gemeinschaft sind und nicht repräsentiert werden, aber von Handlungen der politischen Gemeinschaft betroffen sind. Wenn also ein Staat ausländische Staatsbürger zum Tode verurteilt und hinrichtet, wie etwa die USA dies immer noch tun, dann muß die Legitimität dieses Justizaktes in doppelter Weise geprüft werden. Gegenüber den Betroffenen selbst als Nichtstaatsbürgern der USA und gegenüber den Staatsbürgern der USA in deren Namen die Hinrichtung erfolgte. Nur beim zweiten Aspekt handelt es sich um eine Frage der Repräsentation, die deshalb spezifischen Legitimitätsvoraussetzungen unterliegt. Beim ersten Aspekt ist die Situation derjenigen vergleichbar, wenn eine Privatperson oder eine Gruppe von Privatpersonen einen Menschen tötet.

Als Ergebnis der hier vorgetragenen Überlegungen läßt sich festhalten: Politik besteht in gemeinschaftsbildendem und gleichzeitig repräsentativem Handeln, sofern durch dieses Handeln zumindest für bestimmte Sachverhalte mit gewisser Aussicht auf Erfolg die Möglichkeit einer Letztentscheidung in Anspruch genommen wird, sowie dem Prozeß, der auf derartige Entscheidungen hinzielt. Politisches Handeln läßt sich also in drei Stufen von einfachen sozialen Beziehungen im Sinne der 3. Stufe von Max Webers Kaskade abgrenzen. Es ist:

1. gemeinschaftsbildendes Handeln, d.h. kooperativ,[38]
2. Handeln für eine Gemeinschaft, d.h. repräsentativ
3. und erhebt schließlich den Anspruch auf die Möglichkeit der Letztentscheidung mit Aussicht auf Erfolg, d.h. potentiell ultimativ.

Staaten lassen sich gegenüber bloßen politischen Gemeinschaften durch zwei zusätzliche notwendige, wenn auch möglicherweise nicht hinreichende Merkmale kennzeichnen: (1) eine notwendige Territorialbindung, sowie (2) die Inanspruchnahme der Letztentscheidungsmöglichkeit für alle oder zumindest einen wichtigen und großen Teil von Sachfragen.

Zur abschließenden Illustration soll der hier erarbeitete Vorschlag zur Bestimmung des politischen Handelns noch einmal als Folge aller Stufen aufgeführt werden:

Typ der Handlung	Beispiele	Abgrenzung gegen vorherige Stufe
1) Natürliche Tatsache, Verhalten	Armbewegung	
2) Einfaches, individuelles Handeln	Individuelles Gebet; Aufspannen eines Regenschirms	Handlungsintention
3) Soziales Handeln	Rache für frühere Angriffe; Versuch, dem anderen auszuweichen; Schimpfen	Orientierung des eigenen Verhaltens am vergangenen, gegenwärtigen oder künftigen Verhalten anderer.
4) Soziale Beziehung = Tatsache/partiell gemeinschaftliches Handeln	Freundschaft, Feindschaft, Marktaustausch	Handlungsbezogene Wir-Intention
5) Gemeinschaft	Skatrunde, Wohngemeinschaft, Gesprächskreis, Band	Gemeinschaftsbezogene Wir-Intention
6) Handeln für eine Gemeinschaft/Gemeinschaft mit Repräsentation	Der Vorsitzende eines Vereins kauft für den Verein ein.	Repräsentation
7) Politisches Handeln/ Politische Gemeinschaft	Der Bundeskanzler unterschreibt ein Gesetz, der Richter verkündet ein Urteil, das Parlament erläßt ein Gesetz.	Anspruch auf die Möglichkeit der letzten Konfliktentscheidung wird mit gewisser Aussicht auf Erfolg erhoben.

---

[38] Vgl. zu diesem Begriff als Zentralbegriff der Demokratie: Julian Nida-Rümelin, Demokratie als Kooperation, Frankfurt a.M. 1999.

Literatur

Baltzer, U.: *Gemeinschaftshandeln. Ontologische Grundlagen einer Ethik sozialen Handelns*, Freiburg/München 1999.
Grimm, D.: *Wachsende Staatsaufgaben – sinkende Steuerungsfähigkeit des Rechts*, Baden-Baden 1990.
Hobbes, T.: *Leviathan*, hrsg. von R. Tuck, Cambridge 1991.
Jellinek, G.: *Allgemeine Staatslehre*, 3. Aufl. Darmstadt 1959.
Lepsius, O.: *Steuerungsdiskussion, Systemtheorie und Parlamentarismuskritik*, Tübingen 1999.
Locke, J.: *Two Treatises of Government*, hrsg. von P. Laslett, Cambridge 1960.
MacCormick, N., Weinberger, O.: *Grundlagen des Institutionalistischen Rechtspositivismus*, Berlin 1985.
Nida-Rümelin, J.: *Kritik des Konsequentialismus*, München 1993.
Nida-Rümelin, J.: *Demokratie als Kooperation*, Frankfurt a.M. 1999.
Nozick, R.: *Anarchy, State and Utopia*, New York 1974.
Rawls, J.: *A Theory of Justice*, Oxford 1972.
Rousseau, J.-J.: *Du Contrat Social*, Paris 1992.
Schmitt, C.: *Der Begriff des Politischen*, Nachdruck der 1963 erschienenen Auflage, Berlin 1987.
Schmitt, C.: *Verfassungslehre*, 8. Aufl. Berlin 1993.
Searle, J.: Collective Intentions and Actions. In: *Intentions in Communication*, hrsg. von Cohen, Morgan und Pollack, Cambridge 1990, 401–415.
Searle, J.: *The Construction of Social Reality*, Harmondsworth 1995.
Tönnies, F.: *Gemeinschaft und Gesellschaft*, 3. Aufl. Darmstadt 1991.
Tuomela, R.: *The Importance of Us*, Stanford 1995.
Tuomela, R., Balzer, W.: Collective Acceptance and Collective Social Notions, *Synthese* 117 (1999), 175–205.
Weber, M.: Wirtschaft und Gesellschaft, 5. Aufl. Tübingen 1985.
Weinberger, O.: Das philosophische Framework der Handlungs- und Institutionentheorie, *Rechtstheorie* 31 (2000), 47–66.

Teil IV
Ästhetik

Catherine Z. Elgin

Originals, Copies and Fakes

Abstract

I argue that attribution is a mechanism for locating paintings in bodies of works whose interpretations shed light on one another. Since they are bound to diverge from their originals somewhere, forgeries corrupt those bodies of works, increasing the likelihood of misunderstanding. This raises the question: why is it acceptable to use slides and reproductions in studying art? I argue that because slides and reproductions are recognized as pictures *of* their originals, they are not mistaken *for* the originals. I discuss the semantic and epistemic functions such copies perform and show how they advance understanding.

Things are not always what they seem. Paintings purporting to be by Rembrandt get disattributed. Works ascribed to Vermeer turn out to be forged. Do such changes in attribution matter aesthetically? Or is it, as Arthur Koestler charges, sheer snobbery to care who painted a given work?[1] The painting is, after all, the same painting it always was, whether it was painted by Rembrandt or Droste, Van Meegeren or Vermeer. If we really care about art, we should attend to the painting itself, and not let peripherals distract us. This last claim is uncontroversial. But it does not tell us whether, as Koestler implies, authenticity is peripheral. It is aesthetically irresponsible to look at the caption rather than the picture, to care about the attribution instead of the work, to let the reputation of the artist determine the value of the painting. But we should not too quickly conclude that authenticity is aesthetically irrelevant. Even if it is wrong to focus on the artist instead of the work, it may be right to allow considerations of authorship to inform our responses to the work. The question is then whether it is appropriate to look at a work differently, or see different things in it, if we understand it to be or not to be by Rembrandt.

---

[1] Arthur Koestler, *The Act of Creation*, New York: MacMillan, 1969, p. 404.

Koestler's concern is no doubt fueled by the recognition that disattributed paintings typically plummet in value – not just in financial value, but in what purports to be aesthetic value as well. People seem to think less of *Anna and the Blind Tobit* as a work of art once it is attributed to Dou rather than Rembrandt. This does not seem fair. Nor does it seem inevitable. Rather than thinking less of the painting, perhaps we should think better of Dou. Indeed, one side-effect of the reattributions of the Rembrandt Research Project may be a major reassessment of the general level of talent in Rembrandt's circle. The question I want to focus on, though, is not primarily a question about value. I do not want to argue that we should think less of *Anna and the Blind Tobit* once we conclude that it is not by Rembrandt, only that we should think differently about it.

It would be nice if my argument began with uncontroversial premises and led inexorably to the conclusion I favor. Unfortunately, it does not. Little in aesthetics is beyond dispute. Presuppositions tend to be tendentious. Arguments branch, and the attractiveness of alternatives varies with the background commitments used in assessment. None of this is surprising, but it does suggest that there is no hope of conclusively solving any one problem in aesthetics without developing and successfully defending a comprehensive philosophy of art. I am not going to attempt anything nearly so ambitious. Rather I will argue from Goodmanian premises and attempt to show the attractiveness, if not the inevitability, of particular choices, when choices must be made. My goal is not so much to show what Goodman's theory contributes to aesthetics as how aesthetics, as Goodman conceives it, contributes to epistemology.

My efforts might seem superfluous. Anyone who has read Chapter III of *Languages of Art* knows that Goodman thinks authenticity matters and has a pretty good idea why he thinks it matters. Anyone inclined to accept Goodman's account might consider the matter closed. But the account faces a pair of potentially devastating objections. The first is that it does not evade Koestler's criticism. If authorship is aesthetically irrelevant, then the fact that one mistake about authorship is apt to engender other mistakes about authorship should be aesthetically irrelevant as well. The second is that Goodman's reasons for rejecting forgeries seem to discredit the practice of using reproductions and copies in studying art and art history. Since this widespread practice appears pedagogically valuable, the tension between theory and practice, if unresolved, would seem to tell against Goodman's position. I will argue that Goodmanian aesthetics has the resources to rebut these objections. But my aim is not just to save Goodman from a pair of embarrassing gaffes. That would be of limited interest. I suggest that the payoff is considerably greater. For a proper understanding of how misattributions mislead, and why copies and reproductions do not, shows something of the rich texture of the epistemological conception of aesthetics, and provides additional reason to take it seriously.

Discussions of the aesthetic importance of authenticity are often cast as worries about forgery. But forgery *per se* should not be the locus of concern. Let us call someone who is qualified to tell whether a work of art is authentic an authenticator. A work of art is a forgery just in case an authenticator purports that it is authentic, knowing or having good reason to believe that it is not. The authenticator need not be the artist who painted the forgery. As I am using the term 'forgery', a work can be a forgery even if the artist was no forger. A dishonest dealer or curator or collector who passes off a copy as an original, or passes off the work of one artist as the work of another converts the picture in question into a forgery. A forgery is in effect a lie. It conveys false information with the intent to deceive. All misattributions convey false information, but not all are intended to deceive. Whenever an authenticator purports that a work is authentic, and in fact it is not, that work is misattributed. Authenticators are not infallible. Many misattributions are honest mistakes. Ethically, the difference between lies and honest mistakes is crucial. Epistemologically, it is not. For both misinform. Whatever the intent behind them, unrecognized misattributions impart false beliefs.

Imparting false beliefs is epistemologically objectionable, regardless of motive. Since, like Goodman, I construe aesthetics as a branch of epistemology, I suggest our concern should be with misattributions generally, not just with those that are intended to deceive. But even if we adopt this stance toward aesthetics, it does not immediately follow that misattribution is an aesthetic mistake. To show that misattribution matters aesthetically, we have to demonstrate not merely that it engenders false beliefs or inhibits true beliefs about works of art, but also that at least some of those beliefs concern aesthetic properties or functions of the works. Not all false beliefs about art do so. The false belief that a given painting once passed through the Gare du Nord has, as far as I can tell, no aesthetic import. Perhaps the identity of the artist, like the route to the gallery, is a matter of aesthetic indifference. I will not try to settle that question here. For whether or not misattributions are themselves aesthetic mistakes, if they lead to mistakes that are manifestly aesthetic, we have good aesthetic reasons to care about authorship.

A belief is misleading to the extent that it occasions misunderstandings. It is aesthetically misleading to the extent that it occasions misunderstandings about works of art functioning as such. So to show that misattributions are aesthetically misleading, we need to show (1) that they engender misunderstandings, and (2) that some of those misunderstandings bear on the aesthetic functions of works of art – either the misattributed works or others. The first part is relatively easy. The second is not, for there is wide disagreement about how works of art function. As a result, there is disagreement about which misunderstandings qualify as aesthetic misunderstandings. Rather than trying to settle that issue, I will attempt to show that some of the misunderstandings misattributions engender concern matters that are widely conceded to fall within the aesthetic realm.

Faced with a work of doubtful provenance, the problem of authentication is a problem of projection. Given a precedent class consisting of works acknowledged to be by N, an authenticator identifies features that she takes to be distinctive of N's work. She then attempts to project those features onto the work in question. If the work shares enough of the distinctive features, and lacks features which the precedent class shows to be decidedly uncharacteristic of N, it will be counted as an N and incorporated into the precedent class against which further cases will be judged. The constitution of the precedent class is thus crucial. If the precedent class is corrupt, features that are not features of N's work, or that are not distinctive features of N's work, may be used as a basis for projection. Projection from a corrupt precedent class is apt to lead to further misattributions.[2]

This might be doubted. It assumes that the misattributed picture either lacks the distinctive features of N's work or that it has distinctive features that are not distinctive of N's work. The mere fact that the picture is not by N, one might argue, is insufficient to show that. Deceptive forgeries and other unrecognized misattributions owe their acceptance to the fact that they evidently have the requisite features. That is what makes them deceptive. I want to set this worry aside for now. Unless we can rebut the charge that authenticity is aesthetically irrelevant, we need not address it. Let us then provisionally concede that a corrupt precedent class increases the likelihood of further errors.

The problem is not just that one misattribution increases the probability of a second. Errors compound, for each accepted work alters the precedent class against which further pictures will be judged. The greater the number of Van Meegerens that we accept as Vermeers, the more likely it is that the next Van Meegeren will be accepted as a Vermeer.[3] Eventually, Van Meegerens could dominate the precedent class, making new Van Meegerens more likely to be accepted as Vermeers than that newly discovered works by Vermeer. This, no doubt, is a serious practical and epistemological problem. The question is whether it is an aesthetic problem. Goodman takes for granted that it is. But if, as Koestler's challenge implies, it makes no aesthetic difference who

---

[2] Nelson Goodman, *Languages of Art*, Indianapolis: Hackett, 1976, pp. 109–110.
[3] Goodman 1976, p. 111.

painted one work, it is hard to see why the fact one misattribution leads to other misattributions should concern aesthetics.

In matters of attribution, we try to be as precise as we can responsibly be. But not all attributions are maximally precise. A glance at imprecise or unspecific attributions sheds light on how attributions function. The attribution of the Flemish Altarpiece to the Master of the Flemish Altarpiece is utterly uninformative. The caption simply tells us that whoever did it did it. But to learn that a second panel was also painted by the Master of the Flemish Altarpiece is far from uninformative. Once we know that the two works were painted by the same artist, we can look from one to the other for interpretive cues. We can investigate how a particular artist approached his subjects, what his concerns were. We can learn about his technique, his talents and limitations, his imaginative range, and so forth. By playing the works off against each other, we often discover aspects that we would otherwise overlook. Features that initially seem insignificant acquire salience when we find or fail to find resonances in other works by the same artist. As more pictures come to be accepted as by the same artist, we gain access to evidence for increasingly nuanced, more highly textured interpretations of individual works. Whether we know the name of the artist makes no difference.

For example, an ambiguous light source is often considered a weakness in a genre painting. But if the other works the artist painted in the same period reveal that he is adept in his treatment of light, we might hesitate to draw that conclusion. Knowing that he usually provides a clear indication of where the light is coming from, we wonder why he fails to do so in this work. This prompts us to attend to the function of light in the painting. We may conclude that the ambiguity plays a metaphorical role that converts it from a weakness to a strength. We discover the metaphor then only because the artist's other works give us reason to question the seemingly obvious reading of this one. Still, one might argue, knowledge of the artist's other works is only of heuristic value here. If we seriously attended to the role of light in the painting in question, we would have ample resources for our interpretation. This may be so. But even if we could vindicate our interpretation without appeal to the artist's other works, it does not follow that the painting's membership in a particular body of work is aesthetically irrelevant. Knowing that the work was painted by the artist who painted certain other works equips us to formulate and test interpretive hypotheses that might otherwise never come to mind.

In other cases, the relationship among the various works of a single artist is even more intimate. Cross references or thematic links sometimes connect distinct works. Suppose, for example, that like other religious artists of his time and place, an artist painted saints with halos. There would be nothing remarkable about that. But as we consider his works in light of one another, we realize that not all his halos are alike. They vary in color, intensity, and definition. We may come to understand that the variations are not idle. Nor are they just separate commentaries on the characters of the particular saints who wear the different halos. Rather, they constitute a sustained meditation on variations in the strength, stability, and intensity of virtue. Although all saints are holy, the artist's œuvre suggests, the depth of their holiness varies and their hold on holiness is not equally firm. Taken in isolation, no one of the pictures suggests or sustains such a reading. But seen in the context of the other works, each one admits of, and gains resonance from this interpretation. If we insist that each painting be considered only in isolation, we rule out in advance this sort of understanding of an artist's works. We do something similar in philosophy as a matter of course. When interpreting a passage from Kant, we consider it in light of relevant passages in Kant's other works. If we had to consider each work in isolation, we would have a far more impoverished and tentative understanding of both the individual works, and Kant's entire œuvre. I suggest that the same holds in the interpretation of works of art. It is, I believe, no more reasonable to demand that we interpret each of Rembrandt's works in isolation, than it is to demand that so interpret each of Kant's.

As I have stated them, the examples highlight the significance of the fact that several paintings are by the same artist. With minor revisions, they could be used to show the significance of works of the same period or the same school. Attributions like 'School of Caravaggio', or 'Fourteenth Century Siennese' inform our readings of the works that bear them. If we know what artists in those groups were up to, what techniques they employed, what issues gripped them, what resources they had, and how they adapted, rejected, or positioned themselves with respect to one another's works, we have some idea how to look at their paintings. So do more specific attributions. Knowing where a work fits in an artist's œuvre may contribute to our understanding of it and of his other works. We see how his style develops, what is gained and lost and modified along the way.

One could grant everything I have said about the cognitive value of knowing what artist, school, or tradition a painting belongs to, and still deny that I have demonstrated the *aesthetic* relevance of attribution. Why not say that my points only show the importance of attribution for art history? After all, a variety of facts about when and where and why a work was done are historically significant. But that does not make those facts aesthetic. The price of canvas in sixteenth century Ghent may figure in the explanation of a painting's dimensions, but that would hardly show that the price of canvas functioned aesthetically. The difference is this: knowing the œuvre, school, or tradition a work belongs to aids us in interpreting the symbols that constitute the work.

An example may bring this out. Although *The Polish Rider* has long been attributed to Rembrandt, many art historians expect the Rembrandt Research Project to disattribute it. The central figure in the painting is a young, vibrant rider on a moribund, skeletal horse. There are many ways of interpreting the painting. Some are viable regardless of who painted it; others, I suggest, are not. Despite the uncertainty about its authorship, art historians generally agree that *The Polish Rider* was painted in about 1655, a time of personal turmoil, financial difficulty, and great creativity in Rembrandt's life. The church was criticizing the artist for his irregular relationship to Hendrickje Stoffels, he was going bankrupt, and he was painting masterpieces.[4] A young, vital rider, full of promise and looking for adventure, astride a horse nearly dead on its feet is a powerful metaphor for Rembrandt's situation. It is even more powerful if we read the picture as a self-portrait. *The Polish Rider* admits of such a reading if it was painted by Rembrandt. If it was not, then clearly we ought not construe it as a Rembrandt self-portrait. Our understanding not only of *The Polish Rider*, but also of Rembrandt and his other works is affected by whether we think he made that metaphor. For that metaphor, if Rembrandt made it, affords insight into his conception of himself as an artist. Inasmuch as many of his works are profoundly self-reflective, insights about his artistic self-image should inform our interpretations of these other works as well. Either way there are dangers. If we wrongly think he did, or wrongly think he did not paint *The Polish Rider*, our understanding of Rembrandt's œuvre will be skewed. It would not be enough to show that *The Polish Rider* displays the distinctive features of a Rembrandt. The appropriateness of the interpretation I have suggested depends on whether or not Rembrandt actually painted the work.

Although telling, the example may seem too limited to be helpful. Something is a self-portrait only if it is painted by its subject. We cannot then know the identity of the subject of a self-portrait and know that it is a self-portrait without knowing about who painted it. Authenticity plainly matters in such cases. Still, this seems to be a special feature of self-portraits that does not extend to still lifes, genre scenes, landscapes or abstracts. But as we have seen, the consequences of taking a work like *The Polish Rider* to be or not to be a self-portrait spill over to affect the interpretations of other works. So the point may be less narrow than it looks. Moreover, if the important question is whether Rembrandt made a particular metaphor at a certain point in his life, then the issue of putative self-portraits is peripheral. One could ask of any

---

[4] Anthony Bailey, *Responses to Rembrandt*, New York: Timken, 1994, p. 106.

symbol in any work, whether a particular artist's having used that symbol in that work affects how his other works should be interpreted. Whenever the answer is 'yes', the authenticity of the work containing that symbol matters aesthetically.

I have not yet shown that the answer is generally 'yes'. So let us extend our discussion of *The Polish Rider*. Suppose, for the moment, that *The Polish Rider* is not by Rembrandt, but is a metaphorical portrait of Rembrandt by one of his followers. Call the actual artist X. X was evidently steeped in Rembrandt's style, and was knowledgeable about and sensitive to Rembrandt's circumstances. He used his knowledge, sensitivity, and skill to paint an extraordinarily empathetic portrait. He has, as it were, feigned the first person perspective, painting the metaphorical portrait "as though from the inside". The fact that experts are undecided about whether the work is by Rembrandt shows that he did an extraordinarily good job. Those who consider undetected misattributions aesthetically equivalent to originals might argue that he did a good enough job that it makes no aesthetic difference whether the work was painted by X or by Rembrandt, hence that it makes no aesthetic difference whether it is a genuine self-portrait or a successful pseudo-self-portrait. Since it is close enough to Rembrandt's work in all relevant respects, the insights we glean about Rembrandt and his work are exactly the ones we would have gleaned if Rembrandt had painted *The Polish Rider*.

The problem, as Goodman makes clear, is that we have no standard of *close enough*. Because paintings belong to syntactically and semantically dense symbol systems, there is no lower bound beyond which further differences do not matter. In principle, any difference between symbols and any difference between referents, no matter how small, may be significant. Because paintings belong to relatively replete symbol systems, we can never purport to have identified all the dimensions, literal and metaphorical, along which a given symbol functions.[5] A Rembrandt self-portrait is a vivid illustration, since both the self-understanding and the ways of exhibiting that self-understanding seem infinitely nuanced in Rembrandt's portrayals of himself. But the same point applies to other paintings. In a dense and replete system, there is no standard for being close enough to the way Monet painted water lilies or to the way Mondrian painted squares that further differences do not matter. If we wrongly incorporate a picture of water lilies into Monet's œuvre, we increase our vulnerability to misunderstanding Monet's works, and the works of other artists he was reacting to or who were reacting to him. The point

---

[5] Goodman 1976, pp. 252–255.

is not that we need to know the name of the artist who painted a particular picture. What we need to know is the bodies of work the picture belongs to.

Languages of Art contends that works of art belong to symbol systems that are similar in structure to languages. Goodman details the syntax and semantics of such systems. I want to focus on pragmatics, for context affects the functions of non-linguistic symbols as well as linguistic ones. I contend that attributions function aesthetically because (a) attributions locate works in an aesthetic context, (b) the context within which a symbol functions influences its interpretation, and (c) interpretation of works of art is an aesthetic activity.

Let us look briefly at language. Utterances and inscriptions are interpreted in context. To understand a linguistic token, we typically need to know something about who produces it, for whom it is produced, what is presupposed, and what is at issue. Context informs content, even for simple declarative sentences like 'The cat is on the mat'. Which cat? Which mat? Why are you saying this to me now? How does this utterance contribute to the ongoing discussion? Is it, for example, a description, a warning, an apology, or a threat? Contextual factors affect whether the extension assigned to this token of 'cat' consists only of house cats, or includes lions, tigers, panthers, and so on. In deciding what extension to assign, the hearer or reader needs to know what extension the speaker assigns to the term, and what extension the speaker thinks the hearer assigns to it. A decontextualized token, even if syntactically and semantically unproblematic, is apt to yield a sparse and tentative interpretation.

We do not necessarily need to know the name of the person who produced the token. But we often need to know that it was produced by the same speaker who produced various other tokens, that it was produced in a linguistic context where certain linguistic resources were available, certain issues were in contention, certain presuppositions were in place, and certain other claims had already been made and accepted or challenged. We may also need to know that it was produced in a particular natural and social milieu. Obviously, merely knowing the name of the utterer is not enough. It would hardly help me to know that Ralph uttered 'The cat is on the mat', if I did not know Ralph. But if I already know a good deal about Ralph, about his background assumptions and linguistic proclivities, the news that he uttered the sentence could be useful, not merely for assigning responsibility for the utterance but also for supplying valuable interpretive cues. Attuned to Ralph's interests, circumstances, assumptions, and tendencies, I have resources to draw on to make sense of the utterance. He cannot tell a possum from a house cat, so we should not assume he has identified the species correctly. He would never call a prayer rug a mat, so we can be reasonably confident that he is right on that score. He is not given to idle asides about of the distribution of wildlife in the neighborhood, so we should take it that he takes it that his comment is relevant to our present concerns. If the literal semantic content is not relevant, we should look for metaphors or implicatures. This is familiar in the study of language. It also applies to the study of symbols of other kinds. Knowing the œuvre, school and tradition a painting belongs to equips us with resources for understanding what symbols it contains, and how they function.

Granted, the brute fact cited on the caption does not do much to advance understanding. If I know nothing of Vermeer, then the fact that a painting bears the caption 'Vermeer' is no more helpful than knowing that Ralph said 'The cat is on the mat', when I am unacquainted with Ralph. But if I have some understanding of the artist, the tradition, or the school, I can activate that understanding, and interpret the painting in light of it. I know what sorts of presuppositions were apt to be made, what sorts of techniques were available, what sorts of aesthetic options were considered live options, and so on. When we consider a work like *The Girl with a Pearl Earring* against the background of the work of Vermeer's contemporaries, we find that using fine lines to define forms was a live option. We may not only notice that Vermeer failed to exercise that option,[6] but begin to understand what effect this had. We come to realize that Vermeer achieved his pellucid clarity by means of blurriness, and begin to wonder why and with what effect he did so. Considering Vermeer's paintings in light of the works of his contemporaries does not dictate an interpretation, but provides resources for interpretation. Such a stance may suggest metaphors, motifs, or themes to be found in the work. In language, a great deal goes without saying, being presupposed by all parties to an exchange. But exactly what goes without saying varies from one linguistic context to the next. Similarly, in painting, much goes without showing. But exactly what remains tacit varies from one tradition, artist or school to the next. Attribution, I suggest, is a mechanism for locating a work in aesthetically significant classes: the class of works by the same artist, by artists in the same school, by artists in the same studio, and so on. There are good reasons for wanting to know which such classes a work belongs to, for it is by reference to common assumptions and points of disagreement within and across such classes that we begin to make sense of what functions the work performs and how it performs them. The information that attribution supplies to someone knowledgeable about such classes informs and enriches interpretation of a work.

My emphasis on the importance of context is not a claim that the way a work functioned in its original context determines how it is to be interpreted

---

[6] Arthur K. Wheelock, Jr. *Jan Vermeer*, New York: Harry N. Abrams, Inc., 1998, p. 118.

now. Nor is it a claim that an interpretation that accords with its original functions is preferable to other interpretations that might be given of it. But if we know the context, we have some idea what the artist was trying to do, what parameters he was working within, what obstacles he faced, and so on. This may give us some purchase on the work. The same thing holds in language. People sometimes say things that they do not mean. But to recognize that an utterance is irrelevant or out of character, or is a slip of the tongue or a malapropism, or to recognize that the speaker said something more or less or different from what he intended, we need to know what the speaker would be apt to say in that context. That requires an understanding of the speaker and the context. My claim then is not that context dictates the correct interpretation of a work of art, or that the interpretation that fits best with the context in which a work was produced is always to be preferred. Rather it is that context supplies potentially valuable resources for the interpretation of works of art, resources that we would – or at least very well might – otherwise lack. If this is so, and if attribution is a vehicle for providing information about aesthetically relevant features of context, then attribution is aesthetically relevant.

This leads to the second problem. I have argued that forgeries and other misattributions are aesthetically objectionable because they are misleading. They are misleading because they inevitably diverge from the originals, and no divergence is small enough to be aesthetically negligible. In that case it seems, copies, slides, and other reproductions should be even more objectionable. They too inevitably diverge from the originals they purport to reproduce. Indeed they diverge far more than deceptive misattributions do. If the practically imperceptible differences between the *Mona Lisa* and a deceptive forgery are grounds for rejecting the latter, shouldn't the glaring differences between the *Mona Lisa* and its reproduction in Jansen's *History of Art* be even better grounds?

The difficulty is that copies, slides, and other reproductions have long been regarded as pedagogically valuable tools in the study of art. Throughout history, art students have learned technique by copying acknowledged masterpieces. Students of art history and criticism spend their formative years staring at reproductions and slides. Connoisseurs, collectors, and curators pore over transparencies and photographs of works they are interested in. Major museums unblushingly display their collections of Roman copies of Greek statues. If Goodman is right, these behaviors may seem benighted. If a deceptive forgery of the *Mona Lisa* is apt to engender misunderstandings, it would seem that slides and other reproductions should do so as well. If, on the other hand, such reproductions afford epistemic access to the ideas embodied in the *Mona Lisa*, then it would seem that the forgery should do so too. Can we in good conscience continue to disparage forgeries and other misattributions on epistemological grounds and maintain that reproductions of various sorts provide insight into works of art?

I think we can. The most glaring difference between a deceptive forgery and a slide of the *Mona Lisa* is that the forgery is practically indistinguishable from the original, while the slide obviously is not. The important difference, however, lies elsewhere – in the symbolic functions of the two images. Since the forgery pretends to be the original, it purports to perform all and only the symbolic functions of the original. If it were successful, it would function as the *Mona Lisa* does – as a picture of a woman with an enigmatic smile, not as a picture of a picture. The slide, on the other hand, is and presents itself as a picture of the *Mona Lisa*. Since the *Mona Lisa* does not denote itself, the slide thus performs at least one referential function that the original does not. The difference is even more vivid in the case of non-representational works. Mondrian's *Broadway Boogie-Woogie* does not denote. Neither does a forgery of *Broadway Boogie-Woogie*. But a slide of *Broadway Boogie-Woogie* denotes the painting. It is a picture *of* the painting. Whatever else they do then, slides and other reproductions denote the works they reproduce.

The difference is real. But is it relevant? Goodman's objection to forgeries concerns the possibility of performing all the symbolic functions of the original, not performing only those functions. Because paintings are dense and replete, Goodman maintains, a forgery's aspiration to perform all the symbolic functions of the original cannot be met. If a reproduction shares that aspiration, then whether or not it performs additional symbolic functions, it inevitably fails to achieve its goal.

But we need not think that merely because a reproduction is expected to look like the original it either does or purports to perform the same symbolic functions as the original. Clearly such is not the case. The slides, transparencies, and photographs that connoisseurs and students study are images that differ in obvious ways from their originals. Normally there are significant differences in size. The image projected in the lecture hall is typically vastly bigger than the original; the image in the art history text is apt to be significantly smaller. The slide differs from the original in luminosity, tone, and texture as well. Books about art contain black and white photographs of colored paintings. There is no pretense that slides and photographs are pictorial equivalents of their originals. Whatever we mean in saying that they look like the originals, we do not mean that they are visually indiscriminable from the originals. The goal of such images is not to duplicate but to depict to the works of art they denote. They do so, not by performing either all or only the symbolic functions of the originals, but by performing a range of symbolic functions that afford avenues of epistemic access to the originals.

Reproductions function in art in the way that paraphrase functions in language. Both *re*-present, that is, present again, the material they concern. Let us look briefly at the linguistic case. Not every description of an utterance or inscription constitutes a paraphrase. If I report that Ralph said something foolish or that he said something in French, I describe his utterance but do not paraphrase it. A statement is a paraphrase only if it affords information about what is said. A paraphrase conveys content. Similarly, a picture of a painting is a reproduction of it only if it conveys the painting's content. That being so, in what follows, I use the term 'paraphrase' in an extended sense to comprehend both linguistic paraphrases and pictorial reproductions.

Many philosophers believe that one locution paraphrases another only if the two express the same proposition. In that case, they are analytic equivalents. Exactly what propositions are is far from clear. So it is hard to know whether two locutions express the same proposition or two similar ones. Nor is analytic equivalence a particularly perspicuous notion. But we need not enter into debates about such matters here. For it is obvious that many acceptable paraphrases do not contain anything like analytic equivalents of the passages they concern. This is what makes paraphrase a useful device for explication, clarification, disambiguation, and diplomacy. Moreover, in the arts at least, equivalence of literal descriptive content (which is what the standard criteria purport to deliver) is not enough. A paraphrase of a poem that failed to reflect dramatic tension or emotional tone would normally be unsatisfactory.

What is valuable in the familiar accounts is not the appeal to propositions or analyticity, but the recognition that a paraphrase must express, not merely describe or possess, the content it conveys. Both the notions of content and expression need elaboration. A symbol's content consists of what it symbolizes. As we have seen, symbolization can be multifaceted and complex. Literal and figurative, denotational and exemplificational, direct and indirect reference all figure in the contents of verbal and pictorial symbols. To be sure, not every symbol refers in all of these ways. To determine the content of a symbol requires deciding what modes of reference it employs, and for each of the modes it uses, what it refers to. Because verbal and pictorial symbol systems are semantically dense, there are multiple admissible candidates for the referent of a given symbol. There is no basis for choosing one rather than any of the others as symbol's referent. Because of the capacity of such symbols for repleteness, a given symbol might symbolize along several dimensions at once. Exactly which aspects symbolize may also be undecidable. As a result, a verbal or pictorial symbol admits of multiple, divergent interpretations, each of which assigns it a different content.

The susceptibility to a variety of divergent interpretations might seem to make paraphrase impossible. The goal of conveying the content of a symbol beset with indeterminacy may seem as realizable as that of delineating the precise boundaries of a cloud. But to say that a paraphrase conveys its subject's content is not to say that any single paraphrase exhausts its subject's content. An oral paraphrase of a technical report might slight the mathematical details that the original imparts through complex equations. A paraphrase for a lay audience might eliminate technical jargon entirely, substituting metaphors where needed to convey the gist. One paraphrase might highlight the magnitude of the finding; another, the meticulousness of the methodology. Yet another might focus on matters of style, treating the paper as a model of scientific writing. Paraphrases are interpretations. Each expresses content that it shares with its subject. But a single paraphrase is not, and does not purport to be, comprehensive or unique. So it neither does nor purports to convey exactly what its subject does. Rather, it conveys something of its subject's content. In so doing, it affords epistemic access to the original.

Although accounts of paraphrase say practically nothing about what expression involves, this much seems clear from their examples. To express content, in the sense of 'express' that concerns us here, is to make content manifest – to display or exhibit it. To express content is, in Goodman's sense, to exemplify it.[7] Exemplification is the mode of reference by which a sample refers to whatever it is a sample of. It does so by both instantiating and referring to the features it samples. A commercial paint sample both instantiates a particular color and refers to that color. The sample not only is an instance of the color, it also highlights exhibits or displays the color. In so doing it affords epistemic access to the color. Likewise, I suggest, a paraphrase not only shares content with the symbol it represents, it also highlights, exhibits, or displays the shared content. It thereby affords epistemic access to the content.

Exemplification is selective. A commercial paint sample normally exemplifies its color, not its size or shape. Some such samples also exemplify sheen. Others do not. So interpreting an exemplar involves determining which of its features function referentially. It also involves knowing how specifically or

---

[7] Goodman 1976, pp. 52–57; Catherine Z. Elgin, *Considered Judgment*, Princeton: Princeton University Press, 1997, pp. 171–183. Note that the discussion in *Languages of Art* (pp. 85–95), concerns a different, but related notion of expression. A painting that expresses sadness, in the sense that concerns Goodman, exemplifies sadness metaphorically. A reproduction or other paraphrase that expresses its subject's content, in the sense that concerns me, literally exemplifies its content.

generally they refer. What range of paints count as matching the sample? One might think that the answer is obvious. The color the sample exemplifies is the unique shade that is visually indiscriminable from the color on the card. This proposal faces the usual objections. Colors that are indiscriminable by one viewer are not always visually indiscriminable by others. Two colors that are indiscriminable from each other may be such that only one of them is indiscriminable from a third. And so on. But the real difficulty does not concern color discrimination. It concerns symbolization. The plethora of options that paint manufacturers offer may suggest that the customer chooses the precise shade of color she wants. In fact, paint samples symbolize more generally. They indicate a range within which the sample and all instances deemed to match the sample fall. Anyone who ever neglected to order enough paint to finish a job knows that indiscriminability is not the standard of matching that commercial paint manufacturers use. Two batches of paint that count as matching the same sample are often readily discriminable from each other. Other exemplars symbolize even more broadly. A Monet painting of a haystack can function as an exemplar of the impressionist style. Then the features it exemplifies are to be found in a wide range of works that differ from one another in a variety of obvious respects – for example, subject matter.

My appeal to exemplification might seem self-defeating. If one symbol is to exemplify the content of another, it must share that content. Since pictorial symbols cannot be replicated, it might seem that their content cannot be shared. But replication is not required for content sharing. As we have seen, because of their density and repleteness, such symbols admit of multiple interpretations, each assigning different content to the work. A reproduction of a picture is an interpretation that assigns content to the picture, shares the content it assigns, and exemplifies that content.[8] Although interpretation is flexible and context dependent, there are constraints on acceptable interpretation. A Raphael Madonna cannot plausibly be interpreted as a picture of a Wivenhoe Park. A reproduction, like any other paraphrase, is correct only if the work has the content assigned to it.

There are such things as loose interpretations. One might interpret the Raphael as a Madonna wearing a midnight blue cloak. Granted, 'midnight blue' is a fairly broad color term that comprehends a range of shades. To

---

[8] This is clearly not sufficient for reproduction. Minimally, I think, the reproduction's exemplification must be literal and must be of literal pictorial properties of the original. Unfortunately, exactly which properties are literal pictorial properties is far from clear. See Goodman 1976, p. 42, and Catherine Z. Elgin, *Between the Absolute and the Arbitrary*, Ithaca: Cornell University Press, 1997, pp. 69–70.

call the cloak 'midnight blue' by no means tells us exactly what shade the cloak is. But the description is not inaccurate on that account. It is merely somewhat general. Nevertheless, it conveys content. It tells us something about what and how the painting represents. Suppose that a reproduction portrayed the Raphael Madonna as wearing a midnight blue cloak. The shade of the cloak in the reproduction might diverge considerably from the shade of the cloak in the original. But if both fell within the scope of the predicate 'midnight blue', and the reproduction was interpreted as portraying the cloak as midnight blue, rather than as portraying the cloak's color more precisely, the reproduction would exemplify content it shared with the original. If reproductions symbolize generally, their manifest divergence from the originals is unproblematic.

Exemplars, like other symbols, require interpretation. An exemplar must possess the features it exemplifies, but even if the features exemplified are visible features, you cannot tell what an exemplar exemplifies just by looking. For an exemplar does not exemplify every feature it possesses. To determine which of its myriad features a given exemplar exemplifies requires not just looking, but reading.

To interpret a paraphrase, we need to determine what features function referentially, and how specifically they refer. Does the paraphrase purport to convey exactly the same information as its referent or only an approximation thereof? Does it purport to preserve the emotional tone? The idiomatic texture? The literary or pictorial or historical allusions? Answers vary from one paraphrase to the next. A linguistic paraphrase has a grammatical structure. It may, but need not, exemplify that structure. If it does, it provides insight into the grammatical structure of its referent; otherwise it does not. A pictorial reproduction has some spatial dimensions. It may, but need not, exemplify them. If it does, it provides insight into the size of its referent; otherwise it does not.

Criteria of acceptability for paraphrase are flexible. They depend on purpose and audience as well as on the limitations of their medium or symbol system. A paraphrase of a technical result suitable for inclusion in a newspaper would not be appropriate for inclusion in a scientific abstract. A reproduction of the *Mona Lisa* that is suitable for inclusion in a guide book would not have enough detail or the right kind of detail to be effective in a seminar on Leonardo's style. A black and white photograph of a Matisse might effectively display design, but cannot convey color. A written paraphrase of an utterance cannot convey nuances of timbre or tone. These points are so obvious that we may overlook the fact that we take them into account in interpreting the paraphrases in question. But that we do take them into account shows that we know how to read the paraphrases.

The crucial difference then between a deceptive forgery or other misattribution and a reproduction is that they are read differently. Undetected misattributions mislead. They beguile us into taking any and all of their symbolic features to be characteristic of the original work, artist, or school that they purportedly belong to. A successful reproduction, on the other hand, leads us back to the original.[9] It is not a replica of the original. It does not have, and does not purport to have all or only the symbolic functions of the original. But if interpreted correctly, it affords insight into what and how the original symbolizes.[10]

References

Bailey, A.: *Responses to Rembrandt*, Timken, New York 1994.
Elgin, C. Z.: *Between the Absolute and the Arbitrary*, Cornell University Press, Ithaca 1997.
Elgin, C. Z.: *Considered Judgment*, Princeton University Press, Princeton 1997.
Goodman, N.: *Languages of Art*, Hackett, Indianapolis 1976.
Koestler, A.: *The Act of Creation*, MacMillan, New York 1969.
Wheelock, Jr, A. K.: *Jan Vermeer*, Harry N. Abrams, Inc., New York 1998.

---

[9] To be sure, not all reproductions are successful. Many are crude, and ham handed, and lead us away from rather than back to the works they set out to illuminate. This is no surprise. To say that a symbol admits of multiple interpretations is not to say that all interpretations of it are correct.

[10] I am grateful to Amelie Rorty and Israel Scheffler for comments on an earlier draft of this paper.

Reinold Schmücker

Sind Fälschungen Originale?

I

Nur Kunstphilosophen zweifeln daran, daß Kunstwerke physische Objekte sind. Und für einige Kunstwerke, für Gemälde und Skulpturen zum Beispiel, scheint dieser Zweifel selbst ihnen mehrheitlich unangebracht. Angesichts der erdrückenden Beweislast, die gegen die Identifikation beispielsweise von literarischen und musikalischen Kunstwerken mit physischen Gegenständen spricht,[1] räumen die meisten Autoren zwar ein, daß sich nicht alle Kunstwerke als physische Objekte auffassen lassen. Einem Roman, der weder mit dem Manuskript des Autors noch mit einem seiner gedruckten Exemplare identifiziert werden kann (und wohl auch nicht mit allen), oder einer Sinfonie, die sich schwerlich mit dem Autograph oder einem anderen Exemplar der Partitur, aber auch nicht mit irgendeiner bestimmten Aufführung gleichsetzen läßt, gesteht die kunstontologische *communis opinio* deshalb den ontologischen Status idealer oder abstrakter Gegenstände zu.[2] Im Hinblick auf die klassischen bildenden Künste dürften jedoch die weitaus meisten Ästhetiker der Meinung sein, daß Kunstwerke physische Gegenstände sind.[3]

Ein solcher auf bestimmte Künste *eingeschränkter Physizismus* wirft allerdings zwei Probleme auf: das Dualitätsproblem und das Abgrenzungsproblem. Als *Dualitätsproblem* bezeichne ich die grundsätzliche Frage, warum wir

---

[1] Vgl. Wollheim 1980, 4 ff.; Patzig 1981, 117 ff.; Reicher 1998, 10 ff.; Schmücker 1998, 169 ff.
[2] Vgl. z. B. Wollheim 1980, 10–34 u. 177 ff.; Wolterstorff 1980; Wolterstorff 1987, 233 u. 249 f.; Gadamer 1993, 82. – Franz von Kutschera sucht diese Konsequenz dadurch zu vermeiden, daß er auch Kunstwerke, die offensichtlich keine physischen *Dinge*, sondern „der gemeinsame *Typ*" bestimmter physischer Dinge sind (1989, 211, Herv. im Original), als physische *Gegenstände* auffaßt. Diese Auffassung ähnelt derjenigen Eddy M. Zemachs (1966; 1989; 1991), die Maria E. Reicher (1998, 89 f.) überzeugend widerlegt hat. Zur Kritik von Kutscheras Position siehe Schmücker 1998, 184 ff.
[3] Besonders nachdrücklich verteidigt Kulenkampff (1983) diese von vielen Kunstwissenschaftlern stillschweigend eingenommene Position. Vgl. auch die Bilanz von Hanfling (1992, bes. 110).

überhaupt eine zweiteilige Kunstontologie annehmen und nicht allen Kunstwerken den gleichen ontologischen Status zuschreiben sollten. Aus welchem Grund sollten wir die Alternative einer einheitlichen Kunstontologie verwerfen, die ein uneingeschränkter kunstontologischer Idealismus böte? Das *Abgrenzungsproblem* ist dagegen ein Folgeproblem der Entscheidung zugunsten einer dualen Kunstontologie. Es bezieht sich auf die Frage, wo genau die Grenze zwischen physischen und nichtphysischen Künsten verläuft. Nelson Goodmans Unterscheidung zwischen „allographischen" und jenen „autographischen" Künsten, die sich Goodman zufolge dadurch auszeichnen, daß für sie „die Unterscheidung zwischen Original und Fälschung bedeutsam" ist,[4] scheint auf beide Fragen eine Antwort zu geben. Denn sie scheint die Existenz zweier Arten von Künsten zu belegen, die so unterschiedlich sind, daß es naheliegt, ihrer Differenz auch kunstontologisch Rechnung zu tragen. Und sie scheint ein Kriterium anzugeben, das physische und nichtphysische Künste voneinander zu unterscheiden erlaubt. Für den Vertreter eines eingeschränkten Physizismus – ich werde ihn der Einfachheit halber als Physizisten bezeichnen – liegt es daher nahe, Goodmans Unterscheidung kunstontologisch auszuwerten und das Vorkommen von Fälschungen als Indiz für eine physische Kunst aufzufassen, ihr Nichtvorkommen hingegen als Indiz für eine Kunst, deren Werke ideale Entitäten sind.[5]

Goodman selbst hat seine Unterscheidung – wie seine Kunsttheorie überhaupt – allerdings von ontologischen Konklusionen freizuhalten versucht, und er hat 1976 ausdrücklich erklärt, daß er die Relevanz der Unterscheidung zwischen Original und Fälschung nicht als Definiens autographischer Kunst verstanden wissen will.[6] Das Vorkommen von Fälschungen scheint jedoch unabhängig davon, ob es autographische von allographischen Künsten abzu-

---

[4] Vgl. Goodman 1976, 113: „Let us speak of a work of art as *autographic* if and only if the distinction between original and forgery of it is significant; or better, if and only if even the most exact duplication of it does not thereby count as genuine."

[5] In diesem Sinn, freilich in kritischer Absicht, hat etwa Günther Patzig (1981, 125) Goodmans Unterscheidung autographischer und allographischer Künste interpretiert.

[6] Vgl. Goodmans Vortrag auf der 5. Philosophischen Tagung in Bristol, 16.–19. Juli 1976 (Goodman 1978, 52). Unklar bleibt allerdings, was genau es dann bedeuten soll, daß „der Unterschied zwischen autographischen und allographischen Künsten [...] *allgemein* mit demjenigen zwischen Künsten, in denen es Fälschungen einzelner Werke geben, und denen, wo es keine solchen Fälschungen geben kann, *verbunden*" sei, wie Goodman im selben Vortrag ausführt (Herv. von mir, R. S.). Soll diese Auskunft nur eine empirisch zwar häufig anzutreffende, gleichwohl aber kontingente Koinzidenz bezeichnen? Woher aber wüßten wir dann um deren Kontingenz? Oder verneint Goodman, wie der Kontext der Äußerung vermuten lassen könnte, die definitorische Qualität der Relevanz der Unterscheidung zwischen Original und Fälschung nur, um der Möglichkeit „einer Welt erfinderischer Engel bar jeglichen Nachahmungsdrangs oder jeglicher bösen Absichten" Rechnung zu tragen (ebd.)?

grenzen erlaubt, ein starkes Indiz für die physische Natur mancher Kunstwerke und prima facie ein triftiges Argument für eine duale Kunstontologie zu sein.[7] Denn es gibt offensichtlich Künste, bei denen wir, wie bei Gemälden, zwischen Original und Fälschung unterscheiden, während uns eine solche Unterscheidung etwa bei literarischen Werken gegenstandslos erscheint. Und es ist unstrittig, daß sich die Wertschätzung, die etwa ein Gemälde in unseren Augen genießt, zwar unmittelbar auf das Original, aber nicht auf eine Fälschung überträgt. Das Faktum der Fälschung scheint deshalb zu belegen, daß es verfehlt wäre, die Werke aller Künste als nichtphysische Entitäten zu begreifen, wie es eine nicht auf bestimmte Künste begrenzte *idealistische Kunstontologie* tut. Ein Gemälde, so scheint es, ist, ebenso wie eine Skulptur oder ein architektonisches Werk, ein physischer Gegenstand und als solcher mit seinem Original identisch.

Muß sich aber der kunstontologische Idealist – wie der Vertreter einer uneingeschränkten idealistischen Kunstontologie heißen soll[8] – wirklich so rasch geschlagen geben? Genügt der simple Hinweis auf das Faktum der Kunstfälschung, um ihm das Zugeständnis abzunötigen, daß es zumindest einige Kunstwerke gibt, die keine idealen, sondern physische Entitäten sind? Ich glaube nicht. Denn der Eindruck, daß das Faktum der Fälschung seinem physizistischen Antipoden einen uneinholbaren Vorsprung verschafft, resultiert aus einer Prämisse, die eine genauere Prüfung verdient. Bevor wir uns ihr zuwenden, sei zunächst jedoch der Begriff der Fälschung selbst präzisiert.

II

In der Kunstphilosophie wie in der Alltagssprache ist von Fälschungen allgemein im Hinblick auf solche Kunstobjekte die Rede, die uns über ihre tatsächliche Entstehungsgeschichte täuschen sollen.[9] Wer von einem gefälsch-

---

[7] Daß es auch in den druckgraphischen Künsten Fälschungen gibt, steht dieser Vermutung nicht entgegen. Vielen Physizisten gilt nämlich die Druckgraphik als eine physische Kunst. Diese Auffassung ist nicht so abwegig, wie sie auf den ersten Blick vielleicht erscheint. Denn zum einen schließt der Physizismus die Annahme pluraler Originale nicht aus, und zum anderen sprechen gute Gründe dafür, bei den druckgraphischen Künsten den Druckstock und bei Werken der Fotografie das Negativ als Original anzusehen (vgl. Schmücker 1998, 182f.).

[8] Kunstontologische Idealisten in diesem Sinne sind z.B. Strawson (1959, 231, Anm. 1; 1966, 10), Patzig (1981) und Reicher (1998; 2002); vgl. auch Schmücker 1998, 264ff.

[9] Vgl. Goodman 1976, 122; Reicher 1998, 40. Die in einer Fälschung sich manifestierende Täuschungsabsicht geht dabei auf deren tatsächlichen Urheber zurück (vgl. Beardsley 1983, 226; Goodman 1986, 291; Stalnaker 2001, 401).

ten Turner spricht, muß damit allerdings kein Duplikat eines bestimmten Bildes meinen, das Turner gemalt hat. Vielmehr kann auch von einem Bild die Rede sein, das in Turners Malart ausgeführt und wahrheitswidrig als dessen Werk gekennzeichnet ist, in Turners Œuvre jedoch kein Gegenstück hat. Wir müssen deshalb zwei Arten von Fälschungen unterscheiden: solche, die lediglich die einem bestimmten Künstler zuzurechnende besondere Technik und stilistische Eigenart imitieren (wobei zur stilistischen Eigenart eines Künstlers beispielsweise auch die Auswahl bestimmter Motive gehören kann), und solche, die ein bestimmtes Kunstwerk reproduzieren. Beiden Arten von Fälschungen ist gemeinsam, daß sie über ihre Entstehungsgeschichte gleichsam falsche Angaben machen. Eine Fälschung des ersten Typs ist jedoch unzweifelhaft selbst ein Original – auch wenn es sich dabei um das Original eines epigonalen Werks handelt und meist zudem um eines, das einen unzutreffenden Urhebervermerk trägt. Han Van Meegerens im Stile Vermeers gemaltes Bild „Jesus Preaching in the Temple" ist dafür ein gutes Beispiel.[10] Weil solche Fälschungen auf der Imitation der Gestaltungs- und Verfahrensweisen beruhen, die für das Werk eines bestimmten Künstlers kennzeichnend sind, möchte ich sie *Imitatfälschungen* nennen.

Im Unterschied zu einer bloßen Imitatfälschung bezieht sich eine Fälschung des zweiten Typs auf ein bestimmtes Werk. Fälschungen dieses Typs können daher *Werkfälschungen* heißen. Solche Fälschungen hat zum Beispiel Miguel Canals von Rossettis „Proserpine" angefertigt,[11] und sie existieren auch von vielen Gemälden Caspar David Friedrichs, bei denen sich oft nicht mehr genau ausmachen läßt, welches Bild das Original und welches die Fälschung ist.[12] Für Werkfälschungen gilt, was Goodman als Kennzeichen von Kunstfälschungen überhaupt erachtet: Sie geben fälschlicherweise vor, „die Entstehungsgeschichte zu besitzen, die für das (oder ein) Original des Werkes notwendig ist".[13] Werkfälschungen sind in der Regel – aber nicht

---

[10] Eine Abbildung findet sich in Beckett 1995 nach Seite 114.
[11] Vgl. die Abbildung in Beckett 1995 nach Seite 114.
[12] Vgl. Wettengl, Hrsg. 1990.
[13] „A forgery of a work of art is an object falsely purporting to have the history of production requisite for the (or an) original *of the work*." (Goodman 1976, 122, Herv. von mir, R. S.) – Goodmans Behandlung des Problems der Fälschung leidet insbesondere darunter, daß er Imitatfälschungen und Werkfälschungen nicht hinreichend trennt und die von ihm diskutierten Fälschungen Van Meegerens im Sinne seines eigenen Fälschungsbegriffs „eben gar keine Fälschungen" sind (Steinbrenner 1996, 95, Anm. 60; vgl. Levinson 1980, 376f.). Bernd Philippis Neuübersetzung von „Languages of Art" sucht diese Inkonsistenz bezeichnenderweise dadurch zu verdecken, daß sie das von mir kursivierte Genitivobjekt am Satzende von Goodmans Fälschungsdefinition unterschlägt: „Die Fälschung eines Kunstwerkes ist ein Gegenstand, der fälschlicherweise vorgibt, eine Entstehungsgeschichte zu besitzen, die für das (oder ein) Original unerläßlich ist." (Goodman 1995, 120f.)

notwendigerweise[14] – mittelbare oder unmittelbare Replikate oder Kopien des (oder eines) Originals des betreffenden Werks. Allerdings sehen wir nicht jedes Replikat und nicht jede Kopie als eine Werkfälschung an. Mitunter werden nämlich Replikate oder Kopien eines Werks von dessen Urheber angefertigt oder autorisiert. Solche derivativen Kunstobjekte bezeichnen wir ebensowenig als Fälschungen wie jene Replikate und Kopien von fremder Hand, die hinreichend als solche gekennzeichnet sind.[15] Denn solche Objekte können uns nicht über ihre tatsächliche Entstehungsgeschichte täuschen, weil sie zu erkennen geben, daß ihre Entstehungsgeschichte eine andere als diejenige ihres Urbilds ist. Werkfälschungen sind also nur solche Replikate und Kopien, die uns vorspiegeln sollen, sie seien das (oder ein) Original des betreffenden Werks. Was sie von ‚bloßen' Replikaten und Kopien unterscheidet, ist ihr zu Unrecht erhobener Originalitätsanspruch.

III

Kunstontologisch sind vor allem Werkfälschungen von Interesse. Denn nur ihr Vorkommen könnte ein Indikator für den Grenzverlauf zwischen physischen und nichtphysischen Künsten sein. Wer im Vorkommen von Werkfälschungen ein Kriterium dafür erblickt, daß eine Kunst eine physische Kunst ist, unterschreibt freilich eine Prämisse, die Goodman mit all denjenigen teilt, die seine Theorie kunstontologisch auszuwerten suchen. Dieser Prämisse zufolge – ich nenne sie (P) – ist die Unterscheidung zwischen Original und Fälschung nur für einige Künste bedeutsam. (P) läßt sich in einem starken und in einem schwächeren Sinn interpretieren.

Interpretiert man (P) im starken Sinn, besagt die Prämisse, daß es nur einige Künste gibt, deren Werke fälschbar sind (P'). Wenn aber (unter anderem) alle diejenigen Replikate und Kopien, die uns vorspiegeln, sie seien das (oder ein) Original des betreffenden Werks, Werkfälschungen sind, dann sind alle Werke, von deren Originalen es Replikate oder Kopien geben kann, fälschbar. Denn jedes Replikat *kann* so präpariert oder präsentiert werden,

---

[14] Weil es von den spezifischen Wahrnehmungsfähigkeiten, Kenntnissen und Überzeugungen des Publikums, das getäuscht werden soll, abhängt, wie stark eine Fälschung dem Original ähneln muß, das sie zu sein vorgibt, sind auch Fälschungen denkbar, die keine Replikate oder Kopien sind (vgl. Bailey 1992, 155).

[15] Allerdings kann es – entgegen der Meinung Sagoffs (1983, 148) – auch Fälschungen geben, die der Urheber des gefälschten Werks selber angefertigt hat (vgl. Bailey 1992, 155). Denn eine Kopie, die nicht als Kopie ausgewiesen ist, sondern den Eindruck vermittelt, sie sei das Original, ist auch dann eine Fälschung, wenn sie von demselben Urheber angefertigt wurde wie das Original.

daß es uns vorspiegelt, es sei ein Original; und für jede Kopie gilt dasselbe. Nun läßt sich aber im Prinzip jedes Original kopieren (wie unvollkommen auch immer): das Originalmanuskript eines Romans ebenso wie die Originalleinwand eines Gemäldes. Wenn man der These zustimmen will, daß es nur einige Künste gibt, deren Werke fälschbar sind, muß man deshalb behaupten, es gebe in einigen Künsten kein Original. Diese Annahme ist jedoch nicht plausibel. Denn ungeachtet der Probleme, die uns die Bestimmung des Originals in manchen Künsten bereitet,[16] behaupten allenfalls unbelehrbare kunstontologische Mentalisten, es könne ein Kunstwerk geben, ohne daß es dazu einer physischen Originalmanifestation bedürfte.[17]

Aber vielleicht müssen wir die Prämisse des Physizisten in einem schwächeren Sinn verstehen. Vielleicht soll sie nur besagen, der Unterschied zwischen Original und Fälschung sei nur in bezug auf einige Künste *relevant* (P''). Die eingangs zitierte Formulierung Goodmans zum Beispiel legt nahe, daß er (P) im Sinne von (P'') verstanden wissen will. Interpretiert man (P) in diesem Sinn, provoziert sie allerdings die Rückfrage, *warum* die Differenz nur im Hinblick auf manche Künste von Bedeutung sei. Will sich der Physizist keiner *petitio principii* schuldig machen, kann er auf diese Frage nicht antworten: weil im einen Fall das Original das Kunstwerk ist und im anderen nicht (P''$_1$). Auch der Hinweis darauf, daß in einigen Künsten für ein Original mehr Geld bezahlt werde als für eine Kopie (P''$_2$), ist kein überzeugendes Argument. Denn es ist nicht nur unklar, inwiefern der Bereitschaft, für ein Original mehr Geld auszugeben als für eine Kopie, kunst*ontologische* Relevanz zukommen soll, sondern vor allem unzutreffend, daß von dieser Bereitschaft bestimmte Künste ausgenommen wären. Wer in Antiquariatskatalogen die Preise für Handschriften von Dichtern und Komponisten studiert, wird das bezeugen.

Könnte der Physizist aber nicht geltend machen, daß sich die Wertschätzung, die ein Original genießt, in einigen Künsten offensichtlich nicht auf eine Fälschung überträgt, und könnte er dies nicht als Indiz für die unterschiedliche Relevanz des Unterschieds zwischen Original und Fälschung werten (P''$_3$)? Auch dieses Argument erscheint als wenig aussichtsreich. Denn erstens überträgt sich auch in Künsten, in denen Fälschungen von Originalen erheblich seltener sind als etwa in der Malerei, die Wertschätzung des Originals nicht auf eine Fälschung. Gefälschte Autographen von Bach werden beispielsweise nicht in gleichem Maße geschätzt wie die Originalpartituren. Das Argument taugt also nicht als Argument für einen auf einige Künste

---

[16] Daß sie nicht unlösbar sind, habe ich andernorts zu zeigen versucht (Schmücker 1998, 178 ff.).
[17] Auch wenn man dem Physizisten nur die These unterstellt, es gebe fälschbare und nichtfälschbare Kunstwerke, ohne daß sich jede dieser Klassen mit einer Klasse von Künsten deckte, ergibt sich das gleiche Resultat.

oder auf bestimmte Kunstwerke eingeschränkten Physizismus. Und zweitens überträgt sich die Wertschätzung, die ein Betrachter einem Original entgegenbringt, *nur dann nicht* auf eine Fälschung, wenn der Betrachter die Fälschung als solche erkennt oder um ihren Fälschungscharakter weiß. Ist sie hingegen so perfekt, daß sie unenttarnt bleibt, kann sie auf ebenso große Wertschätzung rechnen wie das Original. Das Argument belegt also nicht, daß der Unterschied von Original und Fälschung *als solcher* relevant ist – in welchen Künsten auch immer –, sondern es zeigt allenfalls, daß unser Wissen, daß ein Gegenstand eine Werkfälschung ist, unsere Wertschätzung dieses Gegenstands beeinflußt.

Der Physizist könnte jedoch darauf hinweisen, daß es in einigen Künsten keine perfekten, d.h. keine perzeptorisch äquivalenten Kopien von Originalen gibt, in anderen hingegen wohl (P''_4). Diese These trifft gegenwärtig vermutlich zu. Von einem mit dem Computer geschriebenen Romanmanuskript lassen sich problemlos perzeptorisch äquivalente Kopien herstellen, vom Original eines Ölgemäldes kaum.[18] Es ist jedoch wahrscheinlich, daß sich Umfang und Zusammensetzung der Klasse derjenigen Werke, deren Originale perzeptorisch nicht äquivalent reproduzierbar sind, im Zuge der Entwicklung neuer Reproduktionstechniken verändern. Wollte man die aktuelle Zusammensetzung dieser Klasse zur Grundlage ontologischer Zuschreibungen machen, müßte man annehmen, daß der ontologische Status von Kunstwerken einen durch den jeweiligen Stand der Entwicklung der Reproduktionstechniken bedingten Zeitindex trägt. Ein und dasselbe Kunstwerk könnte demnach zum Zeitpunkt t_1 ein physisches Objekt und zu einem späteren Zeitpunkt t_2 kein physisches Objekt mehr sein – ohne daß es selbst sich in irgendeiner Weise verändert hätte. Diese Annahme scheint mir ein zu hoher Preis für einen auf einige Künste eingeschränkten Physizismus zu sein.

Zugunsten des eingeschränkten Physizismus ins Spiel bringen ließe sich indessen auch Goodmans Beobachtung, daß nur einige Künste über ein Notationssystem verfügen, das es in Goodmans Augen ermöglicht, einen bestimmten Gegenstand oder ein bestimmtes Ereignis unabhängig von seiner Entstehungsgeschichte als ein Vorkommnis („token") eines bestimmten

---

[18] Allerdings bereitet die Identifikation von Werkfälschungen auch bei Gemälden oftmals ganz erhebliche Schwierigkeiten. Kunstmuseen und Kunstversicherer treiben deshalb einen ungeheuren technischen Aufwand, um Werkfälschungen wenigstens mit einiger Sicherheit als solche zu erkennen. So wird etwa im Doerner-Institut der Bayerischen Staatsgemäldesammlungen das Alter von Farbpigmenten mit Hilfe von Röntgenaufnahmen bestimmt, ggf. aber auch unter dem Rasterelektronenmikroskop die chemische Zusammensetzung abgekratzter Farbpartikel analysiert (vgl. Spanke 2001).

Werks zu identifizieren.[19] Warum sollten wir nicht annehmen, daß die Unterscheidung von Original und Fälschung für diejenigen Künste bedeutsam ist, denen ein solches Notationssystem fehlt (P''_5)? Ist es nicht so, daß die Identifikation eines Gegenstandes oder eines Ereignisses als Vorkommnis eines bestimmten Werks in bezug auf diese Künste – und nur im Hinblick auf sie – die Kenntnis seiner Entstehungsgeschichte zur Voraussetzung hat? Ich möchte auch das bestreiten. Goodmans Beobachtung, daß nur einige Künste über spezifische Notationssysteme verfügen, trifft zwar zweifellos zu. Die Existenz systematischer Notationskonventionen etwa für Musikwerke und literarische Texte ist aber keine hinreichende Bedingung dafür, daß sich ein Gegenstand oder Ereignis unabhängig von seiner Entstehungsgeschichte als Vorkommnis eines bestimmten Werks identifizieren läßt. So erlegen uns beispielsweise Druckfehler und falsch gespielte Töne – die ja auch gehäuft auftreten können – die letztlich nur mit Hilfe unserer Urteilskraft zu treffende Entscheidung auf, ob es sich bei dem betreffenden Gegenstand oder Ereignis noch um ein Vorkommnis des fraglichen Werks handelt oder nicht. Umgekehrt folgt aus dem Fehlen eines spezifischen Notationssystems auch nicht die Unmöglichkeit einer von der Kenntnis der Entstehungsgeschichte unabhängigen Identifikation. Jedenfalls trauen wir uns in aller Regel auch bei Werken, deren konstitutive Eigenschaften nicht anhand eines Notationssystems standardisiert identifizierbar sind, ein Urteil über die perzeptorische Äquivalenz zweier Gegenstände oder Ereignisse zu. Und es wäre unplausibel, identifizierbare werkkonstitutive Eigenschaften überhaupt nur solchen Werken zuzuschreiben, bei denen sie sich anhand eines Notationssystems standardisiert identifizieren lassen. Denn dann berechtigte uns nichts mehr dazu, die perfekte Kopie eines bestimmten Gemäldes als perfekte Kopie *ebendieses bestimmten* Gemäldes anzusehen. Der Annahme, daß die Unterscheidung von Original und Fälschung speziell für diejenigen Künste bedeutsam sei, denen ein Notationssystem fehlt, liegt deshalb eine zu mechanistische Vorstellung davon zugrunde, was wir tun, wenn wir einen Gegenstand oder ein Ereignis als Vorkommnis eines Werks identifizieren – in welcher der Künste auch immer.

Ermöglicht aber nicht in einigen Künsten nur das Original die adäquate Interpretation eines Werks (P''_6) – oder aber dessen unverkürzte ästhetische Erfahrung (P''_7) –, während es dazu in anderen Künsten des Originals nicht bedarf? Prüfen wir zum Schluß auch diese beiden Hypothesen. (P''_6) macht

---

[19] Vgl. Goodman 1978, 53: „Was aber den Unterschied zwischen allographischen und autographischen Werken betrifft, so zählt einzig und allein das Kriterium für die Bestimmung […], daß ein Gegenstand oder Ereignis ein Anwendungsfall eines Werks ist, das zum Beispiel durch einen anderen Anwendungsfall oder durch eine Partitur spezifiziert werden kann."

zu Recht geltend, daß die Überzeugungskraft der Interpretation eines Kunstwerks oftmals davon abhängt, ob die Interpretation am Original gewonnen oder zumindest geprüft ist oder nicht. Mir scheint das aber kein Spezifikum derjenigen Künste zu sein, die Physizisten als physische Künste betrachten. Auch eine Interpretation von Hölderlins lyrischem Spätwerk, die am handschriftlichen Befund des Homburger Foliohefts geprüft ist, wird nämlich in aller Regel jener anderen vorzuziehen sein, die sich allein auf die Textarbietung der Beißnerschen oder einer anderen geläufigen Edition verläßt. Zurückzuführen ist das meines Erachtens darauf, daß das Original *in jedem Fall* (und also nicht nur in bestimmten Künsten) der Maßstab ist, an dem sich unser Urteil darüber, ob ein Gegenstand ein Vorkommnis eines bestimmten Kunstwerks ist, orientiert. In den sekundärtransitorischen Künsten – bei Kompositionsmusik also und bei dramatischen Werken – kommt diese Maßstabsfunktion des Originals zwar nur vermittelt zum Tragen. Denn hier beziehen sich Interpretationen zumeist auf Aufführungen und nicht auf Dramentexte oder Partituren. Nicht die Uraufführung, sondern das Dramenmanuskript oder die Originalpartitur wird man aber bei sekundärtransitorischen Werken als das Original auffassen müssen. Denn der Status des Originals gebührt jeweils dem ersten Resultat des künstlerischen Produktionsprozesses, das als Vorkommnis eines bestimmten Kunstwerks angesehen werden kann, weil es die Existenz des fraglichen Kunstwerks begründet. Auch für die sekundärtransitorischen Künste gilt jedoch, daß eine Interpretation, die am Original bewährt werden kann, anderen Interpretationen vorzuziehen ist, auf die dies nicht zutrifft. Und ebenso gilt auch für sie, daß perfekte Kopien (und also auch perfekte Fälschungen) das Original ohne Qualitätsverlust für eine auf ihnen beruhende oder an ihnen bewährte Interpretation vertreten können. Ob die Konsultation des Originals für eine überzeugende Interpretation erforderlich ist, hängt deshalb davon ab, ob es perfekte Kopien des Originals gibt. Da dieser Sachverhalt historisch kontingent erscheint, lassen sich auf ihn jedoch keine ontologischen Zuschreibungen gründen. Vielmehr läßt sich (P''_6) auf (P''_4) reduzieren und ist mithin demselben Einwand ausgesetzt wie diese Prämisse.

Was auf die adäquate Interpretation eines Werks zutrifft, gilt in gleicher Weise aber auch für dessen unverkürzte ästhetische Erfahrung. Wenn nämlich unverkürzt eine ästhetische Erfahrung heißen soll, die alle diejenigen ästhetischen Wahrnehmungen umfaßt, die uns ein Werk eröffnet, dann kann eine perfekte Fälschung (ebenso wie jede andere perfekte Kopie) das Original als Bezugspunkt unverkürzter ästhetischer Erfahrung immer vertreten.[20] Im

---

[20] Vgl. Lessing 1983, 76: „The fact of forgery is important historically, biographically, perhaps legally, or [...] financially; but not, strictly speaking, aesthetically." Die gegenteilige Annahme

Fall eines sekundärtransitorischen Werks ermöglicht allerdings auch das Original noch keine unverkürzte ästhetische Erfahrung – denn die Lektüre von Beethovens Partitur stellt noch keine unverkürzte Erfahrung der Hammerklaviersonate dar. Als Bezugspunkt unverkürzter ästhetischer Erfahrung tritt bei solchen Werken eine originalgetreue Aufführung an die Stelle des Originals. Doch so bedeutsam dieser Unterschied ist: Mit der Differenz zwischen Original und Fälschung hat er nichts zu tun.[21] Auch (P''_7) liefert also keine überzeugende Begründung des eingeschränkten Physizismus.

Aus unserer einigermaßen langwierigen Verhandlung geht der kunstontologische Idealist gestärkt hervor. Er konnte den eingeschränkten Physizismus zwar nicht widerlegen – in weiser Voraussicht hat er das auch gar nicht versucht –, aber eine seiner populärsten Begründungen entkräften: Auch wenn wir die Prämisse (P) im schwächeren Sinn von (P'') interpretieren, läßt sie sich, soweit ich sehe, nicht so plausibel begründen, daß sie die These zu stützen vermöchte, das Vorkommen von Werkfälschungen weise bestimmte Künste als physische Künste aus. Goodmans Hinweis auf den Unterschied zwischen Original und Fälschung eröffnet also keine Lösung des Dualitäts- und des Abgrenzungsproblems.

IV

Kann der kunstontologische Idealist noch mehr erreichen? Vielleicht. Wenn nämlich Werkfälschungen ein Prüfstein für die Güte kunstontologischer Hypothesen sind, dann muß diejenige Hypothese als die plausiblere gelten, die ihren Status überzeugender zu bestimmen vermag. Damit steht die Titelfrage erneut auf der Tagesordnung: Sind Fälschungen Originale?

---

verwechselt den ästhetischen Wert eines Kunstwerks mit dem historischen Wert, den ein physisches Objekt dem Umstand verdankt, daß es von einer vergangenen Zeit zeugt (vgl. Meiland 1983, 116), oder – wie Meyer (1983), der dem Original eines Kunstwerks eine Bedeutung zuspricht, die derjenigen wissenschaftlicher Entdeckungen vergleichbar sei, und Sagoff (1983), der Fälschungen als bloße Wiederholungen der Problemlösungen begreift, die sich in den betreffenden Originalen manifestieren – die Kreativität des Künstlers mit einer Eigenschaft seines Werks (siehe Meiland 1983, bes. 123).

[21] Tatsächlich ermöglicht das Original (ebenso wie seine perfekte Kopie) bei den meisten musikalischen und dramatischen, ja sogar bei manchen lyrischen Werken, die durch Rezitation allererst gleichsam zum Sprechen gebracht werden müssen, nur eine verkürzte (!) ästhetische Erfahrung. Meines Erachtens eignet sich dieser Umstand weit eher als die Relevanz des Unterschieds von Original und Fälschung oder die Existenz eines Notationssystems als ein Kriterium zur Abgrenzung unterschiedlicher Arten von Künsten. Indem er transitorische von nichttransitorischen Künsten zu unterscheiden erlaubt, nötigt er aber nicht zur Annahme einer dualen Kunstontologie.

Für Imitatfälschungen ließ sich die Frage umstandslos bejahen. Denn jede Imitatfälschung konstituiert ein – wenngleich epigonales – neues Werk. Sind aber auch Werkfälschungen Originale? Oder, weniger paradox formuliert: Konstituiert auch eine Werkfälschung ein neues Werk? Der Physizist muß diese Frage bejahen – oder Werkfälschungen ganz aus dem Reich der Kunstobjekte verbannen. Ist nämlich eine Werkfälschung Kunst, aber kein Vorkommnis des Werks, als dessen Original sie sich ausgibt, dann muß sie das Original eines anderen Werks sein.

Die Alternative ist unattraktiv: Schlösse man Werkfälschungen aus der Klasse der Kunstobjekte aus, reduzierte sich die Bedeutung des Kunstbegriffs auf die wahrheitsgemäße Offenbarung der Entstehungsgeschichte eines Produkts. Denn alle sonstigen Eigenschaften eines Werks, auf die sich unser Urteil, es sei ein Kunstwerk, beziehen könnte, würden dann im Fall einer perfekten Fälschung von einem nichtkünstlerischen Objekt geteilt. Ein solches Begriffsverständnis stünde aber sowohl zu unserem alltagssprachlichen Kunstverständnis als auch zu allen einflußreichen philosophischen Rekonstruktionen der Bedeutung des Kunstbegriffs in offensichtlichem Widerspruch.

Wer in einer Werkfälschung das Original eines neuen Kunstwerks sieht, erweist hingegen dem Fälscher zuviel der Ehre. Ist nämlich die Fälschung beispielsweise einer Skulptur ein von dieser verschiedenes Werk, dann muß der Fälscher als dessen Urheber gelten – wie illegitim das Maß, in dem er sich von dem Werk eines Kollegen hat inspirieren lassen, uns auch erscheinen mag. Wer eine Fälschung als Original eines neuen Werks auffaßt, betrügt mithin den Urheber eines Kunstwerks um seine mittelbare Urheberschaft an allen Fälschungen seines Werks.

Als Ausweg aus dieser Aporie bietet sich die Bekehrung zum kunstontologischen Idealismus an. Er faßt Kunstwerke als nichtwirkliche Entitäten auf, die unter zwei einschränkenden Bedingungen existieren: Erstens gibt oder gab es mindestens ein raum-zeitliches Vorkommnis, durch dessen Produktion sie konstituiert wurden, und zweitens gibt es mindestens ein raum-zeitliches Vorkommnis, in dem sie sich aktuell (oder virtuell[22]) manifestie-

---

[22] Von einer virtuellen Manifestation spreche ich dann, wenn eine subjektive Kompetenz die Möglichkeit der jederzeitigen raum-zeitlichen Manifestation verbürgt, etwa bei einem Gedicht, das jemand so im Kopf hat, daß er es jederzeit aufschreiben oder vortragen könnte, oder bei einer Tanzperformance, deren Choreographie die Tänzerin so in Kopf und/oder Beinen hat, daß sie sie jederzeit zur Aufführung bringen könnte. Maria E. Reicher (1999, 288) hat gegen diese Annahme virtueller Kunstmanifestationen den grundsätzlichen Einwand erhoben, es sei „schwer zu verstehen, wie eine ‚virtuelle Manifestation' eine nicht vorhandene aktuelle ersetzen kann". Meines Erachtens verliert dieser Einwand seine vordergründige Plausibilität, wenn man sich vergegenwärtigt, daß die für die Existenz eines Kunstwerks konstitutive

ren. Indem der kunstontologische Idealismus Kunstwerke derart von jenen raum-zeitlichen Vorkommnissen unterscheidet, in denen sie sich unserer Wahrnehmung darbieten, eröffnet er die Möglichkeit, Fälschungen ebenso wie jene ‚bloßen' Kopien, die ihren wahren Charakter nicht verhüllen, als sekundäre Vorkommnisse jener Werke zu verstehen, von deren Original sie sozusagen abstammen. Entgegen einem verbreiteten Vorurteil ist der kunstontologische Idealismus dabei nicht gezwungen, das Verhältnis zwischen dem als nichtwirkliche Entität beschriebenen Werk und dessen physischen Vorkommnissen so schematisch zu bestimmen, daß schon ein falscher Ton die Aufführung eines musikalischen Werks zur Uraufführung eines neuen Werks werden ließe. Der kunstontologische Idealismus ist nämlich mit einer Theorie der Werkidentität von Kunst verträglich, die der für alle Künste zu konstatierenden besonderen Bedeutung des Originals Rechnung trägt, ohne das Original physizistisch zum Werk selbst zu hypostasieren.

Dieser Theorie zufolge ist die Werkidentität zweier Kunstobjekte ein Identitätsverhältnis, das (1) in entstehungsgeschichtlicher Verwandtschaft oder numerischer Identität mit dem Original eines bestimmten Werks und (2) in Originaläquivalenz fundiert ist: Ein Wahrnehmungsgegenstand w_1 ist genau dann werkidentisch mit einem von ihm selbst numerisch verschiedenen Wahrnehmungsgegenstand w_2, wenn (1) sowohl w_1 als auch w_2 vom Original eines Kunstwerks K ‚abstammen' oder einer von beiden von ihm ‚abstammt' und der andere mit ihm numerisch identisch ist und wenn (2) sowohl w_1 als auch w_2 Äquivalente des Originals von K sind oder einer von beiden ein Äquivalent des Originals von K und der andere mit ihm numerisch identisch ist.[23] Das Kriterium der Originaläquivalenz ist dabei so zu interpretieren, daß es das Original im Originalzustand meint, d.h. in dem Zustand, in dem es vom Künstler erstmals präsentiert (oder hinterlassen) wird.

Aus dieser Definition erhellt, warum wir grundsätzlich herauszufinden suchen, welches von zwei außerordentlich ähnlichen, aber nicht gleichen Kunstobjekten das Original ist und welches eine Kopie oder Fälschung:[24]

Manifestationsbedingung auf die Möglichkeit der ästhetischen Erfahrung des betreffenden Werks zielt. Diese Möglichkeit wird durch eine subjektive Kompetenz unter Umständen in vergleichbarer Weise verbürgt wie durch die physische Existenz eines Gegenstandes: Wenn ich einem Freund Gelegenheit zur ästhetischen Erfahrung eines Gedichts geben will, das er nicht kennt, kann ich ihm das Gedicht ebensogut auswendig vortragen, wie ich es ihm aus dem Manuskript, aus einem Buch oder aus einer Abschrift vorlesen kann.

[23] Gegen diese Definition spricht nicht, daß es – zum Beispiel bei Kunstwerken, die am Computer erzeugt werden (vgl. dazu Bickel 1992) und sich via Internet zeitgleich und phänomenal ununterscheidbar manifestieren – plurale Originale gibt. Denn alle jene gleichursprünglichen Primärexemplare, die ein solches plurales Original bilden, sind perzeptorisch völlig äquivalent.

[24] Wir tun das auch etwa bei Literatur, wenn uns z.B. zwei Handschriften eines Gedichts nicht

weil das Original der Maßstab ist, anhand dessen wir nicht nur darüber entscheiden, ob ein Kunstobjekt das Vorkommnis eines bestimmten Werks ist, sondern gegebenenfalls auch ermitteln, in welcher Qualität es dieses Werk repräsentiert. Werkfälschungen unterliegen demnach denselben Identitätsbedingungen wie ‚bloße' Replikate und Kopien. Weil aber die Täuschungsabsicht, die sich in ihnen manifestiert, die Erfüllung der Abstammungsbedingung bereits impliziert, sind sie Vorkommnisse des Kunstwerks, als dessen Original sie sich ausgeben, in eben dem Maß, in dem sie Äquivalente seines Originals sind.

Daß eine idealistische Kunstontologie den Status von Werkfälschungen plausibler zu bestimmen vermag als der Physizismus, scheint mir damit offenkundig zu sein. Der Idealismus hat damit gewiß nur einen Punktsieg errungen. Vielleicht ist aber auf dem Feld der Kunstontologie ein besseres Resultat gar nicht möglich.[25]

Literatur

Bailey, G.: [art.] forgery. In: *A Companion to Aesthetics*, ed. by D. Cooper, Oxford/Cambridge, Mass.1992, 155–158.

Beardsley, M. C.: Notes on Forgery. In: Dutton 1983, 225–231.

Beckett, A.: *Fakes. Forgery and the Art World*, London 1995.

Bickel, P.: *Musik aus der Maschine. Computervermittelte Musik zwischen synthetischer Produktion und Reproduktion*, Berlin 1992.

Dutton, D. (ed.): *The Forger's Art. Forgery and the Philosophy of Art*, Berkeley/Los Angeles/London 1983.

Gadamer, H.-G.: Dichtung und Mimesis (1972). In: H.-G. Gadamer, *Ästhetik und Poetik I: Kunst als Aussage (Gesammelte Werke, Bd. 8/1)*, Tübingen 1993, 80–85.

Goodman, N.: *Languages of Art. An Approach to a Theory of Symbols* (1968), 2nd ed., Indianapolis, Ind./Cambridge, Mass. 1976.

Goodman, N.: Kritische Anmerkungen zu Wollheims Vortrag, *Ratio* 20 (1978), 52–54.

Goodman, N.: A Note on Copies, *The Journal of Aesthetics and Art Criticism* 44 (1986), 291–292.

Goodman, N.: *Sprachen der Kunst. Entwurf einer Symboltheorie*, übers. v. Bernd Philippi, Frankfurt a.M. 1995.

---

gleich zu sein scheinen – etwa, weil die eine einige Hinzufügungen oder stilistische Änderungen enthält. Und auch bei zwei Ausgaben eines Romans fragen wir bei Abweichungen danach, welche die größere Originaläquivalenz besitzt.

[25] Christoph Jäger, Marcus Rossberg und Jakob Steinbrenner haben mich durch ihre Einwände von der Notwendigkeit der vorliegenden Neufassung meines Bielefelder Vortrags überzeugt. Dafür gilt ihnen mein herzlicher Dank – auch wenn ich ihren Anregungen nicht in allen Punkten gefolgt bin.

Hanfling, O.: The Ontology of Art. In: *Philosophical Aesthetics. An Introduction*, ed. by O. Hanfling, Milton Keynes/Oxford/Cambridge, Mass. 1992, 75-110.
Kulenkampff, J.: Gibt es ein ontologisches Problem des Kunstwerks? In: *Kant oder Hegel? Über Formen der Begründung in der Philosophie. Stuttgarter Hegel-Kongreß 1981*, hrsg. v. D. Henrich, Stuttgart 1983, 572-590.
Kutschera, F. von: *Ästhetik*, Berlin/New York 1989.
Lessing, A.: What Is Wrong with a Forgery? (1964). In: Dutton 1983, 58-76.
Levinson, J.: Autographic and Allographic Art Revisited, *Philosophical Studies* 38 (1980), 367-383.
Meiland, J.: Originals, Copies, and Aesthetic Value. In: Dutton 1983, 115-130.
Meyer, L.: Forgery and the Anthropology of Art (1967). In: Dutton 1983, 77-92.
Patzig, G.: Über den ontologischen Status von Kunstwerken. In: *Redliches Denken. Festschrift für Gerd-Günther Grau*, hrsg. v. F.W. Korff, Stuttgart-Bad Cannstatt 1981, 114-129.
Reicher, M.: *Zur Metaphysik der Kunst. Eine logisch-ontologische Untersuchung des Werkbegriffs*, Graz 1998.
Reicher, M.: [Rez. von Schmücker 1998], *Conceptus* 32 (1999), 280-289.
Sagoff, M.: The Aesthetic Status of Forgeries (1976). In: Dutton 1983, 131-152.
Schmücker, R.: *Was ist Kunst? Eine Grundlegung*, München 1998.
Stalnaker, N.: Fakes and Forgeries. In: *The Routledge Companion to Aesthetics*, ed. by B. Gaut and D. McIver Lopes, London/New York 2001, 395-407.
Steinbrenner, J.: *Kognitivismus in der Ästhetik*, Würzburg 1996.
Strawson, P.: *Individuals. An Essay in Descriptive Metaphysics*, London 1959.
Strawson, P.: Aesthetical Appraisal and Works of Art, *The Oxford Review* 1, no. 3 (1966), 5-13.
Wettengl, K. (Hrsg.): *Caspar David Friedrich. Winterlandschaften*, Heidelberg o. J. 1990.
Wollheim, R.: *Art and its Objects* (1968). Second Edition. With Six Supplementary Essays, Cambridge 1980.
Wolterstorff, N.: *Works and Worlds of Art*, Oxford 1980.
Wolterstorff, N.: Towards an Ontology of Artworks (1975). In: *Philosophy Looks at the Arts. Contemporary Readings in Aesthetics*, ed. by J. Margolis, 3rd ed., Philadelphia, Pa. 1987, 229-252.
Zemach, E.: The Ontological Status of Art Objects, *The Journal of Aesthetics and Art Criticism* 25 (1966), 145-153.
Zemach, E.: How Paintings Are, *The British Journal of Aesthetics* 29 (1989), 65-71.
Zemach, E.: Art and Identity, *The British Journal of Aesthetics* 31 (1991), 363-368.

Christel Fricke

Kunstwerke und ihre nicht-künstlerischen Gegenstücke

*Ein Kantisch inspirierter Beitrag zur
Debatte über das Ende der Kunst*

Abstact

In *After the End of Art* (1997) vertritt Arthur Danto die Auffassung, daß die Entwicklung der Kunst in dem Moment vollendet wurde, in dem Andy Warhol seine *Brillo Boxes* schuf. Danto beruft sich dabei auf Hegels These vom Ende der Kunst. Eine Analyse der Gründe, die Danto für seine apokalyptische Deutung der kunstgeschichtlichen Rolle der *Brillo Boxes* anführt, läßt Zweifel aufkommen sowohl an der Plausibilität dieser Auffassung als auch an ihrer Verwandtschaft mit Hegelschen Überzeugungen. Danto betont zu Recht, daß wir geeignete Konzepte eines Kunstwerks und seiner ästhetischen Erfahrung brauchen, um den Kunstcharakter von Werken zu verstehen, die nicht-künstlerische Gegenstücke haben. Wenn es für diese Konzepte Anknüpfungspunkte in der Geschichte der philosophischen Ästhetik gibt, dann sind diese nicht bei Hegel, sondern bei Kant zu finden. Denn während Hegel der Ansicht ist, daß sich die ästhetische Qualität eines Kunstwerks in der Anschauung offenbart, analysiert Kant das Verstehen ästhetischer Qualität als einen Prozeß spezifisch ästhetischer Reflexion. Im Ausgang von einer Analyse dieser Reflexion als Zeichenprozeß lassen sich geeignete Konzepte eines Kunstwerks und seiner ästhetischen Erfahrung entwickeln. Aber mit der Ausarbeitung dieses Konzepts wird das Entwicklungspotential der Kunst nicht erschöpft.

In *After the End of Art – Contemporary Art and the Pale of History* (1997) vertritt Arthur Danto die Auffassung, daß die Entwicklung der Kunst – wenn auch nicht die weitere produktive Tätigkeit von Kunstschaffenden – an ihr Ende gekommen sei. Er beruft sich dabei auf Hegels These vom Ende der Kunst. Allerdings stimmt er schon in der Frage der Datierung nicht mit Hegel überein. Während Hegel das Ende der Kunst mit dem Ende der griechischen klassischen Kunst im dritten vorchristlichen Jahrhundert identifiziert, datiert

Danto das Ende der Kunst auf das Jahr 1964. 1964 stellte Andy Warhol erstmals seine *Brillo Boxes* aus, von ihm selbst und von Freunden handgefertigte hölzerne Nachbildungen jener Kartons für Abwaschschwämme der Firma Brillo, wie sie damals in jedem amerikanischen Supermarkt stapelweise zu finden waren. Diese *Brillo Boxes* werden gemeinhin als Kunstwerke angesehen, obwohl sie in ihrer visuellen Erscheinung ununterscheidbar sind von Gebrauchsgegenständen, denen kein entsprechender ästhetischer Status zuerkannt wird. Es sind Kunstwerke mit nicht-künstlerischen Gegenstükken. In welchem Sinn sind Warhols *Brillo Boxes* Kunstwerke, nicht aber die entsprechenden Kartons in den Supermärkten? Was bedeutet die Entstehung derartiger Kunstwerke für die Geschichte der Kunst? Wie begründet Danto seine These, daß mit dem Entstehen von Kunstwerken, die nicht-künstlerische Gegenstücke haben, die Entwicklung der Kunst an ihr Ende gekommen sei? Kann er sich dabei zu Recht auf Hegel berufen?

Von Hegel übernimmt Danto eine teleologische Auffassung der Geschichte: Die geschichtliche Entwicklung wird so lange von dem Unbehagen an einem Erkenntnisdefizit vorangetrieben, bis dieses Defizit endlich beseitigt werden kann. Danto geht es allerdings nicht, wie Hegel, um die Weltgeschichte und den sich in ihr verwirklichenden Prozeß der Selbsterkenntnis des absoluten Geistes, sondern lediglich um die Geschichte der Kunst, insbesondere um die Geschichte der bildenden Kunst. Die Geschichte der Kunst ist, so Danto, bestimmt von der Suche nach einer Antwort auf die Frage, was ein Kunstwerk sei. Er identifiziert insgesamt drei Antworten auf diese Frage und entsprechend drei geschichtliche Entwicklungsstadien der Kunst: Nachahmung, Moderne und das Endstadium der Kunst. Vom 14. bis zum 19. Jahrhundert sei das Kunstwerk als ein Zeichen verstanden worden, das wirkliche Gegenstände oder Ereignisse nachahmt; die interne Entwicklung innerhalb dieses ersten Stadiums sei bestimmt worden von dem Bemühen um eine möglichst wirklichkeitsgetreue, realistische Darstellung dieser Gegenstände und Ereignisse. Von dem Projekt der Nachahmung habe sich die moderne Kunst am Ende des 19. Jahrhunderts verabschiedet. Das Kunstwerk sei nun als ein Werk angesehen worden, das zwar einerseits Exemplar einer der traditionellen Kunstgattungen, wie z. B. der Malerei oder der Bildhauerei war, andererseits aber die traditionellen künstlerischen Gestaltungsmittel nicht mehr zum Zweck der Nachahmung außerkünstlerischer Wirklichkeit verwendete, sondern zum Zweck einer abstrakten Gestaltung des Kunstwerks um seiner selbst willen und damit zum Zweck der Abgrenzung des Kunstwerks von der außerkünstlerischen Wirklichkeit. Den Schritt über die Moderne hinaus habe dann Warhol 1964 gemacht, als er mit seinen *Brillo Boxes* demonstrierte, daß der Status eines Werks als Kunstwerk nicht davon abhängt, daß dieses Werk anders aussieht als alles, was in der außerkünstlerischen Wirklichkeit vorkommt. Warhol habe damit vorgeführt, daß im Prinzip alles ein Kunstwerk sein kann.

Daraus, daß alles ein Kunstwerk sein kann, folgt auch Danto zufolge nicht, daß alles tatsächlich ein Kunstwerk ist. Die Frage, was ein Kunstwerk sei, so Danto unter Berufung auf Warhol, ist die Frage danach, was ein Kunstwerk von nicht-künstlerischen Gegenständen unterscheide, und die richtige Antwort auf diese Frage kann nur geben, wer verstanden hat, daß der fragliche Unterschied kein Unterschied hinsichtlich der jeweiligen sinnlich wahrnehmbaren Gestalten sei.[1] Wie aber lautet die richtige Antwort auf diese Frage?

Bevor ich mich dieser zentralen Frage zuwende, will ich Stellung nehmen zu Dantos These, daß Warhol mit seinen *Brillo Boxes* die historische Entwicklung der Kunst abgeschlossen und damit die Kunstgeschichte vollendet habe, sowie zu Dantos Berufung auf Hegel. Die Plausibilität der Dantoschen These vom Ende der Kunst und ihrer Geschichte hängt wesentlich von der Überzeugungskraft seiner These ab, daß die Frage, was ein Kunstwerk sei, die Geschichte der Kunst seit dem 14. Jahrhundert bewegt habe. Belegt die Geschichte der Kunst vom 14. bis zum 19. Jahrhundert die These, daß das Wesen eines Kunstwerks in der möglichst realistischen Nachahmung wirklicher Gegenstände und Ereignisse gesehen wurde? Zweifel erscheinen mir angebracht. Zum einen ist der größte Teil der malerischen und plastischen Werke, die in dieser langen Zeit entstanden, mythologischen und religiösen Themen gewidmet; in diesen Werken geht es um die Veranschaulichung imaginärer Gegenstände und Ereignisse, nicht aber um die Nachahmung von Wirklichkeit. Zum anderen ist es keineswegs offensichtlich, daß die Perfektionierung von Techniken wirklichkeitsgetreuer Darstellung in der Absicht erfolgte herauszufinden, was ein *Kunstwerk* sei. Große Debatten über die eigentliche Aufgabe der Kunstschaffenden, wie z.B. die literaturtheoretische „querelle des anciens et des modernes" und ihre Gegenstücke in der Theorie der bildenden Kunst und der Architektur, waren bewegt von der Frage, ob die Kunstschaffenden sich an antiken Vorbildern in den jeweiligen Kunstgattungen orientieren sollten. Die „anciens" plädierten für eine solche Orientierung, weil sie der Überzeugung waren, daß die künstlerische Vollendung antiker Kunstwerke nicht mehr zu überbieten sei. Die „modernes" dagegen forderten vor allem eine Natürlichkeit der künstlerischen Darstellung, die sich ohne den Zwang zur Nachahmung antiker Vorbilder sollte entfalten können. Diese Forderung nach Natürlichkeit in der künstlerischen Auseinanderset-

---

[1] Siehe Danto 1997, S. 35: „... what makes the difference between a work of art and something not a work of art when there is no interesting perceptual difference between them?"

zung mit einem Thema sollte jedoch nicht als Forderung nach einer möglichst realistischen Nachahmung wirklicher Gegenstände mißverstanden werden. Denn sie betrifft vor allem die Möglichkeit für die Kunstschaffenden, in ihrer Arbeit ihre künstlerische Kreativität zu entfalten. Erst in dieser Kreativität offenbart sich, so die Idee der „modernes", eine geniale, ihrem Ursprung nach natürliche Gabe künstlerischer Gestaltung. Weder die „anciens" noch die „modernes" propagierten in diesen Debatten das künstlerische Ideal einer möglichst realistischen Darstellung wirklicher Gegenstände oder Ereignisse. Allerdings wurde die Gegenständlichkeit oder Figürlichkeit künstlerischer Zeichen in dieser Debatte von keiner Seite in Frage gestellt. Figürlichkeit und Realismus künstlerischer Darstellung sollten jedoch nicht verwechselt werden.[2]

Die zentrale Frage, um deren Beantwortung sich die „anciens" und die „modernes" stritten, die Frage, nach welchen Regeln oder unter Einwirkung welcher kreativen Kräfte ein Kunstwerk geschaffen werden könne, sollte nicht mit der Frage nach dem Wesen eines Kunstwerks verwechselt werden. Jene Frage verlangte keine Antwort, die für alle Kunstwerke, die zu verschiedenen Zeiten und an verschiedenen Orten entstanden, Gültigkeit beanspruchte. Möglicherweise hat die Tatsache, daß sich die Künste über Jahrhunderte im Rahmen figürlicher Darstellung und im Rahmen der traditionellen Kunstgattungen entwickelt haben, eine epochenübergreifende Antwort auf die Frage nach dem Wesen eines Kunstwerks über einen entsprechend langen Zeitraum nicht als besonders dringlich erscheinen lassen. Solange sich die Kunst im Rahmen figürlicher Darstellung und im Rahmen traditioneller Gattungsgrenzen entwickelte, war leicht zu übersehen, daß es jenseits aller beschränkten Kunstkonzepte eine allgemein verbindliche Antwort auf die Frage, was ein Kunstwerk sei, gar nicht gab. Die Frage, was ein Kunstwerk eigentlich sei, scheint erst in dem Moment akut geworden zu sein, als sich die Kunst aus ihrem traditionellen Rahmen figürlicher Darstellung zu lösen begann und sich außerdem anschickte, die Grenzen der traditionellen Kunstgattungen in Frage zu stellen, um sie schließlich zu überschreiten.

Daß die kunstgeschichtliche Entwicklung von jeher, wie Danto behauptet, vorangetrieben worden sei von dem Anliegen, die Frage nach dem Wesen eines Kunstwerks jenseits aller zeitlich und räumlich beschränkten Erscheinungsformen von Kunst zu beantworten, erscheint daher kaum überzeugend. Hinzu kommt, daß die Antwort auf diese Frage, wie Danto sie in Warhols *Brillo Boxes* verkörpert sieht, sich nicht erst 1964 abzeichnet, sondern schon 1913, nämlich mit den *ready-mades* von Marcel Duchamp. Das

---

[2] Siehe zu den Leitfragen der „querelle des anciens et des modernes" u.a. Jauss 1964.

Datum der ersten *ready-mades* paßt aber nicht in Dantos kunstgeschichtliches Konzept, denn 1913 war das Projekt der modernen, abstrakten Malerei, der zweiten von Danto identifizierten kunstgeschichtlichen Epoche, noch nicht abgeschlossen. Die kunstgeschichtliche Bedeutung von Warhols Ausstellung der *Brillo Boxes* liegt nicht darin, die Kunstgeschichte vollendet zu haben, sondern darin, das von Danto als „modern" charakterisierte Verständnis von Kunst endgültig verabschiedet zu haben, demzufolge ein Kunstwerk sich in seinen sinnlich wahrnehmbaren Eigenschaften, in seiner phänomenalen Erscheinung, von nicht-künstlerischen Gegenständen zu unterscheiden habe. Den Prozeß dieser Verabschiedung hatte Duchamp schon 1913 eröffnet. Die philosophische Ästhetik allerdings hat erst in den sechziger Jahren des vergangenen Jahrhunderts damit begonnen, das Konzept eines Kunstwerks zu erarbeiten, mittels dessen der künstlerische Charakter von Kunstwerken verständlich gemacht werden kann, die nicht-künstlerische Gegenstücke haben und damit eine Verabschiedung des Kunstverständnisses der Moderne verkörpern.[3] Die These Dantos, daß Duchamp und später die Vertreter der pop-art, insbesondere Andy Warhol, mit ihren Kunstwerken, die nicht-künstlerische Gegenstücke haben, eine Antwort auf die Frage, was ein Kunstwerk sei, als besonders dringlich haben erkennen lassen, halte ich für plausibel. Daß sich mit der – künstlerischen und schließlich auch philosophischen – Beantwortung dieser Frage aber die Geschichte der Kunst vollendet habe, erscheint mir nicht überzeugend, denn für die Plausibilität dieser apokalyptischen Auffassung fehlen die historischen Voraussetzungen: Die Suche nach einer Antwort auf die Frage, was ein Kunstwerk sei, hat die Kunst nicht schon immer bewegt, sie ist vielmehr das zentrale Anliegen einer begrenzten Epoche, nämlich der Kunst, die sich von dem Projekt der Moderne verabschiedet. Die historische Funktion dieser Suche läßt sich daher nicht nach dem Modell von Hegels Verständnis der historischen Funktion des nach Selbsterkenntnis strebenden Geistes verständlich machen.

Dies ist nicht der einzige Grund, der mich veranlaßt, an der Berechtigung von Dantos Berufung auf Hegel und dessen These vom Ende der Kunst zu zweifeln. Hegel versteht die Weltgeschichte und ihre teleologische Entwicklung, die sich in der Selbsterkenntnis des absoluten Geistes vollendet, als eine Art Staffellauf. Staffelträger sind verschiedene Institutionen, nämlich nacheinander die Kunst, die Religion und die Philosophie. In einem frühen Stadium der weltgeschichtlichen Entwicklung, in der Zeit der griechischen klassischen Kunst, ist es die Kunst, genauer gesagt die Bildhauerei, die den Stab der weltgeschichtlichen Entwicklung trägt. Daß es die Bildwerke der griechischen

---

[3] Siehe insbes. Nelson Goodmans *Languages of Art*, das 1968 erstmals erschien.

Klassik sind, die in dieser zentralen Phase der weltgeschichtlichen Entwicklung den Stab tragen, erklärt sich aus der Hegelschen Auffassung, daß den Zeitgenossen in diesen Bildwerken der absolute Geist in seiner Konkretheit sinnlich, und d. h. anschaulich erschien. Das Medium der Kunst ist für Hegel die sinnliche Konkretheit, und die angemessene Rezeption dieser Konkretheit ist für ihn die Anschauung. In der frühesten Phase der weltgeschichtlichen Entwicklung kann sich der absolute Geist nur in der Anschauung von Kunstwerken offenbaren. Da aber die Anschauung nicht die dem absoluten Geist eigentlich angemessene Erkenntnisform ist, muß die Kunst den Stab wieder abgeben, zunächst an die Religion und dann an die Philosophie. Ihre Funktion des weltgeschichtlichen Motors ist zeitlich begrenzt. Hegels These vom Ende der Kunst, von der Begrenztheit der Zeit, in der die Kunst den Stab im Staffellauf der Weltgeschichte trägt, ist eng mit seiner These verknüpft, daß die der Kunst allein angemessene Art der Rezeption die Anschauung ist. Sobald Menschen versuchen, über das, was in der Kunst anschaulich gemacht wird, zu reflektieren, um es besser zu verstehen, transzendieren sie den Bereich der Kunst und erkennen, daß sie über die Kunst hinausgehen müssen, um die Selbsterkenntnis des absoluten Geistes weiter zu befördern. In der Perspektive der Hegelschen Auffassung von Kunst und ihrer anschaulichen Rezeption läßt sich nun aber gerade nicht verständlich machen, daß es Kunstwerke geben kann, die nicht-künstlerische Gegenstücke haben. Denn in der bloßen *Anschauung* unterscheiden sich diese Werke nicht von ihren nicht-künstlerischen Gegenstücken. Der künstlerische Status dieser Werke erschließt sich nicht in der Anschauung, es bedarf der *ästhetischen Reflexion*, um diesen Status zu verstehen. Es ist daher irreführend, wenn Danto sich mit seiner These, daß mit den Kunstwerken, die nicht-künstlerische Gegenstücke haben, die Geschichte der Kunst an ihr Ende gekommen sei, auf Hegels These vom Ende der Kunst beruft.

Was aber macht Warhols *Brillo Boxes* (und Duchamps ready-mades) zu Kunstwerken? Was unterscheidet diese Objekte von den nicht-künstlerischen Objekten derselben Art, den Kartons mit Abwaschschwämmen in den Supermärkten, den Schneeschaufeln (den nicht-künstlerischen Gegenstücken zu Duchamps „In advance of the broken arm" (1915)) und den Urinierbecken in den Sanitärgeschäften und Herrentoiletten (den nicht-künstlerischen Gegenstücken zu Duchamps „Fountain" (1917))? Mit welchem Konzept eines Kunstwerks läßt sich der Anspruch dieser Werke auf einen künstlerischen Status rechtfertigen? Und wie universell ist das Konzept eines Kunstwerks, das eine solche Rechtfertigung erlaubt?

Dantos Antwort auf die Frage, was ein Kunstwerk sei, mutet auf den ersten Blick ebenso schlicht wie wenig originell an: Kunstwerke sind *Zeichen*, Träger einer Bedeutung, und was sie von anderen Arten von Zeichen unterscheidet ist, daß sie ihre Bedeutung *verkörpern*.[4] Es ist der Zeichencharakter, der Warhols *Brillo Boxes* von ihren nicht-künstlerischen Gegenstücken unterscheidet. Ich denke, daß Dantos Konzept eines Kunstwerks als Zeichen, das seine Bedeutung verkörpert, weiterer Ausarbeitung bedarf, um das zu leisten, was es leisten soll. Aber auf eine Pointe dieses Kunstkonzepts läßt sich schon hier verweisen: Daß jeder beliebige sinnlich wahrnehmbare Gegenstand ein Kunstwerk sein kann, wenn auch nicht jeder beliebige sinnlich wahrnehmbare Gegenstand ein Kunstwerk ist, läßt sich aus dem Zeichencharakter eines Kunstwerks erklären. Es kann nämlich auch jeder beliebige sinnlich wahrnehmbare Gegenstand als ein Zeichen fungieren. Ob ein gegebener sinnlich wahrnehmbarer Gegenstand als ein Zeichen fungiert oder nicht, hängt nicht ab von seiner konkreten Gestalt. Ein Gegenstand fungiert nur dann als ein Zeichen, wenn er von einer Zeichenverwenderin oder einem Zeichenverwender zu einem Zeichen gemacht worden ist. Der Unterschied zwischen Gegenständen, die Zeichen sind, und solchen, die keine Zeichen sind, beruht nicht auf natürlichen oder phänomenalen Unterschieden zwischen diesen Gegenständen, er ist ausschließlich pragmatischer Art. Entsprechendes gilt für Kunstwerke und nicht-künstlerische Gegenstände. Die Möglichkeit von Kunstwerken, zu denen es nicht-künstlerische Gegenstücke gibt, beruht auf dem Zeichencharakter von Kunstwerken, denn dieser ist wesentlich pragmatisch.

Wie läßt sich das von Danto in Ansätzen skizzierte Konzept eines Kunstwerks weiter ausarbeiten? Es ist zu klären, wie sich Kunstwerke von anderen Zeichen, die ihre Bedeutung verkörpern, unterscheiden. Denn nicht nur sind nicht alle Zeichen Kunstwerke, es sind auch nicht alle die Zeichen Kunstwerke, die ihre Bedeutung verkörpern. Zu den Zeichen, die ihre Bedeutung verkörpern, gehören u. a. alle bildlichen Zeichen, insofern die konkrete Gestalt bildlicher Zeichen im Verhältnis zu dem, was diese Zeichen bildlich bedeuten, nicht willkürlich ist. Die Bedeutung eines Bildes ist mit der Bedeutung eines mehrstelligen Prädikatausdrucks zu vergleichen, allerdings eines Prädikatausdrucks von besonderer Gestalt. Ein Bild wird – ähnlich wie ein Prädikatausdruck – erfüllt von Gegenständen einer bestimmten Art. Die Gegenstände der fraglichen Art sind Raum-Zeit-Regionen, in denen

---

[4] Danto 1997, S. 195: „To be a work of art is to be (i) *about* something and (ii) to *embody its meaning*." Siehe dazu auch Danto 1981, Kap. 6, insbes. S. 147–148.
Das Konzept eines Zeichens, das seine Bedeutung verkörpert, spielt schon in Nelson Goodmans Zeichentheorie und Ästhetik eine zentrale Rolle. Statt von einem seine Bedeutung verkörpernden Zeichen spricht Goodman allerdings von einem „exemplifizierenden" Zeichen (siehe Goodman 1981, Kap. II.3. u. VI.5.)
Zu Goodmans Konzept eines exemplifizierenden Zeichens siehe auch Steinbrenner 1996 und Fricke 2001.

sichtbare Objekte präsent sind. Von Prädikatausdrücken anderer Art unterscheidet sich ein Bild dadurch, daß seine Gestalt die Art der Gegenstände charakterisiert, die es erfüllen: Die Gegenstände, die ein Bild erfüllen, sind so beschaffen, daß ihre visuelle Wahrnehmung bei einer Person visuelle Wahrnehmungsfelder entstehen läßt, die in einem Verhältnis der Isomorphie zu dem Wahrnehmungsfeld stehen, das bei dieser Person entsteht, wenn sie dieses Bild betrachtet. Die Ähnlichkeit, von der im Zusammenhang eines figürlichen Bildes und den auf ihm dargestellten Gegenständen oft die Rede ist, ist keine Ähnlichkeit zwischen diesem Bild und diesen Gegenständen, zumal die Möglichkeit besteht, Gegenstände abzubilden, die in keiner zur wirklichen Welt gehörenden Raum-Zeit-Region existieren. Die fragliche Ähnlichkeit ist vielmehr eine Ähnlichkeit zwischen visuellen Wahrnehmungsfeldern. Visuelle Wahrnehmungsfelder können jedoch nicht nur bei der Wahrnehmung wirklicher Raum-Zeit-Regionen entstehen, sondern auch in der Einbildungskraft oder Phantasie einer Person.[5]

Neben Bildern können beliebige Gebrauchsgegenstände, deren Gestalt den Zweck erkennen läßt, dem sie dienen und im Hinblick auf den sie als Artefakte gestaltet wurden, als Beispiele für Zeichen angesehen werden, deren Gestalt im Hinblick auf das, was sie bedeuten, nicht willkürlich ist. Ein Gebrauchsgegenstand verkörpert seine Funktion, und insofern er als ein Gegenstand angesehen wird, der seine Funktion verkörpert, hat er den Status eines Zeichens für seine Funktion. Die meisten Gebrauchsgegenstände sind keine Bilder, die Raum-Zeit-Regionen abbilden, in denen sichtbare Objekte einer bestimmten Art präsent sind. Nun bin ich der Ansicht, daß sich der Zeichencharakter von Kunstwerken eher nach dem Modell des Zeichencharakters von Gebrauchsgegenständen als nach dem Modell bildlicher Zeichen verständlich machen läßt.

Der historische Anknüpfungspunkt für dieses Verständnis eines Kunstwerks als Zeichen ist nicht in Hegels, sondern in Kants Ästhetik zu finden. Im Unterschied zu Hegel begreift Kant die ästhetische Erfahrung eines Gegenstands, in deren Vollzug wir die ästhetische Qualität und damit den künstlerischen Charakters dieses Gegenstands entdecken, nicht als Anschauung, sondern als einen Prozeß der *Reflexion*. Und der Prozeß der ästhetischen Reflexion, wie Kant ihn analysiert, läßt sich auch als der Prozeß beschreiben, in dem wir einen Gegenstand als ein Zeichen zu verstehen und zu interpretieren versuchen, und zwar als ein Zeichen besonderer Art, als Kunstwerk. Diese These mag auf den ersten Blick verwunderlich erscheinen. Denn zum einen sind für Kant nicht Kunstwerke in unserem heutigen Sinn, also künstle-

---

[5] Zu dem hier unterstellten naturalistischen Verständnis der Bildlichkeit von Zeichen siehe Budd 1993 und Fricke 2001, Kap. 4.

rische Artefakte, die bevorzugten Gegenstände ästhetischer Erfahrung, sondern natürliche Gegenstände; und zum andern analysiert er unsere ästhetische Erfahrung als interesseloses Wohlgefallen, also als ein Gefühl. Aber wir sollten uns davon nicht täuschen lassen. Kant zufolge offenbart sich uns in der ästhetischen Reflexion über einen schönen natürlichen Gegenstand, daß dieser eine Art Artefakt ist, wenn auch kein Artefakt menschlicher, sondern ein Artefakt natürlicher oder göttlicher Provenienz. Und das interesselose Wohlgefallen, in dem uns die (von Kant als „Schönheit" bezeichnete) ästhetische Qualität und damit der künstlerische Charakter eines Gegenstands unserer sinnlichen Anschauung bewußt wird, beruht Kant zufolge auf einem Prozeß ästhetischer Reflexion. Diesen Prozeß beschreibt er nicht nur als ein freies Spiel von Einbildungskraft und Verstand, sondern auch als eine geistige Tätigkeit, bei der wir versuchen, in dem uns anschaulich gegebenen Gegenstand eine „Form der Zweckmäßigkeit ohne Zweck" zu entdecken. Dies ist, so jedenfalls mein Verständnis dieses zentralen Teils der Kantischen Theorie ästhetischer Erfahrung, die Form, die einen Gegenstand auszeichnet, der ein spezifisch ästhetisches Zeichen ist, ein künstlerisches Artefakt. Ein solches Artefakt verkörpert, anders als alltägliche Gebrauchsgegenstände, keine Gebrauchsfunktion, sondern eine gedankliche oder ideelle Bedeutung, die es im Prozeß der ästhetischen Reflexion zu ergründen gilt.[6] Wie dieser Prozeß ästhetischer Reflexion als Zeichenprozeß analysiert werden kann, will ich im folgenden skizzieren.

Im Unterschied nicht nur zu Zeichen einer natürlichen Sprache, sondern auch zu bildlichen Zeichen und Gebrauchsgegenständen sind Kunstwerke, so meine These, wesentlich *freie Zeichen*, Zeichen, die zu keinem bekannten Zeichensystem gehören. Das bedeutet zunächst, daß wir uns, wenn wir die Bedeutung eines Kunstwerks im Prozeß einer ästhetischen Reflexion zu verstehen versuchen, an keinem bekannten Zeichensystem orientieren können. Wegen dieser Orientierungslosigkeit erscheinen uns viele Kunstwerke auf den ersten Blick als bedeutungsopak. Welche Rolle die Bezugnahme auf ein Zeichensystem bei der Interpretation eines bestimmten Zeichens spielt, läßt sich am Beispiel eines Zeichens veranschaulichen, das zu einem kodifizierten Zeichensystem gehört. Ein *kodifiziertes Zeichensystem* besteht aus einer bestimmten, endlich großen Menge von Zeichentypen, deren Zeichenvorkommnisse sich anhand ihrer syntaktischen Klassifikationsmerkmale voneinander unterscheiden und den entsprechenden Zeichentypen zuordnen lassen. Für die Verbindung von Zeichenvorkommnissen zu komplexen Zeichen gelten semantische Regeln, die erlauben, zwischen wohlgeformten und nicht wohlgeformten Zeichen zu unterscheiden. Allen Zeichentypen, die

---

[6] Siehe zur dieser Interpretation der Kantischen Ästhetik Fricke 1990 und 1998.

eine eigene semantische Funktion haben, ist in einem kodifizierten System eine Bedeutung zugeordnet. Die Bedeutungen verschiedener Zeichentypen unterscheiden sich hinsichtlich ihrer semantischen Klassifikationsmerkmale. Wir können die Bedeutung eines Zeichenvorkommnisses eines solchen kodifizierten Zeichensystems verstehen, wenn wir es anhand seiner syntaktischen Klassifikationsmerkmale dem entsprechenden Zeichentyp zuordnen (und von Vorkommnissen anderer Zeichentypen unterscheiden); über diese Zuordnung erhalten wir Aufschluß über das entsprechende semantische Klassifikationsmerkmal und damit über die Bedeutung des Zeichens. Einfache Beispiele für derartige kodifizierte Zeichensysteme sind die Schachnotation und das Morsealphabet.

Die Bedeutung von Zeichen kodifizierter Zeichensysteme ist durch das jeweilige System festgelegt und damit weitgehend unabhängig davon, welcher Sender diese Zeichen in welcher Kommunikationssituation an welchen Empfänger übermittelt.[7] Die Bedeutung alltagssprachlicher Mitteilungen ist allerdings selten derartig systembestimmt und entsprechend unabhängig von den kommunizierenden Personen und ihren Kommunikationsabsichten. Dennoch kann auch aus Zeichen einer natürlichen Sprache ein Zeichenkode erstellt werden. Für ein Verständnis der Bedeutung eines natürlichsprachlichen Zeichens ist dieses Zeichen in allen Fällen auf ein entsprechendes Zeichensystem zu beziehen. Je nach dem Grad der Kodifizierung dieses Systems läßt sich die Bedeutung eines solchen Zeichens in der Beziehung auf das entsprechende Zeichensystem mehr oder weniger eindeutig bestimmen. Wenn eine Person z.B. eine schwarze, merkwürdig gekrümmte Linie auf einem weißen Papier sieht, dann kann sie sich fragen, ob es sich bei dieser Linie eventuell um ein Wort einer natürlichen Sprache handelt. Zur Beantwortung dieser Frage muß sie prüfen, ob diese Linie syntaktische Klassifikationsmerkmale aufweist, die es erlauben, diese Linie als Zeichenvorkommnis eines Typs eines entsprechenden Zeichensystems zu bestimmen. Wenn eine Zuordnung der Linie zu einem solchen Zeichentyp gelingt, dann wird diese Linie als Wort einer natürlichen Sprache erkannt. Diese Erkenntnis bildet den Ausgangspunkt für das Verständnis der Bedeutung des linienförmigen Zeichens. Denn den Zeichentypen eines Systems sind semantische Klassifikationsmerkmale zugeordnet, an denen sich jedes Verständnis der Bedeutung eines entsprechenden Zeichenvorkommnisses orientieren kann.

Daß Kunstwerke freie Zeichen sind, bedeutet nun erstens, daß wir uns zum Zweck ihrer Zuordnung als Zeichenvorkommnisse zu einem Zeichentyp und zum Zweck ihrer Abgrenzung von Zeichenvorkommnissen anderer

---

[7] Die fragliche Unabhängigkeit muß nicht vollständig sein, denn ein kodifiziertes Zeichensystem kann auch indexikalische Ausdrücke enthalten.

Typen, also zum Zweck der Identifikation ihrer syntaktischen Klassifikationsmerkmale, nicht an einem gegebenen Zeichensystem orientieren können. Zweitens bedeutet die Freiheit eines künstlerischen Zeichens, daß wir seine semantischen Klassifikationsmerkmale nicht in bezug auf ein entsprechendes System bestimmen können. Die Freiheit künstlerischer Zeichen stellt jedoch nicht nur ein Problem im Hinblick auf die Bestimmung seiner syntaktischen und semantischen Klassifikationsmerkmale dar. Sie zwingt darüber hinaus zu einer Infragestellung des Zeichencharakters eines Kunstwerks. Ein Gegenstand kann nämlich nur im Zusammenhang eines Zeichensystems als Zeichen fungieren, da sich nur unter Bezugnahme auf ein solches System seine sinnlich wahrnehmbaren Eigenschaften als syntaktische Klassifikationsmerkmale bestimmen und seine semantischen Klassifikationsmerkmale angeben lassen.[8] Inwiefern ist die Rede von Kunstwerken als freien Zeichen, wie ich sie hier vorschlage, dann aber überhaupt noch sinnvoll? Bedeutet die Systembezogenheit jedes Zeichens nicht, daß es freie Zeichen in dem behaupteten Sinn gar nicht geben kann?

Zur Plausibilisierung meiner These, derzufolge Kunstwerke freie Zeichen sind, muß ich auf das Konzept ästhetischer Reflexion bezug nehmen. Als „ästhetische Reflexion" bezeichne ich den Prozeß der sinnlichen Wahrnehmung, Beschreibung und Interpretation eines Gegenstands als Kunstwerk. Wir können jeden sinnlich wahrnehmbaren Gegenstand zum Gegenstand einer ästhetischen Reflexion machen. Am Beginn einer solchen Reflexion steht nicht mehr als die ästhetische Hypothese, daß ihr Gegenstand ein Kunstwerk, ein freies Zeichen sei. Weil ein Gegenstand nur in bezug auf ein Zeichensystem den Status eines Zeichens erhalten kann und weil für das Verständnis eines Gegenstands als freies Zeichen am Beginn einer ästhetischen Reflexion über ihn ein solches Bezugssystem nicht zur Verfügung steht, erwächst aus dieser ästhetischen Hypothese die Aufgabe, ein Zeichensystem allererst zu konstruieren, in bezug auf das sich dieser Gegenstand als Zeichen klassifizieren und interpretieren, also hinsichtlich seiner syntaktischen und semantischen Klassifikationsmerkmale bestimmen läßt.

Das im Prozeß einer ästhetischen Reflexion über einen Gegenstand als freies Zeichen zu konstruierende Zeichensystem kann nun kein beliebiges System sein, sondern es muß ein solches sein, dessen Zeichenvorkommnisse so gestaltet sind, daß ihre Verbindung mit ihrer Bedeutung nicht willkürlich erscheint. Die Zeichen der zu konstruierenden Systeme müssen ihre Bedeutung verkörpern, und das heißt, daß ihre syntaktischen Klassifikationsmerkmale uns Hinweise auf ihre Bedeutung, die ihnen zuzuordnenden semanti-

---

[8] Siehe zu dem Zusammenhang zwischen dem Zeichenstatus eines Gegenstands und dessen Zugehörigkeit zu einem Zeichensystem u.a. Fricke 2001, Kap. 1.4.

schen Klassifikationsmerkmale geben müssen. Für die ästhetische Reflexion über einen Gegenstand bedeutet dies, daß seine konkrete Gestalt mit all ihren sinnlich wahrnehmbaren Eigenschaften dessen Zeichenpotential und damit den Ausgangspunkt für das zu konstruierende Zeichensystem bildet. Bei dieser Konstruktion spielen insbesondere Beziehungen der Ähnlichkeit und Verschiedenheit eine wichtige Rolle, in denen dieser Gegenstand zu anderen Gegenständen steht, insbesondere zu solchen, die als Kunstwerke gelten.

Die Ausgangshypothese der ästhetischen Reflexion über einen Gegenstand kann sich in mehr oder weniger hohem Maß bestätigen oder als unberechtigt erweisen. Sie bestätigt sich in dem Maß, in dem es gelingt, ihren Gegenstand als Zeichen zu verstehen, das seine Bedeutung verkörpert. Je mehr der sinnlich wahrnehmbaren Eigenschaften eines Gegenstands sich im Prozeß einer ästhetischen Reflexion als syntaktische Klassifikationsmerkmale erweisen, die uns Hinweise auf entsprechende semantische Klassifikationsmerkmale geben, desto erfolgreicher ist diese Reflexion, in desto höherem Maß erweist sich dieser Gegenstand als ein Kunstwerk, als ein Werk von ästhetischer Qualität.

Ob es einer Person gelingt, in einem Prozeß der ästhetischen Reflexion über einen Gegenstand diesen als Kunstwerk zu verstehen oder nicht, das hängt zum einen von dem ästhetischen Potential dieses Gegenstands, zum anderen aber davon ab, ob und in welchem Maß es dieser Person gelingt, ein Zeichensystem zu konstruieren, in bezug auf das sich dieser Gegenstand als Zeichen klassifizieren und interpretieren läßt. Es sind vor allem alltägliche Gebrauchsgegenstände, Zeichen bekannter Zeichensysteme und Kunstwerke, die den Fundus bilden, aus dem wir schöpfen, wenn wir in ästhetischen Reflexionen geeignete Zeichensysteme konstruieren. Dabei liegt es an uns, was wir aus diesem Fundus schöpfen und als Zeichen eines Zeichensystems ansehen, an unserer Fähigkeit, uns all dieser Dinge zu erinnern, und an unserer Phantasie, uns geeignete Hinsichten auszudenken, in bezug auf die wir den Gegenstand unserer ästhetischen Reflexion so mit all diesen Dingen vergleichen können, daß wir seine sichtbaren Eigenschaften als syntaktische Klassifikationsmerkmale und seine Gestalt entsprechend als Verkörperung seiner Bedeutung verstehen können.

Wenn es uns gelingt, einen Gegenstand im Prozeß einer ästhetischen Reflexion als Kunstwerk zu verstehen, verlieren wir nicht das ästhetische Interesse daran, diese Reflexion fortzusetzen. Der Erfolg einer ästhetischen Reflexion, die Bestätigung ihrer Ausgangshypothese, bedeutet nicht deren Ende. Denn eine solche Reflexion ist niemals abgeschlossen. Jede Konstruktion eines Zeichensystems, in bezug auf das sich der Gegenstand einer ästhetischen Reflexion als künstlerisches Zeichen verständlich machen läßt, bedeutet einen Vorschlag unter verschiedenen möglichen, für dessen Ausarbeitung es keinen zwingenden Abschluß gibt. In diesem Sinn ist die Interpretation jedes Kunstwerks inkommensurabel. Diese Inkommensurabilität der ästhetischen Interpretation eines Kunstwerks bedeutet, daß es auch im Prozeß einer erfolgreichen ästhetischen Reflexion seine Freiheit als Zeichen nicht verliert. Jede Einbindung eines Kunstwerks in ein Zeichensystem hat den Charakter eines Vorschlags, dem immer etwas Vorläufiges anhaftet.

Wenn wir über einen Gegenstand ästhetisch reflektieren, wenn wir versuchen, ihn als freies Zeichen, das seine Bedeutung verkörpert, d. h. als ein Kunstwerk zu verstehen, dann fragen wir immer, aus welchem Grund dieser Gegenstand genau so gestaltet wurde, wie er gestaltet wurde. Diese Leitfrage der ästhetischen Reflexion über einen Gegenstand sollte nun aber nicht als die Frage nach der mechanischen Entstehungsgeschichte dieses Gegenstands mißverstanden werden, ebensowenig wie als Frage nach den Absichten, mit denen eine Künstlerin oder ein Künstler diesen Gegenstand gestaltet hat. Es ist vielmehr die hermeneutische Frage danach, in welcher Weise der Gegenstand ein Zeichen ist, dessen Gestalt im Verhältnis zu dem, was es bedeutet, nicht willkürlich ist – wobei „Bedeutung" hier nicht im Sinn der Bezugnahme auf etwas verstanden werden sollte, sondern im Sinne der Angabe von semantischen Klassifikationsmerkmalen, d. h. von Kriterien, nach denen wir entscheiden, ob etwas diesem Zeichen entspricht, zu seinen möglichen Erfüllungsgegenständen gehört. Wir dürfen in der ästhetischen Reflexion über einen Gegenstand als freies Zeichen diesem daher nicht willkürlich irgendwelche Bedeutungen zuschreiben, sondern nur solche, die dieser Gegenstand in seiner konkreten Gestalt verkörpert, die uns daher helfen zu verstehen, warum dieser Gegenstand genau so gestaltet wurde, wie er gestaltet wurde.[9]

Im folgenden will ich versuchen, das hier skizzierte Konzept eines Kunstwerks als eines freien Zeichens am Beispiel von Warhols *Brillo Boxes* zu veranschaulichen und zu plausibilisieren. Dabei geht es nicht zuletzt um die Beantwortung der Frage, in welchem Sinn die *Brillo Boxes* Kunstwerke sind, während den entsprechenden Kartons in den Supermärkten kein künstlerischer Status zukommt. Schauen wir uns ein Exemplar der *Brillo Boxes* erst einmal genauer an, studieren wir sein Zeichenpotential. Warhol und seine Mitstreiter haben sich offensichtlich bemüht, einen Gegenstand herzustellen, der hinsichtlich seiner Größe, Form und Farbe eine wirklichkeitsgetreue Nachahmung der Kartons für die Abwaschschwämme der Firma Brillo ist. Warum die Berücksichtigung insbesondere von Größe, Form und Farbe? Das sind diejenigen Eigenschaften der Kartons, die deren visuelle Erscheinung bestimmen. Daß Warhols *Brillo Boxes* geschlossene Kisten aus Holz

---

[9] Zu dem hier skizzierten Verständnis der ästhetischen Reflexion als Zeichenprozeß siehe Fricke 2001, insbes. Kap. 8. u. 9.

sind, also zum Aufbewahren von Abwaschschwämmen gar nicht geeignet, beeinträchtigt ihr Potential visueller Repräsentation in keiner Weise. Indem wir die *Brillo Boxes* bzw. ein Exemplar derselben auf diese Weise beschreiben, vergleichen wir dieses Exemplar zum einen mit den Kartons für Abwaschschwämme der Firma Brillo, zum anderen, wenn auch indirekt, mit anderen, diesen Kartons ähnlichen Gegenständen, die nach dem Vorbild dieser Kartons gestaltet worden sein könnten, mit anderen Kisten, in denen wir etwas aufbewahren könnten, und mit möglichen Vergrößerungen oder Verkleinerungen oder anderweitig verfremdenden Nachahmungen der Kartons für Abwaschschwämme der Firma Brillo. Und schließlich vergleichen wir dieses Exemplar mit anderen Gegenständen, die zum Zweck der visuellen Nachahmung wirklicher Gegenstände geschaffen wurden oder die als figürliche Darstellungen von sichtbaren Gegenständen angesehen werden können. Mit diesem letzten Schritt betrachten wir Warhols *Brillo Boxes* im Kontext u.a. alles dessen, was die Geschichte der Kunst an figürlichen Darstellungen sichtbarer Gegenstände hervorgebracht hat. D.h. wir vergleichen die *Brillo Boxes* auf diese Weise mit verschiedenen Typen von Gegenständen, die entweder den Kartons für Abwaschschwämme der Firma Brillo oder deren Nachahmungen in irgendeiner Hinsicht ähnlich sind. Diese Typen sind, so meine These, als Zeichentypen eines Zeichensystems anzusehen. Und wenn wir die *Brillo Boxes* von Warhol mit Gegenständen dieser anderen Typen vergleichen, können wir fragen, warum sie genau so gestaltet werden mußten, wie sie tatsächlich gestaltet wurden, um ihr Zeichenpotential zu entfalten, d.h. um etwas zu bedeuten und um das, was sie bedeuten, auch zu verkörpern.

Was mit diesen Holzkisten von Warhol figürlich dargestellt wird, ist nichts besonders Schönes oder besonders Heiliges oder besonders Mächtiges, sondern etwas ebenso Profanes wie Nützliches und visuell wenig Interessantes: ein alltäglicher Gebrauchsgegenstand. Warhol leugnet damit die Grundthese der Vertreter der modernen Kunst, derzufolge sich ein Kunstwerk hinsichtlich seiner sinnlich wahrnehmbaren Eigenschaften, seiner phänomenalen Erscheinung von nicht-künstlerischen Gegenständen zu unterscheiden habe. Er stellt sein Werk, insofern es eine figürliche Darstellung ist, bewußt in die Tradition der vormodernen Kunst, demonstriert damit, daß auch eine *Brillo Box* ein Exemplar einer der traditionellen Kunstgattungen ist, nämlich der figürlichen Plastik. Daß er und seine Freunde mehr als eine solche *Brillo Box*, insgesamt 120 Exemplare, hergestellt haben, hat dabei seine besondere Pointe: Die alte Überzeugung von der Einmaligkeit des Kunstwerks wird damit falsifiziert, denn dieses Kunstwerk, obwohl ein Werk, das zu der traditionellen Gattung der Plastik gezählt werden kann, kommt in vielen Exemplaren vor.

Warhol wählt als Gegenstand seiner Darstellung einen profanen Gebrauchsgegenstand, und auch diese Wahl ist nicht von ungefähr. Gebrauchsgegenständen von provozierender Profanität hatte schon Duchamp den Weg in die Kunstwelt geebnet. Seine ready-mades waren und sind jedoch keine Nachahmungen, es sind tatsächlich profane Gebrauchsgegenstände. Duchamp demonstrierte mit seinen ready-mades, daß der Kunststatus eines Werks nicht davon abhängt, als nachahmendes Zeichen von Hand gefertigt zu sein. Auch ein industriell gefertigter Gebrauchsgegenstand kann zum künstlerischen Zeichen avancieren. Warhol wiederholt Duchamps Geste nicht einfach, sondern radikalisiert sie, insofern er ein Zeichen erfindet, das Duchamps künstlerische Einsicht in den pragmatischen Ursprung des Zeichen- und Kunststatus eines Gegenstands wiederholt, sich zum Ausdruck dieser Einsicht jedoch einer traditionellen künstlerischen Strategie bedient, der Schaffung eines figürlichen Zeichens. Dieses Zeichen bedeutet eine Provokation: Auch eine *Brillo Box* ist ein Kunstwerk, ein freies Zeichen, das seine Bedeutung verkörpert – obwohl sie weder schön anzuschauen ist, noch etwas Schönes, Heiliges oder Mächtiges figürlich darstellt, noch ganz anders aussieht als jeder nicht-künstlerische Gegenstand. Sie ist, zusammen mit den anderen der 120 *Brillo Boxes*, dennoch ein Kunstwerk, ein freies Zeichen, das seine Bedeutung verkörpert.

Dies ist nur ein erster, vorläufiger und unvollständiger Vorschlag, wie Warhols *Brillo Boxes* als freie, künstlerische Zeichen interpretiert werden können. Das konstruierte System bleibt vorläufig, es kann jederzeit ergänzt oder ersetzt werden durch alternative Systeme, in bezug auf die dieses Werk Warhols als freies, künstlerisches Zeichen interpretiert werden kann. Ziel der ästhetischen Reflexion über ein Kunstwerk ist es nicht, diesem eine ganz bestimmte, ein- für allemal zu fixierende Bedeutung zuzuschreiben. Entsprechend hat schon Kant die These vertreten, daß die ästhetische Reflexion „sich selbst stärkt und reproduziert", ohne jemals an ein Ende zu kommen.[10]

Es bleibt die Frage nach der Reichweite des Konzepts eines Kunstwerks als freies Zeichen zu stellen. Dieses Konzept eines Kunstwerks erlaubt nicht nur, den besonderen künstlerischen Status jener Werke zu verstehen, die in ganz alltäglichen Gebrauchsgegenständen nicht-künstlerische Gegenstücke haben. All die uns so fremd und unverständlich anmutenden Werke der zeitgenössischen Kunst, wie unschön aussehende oder gar unappetitliche Installationen oder verwirrend flackernde Videos, lassen sich als freie Zeichen interpretieren – wobei wir natürlich immer gewärtig sein müssen, daß nicht jedes Objekt, das vorgibt, ein Kunstwerk zu sein, auch ein Kunstwerk, ein freies Zeichen von ästhetischer Qualität ist. Der Kunstmarkt ist nicht frei von Produkten eines gescheiterten Kunstwollens.

---

[10] Siehe Kant 1924, § 12.

Wenn Kunstwerke als freie Zeichen in dem hier skizzierten Sinn angesehen werden, dann stellt sich im Hinblick auf Zeichen, die zu bekannten Zeichensystemen gehören, die Frage, ob und wie sie den Status von Kunstwerken erwerben können. Und diese Frage stellt sich umso dringlicher, als sehr viele Kunstwerke der traditionellen Kunstgattungen Zeichen bekannter Zeichensysteme sind: figürliche Bilder und sinnvolle Texte. Wie können Texte Kunstwerke sein, Zeichen, die ihre Bedeutung verkörpern, wo sie doch natürlichsprachliche Zeichen sind, zu deren charakteristischen Merkmalen es gehört, daß die Gestalt der jeweiligen Zeichen im Verhältnis zu dem, was sie bedeuten, willkürlich ist? Und wie können figürliche Bilder freie Zeichen sein, wo ihre Gestalt doch bestimmt ist von der Funktion, ein von sichtbaren Gegenständen einer bestimmten Art geprägtes Wahrnehmungsfeld zu veranschaulichen? Die Antworten auf diese Fragen kann ich hier nur noch andeuten. Ein bedeutungsvoller Text ist in dem Maß ein Kunstwerk, in dem die Willkürlichkeit seiner Gestalt im Verhältnis zu seiner Bedeutung reduziert ist. Und ein figürliches Bild ist in dem Maß ein Kunstwerk, in dem ihm neben seiner abbildenden Funktion zusätzliche Bedeutungsdimensionen zukommen, die sich als verkörpert durch seine Gestalt verständlich machen lassen. Einfache Beispiele für die genannten Verfahren sind Gedichte, die klangliche Eigenschaften natürlichsprachlicher Wörter zur Gestaltung einer bestimmten sprachlichen Form nutzen und diese Form in den Dienst der Veranschaulichung ihres Inhalts stellen, und figürliche Bilder, die durch vielfältige Beziehungen der Ähnlichkeit ihrer Gestalt und ihres Gegenstands zu anderen Bildern Bedeutungsdimensionen erschließen, die über die Darstellung von sichtbaren Gegenständen einer bestimmten Art hinausgehen.

Schwierigkeiten ganz anderer Art für das hier skizzierte Konzept eines Kunstwerks ergeben sich im Hinblick auf Werke, die wir als Kunstwerke anzusehen pflegen, die aber in keiner offensichtlichen Weise Zeichen, Träger einer Bedeutung sind. Dazu gehören viele musikalische Werke, Werke der Architektur, aber auch Werke der ungegenständlichen oder abstrakten Malerei und Texte der sogenannten absoluten Poesie. Die Frage, ob und in welchem Maß Werke dieser Art im Prozeß einer ästhetischen Reflexion Zeichencharakter gewinnen können, läßt sich nicht im allgemeinen beantworten. Jedes einzelne Werk ist auf seinen Zeichencharakter zu befragen. Ich kann hier nur darauf hinweisen, daß ein Werk nicht nur dann ein Kunstwerk in dem hier skizzierten Sinn sein kann, wenn sein Zeichencharakter auch unabhängig von einer ästhetischen Reflexion über die Art und Weise, in der es seine Bedeutung verkörpert, ersichtlich ist – wie es bei sinnvollen Texten und figürlichen Bildern der Fall ist. So sind z.B. malerische Werke von Jackson Pollock keine figürlichen, sondern abstrakte Bilder, denen dennoch weitgehend einhellig eine semantische Funktion und damit ein Zeichencharakter zugestanden wird. Und auch den scheinbar unverständlichen Gedichten von Paul Celan wird ein Zeichencharakter zugestanden, der sich nicht auf den Zeichencharakter der einzelnen Wörter reduziert, aus denen sie bestehen.

Es war insbesondere die von Danto als „Moderne" bezeichnete Epoche, in der Kunstschaffende ihren Werken einen offensichtlichen Zeichencharakter verweigerten, in der sie mit Werkformen jenseits aller Zeichen bekannter Zeichensysteme experimentiert haben. Im Bereich der bildenden Kunst waren es vor allem Duchamp und die Vertreter der pop art, die die Kunst von dem Zwang zu dieser Verweigerung befreiten. Als freie Zeichen können Kunstwerke von beliebiger Gestalt sein, sie können Zeichen bekannter Zeichensysteme sein oder ihren Zeichencharakter verbergen. In jedem Fall gilt, daß sich der ästhetische Zeichencharakter eines Werks, die Art und Weise, wie es als freies Zeichen seine Bedeutung verkörpert, erst im Prozeß der ästhetischen Reflexion erschließt. Dabei gibt es für das, was ein Kunstwerk zu seinem Thema machen kann, keinerlei Einschränkung. Insbesondere müssen sich Kunstwerke nicht mit der Frage beschäftigen, was ein Kunstwerk sei.

Die kunstgeschichtliche Bedeutung der Werke von Duchamp und den Vertretern der pop art liegt zum einen darin, daß sie die bildende Kunst befreit haben von der Vorstellung, die künstlerische Legitimation eines Werks ließe sich nur um den Preis seiner Verweigerung jeder Art figürlicher Darstellung retten, und zum anderen darin, daß sie die bildende Kunst befreit haben aus den Grenzen der traditionellen Kunstgattungen. Diese doppelte Befreiung bedeutet keine Vollendung und damit kein Ende der Kunst. Insbesondere die Befreiung der bildenden Kunst aus den Grenzen der traditionellen Kunstgattungen hat jedoch erhebliche Konsequenzen für die weitere künstlerische Entwicklung. Es sind diese Konsequenzen, die Hans Belting vor Augen hat, wenn er vom „Ende der Kunstgeschichte" spricht. Was Belting mit dieser These diagnostiziert, ist jedoch weder ein Ende der Kunst noch ein Ende der Geschichte, sondern lediglich ein Ende jener Kunstgeschichte, die die stilistischen Entwicklungen der Kunst innerhalb der jeweiligen traditionellen Gattungsgrenzen nachzeichnete. Angesichts der grenzenlosen Freiheit künstlerischer Gestaltung und künstlerischer Bedeutung muß sich nicht nur die Kunst, sondern nun auch die Kunstgeschichte immer wieder neu erfinden.

Literatur

Belting, H.: *Das Ende der Kunstgeschichte. Eine Revision nach zehn Jahren*, München 1995.

Budd, M.: How Pictures Look. In: *Virtue and Taste. Essays on Politics, Ethics and Aesthetics*, ed. by D. Knowles and J. Skorupski, Oxford 1993, 154–75.

Danto, A. C.: *After the End of Art. Contemporary Art and the Pale of History*, Princeton/New Jersey 1997.
Danto, A. C.: *The Transfiguration of the Commonplace. A Philosophy of Art*, Cambridge/Mass. et al. 1981.
Fricke, C.: Kants Theorie der schönen Kunst. In: *Kants Ästhetik / Kant's Aesthetics / L'Esthétique de Kant*, hrsg. von H. Parret, Berlin 1998, 674–689.
Fricke, C.: *Kants Theorie des reinen Geschmacksurteils*, Berlin 1990.
Fricke, C.: *Zeichenprozeß und ästhetische Erfahrung*, München 2001.
Goodman, N.: *Ways of Worldmaking*, Indianapolis et al. 1978.
Goodman, N.: *Languages of Art. An Approach to a Theory of Symbols*, Brighton 1981.
Hegel, G. W. F.: *Vorlesungen über die Ästhetik I–III*, Frankfurt 1986 (*Werke* Bde. 13–15).
Jauss, H.R.: Ästhetische Normen und geschichtliche Reflexion in der „Querelle des anciens et des modernes". In: M. Perrault, *Parallèle des anciens et des modernes en ce qui regarde les arts et les sciences*. Mit einer einl. Abhandl. von H. R. Jauss u. kunstgesch. Exkursen von M. Imdahl, München 1964, 8–81.
Kant, I.: *Kritik der Urteilskraft*, hrsg. von K. Vorländer, Hamburg 1924 u. ö.
Steinbrenner, J.: *Kognitivismus in der Ästhetik*, Würzburg 1996.

Teil V

Religionsphilosophie

Richard Swinburne

The New Programme of Natural Theology

Providing arguments – or, more loosely, reasons – for the existence of God has been a concern of many theologians of the Christian tradition over almost the whole of its existence. St. Paul's comment that "the invisible things" of God "are clearly seen, being perceived through the things that are made"[1], gave Christian backing to the message of the middle chapters of the Old Testament *Wisdom of Solomon* that the existence and order of the Universe shows it to be the work of a divine creator. This Biblical tradition merged in the Hellenistic world with the arguments of Plato to the idea of the Good and to the Demiurge, and with the arguments of Aristotle to the existence of the First Mover. And so many Christian theologians of the first millennium had their paragraph or two summarising a cosmological argument or an argument from design. But it is normally only a paragraph or two, and the reasoning is quick. My explanation of why they directed so little energy to this issue is that they felt no need to do more. Most of their contemporaries accepted that there were God or gods. What the theologians needed to argue was that there was only one such God, and that he had certain specifically Christian characteristics and had acted in history in certain particular ways.

With the coming of the second millennium however, the theologians of the medieval west began to produce arguments for the existence of God of considerable length and rigour. It is an interesting historical question why this activity developed. My hesitant suggestion is that the growth of a relatively stable Christian society meant that serious rivals to Christianity (such as Mithraism or Manichaeism) were far less prominent. So there was less need to argue for the specifically Christian doctrines (e.g. of the Incarnation) and more leisure to defend the most central Christian doctrine of all – the existence of God – against the doubts about it which lurked in the minds even of many medieval Christians, and especially in the most educated ones. While the Catholic tradition continued to work on natural theology after the Reformation, the classical Reformers – although believing that the

---

[1] Epistle to the Romans 1.20.

natural world showed abundant evidence of its creator – thought that human sinfulness obscured our ability to recognise this evidence; and that in any case there were better ways of getting to know God.[2] By contrast Liberal Protestants (in particular those of eighteenth century Britain) argued at some length "from nature up to nature's God". So many of them saw the wonders of nature, especially the new ones recorded by microscope and telescope, as new and positive evidence of the existence of God, and they wanted to stir their religiously sluggish contemporaries to wonder. But finally in the mid-nineteenth century a combination of what I regard as very bad reasons deriving from Hume, Kant, and Darwin led to the abandonment of the ancient project of natural theology by so many parts of the Christian tradition. This was unfortunate – for Christianity (and every other theistic religion) needs natural theology.

For the practices of the Christian religion (and of any other theistic religion) only have a point if there is a God – there is no point in worshipping a non-existent creator or asking him to do something on Earth or take us to Heaven if he does not exist; or trying to live our lives in accord with his will, if he has no will. If someone is trying to be rational in practising the Christian (Islamic or Jewish) religion, he needs to believe (to some degree) the credal claims which underlie the practice. These claims include as their central claim, one presupposed by all the other claims, the claim that there is a God. None of those thinkers of the first 1850 years of Christianity who thought that there are good arguments for the existence of God thought that all or even most believers ought to believe on the basis of those arguments, nor that conversion always required accepting those arguments as cogent.[3] Most Christians may well have taken God's existence for granted. Most converts may have believed beforehand that there is a God; their conversion involved accepting more detailed claims about him. And if they did not initially believe that there is a God, they may have come to believe on the basis of religious experience in some sense rather than on the basis of natural theology. But nevertheless, most Christian thinkers before 1850 held that there are these arguments available, and that those who do not initially believe that there is a God and are rational can be brought to see that there is a God by means of them.[4]

---

[2] See John Calvin, *Institutes of the Christian Religion*, Book 1 ch. 5.

[3] Conversion of course involves not merely coming to believe certain propositions, but setting yourself to act on them in certain ways. But my concern here is only with the former necessary but not sufficient element in conversion.

[4] "Not that the same method of instruction will be suitable in the case of all who approach the word [...] the method of recovery must be adapted to the form of the disease [...] [It] is necessary to regard the opinions which the persons have taken up, and so frame your

Most post-Kantian religious thinkers have drawn our attention to the roles of religious experience and religious tradition in sustaining religious belief. It is indeed a basic principle of rational belief – which I call the Principle of Credulity – that what seems to you to be so on the basis of experience, probably is so – in the absence of counter-evidence. If it seems to you that you see me lean on the lectern or hear my voice, then probably you do – unless you wake up and find that it was all a dream, or someone shows you that really there is no lectern there; what seems to be a lectern is really a hologram. And it is also a basic principle of rational belief which I call the Principle of Testimony, that what people tell you is probably true – in the absence of counter-evidence. And so if your teachers told you that the Earth is many millions of years old, or you read in a newspaper that there has been an earthquake in Turkey, these things are probably so – unless you learn something else which casts doubt on them. When doubt is cast, we need more experience or positive arguments to show that there is a lectern there, or that the Earth is many millions of years old. There can be no justification for not extending these general principles of rationality to the case of religious belief. If you have had an experience apparently of God, you probably have; and if your teachers tell you that there is a God, it is rational to believe them – in the absence of counter-evidence. Counter-evidence may take various forms – the fact of pain and suffering may seem incompatible with the existence of God or seem to render it improbable; and rival teachers may tell you that there is no God. Counter-evidence may be strong or weak; and even if fairly strong may (rationally) not disturb the belief of someone who has had an overwhelmingly strong religious experience or believes on the authority of innumerable teachers of diverse backgrounds. But in general the presence of counter-evidence opens up the question of the existence of God which (in the absence of further religious experience) then requires to be backed up by positive arguments (and/or to have negative arguments rebutted) if belief that there is a God is to be rational. But since there is so much more doubt about the existence of God in the sceptical West of today than in most previous cultures and centuries, the need for natural theology is far greater than ever

---

argument in the accordance with the error into which each have fallen, by advancing in each discussion certain principles and reasonable propositions, that thus, through what is agreed on both sides, the truth may be conclusively brought to light. Should [your opponent] say there is no God, then from the consideration of the skilful and wise economy of the Universe he will be brought to acknowledge that there is a certain overmastering power manifested through these channels". – St. Gregory of Nyssa, The Great Catechism, Prologue. (Trans. W. Moore and H. A. Wilson, in Selected Writings of Gregory of Nyssa, Parker and Co., Oxford, 1893).

it has been before – both to deepen the faith of the believer, and to convert the unbeliever.

So various philosophers of today have sought to revive from the past different kinds of argument for the existence of God. Some have revived ontological arguments. Ontological arguments of course differ from all the other traditional arguments in that they start, not from something observable, but from purported logically necessary truths; and they purport to be deductively valid. But a major problem is that if there were such a valid argument, "There is a God" would itself be logically necessary, and so it s negation would be incoherent or self-contradictory. But it seems to me fairly evident that the proposition "There is no God", while perhaps false and even in some sense demonstrably false, is not incoherent. It does not contain any internal contradiction. And from that it follows that there cannot be a sound ontological argument.

Then there is the tradition of attempting to produce deductively valid arguments from premises evident the senses. It is not an unreasonable interpretation of Aquinas's *Summa Theologiae* 1.2.3. that he sought there to give five such arguments. Those in our day who have sought to give such arguments have for the most part tried to do so with the aid of Thomist (or neo-Thomist) terminology. But the enterprise of producing such arguments is also, I think, an enterprise doomed to failure. For if it could be achieved, then a proposition which was a conjunction of the evident premises, together with "There is no God" would be incoherent, would involve self-contradiction. But again, propositions such as "There is a Universe, but there is no God", though perhaps false, and even in some sense demonstrably false, seem fairly evidently coherent.

So my own preference is for the third tradition of natural theology. This begins from premises evident to the senses and claims that they make probable the existence of God. Such arguments purport to be inductively cogent, not deductively valid arguments. Arguments of scientists or historians from their data of observation to their general theories or claims about the past or the future, also do not purport to be deductively valid, merely inductively cogent. Thinkers were not very clear about the distinction between inductive and deductive arguments during the first 1000 years of the Christian era, and not much clearer until the eighteenth century. So it would be anachronistic to say that the patristic writers were seeking to give inductive, or alternately deductive arguments. But the arguments of so many British empiricists of the eighteenth century, culminating in Paley's *Natural Theology*, do seem to me fairly clearly and intentionally inductive.

What I have sought to do in my own natural theology is to give rigorous form to inductive arguments to the existence of God from phenomena evident to the senses, showing the close similarities between such arguments and arguments to a deep theory of physics, such as Quantum theory; or to the arguments of historians or detectives to some particular person having done some deed.

The many such arguments for the existence of God can be ordered by the generality of their premises – the phenomena from which they begin. The most general phenomenon is that there is a Universe; the argument from the Universe to God is the cosmological argument. Then you have arguments of two main kinds from the order in the Universe; these are teleological arguments. One is the argument from the universal operation of natural laws, which I call the argument from temporal order. The other is the argument from the existence of human and animal organisms, which I call the argument from spatial order. Then there is the argument from consciousness – that humans (and animals) are not merely bodily organisms, but are conscious beings (with sensations and beliefs, thoughts, desires and purposes). Then there are arguments from particular miraculous events within history, and above all the Resurrection of Jesus – or rather, since it is disputed whether these events happened, from the public evidence about them. And finally there are arguments from the very widespread phenomena of religious experience. As are arguments from particular phenomena to some deep physical hypothesis, or to some claim of a historian, the arguments are cumulative. Each phenomenon (each clue) gives some degree of probability to the hypothesis. My view, for which I have argued at length elsewhere[5], is that the various arguments for the existence of God taken together, make the latter significantly more probable than not (even when arguments against the existence of God are also taken into account). Constraints of time, however, mean that all that I can hope to do in this paper is to exhibit the pattern of such arguments, and make it plausible that two arguments which I have mentioned – the arguments from temporal order and from spatial order – do give significant probability to their conclusion.

I have sought to show how such arguments work with the aid of confirmation theory (that is, the calculus of probability, used as a calculus for stating relations of evidential support between propositions). I represent by $P(p|q)$ the probability of a proposition p on evidence q. I use Bayes's Theorem,

$$P(h|e \, \& \, k) = \frac{P(e|h \, \& \, k)}{P(e|k)} P(h|k)$$

---

[5] See my The Existence of God, Clarendon Press, revised edition, 1991; and the short simplified version, Is There a God?, Oxford University Press, 1996. Much of this paper uses material published in these places and in shorter articles elsewhere.

to elucidate the relation between the probability of a hypothesis h on evidence of observation e and background evidence k, and other probabilities. To use this calculus does not involve supposing that exact values can be very often given to the probabilities involved. Often, all we can say is that some probability has some rough value – more than this and less than that, and that in consequence some other probability has some other rough value – close to 1, or fairly high, or less than that. The calculus sets out in a formal way the factors which determine how observational evidence supports a hypothesis (or theory). The relevant points can be made easily enough in words, but less rigorously and with their implications less clear. The calculus brings out that a hypothesis h is rendered probable by observational evidence e and background evidence k, in so far as (1) $P(e|h \& k)$ (the posterior probability of e) is high, (2) $P(h|k)$ (the prior probability of h) is high, and (3) $P(e|k)$ (the prior probability of e) is low. Background evidence is evidence about how things behave in neighbouring fields of enquiry (e.g., if you are investigating the behaviour of argon at low temperatures, there may be background evidence about how neon behaves at low temperatures). But when we are dealing with big theories of physics, and above all theories of metaphysics, there are no neighbouring fields of enquiry, and so we can ignore k by putting k as a mere tautology. $P(h|k)$ and $P(e|k)$ will then have values determinable a priori.

We have two different ways of explaining events which we use and think it right to use all the time. One is the way of inanimate explanation, typical of physics and much ordinary-life explanation. Here an explanatory hypothesis consists of initial conditions and purported laws. We explain the expansion of some object by it being copper and being heated (initial conditions) and there being a law that all copper expands when heated. The other way of explaining events is the way of personal explanation, typical of psychology, history and much other ordinary-life explanation. Here an explanatory hypothesis consists of a person (or other rational being), their powers, beliefs and purposes. We explain the movement of my hand by me (person) having the purpose of catching your attention, the belief that I will do so by moving my hand, and my power at will to move my hand.

The first condition above ($P(e|h \& k)$ high) is satisfied to the extent to which you would expect to find e if h is true. Obviously a scientific or historical theory is rendered probable, in so far as the evidence is such as you would expect to find if the theory is true.

However, for any e you can devise an infinite number of different incompatible theories h_n which are such that for each $P(e|h_n \& k)$ is high, but which make totally different predictions from each other for the future (i.e. predictions additional to e). Let e be all the observations made so far relevant to your favourite theory of mechanics – let's say General Relativity (GTR). Then you can complicate GTR in innumerable ways such that the resulting new theories all predict e but make wildly different predictions about what will happen tomorrow. The grounds for believing that GTR is the true theory is that GTR is the simplest theory. When k is a mere tautology, $P(h|k)$ is the intrinsic probability that h is true, that is, the measure of the strength of the a priori factors relevant to the probability of h. These factors are its scope and its simplicity. A hypothesis has large scope in so far as it makes many precise claims; and the larger the scope, other things being equal, the lower its intrinsic probability. But we can ignore this factor if we are comparing theories of similar scope, and, even when we are considering theories of differing scope, scientific examples show that simplicity is more important than scope for determining prior probability – for theories (which satisfy the other criteria well) of large scope are regarded as probable, so long as they are simple. The simplicity of a theory, like its scope, is something internal to that theory, not a matter of the relation of the theory to external evidence.

Let me illustrate the importance of the criterion of simplicity from an example when we are considering rival personal explanations. A detective investigating a burglary finds various clues – John's fingerprints on a burgled safe, John having a lot of money hidden in his house, witnesses reporting seeing John near the scene of the burglary at the time when it was committed (which we summarize by e). He then puts forward a hypothesis (h) that John robbed the safe, which is such that it leads us to expect the clues which were found – $P(e|h \& k)$ is quite high. But there are an infinite number of other hypotheses which have this property. We could, to take but one example, suggest that Brown planted John's fingerprints on the safe, Smith dressed up to look like John at the scene of the crime, and without any collusion with the others Robinson stole the money and hid it in John's house. This new hypothesis would lead us to expect the phenomena which were found just as well as does the hypothesis that John robbed the safe. But the latter hypothesis is rendered probable by the evidence, whereas the former is not. And this is because the hypothesis that John robbed the safe postulates *one* object – John – doing *one* deed – robbing the safe – which leads us to expect the several phenomena which we find. The simplicity of a theory is a matter of it postulating few entities, few kinds of entity, few properties, few kinds of property, and ways of behaving which are unchanging in simple respects. The latter, if we are postulating persons as our entities, involves attributing to them purposes, beliefs, and powers which are constant over time, or only change in regular ways. If we are postulating natural laws, it involves using few mathematical terms and mathematically simple operations.[6] Of course, many accepted scientific theories these days seem to some of us quite complicated, but they are accepted because they are simpler than any other theory which satisfies the other criteria equally well.

$P(e|k)$, the prior probability of e (which for tautological k, is an intrinsic probability) is a measure of how likely e is to occur if we do not assume any particular theory to be true. The normal effect of this term in assessing the probability of any particular theory h, is that e does not render h very probable if you would expect to find e anyway (e.g. if it was also predicted by the main rivals to h which had significant prior probability). $P(e|k) = P(e|h \& k) P(h|k) + P(e|h_1 \& k) P(h_1|k) + P(e|h_2 \& k) P(h_2|k)$ and so on for all the h_n rival to h (where all these together with h are such that at least and at most one of them must be the true theory in the field). This value will clearly be determined largely by the terms n for which h_n has a relatively high prior probability, and which give to e a relatively high posterior probability. To the extent to which rivals to h which give e a relatively high prior probability, themselves have a low prior probability (in comparison with h), the posterior probability of h will be high.

The hypothesis that there is a God is the hypothesis of the existence of the simplest kind of being which there could be. A physical being will have spatial extension and thus consist of parts. Persons, as mental subjects, *need* not have spatial extension. God is the simplest kind of person they could be. A person is a being with *power* to bring about effects, *knowledge* of how to do so, and *freedom* to make choices of which effects to bring about. God is by definition an omnipotent (that is, infinitely powerful), omniscient (that is, all knowing), and perfectly free person; he is a person of infinite power, knowledge and freedom; a person to whose power, knowledge and freedom there are no limits except those of logic.[7] In virtue of his omnipotence he will not be tied down to operating on the world and learning about it by means of

---

[6] For a full account of the nature of simplicity, see my *Epistemic Justification*, Oxford University Press, 2001, chapter 4.

[7] In the Christian tradition God is "three persons in one substance", i.e. three persons each of whom have the listed divine characteristics, and have an essential unity – the Son and the Spirit being eternally and necessarily caused to exist by the Father. Arguments to the existence of God are then best construed as arguments to the existence of God the Father, from which the existence of Son and Spirit follows – in my view by logical entailment. The simplicity of God which I consider in the text is the simplicity of God the Father – that a simple theory has complicated consequences does not make it any less simple. I ignore this complication in subsequent discussion, for the sake of ease of exposition. For my own developed account of the divine nature see *The Coherence of Theism*, Clarendon Press, revised edition, 1993; and *The Christian God*, Clarendon Press, 1994. See chapter 8 of the latter book, for why the existence of the Father entails that of the Son and Spirit.

a body, and so he will not have spatial extension. The hypothesis that there exists a being with infinite degrees of the qualities essential to a being of that kind is the postulation of a very simple being. The hypothesis that there is one such God is a much simpler hypothesis than the hypothesis that there is a God who has such and such limited power, or the hypothesis that there are several gods with limited powers. It is simpler in just the same way that the hypothesis that some particle has zero mass or infinite velocity is simpler than the hypothesis that is has 0.32147 of some unit of mass or a velocity of 221,000 km/sec. A finite limitation cries out for an explanation of why there is just that particular limit, in a way that limitlessness does not. Although the existence of anything at all is perhaps enormously improbable a priori, the existence of God (h) as the existence of the simplest kind of being there could be has a far higher intrinsic probability ($P(h|k)$) than does the existence of anything else (except in so far as the latter is rendered probable by the former). Taking the inductive procedures of science and history seriously forces that conclusion on us.

It follows from God's omniscience and perfect freedom that he will be perfectly good. For being omniscient, he will know which actions are good. The goodness of an action provides a reason for doing it; and being perfectly free, he will be subject to no irrational influences. The worth of an action alone will move him to perform it. So if there is a God, he will seek to bring about good things; and being omnipotent, he will be able to do so. So it is not improbable that he should create a universe, an orderly universe, and within it embodied rational creatures such as humans. It is good that there should be a beautiful universe. Beauty arises from order of some kind – the orderly interactions and movements of objects in accord with natural laws is beautiful indeed. It is a further good thing that there should be human beings who can choose between good and bad, make differences to themselves, each other, and the world; choose whether to grow in power and knowledge, and so choose whether or not to enter into a loving relationship with God himself. Limited power means power over a limited region of the world, that is a body; and growing in power involves using our bodies to control things at a distance. But we have to know which bodily movements will make what difference to the world, in order to have an effective choice of which differences to make to the world – and that involves there being regularities in the world which are simple enough for us to detect. We can then use them to mould the Universe for good or ill – to develop an agriculture, and to make houses and bridges or bombs and prisons, and to send humans to the moon. With e as the operation of laws of nature, and their being such as (with initial conditions) to lead to the evolution of humans, $P(e|h \& k)$ is not too low. But unless there is a God, it is immensely unlikely that any Universe would be governed by simple natural laws. For natural laws are not entities. To say that all objects obey Newton's laws is just to say that each object in the Universe behaves in a way that Newton's laws state, i.e. has exactly the same properties of movement in reaction to the presence of other objects, as does every other object. It is immensely unlikely that every other object should behave in exactly the same way – a priori, unless there was a common cause of their having the properties they do. And any other possible cause (e.g. many gods) is much less simple than God. (Even if you suppose some impersonal cause to be just as simple a postulate as God, the simplest kind of person there could be, there is no reason why it should bring about this sort of universe.) And, in a world with natural laws, it is immensely unlikely that there would be humans unless either God made them by a special creation, or made just those natural laws and provided just those initial conditions which would allow the evolution of humans from some initial state of the Universe.

In 1859 Darwin produced his explanation of why there were complexly organised humans and animals in terms of the laws of evolution operating on much simpler organisms. His explanation is surely correct. But the question then arises as to why there are laws of evolution which have the consequence that over many millennia simple organisms gradually give rise to complex organisms. No doubt because these laws follow from the basic laws of physics. But then why do the basic laws of physics have such a form as to give rise to laws of evolution? And why were there the primitive organisms in the first place? A plausible story can be told of how the primeval 'soup' of matter-energy at the time of the 'Big Bang' gave rise over many millennia, in accordance with physical laws, to those primitive organisms. But then why was there matter suitable for such evolutionary development in the first place? With respect to the laws and with respect to the primeval matter, we have the choice, of saying that these things cannot be further explained, or postulating a further explanation. In recent years scientists have drawn our attention to the strength of this argument by showing how 'fine-tuned' is the Universe. It needed a certain density and a certain velocity of recession of its matter-energy at the time of the Big Bang if life was to evolve; and increase or decrease in respect of density or velocity (or some other respects) by one part in a million would have made the Universe non-life-evolving. Likewise the physical constants of the natural laws had to lie within narrow limits if life was to evolve. If God made the natural laws and the initial state of the Universe, then – for reasons already given as to why he might well bring about humans – it is to be expected that he would give the initial state and the laws these features (or make some underlying laws – e.g. those of string theory – such that they gave the initial state + laws these features.) But if God was not responsible, the probability of such an initial state and laws of the requisite kind would be immensely low – even if there are laws of nature of some kind. With e again as the conjunction of the premises of our two arguments, P(e|k) is not going to be too much greater than the top line of the right side of Bayes's Theorem – P(e|h & k) P(h|k) – because hypotheses rival to theism either have a far lower intrinsic probability than theism (e.g. the hypothesis that the Universe was created by a million gods)[8] or do not make it in the very least probable that e would occur (e.g. the hypothesis that chance determined the character of natural laws).

So arguments from the two phenomena which I have considered give significant probability to the existence of God. There is not time to develop the case further here, but my own view (argued elsewhere) is that when we add arguments from other phenomena and even when we bring into the equation arguments against the existence of God (e.g. from evil), we get a strong case for the existence of God.

References

Calvin, J.: *Institutes of the Christian Religion*, Book 1.
St. Gregory of Nyssa: *The Great Catechism, Prologue* (Trans. W. Moore and H. A. Wilson, in *Selected Writings of Gregory of Nyssa*, Parker and Co., Oxford 1893).
Swinburne, R.: *The Existence of God*, Clarendon Press, revised edition, Oxford 1991.
Swinburne, R.: *The Coherence of Theism*, Clarendon Press, revised edition, Oxford 1993.
Swinburne, R.: *The Christian God*, Clarendon Press, Oxford 1994.
Swinburne, R.: *Is There a God?*, Oxford University Press, Oxford 1996.
Swinburne, R.: *Epistemic Justification*, Oxford University Press, Oxford 2001.

---

[8] Among the hypotheses rival to theism which make it probable that e would occur is the hypothesis that there are an infinite number of worlds, each with different kinds of law or different kinds of chaos and different kinds of initial conditions. But that seems a wildly less simple hypothesis than theism – to postulate an infinite number of (causally independent) entities in order to explain the occurrence of one entity runs against all the rules of inductive inference.

Christoph Jäger

Religious Experience and Epistemic Justification: Alston on the Reliability of "Mystical Perception"

1. Introduction

A major topic in current philosophy of religion is the question whether, and if so in what sense, religious belief is epistemically justified. One of the most prominent answers to this question is William Alston's claim that certain forms of religious experience can provide a direct or immediate source of justification of religious belief; that "mystical perception" is indeed among the most important bases of justified religious belief. I greatly admire Alston's work on epistemic justification and his epistemology of religious belief. Indeed, I believe that the theories he has developed in these areas are among the most illuminating work contemporary epistemology and philosophy of religion have to offer. However, I also believe that a main step in Alston's argument for the immediate experiential justification of religious belief does not stand up to scrutiny.

In what follows I shall first (section 2) reconstruct some central principles of Alston's theory of epistemic justification. This theory allows for non-propositional justifiers, combines internalist and externalist ideas, and is cashed out in terms of doxastic practices. Next I will outline Alston's famous skeptical argument to the effect that all attempts to show that the practice of basing perceptual beliefs on sense perception (henceforth: *SP*) is reliable are infected with epistemic circularity (section 3). At first sight this seems to be a devastating epistemological result. But Alston argues that it is nonetheless rational to *suppose* that this doxastic practice is reliable. The same, he argues, holds for the less widely distributed practice of basing religious beliefs on "mystical perception". At this point I part company with Alston. If his analysis of epistemic circularity is correct, I argue, there is no bridge between what he calls the *practical* rationality of engaging in these doxastic practices and the rationality of supposing them to be reliable (section 4).

Should we conclude, therefore, that Alston's project is doomed? Yes and no. His attempt to establish the rationality of supposing the mystical doxastic practice (henceforth: *MP*) to be reliable fails. But I will argue for the conditional claim that, *if* he is right in maintaining that there are also no overriding reasons for regarding that practice to be *un*reliable, it is not epistemically irresponsible to engage in it (section 5). Being responsible in forming or holding a belief *B*, however, is not only a kind of positive epistemic status that must be distinguished from basing *B* on what is in fact a reliable, truth-conducive ground. If Alston is right about epistemic circularity, epistemic responsibility does not require either that the subject be in a position to rationally *suppose* that the mode of belief formation s/he employs is reliable.

Before entering into our main discussion I should begin with a few disclaimers. First, I shall start from the assumption that it is indeed legitimate to pursue questions about the justification and rationality of religious belief in terms of *epistemic* justification. There are traditions in the philosophy of religion in which this assumption is rejected or at least treated with great suspicion. In what follows, however, I will not enter into arguments for and against that position but will simply accept Alston's general methodological starting point.[1]

Second, I shall not make heavy weather over Alston's claim that there are such things as non-propositional justifiers. This is a hotly debated topic, but in this paper I shall set it aside and follow Alston, and many others, in assuming that not only judgments and beliefs, but also non-conceptualized mental states such as "raw" experiences and sensations, can justify doxastic attitudes.

Third, I will not have the time to go into related questions about the phenomenology of religious experience. This too is an interesting and important topic, and Alston discusses it at length (1991, chapter 1). But I shall not pursue, e.g., the question whether religious experience really exists as a distinctive kind of mental state. Criticisms that take issue with this basic assumption of Alston's argument, by claiming for example that what the practice in question really amounts to is simply reading one's prior religious beliefs into experiences that would otherwise be cognitively indifferent, will not be discussed.

Fourth, I will not go into problems of religious diversity. Such problems arise from the fact that, for subjects with different religious backgrounds, phenomenally similar experiences produce different, and typically

---

[1] That this starting point is questionable is argued, e.g., by Friedo Ricken 1995, p. 403, who maintains that ordinary epistemological concepts of rationality should not be applied to religious belief.

incompatible, religious beliefs. This suggests that, as Alston himself acknowledges, the majority of experiential religious practices must be *un*reliable. How, then, can it be rational to favor a particular interpretation of the experiences in question over competing ones? Alston himself regards this as the severest difficulty for his position, and I am not convinced that his attempt to defuse the challenge of religious pluralism is ultimately successful (cf. 1991, chapter 7). For the sake of the argument, however, I shall assume here that challenges from this quarter can indeed be met.[2]

Finally, there are various other (potential) defeaters for the religious beliefs under consideration. Alston explicitly acknowledges that religious experience is not confined to theistic religions (1991, p. 9). Yet he focuses his discussion specifically on the "Christian Mystical Practice" that involves "putative direct experiential awareness of God" (1991, p. 35).[3] In consequence, Alston's account not only confronts general questions regarding the role of culturally shaped background beliefs, but also problems that specifically arise from potential defeaters for those religions whose Ultimate Reality is a personal God. Again I shall assume however, with Alston and others, that none of the traditional potential defeaters of theism – such as problems of coherence, the problem of evil, projection theories à la Freud, Marx, etc. – amounts to a knock-down argument.[4]

To summarize, in this paper I want to meet Alston on his own ground and grant him large parts of his overall picture – except for one crucial step: his argument to the effect that it is rational to suppose that the doxastic practice of basing theistic belief on mystical experience is reliable. In order to understand Alston's complex reasoning leading up to this conclusion, however, we must first turn to some of the main tenets of his general account of epistemic justification.

---

[2] For critical discussions of this problem for Alston's account see Schellenberg 1994 and Quinn 1995. Robert Adams 1994, on the other hand, argues that the fact of religious diversity is less problematic for an account along Alstonian lines than Alston himself believes. Such diversities, Adams argues, are restricted to sophisticated theological superstructures and doctrinal systems. One may accept, however, that in some way the basic doxastic practices of different religions are all "in touch with religious reality" and that "there is something cognitively right as well as practically fruitful about them" (p. 890).

[3] Alston prefers to avoid the term "religious experience" in this context because it is too unspecific. In my reconstruction of his argument, however, I shall often employ this more familiar term.

[4] Alston rejects some of the traditional criticisms of the mystical doxastic practice, such as the objection from naturalistic explanations of that practice, in (1991), chapter 6.

2. Epistemic Justification

In several well-known articles and books, Alston develops the following principle of epistemic justification:

(A) A belief is epistemically justified if and only if it is based on adequate grounds.[5]

This sounds like a plausible enough claim, but the ideas that underlie this principle are by no means trivial or uncontroversial. The term "ground" is meant to range over beliefs as well as non-propositional mental states such as experiences and sensations. Hence it is to be understood in an "internalist" sense, which in Alston's account means that the ground is, under normal circumstances, "accessible on reflection alone" to the subject. Although such a ground need not be an occurrent, conscious mental state, states of affairs that do not supervene on the thinker's neuro-physiological system are ruled out by this constraint.

Alston allows for "mediate" or "indirect" as well as for "immediate" or "direct" justification. To be mediately justified in believing that p is to be justified in so believing by other justified beliefs or items of knowledge. Let us, with Alston, call such mediate justifiers "reasons" and use the term "ground" as an umbrella term that covers both propositional and non-propositional justifiers. A subject S is *im*mediately justified in believing that p just in case S is justified in so believing and this justification is not mediated by reasons. Certain perceptual experiences, for instance, justify me in believing that there is a tree in front of me; others justify me in believing that I am looking at a red tomato, or that someone is playing a trumpet next door, that I'd better go to the dentist, and so on. Alston's case for the justification of basing *religious* beliefs on *religious* experience is thus a case for the claim that religious beliefs can be immediately justified, i. e., justified without being based on other beliefs and discursive reasoning. Hence his account must be sharply distinguished from traditional arguments from religious experience, which typically use religious experience to construct an argument to the best explanation for an Ultimate Reality.

A belief is "based on" a justifying ground, according to Alston, if this ground is something *for which* the belief is held. If something is a ground you merely *have* for a belief, in the sense that it is part of your noetic system, while failing to be "psychologically responsible" for your having the belief, this belief is not based on that ground (1991, pp. 73f.). Suppose you believe you will get the job. Suppose you have received a letter from the Department

---

[5] Cf. especially Alston 1988a. See also Alston 1985 and Alston 1991, pp. 70–76.

telling you that you will get it, and you have no reasons to suspect that there is anything wrong with your evidence. Now imagine that what makes you believe that you will get the post is in fact not these reasons but one hour of concentrated crystal-ball gazing. In that case, although you would have adequate grounds, you would have failed to base your belief on adequate grounds, and thus you would lack justification for your belief.

Now, when is a ground adequate? What makes something a good ground for a belief? Here Alston balances his internalist account of the notion of "basing a belief on a ground" with an externalist constraint on the adequacy condition. The constraint is that the ground must be an objectively reliable indication of the truth of the belief. Justifiably believing something, says Alston, requires getting into a good position with respect to truth. Since it is not accessible on reflection alone to a subject whether this condition is fulfilled or not, this condition is an externalist component of Alston's account of epistemic justification.

Incorporating these points into our above characterization, we can formulate Alston's theory somewhat more precisely:

(A*) A subject S is epistemically justified in holding the belief B at a given time t if and only if S bases B at t on (propositional) reasons or non-propositional grounds that are sufficiently truth-indicative.

This principle is formulated for individual beliefs. Inspired by Wittgenstein and Thomas Reid, however, Alston recommends that we formulate principles of epistemic justification in terms of doxastic *practices*.[6] A belief is justified if it is based on adequate grounds. But a proper assessment of the question whether this condition is fulfilled for a particular belief B must consider the general mode of belief formation that is employed in generating B. When a certain phenomenal presentation makes me believe that there is a red tomato in front of me, I will only be justified in this belief if the general practice of basing such beliefs on this kind of presentation can be approved of from the epistemic point of view.

How should doxastic practices be individuated? Alston construes them as families of belief-forming as well as belief-preserving and belief-*trans*forming mechanisms that are bound together by their inputs and outputs and by the functions that connect the two (1991, pp. 153, 165, 185). When I am "appeared to treely," for example, there is a characteristic perceptual input that normally yields as output the belief that I see a tree. Within such a framework, we may also individuate "wider" practices and look for example at the practice of basing perceptual beliefs on sense perception. We may

---

[6] Alston 1989a; Alston 1991, chapter 4; Alston 1993a.

also individuate doxastic practices with respect to cognitive sources such as memory, introspection, inductive and deductive reasoning, and so-called rational intuition (a practice by which we generate and hold beliefs about self-evident truths). These practices Alston calls the "standard package" (cf., e.g., 1991, p. 176), and his project is to show that *MP* is epistemically on a par with the practices included in the standard package.

Finally, a few words about the notion of reliability. Alston works with an account according to which a belief-forming mechanism is reliable if and only if it would yield mostly true beliefs in a sufficiently large and varied run of employments, where these employments must be restricted to situations of the sorts the epistemic subject typically encounters (1991, pp. 104f., 1993a, p. 9). The restriction to typical situations is required because an unfavorable track record of a mechanism that ranges over unusual situations would clearly not discredit that mechanism. The fact that sense experience, for instance, is not reliable in situations of direct brain stimulation should not be taken as indicating that *SP* is not reliable under normal conditions.

The counterfactual formulation is called for because a favorable track record of actual past employments of a belief-forming mechanism could simply be the result of lucky accidents, as when, for instance, "there have been only five crystal-ball readings all of which just happened to be correct" (1993a, pp. 8f.). Moreover, there could be reliable mechanisms which are never put to work, as when, for instance, someone constructs a reliable instrument that no one ever uses. This consideration suggests that we should not even tie reliability to favorable track records that range over all actual past, present, and future employments of a mechanism.

Alston admits that this characterization is still "less than perfectly precise" (1993a, p. 9). What, for example, does it take for a situation to be "typical" in the appropriate sense? What exactly does talk about "mostly" true beliefs amount to? And when is a chosen run of employments sufficiently large? These questions have no easy answer, but here I will assume that a satisfactory answer may be worked out.

Incorporating this doxastic practice approach into our characterization of Alston's theory of epistemic justification, we may finally summarize the account as follows:

(A**) A subject S is epistemically justified in holding a belief B at t if and only if
  (i) S bases B at t on propositional or non-propositional grounds of type G, and
  (ii) the doxastic practice of holding beliefs of that kind on the basis of grounds type G is reliable.

We are now in a position to look at Alston's central argument regarding the possibility of *assessing* the reliability of doxastic practices and the application of his answer to the practice of basing theistic belief on mystical experience.[7]

3. Epistemic Circularity and the Epistemological Status of the "Mystical Perceptual Practice"

A natural question that arises at this point is whether the doxastic practices of the "standard package" *are* reliable; or whether we can show them to be reliable, or at least present good arguments to the effect that they are reliable. Take, for instance, *SP*. Can we show in an epistemically acceptable way that this mode of belief formation is reliable?

No, says Alston, raising the specter of skepticism. Any consideration to this effect, he argues, will be infected with "epistemic circularity" (cf. 1986; 1991, chapter 3; 1993a). This is a malady that an argument for the reliability of a practice *P* suffers from if the reliability of *P* must be assumed at the outset in order to construct that argument. Consider for example inductive test procedures for the reliability of sense perception that simply gather a suitable sample of outputs of *SP* and check it for the proportion of true and false beliefs. Wouldn't favorable track records of this kind provide good evidence for the reliability of sense perception? Maybe we should say so – except that we'd have to concede, of course, that we must rely on sense perception in order to determine whether the relevant beliefs ("this is a red tomato," "this is the sound of a trumpet," etc.) are true. Or suppose that I believe that there is a red tomato in front of me, but someone challenges that belief. I could then check whether the greenhouse is lit by red lights, ask other people whether

---

[7] The account of epistemic justification outlined in this section is Alston's account from the 1980s and the early 1990s. It should be noted, however, that in (1993b) Alston drastically departs from his original epistemological program and argues that "we should abandon the idea that there is a unique something or other properly called 'epistemic justification'" (p. 527). "Indeed," he says, "I shall be plumping for dropping the question of the justification of belief altogether" (ibid.). Alston's reason for this is that the persistence of the disputes over adequate epistemic desiderata strongly suggests that epistemologists are talking past each other and that there is no common pre-theoretical understanding of the nature of epistemic justification. I am not sure how Alston thinks this new point of view bears upon his project of justifying the practice of basing theistic belief on mystical experience. But I suppose he could answer along the following lines. Since he argues that, even if we abandon the idea of a unique concept of justification, it is still desirable to satisfy the various epistemic desiderata discussed in the literature, he would only have to salvage the idea that the rationality of supposing the mystical doxastic practice to be reliable is a desirable epistemic status with regard to that practice.

they too believe that there is a red tomato at the place in question, and so on. Such confirmation procedures, however, would obviously have to rely on sense perception. Consider next the idea that the "fruits" of sense perception, in particular the way it puts us in a position to predict and control the course of events, provide us with an argument for its reliability. Again, this sounds like a natural and reasonable proposal – except that we will, of course, have to use sense perception in order to determine whether our predictions are successful.

Alston discusses a great variety of attempts to establish the reliability of sense perception, and he argues – quite convincingly, I believe – that none of them escapes epistemic circularity. He then extends his reasoning to other belief-forming mechanisms of the "standard package" and concludes that we should not expect of *any* of these mechanisms that we can show in a noncircular fashion that they are reliable.

Where does this leave us? And what is the consequence for mystical perception? At first sight we would seem to be in a desperate epistemic situation, both with respect to standard belief-forming mechanisms and to the mystical doxastic practice. However, one consequence of all this, says Alston, is the following. If none of our standard belief-forming mechanisms can be shown to be reliable without our falling into epistemic circularity, then, if this is a problem that arises for MP as well, this can hardly be regarded as a good reason for downgrading it in comparison to other, less controversial modes of belief formation. It may be true that the attempt to check the reliability of MP must at some point rely on that very practice. However, if Alston is right in his diagnosis of the universal range of the problem of epistemic circularity, that practice would, in this regard, be perfectly on a par with the practices of the standard package (cf. 1991, pp. 143, 184f.). Call this Alston's "parity claim."

A typical, and at first sight reasonable criticism of this line of thought is that, even if such parity holds with respect to epistemic circularity, there are *other* epistemic asymmetries. In particular it will be pointed out that MP is, unlike SP and other practices of the standard package, not universally engaged in by normal human adults. Mystical experience has, throughout the centuries, only been available to a small minority. Does this not cast doubt upon the epistemic value of MP?

Alston rejects objections from this direction for two reasons. First, he argues, such objections are guilty of *epistemic imperialism*, i.e., of "unwarrantedly taking the standards of one doxastic practice as normative for all" (1991, p. 199). Forming beliefs on the basis of sense perception is a practice that all normal human adults engage in, all right; but why suppose that this is a feature every respectable doxastic practice must share? In fact, there are many doxastic practices that are only employed by a small minority, but which we have no inclination to discredit for that reason. Think, for instance, of higher mathematics, or of theoretical physics, wine-tasting, chicken-sexing, and so on.

Second, the objector who is willing to concede the positive epistemic status of "expert practices" also applies an unwarranted *double standard*. He discredits the mystical practice for not being widely distributed, while allowing that other doxastic practices are confined to a certain elite. These considerations show that objections that simply point to the partial distribution of *MP* are far too superficial.[8]

Nevertheless, one crucial question regarding Alston's parity claim is how the conclusion he draws from the observation of the universal range of the problem of epistemic circularity can possibly be regarded as an argument *in favor* of religious experience. "All right," it might be replied, "there may be a parity here, but only insofar as no doxastic practice whatever can get a clean bill of health!" In other words, is not the consequence of all this that the practice of basing religious belief on religious experience is at least as badly off as other belief-forming mechanisms? Alston believes that that would not be an appropriate conclusion and develops an interesting argument for the positive epistemic status both of ordinary and mystical doxastic practices. It is this argument that lies at the heart of his overall defense of basing religious beliefs on mystical experience. Here are the central steps of his reasoning.

(i) For all that has been said about epistemic circularity, it is nevertheless perfectly rational for us to engage in the doxastic practices we do in fact engage in, as long as we lack overriding reasons for regarding these practices as unreliable. True, there does not seem to be any doxastic practice which can be shown in a noncircular fashion to be reliable. Withholding belief altogether, however, is not a serious possibility. And even if we could abandon some or all of our standard belief-forming habits and adopt instead alternative modes of belief formation, how could we establish the reliability of these newcomers? It seems likely that we would run into exactly the same sort of circularity problems that arise for the standard practices. Our human cognitive situation just does not permit our doxastic practices to be assessed "from the outside." But if that is the case, how could it be irrational to

---

[8] It seems clear, however, that much more must be said in order to offer a satisfactory defense of the parity claim. Evan Fales, for instance, has argued that a crucial problem for Alston arises from the fact that the evaluation resources of mystical practice fail to "display a power, richness, and subtlety at least roughly comparable to those available to *SP*" (Fales 1996, p. 25). I will not go into this question here but instead will in what follows present a problem that arises for Alston *even if* the parity claim is acceptable.

engage in the practices we do in fact engage in, as long as we lack overriding reasons for rejecting them? Given the universal scope of the problem, it seems perfectly rational to stick with what we have (cf. 1991, p. 150). More precisely, says Alston, it is at least *prima facie* rational to engage in doxastic practices that are "socially established," i.e., "established by socially monitored learning" (1991, p. 163). For unlike idiosyncratic doxastic practices (such as, for instance, consulting sun-dried tomatoes to determine the future of the stock market), socially established practices have persisted over many generations and thereby "earned a right to be considered seriously" (p. 170). This status of *prima facie* rationality can be strengthened by two further factors: (a) absence of overriders, such as massive intra- or interpractical inconsistencies; and (b) considerable self-support. If these conditions are fulfilled, a doxastic practice counts as unqualifiedly rational.

(ii) Since it is *doxastic* practices that are under consideration, Alston argues, his argument for the rationality of engaging in socially established doxastic practices also warrants another conclusion. It is this step that relates the results of the discussion of epistemic circularity to the reliability constraint on epistemic justification outlined in section 2. Alston regards his analysis of epistemic circularity as suggesting that it is impossible to *show* in an epistemically acceptable way that the doxastic practices in question are reliable. Yet he constructs an argument according to which the fact that it is, as he believes, nonetheless rational to engage in these practices furnishes us with an indirect argument to the effect that it is rational to *suppose* these practices to be reliable: "in showing it to be rational to engage in *SP*," Alston writes, "I have thereby not shown *SP* to be reliable, but shown it to be rational to *suppose SP* to be reliable" (1991, p. 178). Alston's argument to this conclusion, which is essentially developed in (1991), pp. 178–183, is this.

Just as believing that p commits one to the truth of p, in the sense that it would be incoherent to believe p and abstain from judging that p is true if the question arose, it would be incoherent for a subject to engage in a doxastic *practice* and refuse to attribute reliability to that practice if the question arose.[9] "With many sorts of practices," Alston says, "I can take it to be rational to engage in them without supposing them to enjoy the kind of success appropriate to them. I can take it to be rational to engage in playing squash for its health and recreational benefits, without thereby committing myself to the proposition that I will win most of my matches" (1991, p. 179).

---

[9] "When I say that in judging that p I am thereby *committing* myself to its being the case that q, what I mean is this. It would be irrational (incoherent ...) for me to judge (assert, believe) that p and deny that q, or even abstain from judging that q, *if the question arises*" (Alston 1991, p. 179).

But to engage in a *doxastic* practice [my italics, C.J.] is to form beliefs in a certain way. And to believe that p is to be committed to its being true that p. [...] But what is true of individual beliefs is also true of a general practice of belief formation. To engage in a certain doxastic practice and to accept the beliefs one thereby generates is to commit oneself to those beliefs being true (at least for the most part), and hence to commit oneself to the pratice's being reliable. [...] The rationality of a practice (action, belief, judgment ...) extends to whatever that practice ... commits me to. [...] But, then, if I have shown, by my practical argument, that it is rational to engage in *SP* I have thereby shown that it is rational to take *SP* to be reliable. For since the acknowledgment of the rationality of the practice commits one to the rationality of its reliability, to provide an adequate argument for the former will be to provide an adequate argument for the latter (1991, pp. 179f.).

(iii) *Pars pro toto*, Alston develops this argument for *SP*, but the suggestion is that the same considerations apply to other belief-forming practices, including the practice of basing religious beliefs on mystical experience. First, Alston tries to make a case for the thesis that basing religious beliefs on mystical experience is in the same boat with other doxastic practices because it is a practice that, although not universally engaged in, can still be regarded as socially established. It is by no means idiosyncratic. For centuries it has been engaged in by a vast number of intellectually highly respectable people, and it is socially acknowledged in various religious traditions, among them Christianity, as an important source of faith. Second, Alston argues that the standard attempts to show that this practice is unreliable fail. Moreover, it seems to exhibit a significant degree of self-support. By the argument sketched in (ii) it follows that it is rational for someone who has the relevant experiences to engage in the practice of basing religious beliefs on these experiences, and hence to attribute reliability to that practice.

What are we to think of this argument? A closer look at it, I believe, reveals some serious problems.

4. From Practical to Epistemic Rationality?

Let us summarize Alston's argument as outlined thus far and then analyze it step by step. He believes himself to have shown that, first, despite the problem of epistemic circularity, it is nevertheless rational to engage in *SP* and *MP*. The question is how this result connects up with the reliability condition that Alston found necessary to adopt in his account of epistemic justification. There is a connection, he says, but it is indirect. Engaging in a doxastic practice commits one to attributing reliability to that practice, just as believing that p commits one to the truth of p. Being thus committed does not involve consciously judging the practice to be reliable; such a commitment only means that it would be incoherent not to judge the practice to be reliable when the question arises. In a next step Alston argues that, if he has shown that it is *rational* to engage in the practices in question, he has shown that it is rational to suppose these practices to be reliable.

It will be helpful to isolate the various premises and conclusions involved in this reasoning. The first premise is that believing that p commits one to attributing truth to p. Substituting Alston's characterization of the commitment relation, this gives us:

(1) It is incoherent to believe that p and abstain from judging that p is true if the question arises.

Next, Alston argues:

(2) Engaging in a doxastic practice is related to judging that practice to be reliable (if the question arises) in the same way as believing that p is related to judging that p is true (if the question arises).

From these premises he infers:

(3) It is incoherent to engage in a doxastic practice and to abstain from judging that practice to be reliable if the question arises.

Now this interim conclusion does not yet get us very far. For what about wildly irrational doxastic practices? Suppose I decide from now on to determine the future of the stock market by crystal-ball gazing. Then, by the argument just outlined, I would be committed to regarding that practice as reliable. But clearly, something would be seriously wrong with this judgment. What is wrong is of course that it is irrational to adopt that practice in the first place. This is why we need to assess the prior question whether a given doxastic practice is *rationally* engaged in. Now, Alston argues that he has shown that:

(4) Engaging in SP and MP is rational.

But then, he argues, we can conclude:

(5) These practices can also rationally be judged to be reliable.

There is, I believe, more than one problem with this reasoning. First, as Matthias Steup, who reconstructs steps (1)–(3) along similar lines, has argued, (3) appears doubtful (Steup 1997). Is it really true that engaging in a doxastic practice commits one to its reliability? A positive answer would have the following, highly dubious consequence. If such a claim were true, taking a skeptical stance with respect to the reliability of our standard doxastic practices could simply be dismissed by pointing out that this would be an incoherent or "pragmatically self-refuting" position. But this would be an inadequate reaction. There may be good ways of undermining skepticism; but if Alston were right the skeptic could be refuted just by pointing out that he himself engages in the very practices he questions. "Well," we could say, "don't you yourself engage in the doxastic practices you dismiss as epistemically 'uncredentialed'? Of course you do, and you cannot do otherwise. But then you are committed to supposing these practices to be reliable. Hence you are not entitled to your skeptical position." This can hardly be the right story. A refutation of philosophical skepticism will, if at all possible, not be *that* easy. And the reason is that the mere fact that one engages, e.g., in *SP* does *not* commit one to judge that practice to be reliable if the question arises. Hence, since (3) follows from (1) and (2), at least one of these premises must be wrong.

In addition to this, a serious problem for Alston's account arises from his problematic and unclear use of the term "rationality." Exactly what kind of rationality is at issue? While often talking about rationality simpliciter, Alston also says that, strictly speaking, it is some kind of *practical rationality* that attaches to the doxastic practices in question. How, then, does he think of that practical rationality? It is practically rational to engage in *SP* and other established doxastic practices, Alston argues, because there is no alternative:

> What alternative is there to employing the practices we find ourselves using, to which we find ourselves firmly committed, and which we could abandon or replace only with great difficulty if at all? The classical skeptical alternative is not a serious possibility. In the press of life we are continually forming beliefs about the physical environment, other people, how things are likely to turn out, and so on, whether we will or not (1991, p. 150, cf. also p. 168).

The idea here seems to be that, first, it is practically impossible not to engage in the doxastic practices of the standard package. Second, "what possible rationale could there be for [...] a substitution?" (p. 150) We would not be in a better position, Alston says, when trying to provide non-circular support for the reliability of alternative doxastic practices (ibid.).

Now consider, not the rationality of *engaging* in a doxastic practice, but the rationality of *judging* such a practice to be reliable. Take, for instance, *SP*. It is, Alston admits, "only that same *practical* rationality that carries over, via the commitment relation, to the judgment that *SP* is reliable" (1991, p. 180). The same holds for other doxastic practices. But then what (5) really says is this:

(5*) It is *practically* rational to judge that *SP* and *MP* are reliable.

Now, the fact that it is practically rational to engage in a doxastic practice, says Alston, arises from the fact that there are no alternatives and, even if there were alternatives, there would be no rationale for adopting them. Hence if that kind of practical rationality carries over to the *judgment* that *MP* is reliable, one would expect that judgment to share these two features. But it doesn't.[10] For, first, there *are* alternatives, namely judging the mystical practice to be unreliable, or at least suspending judgment on this question. Second, it is not at all clear that we should not at least adopt this second course. Alston's whole analysis of epistemic circularity seems to give us good reasons to do this.

Finally it should be noted that none of this tells us very much about the crucial question how exactly the practical rationality at issue is to be construed. What exactly does it mean to say that it is "practically rational" to make a *judgment*? I find Alston hard to understand on this point. The problem is this.

Alston explicitly admits that he has shown "at most, that engaging in *SP* [and the other practices in question, C.J.] enjoys a *practical* rationality; it is a reasonable thing to do, given our aims and our situation. [...] We have not shown that it is rational in an *epistemic* sense [to believe(?), C.J.] that *SP* is reliable, where the latter involves showing that it is at least probably true that *SP* is reliable. This must be admitted" (1991, p. 180). However, in the very same paragraph he goes on to say that his argument is by no means without "epistemic significance." For if

> we are unable to find noncircular indications of the truth of the reliability judgment, it is certainly relevant to show that it enjoys some other kind of rationality. It is, after all, not irrelevant to our basic aim at believing the true and abstaining from believing the false, that *SP* and other established doxastic practices constitute the most reasonable procedures to use, so far as we can judge, when trying to realize that aim" (ibid., my italics).

These remarks are puzzling. First, if the kind of rationality under consideration *is* relevant to the aim of believing what is true and not believing what is false, then why are we not dealing with some form of epistemic rationality? Isn't it precisely these aims that distinguish epistemic rationality from other kinds of rationality?

Second, what rationale is there for the claim that supposing *SP* to be reliable is rational with respect to the truth goal of believing? Alston's whole case about epistemic circularity seems to show that there isn't any such rationale. The situation seems to me to be this. (i) Either the "practical

---

[10] Steup 1997 was the first to call attention to this problem as well.

rationality" of supposing *SP* and *MP* to be reliable has nothing to do with getting into a good position with respect to the truth of that supposition. (Alston, as we have seen, explicitly denies this, even though he also denies (inconsistently, I believe) that the rationality in question is some form of epistemic rationality.) (ii) Or the rationality in question does have something to do with truth. Alston explicitly endorses (ii). In that case, however, what is at issue *is* a form of epistemic rationality. But there seems to be no good reason for the conclusion that this status really does attach to "supposing *SP* (and *MP*) to be reliable."

In fact I believe that (ii) is the correct way of looking at the matter. For as Alston himself acknowledges, practical rationality, whatever exactly it is, must be defined with respect to aims. What, then, is the aim of engaging in a *doxastic* practice? It would seem to be the aim to generate (and preserve) true beliefs and not generate (and preserve) false ones. But this is precisely the aim that defines epistemic rationality. The problem is that an epistemic subject situated in what we may call the "informed epistemic position," i.e., a position that acknowledges the problem of epistemic circularity, has no reason to assume that s/he pursues that aim when supposing *SP* or other doxastic practices to be reliable.

For these reasons, and the problems mentioned earlier, I conclude that Alston's central epistemological argument must be rejected. It does not warrant the conclusion that it is rational to suppose that the doxastic practices of the standard package and the practice of forming religious beliefs on the basis of mystical experience are reliable.

What overall conclusion should we draw from this? Should we conclude that Alston's project is entirely lost, and that his account has no bearing whatever on *de-jure* questions about experientially based religious belief? I do not think so, and in the remainder of this paper I will outline an account which I believe can salvage some of Alston's main ideas.

5. Religious Experience and Epistemic Responsibility

Alston's reasoning, I argued, does not license his conclusion that one can rationally suppose *MP* to be a reliable doxastic practice. But perhaps it supports a different conclusion. Perhaps it supports the conclusion that engaging in that practice enjoys some other kind of positive epistemic status. A status that seems to me to be a good candidate is *epistemic responsibility*. Let us say that:

(R) A subject S is epistemically responsible in generating or sustaining the belief B at t if and only if
  (i) in generating or sustaining B at t S engages in a doxastic practice that does not violate any reasonable epistemic norms that S is able to conform to at t, and
  (ii) S is generating or sustaining B at t because S conforms to the relevant norms at t.[11]

In the remaining pages of this paper I shall flesh out this definition, incorporating what I take to be some of Alston's main epistemological insights.[12]

First, some general comments. The reason for saying that the norms must be such that the subject is able to conform to them is that epistemic responsibility is an internalist notion of epistemic justification. It has something to do with holding beliefs conscientiously, i.e., in a way that is right *so far as the subject can tell*. Hence norms to the effect that one should hold beliefs that originate in objectively reliable doxastic practices are ruled out, for whether this condition is fulfilled or not is beyond a subject's epistemic perspective. We cannot deliberately follow externalist norms of epistemic excellence.[13]

The reason for saying that the subject must hold the belief *because* it conforms to the relevant norms is that it does not suffice for responsible belief formation that the belief is merely in *accordance* with the relevant norms. This has been pointed out by John Greco (Greco 1990, p. 255f.). Compare the Kantian distinction between doing something merely in accordance with the moral law, which can be a lucky accident and is independent of moral motivations, and doing it *for the sake of the moral law*. Just as it is only the

---

[11] For a similar idea cf. John Greco's account of epistemically responsible belief, as developed in Greco 1990.

[12] Norman Kretzmann offers an analysis of Alston's argument that goes in a similar direction as the one I am suggesting. Kretzmann, too, believes that Alston's practical rationality argument does not warrant the desired conclusion, but that it is dependent on some kind of deontological concept of justification. Kretzmann, however, seems to think of that concept not in terms of epistemic, but in terms of practical justification. In order to bring home his point about rationally supposing the mystical practice to be reliable, Kretzmann argues, Alston would have to admit that Natural Theology is needed. Cf. Kretzmann 1995.

[13] Pollock and Cruz 1999, chapter 5, argue that on closer inspection it becomes clear that an internalist interpretation of the notion of an epistemic norm is the only acceptable interpretation. I cannot go into the arguments for this position here, but my reason for explicitly saying that it must be possible to deliberately act in conformance with the norms is that *prima facie* there is also an "objectivist" reading of the concept of a norm, according to which we may say, for instance, that generating perceptual beliefs on the basis of *un*reliable mechanisms falls "outside the norm."

latter kind of action that is morally praiseworthy, it is only the formation of belief in such a stronger sense of *conformance* with the relevant norms that makes a doxastic process responsible.

What makes an internalist epistemic norm reasonable? This is a complex question that cannot be fully answered in the remaining pages of this paper. I want to conclude, however, by outlining a few desiderata that are strongly suggested by the foregoing discussion. At least the following conditions should be integrated into those norms.

1. *Grounds must exist.* First, if we accept, with Alston, that epistemic justification requires that there *be* internal grounds for a belief, i.e., other beliefs or non-doxastic mental states that serve as justifiers, then holding a belief without having any such grounds is epistemically irresponsible. The set of reasonable epistemic norms will have to include the requirement that a belief B be supported by reasons or non-propositional grounds.

2. *The belief must be based on grounds.* Second, for reasons mentioned in section 2, the norms we are looking for should include the postulate that beliefs be *based* on reasons or non-propositional grounds, in the sense that they function as psychological motivations for holding the beliefs. Thus our first two conditions exclude two different kinds of situations. Case one: S does not have any grounds at all for holding a given belief – the belief is literally groundless, it has just come to S's mind. Case two: S "has" an internal ground, in the sense that there are other beliefs or non-propositional grounds in S's noetic system that *could* function as justifiers, but S does not base the belief on these grounds.

3. *The subject need not be able to show in an epistemically non-circular way that the doxastic practice s/he engages in is reliable.* This is a crucial point. If Alston is right in his analyses of epistemic circularity, the norms in question should *not* include any requirements to the effect that the subject has good non-circular reasons for supposing the relevant doxastic practices to be reliable. If that is impossible, it cannot be a reasonable normative requirement to have such reasons. Still, it may be asked, how can it possibly be maintained that it is not epistemically irresponsible to engage in a doxastic practice that one has no non-circular reasons to regard as reliable? Is this not a highly counterintuitive claim? I do not think so. Compare a situation where your choice is limited to a number of actions each of which is *morally* just as bad as any other. If there is no better alternative, it is not irresponsible for you to choose one of these actions, even if you would wish there were a better one.

4. *The subject must believe that there are no overriding grounds for supposing the doxastic practice to be unreliable.* It is epistemically irresponsible to engage in a doxastic practice that one believes to have overriding reasons for rejecting as unreliable. If, for instance, S realizes that a doxastic practice yields significant intra- or interpractical inconsistencies, it would be epistemically irresponsible for S to engage in that practice.

Much more would have to be said about each of these desiderata, and the list is by no means exhaustive. But in the present context I must leave matters at this point. I want to conclude with a few remarks on three potential objections to what has been said in this section.

6. Mistaken Objections against the Notion of Epistemic Responsibility

"The account of epistemic responsibility you present," it may be criticized, "is a deontological account of epistemic justification. But for familiar reasons, accounts of this family must be rejected." Well, I don't agree that deontological notions of epistemic justification should be rejected *tout court*. The most influential objections to such notions are these. (i) The fulfillment of deontological requirements does not suffice to turn a true belief into knowledge; (ii) there are kinds of mental states to which such requirements cannot be applied; (iii) deontological theories of epistemic justification imply an untenable commitment to doxastic voluntarism.[14] None of these points undermines the position I have advocated.

First, knowledge has not been at issue. Following common practice, I have indeed been talking about *epistemic* justification, and this term, to be sure, is etymologically rooted in the notion of knowledge. This should not obscure the fact, however, that our topic has only been what, perhaps more appropriately, may be called *doxastic* justification. The question was what kind of valuable status certain beliefs might have, independently of the question whether that status suffices to turn these beliefs, if true, into knowledge.

The "objection from inapplicability" fails as well. This objection draws upon the fact that deontological concepts of epistemic (or doxastic) justification presuppose that the subject has a choice when forming a belief. But this, it would seem, is often not the case. Consider, for example, beliefs I form about my own conscious mental states. Such states are "self-

---

[14] The first two objections are, e.g., extensively developed in Plantinga 1993, chapter 2; the classic presentation of the objection from doxastic voluntarism is Alston 1988b.

intimating": when I have a certain perceptual experience I just can't help believing that I have it. But how, then, can such beliefs be formed responsibly or irresponsibly? That is indeed a problem for an unrestricted deontological account of epistemic justification. But again, this problem has no bearing on the topic of this paper. For what is at issue is not people's beliefs to the effect that they have certain experiences, but the epistemic legitimacy of moving from certain experiences to the belief that it is some supernatural reality that causes them. And, as argued earlier, as regards such moves there certainly is a choice, namely to withhold a religious interpretation of these experiences or even to believe that they have no super-natural cause.

Finally, what about doxastic voluntarism? Here the challenge is defused by the fact that we are dealing with doxastic *practices*. It seems clear to me that we have at least considerable indirect control over our belief forming habits. I could easily train myself, for example, not to be too gullible regarding the stories my neighbor to the right tells me about my neighbor to the left. Contrary to what some epistemologists claim, we can even influence our perceptual doxastic practices. Consider Alexius Meinong's example of the aging Austrian.[15] A man has been living for many years next to a garden where, when the wind blows, an Aeolian harp is whistling and thereby keeping the birds away. The man's hearing deteriorates, but at the same time he develops, unbeknownst to him, a tendency to have auditory hallucinations. It thus happens that he sometimes hallucinates the sounds of the harp just when it is actually whistling. Now, I agree that this example (which is a kind of Gettier-case) undermines the idea that deontological justification suffices to turn a true belief into knowledge. As pointed out above, however, knowledge is not our present concern. Our focus is on doxastic justification. Suppose that one day our aging Austrian is presented with good evidence to the effect that in fact he cannot hear the harp any more, and that, unfortunately, all the auditory experiences he still has are hallucinations. In that case it would be epistemically irresponsible for the man not to change his auditory doxastic practices, and I cannot see what would prevent him from doing so. Why should it be beyond his powers to train himself from now on to abstain from moving from the characteristic auditory experience to the belief that the harp is whistling? In general it seems that we *can* voluntarily revise or abandon a doxastic practice, and we should do so if we have good reasons for revising or abandoning it.

---

[15] Meinong 1906, p. 398. This example has been rediscovered for epistemological discussions by Roderick Chisholm 1989, p. 92.

7. Conclusion

I have argued that Alston's argument for the rationality of supposing that the doxastic practice of basing theistic belief on mystical experience is reliable fails. I have argued for the conditional view, however, that, *if* it is true that, even when being in an "informed position" regarding epistemic circularity, people have no overriding reasons for believing that practice to be unreliable, they are epistemically responsible when forming religious beliefs on that basis. Whether the antecedent of that conditional is true is a complicated and controversial question. But if it is true, the mystic is within his epistemic rights. He cannot be blamed for engaging in that practice, because he acts responsibly from an epistemic point of view.

Alston insists that he has shown "that it is rational to take *SP* and other established doxastic practices to be reliable" and hence rational to suppose that beliefs formed within these practices "are justified in the stronger, truth-conducive sense" (1991, p. 183). I have argued that this conclusion is unwarranted. On the other hand, Alston explicitly agrees that his results may also "be couched in terms of a weaker, non-truthconducive concept of epistemic justification." "I have no objection to doing so," he writes, "provided the rest of the picture is not neglected" (1991, p. 182). It is just such a weaker concept of epistemic justification with which Alston began his examinations of the epistemology of religious belief in the 1980s.[16] I am happy to conclude, therefore, that the argument developed in this paper does not amount to a root-and-branch dismissal of everything Alston has ever said about the epistemology of religious experience. Instead, it can be read as a defense of a position Alston himself favored in the early 1980s against a position he adopts ten years later.[17]

References

Adams, R.M.: Religious Disagreements and Doxastic Practices, *Philosophy and Phenomenological Research* 54 (1994), 885–888.

Alston, W.: Religious Experience and Religious Belief, *Nous* 16 (1982), 3–12. German version in *Analytische Religionsphilosophie*, ed. by C. Jäger, UTB, Paderborn 1998, 303–316.

Alston, W.: Christian Experience and Christian Belief. In: *Faith and Rationality*, ed. by A. Plantinga and N. Wolterstorff, The University of Notre Dame Press, Notre Dame 1983, 103–134.

---

[16] Cf. Alston 1982 and Alston 1983.

[17] For helpful discussions or comments on an earlier draft of this paper I am grateful to Thane Naberhaus and Richard Swinburne.

Alston, W.: Concepts of Epistemic Justification, *The Monist* 68 (1985), repr. in Alston 1989b, 81-114.
Alston, W.: Epistemic Circularity, *Philosophy and Phenomenological Research* 47 (1986), repr. in Alston 1989b, 319-349.
Alston, W.: An Internalist Externalism, *Synthese* 74 (1988a), repr. in Alston 1989b, 227-245.
Alston, W.: The Deontological Conception of Epistemic Justification. In: *Philosophical Perspectives 2: Epistemology*, ed. by J. Tomberlin, Ridgeview Publishing Company, Atascadero 1988b, repr. in Alston 1989b, 115-152.
Alston, W.: A 'Doxastic Practice' Approach to Epistemology. In: *Knowledge and Skepticism*, ed. by M. Clay and K. Lehrer, Westview Press, Boulder, Colorado 1989a, 1-29.
Alston, W.: *Epistemic Justification – Essays in the Theory of Knowledge*, Cornell University Press, Ithaca and London 1989b.
Alston, W.: *Perceiving God – the Epistemology of Religious Experience*, Cornell University Press, Ithaca and London 1991.
Alston, W.: *The Reliability of Sense Perception*, Cornell University Press, Ithaca and London 1993a.
Alston, W.: Epistemic Desiderata, *Philosophy and Phenomenological Research* 53 (1993b), 527-551.
Chisholm, R.: *Theory of Knowledge*, 3rd ed., Prentice Hall, Englewood Cliffs, N.J. 1989.
Fales, E.: Mystical experience as Evidence, *International Journal for Philosophy of Religion* 40 (1996), 19-46.
Greco, J.: Internalism and Epistemically Responsible Belief, *Synthese* 85 (1990), 245-277.
Kretzmann, N.: St. Teresa, William Alston, and the Broadminded Atheist, *Journal of Philosophical Research* 20 (1995), 45-66.
Meinong, A.: *Über die Erfahrungsgrundlagen unseres Wissens* (first published 1906). Repr. in: *Alexius Meinong Gesamtausgabe*, ed. by R. Haller and R. Kindinger, with R. Chisholm, vol. 5, Akademische Druck- und Verlagsanstalt, Graz 1973.
Plantinga, A.: *Warrant: The Current Debate*, Oxford University Press, Oxford 1993.
Pollock, J. and Cruz, J.: *Contemporary Theories of Knowledge*, Rowman & Littlefield Publishers, Lanham et. al 1999.
Quinn, P.L.: Towards Thinner Theologies: Hick and Alston on Religious Diversity, *International Journal for Philosophy of Religion* 38 (1995), 145-164.
Ricken, F.: Religiöse Erfahrung und Glaubensbegründung, *Theologie und Philosophie* 70 (1995), 399-404.
Schellenberg, J.L.: Religious Experience and Religious Diversity: A Reply to Alston, *Religious Studies* 30 (1994), 151-159.
Steup, M.: William Alston, Perceiving God – The Epistemology of Religious Experience, *Nous* 31 (1997), 408-420.

Namenregister

Adams, R.M. 405, 422
Alston, W. 403–420, 422, 423
Anscombe, E. 168, 192
Aristoteles 260, 262
Armstrong, D. 153, 160, 225, 228, 229, 231, 235, 237, 239

Bailey, A. 345, 355
Bailey, G. 361, 369
Baldwin, J. M. 166, 339
Baltzer, U. 319, 335
Balzer, W. 71, 72, 82, 105, 106, 314, 335
Bartelborth, T. 78, 82
Bayes, T. 395, 401
Bealer, G. 92, 106
Beardsley, M.C. 359, 369
Beckermann, A. 23–27, 30, 31, 65, 242, 256
Beckett, A. 360, 369
Belting, H. 387
Berkeley, G. 44, 54, 224, 369
Bernays, P. 117, 135
Bezboruah, A. 123, 135
Bickel, P. 368, 369
Bieri, P. 242, 256
Birnbacher, D. 259, 260, 272
Blackburn, S. 30, 31
Bleckmann, A. 272
Block, N. 211, 214, 223, 224
Boolos, G. 132, 135
Brandom, R. 13, 14, 20, 21, 29, 31
Bricmont, J. 110, 136
Budd, M. 378, 387
Burge, T. 92, 106, 188, 201

Calvin, J. 392, 401
Campbell, K. 161, 225, 227, 231, 239
Canals, M. 360
Carnap, M. 88, 90, 106
Carrier, M. 61, 62, 65
Cartwright, N. 56, 65
Chalmers, D. 211, 214, 223, 244, 256

Chisholm, R. 421, 423
Clark, A. 157, 216, 223
Crick, F. 58
Cruz, J. 418, 423

Dante Rossetti 360
Danto, A. C. 371–377, 387, 388
Darwin, C. 392, 400
Davidson, D. 30, 31, 169, 172, 175–177, 185
Dennett, D. 176, 178, 183–185, 194, 201, 202
Descartes, R. 51, 52, 54, 210, 214
Devlin, P. 269, 272
Dewey, J. 166
Díez, J. A. 83, 94, 104, 107, 203
Dörner, K. 264
Dou, G. 340
Dowe, P. 249, 256
Dretske, F. 190, 192, 202, 206, 210, 223
Droste 339
Dutton, D. 369, 370

Eilan, N. 179, 185
Elgin, C. Z. 8, 352, 353, 355

Fair, D. 249, 256
Fales, E. 411, 423
Feferman, S. 112, 115–117, 122–124, 126, 128, 129, 135, 136
Feyerabend, P. 102, 107
Field, H. 150, 152, 160
Fodor, J. A. 62, 65, 92, 107
Frege, G. 7, 34, 35, 39, 40, 54, 141–149, 158, 160, 161, 215, 236
Freud, S. 405
Fricke, C. 8, 261, 272, 377–379, 381, 383, 388
Friedrich, C. D. 360, 370

Gadamer, H.-G. 259, 357, 369
Gähde, U. 8, 71, 81, 82
Galen, C.A. von 263

Namenregister 425

Ginet, C. 15
Girard, J.Y. 124, 135
Gödel, K. 109–115, 117, 123, 126, 128–131, 135, 136
Goethe, J. W. von 260, 261, 272
Goldman, A.I. 14, 15, 178, 185
Goodman, N. 163, 185, 216, 224, 340–342, 346, 347, 349, 350, 352, 353, 355, 358–364, 366, 369, 375, 377, 388
Greco, J. 418, 423
Gregor von Nyssa, 393, 401
Grice, P. 224
Grimm, D. 314, 335
Guckes, B. 263, 272

Haack, S. 107
Hájek, P. 115, 116, 120, 123, 130, 135
Haken, H. 65
Hale, B. 152, 160, 189, 202
Hamlyn, D. W. 275, 276, 293
Hanfling, O. 370
Hanson, N. R. 86, 87, 102, 107
Harman, G.: 206, 210, 224
Hart, H.L.A. 29, 31, 150, 152, 269, 273
Hartmann, S. 61, 65
Hasenjaeger, G. 116, 135
Hatfield, G. 166, 185
Hegel, G.W.F. 370–373, 375, 376, 378, 388
Hegselmann, R. 267, 271, 273
Higginbotham, J. 92, 107
Hilbert, D. 110–113, 117, 119, 125, 126, 135, 136
Hobbes, T. 315, 328, 335
Hoerster, N. 260, 264, 265, 273
Hoffman, D. 43, 54
Hornsby, J. 165, 173–176, 178, 179, 182, 183, 186
Horwich, P. 107, 149, 160, 190, 202
Hoyningen-Huene, P. 61, 65
Hüppe, H. 259
Hume, D. 152, 167, 187, 392

Jackson, F. 181, 186, 214, 224
Jacob, P. 8, 201, 202
Jauss, H.R. 374, 388
Jellinek, G. 324, 335
Jeroslov, R. 117, 124, 135
Johnson, G. 52, 54

Kanitscheider, B. 245, 256
Kant, I. 40, 150, 153, 167, 185, 243, 268, 275, 277–280, 282, 283, 285–293, 344, 370, 371, 378, 379, 385, 388, 392, 393, 418
Kaplan, D. 142, 160
Kaye, R. 116, 130, 136
Kepler, J. 235
Kim, J. 65, 243, 256
Kistler, M. 249, 256
Kleene, S.C. 109, 116, 136
Koestler, A. 339, 340, 342, 355
Krantz, D. 104
Kreisel, G. 120, 136
Kretzmann, N. 418, 423
Kripke, S.A. 188–190, 202
Kuhn, T. S. 80, 83, 85, 89, 95, 107
Kuhse, H. 260, 266
Kulenkampff, J. 357, 370
Kutschera, F. von 16–18, 23, 30, 31, 39, 44, 52, 54, 357, 370

Langsam, H. 210, 224
Laufs, A. 262, 273
Lauth, B. 72, 82
Lehrer, K. 18, 19, 423
Leibniz, G.W. 232
Lenzen, W. 8, 23, 31, 52, 54
Lepsius, O. 314, 335
Lessing, A. 365, 370
Levinson, J. 360, 370
Lewis, D. 88, 107, 217, 224
Lindström, P. 115, 136
Loar, B. 215, 224
Locke, J. 210, 222, 233, 236, 240, 260, 315, 335
Lowe, E. J. 8, 239, 240, 242, 244, 250, 256
Lucas, J.R. 110, 112, 136
Luce, D. 104

MacCormick, N. 314, 335
Mackie, J.L. 244
Martin, C.B. 225, 233, 236, 237, 239, 240
Martin, M. 203, 222
Marx, K. 405
Mates, B. 157, 160
McDowell, J. 163, 168–172, 176, 177, 182, 183, 186, 205, 206, 208, 224
Meiland, J. 366, 370
Meinong, A. 421, 423

Meixner, U. 8, 256
Merkel, R. 267, 271, 273, 309, 311
Meyer, L. 366, 370
Millikan, R. 201, 202
Mills, E. 243, 252, 256
Mittelstrass, J. 62, 65
Mondrian, P. 346, 350
Monet, C. 346, 353
Monk, D. 115, 136
Moore, G.E. 7, 187, 198, 393, 401
Mostowski, A. 114, 136
Moulines, C. U. 71, 82, 83, 104–107
Müller, A. 198, 199, 260, 265–267, 270–273

Nagel, T. 53, 57, 170, 171, 174, 186, 289, 293
Neander, K. 201, 202
Newton, I. 68, 91, 94–96, 99, 105, 167, 400
Nida-Rümelin, J. 318, 334, 335
Niebergall, K.G. 8, 111, 116, 117, 125–127, 136
Nozick, R. 313, 318, 335

Oppenheim, P. 55–65

Paley, W. 394
Patzig, G. 8, 54, 357–359, 370
Paulus 391
Peacocke, C. 92, 93, 96, 98, 107, 160
Peirce, C.S. 29, 31
Perkins, M. 213, 214, 224
Place, U.T. 237, 239
Plantinga, A. 420, 422, 423
Platon, 22, 31, 92, 230
Pollock, J. 386, 418, 423
Popper, K.R. 50, 51, 76
Pudlák, P. 115, 116, 120, 123, 130, 135
Putnam, H. 55–65, 92, 107, 164, 186, 188, 202

Quine, W.V.O. 224, 249, 256
Quinn, P.L. 405, 423

Raffael 353
Rawls, J. 163, 186, 315, 318, 335
Recanati, F. 182, 186
Reicher, M. 357, 359, 367, 370
Reid, T. 407
Rembrandt (van Rhyn), 339, 340, 344–346, 355

Rest, F. 69, 262, 273, 288, 298, 309
Rey, G. 164, 165, 186
Ricken, F. 404, 423
Rippe, K.P. 273
Robinson, H. 210, 224
Robinson, R.M. 115, 136
Rogers, H. 113, 124, 136
Rorty, R. 28–31, 259, 355
Rosser, J.B. 114, 120, 122, 130, 131, 136
Roth, G. 33–36, 38–54
Rousseau, J.J. 315, 329, 335
Russell, B. 7, 141–145, 148, 149, 160, 210

Sagoff, M. 361, 366, 370
Salmon, N. 142, 145, 161
Salmon, W. 249, 256
Sartwell, C. 16, 18, 25, 31
Scheibe, E. 63, 65
Schellenberg, J.L. 405, 423
Schiffer, S. 8, 152, 154, 160, 161
Schirn, M. 111, 117, 126, 127, 136
Schmitt, C. 313–315, 329, 335
Schmücker, R. 8, 357, 359, 362, 370
Schöne-Seifert, B. 273, 384, 385
Schultz, W. 287, 293
Searle, J. 192, 200, 202, 318–322, 335
Sellars, W. 13, 14, 22, 23, 31, 163, 224
Shepherdson, J. 123, 135
Shoemaker, S. 179, 186, 213, 215, 216, 218, 224
Simons, P. 231, 240
Simpson, S. 112, 136
Singer, P. 260, 265, 266, 273
Sneed, J. D. 71, 82, 85, 105–107
Soames, S. 142, 143, 161
Sokal, A. 110, 136
Sosa, E. 19, 20, 31, 83
Spaemann, R. 263, 264, 273
Sperber, D. 182, 186, 194, 202
Stalnaker, N. 359, 370
Stalnaker, R. 142, 160, 161
Stegmüller, W. 67, 77, 78, 82, 109, 110, 136
Steinbrenner, J. 360, 369, 370, 377, 388
Steup, M. 414, 416, 423
Stich, S.P. 52, 177, 186, 195, 202, 306
Stöckler, M. 8, 62, 65, 66
Strawson, P. 359, 370
Suppes, P. 104, 107
Swinburne, R. 8, 401, 422

Tait, W.W. 112, 136
Takeuti, G. 120, 136
Tarski, A. 114–116, 136
Tesón, F.R. 301, 311
Thomas von Aquin 394
Tönnies, F. 320, 335
Tuomela, R. 314, 319, 335
Turner, W. 360
Tversky, A. 104
Tye, M. 206, 210, 224

van Fraassen, B. 79, 82, 84, 85, 107, 235, 240
Van Meegeren, H. 339, 342, 360
Vermeer, J. 339, 342, 348, 355, 360
Visser, A. 116, 122, 124, 136
Vollmer, G. 50, 60, 66

Warhol, A. 371–377, 383–385
Watson, J. 58
Weber, M. 314, 316–325, 334, 335
Weinberger, O. 314, 319, 335
Wettengl, K. 360, 370
Wheelock, Jr., A. K. 348, 355
Willard, D. 123, 136
Williams, B. 192, 196, 202
Williamson, T. 208, 224
Wittgenstein, L. 30, 31, 168, 188, 189, 202, 205, 223, 260, 267, 268, 272, 273, 407
Wollheim, R. 357, 369, 370
Wolterstorff, N. 357, 370, 422
Wright, C. 30, 31, 152, 160
Wright, L. 201, 202

Yates, J. 106, 107

Zemach, E. 357, 370
Zoubek, G. 72, 82

Autoren

Prof. Jay F. Rosenberg
  Taylor Grandy Professor of Philosophy, University of North Carolina, CB# 3125, Chapel Hill, NC 27599-3125, USA, jfr@email.unc.edu
Prof. Dr. Wolfgang Lenzen
  Universität Osnabrück, FB 2 – Philosophie, 49069 Osnabrück, Germany, lenzen@uos.de
Prof. Dr. Manfred Stöckler
  Universität Bremen, FB 9 – Philosophie, Postfach 33 04 40, 28334 Bremen, Germany stoeckl@uni-bremen.de
Prof. Dr. Ulrich Gähde
  Universität Hamburg, Philosophisches Seminar, Von-Melle-Park 6, 20146 Hamburg, Germany, gaehde@philosophie.uni-hamburg.de
Prof. Dr. José Díez
  Facultat de Lletres, Universitat Rovira i Virgili, Plaza Imperial Tarraco 1, E-43004 Tarragona, España, jadc@fll.urv.es
Dr. Karl-Georg Niebergall
  Seminar für Philosophie, Logik und Wissenschaftstheorie, LMU München, Ludwigstr. 31, 80539 München, Germany, kgn@lrz.uni-muenchen.de
Prof. Dr. Stephen Schiffer
  NYU Department of Philosophy, 503B Main Building, 100 Washington Square East, New York, NY 10003, USA, ss72@nyu.edu
Prof. Dr. Joëlle Proust
  Institut Jean-Nicod, 1 bis, avenue de Lowendal, 75007 Paris, France, jproust@atacama.ehess.fr
Prof. Dr. Pierre Jacob
  Institut Jean Nicod, 1 bis, avenue de Lowendal, 75007 Paris, France, jacob@poly.polytechnique.fr
Prof. Dr. Manuel García-Carpintero
  Departament de Lògica, Historia i Filosofia de la Ciència, Facultad de Filosofia, Universitat de Barcelona, Baldiri Reixach, s/n, 08028 Barcelona, España, garcia@mat.ub.es

Prof. E. J. Lowe
  Department of Philosophy, University of Durham, 50 Old Elvet, Durham
  DH1 3HN, United Kingdom, e.j.lowe@durham.ac.uk
Prof. Dr. Uwe Meixner
  Universität Regensburg, Institut für Philosophie, 93040 Regensburg, Germany, uwe.meixner@psk.uni-regensburg.de
Prof. Dr. Günther Patzig
  Universität Göttingen, Philosophisches Seminar, Humboldtallee 19, 37073 Göttingen, Germany
Prof. Dr. Peter Railton
  University of Michigan, 1, College of Literature Science and the Arts, Philosophy, 2247 Angel Hall, Ann Arbor, USA, prailton@umich.edu
Prof. Dr. Georg Meggle
  Philosophisches Institut, Universität Leipzig, Burgstr. 21, 04109 Leipzig, Germany, meggle@uni-leipzig.de
Prof. Dr. Dr. Dietmar von der Pfordten
  Universität Erfurt, Postfach 90 02 21, 99105 Erfurt, Germany, Dietmar.vonderPfordten@uni-erfurt.de
Prof. Dr. Catherine Z. Elgin
  Harvard University, Graduate School of Education, 404 Larsen Hall, Cambridge, Massachussetts 032138, USA, catherine_elgin@harvard.edu
Dr. Reinhold Schmücker
  Universität Hamburg, Philosophisches Seminar, Von-Melle-Park 6, 20146 Hamburg, Germany, reinold.schmuecker@uni-hamburg.de
PD Dr. Christel Fricke
  Universität Heidelberg, Philosophisches Seminar, Schulgasse 6, 69117 Heidelberg, Germany, r19@ix.urz.uni-heidelberg.de
Prof. Richard Swinburne
  Oriel College, Oxford, OX1 4EW, United Kingdom, richard.swinburne@oriel.oxford.ac.uk
Dr. Christoph Jäger
  Universität Leipzig, Institut für Philosophie, Burgstr. 21, 04081 Leipzig, Germany, cjaeger@uni-leipzig.de
Prof. Dr. Carlos Ulises Moulines
  Seminar für Philosophie, Logik und Wissenschaftstheorie, LMU München, Ludwigstr. 31, 80539 München, Germany, moulines@lrz.uni-muenchen.de